LIFE IN THE HOMERIC AGE

BIBLO & TANNEN PUBLICATIONS

Abbott, F. F.: Roman Political Institutions

Abbott, F. F.: Society & Politics in Ancient Rome

Budge, E. A. W.: The Mummy

Cave, R. C.: Medieval Economic History

Childe, V. G.: The Bronze Age

Clark, E. D.: Roman Private Law — 4 vols.

Cook, A. B.: Zeus. Vol. 1

Cook, A. B.: Zeus. Vol. II — 2 vols.

Davis, W. S.: A Day in Old Athens

Davis, W. S.: A Day in Old Rome

Dodge, T. A.: Caesar — 2 vols.

Evans, A.: Palace of Minos at Knossos — 4 vols. in 7

Ferguson, W. S.: Greek Imperialism

Hamburger, M.: Morals and Law

Hasebroek, J.: Trade & Politics in Ancient Greece

Henderson, E. F.: Select Historical Documents of the Middle Ages

Judson, H. P.: Caesar's Army

Minns, E.: Scythians and Greeks — 2 vols.

Pausanias   Description of Greece — Trans. J. G. Frazer 6 vols.

Pendlebury, J. D. S.: The Archaeology of Crete

Petersson, T.: Cicero. A Biography

Power, E.: English Medieval Nunneries

Powicke, F. M.: Ways of Medieval Life & Thought

Previte-Orton, C. W.: Medieval History

Reymond, A.: Hist. of Sciences in Greco-Roman Antiquity

Rostovtzeff, M. I.: Out of the Past of Greece and Rome

Sayce, R. U.: Primitive Arts and Crafts

Scott, J. A.: Unity of Homer

Seymour, T. D.: Life in the Homeric Age

Smyth, H. W.: Greek Melic Poets

Thomson, J. O.: History of Ancient Geography

Tozer, H. F.: A History of Ancient Geography

Wace, A. J. B.: Mycenae

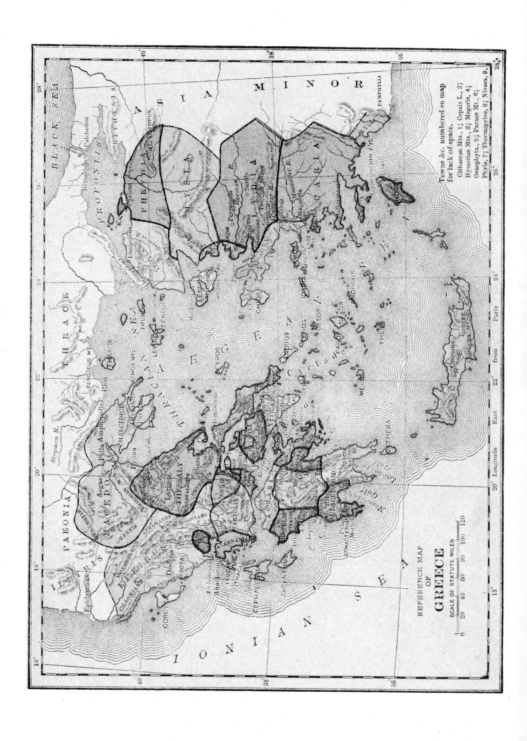

REFERENCE MAP
OF
GREECE

SCALE OF STATUTE MILES

0 20 40 60 80 100 120

Towns &c. numbered on map
for lack of space.

Cithaeron Mts., 1; Oeta L., 2;
Hymettus Mts., 3; Megaris, 4;
Oenophyta, 5; Parnes Mt., 6;
Phyle, 7; Thermopylae, 8; Nisaea, 9.

LIFE

IN THE

HOMERIC AGE

BY

THOMAS DAY SEYMOUR

HILLHOUSE PROFESSOR OF THE GREEK LANGUAGE AND LITERATURE
IN YALE UNIVERSITY

BIBLO and TANNEN
New York
1965

BIBLO and TANNEN
BOOKSELLERS and PUBLISHERS, Inc.
63 Fourth Avenue   New York 3, N.Y.

Library of Congress Catalog Card Number: 63-12451

Second Printing

Printed in U.S.A. by
NOBLE OFFSET PRINTERS, INC.
NEW YORK 3, N. Y.

PREFACE

THIS book is based upon a careful study of the Homeric poems. The earlier works on the same subject have not relieved the author from the obligation of collecting his own material for an independent examination of the questions involved. To Buchholz's *Homerische Realien*, however, he is greatly indebted for collections of material which have enabled him at times to check the completeness of his own. In the main, he has followed Reichel in the chapter on Homeric Arms. Wherever special acknowledgment was due, he has intended to give it in the foot-notes, as a convenience to the reader, as well as the right of the original author. A list of works important for the study of Homeric antiquities is given on pages xiii-xvi, but the author cannot attempt to give a list of all the works which he has consulted.

The author's point of view has been philological, not archaeological. From the poet's language he has attempted to discover what was before the poet's mind. Such a systematic attempt from the philological side to present an account of the life of the Homeric age, has not been made for more than a generation. This book should prove a complement to works like those of Tsountas and Manatt, *The Mycenaean Age*, of Ridgeway, *The Early Age of Greece*, and of Hall, *The Earliest Civilization of Greece*,—which look at nearly the same period from the archaeological point of view. Archaeologists can easily supply from the monuments many more parallels than have been adduced in illustration of life in the Homeric age. As the author has read the printer's proofs, many more such illustrations have occurred to him, which he has been inclined to add, but he has deliberately thrown all the emphasis on the careful interpretation of the poems themselves. This is not intended to be a general work on the Mycenaean age.

The author hopes that the references, which have seemed necessary to support his statements before scholars, will not interfere unreasonably with the comfort of the reader who may be ready to accept his statements without verification. References to the books of the *Iliad* are made by the large letters of the Greek alphabet (A, B, Γ, κτλ.), and references to the books of the *Odyssey*, by the lower-case letters (α, β, γ, κτλ.).

According to the original plan, this book was not to be nearly so large as it has become. The extension of the plan may not have been entirely uniform, and some details may have been omitted for which the earlier plan seemed to afford no room, but which should have found a place in the larger volume. In order to give greater completeness to the discussion of each topic, without an excessive number of cross-references, a considerable amount of repetition has been allowed.

After most of this book was in type, appeared Mr. Andrew Lang's book on *Homer and his Age*, and Mr. Bréal's *Pour mieux connaître Homère*. The author is glad to agree with Mr. Lang in his contention that Homer was not an archaeologist, and he would have counted himself happy if he had used some of Mr. Lang's literary illustrations. Mr. Bréal's work is very suggestive, but the author cannot consider it in detail.

Four or five of the author's friends have read the printer's proofs of different parts of the book,—each that in which he was most interested. For such services, however, the author is particularly indebted to Professor Washburn Hopkins, his colleague, and to Professor Samuel E. Bassett of the University of Vermont.

For the illustrations,—the author is indebted :

To Professor DÖRPFELD for permission to use his map of the Troad in *Troja und Ilion,* and for the use of photographs of Ithaca and Leucas ; to Professor DIELS for the cuts of locks and doors ; to Professor PERCY GARDNER for five cuts from his *Grammar of Greek Art* ; to Professor ERNEST GARDNER for four cuts from his *Greek Sculpture* ; to Professor RIDGEWAY for five cuts from his *Early Age of Greece* ; to Mr. JOHN MURRAY for the use of nine cuts from Schuchhardt's *Schliemann's Excavations.* Figure 6 was copied from Studniczka's *Studien zur altgriechischen Tracht* ; figures 2 and 17 from Engelmann's *Bilderatlas zur Ilias und zur Odyssee* ; and figures 27, 28, 30, 31, 33, 34, 36, and 37 from Reichel's *Homerische Waffen.* The Map of Greece is borrowed from Botsford's *History of Greece.*

YALE UNIVERSITY,
July 1, 1907.

TABLE OF CONTENTS

LIST OF ILLUSTRATIONS

BRIEF BIBLIOGRAPHY[1]

ALBRACHT, FRANZ, Kampf und Kampfschilderung bei Homer, *Naumburg*, 1886, 1895.

ARZ, FRANZ, die Frau im homerischen Zeitalter, *Hermannstadt*, 1898.

ASSMAN, ERNST, das Floss der Odyssee, *Berlin*, 1904.

BARKER WEBB, P., la Topographie de la Troade ancienne et moderne, *Paris*, 1844.

BÉRARD, VICTOR, les Phéniciens et l'Odyssée, *Paris*, 1902, 1903.

BERNHARDI, KURT, das Trankopfer bei Homer, *Leipzig*, 1885.

BLASS, FRIEDRICH, die Interpolationen in der Odyssee, *Halle*, 1904.

BOHSE, PAUL, die Moira bei Homer, *Berlin*, 1893.

BRAUMÜLLER OTTO, Krankheit und Tod bei Homer, *Berlin*, 1879.

BRÉAL, MICHEL, Pour mieux connaître Homère, *Paris*, 1906.

BROWNE, HENRY, Handbook of Homeric Study, *London*, 1905.

BUCHHOLZ, EDUARD, die Homerischen Realien, *Leipzig*, 1871-85. [I. Welt und Natur ; II. Oeffentliches und privates Leben ; III. Götterlehre, Psychologie, Ethik.]

BUTLER, SAMUEL, The Authoress of the Odyssey, *London*, 1897.

CAUER, PAUL, Grundfragen der Homerkritik, *Leipzig*, 1895.

CHAMPAULT, PHILIPPE, Phéniciens et Grecs en Italie d'après l'Odyssée, *Paris*, 1906.

CLERKE, AGNES, Familiar Studies in Homer, *London*, 1892.

DAREMBERG, CHARLES, la Médecine dans Homère, *Paris*, 1865.

DECKER, FRIEDRICH, über die Stellung der hellenischen Frauen bei Homer, *Magdeburg*, 1883.

[1] Many works are omitted from this list since the author believes them to be without value now ; from some of these that are mentioned, however, he is not conscious of having derived an idea. Doubtless, on the other hand, some works have been overlooked. The author assumes that scholars do not need to be reminded of the great dictionaries of Greek Antiquities,—of SMITH, of DAREMBERG AND SAGLIO, and of PAULY-WISSOWA,—nor of the great histories of Greece,—of GROTE, of EDUARD MEYER, and of BUSOLT.—To include articles in periodicals has seemed impracticable.

DELORME, S., les Hommes d'Homère, *Paris*, 1861.

DÖRPFELD, WILHELM, Troja und Ilion, 2 vols., *Athens*, 1902.

DÖRPFELD, WILHELM, Leukas, *Athens*, 1905.

DRERUP, ENGELBERT, Homer, *Munich*, 1903.

EGERER, P. GISLAR, die homerische Gastfreundschaft, *Salzburg*, 1881.

ENGEL, FR. JOSEPH, zum Rechte der Schutzflehenden bei Homer, *Passau*, 1899.

ENGELMANN, R., Bilderatlas zu Homer, *Leipzig*, 1889.

FANTA, ADOLF, der Staat in der Ilias und Odyssee, *Innsbruck*, 1882.

FEITH, EVERHARD, Antiquitatum Homericarum libri IV., Editio nova, *Strassburg*, 1743.

FELLNER, STEPHAN, die homerische Flora, *Vienna*, 1897.

FORCHHAMMER, P. W., Homer : seine Sprache, die Kampfplätze seiner Heroen und Götter in der Troas, *Kiel*, 1893.

FRÖLICH, H., die Militärmedicin Homers, *Stuttgart*, 1879.

GANDAR, E., Homère et la Grèce contemporaine, *Paris*, 1858.

GARDNER, PERCY, New Chapters in Greek History, *London*, 1892.

GEDDES, WILLIAM D., The Problem of the Homeric Poems, *London*, 1878.

GLADSTONE, W. E., Studies on Homer, 3 vols., *Oxford*, 1858.

GOESSLER, PETER, Leukas-Ithaka, *Stuttgart*, 1904.

GRASHOF, K. H. F., das Schiff bei Homer und Hesiod, *Düsseldorf*, 1834.

GRASHOF, K. H. F., das Fuhrwerk bei Homer und Hesiod, *Düsseldorf*, 1846.

GÜNTHER, FRIEDRICH, der Ackerbau bei Homer, *Bernburg*, 1866.

HALL, H. R., The Oldest Civilization of Greece, *London*, 1901.

HELBIG, WOLFGANG, das homerische Epos aus den Denkmälern erläutert, 2 Aufl., *Leipzig*, 1887.

HELBIG, WOLFGANG, zu den homerischen Bestattungsgebräuchen, *Munich*, 1900.

HEPP, LEO, Politisches und Sociales aus der Ilias und Odyssee, *Rottweil*, 1883.

HORT, MAX, vom Weine bei Homer, *Straubing*, 1871.

INGHIRAMI, FRANCESCO, Galleria Omerica, o raccolta di Monumenti Antichi per servire allo Studio dell' Iliade e dell' Odissea, 3 vols., *Florence*, 1827-31.

ISHAM, NORMAN M., The Homeric Palace, *Providence*, 1898.

JEBB, RICHARD C., Homer, *Glasgow*, 1887.

JOSEPH, D., die Paläste des homerischen Epos, *Berlin*, 1893.

JUBAINVILLE, H. D'ARBOIS DE, la Civilisation des Celtes et celle de l'Épopée Homérique, *Paris*, 1899.

KELLER, ALBERT G., Homeric Society, *New York*, 1902.

KLÖTZER, R. F. J., die griechische Erziehung in Homers Ilias und Odyssee
Zwickau, 1891

KOERNER, OTTO, die homerische Thierwelt, *Berlin*, 1880.

KOERNER, OTTO, Wesen und Wert der homerischen Heilkunde, *Wiesbaden*,
1904.

KÜCHENMEISTER, über das in Homer . . . physiologisch-medizinische
Material, *Breslau*, 1855.

LANG, ANDREW, Homer and his Age, *London*, 1906.

LAWTON, WILLIAM C., Art and Humanity in Homer, *New York*, 1896.

LEAF, WALTER, A Companion to the Iliad, *London*, 1892.

LE CHEVALIER (*Citoyen*), Voyage dans la Troade, 2me éd., *Paris*, l'an vii.

LINDNER, ROBERT, RITTER VON, das Eingreifen der Götter in die Hand-
lung der Ilias, *Landskron*, 1882.

LÖWNER, HEINRICH, die Herolde in den homerischen Gesängen, *Eger*, 1881.

MANGOLD, B., la Ville Homérique, *Berlin*, 1887.

DE MARÉES, H. W. A., Versuch über die Cultur der Griechen zur Zeit des
Homer, *Berlin*, 1797.

MIEHE, GUSTAV, Verwandtschaft und Familie in den Homerischen
Gedichten, *Halberstadt*, 1878.

NÄGELSBACH, CARL FR. VON, Homerische Theologie, 3te Aufl., *Nuremberg*, 1884.

NICOLAÏDES, GEORGIOS, Ἰλιάδος στρατηγικὴ Διασκευή, *Athens*, 1883.

NIESE, BERNARD, der homerische Schiffskatalog, *Kiel*, 1873.

NOACK, FERDINAND, Homerische Paläste, *Leipzig*, 1903.

PERRY, WALTER COPLAND, The Women of Homer, *New York*, 1898.

PLATNER, EDUARD, Notiones Juris et Justitiae ex Homeri carminibus,
Marburg, 1819.

PROTODICOS, JOANNES, de Aedibus Homericis, *Leipzig*, 1877.

REICHEL, WOLFGANG, über Homerische Waffen, 2 Aufl., *Vienna*, 1901.

RHANGABÉ, C. R., ὁ καθ᾽ Ὅμηρον οἰκιακὸς Βίος, *Leipzig*, 1883.

RIDGEWAY, WILLIAM, The Early Age of Greece, I., *Cambridge*, 1901.

RIEDENAUER, ANTON, Handwerk und Handwerker in den homerischen
Zeiten, *Erlangen*, 1873.

ROBERT, CARL, Studien zur Ilias, *Berlin*, 1901.

RUMPF, J. H. S., de Interioris Aedium Homericarum partibus, *Giessen*, 1858.

SCHENKL, HEINRICH, die homerische Palastbeschreibung, *Vienna*, 1893.

SCHLIEMANN, HEINRICH, Ithaka, der Peloponnes, und Troja, *Leipzig*, 1869.

SCHLIEMANN, HEINRICH, Trojanische Alterthümer, *Leipzig*, 1874.

SCHLIEMANN, HEINRICH, Ilios, *New York*, 1881.

SCHLIEMANN, HEINRICH, Troja, *New York*, 1884.

SCHLIEMANN, HEINRICH, Tiryns, *New York*, 1885.

SCHOEMANN, G. F., Griechische Alterthümer, 4te Aufl., neu bearbeitet von J. H. Lipsius, I., *Berlin*, 1897.

SCHUCHHARDT, CARL, Schliemann's Excavations, translated by Eugenie Sellers, *New York*, 1891.

SORGENFREY, TH., de Vestigiis Juris Gentium Homerici, *Leipzig*, 1871.

SPOHN, FR. A. G., de Agro Trojano in Carminibus Homericis descripto, *Leipzig*, 1814.

STUDNICZKA, FRANZ, Beiträge zur Geschichte der altgriechischen Tracht, *Vienna*, 1886.

TIMAYENIS, T. T., Greece in the Times of Homer, *New York*, 1885.

TSOUNTAS, CHRESTOS, and J. IRVING MANATT, The Mycenaean Age, *Boston*, 1897.

TYLER, W. S., The Theology of the Greek Poets, *Boston*, 1867.

VECKENSTEDT, A. E., Regia Potestas quae fuerit secundum Homerum, *Halle*, 1867.

VÖLCKER, K. H. W., über homerische Geographie und Weltkunde, *Hannover*, 1830.

WARREN, WILLIAM F., Homer's Abode of the Dead, *Boston*, 1883.

WARREN, WILLIAM F., Homer's Abode of the Living, *Boston*, 1885.

WEGENER, WILHELM, die Tierwelt bei Homer, *Königsberg*, 1887.

WEISSENBORN, EDMUND, Leben und Sitte bei Homer, *Leipzig*, 1901.

WEISSENBORN'S Homeric Life, translated by G. C. Scoggin and C. G. Burkitt, *New York*, 1903.

WOOD, ROBERT, Versuch über das Originalgenie des Homers (aus dem Englischen), *Frankfurt*, 1773.

CHAPTER I

INTRODUCTION

A HANDBOOK which endeavors to cover the whole field of Homeric antiquities, must be content with registering the most important facts in regard to the life which the poet depicts, and seeking to make clear the *This not a* relation between these facts. It cannot enter *Study of Origins.* into the question of origins and pursue inquiries as to the connexion between these facts and an earlier period of civilization. We cannot ask here whether the Trojans were Phrygians or of Greek stock,—which would be a rather fruitless effort with our present material and at the present stage of science,—nor even who were the Achaeans or Greeks, and how long they had been in the Balkan peninsula. That the poet draws no distinction between the language and customs of the Greeks and those of the Trojans, may indicate his *naïveté* rather than the identity of race of the peoples. A recent endeavor[1] to prove that the Achaeans were a light-haired race which not long before had come down from the north of Europe and had overcome the old Mycenaeans, does not seem to have been successful; the Achaeans, so far as we see, may have been the descendants of a race which had lived in Greece for a thousand years before Homer. Nor is it within our province to endeavor to determine under what special influences the Achaean civilization was developed and where its centre lay, whether in Crete or on the mainland of Hellas. Nor can we discuss the exact relations of Zeus and Hera to their Roman

[1] Ridgeway, *The Early Age of Greece*, i., 1901 ; see also Tsountas and Manatt, *The Mycenaean Age*, 1897.

cousins Jupiter and Juno, nor whether Apollo was borrowed from the predecessors of the Greeks in Asia Minor, or rather was a near kinsman of the Roman Mars, nor how much of the myth and worship of Aphrodite is due to the nations of the East, nor whether Ares was a god of the lower world or (as Homer believed him) a war-god of Thrace. Nor shall we consider the relation of these higher divinities to the popular religion and the lower, local divinities of Greece, who are ignored for the most part in the Homeric poems. Nor for our purpose do we need to know who the Amazons were, though they are mentioned by the poet once or twice. Nor can we study here the early Phoenician trade-routes in Greece, nor attempt to determine the debt of Greece for art and science to Phoenicia and Egypt, except so far as these are indicated in the *Iliad*

Elements and *Odyssey*. For our purpose we need not
of Myth, determine even approximately the proportions of
Tradition, the elements of myth, historical tradition, and
Imagination. imagination in the story of the poems. Probably the poet himself could not have distinguished clearly between the mythical and the historical elements. For him, Agamemnon was certainly a "king of men," and not a god ; he was as real and actual as any of Homer's contemporaries. We need not even examine the evidence for the theory that originally Agamemnon was a Thessalian and not king at Mycenae. Whether Telamonian Ajax was the double or the original of the lesser Ajax, the son of Oïleus, has no importance for the work before us now. For Homer, Helen was certainly a fair woman and not the Dawn, nor the moon which wanes and disappears from the heavens. To introduce into our discussions the consideration of origins would lead to endless confusion and to no clear result. These must be determined by detailed investigations before any summary statements about them can have any value. If Diomed is wounded in the foot by Paris, this in Homer's eyes is no allegory for the god of light attacked by a god of darkness, nor is any sound indication to be found that the quarrel in the first book of the *Iliad* between Zeus and Hera seemed to the poet a natural failure of agreement between the starry heavens by night

and the sunlight of day.[1] No one understands the Homeric poems the better for any such allegorical explanations, and our present inquiries must be limited to what may be learned from, and what in turn directly illustrates, the poems. This is said with no lack of respect for the questions which have been suggested, but only to indicate the aim of the present work.

Still less than the questions of prehistoric archaeology, may we discuss here the so-called Homeric question, as to the manner of the composition of the poems, although the general attitude of the writer must be briefly stated.

The final solution of any one of the problems to which reference .has been made, will require many more years of patient investigation on the part of many scholars. Some of these questions are insoluble with our present material. A better understanding of the facts of the civilization which is depicted by the Homeric poems, is needed before scholars are free to draw full and absolute inferences from this civilization. The time has not come for drawing sweeping conclusions for Homeric culture from other races which in certain respects have similar customs. This book *Merely a* seeks to set forth with regard to Homeric *Statement of* antiquities simply what may be learned from *Facts.* the Homeric poems themselves, with such illustration as is obvious or naturally presented from other sources.

Within the memory of many living scholars, the Homeric poems were thought to preserve and to present to us the earliest extant pictures of European civilization, just as they themselves are the oldest remains of European literature. They were thought to give, if not the very first, yet the clearest and most complete views of early life in our Indo-European family. The fidelity of the pictures of human life presented in the poems was not doubted, although the historic character of the war was either doubted *Historical* or entirely disbelieved, Only a bold man half *Basis of the* a century ago dared to hold that a substantial *Homeric* basis of fact underlay the stories of the battles *Story.* before Troy,—not to speak of the wanderings of Odysseus ; and archaeologists believed that the poet had not simply

[1] Weissenborn's *Homeric Life*, page 62.

idealized but also exaggerated freely the wonders of the works of art and craft to which he refers. When, little more than a third of a century ago, Dr. Schliemann began to dig for indications of early settlements on the chief Homeric sites,—first at Hissarlik on the shore of the Hellespont, which had been held by the ancients to be the site on which Homeric Troy had stood, and then in Argolis, at Mycenae and Tiryns,—many mocked just as they would have done if the enthusiastic German had sought to determine the sites of the exploits of Jack the Giant-killer. Mycenae was a place of no interest to the historian Grote, in spite of his careful study of Homer, and Minos in his palace at Cnosus on Crete seemed to many to be, as unreal as Minos with Rhadamanthys on the Asphodel Plain of the nether world. Not long ago the saying of Pascal was quoted with approval, that no one could believe Troy and Agamemnon to have had any truer existence than the apples of the Hesperides. The story of the Trojan War, many of us were taught, and handbooks are still repeating the doctrine, was only a highly imaginative and anthropomorphized account of the ever-renewed and unending contest between Darkness and Light, between the West and the East, and so between Europe and Asia, for the possession of the beautiful Dawn, which seemed to belong partly to each. Those who were most ready to acknowledge a historical basis for the story, held that the conflicts of the *Iliad* were only a sort of personification of the struggles of the early Greek colonists to secure a foothold on the shores of Asia Minor. Scholars were divided in opinion as to which of the two sites, Hissarlik and Bunárbashi, the poet had chosen for the Troy of his story, but they no more expected to find a real Troy than a real Avilion. But, as every reader now knows, Schliemann found, both at Troy and at Mycenae, evidence of ancient, contemporary,

Kingdoms of Troy and Mycenae. powerful, and wealthy settlements or kingdoms, of similar civilization. The gold, in which the Homeric poet had declared Mycenae to be rich, had been thought to be as unsubstantial as the treasure of the Nibelungs, or the abundant red gold of German fairy tales. Gold was a rarity in Greece, we were told ; the

Spartans were obliged to send to Lydia for it when they desired to dedicate a splendid offering to Apollo (Herodotus, i. 69), and even after the battle of Plataea, 479 B.C., the ordinary Greek thought that the Persian general's gold plate was brass (Herodotus, ix. 80). But the Homeric epithet " rich in gold " ($\pi o\lambda\acute{v}\chi\rho v\sigma o\varsigma$, H 180) was found by Schliemann to be fully justified as applied to Mycenae. The fortifications of " well-walled ($\epsilon\grave{v}\tau\epsilon\acute{\iota}\chi\epsilon o\varsigma$, B 113) Troy," too, were seen to be worthy of their Homeric builder, the god Poseidon. But an unexpected difficulty arose : the works of art discovered seemed to be superior to those which were familiar to the Homeric poet. So archaeologists no longer held that the poet's imagination far transcended what he had seen, but were inclined on the other hand to say that he lived in a period of decadence ; otherwise his heroes would have carried more magnificent swords and shields, and their palaces would have been adorned with more splendid decorations,— although we must grant that from detached references or even from a description the hearer cannot judge well of a picture or any other work of art, unless he knows exactly the narrator's standard. Archaeologists and philologists were perplexed also by the difference of style between the Mycenaean and Trojan remains and what had been expected on the basis of the preceding study of the Homeric poems. Many saw no tie of connexion between the Homeric and the Mycenaean civilizations, and some have gone so far as to declare the Mycenaean remains to be un-Hellenic,—not to recall the extravagance of the one or two who asserted the Mycenaean tombs to be the work not of a prehistoric people, but rather of foreign invaders of Greece since the beginning of our era.

The question of the relation of the monuments of the Mycenaean age to the life depicted in the Homeric poems is still before the archaeological courts and cannot be discussed in detail here, but we may say that *Mycenaean Antiquities and the Homeric Age.* the study of Mycenaean antiquities has done more than anything else of recent years to throw light on the life of the Homeric age, and that much in them which at first seemed wholly strange and un-Homeric is now found to be our best illustration of Homeric usage, and in further points, too, philologists will be glad to modify their interpretation of the Homeric poems at the suggestion of Mycenaean and Cretan monuments. Not for more than a dozen years after Schliemann's excavations at Mycenae did scholars see that the Mycenaean shield was admirably adapted to the conflicts as described by Homer, while at present prominent scholars would consider as comparatively late additions to the poems any passages which assume the use of the round and not the Mycenaean shield ; and no one showed how the Homeric shield was worn or carried until the hint was given by figures inlaid on Mycenaean swords, although since that time illustrations of this usage have been multiplied. The ruins of the palace uncovered at Tiryns were declared at first to afford no hint for the understanding of the Homeric palace of Odysseus, but more recently scholars have derived from Tiryns much light for the appreciation of the homes of Homeric princes. The opening in the roof near the middle of the great hall for the passage of smoke, the columns near the fire, the use of blue glass paste (*cyanus*) for a frieze, and of stucco for a covering of stone seats, may be cited as examples. For our knowledge of Homeric dress, on the other hand, little has been gained from the Mycenaean monuments,—with the exception of emphasis laid upon a loin-cloth for the men, which on early monuments appears sometimes in the form of an Indian's breech-clout, and sometimes like a boy's bathing drawers. As for religion, again, the Mycenaean age sheds little light on the Homeric poems. Shrines indeed are found in the palace at Cnosus, and a town or village shrine, only a few feet square, has been uncovered at Gournià, but no figure or monument which could be associated naturally and closely with Zeus, Apollo, or Athena. As for political life, the kings who built the fortresses, palaces, and tombs of Mycenae, Tiryns, and Cnosus, must have had more absolute power than Agamemnon seems in general to possess. These palaces were built for the use of royal families, not for the enjoyment of the people, and Tiryns and Cnosus still show immense store-rooms which must have been used for treasures of grain, brought more or less willingly by subjects to their lord. Such stores of grain are not mentioned in the poems. The lord of Mycenae, on the

other hand, cannot have gained his wealth of gold directly
from the tribute of his vassals: he is more likely to have
exacted this from the merchants who passed near his castle
in following the trade route by land from Nauplia to Corinth,
from the Argolic to the Corinthian Gulf, although such robber-
barons do not appear in the Homeric poems. Archaeologists
long disputed about the technical processes before the poet's
mind in the composition of the Shield of Achilles (Σ 478-608),
but the richly ornamented sword blades, inlaid with several
different colored metals, found at Mycenae, show that the
difficulty and dispute had arisen simply because the poet
assumed the familiarity of his hearers with a well-developed
technical process,—not because of any vagueness in his own
mind.

On the whole, then, the relations between the life depicted
in the Homeric poems and that which is indicated by the
Mycenaean remains, are much closer than were *Views of the*
supposed a quarter of a century ago. Scholars *Classical*
had projected into the early ages of Greece their *Period*
views of Greek life which were based on the *projected into*
remains and literature of the classical period,— *Homeric Age.*
making in archaeology exactly the same mistake as was made
in philology until very recent times, since Attic meanings,
forms, and constructions, so far as possible, were long taken
as the norm also for Homeric usage. Thus through much of
the nineteenth century any work of Greek or Roman art
might be used to illustrate Homeric life. Modern artists were
left free to follow their own bent in depicting Homeric scenes,
and Flaxman seems to have " builded better than he knew,"
when he represented the Achaean warrior as ready to go into
battle without bronze cuirass, and in fact without much clothing.
Scenes from Greek vases of the sixth and fifth centuries
B.C. were used, as freely as publishers would admit, for the
elucidation of the Homeric poems.[1] A third of a century
ago, illustrations from Egyptian and Assyrian monuments were
introduced in large numbers in works on the life of the
Homeric age, often bringing in, as is seen now, a mass of

---

[1] The Homeric manner of stringing the bow (see fig. 34) is perhaps the most
important lesson learned for Homeric warfare from a Greek vase, but this lesson was
learned long after the publication of the vase.

matter which would have seemed strange not only to our poet, but also to the Greeks of any other century. These so-called illustrations had little reference to early Greek monuments, and their connexion with early Greek literature was not much closer; they had slight relation to either the earlier or the later civilization of Greece.

As to the time in which the Homeric poems were composed, any brief statement must be vague or over dogmatic.

Date of the Composition of the Homeric Poems. Archaeologists believe that Mycenae and Troy, the home of Agamemnon and that of Priam, both were at the height of their power and magnificence in the latter half of the second millenium B.C.,— thus agreeing essentially with the ancient chronologists who set the fall of Troy at 1184 B.C. (with Eratosthenes) or twenty-four years earlier (as the Parian Chronicle). Recently Troy and Mycenae have so been brought back from the realm of fancy to that of fact, that scholars are more ready than before to believe in the reality of such a siege of Troy as is narrated in the Homeric poems. The supposition that in the original form of the story, Troy was not sacked because the earliest efforts of Aeolian colonists to secure a foothold in the Troad were unsuccessful, is less important than it was before the site of Troy was carefully examined. Without rendering ourselves liable to ridicule from those who have a right to an opinion on the subject, we may believe that Troy was sacked about 1200 B.C. (which agrees closely with the beliefs of the ancients) by an expedition from Hellas under the leadership of the king of Mycenae,—whatever may have been his name and the cause of the war. Details like the length of the war, the number of men and ships on the expedition, and the manner of the capture of the city, are of secondary importance. That the names of Ilium and Dardanians are historical, seems probable. Priam and Hector, too, may be real persons.

Those who doubt the historic basis for the Homeric story have not explained fully why the lays of Thessalian and *Prominence of Peloponnesian Warriors.* Aeolian poets, developed and perfected in Asia Minor, should have as central figures the kings of Mycenae and Sparta, or how Agamemnon and Menelaus should have been brought from northern to southern Greece after the story was well developed.[1] If we agree that the name Argos has been transferred from Thessaly to Peloponnesus, we are still in ignorance of the motive which might have led the Aeolian or Ionian poets to make this transfer. To say that Agamemnon was originally a local Spartan divinity, does not cast even a single ray of light upon this problem. The very latest hypothesis offered to explain the origin of the story of the war is that at first Telamonian Ajax was the chief Achaean warrior, and that his home was not on the island of Salamis but at the Aeanteum on the Hellespont, within four miles of Priam's palace, so that the war was between immediate neighbors. This hypothesis cannot be proved, and seems to leave as many difficulties as before, but the important consideration for us in the present work is that such hypotheses do not affect in the least our understanding or appreciation either of the Homeric poems or the life depicted in the poems. However important and interesting such inquiries may be, until the results are finally determined, they do not affect seriously a hand-book of Homeric antiquities.

If the story of the *Iliad* was based upon actual conflicts, then we may believe it to have been begun within a century or so of the war, since after that time new events would have displaced that war in the public mind. The early elements of the Homeric poems may be as old as the close of the second millenium B.C.

Just as "many brave men lived before Agamemnon," so also many bards lived before Homer. In the *Odyssey*, we

---

[1] Cf. "The importance of Achilles and Thessaly in the heroic age has been vastly exaggerated during the last fifty years. Critics have brought themselves to believe in a Thessalian Epos, a Thessalian Argos; and in a subsequent transference of place and interest to Mycenae and Agamemnon. Archaeology has swept away these cobwebs of the professorial brain. The coincidence of the Mycenaean monuments with Epic tradition is a chain not to be broken. . . . In Homer there was no Thessaly. That region was in various hands. . . . There are local legends, Lapiths and Chiron, but nothing to suggest a once ruling race, a centre of gravity of Greece. . . . Homer, the dramatist, by selecting the portion of chronicle to which Achilles' quarrel belonged and treating it with his art, raised Achilles to the place where he stands. . . . The potentate of Mycenae, installed on the isthmus, with his 100 ships, his brother at Sparta, the Arcadians on his transports, was the Emperor for which Thucydides recognized him." T. W. Allen in *Classical Review*, xx. 201.

read of a bard Phemius at the home of Penelope, singing under compulsion for the suitors at their feasts (α 154), of

Bards before Homer.

another bard, Demodocus, at the palace of the Phaeacian king (θ 43), and of a third who was left by Agamemnon as an adviser for his queen Clytaemestra, but was removed and slain by Aegisthus (γ 267). In the *Odyssey*, too, we have the figure of a bard reciting his lay as a comparison for Odysseus telling of his adventures (λ 368). In the *Iliad* we read of no professional bard,—the scene of active war was no place for him,—but when the embassadors of the Achaeans go to Achilles, begging him to return to the field of battle, they find him cheering his heart in singing of the "glorious deeds of men" (κλέα ἀνδρῶν, I 189), with his comrade Patroclus by his side "waiting until he should cease his song," when perhaps Patroclus would take up the strain. Whether the songs of the Trojans as they bivouac on the plain before the Achaean camp (K 13), are lyric or epic, no one can say,—indeed this music may have been simply instrumental; and the songs of the young Achaeans in honor of Apollo at Chrysa, and the lays of Apollo himself and the Muses, at the feast of the gods on Olympus, may have been lyric (A 472, 604). But the songs of the *Odyssey* are clearly epic,—one is a little *Iliad* (θ 73, 500), telling of a quarrel between the leaders of the expedition against Troy and of the sack of the city; another is a little *Odyssey* (α 326), telling of the sad return of the Achaean leaders from Troy; still another sings of the loves of Ares and Aphrodite (θ 266). Indications of other epic poems are found in Homer, notably of lays with regard to the Argonautic Expedition (as μ 70), the labors of Heracles (as Θ 363), and the Calydonian Hunt (I 529). Many expressions convenient for the verse became fixed as formulas, and many ornamental epithets became attached to the names of warriors or divinities. For many generations in Hellas all literary impulses turned to epic poetry. A vast mass of epic material, narrations and descriptions of conflict and adventure, was gathered and handed down from age to age. Some bards may have sung only the lays which they had learned. Others, doubtless far more numerous, not only amended and revised what they had received as their inheritance, but also composed lays of their own; thus

Phemius of Ithaca says that he is " self-taught " (αὐτοδίδακτος, χ 347), which is understood to mean that he was no mere rhapsodist,—a singer of other men's songs,—but was himself a composer. The idea of literary property, of course, was still entirely unknown. These lays then became a kind of common possession, since no one of them bore its maker's name, and doubtless an old bard would have been sore perplexed in many cases to distinguish his own compositions from those of others.

Very likely the *Iliad* contains narratives of combats between mighty warriors who never saw the plain of Troy,—or, if the reader prefers, scenes originally invented for a lay which told of battles in other lands,—the field of *Old Material* conflict being transferred from Crete or Thessaly to *in New* the plain of the Scamander. An instance of old *Lays.* material used in new lays is found by scholars in the tenth book of the *Iliad.* This book is thought to be of comparatively recent composition, but it contains the clearest description in the poems of the old Mycenaean form of helmet, and the most frequent mention of the use of the skins of animals as light shields for nobles, and it nowhere mentions either cuirass or greaves, which at least were more common in later than in earlier times. The *Odyssey*, too, is held to be of later composition than most of the *Iliad*, but it nowhere names the cuirass, though several opportunities exist for its mention. Grammatical forms and syntactical constructions of successive ages are found in the poems, the old and the new, side by side. Why should we not expect to find also in the *Iliad* and the *Odyssey* older and newer customs of war and peace, of sentiment and of dress, in close juxtaposition? Some parts of the poems may be two or even three centuries older than others.

Different strata doubtless exist in the Homeric poems, but their limits have not yet been determined to the satisfaction of the community of scholars. Hardly a beginning has been made in this investigation. *Strata in the* Paul Cauer showed in his careful discussion of *Homeric* the use of bronze and iron in Homer (*Homer-* *Poems.* *kritik*, 1895) the possibility of applying archaeological tests to determine the relative age of parts of the poems, but these indications have not been shown to agree with those derived from philological scrutinies. Rather recently, Professor Robert of Halle (*Studien zur Ilias*, 1901) has made a vigorous attempt to distinguish strata in the *Iliad* by uniting archaeological with philological arguments : the presence of both the Mycenaean shield and Aeolic forms of words, indicated to him an early stage, while the mention of the round shield and firmly established Ionic grammatical forms, proved a later stage of the poems. But Robert was obliged not only to assume that earlier formulas and epithets had been used by later poets, which is entirely credible, but also to hold that in the tradition of the poems certain later epithets had been introduced in earlier lays, and to eject some passages which did not suit his theory. His argument was touched by the remark that any theory can be made to fit the poems if all passages which are inconsistent with it may be cast out. As for the study of mythology in relation to these poems, Gruppe (*Griechische Mythologie*, p. 610) is explicit in declaring that conclusions of different strata in the Homeric poems, inferred from supposed aesthetic inconsistencies, have been almost regularly worthless,—and this in spite of his belief that these poems did not receive their present form until near the close of the seventh century B.C. Not even in the picture of the realm of Hades in the eleventh book of the *Odyssey*, does Gruppe recognize strata of composition. In the Catalogue of Ships (B 549), Athena has a temple in Athens and gives Erechtheus a place in it, while in the *Odyssey* (η 81) her Athenian shrine seems to be in the home of Erechtheus,—but the Catalogue of Ships has long been recognized as of late composition. That in the early Aeolic lays the palace of Priam stood on the acropolis of Ilium, while in the later Ionic lays Athena had a temple there (Z 297), has not clearly been made out.

The archaeological arguments to show that the *Odyssey* is of later composition than the *Iliad* are but slight. Some scholars have thought the *Odyssey* to show a more advanced stage of civilization than the *Iliad*, neglecting the rather obvious truth that the action of the *Iliad* is in a military camp, and on the field of battle, in the last year of a demoralizing war, while the *Odyssey* tells of adventures in times of peace, when milder manners and a less auto-cratic government are expected. In point of fact, *Arguments* the popular assembly has no more authority in *for the* the *Odyssey* than in the *Iliad*, and the few *Earlier* indications in the *Odyssey* of the increased *Composition* power of the nobility may be explained by the *of the Iliad.* peculiar state of affairs on Ithaca during the twenty years' absence of its king.[1]   The ceremonies and routine life of men away from home, like the Achaeans before Troy, may have varied somewhat from those at home.   Little con-straining force as evidence of different authorship is to be drawn from the two stock observations that in the *Iliad*, Olympus is always the name of a mountain, the seat of the Gods, while in the *Odyssey* it seems at times to be used in a general way for heaven ; and that in the *Iliad* Iris is the messenger of the gods, but Hermes in the *Odyssey*,—although Hermes is a messenger of Zeus in the last book of the *Iliad* (Ω 333), and in the *Odyssey* (σ 6) the Ithacan professional beggar is called *Irus* because he is ready to run errands.   The evidence for the later date of the *Odyssey* as yet is philological, not archaeological.[2]

At present, and for the chief questions before us, we are obliged to consider the Homeric poems as units, *For our* although we may hope that in secondary matters *purpose the* archaeology will come to the help of philology *Homeric* in determining what passages are to be regarded *Poems* as containing particularly ancient material, and *are Units.* what must be recognized as of comparatively late composition.

[1] In the *Neue Jahrbücher*, 1906, pp. 313 ff., 393 ff., Finsler argues that the State of the *Odyssey* is an aristocracy rather than a monarchy, but he believes the poet of the *Iliad* to have had a like aristocratic state before his eyes, although he depicts a monarchy.

[2] That the cypress, palm, laurel, and fig are mentioned in the *Odyssey*, but not in the *Iliad*, is not important.   Nor that oracles are mentioned twice in the *Odyssey*, but not in the *Iliad* ; nor even that Sicily is not named in the *Iliad*, and Egypt only at I 382. An examination of the passages allows these to be brought easily into the realm of chance or to be explained from the difference of theme. Indeed Sicily is mentioned in the *Odyssey* only in passages (v 383, ω 211, 366 ff.) which are clearly of later composition than most of the rest.   In Helbig's great work on the Homeric poems as elucidated by the monuments, the author declared that for his purposes he was obliged to treat

The laws of the epic verse were fixed very definitely in the Homeric period.   For example, a pause was favored *Laws of Epic* particularly between the two short syllables of *Poetry already* the third foot of the verse (as in the first verse *fixed in* of Longfellow's *Evangeline*, after " This is the *Homer's Time.* forest primeval "), but was never allowed in the same place in the fourth foot ; while a pause was approved at the close of the fourth foot, but forbidden at the close of the third foot.   The verse was clearly past the experimental stage, and the comparatively few deviations from the fixed practice which remain in our editions of the Homeric poems are chiefly due to errors in transmission, though they are partly to be ascribed to unreasonable applications of the principle of analogy by rhapsodists.   The Homeric poet was not " cabined, cribbed, confined " by such intricate rules as those of the Master-singers of Nuremberg, but he was an artist well trained in his art, following approved precedents, and he did not sing untaught, like a bird, simply because of his instinct, the spirit of song within him.   He was not such an untrained and unreflective child of nature as some have thought him.   Many generations of less skilful singers had preceded him.   The certainty of the laws of Homeric verse is particularly marked when we contrast the distinct development of the laws of the Latin hexameter as this is used by Ennius, Cicero, Vergil, and Ovid, and as we observe the individuality of the verse of Theocritus.

The *Iliad* and the *Odyssey* are surely not due to a single poet in the sense in which *Paradise Lost* and *Paradise* *The Iliad* *Regained* are the work of John Milton, and a *a Combination* third of a century ago, most scholars who were *of separate* considered to be entitled to an opinion on the *Songs ?* subject, believed with Lachmann that the *Iliad* was made up of a number of originally independent lays, skilfully united, but still showing to a careful observer the seams of juncture.   Of recent years, however, scholars are abandoning the view of Lachmann, and believe in the organic

the poems as a unit.   Several years ago, however, he stated that in the forthcoming third edition of his work, he would distinguish between passages of earlier and later composition, as containing earlier and later customs.   But this new edition has not appeared.

development of the Homeric poems rather than in their formation by a "fortuitous concourse of atoms." Many are now ready even to accept the necessary inference from the principle that a great poem implies a great poet, though no one doubts that the poet whom the Greeks and we call Homer used with absolute freedom the poetic material which he in common with other bards had inherited, and which had been gathering for generations by a process of gradual accretion, and that additions were made to the poem by his successors. Some of the apparent sutures, indicated chiefly by slight inconsistencies, may be due not so much to the original lack of finish at the junctures, as to the fact that the poems were long sung as separate lays, selected according to the special occasion by the bard, or as desired by the hearers, and that the rhapsode made slight modifications of his text at the beginning and the close of his recitation in order to give to his story greater completeness and independence of form.[1] Certain other changes may have been made to adapt the lay more perfectly to the audience or to the occasion on which it was sung. The poems were thus in a manner "sung to pieces," rather than composed separately and stitched together. How thoroughly the poet, whom we may call Homer, revised and digested and modified and used the epic material which he inherited, of course no one can say, but the stamp of a great personality seems to lie upon each of the two great poems. These poems have such unity as cannot easily be explained if they are the work of several poets. Pains are taken in advance to arouse the hearer's sympathy for Hector, and to justify the slaughter of Penelope's suitors. But during recent years, scholars have been so busy in searching for proofs of the different authorship of different parts of the poems that they have overlooked indications of unity of purpose, of spirit, and of execution.[2]

For centuries, more than seven cities, among which

---

[1] With this we may compare the slight changes, additions in particular, made at the beginning of the ecclesiastical *pericopae* or Scripture lessons, in order to secure a better opening for the passage read.

[2] For the latest, and an admirable, defense of the unity of the Homeric poems, see Blass, *Interpolationen der Odyssee*, Halle, 1905.

Smyrna and Chios were prominent, contended for the honor of being Homer's birthplace. But scholars no longer ask where Homer was born,—the poet maintains his impersonality too perfectly to encourage this question,—but where

Aeolic Source of Greek Epic Poetry. Greek epic poetry had its rise and development. This seems to have been on the slopes of Mount Olympus, the seat of the gods, near Mt. Ossa and Mt. Pelion, not far from the home of Peleus and Achilles. There, in Pieria, the Muses were born. The germ of the epic went with the Aeolians to Asia Minor, but here the art passed to the Ionians, who perfected it. Why the cause of this expedition should be the rape of Helen, a Spartan woman, and why the commander-in-chief should be the king of Mycenae, are not explained on this hypothesis, however, unless in these matters the poet was simply following tradition. Many dialectic peculiarities of the Homeric poems are explained most easily on the theory that phrases and epithets of the old Aeolic material were preserved in the early form because they could not readily be transferred into Ionic metrical equivalents. The dialect of the poems as we have them is not such as was ever spoken by any people. This linguistic fact of itself would refute the view, which for a time was popular, that the poems were composed by the people rather than by a poet. Some of the peculiarities of dialect, however, may be explained not so well by the use of still earlier material nor by the oral transmission of the poems by successive generations of rhapsodists, as by the life of the bard, wandering from land to land and desiring to appear nowhere as a complete stranger. The fact that not only the personality but even the country of the poet, is not indicated in the poems, may be explained if we think of him as without strong local attachments, a man who did not care to glorify one land or tribe and revile another. Such a bard might have won for himself familiarity with the geography of Greece and with local stories ; though born and trained in Asia Minor, he might be no stranger even to the western coast of Peloponnesus and the island of Ithaca. The bard is mentioned (ρ 385), with the seer, the surgeon, and the carpenter, as one who might be called from one

town or settlement to another, sure of a welcome everywhere.

In early historical times several of the noble or princely
families of Asia claimed descent from Homeric warriors, and
we may suppose the Homeric poems to have
been sung and honored particularly at these *Early*
Audiences
courts. Not impossibly some of the neighbors of *for Homer.*
these families were the avowed descendants of
the Trojan royal family, and cherished the old traditions
and the newly composed lays. These courts supplied
audiences which were often at leisure to listen to such
poems. In democratic times and countries such audiences
could be had only on festival days. That a bard seldom
could have an opportunity to recite so long a poem as the
Odyssey, is no argument against his composing such a poem
for his own satisfaction and that of those who listened to
him often enough to have familiarity with it as a whole,
but he would be encouraged and stimulated by the audiences
at the courts of Asiatic princes.

The question is raised with much persistency, and often
with the implication of a negative answer, whether we have
a right to assume that the epic poet is telling of
life as it appeared to his own eyes. The life and *Did the Poet*
tell of the Life
culture of his poems, some urge, may be just as *which he saw?*
unreal as the Chimaera dire or the Cyclops
Polyphemus, and we may no more expect to find the
customs of his time mirrored in the poet's page, than to
identify the cobbler who stitched the leathern bag in which
Aeolus imprisoned his winds for the safety of Odysseus.
Homer's aim and work were not to instruct but to please
even his own hearers,—in this Eratosthenes was right as
against the geographer Strabo (7 c). Still less did the poet
think of teaching archaeologists who were to live nearly
three thousand years after him. His poems were composed
for his contemporaries, not for the present generation ; and
for us, some say, they have no value as a source of archaeological knowledge.

Some scholars are inclined to treat the archaeological
element in the Homeric poems as quite as likely to be
due to the imagination of the poet as the narrative itself.

This view seems clearly wrong.   The poems contain mythical, historical, and imaginative, as well as archaeological, elements. The three former cannot easily be distinguished from each other, but they can be separated from what is archaeological. One scholar thinks Agamemnon to have been a form of Zeus, a second holds him to have been a Thessalian prince, another believes him to be the invention of the poet, as truly as Mr. Pickwick and Sam Weller were the products of Dickens' imagination ; while a fourth scholar, a peer of the other three, would not be surprised by the discovery of evidence that Agamemnon was the name of an actual king of Mycenae who led a military expedition against Ilium. At present each of these scholars has fair grounds for his opinion and no one can determine positively which is right, though a scholar may be satisfied for himself.   No device has been found for the separation of the mythical from the historical, and even sceptical critics who believe that Agamemnon was a Lacedaemonian god, still think that the name of Priam may be historical, while others who hold that Agamemnon was a historical character, accept the view that Helen was transferred from the company of divinities to that of mortal women.   Much that was originally mythical may later have been stripped of its mythical character.   But with regard to Agamemnon's armor, dress, and way of life, we may expect to reach a more stable

How much is True ? position.   We cannot determine indeed how much of the Homeric story itself is truth and how much is fiction.   That cities of wealth and power and similar civilization are proved to have existed at the same time on the sites of Troy and Mycenae, near the close of the second millenium B.C., certainly lends strong support to the belief that the war of which Homer sings was an actual war, really fought.   The general credibility of Hellenic tradition has been further increased in recent years by finding that the king of Cretan Cnosus had quite as much wealth and power as Thucydides seems to assume for Minos ; and in lesser matters, the American excavations at the Argive Heraeum confirm the old tales of the importance of the worship of the Argive Hera, and our excavations of twenty years ago at Icaria have made easy the belief in the old stories about Thespis of Icaria as the founder of the Greek drama. Doubtless the Homeric poet would have been greatly surprised if he had been told that Helen was the Dawn, and that Hector and Paris were demons of Darkness. But this thought removes the difficulty only a step further from us : perhaps Homer himself was as unable as we are to separate the mythical in his story from the historical and from that which had been added by the free imagination of earlier bards.

Must we acknowledge also that we cannot separate the archaeological from the imaginative and mythical elements? The question has importance.

With regard to the picture of life presented by the Homeric poems, three views are possible :

First, that the poet, conscious of his office to please rather than to instruct, depicted a life such as *Three Views* had never been on land or sea, drawing from his *of the Homeric* imagination his colours as well as his forms. His *Picture of* hearers were pleased with accounts of Utopia. The *Life.* very oddity and novelty of the life depicted added interest to the story.

Second, that the poet painted the life of the earlier generation of which he had heard,—the generation which saw the fall of Troy and knew Odysseus.

Or, third, that the poet represented the life which was familiar to himself and his hearers. Each action, each event might be given by tradition, or might be the product of the poet's imagination, but the details which show the customs of the age, and which furnish the colors for the picture, are taken from the life of the poet's time. His interest is centred in the action of the story, and the introduction of unusual manners and standards of life would only distract the attention of his hearers.

That the poet recognizes himself as of a later and degenerate age, as compared with his heroes, is *Poet* manifest. Nowhere does he claim direct or even *recognizes* indirect knowledge of the events which he nar- *Himself as of a* rates, but always he appeals to the Muse for *later Age.* inspiration and instruction. His eyes have not seen, and no forbears have told him of the Trojan war. He has heard his story from no survivor of the generation of those who fought on the shores of ·the Hellespont. No word of the poem implies that he has seen the Scaean Gate and the palace of Priam. The Muse herself tells the story, and the poet is but her mouthpiece. He begs her to tell of the wrath of Achilles (A 1), of the wanderings of Odysseus (α 1, 10), and of the forces before Troy (B 484), since "we mortals know nothing, but hear only report." Odysseus says to the bard Demodocus in the palace of the Phaeacian king, that " Apollo or the Muse must have taught him," for he sings so truly of the woes of the Achaeans (θ 488); he does not say that the bard must have known personally some veteran soldiers who had served in that war. Acknowledging the inferiority of his own generation, the poet speaks often of one of his heroes as doing what two men could not do, "such as men now are" (M 449), but he nowhere indicates the consciousness of a change of custom, as that one fashion of dress is newer or older than another, or that men used to wear different arms, or fight in a different way, or have a different form of government, or ever had other ways of worshipping the gods, or other standards of action.

Doubtless customs were changing. The Homeric kings no longer had the power of their predecessors in Greece who built

Change of Customs.

the fortresses of Mycenae and Tiryns. We may suppose the power to be passing from the kings to the nobles. Occasionally, Agamemnon arrogates to himself just as absolute power as a monarch ever had, while again he is simply first among his peers, and is rebuked in open council for proposing plans which are both foolish and cowardly. But this may indicate uncertainty in the position and authority of individual kings, rather than a distinct change in their relation to the nobles during the period of the composition of the Homeric lays. Some scholars have claimed to discern a change of custom with regard to dowry and wedding gifts, discussed in connexion with Penelope and her suitors; but if such a difference of custom existed, it may have been local rather than temporal. In Greece, as well as elsewhere, we may believe copper and bronze to have been used before iron for tools and arms, but we are not justified in judging to be of late composition all passages which imply or clearly state the use of iron ; nor, conversely, may we believe with certainty that a passage is of early composition because in it bronze is said to be used and not iron. Both metals seem to have been in use during the Homeric period.

Against the first of the three views suggested, an important consideration offers itself at once, viz. : the general consistency of the views of life found in the Homeric poems. One action at times may seem inconsistent with *Consistency of Views of Life.* another, but, as we have already seen, we are as yet unable to say that one custom prevails in one part of the poems and another custom in another part of the poems. And the more poets we suppose to have had to do with the composition of the *Iliad* and *Odyssey*, the greater difficulty meets the assumption that all these poets united in making a consistent picture of an unreal life. Sir Thomas More and Dean Swift could draw consistent pictures separately of a wholly imaginary life, but for later writers to combine the stories of Lilliput and Utopia, without rewriting the stories or leaving very obvious seams, would not be easy, particularly with collaboration so indefinite as that of the Greek epic poets.

In this connexion we must observe that the Homeric pictures are not painted directly by descriptions such as More presents in his *Utopia*, and as Sir John *Painted Incidentally.* Maundeville gives of the several countries which he visits, but wholly incidentally. In order to form a clear picture of Homeric life, scattered hints or incidents have to be gathered from different parts of the poems. A recent writer has declared that Homer intentionally makes the home of Odysseus to be far ruder and less attractive than such a hall must have been ; the Ithacans, on this theory, are falsely represented as semi-barbarians, just as Odysseus himself, several centuries later, is depreciated and treated with contempt in the Attic drama. We must bear in mind, however, that a certain amount of rudeness of life is entirely consistent with a kind of magnificence,— for even in Asia Minor in the time of Mimnermus, guests at an Ionian banquet apparently felt free to drop upon the floor any bones from their meat and other refuse from their food ; and we must remember also that the house of Odysseus, although it is large, is but a country farm-house, and is nowhere stated to have such splendor as the palace of Menelaus,—Telemachus and Nestor's son are fairly dazzled by the radiance of the Spartan palace.   But observe how widely scattered are the details from which we must gather our pictures of the rudeness of Odysseus's house.   Within the courtyard, before the door of the house, Penelope's suitors flayed goats and singed swine (β 299) ; not far away, also in front of the house, was a heap of manure (on which the dog Argos lay) waiting to be carried to the fields (ρ 291). In this courtyard (σ 105), Odysseus leaned the beggar Irus against the outer wall, and put in his hand a stick, that with this he might " keep off both swine and dogs,"—clearly implying that swine were wandering there at large.   The night before his slaughter of Penelope's suitors, Odysseus slept on an untanned ox-hide, which he found in the court (υ 2, 96).   The goats and the cow which were brought for the suitors' feasts were bound in the corridor (υ 176, 189). One of the suitors, Ctesippus, took a hoof of an ox from a basket by his side, as he sat feasting in the great hall, and hurled it at the disguised Odysseus (υ 299).   Raw meat seems to have been at hand in the hall, for the suitors, dazed by Athena, ate meat mingled with blood ($\alpha\grave{\iota}\mu o\phi\acute{o}\rho\upsilon\kappa\tau a$, υ 348), i.e. took up uncooked flesh instead of a roasted portion.   The herald Medon wrapped himself in an ox-hide in the hall (χ 362), while Odysseus was slaying the suitors ; and this hide must have been lying on the floor.   That the floor of the hall was not kept neat is indicated further by the act of the maids in the evening after Penelope's suitors have departed,—the women throw upon the floor ($\chi a\mu\acute{a}\delta\iota\varsigma$ $\beta\acute{a}\lambda o\nu$, τ 63) the ashes and coals from the basins or torch-holders.   That the hall of the house had no floor of wood or stone, is shown first by the act of Telemachus in digging a trench there for the purpose of setting up the axes which were to serve as a mark in the contest of archery (ϕ 120), and again by the manner of cleansing the great hall after the death of the suitors, when the upper part of the earth, which was stained and soaked by the suitors' blood, is removed with hoes (χ 455). Now if the poet had intended to call special attention to the rudeness and squalor of this house, he would not have been satisfied with scattering the details of his picture over books ii., xvii., xviii., xix., xx., xxi., and xxii. These traits are all incidental, and have to be collected by pedants in order to form the picture, and for our purpose this incidental testimony is more, not less, trustworthy than direct evidence. When the old priest Chryses prays to Apollo for vengeance upon the Greeks who refuse to restore to him his daughter, and asks the god to remember if ever his priest had roofed for him a pleasing temple or had burnt on his altars the fat thigh-pieces of bulls and of goats (A 39), this last incidental clause is completely satisfactory evidence both for the existence of temples in the poet's time, and for their being so small that the priest himself could roof them.[1] Another familiar example of the poet's indirect, incidental testimony to a custom is found in several of his epithets : *e.g.* when *Incidental Testimony of Epithets.* Hera is called white-armed (λευκώλενος, A 55), no one doubts that the Homeric dress of women left the arms bare ; and when Telemachus, on rising in the morning, binds his sandals under his sleek (λιπαροί, β 4) feet, the poet assumes that the uncovered feet were seen more generally than in our day. The poet assumes that his hearers are familiar with the ordinary form of the shield, the construction of the chariot, the manner of dress. As we must always remember, he does not describe,—he narrates,[2] and the charm of his story for his first hearers must have rested largely on their familiarity with the materials of which this tale is composed. Just such actions, under similar circumstances, many a one of them had beheld. The collection of the poet's indications of the life of his time has been left to scholars of the nineteenth and twentieth centuries. But though our picture of the life of the Homeric age is

---

[1] Of course the assistance of others for the roofing is not excluded, any more than for the sacrifices ; but the parallelism clearly implies that the roofing was a repeated act. (See p. 491.)

[2] The description of the Garden of Alcinoüs (η 103-131) is the only description in the poems, and as such has been suspected to be of late composition. In another form of the poems, this passage might have been put into the mouth of a speaker.

thus largely drawn from indirect evidence, this picture seems
to be even more complete than that of the life of the
ancient Hebrews which may be derived from the much more
voluminous Old Testament.

Closely akin to the argument which has just been presented,
is the consideration that a large part of the archaeological
Evidence from information to be found in the Homeric poems is
Comparisons. contained in the nearly three hundred comparisons,
drawn from all departments of life, which are
designed to throw into high relief some detail of the action
narrated, as where the seething of the waters of the Scamander
is compared to that of hog's fat in a kettle (Φ 362), or where
Achilles's horses trampling on the bodies and the armor of the
slain, are compared to cattle treading out the grain on a
threshing floor (Υ 495), or, again, where Achilles's grief at the
death of Patroclus is likened to that of a lion whose whelps
a hunter has stolen (Σ 318).

In its very nature a Homeric comparison, like the parables
of the New Testament, is intended to throw light from the more
Comparisons familiar upon what is less familiar.   The poet
throw Light cannot intend to illustrate the moderately familiar
from the more by what is wholly strange.   Where the Trojans
Familiar. are described as following their leader just as sheep
follow the ram of the flock (N 492), or where Athena turns
the arrow of Pandarus aside from Menelaus as a mother
brushes away a fly from her sleeping infant (Δ 130), or where
Achilles says that Patroclus weeps as a little girl who runs
by her mother's side, clinging to her gown and begging to
be taken up in her arms (II 8), or where Ajax yields only
slowly before the Trojans, as a stubborn ass, on whose back
many sticks have been broken, leaves a cornfield only when
his appetite is sated, though he is assailed by small boys
with clubs (Λ 558), or where Paris, at sight of Menelaus on
the field of battle, starts back as a man starts back at the
sight of a serpent on the mountain, while Menelaus is gladdened
at sight of Paris as a hungry lion on finding a stag or wild
goat (Γ 33),—in these instances and dozens like them we
can have no doubt that what is used as an illustration was
well known to the hearer.   The fact that the ass is not
mentioned elsewhere by the poet, would not cause us to

doubt the existence of that animal in Greek lands, even if mules were not named often. But if we believe that in the examples cited the poet is using familiar illustrations, then we may reasonably hold also that since the poet compares Menelaus's fair skin, with the blood from his wound flowing over it, to an ivory cheek-piece for horses, stained with crimson by a skilful woman of Maeonia or Caria (Δ 141), the poet and his hearers had seen not only ivory but also ivory cheek-pieces for horses, and that Carian and Maeonian women were known to be skilled in the decoration of these. So also when Homer compares the stanching of Ares's wound to the curdling of milk by the use of the sap of the wild fig tree (E 902), we need not doubt that many of the bard's hearers had seen milk curdled and cheese made by that process. To say that the waters of the Scamander seethed like lard boiling in a kettle (Φ 362), would be entirely absurd,—certainly contrary to all our notions of the principles of the natural epic,—if the hearers had never seen or heard of lard thus boiling. That a thing or a custom appears only in a comparison, and not in the action of the poems, does not prove that it belonged only to the poet's age and not also to that of his heroes. For example, lions are mentioned in comparisons thirty times in the *Iliad*, but naturally do not appear in the action, which has no place for them, and no one dreams that lions became more numerous in Greece or Asia Minor after the Trojan War. And why and where should the process of trying hog's fat have a place in the action? The same is true of many other matters. Only in the case of an article or custom which naturally would appear in the action of the story, such as the trumpet (which appears only in a comparison, Σ 219, and in a verb, Φ 388), has the negative argument considerable weight.

That all Homeric peoples are represented as having the same customs, has been observed already. Only one exception is obvious, out of fairy land,—the Hippemolgi who *Customs the* live on mare's milk (N 5). Even in fairyland the *same in all* exceptions are not very many,—the Lotus Eaters *Lands.* who are vegetarians (ι 84), the Laestrygonians, who are cannibals (κ 116), and the Cyclopes, who are savages and have no government (ι 106). The poet does not declare indeed, that all customs of all men agree, just as he does not assert that all men have but one language ; but just as the Trojan Priam is represented as talking with the Achaean Achilles, without embarrassment from lack of an interpreter, and the Lycian Glaucus converses with the Argive Diomed, and even Odysseus with the Cyclops Polyphemus, so, on his wanderings, Odysseus is never struck by difference of customs, whether among the Phaeacians or at Circe's palace, though difference of splendor is noted.   He " learns the mind of many men," as he sees their cities, but he does not learn of new forms of government, nor of new forms of architecture, nor of new manners of worshipping the gods.   That the culture of the Trojans cannot be distinguished from that of the Achaeans is an old remark.   Even the customs of the gods are like those of men, though for half-a-dozen objects their vocabulary differs.   The gods have not only human weaknesses and passions but human fashions and standards.   Since men mix their wine with water, the gods dilute their nectar (ϵ 93). The dress of the gods and their armor seem to agree with those of men.   Even the water-nymphs have looms and weave (ν 107), though they might seem the last persons in the world to need garments, and to have ordinary feminine occupations. Old critics tried to maintain that the Trojans are represented as less civilized than the Achaeans, but their chief arguments were but three ; firstly, that the Trojans advanced to battle with a cry, while the Achaeans came on in silence (Γ 2),— though elsewhere the Achaeans are " good at the war-cry " ; secondly, that Priam did not allow his people to weep for their dead when these were taken up from the plain (H 427),—as if they would go to excess in their emotion if they were not repressed entirely ; and, lastly, that Priam is a polygamist,— but he is the only polygamist in Troy, too.   Another point has been considered sometimes : the sacrifice of horses to a Trojan river-god is once mentioned (Φ 132), but this too is unique for the Trojans as well as in the poems.   These three or four are the only indications which have been found of a difference of culture between Argos and Troy, and scholars of to-day would lay little stress on such evidence.   This apparent agreement of customs in the different Homeric peoples is altogether natural, since to the poet the action was everything, and all else had importance simply as it illustrated this. He cared nothing for "local color,"—and if he did not value *local* color, why should he have heeded *temporal* color, and carefully have avoided anachronisms?

A special argument against considering Homer an archaeologist, is the remark that while he is artistic, he is never artificial, as in his age he would need to be if he *Homer is* were to avoid systematically the mention of what *never* was familiar to his contemporaries. The fact that *Artificial.* much in the poems is conventional, does not indicate that it was untrue to the life of his day. The manner of his references to customs and life generally, differs widely from those of Apollonius Rhodius and of Vergil, both of whom were in a sense archaeologists, with the desire to paint pictures of an age of which they had only literary knowledge. The later poets desired to follow the earlier in archaeological as well as in philological matters, but in both alike they proved themselves mere imitators. Thus, in his references to customs, Vergil is commonly either laboriously explicit or else vague. His remark with regard to the Italian name of reefs (*altars*,— *saxa vocant Itali . . . aras, Aen.* I. 109) is foisted into the story, delaying the narrative, for which it has no value. Thus, a few verses later (I. 318) Venus is described with more detail than Homer would have used, with quiver on her shoulder, hair floating in the breeze, and garments so girt as to leave her knee bare. But between these two passages, a sentence with regard to the bronze kettles placed on the shore in preparation for a long-delayed meal, is too indefinite to be interesting; Vergil does not tell us, as Homer would have done, what was cooked in these kettles,—whether vegetables, fish, fowl, or flesh. Thus also Apollonius of Rhodes, learned in archaeology as well as in philology, while almost painfully elaborate in some descriptions, fairly forgets to give to his readers clear indications of the ordinary course of his heroes' life. In his story, indeed, the Argonauts seem to care little for either food or sleep; not infrequently they row all night long, they are without water for twelve days, and no particular kind of food but mutton appears to be mentioned in the long poem. Like Vergil, Apollonius gives comparatively little incidental archaeological information. If one tries to form a view of life in the

heroic age according to either of these learned poets, he will
secure but a dull picture, with many broad gaps.

Bearing in mind our observation that the Homeric poet uses
his references to customs of life chiefly as by-work for his
story, to brighten and illustrate his narratives of action, we
may find a positive argument for the third of the possibilities
presented,—viz. that the poet paints a picture of the life of his
own time,—in the manner of painters at a simple stage of
culture. The Greek vase painters of the classical period used

The Manner of Early Painters. the dress and manners of their own time in depicting scenes of the heroic age,—a custom which, as
we have seen, misled many modern scholars. Thus
also the illustrations of Vergil and Terence published
in the fifteenth and early sixteenth centuries, may be (and
generally are) particularly interesting as representations of the
dress, manners, and architecture of the age of the artist,—not
of the classical period. A German engraver of that time
would give to the Athens of Pericles, Gothic cathedrals and
German scenery, with inhabitants attired in German garb, while
a Dutch artist would give to the same city the general appearance of Leyden and Utrecht. Even Raphael depicted Plato in
the School of Athens with a folio book under his arm. In a
well-known edition of Terence, printed at Strasburg in 1496,
the scenery is made more natural to the reader by the introduction of a little wayside shrine with a crucifix, just such as
the traveller still sees in southern Germany or the Tyrol.
Woodcuts in editions of Vergil published four centuries ago
show very slight effort to recall the scenes at Troy and at
Carthage, such as archaeologists would depict them now. One
woodcut even introduces a cannon into the heroic age. An
old set of illustrations to Ovid shows a great four-poster bed,
such as are preserved in castles and museums, but had not
been invented in Ovid's time. The woodcuts which illustrate
a German translation of the historical work of Diodorus Siculus,
exhibit the Amazons in their conflicts with the Greeks as
carrying German lances and wearing the garb of German
peasant women of the sixteenth century of our era. Doubtless
no one of these artists supposed that his picture was historically
correct, but, like Homer, he was more interested in the action
which he was depicting than in any archaeological details.

The early American illustrator of Milton's *Paradise Lost* who represented the fallen angels as clad like British red-coats while the heavenly host wore the garb of the Continental army, was neither jesting nor so ignorant as to believe the angelic hosts to have been so arrayed,—he was catering to the tastes of his patrons; and after all is this much worse than the representation of the archangel Raphael "in the tilting garb of a knight of the fourteenth century"? And a high authority recently has called attention to the absurdities of the equipment of King Arthur's knights in both poetry and painting. The engraver's habit to which reference is made, is most familiar to us in Biblical scenes. For these, artists for the most part have now adopted conventional dress and architecture, but in early times of art, local usages prevailed. For instance, a Dutch painter would depict a thoroughly Dutch Ishmael in the costume of the small boy of the painter's period and country, while a Roman painter would make an Italian of the outcast. Many a "Holy Family" in the art galleries of Europe shows the dress and furniture of the artist's day and country. Only within recent years has an earnest effort been made to attain historical and archaeological accuracy in depicting Biblical scenes, and even now no such picture with archaeological truth would be used as an ordinary aid to devotion. Why not? Simply because the strangeness of the dress or of the other surroundings distracts the mind from the real motive and subject of the picture. A realistic painting of Christ before the judgment-seat of Pilate, depicting with perfect accuracy the dress of the Roman soldiers and the Jewish onlookers, may be impressive, but it calls the beholder's attention to a dozen other things than the central figure, and would draw his mind away from the scene as he had pictured it. Just so, if Homer had depicted a life of Greeks, and yet a life markedly different from that of his own day, the attention of his hearers would have been distracted from that which he thought of prime moment to that which was to him merely incidental,—from the chief action to the background or setting of the picture. The poet would in this manner have confused and darkened his story and not enlightened it. Thus even if he himself had been familiar with a difference of customs, he would not have assumed this knowledge on the part of his hearers, and would have avoided drawing their attention away from what was of primary interest to both, the events which he was narrating. No one would argue seriously that the poet and his hearers cared more for the very scattered hints of customs to be found in his story than they did for the deeds of which he told.

But analogies for our argument may be drawn not merely from the painter's art in simple times, but also from classical *Analogies from Classical Literature.* Greek literature. The Athenian dramatists are not sticklers for archaeological accuracy nor for exact local coloring. Just as Aeschylus ascribes Athenian customs to the Persians, and represents these as worshipping Greek divinities, and even gives to many of them good Greek names, so he gives to his heroes of the war before Thebes devices for their shields (which were unknown to the Homeric period), ascribes a democratic polity to the gods of Olympus, and makes even the ocean nymphs familiar with the art of writing. Evidently he takes no pains to secure archaeological accuracy. In Sophocles, the story of the death of Agamemnon's son in the Pythian games is offered as reasonable, although all the spectators knew that these games were instituted only a century or so before the time of Sophocles, instead of five hundred years earlier, in the time of the Trojan War; and at these games two Libyans are represented as contending in the horse-race,—coming from a city which was founded long after the Trojan War and the death of Orestes. Euripides makes Phaedra write a note to explain her suicide, and makes Medea complain that women must buy themselves husbands, or, as she puts it, they buy themselves masters. But in Medea's day, brides, not husbands, were bought, and though an art of writing was known in Phaedra's time, women were not likely to use it for their communications. Indeed, the spirit of the age of Pericles is manifest frequently in the tragedies of Euripides, although the action of the drama is supposed to lie in the remote past. All are familiar with Shakespeare's contempt for anachronisms and his disregard of local color, which went so far as to allow modern time-pieces to the ancient Romans. And Vergil, though something of an archaeologist, did not shrink from making his warriors use battering rams and storming-ladders. Were Homer's hearers more reflective, learned, and archaeological than Shakespeare's and Vergil's? Why should we suppose that the Homeric poet took more pains than Aeschylus, Vergil, the poets of the Nibelungenlied, and Shakespeare, to secure an exact reproduction of the customs of the age of his warriors?

Analogy, then, does not encourage us to believe that the Homeric poet was an archaeologist, composing a species of historical novel, and carefully refraining from the introduction of any kind of anachronistic arms or *Homer not an Archaeologist.* customs,—not mentioning the art of writing, just as one of our own generation would not mention the use of telephone or telegraph in composing a story of the Revolutionary War. That he does not picture such a dismal country life as Hesiod knew in Boeotia, is not important for our purpose. The difference between the spirit and tone of the *Iliad* and *Odyssey* on the one hand, and of the *Works and Days* of Hesiod on the other, lies not so much in the changed conditions of Greece, nor, as is often said, with the audience—that one sings for warriors and chieftains, while the other sings for hard-working peasants,—as in the poets themselves. The temper of Hesiod was soured by his disappointments,—as truly as that of Archilochus was embittered by his rejection by his mistress's father,—and by his life in Ascra, which was "miserable in winter, wretched in summer, and never good" (*Works*, 640), while the Homeric poet in general is buoyantly optimistic in spite of a very few pessimistic sayings which are put into the mouths of his characters when these are in dire distress. The life of Hesiod's farmer seems much more wretched to us, since Hesiod himself hated it so bitterly. How is the Homeric Eumaeus, the "divine swineherd," better off? Yet the latter complains only of the troubles caused by the absence of Odysseus and the presence of Penelope's suitors,—not of his being made a slave, nor of his hard work, nor of his plain fare. He makes no hardship of taking a sharp javelin and his goatskin cloak, and leaving his hut in order to sleep near his swine, as their guard on a stormy night, and he does not grumble over the lack of chairs, bed, table, or other furnishings for his hut.

Quite as noteworthy as the sordid nature of the life depicted in Hesiod's poem in comparison with the largeness of heart of the Homeric heroes, is the impersonality of Homer in contrast with the distinct personality of Hesiod. We should expect only a limited audience to be interested in the latter's accounts of his quarrels with his brother and of his failures in his law-suits. The personality of the poet is as distinct in his verses as in those of the iambic and lyric poets, Archilochus, Hipponax, Stesichorus, and Timocreon. Hesiod was a prophet rather than a popular poet, while Greeks of all classes and of all times listened gladly to Homer.

True it is that while the Homeric poet tells of, or at least alludes to, nearly every side and department of human

Homeric Poems, and Princes.

life, yet his poems have to do chiefly with princes and kings. The life of the ordinary plain farmer or shepherd is not depicted quite so distinctly as that of the nobles, except in the case of the swine-herd Eumaeus,—just as in the Homeric battles, the common soldier is a forgotten man, on whom the failure or the success of the expedition does not depend. But even in comparatively recent times our histories, for whatever readers designed, were chiefly accounts of wars and dynasties, and only of late years has more attention been paid to the history of the life of the people. We need not wonder, then, that in the Homeric poems the palaces of the Phaeacian and Spartan kings are presented to the hearer in fuller detail than the country home of the old Laërtes. The inventory of Laërtes's cabin and of Eumaeus's hut would have been brief, and yet the poet interests his hearers in the life and personality of the swine-herd and of Laërtes on his farm. That Homer calls the swine-herd "godlike," does not indicate that his hearers had contempt for swine-herds and other common men. Doubtless many, if not most, of his hearers were common men, though as few "peasants" could be found in a Homeric community as in Scottish Perthshire.

While we bear in mind the truth that not all Homeric verses are of the same age, we must remember also that in primitive times customs change very slowly, and in par-ticular that in Asia Minor these changes in many details have been slight in the last three thousand years, although the region has been overrun by many armies.   Only a couple of hours by railway train from Smyrna, ploughs of the same pattern and manufacture as in Homer's day are still in use, and a little further to the *In primitive* interior the ordinary bread is still of the Homeric *Life, Customs* *change slowly.* order, and meat is sold at railway stations, served on just such spits as we may suppose Achilles to have used. Henry Clay Trumbull has shown the persistence of old customs of daily life in Palestine, and Samuel Ives Curtiss has proved the survival there of very old, indeed primitive, Semitic beliefs and religious practices.   The outward life of an Arab sheikh is very much like that of his predecessor, the patriarch Abraham, and the Wallachian shepherds of to-day live much in the same way as the Homeric Cyclopes.   The necessity for supposing rapid changes in the manners of life in the early ages is less, also, since scholars are allowed indefinite time for the development of civilization from barbarism, and since the remains of the fifth millenium B.C. show a condition of life with arts not very different from what had been assumed for the beginning of the first millenium B.C.   Of gradual changes no tradition is preserved in a simple state of society.   Most of the old farmers of New England would say that they speak exactly the same dialect now as fifty years ago, although the changes may have been considerable.

When epic poetry passed from the Aeolians to the Ionians new manners may have been introduced into the life represented in the poems, but no proof of this has been found.   No one, I think, has even seriously *Aeolian and* suggested that one custom may have been Ionian *Ionian* *Customs.* and another Aeolian, except with regard to the form of the shield and the use of the cuirass, and for this the evidence is not yet convincing.   As has been remarked in another connexion, the suggestion that in the Aeolian form of the *Iliad*, Priam's palace stood on the summit of the Trojan citadel, while in the Ionian form, Athena has her temple there, is entirely unsupported by philological or archaeological evidence.

Next to the impersonality of the poems we may place their Pan-Hellenic, almost cosmopolitan character.   The poet

has no personal local patriotic prejudices.   In his accounts of
the battles on the plain of Troy, he is clearly a Greek ;
he thinks of himself as standing on the Achaean
Pan-Hellenic
Character of
the Poems.
side of the fight,—the left of the battle to him,
is the left of the Achaean line,—but many
readers of the *Iliad* have felt that his sympathy
was with Hector quite as strongly as with Achilles, and a
vigorous effort has been made to prove that he was a poet
at the court of the Trojan Priam.   Certainly no contrast
is noted as yet between the Greeks and all foreigners,[1] such
as was felt strongly in later times, and such as existed
between the Israelites and all other peoples.   And in Greece
itself, the poet shows no special local affection or interest.
He glorifies no particular people and has no enmities to
gratify.   His omission to record the home of the buffoon
Thersites is probably intentional ; none of the Greeks would
have been pleased if this disagreeable character had been
assigned to their country.   Old traditions and the dialect
of the poems are the only evidence that epic poetry had
its development in Asia Minor rather than on the mainland
of Greece.   Even the great critic Aristarchus believed that
Homer was an Athenian.

Long ago attention was called by scholars to the impropriety
of drawing important inferences from the Homeric poet's failure
to mention a certain thing or custom.   One quarter
Inferences
ex Silentio.
of the vocabulary of the poems is said to be made
up of words which are used but once by the poet.
This of itself indicates the large element of chance, and the
possibility that some of these words might not have been used,
while the names of just as familiar articles in fact have been
omitted.   Many words of common life must have been of a
metrical form either impossible or inconvenient for the verse.
But recently attention has been called anew to Homer's
"silences," and to the danger of assuming that he did not
know a custom or a thing simply because he does not mention
it,—and this in connexion with the view which has regained
credence, that the poems were not "composed by the people,"
as one scholar would put it, but by a poet who was fully
conscious of his art.   For example, the art (or, *an* art) of

[1] This remark is made by Thucydides, οὐ μὴν οὐδὲ βαρβάρους εἴρηκε κτλ., i. 3. 3.

writing was known in Greek lands long before Homer's day, but only once (Z 169) does he refer to it. There the reference is distinct enough, a folded tablet *The Art of* is given with "destructive signs," as a letter of *Writing* introduction with instructions to kill the bearer, *mentioned but* a "Uriah's letter," as the Germans say; the poet *once.* here does not avoid the mention of an art of writing. The art was known, indeed, but how much was it used except for records and commercial purposes? No one can tell.

Philologists are familiar with the fact that Demosthenes and the other Attic orators rarely appeal to historical documents, but often to oral tradition. Aeschines refers to the stories which his very aged father had told him of the past, rather than to the records in the Metroüm or to the histories of Herodotus and Thucydides. Yet in that fourth century B.C. the Athenians seem actually fond of writing. Herodotus himself rarely refers to written sources of information. He tells his tale as it was told to him, with no references to chapter and verse for his authority, and generally implying that he heard his story, and did not read it. This is his manner. We need not infer that he was consciously and intentionally ignoring the annalists who were his predecessors, and that he saw no records on skin, bronze, or stone.

The art of writing was well known in England centuries before King Alfred's time, but doubtless few of his knights made use of it. That no letter was sent from Troy to Greece, or was brought from Greece to Troy, during the ten years' war, need excite no more surprise than the failure to send a messenger, since there was no postal service.[1] The Crusaders lived in an age of clerks, but they sent few letters from Palestine to their homes, and seem to have made slight use of the art of writing. Though they occupied Palestine for many years, they left few inscriptions behind them. But no scholar now would set the Trojan War before the age of the palace of Cnosus in which thousands of written documents are found. The art of writing was known, then, not merely in

---

[1] Possibly this lack of connexion between Greece and the camp before Troy, in the Homeric story, may be taken as another indication that in the original form of the story the war was not of ten years' duration. (See page 571.)

the poet's own age, but also in that of his warriors and his warriors' grandfathers. What motive could he have had for the intentional omission of the mention of this art?

Similarly, we are told that coined money was known in Homer's day, but that he passes it by in silence in order to give to his story a more antique coloring. *Coined Money in Homer's Day.* Probably the "talent of gold" of which the poet speaks (Ψ 269, 751) was a Babylonian shekel, and here he recognizes a money standard of value. But neither gold nor silver was coined in Greece until long after his day, and even if foreign coins were known to the Homeric Achaeans, no evidence is offered that they were the ordinary medium of exchange in Hellas. Since the Greeks of that time had no money of their own, the poet may have been quite accurate in representing ordinary trade as barter. Indeed, this is altogether probable. Recent examples furnish American illustrations. In his *Winning of the West*, President Roosevelt writes: " In the backwoods . . . there was hardly any money at all. Transactions were accomplished chiefly by the primeval method of barter. . . . Among the articles which were enumerated as being lawfully payable for taxes were bacon at sixpence a pound, rye whiskey at two shillings and sixpence a gallon, peach or apple brandy at three shillings per gallon, and country-made sugar at one shilling per pound. *Skins, however, formed the ordinary currency* ; otter, beaver, and deer being worth six shillings apiece, and raccoon and fox one shilling and threepence." In this instance shillings and pence were the standard, but this was simply by the force of long tradition, such as that which kept cattle as the standard of value according to the Homeric story. Even in the country towns of Northern Ohio, little more than half a century ago, the amount of cash money in circulation was absolutely insignificant. The farmers brought their produce to the " general store," and received in return the manufactured articles which they required. They " swapped " farms or cattle or produce with each other, equalizing the values not by payments of money but by smaller articles " given to boot." Even now country newspapers advertise many opportunities for exchange, and often receive farm-produce in payment for subscriptions. A

similar state of things still exists in large sections of the
Southern United States, where the negroes have no money
but only accounts at the country store. No one need wonder,
then, that the Achaean warriors,—who received no pay of any
kind, nor even rations, but in compensation for their services
were allowed to plunder freely,—bought wine "some with
bronze, others with bright iron, others with hides, others with
cattle themselves, and others with slaves" (H 472). The
inference that the poet here intentionally avoids the mention
of coined money, is entirely unsound.

Another matter of which Homer's real ignorance is doubted,
is cavalry. He certainly may have known the use of mounted
warriors, although the passages in the poems which
are cited as evidence of this knowledge (ι 49, Λ 51) *Absence of Cavalry.*
are not clear witnesses. But why any one should
care to substitute in his poems cavalry for chariots, is not
obvious. Certainly chariots were used in Greece in the
Mycenaean period. Only "one who was maintaining a thesis"
would interpret otherwise the familiar Mycenaean tombstones,
on which the chariot cut on the stone is thought to indicate
the knightly rank of the man buried beneath it. And the
network of ancient roads about Mycenae seems to have been
intended for wheeled vehicles, since narrower paths would
have sufficed for pack animals and for ordinary expeditions
on foot. The use of the chariot in the national games of
Greece has fairly been considered another indication, as well as
the analogies of Egypt and Asia, of its early employment in
Hellenic wars. Some scholars, indeed, believe that chariots
were used in battle by Thebans and other Greeks until
near the close of the sixth century B.C.

The absence from the Homeric poems of any devices on
the shields, such as were usual if not universal in later Greece,
cannot prove the poet's conscious effort to avoid
the mention of what was familiar to him. Such *No Devices on Shields.*
arguments clearly are of little value, unless both
the poet's knowledge can be shown and a motive assigned for
the omission.

The silence of the Homeric poet with regard to Phoenician
trading stations in Greece is curious, but may not be interpreted as an indication of his desire to give antique color

to his poems.   The burden of proof still rests on those
who maintain that such stations existed in the poet's time.

Phoenician Trading Stations. Archaeological excavations as yet have not supported the belief in ancient Phoenician settlements
on the shores of Greece.   But why should the
poet shrink from mentioning such trading-posts if
he knew them?   He has no hesitation in telling of this work
or that, of art, as brought by the Sidonians.   The Phoenicians
are indeed the typical traders of the poems, mentioned without
reserve, and the wares which they brought were in high repute.
And if the Phoenicians had no stations in Greece in the twelfth
century B.C., about the time set for the Trojan War, they were
not likely to be there two or three centuries later, at the time
of the poet.   Similarly the poet shows no knowledge of
Phoenician trade routes by land, nor of Phoenician religious
rites as introduced into Greece.   That the Sidonians, but not
the younger Tyrians, are mentioned in the poems, is a common
observation, but only a daring spirit would assert that Homer
consciously avoided the mention of Tyre, though the lack of
such mention does not argue that Tyre had not been built.
Phoenicians were Sidonians to him, just as the Persians were
still "Medes" to the Greeks, long after the conquests and
death of Cyrus the Great.

Another matter in regard to which Homer is thought by
some consciously to present a picture at variance with his own
Seamanship in Homer. times, is the seamanship of the Greeks.   In this the
poems are entirely self-consistent.   No scene from
sea-life is wrought on the Shield of Achilles (Σ 483),
on which almost every human activity is represented.   The
wise Nestor needed a portent from the gods before he would
venture to sail across the Aegean Sea from Lesbos to the
southern point of Euboea,—a sail of about eighty miles, finally
accomplished in a long day, with land in sight all the way,—
instead of following the coast of Asia Minor to Cos, at its
south-west corner, and then the coast of Crete, to the west
(γ 170).   Agamemnon himself seems to have followed the
longer course (δ 514).   The Homeric mariners were accustomed to land every night for food and sleep (μ 284, ν 278).
Cape Malea at the south of Peloponnesus was dreaded by the
Homeric Greeks as Cape Horn was feared by the navigators

of two and three centuries ago.   This is not easily believed of
the Greeks of the ninth and eighth centuries B.C.   Shall we
then set Homer late, and say that he and his colleagues were
always mindful to represent their warriors as fearful sailors,
unlike themselves, or shall the poet rather be assigned to a
time when his contemporaries actually feared to round Cape
Malea?   The fleet of nearly twelve hundred boats sent against
Troy, has been urged as sufficient proof that the Achaeans were
good sailors, but philologists generally recognize the Catalogue
of the Ships, on the authority of which part of the poems alone
the notion of the large number rests, as of different, and probably of much later authorship than the bulk of the poems.

In connexion with seamanship may be mentioned the
doubts lately expressed whether Homer may not have known
much more of the lands near Greece than would
appear from his poems.   But Duncker long ago *Homer's*
called attention to the impossibility of a poet's *Knowledge of*
contracting the geographical field of his time.   If *Geography.*
Homer's hearers knew much about Egypt, it would have been
absurd for him to make Menelaus tell of the island Pharos (a
few rods from the site of Alexandria) as a day's sail from
Egypt (δ 355), or Achilles refer to Egyptian Thebes as having
one hundred gates with two hundred warriors coming forth
from each gate (I 383), when in truth it had no wall or gates
at all.   These misstatements prove the vagueness of the
information with regard to Egypt which had reached Greece.
If every hearer could correct the poet, the bard would indeed
have seemed ignorant, but this ignorance of the bard would
not have suggested to any one that the action of the poem
lay in a time when men had less geographical knowledge.
We may believe that the poet knew Smyrna, though he does
not mention it, but we need not hold that he carefully
suppressed all mention of that city.   The action of the story
does not require such mention.

Again, the poet seems to know few temples of the gods.
Only two of these appear directly in his story,
and that to which Chryses refers was hardly *Few Temples*
more than a wayside shrine.   Shall we say that *in Homer.*
the poet deliberately avoids the mention of such temples
as we have reason to believe existed in the eighth or

ninth century B.C., or that he lived earlier, or that archaeologists are mistaken in believing Greek temples to have
been built so early? With the temples may be classed
the great national festivals and oracles at Delphi and
Olympia. Two slight references are made to the Delphian
temple (I 404) and oracle (θ 80), with only a possible
hint of the games at Olympia (Λ 700). A distinguished
scholar seems to assume that if the Phaeacians held athletic
contests (θ 100), and the Achaeans had horse-races and
games in honor of Patroclus (Ψ 258), then the Olympian
festival must have been established already, and familiar to our
poet, but ignored by him. But if brave men lived before
Agamemnon, may not other contests have preceded those
at Olympia? Nothing assures us, or even indicates, that
informal athletic contests were not held elsewhere in Greece
until after the founding of the Olympian games. That in
later times Pelops or Heracles was called the founder of the
Olympian festival, certainly does not prove this to have existed
before the age of Homer.

More important in this connexion may be thought the
poet's omission to say anything about fetish-worship, of

*No Fetish-
Worship.* which many remains existed in Greece for a
thousand years after his time,—many a rude local
worship having a place in the life of the people by
the side of that of the great divinities. Shall we say that in
Asia Minor stocks and stones were not so freely accepted as in
Greece proper, as being the impersonation or abiding place
or representation of a divinity?

And shall we say the like with regard to the poet's omission
to recognize the worship of the dead,—that the Greeks in Asia

*Homeric
Beliefs in
regard to the
Dead.* Minor, having come to new homes, far from the
old tombs of their ancestors, left behind them their
superstitions, and in particular their old beliefs with
regard to the needs and the influence of the souls
of the dead? In general, beyond question, the soul of one
of Homer's warriors, at least after his body was cremated,
was thought not to "revisit the glimpses of the moon."
The Homeric dead had no power to harm or to help, and no
reason existed for propitiating them or for striving to please
them in any way. Only slight indications are found in the

poems of any sort of sacrifices, or offerings to the dead, but
not only were these honors to the dead paid in Plato's time,
when to secure them was a prime motive for marriage, and in
the age of St. Chrysostom, who was scandalized by them, but
the belief in their importance is very real in Greece to-day.
In this matter the poet seems, indeed, as a very high authority
has said, centuries in advance of his age.   But at least it is
clear that Homer does not avoid the mention of superstitious
beliefs in order to give the impressions of an earlier generation
than his own.   These superstitions prevailed through the
second millenium B.C., as well as in later ages.

In this field of religious antiquities, other specifications may
be added, where the poet is unexpectedly reticent.   He says
nothing of "mysteries,"—but perhaps these had not been
founded,—nor of holy days (with a single exception, v 156,
ϕ 258), nor of purification from blood-guiltiness, nor of
divination by the inspection of entrails or by watching
the conduct of the sacrificial flame, though in the later,
so-called Cyclic poems, some of these appear.   Some of
these customs may have arisen later than the poet, though
most are primitive in their nature, rather than of an
advanced stage of culture, but in every case the silence is
to be explained otherwise than as intended by the poet to
avoid the mention of a recent custom.

More important, perhaps, than any of the other matters in
regard to which the Homeric poems may be thought not to
represent accurately the beliefs of the poet's own
age, is one about which dogmatic statement is
still out of place.   Hardly a quarter of a century
ago, every scholar laughed at Herodotus's assertion
that the Greeks owed their theology and theogony *Homeric Influence on the later Conceptions of the Gods.*
to Homer and Hesiod.   Had men not learned, on the contrary,
that Ζεὺς πατήρ was not only *Jupiter* but also *Dyāuspitar?*
That Uranus was *Varuṇa*, Athena was *Ahanâ*, Hermes was
Sārameya, Prometheus was *Pramantha*, the centaurs were
Gandharvas, the Graces were *Harits*, etc., *i.e.* that the gods
of the Greeks were part of their primeval Aryan inheritance,
with the exception of a few divinities who might have been
borrowed, as Aphrodite from the Phoenicians and Ares
from the Thracians.   That these Greek and Sanscrit gods

did not correspond to each other very well in position and influence, and that the etymologies were not in every case beyond dispute, was not allowed much weight in the consideration, and few scholars then had the right to express judgment on these points. But modern mythologists attach little importance to such resemblance or even identity of name, and the study of the primitive religion of the Greeks shows that the epic poets had at least very great influence in fixing the anthropomorphic characteristics of the gods. Not simply for Phidias in his making of the chryselephantine statue for the temple of Zeus at Olympia, but for the ordinary Greek as well, the verses of Homer determined the idea of Zeus. Indeed the Homeric poems fixed the anthropomorphic notions of divine beauty for all western countries during later ages. That Zeus should be recognized all over Greece as the supreme god, and that Athena and Hera were national rather than local deities, is due largely if not chiefly to the Homeric poems. These did not create the divinities, but had much to do with determining their later positions among the Greeks.

That the poet idealized somewhat the life of his age, we may easily believe, just as he has magnified many times the

Poet's Age Idealized. size of the walled city of Troy. Golden goblets may not have been used so freely in Homeric Hellas, as the poems would lead us to suppose, and such feasts as Homer describes may not have been of daily occurrence. Idealization and exaggeration are natural to story tellers in a simple age,—not to say, in all ages. But where the poet directly mentions an object or a custom, we may believe this to have been known and somewhat familiar to the Greeks of his own day, unless other evidence appear (and none has appeared as yet) to the contrary. But though the poet endeavoured to depict the manners and life of his time, he may not have cared, or indeed have been able, so to revise all the allusions to earlier customs in the poetic material which he used, as to make it agree exactly with later usages. So indications of earlier manners of life still might remain. Even the wanderings of Odysseus have archaeological value as presenting in the main such a view of the regions beyond the actual knowledge of the Greeks of the poet's time as might readily be formed on the basis of the stories of Phoenician and Achaean sailors and traders. The accounts of the short nights of the Laestrygonians and the unending nights of the Cimmerians, may have come not by sea but by land, together with amber, over a trade route from the Baltic, but this does not alter the principle.

With the limitations which have been indicated, the *Iliad* and *Odyssey* afford trustworthy evidence with regard to the life of the Greeks at the time of the composition of the poems.

The reader of the present work should not be surprised at the large number of illustrations drawn from the Old Testament. In spite of all its marked differences, no other book depicts a civilization which has *Illustrations* so much in common with that of the Homeric *from the Old Testament.* Greeks in both small and important matters. The relation of Abraham and Lot to their followers, though they were leading a nomadic life, was much like that of Odysseus and Menelaus to their men. The challenge of Goliath of Gath is a fair parallel to those of the Trojans Paris and Hector. The women ground at the mill and pounded grain with the pestle alike in Greece and in the land of Canaan. Even in the matter of religious ceremonies, particularly in their burnt sacrifices and drink-offerings, the two peoples had much in common. The Homeric Greeks, like their contemporaries in Palestine in the time of the Judges or under David and Solomon, had much noble poetry, many lofty sentiments, considerable wealth and splendor, together with many customs and principles which appear to us rude and crude.

Homer's picture of the life of his age is of particular interest to the modern reader since it is the earliest account extant of the culture from which our own is a true lineal descendant. The civilization of the *Homer's* Orient has affected the Occident only through *Picture is the* Greece. The astronomy of Babylonia and the *Extant of the* mathematics of Egypt touched the west only *Civilization* mediately, as their learning was adapted and *from which* perfected by the Hellenes. Just as all western *ours is* alphabets are derived from the Greek alphabet,—for although the Phoenicians traded with all the peoples bordering on the Mediterranean Sea none but the Greeks were able so to modify the Phoenician alphabet as to adapt it to western use,—so no other people but the Greeks was able to receive, employ, and carry further the arts and sciences of the east and of Egypt. The ancients were fond of discovering in the poems of Homer the essence of all wisdom,[1] and often found there knowledge which was foreign to his age. But in fact the beginnings of a large part of our civilization may be studied in the *Iliad* and *Odyssey*. The life of the poet's age in some respects was not very primitive, and though many changes have been made, the various steps of progress may clearly be traced from Homer's age to our own. The oratory of Nestor, like that of the second book of the *Iliad*, where Odysseus urges the Achaeans to remain before Troy (B 284), and that of the ninth book of the *Iliad*, where Achilles is asked to return to the field of conflict (I 225 ff.), is no natural untrained eloquence, but shows that the art had been studied. The arts of war and peace are sufficiently advanced in Homer's picture to be full of interest, and yet the reader may feel that he approaches the cradle of our civilization.

[1] See in particular Plato's *Republic*, 606 E.

CHAPTER II

HOMERIC COSMOGRAPHY AND GEOGRAPHY

THE Homeric poems contain no cosmogony or theogony.[1]
The poet gives no indication of his beliefs with regard to
the creation of the world or about previous races
of men and gods. He knows of no Golden Age *No Cosmogony or Theogony.*
nor golden race in the past, and of no pre-
Hellenic inhabitants of Greece, and of only a few generations
of Greeks themselves, and he nowhere states that Zeus had
a predecessor on his throne. But Zeus and his brothers
Poseidon and Hades cast lots for their realms (O 187), and
so no one of these gods can have been the creator of the
universe.

As to the form of the earth, scholars ordinarily suppose
that the poet and his hearers believed this to be flat, and
oval or circular, since the Ocean was thought to
be a river, encircling the earth with its ceaseless *The Form of the Earth.*
stream. Thus Oceanus is represented as forming
the outer rim of the shield which is wrought by Hephaestus
for Achilles (Σ 607), while on this shield are formed scenes
from so many departments of human life that the whole
seems to stand for the world and the activity of the human
race. A learned and ingenious argument to prove that the
Homeric earth was spherical, has not generally been accepted.[2]

---

[1] The one bit of theogony in the poems is in the so-called "Deceit of Zeus,"
in which Hera twice, in an identical verse, and Hypnos once declare Oceanus
to be the source of the gods (θεῶν γένεσιν, Ξ 201, 246, 302),—and this does not
agree with Hesiod.

[2] *Paradise Found: The Cradle of the Human Race at the North Pole*, by
William F. Warren, 1885, in which the author tries to show "that the voyage of
Odysseus is a poetical account of an imaginary circumnavigation of the mythical

The fact that Odysseus reaches the realm of Hades by sailing in his ship a day's voyage from the island of Circe (λ 11 f.), while elsewhere in the poems the home of the dead seems to lie beneath the earth, has been considered the strongest support for such an hypothesis, but perhaps this allows of some other explanation, or the account of Odysseus's voyage may be by another poet, who had another view of the state of the dead. That the poet who told of the voyage from Circe's island thought of Odysseus as actually entering the home of Hades is not certain.

The Homeric sun sinks into Oceanus in the west (Θ 485, cf. Σ 239), and rises again from the water in the east (γ 1). How it passes from the west to the east, to begin again its daily course, is not stated. The poet by no word implies a knowledge of the later fancy that the sun was borne from the evening to the morning in a golden skiff along the stream of Oceanus (Mimnermus, 11, Stesichorus 6), nor that the sun shines in Hades during the night of gods and men (Pindar, *Frag.* 129). The sun once sets prematurely by order of Hera (Σ 239), for the safety of the Achaeans, and on the other hand the Dawn is detained by Athena near Oceanus, and not allowed to yoke her horses, Lampus and Phaëthon, which bear light to men, in order that the reunited Odysseus and Penelope may have leisure to relate to each other their experiences during the time of their separation (ψ 243). The "turning places of the sun" (τροπαὶ ἠελίοιο, ο 404), above Ortygia, have been interpreted variously. Some identify Ortygia with Delos, and see in the expression an observation of the solstice.[1] More scholars

earth in the upper or northern hemisphere, including a trip to the southern or under hemisphere, and a visit to the ὀμφαλὸς θαλάσσης or North Pole" (p. 122). President Warren claims alone to present a solution of the problem which places the realm of Hades "underneath the earth" and yet "on the surface of the earth" (p. 476).

[1] Thus Professor Geddes supposes that from Ionia Delos was "pointed out as the point in the horizon where the sun sank at the shortest day, that is, at the cardinal point of the winter solstice," and that the story was "transferred into the *Odyssey* from its native *habitat* in Ionia, without any new adaptation to the locality where it is supposed to be uttered" (*Problem of the Homeric Poems*, 294). Miss Agnes Clerke, however, in *Familiar Studies in Homer*, p. 36, says, "This probably meant that Delos lay just so much south of east from Ithaca as the sun lies at rising on the shortest day of winter." But while the former view is a mere hypothesis, the latter is confessedly not very exact, and it assumes for

would give to the Homeric Ortygia a wholly mythical character, remembering that at Circe's island, Aeaea, were the "dwelling and dances of the Dawn and the risings of the Sun" (μ 6).

The sun ('Ήέλιος) is clearly personified (at μ 376) where, on the slaughter of his cattle by the comrades of Odysseus, he demands from Zeus satisfaction, in lack of which he will descend to the realm of Hades and give light to the dead, and also (at θ 270, 302) where he informs Hephaestus of the infidelity of Aphrodite. He is *The Sun and the Year.* the father of Circe and Aeetes (κ 138). Agamemnon swears "by Zeus and the sun, which seeth all things and heareth all things" (Γ 277), but his addition of "ye rivers, and thou earth" shows that the personification here is not complete. The sun is Hyperion ('Υπερίων, as at α 8), perhaps as the "son of the height." In a passage of late composition (ω 12), the gates of the sun (in the west) are hard by the country of dreams. The Dawn, as we have seen, has horses (ψ 243). She is *rosy-fingered* (ῥοδοδάκτυλος 'Ηώς, Α 477), or "with russet mantle clad" (κροκόπεπλος, Θ 1), as well as *fair-tressed* (ϵ 390), *golden-throned* (κ 541), and "bringing light to mortals" (Ω 785). Preceded by Lucifer ('Εωσφόρος, Ψ 226), she rises from the couch of Tithonus (Λ 1) or from the streams of Oceanus (Τ 1). She was the mother of Memnon (δ 188), and loved Orion and Clitus (ϵ 121, o 250). Light and night come to the gods on Olympus just as they do to men on earth. The length of the year seems to be indicated as 350 days by the herds and flocks of the sun,—seven herds of cattle, with fifty kine in each herd, representing the days, and seven flocks of sheep, with fifty in each flock (μ 128), representing the nights; of these none die, and to them none are born,— *i.e.* the number remains the same. No names of months are mentioned, and no indication is given of the length of the month, though this doubtless was well understood. The poet had heard of countries where the nights were unending, as of the Cimmerians (λ 14), and of others where the nights were

---

the Homeric Greek a map with a far more precise designation of latitude and longitude than was attained for several centuries after him. A still more recent suggestion is that Aeaea lay due south of Greece, where the sun turned to go down toward the west.

very brief, as of the Laestrygonians (κ 82), but he knows of no difference in the lengths of the days in summer and in winter in Greece. He shows further no such knowledge of the northerly and southerly course of the sun as Hesiod shows in his *Works and Days* (*cf.* 527, where the sun visits the Aethiopians in winter), and as is postulated by Dr. Penrose's astronomo-architectural observations and theories of the orientation of early Greek temples. No stated beginning of the year as a "New Year" is known, while Hesiod's year seems to begin with January (Ληναιών, *Works* 504),—nor even any anniversary.[1] The month was an older division of time than the year. The division of the year into three seasons— spring, winter, and summer[2]—is not absolutely clear. No indication appears of any exact bound for the seasons, *e.g.* of spring as beginning at the equinox. Even Hesiod gives no more exact limit for the beginning of the spring voyage than "when the fig leaves are as large as a crow's foot,"[3] and the popular division of the seasons was not precise in the time of Thucydides. Homer's mention of the Phaeacian fruit as failing neither in summer nor in winter (η 118) has been interpreted as implying the most primitive division of the year, into but two seasons, the cold and the warm, but the inference is not certain.

Naturally the poet knows no division of the day into hours ; the "Hours" were seasons. High noon is when the sun *Divisions of the Day.* passes the zenith (Π 777), or when the weary woodcutter pauses in his work, for his midday meal (Λ 86). Similarly, late afternoon was the time for "the loosing of cattle" from the plough (ι 58, Π 779).[4]

---

[1] ἐνιαυτός at times may be used for an anniversary, or completion of a year. This is the most frequent word for year, ἔτος being somewhat less common. λυκάβας (ξ 161, τ 306,—*lux* and βαίνω?) was understood by the ancients as *year*, but some modern scholars understand it as *month* or *day*.

[2] ἔαρ, *ver*, as Ζ 148; χειμών, *hiems*, as Γ 4; θέρος as Χ 151, and ὀπώρη (*late summer?*) as λ 192, Χ 27,—clearly four seasons if θέρος and ὀπώρη are to be distinguished,—but ὀπώρη would be a very early autumn, since this is the time of the dog-star (Χ 27).

[3] *Works*, 679. So the Indians of Connecticut planted their maize when the leaves of the "Charter Oak" were as large as a mouse's ear.

[4] *Cf.* Milton's designation of time : "Two such I saw what time the labor'd ox | In his loose traces from the furrow came, | And the swinkt hedger at his supper sat" (*Comus*, 291 f.).

The night was divided into three watches (K 251, *cf.* μ 312, ξ 483). As in later times, it was an object of dread ; light was an emblem of safety (Z 6, Λ 797). Twilight is mentioned once (ἀμφιλύκη νύξ, H 433). As with the Hebrews, the civil day began at sunset.[1] No phase of the moon but the full moon is mentioned, although these phases must have been observed if the moon was to measure and mark the months. The constellation then already *Constellations.* known both as Bear and as Wain, is named as not "bathing in Oceanus," *i.e.* as never sinking below the horizon. Odysseus sails from Calypso's island for seventeen days, keeping this on his left hand, and so clearly sailing from the west (ε 273). Only here in Homer does a mariner direct his course by the stars. The Pleiades are mentioned in the same passage, and, together with the Hyades, as wrought by Hephaestus on the Shield of Achilles (Σ 486). Orion[2] is named in the two passages last referred to, and his dog-star (not yet called Sirius) is the simile for the brightness of Achilles's armor as he assailed the Trojan city (X 29),—most brilliant, but an evil sign, for it "brings much feverish heat to mortals." Sirius is thought to be in the poet's mind on two other occasions where a bright or destructive star is mentioned (E 5, Λ 62). The constellation Boötes is named among the stars watched by Odysseus on his voyage from Calypso's island (ε 272). Its epithet "late-setting" has been explained as derived "from the perpendicular position in which it descends below the horizon." If it refers to a time of year, it affords the only instance in Homer of the determination of the seasons of the year by the change of constellations. The same constellations appear in Hesiod, *Works*, 615 f. The evening star, Hesperus, is the fairest star in heaven (X 318), and serves as a simile for the brightness of the spear-point of Achilles. The identity of the evening with the morning star had not been observed. "Starry" is so characteristic an epithet of the sky that it is applied even by day, as where Polyphemus lifts his hands toward the starry heavens invoking

[1] Thus "yesterday" (χθιζός, T 141) is used properly of an offer made on the evening of the second preceding day (I 262).

[2] Since Ὠαρίων was the earlier (and probably Homeric) form of the name, the suggested connexion with the Accadian *Ur-ana* is quite impossible.

vengeance on Odysseus (ι 527, cf. Δ 44). The planets were not yet distinguished from the fixed stars. No Milky Way was observed. No Pole-star is known. Naturally the precession of the equinoxes had not yet brought our pole-star to its present eminent position. No omens were taken from the stars, which had as yet no "influence," either baleful or precious. For the beauty of the infant son of Hector (Z 401), no better simile is found than a "fair star."

Meteors. The fall of a meteor or shooting star serves as a comparison for the descent of Athena from Mt. Olympus to the Trojan plain (Δ 75). To the English poet Pope this did not seem sufficiently magnificent, and in his translation he substituted a comet, but no comet is mentioned by Homer.

An eclipse of the sun is found by a German scholar in the darkness which attends the death of Sarpedon (Π 567), but this is by no means certain.

A rainbow is said to be stretched by Zeus as a portent for mortals, of war or of chilling winter (P 547), and the blue serpents on the cuirass of Agamemnon are likened to the rainbows which the son of Cronus fixes in the cloud (Λ 27).

Air and Aether. The denser atmosphere about the earth is air;[1] the purer atmosphere in the heights where the gods live is *aether*. Thus a very tall pine on Mt. Ida reaches through the air to the *aether* (Ξ 288). So Zeus dwells in the *aether* (αἰθέρι ναίων, B 412), and the clear *aether* (αἴθρη, ζ 44) lies ever about the summit of Olympus. But "out of the *aether*," that is, out of the sky (Π 365), come storms. Clouds form the outer walls and gates of the dwellings of the gods on Olympus. Of these gates the Hours are the keepers, to open or to close them (E 749 = Θ 393), and as such they unharness the horses of Hera on her return from earth (Θ 433). That these gates are said to grate or bellow when they are opened, is a mere transference of a characteristic of ordinary gates to those of the gods,—the ordinary gate rubbed on the threshold. That the summit of Mt. Olympus was invisible to men, of course did not indicate that the clouds extended over this summit, but only that the Hours had closed the gates, leaving the divinities in the bright aether,

---

[1] ἀήρ, which is sometimes equivalent to *mist*, as Γ 381, E 776, 864.

whatever weather prevailed among men. Since the clouds form the walls of Olympus, Zeus may fitly be said (O 192, cf. π 264) to receive as his special realm the broad heaven in the *aether* and clouds, *i.e.* to dwell in the aether surrounded by clouds. Occasionally the heaven is said to be of bronze or of iron (P 425, γ 2, o 329), but this does not necessarily imply belief in a "metal hemisphere" above the world, as a firmament. The reader will remember Coleridge's "copper sky."

Dew and hoar frost (στίβη, ἐέρση, ε 467) are feared by the shipwrecked Odysseus as he lies down to sleep on the Phaeacian shore. The glistering dew on the growing grain serves as a comparison for the glad heart of *Dew and Snow.* Menelaus on receiving a prize in the horse-race (Ψ 598). Dew and rain together promote the fertility of Ithaca (ν 245). Snowstorms are familiar to the poet. Words drop like snowflakes from the lips of Odysseus (Γ 222), stones fall like snowflakes from the defenders upon the assailants of the wall about the Achaean camp (M 156), and as the Achaeans prepare for battle, on the reconciliation of Achilles with Agamemnon, helmets as many as snowflakes are brought forth from the tents (T 357). The horses of Rhesus are whiter than snow (K 437). Not only Mt. Olympus and Mt. Tmolus, but the mountains of Thrace and Crete are snowy.[1] Ice[2] is mentioned twice, once as a standard of cold, and once as forming on the shield of a warrior by night on the Trojan plain. Hail is mentioned three times, once with ice as a standard of cold, and twice in company with snow (χάλαζα, K 6, O 170, X 151). No rain is said to fall except in a storm. In general little is said about the climate or of suffering from cold or heat.

Atmospheric phenomena are primarily under the direction of Zeus, who is the "cloud-gatherer" (νεφεληγερέτα, A 511), who thunders and hurls the bolt of lightning (Θ 133, μ 415), who sets the rainbow in the clouds *Atmospheric Phenomena.* (Λ 27) and gathers storms (ι 67). But any divinity may control the winds. Not merely Apollo (A 479) and Athena (β 420, o 292), but also the lesser divinities, Circe

---

[1] ἀγάννιφον, A 420; νιφόεις, Τ 385, Ξ 227, τ 338.
[2] κρύσταλλος, X 152, ξ 477 ; cf. *crystal*, and κρύος *cold*.

(λ 7) and Calypso (ε 268 ; *cf.* ο 34), send favorable breezes to mariners, while Poseidon not only stirs the sea, but gathers the clouds and rouses the winds for the wreck of Odysseus (ε 291). Aeolus is master of the winds (κ 21), but when a breeze is needed to fan the flame of the funeral-pile of Patroclus, the winds are feasting at the home of Zephyrus in Thrace (Ψ 200, *cf.* 230 and I 5). Zephyrus is no modern zephyr, but is a stormy blast (except δ 567), associated with Boreas in fury. Two winds are needed to make a storm,[1] which is a "conflict of opposing blasts" (Aeschylus, *Prom.* 1087). The Homeric Greeks as well as the old Hebrews were familiar with the sulphurous odor of ozone as accompanying the thunderbolt, and thus thought of "fire and brimstone" as coming from Zeus.[2]

Intimations of earthquakes appear in Poseidon's frequent epithet *earth-shaker* (ἐνοσίχθων, α 74, ἐννοσίγαιος, ε 423). The

Earthquakes. tidal waves which accompany and follow an earthquake were thought to have caused it. The earthquakes in Cilicia were ascribed to the struggles of the monster Typhoeus, smitten by the bolts of Zeus (B 782). The earth was believed to rest upon the water (see page 440), but the only floating island is that of Aeolus (κ 3). Atlas certainly did not support the world on his shoulders, and appears still to be a sea-divinity, on whose element both the earth and the heavens were thought to rest. No indication is found in the poems of his being or even steadying a mountain.

The Elysian Plain is mentioned once, as the happy region

The Elysian Plain. to which Menelaus should be translated (δ 563). It lies near Oceanus, which sends refreshing west winds for the comfort of its inhabitants, but whether it is on an island is uncertain. The Isles of the Blest and the Garden of the Hesperides are not Homeric.

The Homeric determination of the points of the compass was by no means exact. The poet's ordinary and natural

Points of the Compass. orientation was from east to west, "from the dawn to the darkness," "from the rising of the sun unto the going down of the same" (κ 190, θ 29, M 239). The line from north to south was far less important. No attempt was made to subdivide the four cardinal points of our compass. For example, only four

[1] I 4, ε 292, 317, 331.   [2] Θ 135, Ξ 415, μ 417, ξ 307. *Cf. Genesis* xix. 24.

winds are mentioned. Thus a west wind might be a north-west or a southwest wind. Following the shore closely as the Achaean mariners were wont to do, their notions of the geographical relations of different places were often inexact. So Athena gives to Telemachus a west wind (β 421), to bear him from Ithaca to Pylus, though a modern map would show that a wind northwest by north would answer the purpose better.[1] A modern map with a designation of Homeric places does not then really represent the Homeric idea of the known world, any more than modern maps of the western hemisphere can be made to agree precisely with those drawn by the early navigators in the age of exploration.

The limits of geographical knowledge were narrow, and we cannot suppose that the poet claims ignorance on matters which were familiar to his hearers. *Limits of Geographical Knowledge.* He had nothing to gain by appearing to be ignorant of what others knew. As in most other matters, Homer was a man of his times, not an archaeologist nor a modern scientist.

Homer had no recondite sources of knowledge nor new information with regard to distant lands, though he may have travelled more widely in Greece than most of his contemporaries. The argument to prove the home of the poet from his geographical knowledge would tend, so far as it goes, to support the belief that early epic lays were sung in Thessaly, the home of Achilles, and near to the haunts of the Pierian Muses and to the seat of the gods on Mt. Olympus, but this evidence is neither clear nor strong. The view that the poems as we have them were first sung at the courts of princes in Asia Minor, rests entirely on other grounds. The poet shows no special acquaintance with that region, outside of the Troad, and certainly evinces no impulse to celebrate the local myths of Asia Minor. If he would glorify the descendants of Nestor by his stories of the sweet-voiced orator of the Pylians, his purpose is well concealed.

[1] That the points of the compass to the Homeric mind were all a little askew, so that Boreas blew from the northeast, and Eurus from the southeast, is a fancy which cannot be proved.

The name Europe does not appear in our poems, but occurs first in the *Hymn to Pythian Apollo* (73, 113), where *Europe and Asia.* it may mean Northern Greece. Asia in Homer is only a plain of Asia Minor (B 461). As the Greeks were not yet contrasted with "barbarians," so the poet has no one word for Greece. Hellas is no more than Central Greece, if indeed it is not restricted to Thessaly. Argos sometimes stands for Greece, sometimes for Peloponnesus, and sometimes for the town in Argolis. Argives, Achaeans, and Danaans are names used indiscriminately for the Greeks, according to the poet's convenience, differing only in metrical value. Of these, the Danaans have no place in Greek history. Pelasgian Argos is in Thessaly, and Achaean Argos is Peloponnesus, which does not bear its later name. "Through Hellas and Argos "[1] is a periphrasis for all Greece, with which may be compared "from Dan to Beersheba," and "from John o' Groat's to Land's End." Dorians are named but once (τ 177), and that in Crete. Ionians also are named but once (N 685), and that in connexion with Boeotians and Locrians. The name of Aeolians does not occur. Greece naturally was the centre of the poet's world of thought, but no trace appears of a belief that Greece was the actual centre of the earth, such as was found at Delphi in later times.

India and China, Assyria and Babylonia are far beyond the poet's ken. His knowledge of Egypt is vague. Nestor's expression with regard to the travels of Menelaus, that he had visited lands so remote that not even a bird could go and return in the same year (γ 321) doubtless is hyperbole; the poet shows his familiarity with the migrations of cranes to the land of pygmies in order to escape the winter and storm (Γ 3),—the only indication of knowledge that southern countries had a warmer climate. But the island of Pharos is set at a day's sail from Egypt, instead of within a few

---

[1] καθ' Ἑλλάδα καὶ μέσον Ἄργος, α 344. But scholars who hold to the Thessalian origin, not merely of Greek epic poetry but also of the story of the *Iliad*, believe that Achaea and Argos were both originally Thessalian, and that Agamemnon was transferred to Mycenae in Argolis after epic poetry had passed to the Ionians, when Argolis was more prominent than Thessaly. See Cauer, *Homerkritik*, 153 ff. But see note on p. 9.

rods of the shore,[1] and Egyptian Thebes is believed to be a walled city with an hundred gates, which it never had.[2] Libya is only a narrow tract west of Egypt (δ 85, ξ 295), and the Syrtes and the Lake Tritonis are unknown.   Ithaca is on the very western frontier of the Greek world.   Once, it is true, a story is told of a Taphian king on his way to Temesa in Bruttium, on the west coast of Italy, to exchange his iron for copper (a 184).   But the poet's knowledge of Sicily is slight.   The old woman servant who cared for the aged Laërtes was a Sicilian woman (γυνὴ Σικελή, ω 211—a passage of late composition), and the Sicels were noted slave traders (v 383), but no more is heard of the race, and no one knows even whether they yet had come to dwell on the island of Sicily.   In general, every country to the west of Ithaca is in fairyland.   Very probably *Knowledge of the West.* the dangers and horrors of the western sea were exaggerated not simply to indulge the hearer's love of the marvellous, and from the roving mariner's desire to excite surprise and admiration, but also by the natural wish of the traders who had visited the far west, to enjoy the monopoly of trade with the peoples which they had discovered.   If they had found a region where the inhabitants were glad to give large stores of purple, of metal, or of grain, in exchange for baubles from the east, they desired no rivals in this commerce.

On the north of Greece, Homer knows not only Mt. Olympus, but also Ossa and Pelion, and the story that Otus and Ephialtes sought to place Ossa on Olympus and Pelion upon Ossa, in order to scale the heavens (λ 315), shows that the shapes of these mountains were familiar to him ; the poet knows which should form the base, and which the apex of this pile.   In general, however, the poet has no Thessalian tales which would lead us to believe that his predecessors had brought a large stock of stories and

---

[1] δ 354. A recent explanation, that the poet knew that the Delta of the Nile was alluvial, and represented the distance of the island from the shore as so great in order to indicate the remoteness of the period of Menelaus, is devoid of probability.

[2] I 383 f. The chariots mentioned in the same passage on the other hand might well be Egyptian. The gates may have been suggested by a story of the great *pylones* of the Egyptian temples. See Introduction, p. 39.

geographical knowledge with them from Thessaly to Asia Minor.[1] Pieria and Emathia are mentioned (Ξ 226), but northern Macedonia and western Thrace seem to be unfamiliar. But the river Axius, which flows into the Gulf of Salonica, is named three times (B 849, Π 288, Φ 141 f.). On its banks dwell allies of Priam. The Cicones, who also were allies of the Trojans (B 846), and whose land was wasted by Odysseus on his leaving Troy (ι 39), throughout antiquity were assigned to the shore north of Samothrace, somewhat to the west of the modern Dede Agatch. The shores to the east of the Cicones naturally were held by friends of Priam,—associated with the east rather than with the west.

Thrace is the home of Ares (N 301, θ 361), but it is a fertile land, rich in flocks and not lacking wine (Λ 222, I 72). The Hippemolgi, who use the milk of mares, and the Abii, "justest of men" or "most cultured of men" (N 6), seem to be the Homeric equivalents of the Hyperboreans, who are not mentioned by our poet.

Thrace.

The Paphlagonians (B 851) represented the northernmost region of Asia Minor known to our poet, who does not mention the Black Sea nor any of the rivers which flow into this, while the southern Lycians represent the limits of his knowledge in that direction. Some places, however, may not have been named simply because they were not important for the story. For example, we are not obliged to accept the alternative that Homer either did not know Smyrna, Ephesus, and Sardis, or else deliberately avoided the mention of them. Miletus appears but once, as a Carian city in the Catalogue of Ships (B 868). The relation between the historic and the Homeric Cilicians (Z 397), is not clear. In general surprisingly little knowledge is shown of Asia Minor. Of this, as well as of all other countries than Greece proper, the poet knows only the coast. The Phrygians were Priam's neighbors on the east. His queen, Hecuba, seems to have been a Phrygian (Π 718 f.), and Priam went to the defence of the Phrygians against the Amazons (Γ 189). The Amazons appear in the poems only in the passage

Asia Minor.

[1] T. W. Allen, in the *Classical Review*, xx. 197 ff., discusses and elucidates the Homeric geography of Thessaly.

just cited, and as overcome by Bellerophon (Z 186) in or near Lycia. Myrina, whose tomb formed a landmark and look-out on the Trojan plain (B 814), was declared in later times to have been an Amazon ; this story, if Homeric, would imply an Amazonian invasion of the Troad.

Cyprus has been thought by some scholars to lie beyond the limits of the original Homeric story, although not only is it mentioned in several connexions,[1] but a considerable number of Homeric words continued in ordinary use down to classical times only in the dialect of that island. Little importance in the poems is given to the islands of the Aegean Sea. Chios is mentioned but once (γ 170), and that in the account of the return of the Achaeans from Troy. Hera's island of Samos is not named. Delos appears once (ζ 162), with a mention of an altar of Apollo. Lesbos is named four times (*cf.* I 664, Ω 544, γ 169). This was taken by Achilles (I 129), and in the earliest form of the story, Briseïs very likely was only "the maiden from Brisa" or Bresa, on that island. Phoenicia was visited by Paris and Helen on their way from Greece to Troy, and by Menelaus on his wanderings after the siege (Z 291, δ 83 f.).[2] But who were the Erembi, who are named in the latter of these passages, between the Sidonians and Libya? The ancient scholars could not answer this question with knowledge. The Stoic Zeno thought they were Arabians, and Crates read *Eremni*, the *dark*, and supposed them to be Hindoos.[3]

Cyprus and the Islands of the Aegean.

As for the countries visited by Odysseus on his wanderings, the poet does not afford sufficient indications for their identification, either in their direction or in their distance from known points, or in his description of the places themselves. The land of the Lotus Eaters is in the south, and the island of Calypso is in the

Wanderings of Odysseus.

---

[1] E 330, etc., Λ 21, δ 83, θ 362, ρ 442 f.

[2] The Phoenicia of δ 83, which is distinguished from the land of the Sidonians, may be Caria. See Athenaeus, 174 f. ; Fick, *Vorgriechische Ortsnamen*, 124.

[3] For the geographical interpretation of Homer by the scholars of the Alexandrian and Pergamenian Schools, see Berger, *Geschichte der wissenschaftlichen Erdkunde der Griechen*,[2] 386 f., 443 f., 535 ff., 576 f. Also Neumann, *Strabons Urtheil über Homer*, in *Hermes*, xxi. 134.

far west, but the other places might be almost anywhere in
the west.   In spite of this difficulty, however, many attempts
have been made to establish these identifications.   Only a
few years ago, an Englishman, Mr. Butler, maintained not
only that Trapani on the northwest coast of Sicily was
Scheria, the home of the Phaeacians, but also that Nausicaa,
the Phaeacian princess, was herself the author of the *Odyssey*.
A little later, M. Bérard, in a sumptuous book[1] intended
to prove that the *Odyssey* was only a Greek poetic para-
phrase of the Sailing Directions of Phoenician Mariners,
maintained that the home of Nausicaa was on the western
coast of the island Corfù, while the ancients found it at
the harbor on the eastern side of this island.   Still more
recently another Frenchman[2] identifies Scheria with Ischia,
at the entrance to the bay of Naples.   M. Bérard identifies
Calypso's island at the foot of Monkey Mountain, just
outside the straits of Gibraltar, while a still more distinguished scholar is inclined to find it at the heel of Italy.
Similarly while the ancients agreed in placing the Cyclops
Polyphemus on Sicily and brought him into relations with
the volcano of Mt. Aetna, the two French writers just
referred to, place him at Posilippo, the well-known suburb of
Naples, and explain his round eye from the craters of the
small extinct volcanoes of the Solfatara region.

To discuss these theories here is impossible.   We need
not be more definite than Homer himself.   On their return
from Troy, as they are rounding the southeastern promontory of Peloponnesus, Odysseus and his ships were driven
for nine days by Boreas to the land of the Lotus Eaters,
which is not further identified, but clearly is in or near
Africa (ι 83).   Thence they sailed for an unspecified time
in an unspecified direction until they came to the country
of the Cyclopes, and landed on a small island which was
stretched outside the harbor (ι 105).   From this island,
after visiting the cave of Polyphemus, they sailed, again for an
unspecified time, in an unspecified direction, to the floating
island of Aeolus, master of the winds, who received them with
kindness and gave to them a favorable west wind to convey

[1] V. Bérard, *Les Phéniciens et l'Odyssée*, 2 vols., Paris 1902, 1903.
[2] P. Champault, *Phéniciens et Grecs en Italie d'après l'Odyssée*, Paris 1906.

them to Ithaca, but the folly of Odysseus's comrades undid
the bag in which the other winds were confined, and these on
being released hurried back to the home of Aeolus, and carried
the Ithacans with them (ι 565. ff.). From the island of
Aeolus the comrades of Odysseus rowed, in an unspecified
direction but presumably east, until they reached the land of
the Laestrygonians on the seventh day (κ 77). There eleven
of the twelve ships were destroyed, but Odysseus sailed on for
an unspecified time in an unspecified direction, until he came
to the island of Circe (κ 133), from which he sailed (apparently
in a single day, λ 11) in an unspecified direction, to the
bounds of Oceanus, the country of the Cimmerians, and the
realm of Hades, and to which he returned. Circe gave to
Odysseus on his departure from her island an unspecified
favorable breeze (μ 149) which bore the Ithacans by the
island of the Sirens (μ 167), and between Scylla and
Charybdis (μ 235) to the Island of the Sun (μ 261), where
the comrades killed some of the Sun's kine and therefore were
punished by shipwreck as soon as they put to sea again
(μ 403). Odysseus was saved by binding the mast to the
keel of the wrecked boat and using these as a raft. This
raft was swallowed by Charybdis, to which he was borne by a
south wind, but he clung to a wild-fig tree which hung over
the abyss, and waited patiently until his raft reappeared.
Thence he was borne on this raft in an unspecified direction
for nine days, and on the tenth night reached Calypso's
island, the "navel of the sea" (μ 420).

On his return from the island of Calypso Odysseus was borne
on his raft by a favorable breeze, keeping the Great Bear
upon his left (*i.e.* sailing due east), until on the eighteenth
day, when he was already in sight of the mountains of the
Phaeacians, Poseidon observed him and wrecked his craft
(ε 268). Then Athena sent a strong north wind which bore
him for two days and nights toward the land of the
Phaeacians (ε 385). From Scheria Odysseus was borne,
while he slept, to his Ithacan home (ν 73), in a single
night, but the Phaeacian ships were swifter than a hawk
(ν 86), and the poet does not intend to indicate that the
distance from Scheria to Ithaca was only a night's sail for
ordinary craft; the Phaeacians had sailed to Euboea and

back on the same day (η 321), which implies a speed much greater than that of any steamer.

The foregoing sketch of Odysseus's wanderings clearly does not encourage us to attempt the positive identification of many of the sites of the story. Charybdis and Scylla have always been found at the Strait of Messina, but the basis of the story of Charybdis has generally been thought to be some mariner's report of the ebb and flow of the ocean tides; that Charybdis gulped down the water thrice and not twice a day, was "poetic exaggeration" (Strabo, 43 C). The Cyclops Polyphemus has been associated ordinarily with Mt. Aetna; but this may have been due to the disposition of the early Greek colonists in the west to identify Homeric sites with the lands visited by them, finding the promontory of the Sirens, the home of Circe, and the entrance to Hades, all on the western coast of Italy.[1]

That the Phaeacians were Phoenicians has been a common belief, but it is based on a superficial view which overlooks

Phaeacians not Phoenicians. the important truth that the Homeric Phoenicians were more noted as traders than as seamen, while on the other hand the Phaeacians delighted in the sea but despised trade; the most stinging insult which one of these can offer to Odysseus is that he looks not like an athlete, but like a trader, "a commander of sailors who are traders,—one mindful of the cargo and of eagerly sought gains" (θ 159). Such a word would be no reproach in Homeric Phoenicia, but the Phaeacian who utters it is bidden not merely to apologize but to make reparation by a gift of value (θ 396). To say with M. Champault that they were a rich Phoenician settlement which despised small trade and formed a great "Transportation Company," does not bring them nearer to the Homeric Phoenicians. That the Phaeacians are the special favorites of the gods, who often

---

[1] The epithets given to the localities visited by Odysseus do not assist greatly in their identification. No epithet is assigned to the land of the Lotus Eaters. The island which lay off the land of the Cyclopes is low and well wooded, it has good soil and a good harbor, with a spring, and it lies not very far from the mainland. About the floating island of Aeolus stands a bronze wall and a sheer rock. The land of the Laestrygonians has a harbor surrounded by steep rocks, with a narrow entrance between projecting headlands. A layman would be surprised to learn what inferences have been drawn from the poet's simple statements.

have sat *in propriis personis* at their feasts, and appear openly at their sacrifices (η 201), does not tend to connect them with the tricky Phœnicians.

The relation of the Phoenicians to early Greece cannot be discussed in this place, but one may say with safety that the current views of the wide and deep influence of Phoenicia on Greece receive no direct confirmation *Phoenicians.* from the Homeric poems. Homer knows of no Phoenician trading station in Greece proper. The "divine swine-herd" Eumaeus was kidnapped when a child by Phoenician traders, who spent a year at his home (o 455) and later brought him to Ithaca and sold him to Laërtes (o 482), but no one dares say with confidence where lay this island of Syrié, on which Eumaeus was born. It is not mentioned elsewhere, and seldom elsewhere do we read in Homer of a purchased Greek slave (p. 272), so Syrié may not be a Greek island ; Eumaeus notes that he had a Phoenician nurse, who curiously enough had been stolen from her home by Taphian pirates (o 427). These Taphians must have gone to Sidon as traders, and the incident shows that the Greeks went to the east as well as the Phoenicians to the west. A Phoenician ship called at Lemnos, however, in the generation next preceding the Trojan War, and gave to the king of the island a beautifully-fashioned silver bowl, evidently as a kind of harbor dues, in return for the privilege of trading there (Ψ 744). In the *Iliad*, Phoenicians are mentioned only in this passage and in the account of old Hecuba's bearing as an offering to Athena a robe made by Sidonian women who were brought to Troy by Paris (Z 290), who seems to have called at Sidon when on his way with Helen from Sparta to Troy. In the story of the disguised Odysseus (ξ 288) Phoenicians appear in the same character as in the story of Eumaeus, tricky tradesmen who united kidnapping with their other occupations. A silver bowl similar to that given as harbor dues to the Lemnian king, is bestowed by the Sidonian king on Menelaus, who in turn gives it to Telemachus (o 115), but this is said to be the work of Hephaestus. These incidents, thus collected, are seen to form only a slight basis for the belief that the Phoenicians had a wide influence on the art and culture of Greece in the

Homeric period. That the Phoenicians are called Sidonians, while Tyre is not mentioned, must not be understood as ground for the inference that Tyre had not yet been founded. As has been observed already, the old name was used, after the later city had gained power, just as the Persians were called " Medes " by the Greeks not only in the time of the Persian wars, but even in the age of Demosthenes. Carthage, naturally, is not mentioned.

Of the Aethiopians the poet gives no exact information. They dwell by the streams of Oceanus, and are beloved by *Aethiopians.* the gods, who repeatedly go thither to share in their feasts. Zeus and the other divinities go to the Aethiopians for a twelve-day visit early in the action of the *Iliad* (A 423), the goddess Iris makes a special trip by herself to share in their sacrifices (Ψ 205), and at the opening of the action of the *Odyssey*, Poseidon is with them (α 22), making a considerable visit, for he seems not to return for at least twelve days. Evidently they live so far from Greece that it is not worth the while to go thither for a single dinner or a brief call. Some of the Aethiopians dwell in the east and others in the west (α 24),[1] and those visited by Poseidon seem to have been the eastern people, since he is on his return and near the mountains of the Solymi, in Lycia, when he catches sight of Odysseus on his raft approaching the land of the Phaeacians (ε 282) from the west. Menelaus reports that on his wanderings he visited the Aethiopians (δ 84), but gives no detail with regard to them.[2] That Memnon (who is not called an Aethiopian by Homer) comes to the aid of the Trojans (δ 188, λ 522), has been thought by some to prove that the Aethiopians cannot have lived very far from Troy. The Aethiopians who live by Oceanus, so far away from Olympus that the gods go to them for a twelve-day visit (A 425), would hardly send

---

[1] Herodotus also (vii. 70) recognizes two races of Aethiopians,—straight-haired Aethiopians of the east, and wooly-haired Aethiopians of Libya. The geographer Strabo exerts himself (30 c f.) to justify the expression of Homer and to accommodate it to the knowledge of his own day.

[2] The ancients discussed seriously the routes by which Menelaus could have reached the Aethiopians, whether (1) through the Straits of Gibraltar, or (2) over the Isthmus of Suez (not then covered by water), or (3) through a canal from the Nile to the Red Sea. Strabo, 38 c.

an army to aid the Trojans. That Memnon is called the most beautiful of men, with no reference to his complexion, might show that he was at least not one of Herodotus's western Aethiopians. Some scholars would connect him with the Assyrians, but this is seeking the basis of the Homeric story, not declaring what the poet believed, or would represent him.

Egypt appears in the *Iliad* only once (I 382), where Egyptian Thebes is named as famed for its wealth and power. In the *Odyssey* it appears more frequently. *Egypt.* Thither Menelaus was driven by a storm on his way home from Troy (γ 300); there he and Helen were entertained and received gifts—including silver bath tubs—at the palace of the king of Thebes (δ 125 ff.); and near Egypt he was detained, on the island of Pharos, because of his failure to offer proper sacrifices to the gods (δ 351). The disguised Odysseus tells a fictitious story of leading a marauding expedition to Egypt, of wasting the fields, but then being worsted by the inhabitants (ξ 258, ρ 427). The wealth of Egypt is noted in the *Odyssey*, too (δ 127), and that this land bears many medicinal herbs and here every man is a physician (δ 229). The river of Egypt has the same name as the land (δ 581); the name Nile does not appear. An old Ithacan is called Aegyptius (β 15),—probably because he or his father had made a voyage thither. At the home of Odysseus is a *byblinon* ship's cable (φ 391),— which seems to be of papyrus—but the poet mentions no trade ·between Greece and Egypt. This may be significant with regard to his relations to Crete, since the recent archaeological discoveries show the connexion between Crete and Egypt to have been rather close.

Of the pre-Hellenic inhabitants of Greece, Homer says nothing distinctly. Pelasgians are among the allies of the Trojans (B 840, K 429, P 288); others are among the inhabitants of Crete (τ 177), with the Dorians *Pelasgians.* and Cydonians. "Pelasgian Argos" seems to be Thessaly (B 681,—it may mean only the Pelasgian Field),—and as Patroclus sets out for the field of battle, Achilles invokes "Pelasgian Zeus, of Dodona" (Π 233). The name Larissa, which has been thought to be a Pelasgian name for city, occurs only twice, in the passages mentioned above (B 841, P 301). So the Homeric poet affords slight grounds for inference with regard to the relations between the Hellenes and the Pelasgians.

As for Greece proper, the poet shows a wide acquaintance with names of countries and places, but gives no descriptions and but few specially characteristic epithets. *Homer's Acquaintance with Greece.* Mycenae is "broad-streeted" and "rich-in-gold" (Δ 52, H 180), but no reference is made to the walls of her citadel, with the Lion Gate, which has never fallen nor been concealed, nor to the bee-hive tombs which have been excavated there in recent years. An epithet applied to Lacedaemon is not quite clear (κητώεσσα or καιετάεσσα, δ 1); it seems to mean "full of ravines or chasms," and then would refer to the well-marked deep hollows worn by mountain torrents on the steep slopes of Mt. Taygetus. Not a word is said of Acrocorinthus, nor of the Palamidhi of Nauplia, nor of the Athenian Acropolis, though the poet knows the palace of Erechtheus which stood on the Acropolis. Athens indeed is mentioned only half a dozen times in the poems, and receives no epithets except "broad-streeted," "sacred," and "a well-built town"; while Corinth is called "wealthy" in the Catalogue of Ships, but is mentioned only once more by that name, and once by its older name Ephyra (B 570, N 664, Z 152). Amyclae is named but once, and that without an epithet (B 584), in the Catalogue. The ancient fortress of Gha or Gla by the Copaïs lake is not mentioned, and no reference is made to the great engineering works which drained Lake Copaïs, reopened only in recent years. No Thebans took part in the war before Troy, and the ancients offered in explanation the theory that their city had not yet been rebuilt after its capture by the Epigoni. But Megara and Eleusis, too, are not named at all. The site of Nestor's Pylus was disputed by scholars two thousand years ago, as we shall see, and modern scholars dispute whether the classical Ithaca was the Ithaca of Odysseus. The traditional praise of Homer's exact geographical knowledge applies in strictness only to three or four epithets in the Catalogue of Ships (B 484-779), in which Aulis is called "rocky," as indeed it is, Thisbe "abounding in doves," and Haliartus "grassy" (B 496, 502, 503). That Ilium is "fair-towered" (εὔπυργος, H 71), might seem an easy inference from the fact that it endured a long siege.

The Catalogue of Ships was recognized as an important geographical document long ago. Some ancients charged the wise Solon or his younger contemporary Pisistratus, the Athenian ruler of the sixth century B.C., with interpolating in this a verse to indicate *The Catalogue of Ships.* the close relations existing between Athens and Salamis in the heroic period, as the basis of a claim to the control of Salamis. The relation of the Catalogue to the rest of the *Iliad*, however, is not clear, and certainly no violence should be used to bring the rest of the poems into harmony with this document. More discrepancies exist between it and the story of the battles than between any other parts of the poems. The troops from Rhodes and the other islands of Asia Minor (B 653-680), the Arcadians (B 603-614), the Magnetes (B 756), and others, appear only in the Catalogue and not in the battles, while on the other hand Agamemnon offers to Achilles if he will return to the conflict (I 149 f.) seven Messenian cities of which no one is mentioned in the Catalogue. A probable theory is that an early geographical register in poetic form, which bore no relation to the war against Troy, was made the basis for the present Catalogue,—the names of the leaders, the numbers of ships, and a few brief episodes being added.[1]

[1] Niese, *Der homerische Schiffskatalog*, Kiel, 1873.—Mr. T. W. Allen, in the *Classical Review*, xx. 193 ff., presents a strong argument for an earlier date for the Catalogue than has been accepted in recent years : " In itself, as a table, it bears every mark of venerable antiquity. . . . What is the one simplest test of the antiquity of a document of this sort? Surely the portrayal of a state of things, political and topographical, which never recurred in later history ; and which no one had any interest to invent, or even the means for inventing. This character is written all over the Catalogue ; the absence of the States of Megara and Messenia, the separation of Orchomenus from the rest of Boeotia, Thebes represented by Ὑποθῆβαι and in no sense predominant, the vanished kingdom of Nestor (Pylos and the ford of Alpheus),—none of these conditions ever existed again in the world, and it never became anyone's interest to invent or restore them. . . . Agamemnon, king of men, is seated at Corinth : he holds Corinth, Sicyon, and the whole of the later Achaean riviera ; to the south of Corinth he has his castle Mycenae at the south foot of the pass, but of the plain of the Inachus not an inch, and no access to the sea. Argos the town, Tiryns, Asine, the whole of the Hermionic peninsula round to Troezen and Epidaurus, even Aegina, are in the hands of Diomed (son of the Aetolian fugitive), Sthenelus (who represented the old Argive house), and Euryalus."

In this process, to make provision for warriors who were already well known in the story of the expedition, some kingdoms were broken up and divided. For instance, Diomed reigns over Argos, Tiryns, Epidaurus, and so on (B 559), and Agamemnon over Mycenae, Corinth, Sicyon, etc. (B 569), although elsewhere Agamemnon is king "over all Argos" (B 108), and where the frontier line should run between these two kingdoms is not easily seen.

In one passage which has to do with the topography of Argolis, the text seems to be confused. According to the *Confusion in Topography of Argolis.* manuscripts (δ 515), winds drove Agamemnon from his course as he was approaching his home on his return from Troy, and carried him to the confines of the land where Aegisthus dwelt. Then the wind changed and a favorable breeze brought him to his own land, where, on disembarking, he was met by his false-hearted cousin Aegisthus, with an invitation to dine with him before proceeding to Mycenae. Probably verses 517, 518 originally stood after 520, and the favorable breeze brought Agamemnon to Argolis indeed, but to the confines of the land of Aegisthus, who naturally in these circumstances met him and invited him to dinner. Why, if he had landed nearer Mycenae than to the home of Aegisthus he should have dined with Aegisthus instead of proceeding at once to his own palace, cannot be shown. Probably the verses were transposed by some one who failed to notice that here, as consistently in Homer, Aegisthus takes Clytaemestra to his own home, instead of going to Agamemnon's palace as in the story of the tragic poets. That this story makes Agamemnon approach his home by way of Cape Malea, should cause no trouble. If Nestor had not received a special omen he, too, would have followed the same route, coasting along the shores of Asia Minor and Crete, instead of taking the short course across the Aegean Sea (γ 174), from Lesbos to Euboea.

Crete is fairly prominent in the *Iliad* as the home of Idomeneus, who, though half-grizzled, is one of the more important Achaean leaders,[1] and of Meriones, his valiant lieutenant. Idomeneus was son of Deucalion and

---

[1] Γ 230, Δ 251, M 117, N 449 f., P 608, Ψ 450.

grandson of Minos, who was son of Zeus, and he seems like his grandfather to have reigned at Cnosus. The Catalogue of Ships says that Crete had an hundred cities (ἑκατόμπολις, B 649), and enumerates Cnosus, *Crete.* well-walled Gortyna, Lyctus, Miletus, gleaming Lycastus, Phaestus, and Rhytius. It adds that eighty black ships accompanied Idomeneus,—a number exceeded only by the fleets of Agamemnon and of Nestor. Only a prosaic mind sees an inconsistency between the hundred Cretan cities of the Catalogue and the ninety cities assigned to the island by the *Odyssey* (τ 172), in a passage which names no city but Cnosus, though it enumerates the peoples: Achaeans, Eteocretans, Cydonians, Dorians in three sections, and Pelasgians. Scholars are nŏt in agreement as to the local divisions of these peoples. Recent excavations, familiar to every reader, have shown the poet's right to give prominence to Cnosus and Phaestus, which are the only two Cretan towns named in the *Odyssey*. Doubtless he knew more than he told about their wealth and power, but here as in Greece proper he gives us no illuminating epithets, to say nothing of descriptions, and shows no exact knowledge of the island. In the *Odyssey*, Crete receives distinction from the stories told by the disguised Odysseus, who says to the swine-herd Eumaeus that he is the son of a noted Cretan by a slave woman, and had been a leader in the siege of Troy (ξ 199), and to.Penelope that he is a brother of Idomeneus, and that he received as his guest Odysseus on his way to Troy (τ 172 f.). A lying Aetolian had reported, also, that he had seen Odysseus in Crete at the palace of Idomeneus, repairing his ships (ξ 382).

The bounds of the kingdom of Odysseus, like those of the realm of Agamemnon, are not distinct (B 631 f.), but it well may be that in western Greece in the Homeric Age, limits were not exactly determined for every ruler. Boundary lines were subject to variation with the power and energy of kings and peoples ; and since the harbors of Greece were opened to the east rather than to the west, the towns and countries in western Greece were relatively unimportant. Not all the land may have been required for the population there, and broad neutral zones may have remained.

According to Strabo three sites were proposed for Pylus, the home of the wise and eloquent Nestor : (1) in Elis,

Three Sites proposed for Pylus. (2) Triphylian Pylus, on the coast a little to the south of the mouth of the Alpheüs, of which no remains existed in Strabo's time, and (3) Messenian Pylus, by the north entrance of the Bay of Navarino, opposite the island Sphacteria.[1] The exact sites of the first two are unknown, and scholars have been inclined to accept the identification with the third, but in addition to the fact that no remains of a Homeric palace have been found on this site, a serious difficulty has appeared in recent years. Telemachus and Nestor's son Pisistratus drive in a chariot from Pylus to Pherae, and thence in a single day to Sparta (γ 485 f.). No mention is made of any mountain range. But those who have set Pylus by Sphacteria have also set Pherae on or near the site of the modern Kalamata, at the head of the Gulf of Messene. From Kalamata a path runs to Sparta, it is true, but a path, as Bérard says, better fitted for goats and bandits than for chariots, over Mt. Taÿgetus, through the noted Langadha pass. No horses ever drew a chariot briskly along this route. On the ordinary map, Pherae or Kalamata seems to be the natural half-way stopping-place between Navarino and Sparta, but in reality this route is seen to be impossible, and Homer had no map by which he might have been deceived. The inference is necessary, that either Homer knew nothing of the route which he makes Telemachus traverse, or the Messenian Pylus cannot have been Nestor's Pylus. Bérard sets the Triphylian Pylus at Samicum, where are some ruins of classical times which have not yet been thoroughly examined, and holds Pherae to have been the classical Aliphera in Arcadia, fourteen or fifteen miles from Samicum on the way to Sparta. Another station on this trade-route from the harbor of Sparta to the west coast of Peloponnesus, according to Bérard, was Lycosura, but here Telemachus did not tarry, although the length of his second day's drive, from Aliphera to Sparta, seventy miles or more, would seem excessive. Dr. Dörpfeld agrees with Bérard in placing Nestor's Pylus at or near Samicum,

---

[1] For a recent discussion, see Bérard, *Les Phéniciens et l'Odyssée*, i. 61 ff.

but would set Pherae at or near the modern Leondari, in the upper valley of the Alpheüs, overlooking a narrow pass which separates Messenia from Arcadia, about mid-way between Samicum and Sparta,—eight hours and a half from Sparta according to the *Guide-Joanne*. Two routes were possible from Samicum to Sparta,—one following the river Alpheüs to the water-shed of the Eurotas, and another further to the south, following in general the course of the railroad which has recently been constructed. If the view of Bérard is accepted, Pylus received its name as the gate (πύλη) of Peloponnesus, at the extremity of an important route. A further argument for the Triphylian rather than the Messenian Pylus, is that the voyage from Ithaca to the Bay of Navarino is too long to be accomplished in a single night (β 434).

Alternatives not wholly unlike the dilemma presented by the Messenian Pylus are offered with regard to Ithaca: either the poet, living in Asia Minor, had no accurate knowledge of the Ionian islands, and chose Ithaca at random for the home of his hero, or the classical Ithaca was not the Homeric Ithaca.[1] Even if the Homeric bard's home was in Asia Minor, he might have visited Pylus in Peloponnesus, and even have passed a year with Telemachus or his successor, on Ithaca.

Was the Classical the Homeric Ithaca?

Recently Dr. Dörpfeld has urged with great force and ingenuity the view that Leucas was the Homeric Ithaca, taking as his text verses spoken by Odysseus to the Phaeacians : " I am Odysseus, son of Laërtes,—my fame reaches heaven. And I dwell in Ithaca, a land seen from afar, in which is a mountain, Neritos, conspicuous. About lie many islands near each other,—Dulichium and Samé and woody Zacynthus But my island lies low in the sea, uppermost of all,—to the west, while the rest lie apart towards the dawn and the sun " (ι 19 f.). Four islands are named here, but according to the prevalent view only three appear on the map,—Zante, Cephallenia, and

---

[1] The first horn of the dilemma is maintained by Wilamowitz, *Homerische Unter-suchungen*, 24 f. ; the second, by Dörpfeld, *Leukas*, Athens, 1905 ; Goessler, *Leukas-Ithaka*, 1904. The monograph by Manly, *Ithaca or Leucas*, 1903, was published before Dörpfeld's theory was fully presented.

Ithaca.   Zante is clearly Zacynthus, off the coast of Elis, and Cephallenia has been thought to be Samé, but what has become of Dulichium?   Several explanations were offered even two thousand years ago, among them being the suggestion that Dulichium might have sunk beneath the sea.   No one seems to have thought of considering Leucas one of these islands, since scholars remembered the tradition that this was connected with the mainland until the Corinthians, about 700 B.C., dug a canal to facilitate the passage of ships on the east of this country.   But practically Leucas is and has been considered an island.   So it is represented, for instance, by Kiepert, not only on his wall-map of Greece, and in the small *Atlas Antiquus*, but also in his larger *Atlas von Hellas*.   The ancients were not prevented by the Isthmus of Corinth from speaking of the Morea as the Island of Pelops.   But no firm isthmus ever connected Leucas with the mainland, and the digging of the Leucadian canal by the Corinthians may be compared more fitly to the dredging of the channel in a harbor filling with silt, or of a river, than to the cutting of the Corinthian canal a few years ago.   It is true that the level of the sea in that region seems to have risen about ten feet in the last three thousand years, but this has barely kept pace with the rise in the bed of the sea near to the shore, due to the silt brought by the rivers and mountain torrents, and made by the action of the waves.

But if Leucas is accepted as one of Homer's four islands, it must be his Ithaca, for this was the "uppermost of all, to the west."   That the west is named here instead of

Or Leucas?   the north-west, should cause no difficulty.   The ancients seem to have considered the line of navigation along these islands as running east and west, rather than north and south, or north-west and south-east.   We have seen that the Homeric Greeks did not divide the cardinal points of our compass, and that a west wind conveyed Telemachus from Ithaca to Pylus.   The fact that these islands lay on the route from the eastern end of the Corinthian Gulf to Italy in the west, may have encouraged the habit of thinking of them as lying in an east and west line.   In this respect then, Leucas corresponds well to the description given by Odysseus, while the classical Ithaca corresponds ill, for this

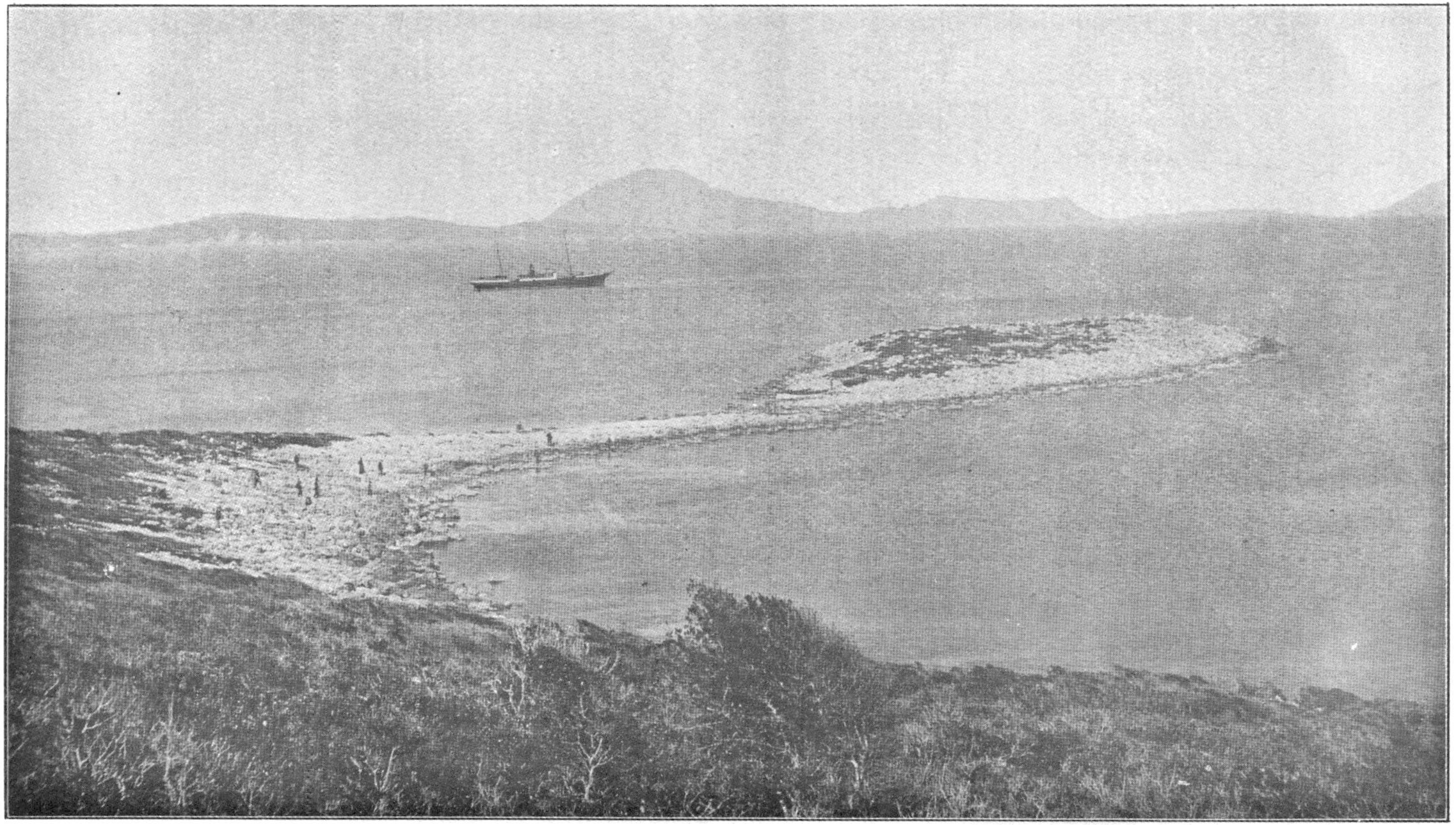

PLATE I. THE TWIN HARBORS OF ARKUDHI (ASTERIS ?). Facing p. 70.

lies not so far to the west as Cephallenia, and only a trifle further to the north. To speak of Cephallenia as lying to the east of Ithaca would be sheer ignorance.

A second important argument for the identity of the classical Leucas with the Homeric Ithaca, is found in the story of the possessions of Odysseus on the mainland (ξ 100 f.): there he kept twelve herds of *Classical* kine, twelve flocks of sheep, twelve droves of swine, *Ithaca too far from* and twelve herds of goats, while on Ithaca itself he *Mainland.* had eleven herds of goats and 960 swine. That is, most of his herds are on the mainland, not on the island. Philoetius, on the day of the killing of Penelope's suitors, brought from the mainland (υ 185) a cow and goats for the feast, carried across the water by ferry men.[1] But the classical Ithaca lies more than twenty miles from the mainland, and at no time in the year would so long a voyage for the daily supply of beef and pork be convenient, while during several months of the year it would be entirely impracticable.

A further difficulty in supposing the classical to be the Homeric Ithaca has lain in the identification of the little rocky island Asteris, with twin harbors (δ 846), between *The Island* Ithaca and Samé, on which Penelope's suitors *Asteris.* watched for the return of Telemachus from Pylus, that they might kill him. A rock is found, it is true, in the strait between Ithaca and Cephallenia, but in no way suited, either by its situation or by its size and form, to be the place of ambush for the suitors. It would have been quite unnecessary, for instance, for Telemachus to take pains to pass this in the night ; he might have landed on the southern shore of Ithaca before reaching this place. On the other hand, between Leucas and Ithaca lies a small island, Arkudhi, with a hill more than 400 feet high, which is admirably placed to watch the approach of craft from the south. This island also has on the east a small peninsula, with harbors on either

---

[1] πορθμῆες, υ 187. The ordinary translation of this word is not to be pressed, however, for Herodotus uses the word twice for sailors on the voyage from Tarentum to Corinth (i. 24), and πορθμήϊα for the barges used to carry grain from Asia to Mt. Athos (vii. 25), and Euripides (*Iph. Taur.* 355) uses πορθμίς of a ship which should bring Helen from Greece to the Taurians. So Pythagoras διεπορθμεύθη from the foot of Mt. Carmel to Egypt, ὑπό τινων Αἰγυπτίων πορθμέων, Iamblichus, *Pyth.* iii. 14. But the general force of the argument remains.

side of its isthmus, so near each other and so much alike that they may be called twins.[1] Dr. Dörpfeld draws another argument from the epithet of Ithaca, "lies low in the sea" (χθαμαλή, ι 25), which he understands as "near the ground," and so as "near to land," as opposed to the high sea.   In this he has the support of ancient interpreters (Strabo, 454 C), and of analogous expressions in modern Greek.[2]

The general epithets applied to the island of Ithaca cannot be used in its identification, since they might be applied to most Greek islands.   It is "rocky," "rugged," "sea-girt," "seen from afar," but the Greeks them-selves were well aware that most of their islands were simply the summits of mountains, of which the bases were submerged. Telemachus declines Menelaus's proffered gift of horses and chariot (δ 590, 601), since Ithaca has no broad roads nor meadow ; it is a land for goats and not for horses.   In its characterization by the disguised Athena (ν 244), it is said to have abundant grain, and grapes, and woods ; it has continual dew and showers, and its springs are perennial.   Manifestly these characteristics do not apply to one island rather than to its neighbor.   At present the modern Ithaca has good roads, due largely to the British government of the first half of the last century, while Leucas is still without them, but the latter has the broader plains, none however more than two or three miles in length.

Character-istics of Ithaca.

In the expression, "About it lie many islands" (ι 22),— *about*, if it means strictly *on both sides of*, is better suited to

---

[1] ἀμφίδυμοι, δ 847, however, may mean "with a double entrance," like that by Sphacteria.

[2] Bringing Ithaca near to the mainland, Dörpfeld understands the words, "for I do not think you came here on foot" (α 173, ξ 190, π 59, 224), addressed by an Ithacan to a new-comer in explanation of a question as to the manner of his arrival, not as a *naïve* or slightly humorous remark by the islander, but as expressing the opinion that for some reason or other the stranger probably had not come by land. If a beggar (ξ 190), he would have stopped at the town ; if well dressed (α 173), he did not appear as if he had had a long journey.

Another argument in favor of his theory Dörpfeld draws from the story of the disguised Odysseus of his journey from the land of the Thesprotians (ξ 335). The sailors were on their way to Dulichium, but stopped at Ithaca for supper. This would be natural if Ithaca were Leucas and Dulichium were Samé. According to the old theory, the situation of Dulichium is unknown, and therefore the relative positions of Thesprotia and Ithaca to it cannot be discussed.

PLATE II.

THE CLASSICAL ITHACA, LOOKING NORTH.

Facing p. 72.

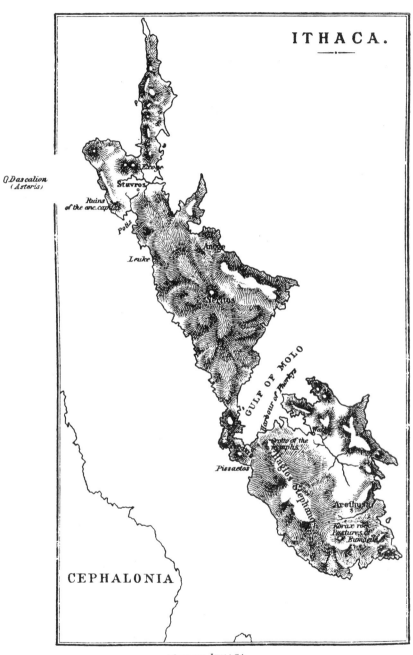

ITHACA.

Q.Dascalion
(Asteris)

Stavros

Ruins
of the anc.capital

Polis

Leuke

Anoge

Neion

GULF OF MOLO

Harbour of Phorty

Pissaetos

Grotto of the
Nymphs

School of
Homer

Arethusa

Korax rock
Pastures of
Eumaeus

CEPHALONIA

MAP OF ITHACA.

the classical Ithaca ; but the "many islands" is well suited
to Leucas, and not at all to the traditional island.

As to local sites on Ithaca.   The Homeric island has two
mountains, of which the larger seems to be Neritos (ι 22, ν
351), while the town itself lies at the foot of Neïos
Sites on
Ithaca.
(γ 81).   A crest immediately above the town is
called the hill of Hermes (π 471).   The town
seems to lie near the harbor, for Telemachus on leaving the
Ithacan assembly (β 260) goes to the shore before going to the
palace.   He washes his hands in the sea, and prays to Athena,
but nothing indicates that he went thither expressly to pray ;
he apparently is on his way home.   Not only from Eumaeus's
herds of swine, but also from Laërtes's farm, one descends to the
town.[1]   The swine kept by Eumaeus fed by the rock of Corax
(Raven Rock) and the spring Arethusa (ν 408).   In addition
to the fountain Arethusa, one, or possibly two, other springs
are mentioned by the poet.   On their way to the city (ρ 205),
Odysseus and the swine-herd Eumaeus were overtaken by the
goat-herd Melanthius at the spring near the city, from which
the people fetched their water.   A grove of alders grew round
about, and the cool water flowed down from above.   An altar
of fountain-nymphs was near at hand, on which all wayfarers
were wont to sacrifice.   The curb of the spring had been built
by Ithacus, Neritus,[2] and Polyctor.   On the morning of the
day in which Penelope's suitors are slain, twenty maid-servants
are sent from her palace to fetch water from the spring,[3] and
nothing indicates that the supply of the palace is from
a different source than that of the city generally.   Three
harbors are mentioned : not only the ordinary harbor, but also
Rheithron (which implies a brook flowing into the sea), away

---

[1] ο 505, υ 163, λ 188.   That at ω 205, on the other hand, Odysseus's party
descended to the farm of Laërtes, on coming from the city, is explained by Goessler
as indicating that a ridge of hills lay between the two places, so that one must both
ascend and descend in going in either direction.

[2] These names are to be understood as formed from those of the island and the
chief mountain rather than (with Goessler) as of three successive kings, who in turn
had beautified this fountain.   The poet nowhere else has any knowledge of these
persons, and they may be represented only as public-spirited citizens.

[3] ἐπὶ κρήνην μελάνυδρον, υ 158.   The epithet μελάνυδρον need not be taken as a
proper name, or as distinguishing this from another spring ; cf. ἀφυσσάμενοι μέλαν
ὕδωρ, δ 359.

PLATE III.   THE HARBOR OF MODERN ITHACA.   Facing p. 74.

from the town, but like it at the foot of Mt. Neïos (a 186), and the harbor of the old sea-god Phorcys (ν 96). Into this last, Odysseus is brought by the Phaeacians. It is formed by projecting headlands which give perfect shelter from winds and waves, so that a boat there may lie at rest without moorings. From it Mt. Neritos can be seen. At its head stands an olive tree, and near at hand is a cave of the naiad nymphs, in which are stone bowls and jars, where bees store honey, and there stand stone looms at which the nymphs weave their mantles. There too is a perennial spring of water. The grotto has two openings, one on the north for men, and the other on the south (presumably higher than the former) for immortals. From this harbor a rocky path led through the forest, along the heights, to the home of the swine-herd Eumaeus (ξ 1). On what part of the island this lay, cannot be said with confidence. If Scheria was the modern Corfù, then the Phaeacians could have landed Odysseus most conveniently on the northern end of the island, but on the other hand, Telemachus coming from Pylus stops at the southern end of the island in order to go to the hut of Eumaeus (o 497 f.), while he sends his boat on to the town. The latter passage seems to have more constraining force than the former, since the Phaeacian ship would not have minded a trifling additional distance. Telemachus needed no harbor in the strict sense, for his landing, since the Homeric boat could land on any smooth beach.

All the sites mentioned in the foregoing paragraph have been found by travellers on the traditional Ithaca, but have not been identified convincingly.[1] For instance, the grotto of the nymphs has been identified *Identifications Unsatisfactory.* with a small unimpressive cave nearly an hour's climb from the main harbor of the island. One may say more reasonably that the poet added the grotto from his own imagination and observation elsewhere than that it was suggested to him by such a hole as is shown on Ithaca. According to another favorite identification, the hut of the

---

[1] For a clear statement with regard to the topography of the classical Ithaca, see Von Marée's *Die Ithakalegende auf Thiaki* in the *Neue Jahrbücher* (1906), xvii. 233.—The map on page 73, from Schuchhardt's *Schliemann's Excavations*, gives the ordinary modern identifications, not those of M. Bérard.—The so-called Cave of the Nymphs is not even beyond the suspicion of having been "improved" in modern times in order to adapt it better to the Homeric story.

swine-herd Eumaeus lay more than ten miles from the home of Odysseus,—which is a long distance to drive swine daily, —and yet the swine arrive before the preparations for the feast are begun (υ 162).

On Leucas Dr. Dörpfeld finds mountains and sites which satisfy fairly well the Homeric requirements. In particular *How does Leucas meet the Requirements ?* Syvota Bay, on the southern shore of the island, forms a beautiful harbor of Phorcys. From it may be seen a bit of the principal mountain of the island, which is nearly 4000 feet high. Small caves are found, with stalactites and stalagmites, but apparently not answering very well to the Homeric description of the Cave of the Nymphs.

Archaeological excavations have shown that Leucas was inhabited in pre-Doric times, but from the nature of the case excavations cannot prove the identity of Leucas with the Ithaca of Odysseus. Nothing but the discovery and decipherment of a Mycenaean inscription on stone or clay or bronze could do this, for even if the remains of an ancient palace should be discovered there, who could testify positively that this was the palace of Odysseus and not another built on a like plan? Scholars who assume that the home of Odysseus was firmly fixed on Ithaca by the early story, and that the poet who inherited and embellished the tale lived only in Asia Minor, and was ignorant of Ithaca and its exact situation, probably will continue to believe that the classical was also the Homeric Ithaca. But those who have been led by the archaeological discoveries of recent years to believe in a firmer basis of fact than was formerly assumed for the story of the *Iliad*, and hold that the poet was operating with known quantities, and see no difficulty in thinking that he may have visited Pylus and the Ionian Islands,—these will be inclined to accept Dr. Dörpfeld's theory.

Perhaps the most vigorous opposition to Dörpfeld's theory has been directed against the assumption of a dislocation of *The Dislocation of Names.* names. This dislocation he is disposed to ascribe to the Dorian migration. The poems in general represent the pre-Dorian situation. That the Dorians came down from the north into Peloponnesus, about one thousand years B.C., and crowded many of the

PLATE IV. SYVOTA BAY (LEUCAS), FROM THE NORTHWEST. Facing p. 76.

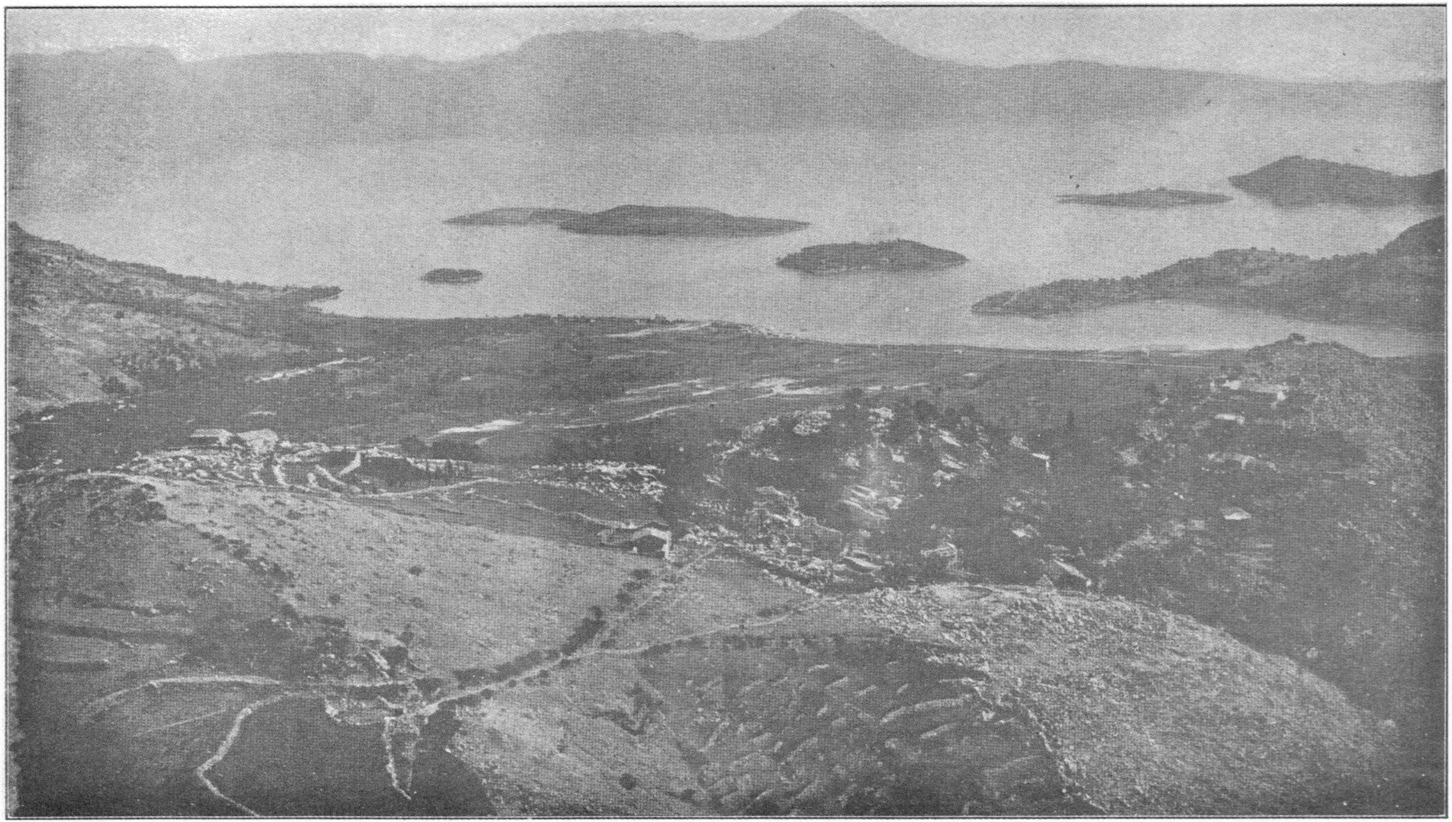

PLATE V. NEOCHORI (LEUCAS), PLAIN OF THE NIDRI, AND THE LITTLE ISLANDS.

Facing p. 77.

Achaeans to the shores of Asia Minor, is generally believed. Dörpfeld thinks that a similar movement of peoples, about the same time, drove before it the Cephallenians of the mainland and the Ithacans from Leucas, the island most accessible from the continent. He observes that of these islands in classical times Leucas alone was inhabited by Dorians. The Cephallenians crossed to Dulichium, and founded a new Cephallenia. The Ithacans crossed to Samé and built there the new Ithaca. Some of the inhabitants of Samé were in turn driven out by the new Ithacans, and founded on Dulichium a city Samos, named from their former home. That emigrating parties often give the old names to their new homes is shown not only by Northern Greek names in Peloponnesus, but also by names of English towns in New England and all over the United States.

If Leucas is accepted as the Homeric Ithaca, then the home of the Taphians (a 105, 417, ξ 452, o 427) cannot be the large island near to Leucas, but must be a like island, Carnus, or Calamos, nearer the shore of Acarnania. On Calamos iron mines have been opened recently, which would show where the Taphian king might have acquired his cargo of iron (a 184).

The Leucadian Rock (Λευκὰς πέτρη, ω 11) is named with the streams of Oceanus, the gates of the sun (through which this passed into darkness), and the country of *The Leucadian Rock.* dreams (which were next of kin to the shades of the dead), as on the route of the souls of Penelope's slain suitors to the home of Hades. But this cliff may not have been conceived as identical with that from which Sappho was fabled to have leaped, although the later story may have been suggested by this cliff, which long stood at the western extremity of the Greek world. The passage in which this expression is found, however, is certainly of late composition.

In the Catalogue of Ships (B 632 f.), according to Dörpfeld, Ithaca is the modern or classical Ithaca, Neritus is Leucadia, and Samos the modern Cephallenia; but in the older parts of the poems, representing the pre-Dorian situation, Ithaca is the classical Leucas, Samé is the historical Ithaca, Dulichium is Cephallenia, and Zacynthus is Zante.

CHAPTER III

THE HOMERIC STATE

THE state in Homeric times was extremely simple and the government depended chiefly on the ruler for the time.
The King was the State. Indeed the government was the king.[1] It had no organization into executive, judicial, and legislative departments. The state neither had legislature nor enacted laws. The king was the leader in both peace and war; he was the general in the field, the presiding officer at all gatherings of the nobles or the people, and the priest at public festivals,—Zeus omnipotent had honored him, and loyalty was due him,—but he had no regular cabinet or staff. He and his heralds were the only public officials. Monarchy prevailed both on earth and on Olympus. Zeus is indeed the type of a Homeric king. We hear of no other kind of government, and of no land without a king,[2] but we must

---

[1] βασιλεύς,—probably in derivation *leader of the people*: cf. duke (*dux*) and the German *Herzog* (*Heer* and *ziehen*). δεσπότης and τύραννος (*despot* and *tyrant*) do not appear in Greek literature until after Homeric times.—Finsler,—*Das homerische Königtum*, in the *Neue Jahrbücher* (1906), xvii. 313 ff., 393 ff.,—argues that the *Odyssey* knows no true monarchy, but the aristocratic form of government prevails. But in Teutonic fashion, he denies the name of monarch to one who does not rule strictly by *divine right*; a king who derives his powers from the people, according to his view, is a mere officer of state. Under these limitations Finsler is right. The poet does not tell us even that Odysseus's father Laërtes, to say nothing of his grandfather Arceisius, ever reigned, nor how the throne came to the family. Alcinoüs inherited his kingdom from his father, but how his father gained it, is not stated. Of course, Finsler's criterion would rule out of the company of monarchs not only Shakespeare's Fortinbras of Norway but also the twentieth century king of Norway, as well as the Polish kings who were elected by the nobles. That the Homeric king does not answer in all things to the state of the modern king, is very true.

[2] The Cyclopes form an apparent exception to this rule, but they not only live in fairy-land but also are savages: "they have no counselling assemblies, either, nor

beware of supposing the Homeric king to have exactly the
same power and dignities as his successor of modern times. No
treasury, standing army, or navy existed. Taxes in
the modern sense were unknown. Troops, boats, *Monarchy prevailed.*
and supplies were provided by special requisition
as occasion demanded. No regularly appointed courts determined justice according to fixed laws. Here, as in many other
matters, we may compare the situation in Israel at almost the
same period, in the reigns of Saul and David. Saul had his
cousin Abner as the captain of his host (1 *Samuel* xiv. 50),
but he had no organized government, and his authority was
limited not by precedents, but only by the bounds of his
power. In the Homeric poems the later word for justice
meant rather manner or precedent than justice in the modern
sense. A just man was one who did as was the wont of the
best of the people, and a good man was a man who was useful
in war or in peace.[1] Custom was law, and the common people
and the nobles may have had a larger part than the kings in
determining custom. At times and in certain places the king
would be more potent than the nobles, and the people would
have little weight in affairs, while again or in another land the
king might be so weak that the government would seem an
aristocracy or a democracy rather than a monarchy,—the
king would be only first among his peers. The unwritten
constitution was subject to great and rapid changes according
to the personal power of the king or of the nobles, but in
general the king seems to have had less absolute power in the
poet's day than is indicated for the king of the Mycenaean age
by the great fortresses and palaces of that time. The subjects
of Menelaus might have refused the toil necessary to build a
citadel like that at Tiryns, and no democratic community
would have constructed the vaulted tomb which was long
known as the Treasury of Atreus. The kings who built the
fortresses at Mycenae must have had some such control over
their subjects as Cheops of Egypt had over his; Cheops'

principles of right, but they dwell in hollow caverns along the summits of high
mountains, and each gives law to his wife and children, nor do they regard each
other" (ι 112).

[1] *Cf.* δίκαιος, *courteous,* γ 52; δίκη, *manner, way,* γ 244; ἀγαθός, *brave, mighty,*
Α 131; ἐσθλός, *brave,* Ζ 489.

pyramid, too, was not built for love.   The royal authority was
limited somewhat by the traditions of former generations, but
doubtless much more by the considerations of policy and
possibility.   The character of the government thus depended
chiefly on the ruler for the time.   One king would consult his
nobles more than his ally might be disposed to do, or more
than his father had done before him.   His rule was analogous
to that of a father in his family (Arist. *Pol.* i. 12), with powers
not clearly defined.   His subjects might decline to obey his
orders, as a son might refuse to obey his father's commands,
and he had no troops, not even a body-guard, either in peace
or in war, at his special command to enforce his will,—not to
speak of having constables or policemen.   Physical, as well as
mental and moral force therefore was important for a powerful
king.   A king had an advantage who, like Telamonian Ajax
(Γ 227) and king Saul (1 *Sam.* ix. 2), was " from his shoulders
and upward higher than any of the ' people."

   How little government was necessary, is shown by the fact
that on the island of Ithaca during the twenty years' absence
of the king, Odysseus, no regent was appointed,
Little Government Necessary. and no session was held either of the assembly of
the people or of any council of nobles (β 26) ; that
is, the island had no government whatever during
this long period.   That the people should do what was good
in their own eyes for so long a time without utter confusion
and demoralization, shows that public opinion and sense of
right was the chief controlling force also during the presence
of the king.   Laërtes, who seems to have been the former
king of Ithaca, was still alive, but he appears to have taken no
steps to resume the reins of government which he had delivered
to his son.   His abdication cannot have been due so much
to his desire to be freed from the burden of civil government,
which must have been light, as to his growing too old to be a
leader on ordinary occasions in war : though even on Odysseus's
return, after an absence of twenty years, Laërtes still has
sufficient vigor to head the party of defense against the attack
of the friends of Penelope's slain suitors (ω 498, 521).   Not a
word indicates that this anarchy in Ithaca was an unusual or
dangerous condition.   The occasion for its mention in the
story is simply the surprise felt at the call of an assembly of

the people by Telemachus. No one of the aspirants for the throne urges that since the return of Odysseus is no longer expected, the vacant throne should be filled at once,—that a delay of a score of years is unusual and dangerous. The poet does not intimate that extraordinary disorder prevailed in Ithaca, except in the one matter,—Penelope's suitors were abusing their position as guests, and were wasting the king's substance, as "if they were masters of the house"; we hear of no murders, robberies, thefts, fraud, or quarrels in the town of Ithaca. The king, then, does not seem so necessary in peace as in war. If Ithaca had been attacked by an enemy during these years, a leader of its army would have been required. On the departure of Odysseus, he had committed to the charge of his old friend Mentor the care of his personal affairs ($οἶκος$, β 226), under the oversight and with the advice of Laërtes, but Mentor had no special authority in the government of the island. The poet nowhere indicates *No Viceroys.* that regents were appointed in other states than Ithaca, either, during the absence of the kings at the siege of Troy. Agamemnon, on embarking for the war, left at his palace a bard as adviser for Clytaemestra, but she held no proper regency, according to Homer, although she did according to Aeschylus (*Agamemnon*, 245). Aegisthus simply usurped the throne of the king when he persuaded the queen to join him (γ 305). Menelaus, too, left no viceroy at Sparta.[1] Similarly, the gods leave Olympus for twelve days to feast with the Aethiopians (A 423), without provision for any temporary government of their subjects, men, during this absence. The importance of the king's part in peace, however, is indicated by the praise bestowed *Kings Dei Gratia.* on Agamemnon (Γ 179, the favorite verse of Alexander the Great),—that he was "both a good king and a mighty man of valor"—"first in war and first in peace." The divine right of kings is recognized at times.[2] At least

---

[1] Fanta thinks that at P 245 Ajax recognizes Menelaus as commander-in-chief in the absence of Agamemnon. But not at all. Ajax appeals to Menelaus only because the latter can be spared better than himself from the conflict over the body of Patroclus.

[2] One of Penelope's suitors warns his associates who are plotting to kill Telemachus that "it is a dreadful thing to shed royal blood" (π 401).

they are "sprung from Zeus,"[1] the king of the gods, and
they are "cherished by Zeus," and "servants of Zeus," just
as warriors are "servants of Ares." Zeus bestows upon them
the sceptre (B 197, 205). The princes Achilles, Ajax,
Agamemnon, Idomeneus, and Priam trace their descent
directly to Zeus, but such a genealogy is not necessary for
a king; Nestor is a grandson of Poseidon.

The right to rule in general is hereditary.[2] Even Penelope's
suitors, each of whom sought the kingdom of Ithaca for himself, acknowledge that by right of inheritance it belongs to
Telemachus (α 387). So Aeneas is told that he may not
hope to succeed Priam, who has sons (Υ 183). If the king
has no son, the sceptre may be given to his daughter's
husband. Thus Tydeus, though an exile from Calydon,
follows Adrastus, as king of Argos (Ξ 119), and Bellerophon,
coming from Corinth, receives a share in the kingdom of
Lycia (Ζ 192 f.). This seems to be the explanation also for
the reign of Menelaus at Sparta,—he wedded the daughter of
Tyndareüs, and succeeded him; but this is not a clear case,
for, according to Γ 236, Helen's brothers were still alive when
she left Sparta, and one of them should have inherited the
sceptre. Atreus was followed directly by his brother Thyestes
(B 106), not by his son Agamemnon, who at the death of
Atreus may not have been old enough to reign, and thus
Agamemnon receives the sceptre later from his uncle. The
situation in Ithaca at the opening of the *Odyssey* was much
like that in Shakespeare's Denmark on the death of the elder
Hamlet. The succession to the throne belonged by customary
right to the late king's son, but the suitors of Penelope hoped
that it would follow the king's widow, just as it went with
Hamlet's mother to her new husband. Evidently, too, an
election in some form, though not by formal ballot, might be
held, just as there was to be a vote in Denmark on the death
of the king and of Hamlet, who gives his vote for Fortinbras.
Eurymachus hopes to be king, for " the people look on him as

---

[1] διογενής is applied to Ajax, Odysseus, Peleus, and others, as Δ 489. For
διοτρεφέων βασιλήων, cf. A 176, B 98. For θεράποντε Διός, meaning simply kings,
of Pelias and Neleus, see λ 255.

[2] Cf. ἐπὶ ῥητοῖς γέρασι πατρικαὶ βασιλεῖαι, Thuc. I. 13, *hereditary monarchies with
fixed privileges, i.e.* limited monarchies.

a god " (o 520). The three divine sons of Cronus divided the kingdom of their father (O 186), but the poet tells of no other such division, unless (what is improbable) Sarpedon and Glaucus have shared the Lycian kingdom (M 313).[1] In default of direct heirs, remote kinsmen might succeed to the throne. Thus on the death of Priam and his sons, Aeneas, by virtue of his descent from Dardanus, was ordained by the gods to reign over the Trojans (Υ 303).

The privileges of the king, like his power and duties, were indefinite, and varied not only in different states, but also at different times in the same state. Telemachus says merely, " It is not a bad thing to be king ; his *King's Privileges Indefinite.* house grows rich and he himself is more highly honored " (α 392). The king has a royal domain (τέμενος, Z 194, Σ 550, ζ 293, λ 185) in addition to his house and private fields,—although no such domain is mentioned as belonging to Odysseus (α 397, δ 757). The king cared for his home and fields, like any other rich man ; Odysseus built his own bed (ψ 189), and had skill to build a barge (ε 243) or to mow a field (σ 366). The princess Nausicaa joined with her maids in laving the family linen (ζ 74), and the princess of the Laestrygonians went to the town-spring to fetch water for the royal household (κ 107). The king receives gifts as tribute from his subjects,—but these gifts are not fixed and definite. Money payments would not be expected at a time when trade was barter, and no fixed ratio, as a tenth of the produce of flocks or fields, was determined for tribute,[2] but more than occasional presents are implied in the words of Agamemnon, in offering to Achilles, if he will return to the work of battle, seven well-built cities, in which dwell men who " will honor him as a god with gifts, and under

---

[1] This, if true, would be not exactly such a division as the former, for Zeus and his brothers each had undivided authority over his own domain, while Sarpedon speaks as if he and his cousin had a common domain. These Lycian kings might be compared more justly to the two kings of Sparta in historical times.

[2] Herodotus, iii. 89, says that down to the time of Darius, the Persians paid no regular taxes, but brought gifts to the king. The Spartan king received the hides of the victims sacrificed at the public festivals, and a suckling from every litter of pigs, in addition to a few other similar tributes, but his domain seems to have been his most important source of income. In 1 *Sam.* x. 27, we read that the children of Belial brought to Saul " no presents," *i.e.* they did not recognize his authority.

his sceptre will pay delightful dues" (θέμιστας, I 156). The king receives a share, a "gift of honor" (γέρας, A 163), in the spoils of forays, even of those in which he had no personal part. Achilles complains that of the booty which he had brought back from his many expeditions near Troy, Agamemnon, though he had remained in the camp, had retained much and had divided little (I 333), and Thersites says that the king's tents are full of bronze and of slaves which the Achaeans give to him first when they capture a town (B 226). Doubtless both these speakers exaggerate their causes, though the king's portion of the booty was not fixed by law, but depended on his will and power,—which included his favor with the people. Briseïs, the cause of the quarrel between Achilles and Agamemnon, was such a gift of honor to Achilles, while Chryseïs was taken by Agamemnon as his prize. Sometimes Briseïs is called the gift of the people (A 299), and sometimes the gift of the king, since he had acted as their agent in dividing the spoil (I 367). Nausicaa's old nurse was such a gift to Alcinoüs (η 10), and Hecamede was selected as a present for Nestor (Λ 627). If the king went on the foray in person he had a right to his ordinary share of the booty, as well as to his special gift of honor, which was set aside before the general division of the spoil. He had also an apparent right to an invitation to all feasts made by his subjects (λ 187), and the Ithacans recognized Telemachus's claim to the throne, or at least his right to act as a representative of his father, by thus inviting him. So the seat of honor, the best piece of flesh at the feast, and full cups of wine (M 311) are named as royal emoluments.

Some scholars have thought that the king received large court-fees for his services as judge, but this seems to be putting late Athenian notions into Homeric times, *Duties to King in Peace and War.* and is unsupported by the poems. Once the poet speaks of a silver cup as given by Sidonians to the Lemnian king (Ψ 745), clearly as a kind of harbor dues, but this was exceptional, though naturally strangers calling at the port for trade would seek the king's favor. Doubtless the king could call upon his subjects for certain services in peace. Nothing is said about payment to the smith who gilded the horns of a heifer which Nestor sacrificed to Athena (γ 425 ff.), and probably the smith was bound to do such work for his king in return for the privilege of exercising his craft at sandy Pylus.[1] Certainly the king could call upon his subjects for service in war. For the expedition against Troy, each household was expected to furnish at least one warrior. Hermes, in the guise of a comrade of Achilles, says that he was chosen by lot from among his father's seven sons, to join the army of the Achaeans (Ω 400). In lieu of service in the army a rich vassal of Agamemnon gives to him a swift mare (Ψ 296). Another comes to the war, though his death in battle was foretold, "avoiding the heavy fine" (θωήν, X 669), which evidently would have been imposed upon him by the king for failure to perform military duty.

The sceptre (σκῆπτρον,—a long staff as it is represented on the monuments of later times) was already the symbol of royal power, although it was borne also by some other officials. Zeus gave to Agamemnon the "sceptre *The Sceptre.* and rights" (σκῆπτρόν τ' ἠδὲ θέμιστας, I 99), and "to be honored above all others with the sceptre" (I 38). Similarly Zeus subdued the Argives under the sceptre of Proetus (ὑπὸ σκήπτρῳ ἐδάμασσεν, Z 159). Agamemnon's sceptre was made by Hephaestus and given to Zeus, who sent it by Hermes to Pelops, who gave it to his son Atreus, at whose death it passed to the brother Thyestes, and then to Atreus's son Agamemnon (B 101). Odysseus receives from the king this sceptre as a token of royal commission, like a royal ring or the king's seal, when he sets out to check the disorderly rush of the Achaeans to their ships (B 186). "Sceptre-bearing" (σκηπτοῦχοι, B 86) is eight times an epithet of kings. Naturally, the king did not always have this staff with him, but Nestor sits before the door of his palace holding his "sceptre" (γ 412). In its origin, of course, the sceptre was only a staff ("that on which one leaned"—σκήπτω), and it is borne and held as a mark of authority also by men acting as judges (Σ 505), by speakers before assemblies (A 234, Γ 218, β 37), and by priests (A 15, 28), as well as by heralds (Σ 505). Even a beggar might have a σκῆπτρον, but this would be a mere stick,

---

[1] *Cf.* the "duty-work" and "duty-chickens" which the Irish tenant of the eighteenth century owed to his landlord.

and no one would suspect it in his hands of being a badge of office.[1] The staff with which Priam in his access of grief drives forth the Trojans from his halls, is certainly not then held as a badge of authority, but is used as any staff might be wielded (Ω 247).

No special royal robe was customary ; purple and saffron were not yet kingly colors. No crown was worn ; no crowns

Royal Array. or even garlands are mentioned by the poet. The word from which our *throne* is borrowed designates a heavy chair, with back, arms, and foot-stool. Several of these, however, would stand in every great hall, and were not limited to royal use.

In two passages the power of the king seems unexpectedly absolute. Agamemnon offers to Achilles, on

King's Power Absolute. condition of his return to the work of battle, seven cities near the sea, on the frontier of Pylus (I 149), and Menelaus says that if Odysseus had returned from the Trojan war, he would have brought him from Ithaca with his wife and child and people, and have given him a city in Argos, " clearing out " (ἐξαλαπάξας, δ 176) one of the cities under the speaker's rule. Scholars have called attention to the facts that the cities to which Agamemnon and Menelaus refer are in the same region, and that here were subject towns in later times also ; these may have been captured rather than inherited cities. The king could hardly have treated an ordinary town or district of his country in so summary a fashion, though he was irresponsible to anybody. The Lycian king gives to Bellerophon the half of his kingly honor (τιμῆς βασιληίδος, Z 193), but this gift is made with the approval of the people, for these bestow on Bellerophon a royal domain. Probably the king took the new-comer, to whom he gave his daughter's hand and thus designated him as his successor, as his associate in the government. Peleus gives to Phoenix the rule of a district (I 483), but doubtless this was a government wholly subordinate to his own.

The words of Menelaus to which reference has been made

---

[1] Fanta thinks that in the later lays of the *Odyssey*, the sceptre is no kingly sign ; but it is better to understand that the original meaning of the word (*staff*) is retained in the language by the side of the later.

in the preceding paragraph, raise the question of the mutual
relation of superior and inferior kings.   The Spartan king could hardly have meant that Odysseus *Superior and*
should abandon entirely his sovereignty ; he must *Inferior Kings.*
have meant that Odysseus should live on his land
and retain his authority over his people ; and so he would
have been a king in a part of another's kingdom.   The
physical geography of the Argolid does not suggest how and
where a line of separation should run between the kingdom of
Diomed at Argos and that of Agamemnon at Mycenae, yet
only Agamemnon and Nestor led more ships to Troy than
Diomed, and nothing indicates any special subordination on
his part to the king of Mycenae.[1]   When the king's rights and
authority were so loosely defined, his power was felt of
necessity more distinctly at his immediate home than in a
village thirty or fifty miles distant.   Odysseus ruled over the
mainland near Ithaca (B 635), and had flocks and herds there
(ξ 100), but the poet tells his hearer nothing of the government on the mainland ; in ordinary times it may have been
nearly as inactive as that in Ithaca during the king's absence.
Even the extent of Odysseus's kingdom is left entirely indefinite by the poet.   Suitors for Penelope's hand came from
Zacynthus, Samé, and Dulichium (π 245), which thus seem
to have been included in his domain ; but on the mainland
his authority is undefined.   On the island of Syrié were two
cities, and the father of Eumaeus reigned in both (o 412),—
but these may have been situated near each other.

The king was the natural leader of his subjects in war.
This was his principal office.   Agamemnon and Menelaus
were " marshallers of the people " ($\kappa o\sigma\mu\acute{\eta}\tau o\rho\epsilon$ $\lambda\alpha\hat{\omega}\nu$,
A 16).   If the king lived to be too old for this *King the*
service, he might abdicate his throne, like Laërtes *Leader in*
on Ithaca,[2] or he might be represented on the field *War.*
of battle by one of his sons, as Priam is represented by Hector

---

[1] See, however, note on page 65.

[2] The poet nowhere expressly states that Laërtes was king before Odysseus, but on
the other hand nothing indicates that a violent change of government had taken
place, and the throne of Ithaca is hereditary (a 387).   That Laërtes on his withdrawal from the town lives a wretched life, and labors with his own hands (having
nothing else to do), of course does not show that his reign has been contemptible.

and Peleus by Achilles.[1]   Nestor, in spite of his advanced
age, being more than sixty years old, is still vigorous ; he
brings ninety ship-loads of warriors against Ilium (B 602),
and takes part in the battles, though he is not stated to kill
any Trojan, and he leads no onset.   Whether the king had the
right to declare war on his own responsibility, is an academic
question which cannot be answered.   He certainly would not
undertake a war without the assured support of his chieftains.

"Minister of justice" (δικασπόλος, λ 186) is used once as
nearly equivalent to *king*, and a blameless king is one who
The King as "fears the gods and maintains right" (εὐδικίας
Judge. ἀνέχῃσι, τ 111), yet the king does not seem to be
a judge by virtue of his office.   As representative
of the government, he had to take account of but few offenses.
Formal laws did not exist, and *justice*, as we have seen, was
custom and precedent.   Most crimes and misdemeanors which
are offenses against a modern state, were private matters and
details of private quarrels in the Homeric age.   Even a murder
was not yet a public crime ; it was a private wrong against the
murdered man and his family.[2]   The murderer withdrew from
his country in order to escape vengeance, not legal prosecution,
Murder or punishment in the strict sense.   The presence of
brought no a murderer then constituted no such pollution to
Pollution. the people of the land as it did in later times in
Greece, and thus the act of killing in itself was
no offense against either state or gods ; just as, even to-day,
among the Mainotes in southern Sparta, homicide is said to be
regarded simply as a matter between man and man.   No ceremonial act of religious purification for the defilement of homicide
is known, such as was absolutely necessary in the classical period.
The Homeric Orestes, on killing Aegisthus, has no such cleansing
process to undergo as is assumed by the *Eumenides* of Aeschylus.[3]

[1] The ghost of Achilles in Hades inquires of Odysseus whether Peleus still retains
his royal honor (λ 495), or whether he is slighted in his old age, with no living son
near him to support his rights.

[2] In Attica, much later, the murderer could not be prosecuted if he had been
forgiven by the murdered man when dying, or even were forgiven by the next of kin.
No public officer was charged with the duty of discovering and punishing a criminal.

[3] Probably the Homeric version of the story of Orestes allowed Clytaemestra to
hang herself in desperation and shame.   The deed for which Orestes is praised by
our poet is his killing of Aegisthus, not that of Clytaemestra (α 299).

But circumstances might make a homicide a dread offense against the gods, especially if the tie of kinship or "guest-friendship" existed between the slayer and the slain. The Erinyes, or Furies, avenge wrongs to kindred, though they do not punish ordinary homicide; they might have followed Orestes if he had killed his mother, but they did not harass Aegisthus for killing his cousin Agamemnon. The only court-scene which is depicted by the Homeric poet is between two men after a murder: one declares and the other denies that the "ransom" or fine has been paid (Σ 498).[1] No question arises as to the execution of the murderer, for which, indeed, the state had no provision. Evidently, extenuating circumstances have persuaded the friends of the man who has been killed, to accept a payment of property in satisfaction of their loss, and the only question before the court is whether this payment has been made. Ajax, reproaching Achilles for his stubborn anger on account of a captive, says that many a man receives compensation ($\pi o \iota \nu \acute{\eta} \nu$, I 633) from the slayer of his brother or his son, and that this murderer remains in the land, on paying a heavy penalty as "damages."[2] In general, however, the murderer believed it wise for him to flee the land.[3] The friends of the slain man under ordinary circumstances were bound to avenge his death, and might pursue the murderer even into distant lands (o 224). Nestor in speaking of Orestes's vengeance on his father's murderer, says "What a good thing it is when a son remains to take vengeance for a slain father" (γ 196). Achilles does not care to live if he cannot avenge the death of his comrade Patroclus (Σ 101), and he

---

[1] See below, page 91. The interpretation that one desires to pay, while the other refuses to receive, a ransom for blood-guiltiness, is improbable, for the injured family could not be compelled by a court to receive gold as "damages,"—the matter rested entirely with their will.

[2] This custom of accepting a fine in satisfaction for a homicide, existed among the ancient Germans also. Cf. Tacitus, *Germania*, 21.

[3] So Patroclus as a boy killed a playmate, in a quarrel about their game, and was taken by his father at once to the home of Peleus, where he and his father remained (Ψ 85, Λ 771). Tydeus, as is made clear in the later story, went to Argos as a suppliant because he had killed his uncle (cf. Ξ 119). Tlepolemus killed his grand-uncle, and withdrew to Rhodes because of the threats of his kinsmen (B 662). Cf. N 696, O 432, II 573, Ω 481, ν 259, ξ 380, o 272, ψ 118.—Even assassination seems no great cause of shame (ν 267).

begs the soul of his friend to forgive him for yielding to Priam
the body of Hector (who slew Patroclus) ; he will share with
his dead friend the ransom for this body (Ω 592). This spirit
of vengeance is the more remarkable since Patroclus had not
been murdered by Hector, but had been killed in open battle.
But in the fight, warriors often seek to avenge the death of a
friend (*cf.* N 414),—introducing a strong personal element into
the conflict. If the exile, fleeing from vengeance, proved
himself a mighty man of valor, he might receive honor and
citizenship in his new home. Otherwise he had no rights
whatever.

If homicide was a private offense, still more were all minor
personal assaults matters of which the state as such took no
cognizance. Theft as well as murder was a purely
personal cause, and each man had to protect the
rights of himself and his family, although as in
rude societies of the present day the neighbors of
the injured party might be willing on their own account to aid
in the punishment of one who might steal from them next.
Telemachus was considered particularly unfortunate, since he
had no brothers who would be his natural supporters (*cf.*
δ 164, π 115). Andromache, in speaking of the helpless fate
of an orphan, says that "others will take away his fields"
(X 489); from such a wrong the orphan had no appeal to
the law, but he might turn to the people (as Telemachus did
when his mother's suitors were wasting his substance, and he
was unable to defend himself, β 49), or he might seek the
personal sympathy of the king or other powerful men. Priam's
grandson might be supposed to be fairly secure in his rights,
but Andromache anticipates that he will be wronged on the
death of Hector. Most of the private lawsuits of the present
day were necessarily absent from the Homeric world. The
Achaeans had no written documents, and no mortgages to
foreclose. Debts there were, however, and disputes about
property, and doubtless other grounds of difference. The
Achaeans had a place set apart for a court in their camp, near
the *agora* (Λ 807). In a comparison, the poet speaks of a
man as returning to his evening meal from the place of
assembly where he had been "deciding the contentions"
($\kappa\rho\acute{\iota}\nu\omega\nu$ $\nu\epsilon\acute{\iota}\kappa\epsilon\alpha$, μ 440) of young men. Nothing indicates that

Assault and Theft Private Offenses.

this judge was a king. Doubtless most trials were really arbitrations, both parties consenting to such a determination of their claims, since no court had the means to see that its decisions were executed, nor even that a delinquent debtor was brought before it. No *subpoena* could be issued for offender or witness. The parties to the suit must both be " willing," as they were in the scene depicted on the Shield of Achilles, to attain a decision,—not as in our courts, into which one of the litigants may be brought sorely against his will. The king, as the chief man of the state, may have been the natural and usual arbitrator[1] in case of a quarrel, but he does not seem to be the judge *ex officio*,[2] and nothing indicates that a special class of causes was reserved for his decision. The poet notes particularly that Arete, Alcinoüs's queen, settles even disputes of men (καὶ ἀνδράσι νείκεα λύει, η 74). On the Shield of Achilles Hephaestus wrought a representation of a court in which the elders (γέροντες, Σ 503), sitting in a circle on seats of polished stone, with heralds' staves in their hands, were acting as judges. The king is not mentioned as present. The people are present, however, actively making known their approval of one side or the other, although they are restrained by heralds. One of the contesting parties claims that he has paid a recompense for a man whom he has killed ; the other, a representative of the family of the murdered man, declares that he has received nothing, and both are eager to attain a decision before a judge (ἐπὶ ἴστορι, Σ 501, *cf.* Ψ 486). Two talents of gold lie before the court, to be given to him " who shall speak justice most straightly." [3] These seem to have

---

[1] According to the story of Herodotus, i. 96, Deïoces, the first king of the Medes, gained his throne by his impartiality in deciding cases submitted to his decision in a time of great injustice, so that men came from other villages to lay their causes before him,—clearly as an arbitrator. So in Israel (2 *Sam.* xv. 2) the people "came to the king for judgment."

[2] Aristotle says that the kings in the early age of Greece were judges in lawsuits (τὰς δίκας ἔκρινον, *Politics*, 1285 b 11).

[3] This passage is ambiguous, and has been much discussed. Some scholars believe that the gold was a court-fee, and was to be presented as a reward to the special judge who should give the best opinion ; but who would decide which of the judges pronounced the wisest opinion ? Was this likely to be obvious ? Was the applause of the bystanders (repressed by the heralds) to decide ? If no Solomon or Daniel came to judgment, a second trial would be necessary for the determination of the several claims of the judges. Other scholars have thought the gold to be the sum at

been deposited by the contestants, one by each, to be in a manner a compensation for the trouble of the suit, as costs for the litigants. If the murderer lost his case, his money as well as the price of blood would be given to the prosecutor ; if he won his case, he received the two talents.

The active sympathy of the people in this suit is noticeable ; indeed, the expression "laying his case before the people" (δήμῳ πιφαύσκων, Σ 500) is used, and the case is really tried before the popular assembly, and the reader remembers that the heliastic courts at Athens were really only committees of the ecclesia.

Appeal to Public Opinion.

This appeal to public opinion is important, since the state has no machinery to enforce a judgment. The contestants desire the sympathy of their neighbors, and their acquaintance with the facts, since the aid of the neighbors may be necessary in order to enforce the judgment. Again the poet assumes a court of judges, rather than the king as a single judge, when he speaks of Zeus as angry with those "who, with violence, in the place of assembly give crooked judgments (σκολιὰς θέμιστας, Π 387) and drive out justice, not considering the watchful eye (ὄπιν) of the gods,"[1] where the decision seems to rest with the people, rather than with the nobles. The king's office, then, did not bind him to see justice done and wrong punished, although a sense of decency as well as self-interest required him, as the most powerful man in a community, to make right prevail so far as practicable. A righteous reign brought manifold blessings (τ 107). If a king was with full purpose (πρόφρων, β 230) gentle and kindly, he deserved praise. Odysseus was gentle (ἤπιος, β 47) as a father to his people. In Hades, Odysseus sees Minos "giving judgments to the dead" (θεμιστεύοντα νέκυσσιν, λ 569). This certainly does not mean that he was judging them for the deeds done in the body, and still less that he was assigning them to future abodes in Elysium or Tartarus, but rather

issue between the parties at variance ; but "two talents of gold" are the fourth prize in the horse race, Ψ 269, in which a mare was the second prize, and the value seems too little to be the price of blood. Others still have suggested that the gold was to pay the expenses of the court ; but a court had no expenses at that time. If the court had but a single judge, he might have received the gold as a fee for his trouble ; but here a company of elders was sitting as judges.

[1] In Hesiod's *Works and Days*, the princes (βασιλῆες, 38, 261), are the judges.

that he was determining their dues or duties in their present shadowy existence. Whether, however, the poet thought of Minos as exercising executive or judicial functions, serving as a king or as an arbitrator, is not clear.[1] According to Aristotle, Agamemnon claimed the right to put to death (παρ' ἐμοὶ θάνατος, *Politics* 1285 a 14,—words not in our Homeric MSS.), but this may refer only to his power, not to his pre-rogative ; so when Hector threatens death to Pulydamas for opposing his will (M 250), this is a violent measure. Clearly a Homeric court had no sheriff or other officers to carry out its decisions, and the state had no prison in which an offender could be confined. Probably a Homeric king would make a special officer of the most convenient person at hand, but no punishment is adjudged by a court or inflicted by the people in the Homeric poems. The stoning[2] which is sug-gested for Paris (Γ 57) would have been mere mob violence. The person in whose favor a sentence had been given would himself see to its execution.

The king not only is leader in war and the first in the council, but also represents his people before the gods.[3]   At the feast of the Achaean council before setting out *King* for the first battle of the *Iliad*, Agamemnon offers *represents his* the prayer for the sacrifice, as the head of the *People before* public family (B 402) ; and at the making of the *the Gods.* truce for a single combat, he prays to the gods and cuts the throats of the lambs (Γ 271 ff.). Thus also Alcinoüs seems to offer sacrifice for his people to Poseidon (ν 181). No priest is mentioned in these connexions, nor at the great sacrifice of the Pylians to Poseidon (γ 5), nor at the harvest-home festival of Oeneus (I 535). Indeed the services of priests seem limited to their temples, and thus no priest is found in the Achaean army before Troy. The sacrifice, on the other hand, which Agamemnon performs at his recon-

---

[1] The word *judge* seems at times to mean simply rule ; *cf.* Τρωσί τε καὶ Δαναοῖσι δικαζέτω, Θ 431, "let [Zeus] rule as he will." We remember that the *Judges* of the Israelites were rulers, and that the Psalmist (*Ps.* xcviii. 9) in "for he cometh to *judge* the earth," means simply that the Lord will *rule* the world.

[2] If the Homeric expression means simply "a stone coffin," yet death is implied and the above remark holds good.

[3] τὰ πρὸς τοὺς θεοὺς ἀποδέδοται τοῖς βασιλεῦσιν, Aristotle, *Politics*, 1285 a 6 ; κύριοι δ' ἦσαν (*sc.* οἱ βασιλεῖς) . . . καὶ τῶν θυσιῶν, ὅσαι μὴ ἱερατικαί, *ib.* 1285 b 10.

ciliation with Achilles (T 252 ff.), is personal rather than public, and those of Peleus in his palace (Λ 772) and Nestor at Pylus (γ 444) are domestic in their nature. Penelope's suitors had with them one who had the special duty of attending to the sacrifices (θυοσκόος, φ 145),—but this was in the house of Odysseus, who was absent from home. The priestly office of the king seems another survival from the early patriarchal form of government, and it is noteworthy in this connexion that at Athens the Archon Basileus represented the state in relation to the gods, and had charge of all matters of public worship. Elsewhere in Greece the monarchy at times degenerated into an hereditary priesthood.

Title of King Bestowed Freely.   The title of king or prince (βασιλεύς) is bestowed freely. Telemachus, in speaking of his hopes, says that there are many other princes of the Achaeans in sea-girt Ithaca, some one of whom may have the royal honor ; but he will be the master (ἄναξ, α 397) of his house and servants. The island of Ithaca is reported to have only 12,500 inhabitants now, and very likely had no more in the Homeric age. It could have few princes in the modern sense, especially since no kinsmen of Telemachus are named on the island. On Scheria were twelve princes in addition to Alcinoüs (θ 390, ζ 54),—certainly with no definite sphere of authority. Some old writers dreamed that these princes might have ruled successively, as the "command of the day" came to each in turn, but this is unsupported by evidence. They seem to have received prerogatives from the people (η 150), but what these privileges were, is not clear. They formed a council, but this, too, had only indefinite powers. Apollo, in the form of a son of Priam, taunts Aeneas with the contrast between his withdrawing before Achilles and his previous boasts to the princes of the Trojans (βασιλεῦσιν, Υ 84),—certainly including others than Priam's sons. The feminine form is used of the *princess* Nausicaa (ζ 115).

The title *anax* (ἄναξ, *protecting lord, lord, master*) is broader and more frequently used than that of *king*. Thus it is given to the gods (especially to Apollo), who are never called kings. It is applied particularly to Agamemnon, as "king of men" (ἄναξ ἀνδρῶν, nearly fifty times), though even this phrase is used of others, as of Anchises and Aeneas (E 268, 311), but it is applied also to the owners of flocks (δ 87), and to Polyphemus in relation to his pet ram (ι 452). The verb formed from it sometimes retains distinctly the meaning of *protect, defend*, as in Chryses's prayer addressed to Apollo, "who art the mighty protector of Tenedos" (Τενέδοιό τε ἶφι ἀνάσσεις, A 38, not "who dost rule Tenedos with a rod of iron"), and in Hector's prayer for his son, that he might be "the great defender of Ilium" ('Ιλίου ἶφι ἀνάσσειν, Z 478). Thus the infant son of Hector was called by the people Astyanax (*Defender of the City*, Z 403), because Hector himself was the main defence of Troy.[1]

The Title Anax.

A similar idea to that of *anax* is in the descriptive title *shepherd of the people* (ποιμένι λαῶν, γ 156), which is applied to kings and chieftains more than fifty times,[2]—to Agamemnon more frequently than to any one else. Compare "He shall feed his flock like a shepherd" (*Isaiah* xl. 10).

Shepherd of the People.

The term κοίρανος may be translated freely as sovereign. It is used eight times,—notably in the words of Odysseus: "The sovereignty of many (πολυκοιρανίη, B 204) is not good ; let there be one sovereign (κοίρανος), one king (βασιλεύς),—the one to whom the son of Cronus gave it." This remark has been thought to indicate a knowledge of a democratic rule, but it refers rather to anarchy, and is suggested naturally by the situation, "We cannot all be masters here." The corresponding verb (κοιρανεῖν) means *hold sway over, rule*. The disguised Odysseus warns the beggar Irus not to play the sovereign (κοίρανος εἶναι, σ 106) over strangers and beggars.

"Sovereign."

The word *ruling, ruler* (κρείων), is used about seventy times. The expression *wide-ruling* (εὐρὺ κρείων) is used twelve times of Agamemnon, and once of Poseidon. The feminine is used once, *queen of women* (κρείουσα γυναικῶν X 48), by Priam of his wife Laothoë. In later stories this

"Ruler."

---

[1] For the epithet of the father given as a name to the son, cf. Telemachus (*Fighting far from home*), Eurysaces (*With broad shield*) for the son of Ajax, and Gershom, (*Stranger*, in *Exodus* ii. 22) for Moses's son born in the land of Midian.

[2] Less significance is to be attributed to the comparative frequency of the use of such epithets, because of the influence of the convenience of the verse on the poet's choice of words or phrases.

word was used as a proper name for several princes and princesses, as Creon of Thebes, Creüsa of Corinth, and the wife of Aeneas.

The term *counsellor, ruler* (μέδων), is generally connected with that for leader and applied to chieftains (ἡγήτορες ἠδὲ μέδοντες, B 79), *leaders in both war and peace.* Once it is applied to Phorcys as the ruler of the sea (α 72). A cognate form is addressed to Zeus as "ruling from Mount Ida" (Ἴδηθεν μεδέων, Γ 276).

The story of the poems does not require exact statements with regard to governments, and we may believe that the law of the Achaean soldiery before Ilium, and of *Martial Law.* the Trojans in their city during the siege, was stricter than prevailed in countries which were at peace—it was "martial law,"—and that the royal authority on Ithaca had been weakened by the long absence of Odysseus. So Aristotle (*Politics*, 1285 a) believed that the power of the Homeric kings on the field in war was greater than at home. So far as we can judge, however, the government of the Achaean army before Troy was much like that of the Achaean people in Greece. Meetings of the council (βουλή) and of the assembly were held as usual (γ 127). Agamemnon was "king of men," and the commander-in-chief of the expedition, in one sense : he had gathered the forces and he had furnished more men and far more ships (B 576, 612) than any other ruler. He was "most royal," he "ruled mightily over all the Argives"[1] and he was expected to lead both in counsel and in action ; all depended on him, whatever prevailed (I 97 ff.). Yet not Agamemnon, the commander-in-chief, but Achilles, a leader of auxiliary forces, calls an assembly of the Achaean soldiery when the pestilence has been raging in the camp for nine days (A 54), and the notion that Agamemnon is offended by this act of Achilles, is not supported by any word in the poems, but solely by modern views of military propriety. After the quarrel and Achilles's withdrawal from the field of battle, Agamemnon cannot have him tried by court-martial for insubordination, or punished in any other way. Achilles is an independent prince in the army on the plain of Troy, just as he is when at home in Thessaly. He has come to

---

[1] βασιλεύτατος, I 69 ; ἄριστος Ἀχαιῶν, B 82 : μέγα πάντων Ἀργείων κρατέει, A 79.

Troy as a volunteer, to aid Agamemnon in securing satisfaction for the rape of Helen, but retains his independence, and may return to his home at his pleasure (I 356 f.); he even threatens to advise the other chieftains to return to their homes. The other Achaean princes were doubtless just as untrammelled as Achilles. So also Nestor in his early years fought as an independent ally of the Lapithae (κατ' ἔμ' αὐτόν, A 271), and the disguised Odysseus, claiming to be a Cretan, says that he was not subordinate to the Cretan king Idomeneus on the plain of Troy (ν 265, ξ 238), but was an independent commander. Even Menelaus, in the preparations for the return of the soldiery after the capture of the city of Troy, refuses to follow Agamemnon's wishes (γ 141), but sets sail at his own pleasure.

A council of Achaean chieftains is held at the opening of the first day of battle, to discuss the delusive dream which Zeus has sent to Agamemnon (B 53); another a little later, just before the battle (B 404); a third at the close of the same day, which determines *Council of Achaeans.* plans for the burial of the dead and for the building of a wall about the camp (H 313); a fourth at the close of the second day of the battle (I 89), which sends an embassy to Achilles, begging him to return to the conflict; and another, perhaps a smaller gathering, a little later in the same night (K 195), which sends Diomed and Odysseus as spies into the Trojan bivouac. In no one of these is a word said about any plan of battle. In all, Agamemnon is rather the presiding officer than an absolute commander. Thrice the wise Nestor makes the proposition which is carried (H 324, I 93, K 203), and he says the decisive word also at the close of the first council (B 83), while at the close of their common breakfast (B 435) he gives the command for action, just as the old Echeneüs in the palace of Alcinoüs suggests to the king the course which is then followed (η 159). The poet tells of an Ithacan envoy sent in early days by "Laërtes and the elders" (φ 21), which shows the latter's influence, if not their power. Hector declares that he has been unable to follow the "offensive" plan of war, because he has been hindered by the elders of the city (O 721). The princes take part in the sacrifice for the truce made between Priam and Agamemnon on the first day of the battles (Γ 270); they are too many to lay hands directly upon the heads of the victims, and therefore Agamemnon cuts wool from these, which wool, clearly representing the victims themselves, the heralds distribute to the Trojan and Achaean chieftains before the prayer to the gods.   A more or less formal vote of the councillors is taken at H 344, I 173, 710, η 226, ν 16, 47.   On Olympus too, Zeus, though absolute and almighty, and sometimes outspoken in the statement of his sovereignty, does not desire to act without the approval of the other gods, and not infrequently yields his personal preference (α 65 ff., Δ 14 ff.).

That the council of chieftains is an informal body rather than a cabinet or senate with definite rights, is indicated by *Membership in Council Variable.* the fact that its membership seems variable.   Who are present at the first council before Troy is not stated.   In the meeting just before the first battle, Agamemnon has to breakfast with him not only his brother Menelaus, but also Nestor, Idomeneus, the two Ajaxes, Diomed, and Odysseus (B 404).   These would form a council of seven, a not improbable number in itself, although Achilles must have been included except during the sixteen days of his wrath, as is seen from his presence at the breakfast in Agamemnon's tent on the morning after Hector's death (Ψ 35); but in the fifth council, six chieftains volunteer to go into the Trojan camp, including Meriones who was not in the former company (K 227), and the terms of the story forbid the supposition that all the captains present volunteered for the service.   Evidently also, Agamemnon is not clear in his mind as to the persons who should be called to the meeting ; the chieftains do not constitute a distinctly defined body.   Menelaus comes to the breakfast without invitation, and the others would need only a notification if they formed the council.   If we suppose the commanders of the several contingents to form a senate, we have a company of twenty-nine (according to the Catalogue of Ships), but some of the contingents have two or more heads, while other commanders named in the Catalogue have no prominence in the action of the *Iliad.*   At Γ 146, seven elders (δημογέροντες) of the Trojans are sitting with Priam on the tower by the Scaean gate,—and these have been thought by some to constitute his council.   But was no one of the sons of Priam, not even Hector, nor one of the sons of Antenor, nor Aeneas, a member of the Trojan council? This would seem unreasonable; at this moment the younger nobles and members of the council naturally are engaged on the field of battle. Alcinoüs, king of the Phaeacians, had twelve princes to form a council with himself (θ 390); at η 189 several of the elders are feasting with him, but he says that on the following morning he will call more elders for the discussion of the succor to be given to Odysseus. A council of Trojan leaders is held by Hector on the field after the second day of battle,— to ask who would go into the Greek camp (K 301). This company cannot have been very select, for Dolon, a man of no distinction, is present, and of course it includes none of the elders who were with Priam by the Scaean gate. To say that Dolon may have been present simply as a bystander, makes the meeting of the council informal.

In the story of Eumaeus, the nobles had been dining with his royal father, and had gone to the "session and speech of the people" ($\dot{\epsilon}$ς θῶκον δήμοιό τε φῆμιν, ο 468),—where the "session" is thought to refer to a meeting of the council. Perhaps, however, the council *Common Table.* had met at the king's table, and the "session" refers to the general assembly. A "common mess" at the expense of the people, like the common dinners of the *archons* and *prytanes* in later Athens, seems to be assumed in P 250 for the Achaeans, and at M 319 for the Lycians.[1] To give a feast to the elders (I 70) is equivalent to holding a session of the council. According to four verses which Wolf rejected as un-Homeric (δ 621 f.), feasters come to the palace of Menelaus, bringing sheep, wine, and bread. This would be

[1] The princes drink the wine "of the people" (δήμια πίνουσιν, P 250) in the tents of Agamemnon and Menelaus, and the chieftains of the Atgives mix "aldermanic wine" (γερούσιον οἶνον, Δ 259; cf. ν 8). Some of these feasters have a limited portion of wine (δαιτρόν, Δ 262), as may have been the case also in the *Syssitia* of Sparta, while others have their cups "always full." That is, as is seen elsewhere, men of all ranks and deserts sit together in the same hall, but are not treated exactly alike. That entertainment for public guests also should be at the expense of the people is shown by the expectation of the Phaeacian nobles to reimburse themselves for their gifts to Odysseus by collections among the people (ν 14), and by the story of the disguised Odysseus of gifts bestowed by a brother of Idomeneus "from the people" (δημόθεν, τ 197). But the king acted as host, being the natural representative of his folk.

for a feast of "the elders," the council, but not at the public expense ; it is an ἔρανος (α 226). Before Troy, also, the Achaeans " make ready a feast for the elders " (δαῖτα γέρουσιν ἐφοπλίζωμεν, Δ 344). That the queen Arete and the prince Laodamas are present at the Phaeacian feast is not decisive evidence against its official character. This queen had great influence with all the people as well as with the king, and in times of profound peace these feasts inevitably would become informal.[1] A justification for the presence of Penelope's suitors at the palace of Odysseus, has been found not so much in their aspirations for Penelope's hand as in the hospitality expected of the king by all his nobles, and indeed by the people generally. The door of the palace was always open for the chieftains of the people. Penelope's suitors only abused the privilege which was theirs of right.

The gathering of the nobles at dinner in the king's hall, in the land of the Phaeacians (η 49, ν 8) as well as in Syriė (ο 467), and in the tent of Agamemnon (B 404, H 313, I 89, Ψ 38), finds a perfect analogy in the company of gods in the hall of Olympian Zeus, as we see them at the close of the first book, and at the beginning of the fourth book, of the *Iliad*, and at the opening of the action of the *Odyssey* (α 26, ε 3). At the beginning of the eighth and twentieth books of the *Iliad*, Zeus calls an assembly, but on the other occasions the divinities are present without special invitation. They have their own separate dwellings (A 606, Σ 369, θ 268), just as Paris and Hector have their own homes, but they gather in the hall of Zeus for a common feast. Such common feasts are assumed also by the twenty small tables which Hephaestus makes (Σ 373) for the use of the gods in their great hall, though the statement that these tables were only to be lent to Zeus, would imply that on some occasions he had more guests than on others. These feasts are a survival from the earlier patriarchal life ; the sons gather about the father, and kinsmen come into the great hall to discuss all matters of common interest.

Council of Gods.

---

[1] The invitations which Telemachus is reported to Odysseus in Hades as receiving (λ 185), are thought to imply that the public feasts were not always held at the king's palace, but successively at the homes of the princes.

The relation between the council of elders (βουλὴ γερόντων, B 53,—where γέροντες already has a technical sense, and refers to age little more than *senators* or *aldermen* in English),—and the assembly of the people (ἀγορὴ λαῶν), is not precisely stated by the poet. According to Aristotle (*Nicomachean Ethics*, iii. 1113 a), the Homeric princes announced to the people what they had determined to do, but this statement is not sustained by the poems. At the opening of the *Iliad*, after the plague has raged in the camp for nine days, Achilles calls an assembly of the soldiery (A 54). This, at least, was for deliberation ; the council had not met, *Assembly of the Achaeans.* the commander-in-chief does not seem to have been consulted, and no one had an order to promulgate. The question before them, is what shall be done in order to secure relief from the plague, and Achilles proposes that they seek to learn from some seer the cause of the god's anger. No one raises the point of order that this matter belongs to the council of elders or to the commander-in-chief, and not to the people. After the meeting of the council at the beginning of the first day of battle, another assembly is held, which indeed at first seems to be for the purpose of making known to all the council's decision to arm the soldiers for battle. But Agamemnon,—far from presenting the plan as voted by the council,—says nothing about a previous discussion and decision, and closes his speech with the exhortation : "Come ! as I say, let all obey ; let us return with our ships to our dear native land."[1] The men start for the ships before another word is said,—no formal vote was usual in a Homeric assembly,—but are brought back to the *agora*, and Odysseus and Nestor propose for action plans which are adopted. On the next following morning, a Trojan herald comes to the Achaean camp to ask a truce for the burial of the dead, and to offer the

[1] B 139. To say with Fanta, that this assembly is not for deliberation, but for a trial of the sentiment of the soldiery, is misleading. The people suppose it to be a deliberative gathering. The circumstance that Agamemnon hopes to lead them to an end different from that which he attains, is not important in this connexion. The form of Agamemnon's words may seem like a mild command, but if the soldiery had not been so impetuous he would have been met by the opposition which Diomed expresses in the gathering at the close of the second day of battle.

proposition of Paris, looking toward a peace. The Achaeans are assembled by the stern of Agamemnon's ship (H 383), *i.e.* at the door of Agamemnon's tent. After hearing the message, Diomed states his opinion, and "all the sons of the Achaeans" shout in approval. Agamemnon understands this as a *viva voce* vote,[1] settling the question, and says to the Trojan herald, "You yourself hear the answer of the Achaeans." At the close of the second· day of battle, the heralds call an assembly (I 11), which is distinguished from the council of elders (I 89) held later, not before it. Here again no order is to be promulgated, but again Agamemnon urges the return to Argos. Diomed rebukes him severely, and the proposition is withdrawn; Nestor directs the station-ing of a guard, and asks that a meeting of the elders be held. Again, at the opening of the last day of battle, all the Achaeans come together (T 45) simply to witness the reconciliation between Achilles and Agamemnon. No orders are to be promulgated. Finally, after the capture of Troy, the .sons of Atreus call an assembly at evening (γ 137),— not to give directions, but to lay their matter of dispute before the soldiery, in order to secure a decision between two plans, since Menelaus desires to hasten home, while Aga-memnon thinks it better to remain and offer propitiatory sacrifices to Athena. The adherents of Menelaus show their mind by departing.[2] In no instance, then, is an Achaean assembly called that the people may learn the will of the chieftains.

The assemblies of the Trojans, also, are deliberative.

Assembly of the Trojans. Coming as embassadors of the Achaeans to demand the return of Helen, before the opening of actual hostilities, Menelaus and Odysseus state their case before the assembled Trojans (Γ 209), who must have been gathered to decide between war and peace, not simply to gratify their curiosity. At this meeting of the people, Antimachus (who was not one of the princes) urged that the envoys be put to death, and not allowed to

---

[1] So in Sparta in the fifth century B.C., the assembly voted with a shout, and if the ephor was not certain of the majority, he called for a literal division, directing the "ayes" to go to one side, and the "noes" to the other. Thucydides, i. 87.

[2] *Cf.* ω 426 ff., where again there is a literal "division" of the assembly.

return to the Achaean camp (Λ 123, 139); *i.e.* a debate was held and different propositions were presented, concluding with the decision to refuse the demand of the envoys, but to allow them to depart. Before the first battle of the *Iliad*, the Trojans are assembled in front of the gates of Priam's palace (B 788). The subject of discussion does not appear, but no orders are mentioned as given; when the assembly is dismissed, the men hasten to take their arms,—but this was because of the tidings brought of the Achaeans' approach. At the close of that day's battle, the Trojans are gathered again by the gate of Priam,—in confusion and fear because of the unexpected strength shown by the Achaeans (H 345),—yet evidently for a discussion of the situation. Antenor proposes to surrender Helen and her possessions; Paris refuses to give up Helen, but consents to surrender the treasures. Then Priam directs the herald to bear to the Achaean camp the proposition of Paris, and to ask for a truce for the burial of the dead. In one sense, this is an order; but it is a result of the assembly,— the people were not called together to hear it. In modern parlance, one might say that Antenor offered a motion to give up Helen and her treasures; that Paris then proposed an amendment to the motion, and Priam declared the motion adopted as amended. If Priam did not care for the vote, or at least to know the mind of the people, he would have settled the question in private. On the next following morning, the Trojans assemble again to hear the reply of the Greeks, and to act accordingly (H 414). The Trojan soldiers are called to an assembly on the field at the close of the third day of battle, when Achilles has appeared before them (Σ 245). This can be for nothing but deliberation. Pulydamas urges that they should return to the city; but Hector insists that they remain by the Greek camp,— saying, indeed, that he will not permit anything else,—and he has the whole army with him (ἐπὶ δὲ Τρῶες κελάδησαν). "Pallas Athena took from them their senses, for they praised Hector though he devised an evil plan, and no one praised Pulydamas who framed excellent counsel." Here Pulydamas makes a motion which is rejected under the influence of Hector.

In the assembly of Ithacans (β 10 ff.), the old Aegyptius, who speaks first, expects not orders but information. He asks who has brought them together. " Has this man tidings of the return of our army, or does he lay some other matter of public interest before us ? " Telemachus then asks the people to relieve him from the oppression of his mother's suitors, but lays no commands upon the assembly,—which would be futile. This assembly is summarily dismissed by one of the suitors of Penelope, who tells the people to go home and leave Telemachus to the care of his friends, and they think it wise to do so (β 252).

Assembly of Ithacans.

The Homeric poems tell of two other popular assemblies, one at Mycenae to determine the sending of troops against Thebes (Δ 380), where the men of Mycenae (not the king) " were willing " to grant the request for aid ; and the other of the Phaeacians (θ 5), where Odysseus is introduced by Alcinoüs, who begins, " Hear me, that I may say what my soul in my breast bids me," which does not sound like the promulgation of a formal order. The importance attached to oratory (θ 170), the epithet of Nestor, " the clear-voiced man of the assembly " ($\dot{a}\gamma o\rho\eta\tau\dot{\eta}s$, A 248), and the epithet of the assembly itself, " which brings glory to men " ($\kappa\nu\delta\iota\acute{a}\nu\epsilon\iota\rho a\nu$, A 490), all imply that the people were gathered for deliberation. Nestor's oratory was useful for persuasion, not for the conveyance of commands.

Thus the Homeric assembly of the people is clearly for deliberation and action,—even in the midst of a military campaign, when the discipline is necessarily stricter than at home, in peace,—although the right of the common man to speak and propose measures as well as to vote, is not absolutely certain. According to Tacitus (*Germania*, xi.), the assemblies of the ancient Germans also were attended by all men of the tribe in arms,—who listened seated, and showed approval or dissent by applause or murmurs. Thersites is severely rebuked by Odysseus for his ribald attack on Agamemnon (B 212 ff.), but this brawler is chastised apparently not for having spoken when he had no right, but for being repeatedly a noisy disturber of the peace. " He was wont

Homeric Assembly for Deliberation.

to affront Achilles and Odysseus" (B 221), which implies several speeches in the past. Even in a town-meeting in democratic America, where every citizen has a right to be heard, a ribald brawler may be rebuked with severity. The Trojan Pulydamas is not one of the chief commanders (M 213), but he makes and urges the proposal to return to the city at the close of the third day of battle (Σ 249 ff.). The Antimachus who proposed to put to death the Achaean envoys (Λ 138), appears nowhere else in the Trojan story, and cannot be held to be one of the princes. Nothing indicates, either, that the old Aegyptius who asks why the assembly of the Ithacans has been called (β 15), is a noble, except that one of his sons is a suitor of Penelope ; his other two sons "keep his farm," and the one who perished on the expedition with Odysseus had no special distinction.

The freedom of discussion at these gatherings of the people is shown by Diomed's open and severe criticism of Agamemnon (I 32),—though they are in the field before the enemy,—and by the speeches in the Ithacan assembly (β 40 ff.). This gathering in Ithaca arrives at no decision, but this is only because it is overawed by Penelope's insolent suitors. That the comrades of Odysseus overrule his desires to leave Ismarus promptly (ι 44), and not to land on the island of the Sun (μ 294), has been cited to prove the independence of the assembly, but these seem rather excep-tional cases of mutinous disobedience, although in form the second instance is one of public discussion and decision. Whether the king had a formal right of veto, cannot be made out with certainty. Under ordinary circumstances, however, we may be sure that nothing could be carried out without his approval, for if the assembly were supreme, he would be no longer king. An instance of such a veto would be the refusal of Agamemnon to grant the request of the old priest Chryses for the return of his daughter, to which the people assented (Λ 22). The fact that the speaker in addressing the assembly of the people directs his words to the "leaders and counsellors of the people" (I 17, θ 26), does not imply the insignificance of the masses, any more than the modern custom of addressing one's remarks to the chairman of the meeting, though these are intended primarily to influence the votes of the assemblage, rather than the mind of the chairman, who has no vote. Odysseus in the gathering of the Phaeacians appears as a suppliant "of the king and all the people" (θ 157), just as the old priest Chryses beseeches "all the Achaeans, but especially the sons of Atreus, the two leaders of the people" (A 15). Idaeus is sent to lay the Trojan proposition for peace before "the sons of Atreus," but he presents it to the whole people (H 385).

The distinction between the nobles[1] and the common people (δῆμος, B 198) is sometimes manifest. Odysseus, when he desired to recall the Achaeans to their assembly (B 188 ff.), checked the princes by courteous words, "but whatever man of the people he saw, and found him shouting, him he struck with his staff and upbraided him with words." Again, however, Pulydamas, a man of standing and even better in counsel than Hector, is "one of the people" (δῆμον ἐόντα, M 213). To pass from the masses to the company of chieftains was possible for a man of physical force and the qualities of a leader, as is shown by the story of the disguised Odysseus (ξ 199 ff.) : the son of a Cretan slave woman led nine expeditions before the Trojan War, and in this war he was a peer of the king Idomeneus.

A Man of the People becomes a Leader. The distinction gained by a brave and mighty man might be a kind of patent of nobility which could be inherited by his children.[2] Thus Bellerophon's descendants ruled after him in Lycia (Z 196 f.); that he was son of a Corinthian king, was of little consequence to him in securing and transmitting this throne, compared with his personal prowess ; he was an exile, and the result would have been the same if he had been the son of an

---

[1] ἄριστοι, Γ 250; ἀριστῆες, Ψ 236; γέροντες, Σ 448; βουληφόροι, Ω 651; δημογέροντες, Γ 149; δικασπόλοι, λ 186.

[2] Fanta holds that the noble like the king had a domain, a τέμενος, as the gift of the people. This view is based chiefly on Odysseus's prayer for the Phaeacian princes, that they might live long and happily, and that each on his death might bequeath to his children his possessions in his hall, and the gift (γέρας, η 150) which the people bestowed. That the people might bestow a domain from common land in return for eminent public service, is clear from I 578; that every noble had what deserves the name of domain, in addition to his private fields, is improbable. See Chapter VIII.

ordinary man. The Lycian king was convinced that Bellerophon was of divine lineage by his success in battling with
the Chimaera, the Solymi, and the Amazons (Z 191), rather
than by any certified accounts of his ancestry. The word
hero (ἥρως) in general means simply *soldier, brave warrior*,
or *brave man*,—not *demi-god* as in later Greek, nor is it
used in the modern sense;[1] it was not restricted to the
chieftains. How the nobles were designated is not clear,—
perhaps only by the invitation proceeding from the king to
the feasts. They had no patents of nobility.

The place of assembly in the Achaean camp before Troy
was by the tent of Odysseus, at the middle of the line
(Θ 223, Λ 807), though once the Achaeans
gather by the ship of Agamemnon (H 383).
Near or in the *agora* was the chief altar of
Zeus. In Troy the people gathered before Priam's palace
(B 788, H 345, *cf.* θ 503). Ithaca (β 7), Scheria (η 44), and
even Laestrygonia (κ 114), as well as Ilium (θ 503), had
agoras, but the situation of these in each town is not
determined. The members of the assembly were seated
(B 99; *cf.* Σ 246), as was the Athenian custom in later
times, and also the wont among the ancient Germans.
Wooden seats can hardly have been provided in the Achaean
camp for the immense number of men assumed by the
Catalogue of Ships, and most must have sat directly upon
the ground. But just as the accounts of battles show that
the poet had before his mind conflicts of small bodies of
men, so in the accounts of the assemblies for deliberation
the poet clearly was thinking of hundreds, and not tens of
thousands of men. Thus at the close of the second day
of battle, Agamemnon bids the heralds to summon each
man severally to an assembly, and not to cry aloud (βοᾶν,
I 12),—wishing apparently not to attract the attention of
the enemy who are bivouacking not far away. Manifestly
such a secret summons would be both unnecessary and
impossible in a great army,—unnecessary since the enemy

The Place of Assembly.

---

[1] In parts of the *Odyssey* it has been thought to have an honorific sense, as in
γέροντα Λαέρτην ἥρωα, α 188 f., "the old warrior Laertes," or in ἄλλῳ εἴπῃς
ἡρώων, θ 242, but this may be only "tell one of the older warriors." *Cf.* also
ἥρως Αἰγύπτιος, β 15; ἥρως Ἀλιθέρσης, β 157.

could not be near enough to hear, and impossible because of the great numbers. And when all, even the stewards and the steersmen, come to witness the reconciliation of Achilles and Agamemnon, the company would be too great to hear and see what was said and done, if nearly 1,200 ships had come to Troy.

The assemblies were summoned by the heralds, generally at the command of the king (B 50, I 10, *cf.* β 6),—but, as has been seen, not the king but Achilles called the assembly in the time of the plague (A 54).
No stated days are appointed for the meetings.
The heralds also maintain order (B 97, Σ 503). The king, as we should expect, has a special seat (β 14), which the elders of Ithaca yield to Telemachus when he appears in his father's absence, to address the people. The time for meeting, as in Athens, is early in the morning (B 48 f., β 5 f., θ 7 f.). The gods, too, gather at dawn (Θ 2). Only three assemblies are reported as held at evening,—one, of the Trojans, after the first day of battle, when the Achaeans have shown unexpected strength (H 345); another, of the Greeks (I 11), after the second day of battle, when Agamemnon believed further conflict useless; and a third (γ 137), after the capture of Troy, when Nestor notes that the hour was unfitting,—the Achaeans were heavy with the wine drunk in their joy. In the assembly, the speaker rose and received from the herald a staff (σκῆπτρον, β 37), which gave him a quasi-official character, indicating that he had the right to speak, or in modern parlance, that he "had the floor,"— the authority of the people was his. In his quarrel with Agamemnon, Achilles casts this staff upon the ground at the close of a speech, thus declaring that he has nothing more to say (A 245). Similarly, when he has ended laying his grievances before the Ithacan people, Telemachus throws the staff upon the ground and bursts into tears (β 80).

An epithet of the assembly is "which brings glory to men" (κυδιάνειρα, A 490), and again it is the assembly "where men are distinguished" (ἀριπρεπέες τελέθουσι, I 441).
Men look upon the skilled orator as a god (θ 173). The voice of Nestor "flows sweeter than honey from his tongue" (A 249), and he is known as the

Conduct of Assemblies.

Distinction of Eloquence.

clear-toned orator of the Pylians (ἀγορητήν, Δ 293); the elders of Troy were skilled orators (ἀγορηταί, Γ 150); words fell like snowflakes from the lips of Odysseus (Γ 222). The perfect man was ready to lead "both in battle and in the council," "in war and in peace."

From the meeting of the assembly no man seems to be excluded. Even the stewards and helmsmen attend that in which Agamemnon and Achilles are reconciled (T 43), but these stewards are mentioned nowhere else; and if beggars found a place in the hospitable palace hall (σ 2) they were not likely to be excluded from the place of assembly, where strangers also might go and be (ρ 72), though they might not be allowed a part in the discussion, since they had no stake in the action. An old formula, "Come hither, all ye people," appears in Plutarch (*Theseus*, 25), as an invitation to the assembly.

Heralds, as has been stated, were the only official attendants of the king, and the only officers of government. As messengers both of Zeus and of men (A 334), their persons seem inviolable, and they served as *Heralds Officers of Government.* a "flag of truce,"—which was unknown, like all other banners and standards. The Trojan herald Idaeus was sent to the Achaean camp (H 372) with the proposition for peace and (failing that) for a truce, that the dead might be buried. The same herald attends king Priam when he goes to the tent of Achilles to ransom the body of his son Hector, and is called the "summoner" of the king (καλήτωρ, Ω 577), and "crier of the city" (ἀστυβοώτης, Ω 701, *town-crier*). On another day he fetches the bowl and golden cups for the libation, and calls Priam to descend to the plain to make a truce for the single combat of Paris and Menelaus (Γ 248 ff.). At the close of the same day, he joins with Agamemnon's herald Talthybius in stopping the single combat of Hector and Ajax, when night has come on (H 274 ff.). Odysseus sends a herald with the two scouts who go to investigate the land of the Lotus Eaters (ι 90), and with those who are dispatched to the city of the Laestrygonians (κ 102). Agamemnon sends his heralds Talthybius and Eurybates to the tent of Achilles with the demand for the captive Briseïs (A 320), and sends Talthybius from the field of battle to the camp, for a lamb for sacrifice, before the single combat of Menelaus and Paris (Γ 118). When Menelaus is wounded by the treacherous arrow of Pandarus, Talthybius is sent by his king to fetch the surgeon Machaon (Δ 192); and when Agamemnon and Achilles are reconciled, Talthybius prepares the boar for the solemn sacrifice (T 196), and at the close of this service he hurls the body of the victim into the sea (T 267). Before the sacrifice which accompanies the truce of the first day of battle, heralds pour water on the hands of the princes (Γ 270). In the only stated religious festival of which the Homeric poems tell us, on Ithaca, "heralds lead through the city the sacred hecatomb of the gods" (υ 276).

Heralds call the Achaeans before Troy to the place of assembly (B 50), summon quietly the warriors to a council (I 11), convoke the assembly on Ithaca at the *Heralds in the Assembly.* command of Telemachus (β 6), and convey from the army to the Trojan city Hector's command that the old men and boys shall stand guard during the absence of the soldiery (Θ 517). Athena assumes the guise of a herald to urge the Phaeacians to go to the assembly at which Odysseus is introduced (θ 8). Seven heralds, as sergeants-at-arms, strive to bring to order the assembly of Achaean soldiers (B 97), and on the Shield of Achilles is depicted a court-scene in which heralds are maintaining decorum (Σ 503). The speakers in the court-scene hold heralds' staves (Σ 505); as Telemachus rises to address the Ithacan assembly, the herald Peisenor puts a staff (σκῆπτρον, β 37) into his hand; and when Menelaus rises to claim a certain prize in the horse-race, a herald places a staff in his hand and commands the people to be silent (Ψ 566). When the Achaean chieftains cast lots to determine who shall fight with Hector in single combat, Nestor shakes the helmet which contains the lots, but a herald bears the successful lot through the throng, seeking the owner (H 183). The heralds, then, deserve the name which Penelope gives them, of "public servants" (δημιοεργοί, τ 135).

The herald did for the king what ordinary trusted servants did for ordinary men. Agamemnon's prize in the games is taken to his quarters by a herald (Ψ 897), and in his tent the

heralds are bidden to place the tripod over the fire and make
ready the bath (Ψ 39). So in a scene on the Shield of
Achilles, a herald prepares the king's dinner   *Heralds*
(Σ 559). In the palace of the Phaeacian king,   *Personal*
the herald Pontonoüs is ordered to mix and dis-   *Attendants of*
tribute the wine (η 179). This he does again on   *the King.*
the departure of Odysseus (ν 53), and then conducts the Ithacan
of many wanderings to the ship which is to bear him to his
home (ν 65). He also cares for the blind bard Demodocus
at the feast (θ 65). He or another herald leads Demodocus
to the place of games, conducts him back to the palace,
and bears to him Odysseus's present of a choice portion
of meat (θ 106, 471, 477). The poet calls Agamemnon's
heralds his "ready attendants" (ὀτρήρω θεράποντε, A 321).
At the home of Odysseus, the heralds mix the wine and
water (α 109, σ 423), bring it to the guests (α 143), and
pour water on the hands of the suitors (α 146 = γ 338).
Menelaus's herald conducts the guests to their sleeping-
place (δ 301). Each prince seems to have had his own
herald. Anchises had a herald Periphas (P 323). Eurybates, the Ithacan herald who cares for the cloak cast off
by Odysseus as he set out to stop the impetuous Achaeans
from their thoughtless impulse to return to Hellas (B 184),
and who serves as his personal attendant, is described by
the disguised Odysseus as having a dark complexion, thick
curly hair, and round shoulders, and as being rather older
than his master. Odysseus valued him more highly than
any other of his companions (τ 246). He and Odius
accompany Odysseus and Ajax on their embassy to the
offended Achilles, to beg him to return to the battle
(I 170). Each Phaeacian prince sends a herald to his
home to fetch a gift for the guest, Odysseus (θ 399), and
heralds bring presents for the suitors to bestow on Penelope
(σ 291). The young Ithacans who accompany Telemachus
to Pylus, dispatch a herald to notify his mother of his
return (π 328). Medon acts as herald for Penelope's suitors,
though he is in sympathy with Odysseus's household, and
his life is spared when the suitors are slain (χ 356).

The Trojan Dolon, whose name is given to the tenth book of
the *Iliad* ("Doloneia"), is the son of a herald, "rich in gold and

rich in bronze" (K 315), and he is present at the council of chieftains. This indicates that the service of a herald was not despised or unprofitable. Heralds very rarely appear on the field of battle, but the Athenian Menestheus being hard pressed in the fight, having no aid or adjutant, sends a herald Thoötes to fetch Ajax (M 342). The proper names given to heralds seem to have nothing to do with their occupation,—as Idaeus, Talthybius, Eurybates, and Medon,—and nothing indicates that the service was hereditary, although in later times the Spartan heralds counted themselves to be the descendants of Talthybius (Herodotus, vii. 134).

Social Position of Heralds.

In relation to other peoples, the men of Homer's day were not so barbarous as to consider all strangers enemies, although they made no formal treaties. The poet's good words for the Abii and the Ethiopians, "most just of men" and "blameless" (N 6, A 423), indicate that he had no prejudice against foreigners. The distinction between "Greeks and barbarians" is not yet known, and the poet did not think of the Trojan War as a stage in the great conflict between Europe and Asia (Herodotus, i. 3). The Achaeans had no common festivals, like those at Olympia and Delphi in later times, and the poet lays no stress on the tie of a common language,—hardly seeming conscious of any linguistic differences. Nor does he indicate differences of religion in other lands : the Cyclopes indeed care nothing for Zeus and the other gods (ι 275), but this only testifies to their savage nature,—Polyphemus himself is the son of Poseidon and when in trouble prays to him (ι 528). "Strangers and suppliants" (ι 270) are under the special care of Zeus. The inhabitants of an island city attacked suddenly by an enemy, light beacon fires at night in the hope that their neighbors may come with ships to their defence (Σ 212). The same principle of self-interest which prompts one neighbor to aid another against a thief or a robber, would incline one hamlet to come to the succor of another in distress. Furthermore, the impulse of unselfish generosity and hospitality seems to have been quite as vigorous in Homer's time as now: for instance, Menelaus received many gifts in Egypt and Phoenicia (δ 128 ff., 617), Odysseus received many presents and a convoy

International Relations.

to his home from the Phaeacians (ν 10 ff.), and the Mycenaeans were disposed to aid Polyneices to recover Thebes, although as a people they had only the slightest interest in his success (Δ 376). A truce is made between the Achaeans and the Trojans after a hard day's fight, for the burial of the dead (H 375, 408). The making of a truce or armistice, and of an agreement by which a single combat shall determine the issue of the war, is described in detail in Γ 250 ff., and the indignation of the Achaeans at the breach of the truce is great (Δ 157); that the Trojans also regarded this breach as a crime, is manifest (H 351). Menelaus and Odysseus went to Troy as embassadors, before the beginning of hostilities, to demand the return of Helen, and probably to declare war in case of a refusal (Γ 205, Λ 139). Diomed's father, Tydeus, was sent as an embassador from Argos to seven-gated Thebes, before the expedition of the military forces against that city (Δ 384, E 803, K 286). Odysseus, when a youth, was sent as an envoy extraordinary to Messenia, to enter a protest against an act of men of that country, who had landed at Ithaca and carried away three hundred sheep and their shepherds (φ 20): the whole Messenian people were in a sense held responsible for the wrong. On the other hand, the father of Antinoüs, one of the suitors of Penelope, had joined Taphian pirates and plundered the Thesprotians who were on good terms with the Ithacans (ἄρθμιοι, π 427), and Odysseus had difficulty in appeasing the Thesprotians. Priam once went to Thrace on an embassy, but the poet does not tell his errand (ἐξεσίην ἐλθόντι, Ω 235); that it was one of peace, is indicated by the present of a beautiful cup then given to him. Menelaus asks Telemachus what has brought him to Sparta,—affairs of the people or his own (δ 314),—and Nestor's similar question (κατὰ πρῆξιν . . . οἷά τε ληϊστῆρες, γ 72) does not mean, "Are you a pirate or a trader," but asks merely whether he comes on an errand (cf. πρῆξις, γ 82). A herald, as has been seen in detail, might serve as messenger between two armies at war (H 372), or attend envoys on a peaceful commission (as κ 102, I 170).

An extraordinary instance of clemency to a foreigner is related by the disguised Odysseus, who represents himself as a Cretan who had led a marauding party to Egypt: they had killed the men, devastated the fields, and carried away the women and children, but then a stronger body of Egyptians appeared who killed or enslaved most of the marauding party,—but this Cretan leader besought the king for mercy, and not only his life but his liberty was spared (ξ 278). That an exile sometimes attained high position in another country, has been seen in the cases of Tydeus and Bellerophon, who became kings of Argos and of Lycia. A foreigner had no rights, however, except as under the protection of Zeus, and Achilles complains that Agamemnon has treated him as an immigrant without rights ($\dot{a}\tau\dot{\iota}\mu\eta\tau o\nu$ $\mu\epsilon\tau a\nu\dot{a}\sigma\tau\eta\nu$, I 648, II 59).[1] When the suitors jeer at the disguised Odysseus and rebuke Eumaeus for bringing him to the town, the swine-herd replies that he has not sought the stranger, and asks, "Who would call one from another land, except those who are workers for the people ($\delta\eta\mu\iota o\epsilon\rho\gamma o\dot{\iota}$, ρ 383), a seer or a healer of ills, or a worker in wood, or an inspired bard?" Craftsmen, then, were likely to find a welcome in another tribe, and might receive special inducements to establish their homes there, just as in the newer American settlements inducements were offered to physicians, teachers, or handicraftsmen to join the settlement, and many cities are ready to give special privileges to manufacturing establishments in order to encourage these industries within their borders.

Clemency to Foreigners.

The Achaeans dwelt together in villages and small towns, like the European villages of the last century, and the Utah hamlets of even more recent times, rather than scattered over the country as in an ordinary new American settlement; they lived together not only for mutual comfort but also for protection against marauders and possibly wild beasts. Only herdsmen like Eumaeus (ν 408) and Melanthius (ρ 223), and a few who, like old Laërtes, had a large establishment of their own (a 190, ω 205) lived away from the town. The pastures were often on the mountain slopes, where the land was not suitable for cultivation. That a man takes his wife and daughter to see his herds (Δ 476) of course implies that these were kept at a distance from the dwelling. In the chapter on

Village Life.

---

[1] Ridgeway interprets this as "one whose life has no $\tau\dot{\iota}\mu\eta$,—is worth no blood-gelt."

property, the suggestion is made that each citizen had a town-lot and a farm-lot, in addition to the right of pasturage on the common lands of the district. What proportion the common lands bore to the land held in severalty, the poet does not tell, nor give any grounds for an inference.[1] The poet has no special word for village (Attic κώμη).

The terms *asty* (ἄστυ) and *polis* (πόλις) have no clear distinction in ordinary usage,[2] but are not absolutely synonymous.[3] ἄστυ is used of a small number of towns,—of Ilium (Γ 116), Ithaca (ο 308), and *Cities.* the city of the Phaeacians (ζ 296). πόλις is used far more freely. Crete alone has ninety or a hundred cities (ἐννήκοντα πόληες, τ 174, ἑκατόμπολιν, B 649), and about three hundred cities in all are said to be named in the poems. Aeolus, the master of the winds, has a πόλις (κ 13), but apparently he and his family are the only inhabitants. This would be an example of an early type. Tiryns, to judge from the ruins, seems to have been a stronghold about which many vassals dwelt who tilled the fertile plains. About Mycenae, too, lived far more people than found room within the wall of the acropolis. But often the château of the master was not so much of a stronghold as were Tiryns and Mycenae. The epithets *high, lofty, wind-swept*,[4] applied to ten towns, imply that a strong position on a height was chosen, as we should expect in view of the danger of hostile invasion. Athens, Ilium, and Mycenae are *broad-streeted*

---

[1] According to Mangold's reasonable view, δῆμος originally referred to the divided land, and ἀγρός to common lands or pasture. But Laërtes lived ἐπ' ἀγροῦ (α 190), and the Egyptian ἀγρός was inhabited (ξ 263). When Telemachus goes to Pylus, Penelope's suitors, who know nothing of his voyage but have noticed his absence, suppose him to be in the fields (ἀγρῶν, δ 640), with the flocks or the swine-herd. ἄστυ is a *dwelling-place*, cf. ἑστία (*Vesta*) hearth. πόλις seems to be in its origin *fortified place, citadel*, nearly equivalent to *acropolis*. πολίτης is not used by Homer in a technical sense for *citizen*, as contrasted with one who had no civil rights, but is simply a *dweller in the city*.

[2] Cf. ἦλθον | ἀσπάσιοι προτὶ ἄστυ, πόλις δ' ἔμπλητο ἀλέντων, Φ 607 ; εὐχωλὴ κατὰ ἄστυ . . . πᾶσί τ' ὄνειαρ . . . κατὰ πτόλιν, X 433.

[3] Cf. ὅππως κε πόλιν καὶ ἄστυ σαώσῃς, P 144.

[4] Ἴλιος αἰπεινή, N 773 ; Πήδασον αἰπεινήν, Z 35 ; Πήδασον αἰπήεσσαν, Φ 87 ; Πύλου αἰπὺ πτολίεθρον, γ 485 (cf. κ 81) ; ἠνεμόεσσαν Ἐνίσπην, B 606 ; Ἴλιον ἠνεμόεσσαν, Γ 305 ; ὑψηλοὺς Ἐρυθίνους, B 855.

(εὐρυάγυια, η 80, B 12, Δ 52). Ilium is *high-towered* (ὑψίπυλον, Π 698,—applied to Hypoplacian Thebes in Z 416) and *well-towered* (εὔπυργον, H 71). Ilium, Tiryns, and Gortyna have notable walls.[1] The epithet *spacious* (εὐρύχορος) is applied to six towns and to Hellas. Scheria is surrounded by a wall (ζ 9), though this is not specially needed since the city is far removed from neighbors. Perhaps this indicates a custom of fortifying cities, but Sparta and other towns have no walls, at least no wall or gate is mentioned as passed by Telemachus (δ 2) on his visit to Sparta, as he approaches the palace.

The palace seems to have been the personal property of the king (α 397), and no court-house, senate-house, "city-hall,"

Public Buildings. or jail existed. The courts and public meetings were held in the open air, as they were in later times also. In addition to the temples in a few towns, the only public building seems to have been the *lesché*, or *loitering place*, to which allusion is made but once: Melantho, Penelope's wanton maid, would send the disguised Odysseus away from the palace to sleep in the smithy or the *lesché*.[2]

As a geographical term, *demus* [3] was applied to the land possessed by a community, and connected with a town, and thus meant country.[4]

---

[1] πόλιν Τροίην ἐυτείχεον, A 129 ; Τίρυνθά τε τειχιόεσσαν, B 559 ; Γόρτυνά τε τειχιόεσσαν, B 646.

[2] λέσχην, σ 329. In Hesiod too (*Works and Days*, 493), the smithy and the *lesché* are the ordinary lounging places in cold weather.—The reader may remember that in later times the most noted λέσχαι were at Delphi and Cnidus (both adorned with paintings by Polygnotus), and at Sparta, where the elders spent much of their time (Plutarch, *Lycurgus*, 25).

[3] δῆμος, B 828, Γ 201, α 103, E 710, Z 158, 225, Π 437.

[4] The Homeric meaning is preserved in the Attic terms ἐπιδημῶ, *am in the country*, and ἀποδημία, *going abroad, departure*.

CHAPTER IV

WOMEN AND THE FAMILY, EDUCATION AND RECREATION

EIGHT types of women are clearly drawn by Homer, though for some he has used but few lines, and *Eight Types* no one of these is repeated : Helen, Andromache, *of Homeric* Penelope, Hecuba,[1] Arēté, Nausicaa, Clytaemestra, *Women.* and Euryclea.

Fair Helen of Troy,—often called Argive Helen (Z 323) from her early home,—is beautiful, fascinating, with great tact but little conscience, the quick-witted mistress of her household and yet easily influenced. She *Fair Helen of Troy.* is not greatly troubled in soul by the fact that she is the cause of the war, but she applies to herself such harsh epithets (*dogfaced woman*, κυνώπιδος, Γ 180 ; *dog*, κυνός, Z 356), and so wishes that she had died before causing all this trouble (Γ 173), that in general no one else has the heart to reproach her, though Achilles, addressing the dead Patroclus, calls her *horrible* (ῥιγεδανῆς, T 325). When she goes to the great tower by the Scaean gate, on the first day of battle, for a view of the conflict on the plain, Priam calls her : " Come hither, dear child, and sit by me that thou mayst see thy former husband, thy kinsmen, and thy friends. Thou art not to blame in my sight ; the gods are to blame, who brought upon me the tearful war of the Achaeans " (Γ 162). Similarly Hector, though he curses his brother Paris for bringing Helen to

---

[1] Consistency would require here the Greek form *Hecabé*, since *Heracles* is used for *Hercules*, *Asclepius* for *Aesculapius*, etc. But no rule for the modernizing of ancient names is satisfactory to all.

Troy,—wishing that he had never been born (Γ 40), and even praying for his death (Z 281),—yet has no word of reproach for Helen herself.   When Hector's body is ransomed and brought back to the city, Helen says that in the twenty years of her life in Troy she never heard a harsh or reproachful word from him ; but that " whenever any other reproached her,—one of his brothers or sisters, or brothers' wives, or his mother ; for his father, as a father, was always kind,"—he checked them by his kind spirit and kind words (Ω 765).   Menelaus, too, has no rebuke for Helen, but welcomes her back to his home, with no reproaches, and accepts the view which Helen herself presents when she says that Aphrodite inspired in her blind infatuation, " when she led her to Troy, away from her fatherland, leaving her daughter, her home, and her husband, who was inferior to no one either in mind or in beauty " (δ 261). Helen presents a similar view to Hector when she says that Zeus put an evil fate upon her and Paris, that they should be the subject of song for men of coming time (Z 357).

The poet gives no description of Helen's beauty.   Nor indeed does he mention the stature, complexion, color of *No Details of* hair or eyes, or weight, of any of his chief female *Beauty.* characters, except as he implies that Nausicaa is tall and slender (ζ 151), by a comparison with Artemis and a young palm tree.   That tall stature was necessary to beauty in Homer's day as well as in Aristotle's, is indicated by Odysseus's words to Calypso when she wonders that he longs to return to Ithaca and Penelope though the goddess offers him a life of undying ease, and she counts herself not inferior to Penelope in stature and form (ε 209).   Not once in all the poems is the age of man or woman given in terms of years : Nestor is old, but Homer does not care how old ; Nausicaa is young, but he does not tell us how young.   Helen and Penelope are ageless in their beauty, as truly as the gods themselves. Lessing observed that no more satisfactory evidence of Helen's beauty could be given than the words of the aged counsellors of Troy, as she approached the Scaean gate : " It is no matter of blame that for such a woman the

Trojans and well-greaved Achaeans suffer long; mightily is she like the immortal goddesses in countenance. But yet, such though she is, let her go in the ships and not remain as a bane to us and our children after us" (Γ 156).

When Hector goes to the house of Paris to summon him to return to the field of battle, he finds him sitting with Helen in her room, and the maids busy with their work of weaving and spinning (Z 321). On learning of the arrival of guests at the palace of Menelaus (δ 121), Helen, "like to Artemis," comes to the great hall "from her fragrant, high-roofed chamber." One attendant sets for her an easy-chair, over which another throws a rug, while a third brings her basket of wool, for she continues her spinning, as modern ladies do their fancy-work, in the evening. Menelaus had refrained from inquiring the names and errand of his guests, until they had finished dinner, but he had been puzzled by their reception of his remarks about the heroes of the Trojan War, and particularly about Odysseus. But Helen, immediately on entering the hall, says, "Why, this must be Telemachus." She has never seen a son resemble his father so strongly as this young guest resembles Odysseus (δ 141). Then Menelaus says that now he, too, sees the resemblance. A little later, Helen tells of Odysseus's exploit in entering Troy in disguise, and Menelaus chimes in, "Yes, wife, all this is very true" (δ 266). Just as Telemachus is leaving Sparta, an eagle carries away a goose from the courtyard, and he turns to Menelaus and asks for whom this omen is sent; Menelaus is still pondering when the quick-witted Helen gives the right answer (o 172).

Helen's tact is shown by her courteous reference to Menelaus in connexion with her going to Troy, already quoted (δ 261): "she must have been infatuated, or she would not have left such a husband." She is charming, too, when she gives to the young Telemachus on his departure a robe which her own hands have wrought, for him to give to his bride on his marriage (o 126). She never is made to utter a harsh or cutting word, except indeed to Paris on his shrinking from the battle (Γ 428, Z 350).

Andromache is the young mother of an infant son, and the wife of the bravest of the sons of King Priam of Troy.

Her father was king of the neighboring Thebes, but he
and his six sons have been killed by Achilles. Her mother

Andromache. was taken captive by Achilles, but was ransomed and died peacefully in her father's home.
Hector and the little Astyanax are Andromache's all
(Z 429). Hector is the chief of the Trojan leaders, and
she shares his cares and anxieties. Interested in all that is
his, she often even feeds his horses on his return from the
field of battle (Θ 187). On the first day of battle, with her
infant son and the nurse she has gone to the Scaean
Gate of the city in the hope of learning tidings of the
conflict and her husband; there she learns that he has
come to the city, with a message for Queen Hecuba, and
she hurries to meet him just after he has sought her in
vain at their home, and is hastening to the field of war.
Hector smiles, looking upon his child in silence, but Andromache, shedding tears, stands by him, clasps his hand,
and says, "My dear husband, this courage of thine will be
thy death, nor dost thou pity thine infant son and me,
hapless woman." She then reminds him that he is to her
not only husband but also father and brother, and urges
him to take his stand within the city and from the wall to
direct its defense. He replies that he remembers all this,
but he cannot remain away from the battle. He knows
that the time will come when Ilium shall perish, and he
grieves not so much for Hecuba herself, nor Priam, nor his
brothers, as at the thought of the lot that is to befall her,—
to weave at the bidding of another, or to fetch water from
the springs of Argos or Thessaly. He caresses her and bids
her grieve not too much for him; he cannot escape death
if the gods have willed it, nor will he be slain unless this is
fated (Z 486). He reminds her, too, that "war is the care
of men," and she departs to her home, often turning about
(ἐντροπαλιζομένη, Z 496) for a last look at her husband.

Andromache appears twice again in the poems. At
the close of the last day of battle, she is weaving in
her hall a double purple cloak, interweaving bright flowers,
and bids the maids place the tripod over the fire that the
warm bath may be ready for Hector on his return from
the battle, when she hears the shrieks which betoken that

some calamity has befallen the Trojans. Her heart fears
the truth, and she hastens to the Tower only in time to
see Hector's body dragged to the Achaean camp behind
the chariot of Achilles. She faints, and on her recovery
bewails the fate of her son, left without a father (X 440 ff.).
And at the close of the *Iliad*, holding Hector's head in
her arms, she bewails him, herself, and their son,—and the
city, too ; for this "will be sacked, since thou hast fallen, its
guardian, who didst save the city itself, and the faithful
wives and young children" (Ω 728). The mutual affection
and confidence of Hector and Andromache is ideal.

Penelope of Ithaca has long been recognized as the type
of a faithful wife. For twenty years no tidings have been
received from her husband Odysseus. The other *Penelope.*
Achaeans have returned, or at least are accounted
for. She is in the midst of troubles,—anxious for her son and
his future, urged to marry by a large number of importunate
suitors, and seeing the estate of her husband wasted,—but she
yet clings to the hope of Odysseus's return. On his arrival
she requires full evidence of his identity ; the change in him
has been great, and she has feared the deceit of men
(ψ 216) ; but on recognizing him the tears of joy fall freely.
" The gods had grudged their happiness, that they two should
remain together, to enjoy their youth and come to the
threshold of old age" (ψ 211). During Odysseus's absence,
Penelope is the undisputed mistress of his house, being under
no guardian, and she does not allow her son Telemachus
to give directions to the women. The swine-herd Eumaeus
delights greatly in going to the palace " to talk with her,
to have something to eat and to drink, and to bring some
gift back to the field " (o 376). She is honored for her good
judgment ; she is wiser even than the famous women of
earlier times (β 117) ; and she is sought in marriage not
simply because she would bring the kingdom as dowry (and
this of itself would show her importance), but also because of
her beauty (σ 245).[1] Her ingenuity is manifested in the

[1] Another instance of the kingdom's going with the late king's widow is that of
Epicasta (the Iocasta of Sophocles), whom Oedipus wedded when he received the
kingdom of Thebes (λ 271). The Homeric poet only alludes to the story, but clearly
agrees in this with Sophocles.

familiar device of her web,—she would not marry until she had completed a fitting death-robe for her husband's aged father Laërtes (β 97); and she unravelled by night all that she had woven by day. Thus she postponed the importunity of her suitors for three years, before her device was discovered. On the first day of the action of the *Odyssey*, she hears from her upper room the lay of the bard, as he sings to her suitors at their feast, of the sad return of the Achaeans from Troy, and she descends to the great hall to bid the minstrel choose some other subject of song (α 328). A second time, at the suggestion of Athena, she appears to her suitors (σ 158 ff.), rebuking them for their insolence and reminding them of the proper manner of conducting a suit for marriage. The suitors acknowledge the justice of her reproach. Each is filled with fresh eagerness to win her hand, and sends to his home for gifts to bestow on her. Finally, on the next day, again on the suggestion of Athena, she appears to the suitors, and promises to wed him who most easily shall string the old bow of Odysseus, and shoot an arrow through a mark which her husband used to set up (φ 1 ff.). When Telemachus sails away to Pylus, he takes care that his mother may not learn of his absence, but may suppose him to be somewhere on the farm, that she may not waste away in anxiety for him (β 373).

In Hecuba we see the aged mother of nineteen sons,— Priam's "mobled queen,"—mourning for Hector, "far the

Hecuba. dearest to her heart of all her children." On the first day of battle, Hector comes from the battlefield and bids her assemble the Trojan matrons, and make prayers and vows to Athena. She bids him wait until she shall bring a cup of wine that he may pour a libation to Zeus, and may himself be cheered by drinking,—but he declines; he may not raise to Zeus hands bespattered with blood and gore, and he fears that the wine may weaken rather than strengthen him (Z 258). Then Hecuba sends for the matrons, and herself chooses the most beautiful robe in her store to "lay on the knees of Athena." She appears next at the close of the last day of battle, on the tower by the Scaean Gate, watching the Trojans driven by Achilles within the city walls. And when Hector alone remains outside the gate, to withstand Achilles, and Priam in vain has begged him to retreat for safety, old Hecuba bares her breast and bids him remember her care, and pity the breast which she had held to his lips in his infancy (X 80). When Hector is slain, Andromache in her hall "hears the voice of her husband's honored mother," and knows that "some ill is near to the children of Priam" (X 451). Hecuba asks why she should live now that Hector has fallen,—he who was her boast both night and day, and a strong defense to the Trojans, who looked upon him as a divinity (X 431). On Priam's receiving a message from Zeus, bidding him go to the Achaean camp and ransom Hector's body, he asks Hecuba's advice. With all her love for her son, she now thinks only of Priam's danger, and endeavors to dissuade him : " How dost thou desire to go alone to the ships of the Achaeans, before the eyes of a man who has slain for thee many and noble sons? Thy heart is of iron. . . . Now let us weep in our halls, apart from Hector. To him mighty fate spun this lot at his birth,— that he should sate the dogs, away from his parents, at the tent of that mighty man, to whose very heart I should like to cling, and devour it " (Ω 203). But since Priam is resolved to go, she brings him a cup of wine on his departure, that he may pour a libation and seek an omen from Zeus (Ω 283). She and Andromache meet the king returning with the corpse of Hector, at the Scaean Gate, and her dirge follows that of Andromache,—" Hector was surely dear in his life to the gods who care for him thus in his death " (Ω 748).

Arētē, wife of Alcinoüs, king of the Phaeacians, on the other hand, is a queen in the midst of peace and prosperity. She guides her household, and settles disputes of her people, even the quarrels of men (η 74),—being *Arētē.* honored as no other woman in the world is honored by her husband. Nausicaa and Athena both give to Odysseus the same advice (ζ 310, η 75) to apply for succor to the queen, —if her favor is secured, the hero may be sure of his return to his home. When Odysseus enters the palace, well on in the evening, he passes by the king and makes his appeal to Arete as she is sitting with her spinning, by her husband and her sons, near the fire, in the midst of the counsellors of the Phaeacians. This was her usual place, clearly the place of honor in the hall.　She recognizes the clothing worn by Odysseus, as the handiwork of her women, and discerns that he must have received aid from her daughter Nausicaa, but discreetly awaits the departure of her guests before making inquiry with regard to this (η 238).　At the conclusion of Odysseus's story of the Fair Women whose shades he had seen in Hades, Arete is the first to break the silence, claiming Odysseus as her special guest, and suggesting that additional gifts be bestowed on him (λ 338).　The oldest counsellor of the Phaeacians takes up the proposition, and says that the queen's words are just what might be expected of her.　It is she, not the king, to whom Odysseus makes his formal adieu (ν 57), and she sends women to bear to the boat his luggage, *i.e.* the gifts which he had received from the Phaeacians (ν 66).

The charming princess Nausicaa, daughter of Arete,—an only daughter, with five brothers (ζ 62); petted but not "spoiled,"—is one of the most attractive characters of the poems, and the only young damsel just reaching the time of marriage (ζ 27, 277) whom Homer depicts.　In order to prepare the way for the kindly reception of Odysseus by the Phaeacians, on the night after he was cast on their shores, Athena visits her in a dream, in the guise of one of her girl-companions, and reminds her that the household linen should be washed, and that the time of her marriage is near, when she should not only be well-clad herself, but also furnish raiment to the groomsmen.　So in the morning, Nausicaa goes to her father, whom she addresses as "Papa dear" (πάππα φίλε, ζ 57), and asks for his wagon and mules that she may go to the river with her women and wash the clothes,—saying nothing about her own marriage, but calling attention to the propriety of his having clean linen as he sits in council, and particularly to her brothers' desire to go to the dance with newly washed raiment (ζ 60).　Her mother prepares the luncheon and adds a goatskin bottle of wine, and also a golden vase of olive oil that she may anoint herself after the bath in the river, which is assumed as part of the day's program.　The maidens make a frolic and sport of the washing (ἔριδα προφέρουσαι, ζ 92), spread the garments in the sun on the clean pebbles, and, while they wait for

Nausicaa.

them to dry, they bathe and take luncheon, and then play a game of ball. At last a maid fails to catch the ball which the princess has tossed, and it falls into an eddy of the river. The maidens shriek, and this rouses the sleeping Odysseus, who appears from under a bush. The other maidens flee, but Athena gives to Nausicaa courage to remain. She bestows on Odysseus raiment and food, and directions for reaching the palace and supplicating the queen. Her sense of propriety and discretion in avoiding notice are shown in her care to avoid the remarks of the Phaeacians, by not herself conducting the wanderer to the palace (ζ 273); this was an unusual case, and her conscience did not reprove her, but she knew that her course might be misinterpreted and misrepresented. The poet very neatly makes Alcinoüs to be less thoughtful for conventionalities than his daughter had been, and to say bluntly and hospitably that she should have brought the stranger directly to the palace (η 299). On her return to her home, her brothers unharness the mules, and her old nurse, who now acts as chambermaid for her, kindles a fire in her room (the only fire in a chamber mentioned by Homer), and prepares her evening meal. She does not sit with the king and queen and their guests, in the great hall, but on the next day she contrives to stand by the door and say farewell to Odysseus, and bid him remember that he owes his life to her (θ 461).

Clytaemestra, Agamemnon's queen, has long been recognized as the Lady Macbeth of the Homeric poems, and the typical unfaithful wife. She is the special foil of *Clytaemestra.* Penelope, but the poet is far from painting her as wholly bad : he says expressly that she had a good heart (γ 266), and that Aegisthus never expected to succeed in persuading her to leave the home of her husband Agamemnon (γ 275). The Homeric story does not represent her either as killing Agamemnon or as being killed by her son Orestes. Very probably the poet thought of her as committing suicide in shame on Orestes's return. But if she did not herself kill Agamemnon, she seems at least to have consented thereto, for his ghost in Hades says that Clytaemestra killed Cassandra by the side of the dying Agamemnon, and did not have the heart to close his mouth and eyes as he died, but departed (λ 422) and left him. The contrast between the early and the later Clytaemestra is so great that some scholars have thought the pictures to be inconsistent, but we need not suppose two forms of the story. When she has once yielded to evil, the elements of good in her are turned to wickedness. So far as Mycenae had any regent in Agamemnon's absence, the rule seems to have been left with her, but with a bard as "assessor"; on taking her to his own home, however, Aegisthus became the ruler of the land (γ 305).

An eighth example of typical Homeric women may be found in the class of servants. Euryclea, "the daughter of Ops who was the son of Peisenor," was bought *The Nurse Euryclea.* by Laertes when she was in the prime of her youth for the worth of twenty cattle (α 429), and had been the nurse of both Odysseus (τ 482) and his son Telemachus (α 435). She still with a torch attends Telemachus to his chamber at night, and smoothes the clothes which he doffs, and hangs them on a peg near the bed, and to her alone he confides his plan of going to Pylus and Sparta (β 356). She holds the key of the storeroom (β 346), and has the general direction of the maids of the house (υ 148, χ 395). During the slaughter of the suitors of Penelope she keeps the door between the apartments fastened, and restrains the women (φ 380). On Odysseus's return, she washes his feet and recognizes him, but does not reveal his secret (τ 475). When the suitors are slain, she tells Penelope of Odysseus's deed (ψ 5), and is bidden by her to prepare the couch for him (ψ 177). That the poet names her grandfather, may indicate that she was a servant by capture rather than by birth, but she never alludes to any earlier condition of life, and is heartily devoted to Penelope and her family.

From the position of goddesses on Olympus, one may fairly draw inferences for the position of women on earth. We note, *Goddesses on Olympus.* perhaps with some surprise, that the chief divinity of war is not Ares or even Apollo, but a goddess, Athena, a favored, almost petted, daughter of Zeus; and her temple at Troy is in the care of a priestess who is also wife of Antenor, and one of the most honored matrons of the city. She may remind us of the warlike maidens, the Amazons, who are mentioned twice in the poems (Γ 189,

Z 186),—as attacking the Phrygians in Priam's early days, and as attacked by Bellerophon, sent from Lycia a few years earlier. Artemis as a huntress reminds the reader of Atalanta in the Calydonian Boar Hunt, and of Cyrene who contended alone and unarmed, even with lions (Pindar, *Pyth.* ix. 26). In physical power and in freedom of action these must have been the match of Spartan maidens. Hera is made to feel her inferiority to Zeus, but she at least speaks her mind to him freely, and is to hear from him what may be heard, before any other of the divinities. She dreads to offend him, but he, too, dislikes to offend her (A 518). The nymphs Circe and Calypso live alone on their islands, attended by other nymphs, and their situation is so different from that of mortals that no inference can be drawn from them, for human conditions, except perhaps that the notion of an unmarried woman at the head of a household was not entirely strange. Since the marriage-state is most clearly indicated as natural for both women and men,—for Homer knows of no unwedded man of middle life,—and a certain obligation rests on every marriageable woman to marry, as is shown in the case of Penelope, we may be surprised that Athena and Artemis remain unwedded, but for this no explanation is given.

The foregoing survey of the most prominent women and goddesses of the Homeric poems shows that the Greek women of the poet's time were far from being kept in semi-Oriental seclusion. Not only do women flock *Women not Secluded.* to the Scaean Gate of Troy, to learn news of the war (Z 238), and form a procession to the temple for public worship (Z 296); they also go out of the town to see a circus rider perform on four horses at once (O 683), to fetch water from the town-spring (κ 107), and to wash clothes at the public troughs and at the river (X 155, ζ 74), and in the harvest-field they prepare the porridge for the reapers (Σ 560). On the last day of battle, Hector says that he and Achilles cannot now "chat together, as a young man and a maiden chat from a rock or a tree" (X 127). Women, evidently neighbors, come into the middle of the street and use harsh language of each other,—" sayings things true and false " (Υ 253). In time of extreme danger, when the warriors are without the gates, the women stand guard on the battlements of the city,

with the old men (Σ 514).   The wife of Antenor, Theano, is
priestess of Athena (Z 300).   The women of Homeric Greece
clearly were far freer and more influential than their daughters
and successors of the historical period.   That the Athenian
historian Thucydides names no woman, is a well-known fact.
Spartan women indeed had more freedom, but in the true
family life they do not seem nearly so influential and important
as the Homeric women.   Nothing in the poems, however,
indicates the existence of a matriarchate in early Greece, but
merely what modern readers would consider the most wholesome and natural family relations of the whole ancient world.
An explanation of the later change of the position of women
in Greece is not certain, but we at least may remember that
while Athens never gave birth to a female poet, and the
Ionian Semonides of Amorgos lampooned women, the Aeolic
race could boast of Sappho, Erinna, and Corinna, and the
indications are clear of a close connexion between epic poetry
and the Aeolians.   The Athenians found such difficulty in
understanding Sappho's freedom of life and song, that their
comic poets most shamefully maligned her.   In this connexion
may be noted also the fact that the Muses, too, are females,
and sing at the feasts of the gods (A 604) as well as at
Achilles's funeral (ω 60), that the Sirens were beguiling
songstresses (μ 184), and that Circe sang while she plied
her loom (κ 221).

We have seen that Arete is the centre of the guests in the
palace hall, and that Helen comes to her hall as soon as she
learns that guests have arrived at the palace.   Certainly
Athena and Hera had honored places in the hall of Zeus,—
apparently one sitting on either side of him.   We may fairly
infer that the great hall was the usual place of the Homeric
wife, and that she was not expected to withdraw to the
women's quarters on the entrance of a stranger.   It was in
the great hall of the palace of Syrié (o 461) that the queen
and her women chaffered with the Phoenicians for their wares.
Doubtless Penelope sat in the hall of her palace until her
suitors became so numerous and importunate that she appeared
to them but seldom (o 516, σ 164).   The loom on which she
wove her noted web was set up in the great hall (β 94), and
there she sat in the morning before the suitors came (ρ 96,

105), and again in the evening after their departure. There she sits by the fire for her talk with the disguised Odysseus on the night before the suitors are slain (τ 55). The situation on the next morning is not quite clear, but she seems to be sitting in the hall while the suitors are feasting; at least her chair is placed where she can hear their words (υ 389). When Penelope appears formally to the suitors, she is attended by two maids (α 331, σ 207), and, similarly escorted, Andromache (X 450) and Helen (Γ 143) go to the tower by the Scaean Gate. Young women, as appears in the case of Nausicaa, are not expected to sit with the guests. As the wishes of Arete prevailed with Alcinoüs, so Cleopatra prevails with her husband Meleager (I 591) when his father and brothers and the elders of the city had supplicated him in vain.[1]

The position of woman in general forbids us to believe that she was bought and sold in marriage, though her father received gifts from her suitor, and Aristotle says that the early Greeks bought their wives (τὰς γυναῖκας ἐωνοῦντο, *Politics*, ii. 8. 12). No one can *Marriage not a Sale.* suppose that Nausicaa was to be given to the highest bidder, and that Arete and Nausicaa herself were to have no voice in the decision. On the contrary, we must believe that the mother and the daughter, and not the father, would determine the suitor's fate. Indeed the poet tells his hearers that Nausicaa has had many noble suitors, but that she (not the father, ζ 283) slights them. Nothing could be more inconsistent with their family life as depicted than to suppose a sale of the daughter, and in particular Alcinoüs is so charmed by Odysseus that he says frankly that this is just the sort of man he wants for his son-in-law, and he is willing to accept him—with no property—as a suitor for his daughter's hand, although many of the Phaeacian nobles are wooing her (η 311, ζ 284). In general, however, the father expected gifts, and the poet applies to maidens the epithet *cattle-bringing* (ἀλφεσίβοιαι, Σ 593).[2] This custom was so general among

---

[1] The large company of fair women whose ghosts Odysseus saw in Hades, of themselves would make it impossible for us to think of Homeric women as of little note (λ 225-329), and with this list we may compare the ἢ οἵαι of Hesiod.

[2] The Thracians of the historical period retained many of the customs of the Greeks of Homer's day (*e.g.* the use of small tables at dinner) and Aristotle

Indo-European peoples that we should expect it as we find it in Greece. The largest specified dowry is that which Iphidamas gives to his grandfather Cisses for the hand of his aunt,—one hundred kine and the promise of a thousand sheep and goats (Λ 244). How this Iphidamas came into the possession of so many cattle is not clear, since he had been brought up by this same grandfather (Λ 223); probably he served for them, as Jacob served his uncle Laban "fourteen years for thy two daughters, and six years for thy cattle" (*Genesis* xxxi. 41). Odysseus's parents gave his sister in marriage to a husband on the island of Samé, and received "countless gifts" (μυρί᾽ ἕλοντο, ο 367), and Achilles's sister was given to a suitor who gave "boundless wedding-gifts" (ἔδνα, Π 178, *cf.* 190, λ 282). The suitor Antinoüs urges that Penelope should marry him "whom her father bids, and who is pleasing to herself" (β 114), but elsewhere she would marry "the man who is bravest and offers the most gifts" (π 77). The question cannot have been simply who would pay the largest price, or the auction would have been soon over. At last, as all know, Penelope demanded no gifts at all, but said she would wed him who most easily should string the old bow of Odysseus, and shoot an arrow through a mark formed by axes (φ 75). Penelope indeed had invited gifts from the suitors (σ 278 ff.): Antinoüs gives her a beautiful embroidered robe with twelve brooches, Eurymachus a long necklace of gold and amber, Eurydamas earrings, and each of the other suitors makes some present to the queen. But these are not to be returned in case of her marriage to another than the giver; they are gifts without condition. Such gifts she declares to be usual, though commonly they would be given to the bride's father, and in principle they are not easily separated from the gifts of cattle by suitors.

Nestor's sister was offered as wife to any one who should drive from Phylace the cattle of Iphiclus (λ 289); in this task the seer Melampus succeeded, but transferred to his

---

(*Frag.* 611. 58) says that Thracian parents receive in exchange for their daughters gifts which are returned in case of an unhappy marriage. But Thracian widows were inherited like the rest of a man's estate, and this is not Homeric: Penelope herself determines the conditions of her marriage.

brother Bias his claim to the hand of Pero. Bellerophon is accepted as son-in-law by the Lycian king, without gifts, when he has killed the Chimaera and rendered other services (Z 192, *cf.* ξ 211). Othryoneus came to the war as a Trojan ally, receiving from king Priam the promise of Cassandra to wife, if he should drive the Achaeans from Troy. He is slain by Idomeneus, who then mockingly says in exultation: "I wonder if you will perform your promise to Priam. We would give you the most beautiful of Agamemnon's daughters to wife, if with us you will sack Ilium. But come and talk the matter over at the ships" (N 366). Similarly, Agamemnon offers to Achilles, when he is sulking in his tent, if he will give up his wrath and fight for the Achaeans, whichever of his three daughters he may choose, without gifts from the suitor (ἀνάεδνον, I 146), while the father will bestow such presents (μείλια, I 147) on the bridegroom as never yet were given with a daughter,—viz. seven well-built towns. In Israel, Saul gave to David his daughter Michal to wife, requiring no "dowry," but that he kill one hundred Philistines (1 *Samuel* xviii. 25). *Cf.* "And Caleb said 'He that smiteth Kirjath-sepher and taketh it, to him will I give Achsah my daughter to wife,'" *Joshua* xv. 16; "And it shall be that the man who killeth him [*i.e.* Goliath of Gath], the king will enrich him with great riches, and will give him his daughter," 1 *Samuel* xvii. 25. Shechem, in love with Jacob's daughter Dinah, said, "Ask me never so much dowry and gift, . . . but give me the damsel to wife" (*Genesis* xxxiv. 12). So the general custom was the same in Israel as in Homeric Greece. Fifty pieces of silver seems to have been the ordinary gift to the bride's father, according to *Deuteronomy* xxii. 29. In modern Palestine, according to Dr. Trumbull (*Oriental Studies*, pp. 9, 20), "Almost universally in the east, a betrothal is based upon an agreement of dowry to be paid by the husband to the family of the wife. . . . It is hardly fair to speak of this 'dowry' as the 'price of a wife,' as though the father were actually selling his daughter. . . . The bride's father is expected to give a like sum with that paid by the groom,—the entire amount being the bride's portion."

Dowry.

A much-discussed passage is contained in the advice of
Athena to Telemachus, "If thy mother's heart urges her to
marry, let her return to her father's house, and they shall
prepare the feast and make ready the wedding gifts" (a 275).
Here the persons who prepare the feast (and these must be
the bride's kinsmen and not the suitor[1]) are also to provide
the gifts. So also Telemachus tells his mother's suitors that
he not only consents to Penelope's marriage, but will give
her untold gifts (v 342).

Apparently the custom is changing, but such gifts, which
developed into the dowry in the modern sense, are implied not
merely in the offer of Agamemnon to Achilles but also in words
of Priam. Two of the old king's sons are missing when the
Trojans are driven into the city, and he says: "If they are
alive and in the Achaean camp, we will ransom them for
bronze and gold, for the renowned Altes gave many treasures
tó his daughter" (X 49), i.e. to Laothoë, who was the mother
of the youths, and one of Priam's wives. Priam clearly had
received gifts with Laothoë rather than paid a heavy price for
her, and her dowry might reasonably be used for the ransom
of her sons. King Alcinoüs expresses his willingness not only
to give his daughter to the wanderer Odysseus, without
presents from the shipwrecked Ithacan, but also to bestow
upon him house and possessions (η 314); and he does not
speak as if this were an act contrary to all precedent, any
more than Penelope does when she consents without further
conditions to wed the suitor who shows like skill in archery
with Odysseus in his young manhood. Very probably, the
father often gave to his daughter the cattle or gold which
he received from her husband, as is customary at present
in some countries of the East; this would amount to a
"settlement" on the wife. The epithet "of many gifts,"[2]
applied to Andromache, Hecuba, and Penelope, is best understood as "richly dowered," i.e. bringing many gifts to her husband
rather than to her father. Naturally such gifts must be repaid
if the wife returned to her father's house, and Telemachus says

---

[1] The latter alternative cannot fairly be accepted on the basis of the apparent
analogy in σ 279, where the suitors bring cattle and sheep *as a feast* for the
maiden's friends (κούρης δαῖτα φίλοισιν) and give splendid presents.

[2] πολύδωρος, Z 394, X 88, ω 294; cf. ἠπιόδωρος, Z 251.

that it would be hard for him to repay Icarius, as he must if he should send back his daughter (β 132).[1] Conversely, the return of gifts made to the bride's father, might be demanded in case of a divorce on the ground of infidelity (θ 318). Naturally, smaller gifts were bestowed more freely by the bride's friends. Thus Icarius gave to Penelope on her marriage with Odysseus a man-slave, Dolius, who later cared for her garden (δ 735), and a serving-woman, Actoris, who served as chambermaid (ψ 228). These seem to have been hers in a peculiar sense. These gifts clearly were simply tokens of love. Such may have been the gifts which Telemachus offered (v 342) with his mother. With these may be compared also the wedding gifts bestowed by the gods. For example, Aphrodite gave a veil to Andromache on her marriage (X 470). That in later times Greek women brought dowries to their husbands, is a familiar fact. Solon, according to Plutarch (*Solon*, 20), already strove to check the practise of giving gifts to daughters, though this regulation may have been rather a sumptuary law to restrict the magnificence of *trousseaus*, and Euripides makes Medea complain of the lot of women in that they are obliged to " buy themselves masters" (*Medea*, 233).

That Homeric women might hold property has been inferred from the gifts which Helen received in Egypt,—Menelaus received two silver bath-tubs and other presents from Polybus, the king of Egyptian Thebes, and *Property of Women.* Helen received a golden distaff and a silver basket, with castors and with gold-plated edges, from the wife of Polybus (δ 130); but this was on the same principle as the gift of a robe by Helen to Telemachus (o 123), though nothing indicates that the Homeric woman was not so free to bestow such gifts as an American woman of to-day. Personal ornaments may be the property of even a Turkish woman. That in general the married daughter inherited a share of her father's estate, is altogether improbable, but no instance to prove this proposition is mentioned by the poet.

---

[1] Keller, p. 226, understands this of a *fine*,—believing this to be "in accord with that phase of the patriarchate where the wife's father can and will stipulate as to her treatment," and holding the interpretation which is preferred above to be "unjustifiable in the face of the elsewhere universal custom of wife-buying."

The cases of Tydeus at Argos and of Bellerophon in Lycia,—
each of whom is an exile, but weds the king's daughter, and
succeeds him on the throne,—show that in lack of a son, a
father might give the right of succession to a daughter's
husband, thus transmitting the throne or property to his
daughter's sons. Thus Hypsipyle's son by Jason, Euneüs,
becomes king of Lemnos (H 468), but this stands by itself,
since the ordinary form of the story represents Hypsipyle

FIG. 2. The Loom.

as queen of the island when Jason and the Argonauts
landed there. Menelaus was even admitted to Elysium
(δ 569,—omitted by some authorities) as the son-in-law
of Zeus.

Antiquarians have observed that, with the single exception
of the "rape of Helen," Homer preserves no trace of the
ancient custom of stealing the bride, of which clear indications
are found in later Spartan legislation.

As for the occupations of women, another chapter shows
that most of the work within the house was done by
women, and that this included not only the care of the

children and the ordinary house-work of modern times, and embroidery, but also much that is now *Occupations of* done by machinery, as the grinding and pound- *Women.* ing of grain, and the carding, spinning, and weaving of wool and flax.

Spinning and weaving were the occupations that were never ended. The employment of the distaff doubtless was much like that still customary in Greece. The loom was upright, and consisted of two perpendicular beams, perhaps three or four feet apart, connected by two horizontal cross-pieces, one at the top and one at the bottom. Near the top of the loom was a roller on which the cloth already woven would be wound. The dependent threads of the warp seem to have been attached alternately to two rods (κανόνες, Ψ 761),—the even threads to one, and the odd threads to the other. The thread of the woof was wound around a shuttle or spool (πηνίον, Ψ 762). The weaver would draw first one of the rods and then the other towards her, and push or throw the shuttle between the alternate threads of the warp.

From the labor of sewing, however, women were relieved, at least for the most part, as is seen in the chapter on dress, and probably in general from the cooking of meat as well as the most of the other cookery of modern times. Women fetched water from the spring : thus a score of women went to the spring from the home of Odysseus (υ 158), and the Laestrygonian princess is on her way to the spring for water when she meets Odysseus's comrades (κ 107). The grinding of grain and the carding of wool were menial, but spinning, weaving, and embroidery were proper occupations for princesses and goddesses,—for Circe (κ 222) and Calypso (ε 61) and Athena (E 735), as well as for Penelope (β 94), Helen (Γ 125, δ 124), Andromache (X 440), and Arete (ζ 306). The Phaeacian women were as proud of their weaving as their husbands were of their ships (η 110). Penelope's web must have been very elaborate if her suitors were satisfied to wait three years for its completion (β 106 ff.). Nausicaa's joining with her maids in " laving the linen," not as a weekly return of menial toil, but as part of a day's pleasant exercise by the river side (ζ 26 ff.), is referred to elsewhere. Even the carrying of a considerable burden is assigned to women, as when Arete sends three women to bear to the ship the gifts which have been bestowed on Odysseus (ν 66). Similarly Telemachus is asked to send women to fetch the presents which he had received at Sparta (ρ 75). Whether women served as shepherdesses, is not clear. They seem to have done so in the time of Daphnis and Chloë, and certainly have done so in Modern Greece,[1] where in general they are more secluded than their mothers were in Homer's time; and two fair-tressed nymphs, daughters of the sun-god, watched his herds and flocks (μ 131). If the sun-god's daughters tended his flocks and herds, we may fairly believe that the daughters of many a chieftain would see nothing unmaidenly in such an occupation. Perhaps women were expected to have special skill in the use of healing herbs. Agamedé, the daughter of Augeas of Elis, "knew all the herbs which grew upon the broad earth" (Λ 741); and, not to speak of Circe and her magic charms, Helen brought from Egypt an herb which, put into the wine, dispelled all care and grief (δ 220).

One service rendered by women needs a special remark. A literal translation of the Greek declares that Hebe "bathed

Serving at the Bath.

Ares and put upon him beautiful raiment" (E 905), when he returned, wounded, from the field of battle; that Helen "bathed, anointed, and clothed" Odysseus (δ 252) when he entered Troy as a spy, and that Nestor's daughter Polycaste performed like service for Telemachus (γ 466). But Nausicaa bids her women "to bathe" Odysseus in the river (λούσατε, ζ 210), where they certainly were not expected to "rub him down"; what they actually did was simply to give him oil and clothes, and tell him to go and bathe himself. That the verb need not be understood with perfect literalness is shown by its use by Odysseus himself in telling Nausicaa's parents of her kindness to him: she had given him food and wine, "bathed him in the river" (λοῦσ' ἐν ποταμῷ, η 296), and furnished him raiment. Again, Odysseus says that Circe "bathed and anointed" his twenty-two companions whom she had turned into swine, and clad them in cloaks and tunics (κ 450),—though he certainly did not expect

---

[1] See Snider's *Walks in Hellas.*

his hearers to believe that Circe personally served each ; she merely gave them the use of the bathroom. Neither Alcinoüs nor Arete understands this as meaning more than what we have already seen. Hebe, Helen, and Polycaste also may have done no more than make or oversee arrangements for the bath, but doubtless the Greeks of Homer's time shrank less than the poet's modern readers from the exposure of the person in the bath, being in this like the Japanese, who, though they are shocked at some Occidental pictures, yet are not disturbed by the exposure of the person while bathing. That Odysseus would not bathe in the river until the women had gone away to a little distance (ζ 218), certainly seems inconsistent with his accepting from Helen actual service at the bath, but his story says distinctly that one of Circe's nymphs poured water down over his head and shoulders (κ 362).

The amusements and recreations of women in Homer's time were doubtless very unlike those of women in modern society. Their life was simple. They had few "social events." But they met at the harvest home and at vintage festivals (I 534, Σ 567), and at marriage feasts (Σ 494?), as well as by the washing-troughs and near the river side. *Recreations of Women.* The maidens danced, then as now, and with young men (Σ 593), though very likely the two sexes were in different groups. After killing Penelope's suitors, Odysseus, desiring that the tidings of what he had done should not get abroad that night, bids the bard to strike his lyre, and Telemachus, the swine-herd, the neat-herd, and the maid-servants to dance, in order that any neighbor or passer-by, hearing the sounds of festivity, might be far from suspecting any dreadful deed of death (ψ 132), and might suppose that Penelope was wedding one of her suitors. Polymele (II 180) was noted as "beautiful in the dance," and Odysseus speaks of the joy of Nausicaa's family in seeing such a "fair flower" ($\tau o\iota \acute{o}\nu\delta\epsilon$ $\theta \acute{a}\lambda os$, ζ 157,—*such a young tree*) entering the dance. Nausicaa's brothers, too, the poet says, are "fond of going to the dance, with newly washed raiment" (ζ 64). Aphrodite, urging Helen to come to Paris after his single combat with Menelaus, says, "You would not think that he had come from the fray, but that he was going to a dance, or was just resting from the dance" (Γ 392). Circe sings as she plies her loom (κ 221), and the songs of the Sirens (μ 183) and of the Muses are familiar (A 604, ω 60). Women showed their gift of song, also, by singing dirges (Ω 723), though on such occasions men might be called in as the leaders of the song.

The most frequent epithet applied to women is *fair-tressed* (ἐυπλόκαμος ε 58, more than 25 times, and καλλιπλόκαμος, Σ 407, six times); next in frequency are *fair-cheeked* (καλλιπάρῃος, A 143, sixteen times), *well-robed* (ἐύζωνος, A 429, seven times, *cf.* καλλίζωνος, H 139, and βαθύζωνος, γ 154), and *fair-ancled* (καλλίσφυρος, I 557). Athena is *gleaming-eyed* (γλαυκῶπις, a 44, nearly a hundred times), and Hera is *white-armed* (λευκώλενος, A 55, nearly forty times) and *ox-eyed* (βοῶπις, A 551). Penelope is called *considerate, prudent* (περίφρων, a 329, just fifty times, and ἐχέφρων, δ 111, seven times). Achaea, Hellas, and Sparta are said to *abound in fair women* (καλλιγύναικα, Γ 75, B 683, ν 412). The locks of Achilles, Menelaus, and Odysseus are *tawny* (ξανθῆς, A 197), but only one woman receives this epithet (Agamede, Λ 740), and no woman or goddess is said to have golden hair.[1]

Epithets of Women.

Of children, Homer says little. The infant son of Hector and Andromache is the only child who appears directly in the action of the poems. When Andromache meets Hector as he is hurrying to the field of battle, the nurse accompanying her carries " in her arms the merry-hearted child, a mere infant, the beloved son of Hector, like to a fair star, whom Hector called Scamandrius,[2] but the rest called him Astyanax (*Defender of the City*), for Hector alone defended Ilium " (Z 400). Hector extends his arms to the child, but the boy does not recognize his father in armor, and with a cry turns to the breast of his nurse, " fearing the bronze and the crest of horse-hair." The father and mother laugh, and Hector lays his bright helmet upon

Children.

---

[1] The epithet *golden* (χρυσέη, δ 14) is indeed given to Aphrodite, but probably from her golden ornaments, just as Ares is called *bronze* from his armor.

[2] Named for the Scamander, the chief river of the Trojan plain. Rivers were thought to have an important connexion with the birth and growth of children. The hair of Achilles was vowed as an offering to the Spercheüs, the chief river of his home (Ψ 142).

the ground. Then he "kisses[1] his dear son and tosses him in his arms," and prays to Zeus that " his son, too, may be a mighty defender of Ilium [here playing on his name], and bring back bloody spoil from the battle, rejoicing his mother's heart " (Z 474). Then Hector gives the child, not back to the nurse, but to Andromache herself, as it were committing to her a trust.

A mother's care in keeping a fly from her slumbering infant, serves as a comparison for the care of Athena for Menelaus (Δ 131), as she wards an arrow from a vital part of his body.

No example is found in Homer of the " exposure " of infants, which was legal long afterwards in Sparta, though Hephaestus says that his mother Hera desired to conceal him because he was lame (Σ 397).

Two words are used in the poems for nurse ($\tau\iota\theta\eta\nu\eta$, Z 389, $\tau\rho\circ\phi\acute{o}s$, β 361),—the one, as it happens, used only in the *Iliad* and the other only in the *Odyssey*, but without apparent difference in meaning.[2] The infant *The Nurse.* Dionysus (Z 132), and Astyanax (Z 389), have nurses in the *Iliad*, while Eurymedusa had been the nurse of Nausicaa

---

[1] Kissing is not mentioned very often in the poems, and never on the lips. Agamemnon kissed his land on his return from Troy (δ 522). After his shipwreck, Odysseus kissed the land of the Phaeacians, and after his return he kissed the soil of Ithaca (ε 463, ν 354). Thetis as a suppliant kisses the knees of Zeus (Θ 371), and similarly old Priam, begging for the return of Hector's body, kisses the hands of Achilles (Ω 478), and a captive in battle kisses the knees of his captor (ξ 279). The servants kiss the head and shoulders of Telemachus on his return (ρ 35), and of Odysseus on his recognition (φ 224, χ 499). The old servant Dolius kisses the hands of Odysseus (ω 398), the swine-herd Eumaeus kisses the " head, eyes, and hands " of Telemachus (π 15), and Odysseus kisses the heads and hands of his old retainers (φ 225). Odysseus's grandmother kisses his head and fair eyes, when he visits her in his youth (τ 417), and Penelope so kisses Telemachus on his return (ρ 39). Odysseus kisses Telemachus on his recognition (π 190), and on meeting his aged father Laërtes, is eager to embrace and kiss him (ω 236). Still uncertain as to his identity, Penelope ponders whether she shall kiss the head and hands of Odysseus (ψ 87), and when her doubt has been dispelled, she throws her arms about his neck and kisses his head (ψ 208).

[2] Nothing implies that these nurses were *wet-nurses*. This remark would be unnecessary but for the assumption, especially of German scholars, that " the frequent mention of nurses and their importance in the household shows that very generally a wet-nurse relieved the mother." The support of this assertion is slight ; the number of nurses is not large. The objections to the statement are considerable.

(η 12), and Euryclea on Ithaca had been the nurse of both Odysseus (τ 482) and Telemachus (β 361), and the swine-herd Eumaeus, by birth a prince on the island of Syrié, in his infancy had a Phoenician nurse (o 450). The tie between the nurse and the child might continue strong in later years. Nausicaa's old nurse lights her fire and prepares her evening meal (η 7), and Euryclea is sought as his faithful friend by Telemachus (β 349), and is the first to recognize her old nursling and master, Odysseus (τ 468). On the recognition, Odysseus addresses her by the old name of his childhood, which Telemachus also uses, *mammy* ($\mu\alpha\hat{\iota}\alpha$, β 349, τ 482).

The child received its name soon after its birth (σ 6), and, as in historical times, the name of the grandfather might be given to his oldest grandson (E 546). The name of Odysseus was appointed by his maternal grand-father, who visited Ithaca soon after his birth (τ 409),[1] and with the name gave the promise of presents,— being a sort of godfather. As in the case of Astyanax, an epithet which is due to the father may be used as a name for the son. So Telemachus ($\tau\hat{\eta}\lambda\epsilon$, $\mu\acute{\alpha}\chi o\mu\alpha\iota$) receives his name from Odysseus's being a *fighter far from* home when the son was an infant.

The Child's Name.

Nothing indicates the existence of detailed rules for the bringing up of children. Of the food of young children, all that we learn surprises us. Andromache says that the little Astyanax, though still an infant in arms, " on the knees of his father ate only marrow and the rich fat of sheep " (X 500) ; Aphrodite brought up the daughters of Pandareüs on cheese, honey, and wine (v 69),—which we see elsewhere as a posset ; and Phoenix, in telling of his care for the young Achilles,

---

Hecuba, the poet tells us, suckled Hector (X 83). The nymphs who cared for Dionysus did not "nurse" him in the special sense. Euryclea cannot well have suckled both Odysseus and his son Telemachus, and nothing indicates that she ever bore a child and could have served as a wet-nurse. The expression "at the breast " ($\dot{\epsilon}\pi\dot{\iota}$ $\mu\alpha\zeta\hat{\omega}$, τ 483), on which stress has been laid in this discussion, proves nothing, for the similar $\dot{\epsilon}\pi\dot{\iota}$ $\kappa\acute{o}\lambda\pi\omega$ is used of the infant Astyanax in the arms of his nurse (Z 400), as she hurriedly accompanies Andromache to the Scaean Gate.

[1] Odysseus's grandfather, Autolycus, the reader will remember, was a noted trickster and thief (τ 396) and thus naturally unpopular. So he gives the name Ὀδυσσεύς to his grandson because he himself was πολλοῖσιν ὀδυσσάμενος (τ 407), *hated by many.*

says that he cut up the meat for him and held the wine to his lips, when the child was so young that he often let the wine fall from his lips upon the tunic of Phoenix (I 488). Doubtless marrow is mentioned by Andromache as a dainty,— but such a diet as these stories imply is no modern "health-food."[1]

Of older children the poet tells his hearers still less than of infants, but a touch of nature is seen in Achilles's address to Patroclus (II 7) on the latter's coming to him in tears on account of the rout of the Achaeans: *Older Children.* "Why, Patroclus, art thou weeping as a little girl, who runs along at her mother's side, bidding her to take her up, clinging to her gown and detaining her in her haste, and looks at her with tears until she takes her in her arms?" The archer Teucer, being himself without a shield, on shooting at an enemy, went to his brother Ajax and the defense of his great shield, "as a child to its mother" (Θ 271).

When a boy outgrew the care of a nurse, he might be committed to some elderly friend of much higher rank than the *paedagogus* of later times. Thus Phoenix, who was an exile from his own home, had charge of the young Achilles, and, being without children of his own, devoted himself to the boy, even accompanying him to Troy at the instance of Peleus, to teach Achilles to be "a speaker of words and a doer of deeds" (I 443). That boys and girls were not always separated early, is shown by Eumaeus's growing up with Odysseus's younger sister Ctimene (τῇ ὁμοῦ ἐτρεφόμην, ο 365), until Ctimene was married and Eumaeus was sent to the field to care for the swine. The boy doubtless accompanied his father in many of his occupations and expeditions, and in particular to his feasts, which, as is seen elsewhere, were made by daylight. Thus Andromache, enumerating the trials of a boy who has lost his father (Χ 490), says that he goes to the comrades of his father (at a feast, as the sequel shows), plucking one by the cloak and another by the tunic; most disregard him, but one who pities him holds a cup for a moment to his lips,—it wets his lips, but not his palate; while a boy whose parents are

---

[1] *Cf.* "My soul shall be satisfied as with marrow and fatness," *Psalm* lxiii. 5.

alive, assails him with his fists, and says, "Be off! Thy father is not feasting with us." Clearly, then, no boy might go to the feast without his father, but the father might take his son with him. At these feasts the boy would hear both the tales and songs about the past, and the discussions about the present, the principles of war and of peace. There he would learn the unwritten laws of the people,—which were the foundation of the public life. There, too, he would observe the methods of public sacrifice. Whether the boys were allowed to accompany their fathers also to the place of assembly, the *agora*, is uncertain. No instance of this is mentioned, but opportunities are lacking in the *Iliad* and rare in the *Odyssey*. The welcome which the father received from his children is indicated in the words of Dione, "He is not long-lived who contends against the immortals, nor do his children say 'papa' at his knees [ποτὶ γούνασι παππάζουσιν, E 408, with which compare Nausicaa's πάππα φίλε] as he returns from the battle,"—*i.e.* he will not return from the battle. Girls, as well as boys, would listen to their father's stories, but it was chiefly from their mothers at home, while they were busy with weaving or spinning, that they would learn the customs which served as laws. The mothers, as well as the fathers, had tales to tell and advice to give.

Of children's playthings, our poet mentions but three,—the top (στρόμβος,—which serves as a comparison for a warrior hit by Telamonian Ajax, Ξ 413), the sand of the sea-shore (O 362), and "huckle-bones" (ἀστραγάλοισι, Ψ 88). Anger in a game of huckle-bones led Patroclus, when still a child, to kill his companion, and thus required the exile from his home which brought him to the house of Peleus. Doubtless boys, as well as young men, played draughts (πεσσοῖσι, α 107), which was one of the amusements of Penelope's suitors, and ball, like the young Phaeacians of both sexes (ζ 100, θ 372).

Plays.

With regard to the musical instruments of the time, the Homeric story gives few indications. The name *lyre* (λύρα) is not used. The *phorminx* and the *cithara* seem to be identical (α 153, 155). This probably had but four strings and but four notes. Whether the tortoise-shell was used for the body of the instrument, as in later times

Music.

(*Homeric Hymns*, iii. 25 ff.), is not clear. This cithara had sheep-gut strings, wound about a peg (φ 407). Achilles's lyre, taken from the spoils of Eetion's city, had a bridge (ζυγόν, I 187, *yoke*) of silver. The lyre was used chiefly to introduce a song and as accompaniment for the dance and feast (α 152 f., ρ 271, ω 144). Hector regarded it as rather effeminate (Γ 54) as played by Paris. The flute or clarionet and the shepherd's pipe or *syrinx* appear but twice in the poems (αὐλός, K 13, Σ 495), as played in the Trojan bivouac in the evening after the second day of battle, and, with the cithara, accompanying a marriage procession depicted on the Shield of Achilles. Apollo, with his lyre, and the Muses furnish music to the gods on Olympus (A 603). The young Achaeans who convey Chryseïs to her father, sing a paean in praise of Apollo at his sacrifice (A 472). Circe sings as she plies her loom (κ 221). The Muses blinded the Thracian bard Thamyris, and took away his gift of song, since he boasted to vie with them (B 597).

Athletic contests were often held in connexion with funerals. Thus the greater part of the twenty-third book of the *Iliad* (Ψ 258 ff.) is given to an account of the funeral games in honor of Patroclus,—a chariot-race *Athletic Contests.* (Ψ 262-615), a contest in boxing (Ψ 653-699), a contest in wrestling (Ψ 700-739), a foot-race (Ψ 740-797), a contest in fighting with the spear (Ψ 798-825), a trial of putting the shot (Ψ 826-849), a contest of archery (Ψ 850-883), and finally one is proposed in hurling the spear, but here Agamemnon receives the prize without an actual trial. These contests were all rather informal. The chariots which took part in the race were clearly those which were used in battle. The funeral games of king Amarynceus and of Oedipus at Thebes are mentioned as being of a former generation (Ψ 630, 679), and the Achaeans with like contests honored the funeral of Achilles (ω 87). The custom is referred to also at X 164. Nestor's father had sent a chariot and four horses to Elis for a race,—which seems like a forerunner of the Olympian games,— but the occasion is not specified, though Nestor reports that king Augeas detained the horses, but dismissed the charioteer (Λ 701). The prizes in the games are a woman-slave, a mare with a mule foal, a basin, two pieces of gold (shekels ?), a cup, a mule six years old, a tripod to stand over the fire, a silver bowl, an ox, half a piece of gold, the arms of a fallen foe, a mass of iron, axes, hatchets, and a spear. An ordinary prize in the foot-race is said to be an ox-hide (X 159) or a victim for sacrifice, while a tripod or a woman-slave was often offered for the chariot-race. The Phaeacians had nine umpires (αἰσυμνῆται, θ 258). In the chariot-race in honor of Patroclus, old Phoenix was set at the turning-post to see that the chariots took the right course, but this does not prevent a charge of foul play (Ψ 359). The Phaeacians had games in honor of the visit of Odysseus (θ 118-130): a foot-race, wrestling, jumping, boxing, and a contest with the discus. Saying that a man has no greater glory than is won by his hands and feet, a Phaeacian challenges Odysseus to take part in these contests, and the latter hurls the discus farther than any one else has done. After the games the Phaeacian dancers display their skill, and Odysseus wonders at the twinkling of their feet (θ 265). Finally two dance alone, one tossing a ball into the air and the other leaping and catching it before his feet touch the ground. At the marriage-feast in the palace of Menelaus, and in a scene depicted on the Shield of Achilles, there were not only dancers but also tumblers.[1]

The formal education of the Homeric child was exceedingly limited, and consisted almost entirely in the observation and
Education. imitation of the elders. In the natural imitation of their mothers, the girls learned to card, to spin, to weave, to embroider, and to make bread, while the boys learned from their fathers and from each other to shoot the bow, to hurl the javelin, to put the shot, to hunt, to fish, and to swim. In such a free, untrammelled life, no definite formal lessons were needed. No time was required then to be set apart for the study and practise of reading, writing, arithmetic, geography, modern languages, etc. Some form of writing seems to have been known, but the art was little used. The memories of the Homeric Greeks were not yet impaired by note books, and children were not *set* to reading and writing. The use of the lyre doubtless was considered a privilege, and the children were not held to certain times for practise, by the clock or the hour-glass. The application of the principle of

---

[1] κυβιστητῆρε, δ 18, Σ 605,—an identical verse, suspected in both instances.

imitation sufficed, and parents, being imitated by their children, were not obliged to have recourse to teachers for their instruction. The children learned how to bind up a wound and to use healing herbs, as these were used for their own ailments, and as their own hurts were tended. Thus in country life, even now, the farmer's boy learns to milk a cow, to harness a horse, to plant corn and hoe potatoes, to shoot, to fish, and to wrestle, to swim and to dance, without formal lessons. He needs special instruction in these arts no more than in speaking. So Plato observed with regard to a potter's boys, that these watched and helped their fathers long before they undertook making pottery on their own responsibility. The centaur Chiron on Mt. Pelion had the only "boarding-school" or educational establishment of classical antiquity, and according to the story developed after Homer, he had most of the Achaean warriors in his care during their youth ; but in the Homeric poems, Asclepius and Achilles alone are named as his pupils, and that in medicine (Δ 219, Λ 831), and his special relation to Thessaly and Peleus would explain his teaching Achilles how to care for a wound. Doubtless the fathers told their sons about the deeds of "mighty men of valor" ; and the songs of the "glorious deeds of men" (κλέα ἀνδρῶν, I 189), such as Achilles sang, would tell of the wars of the past, and also of the ways of the gods, and the standards and ideals of men in many matters. Even the bard Phemius was self-taught (αὐτοδίδακτος, χ 347), but often bards might be in the class of professionals (δημιοεργοί, ρ 383), like physicians and carpenters, who received special training. Doubtless in general, a smith's son succeeded him, as the surgeon Asclepius was succeeded by his sons Machaon and Podalirius, whom he taught the lessons which he had learned from Chiron (Δ 219), but at times he might take under his care another boy who showed interest in such work.

To ask when the son came of age, would be idle. The power of the father over his children as over his servants was theoretically unlimited,—he was a despot (δεσπότης, though this word is not used by the poet) ; practi- cally his power seems to have been used mildly. Patria Potestas. The horrible sacrifice of Iphigenia by Agamemnon, and the exposure of the infant Oedipus by his parents, are un-Homeric.

Youths might be sent on important errands, if they were thought trustworthy. Thus Odysseus while still a boy (παιδνός, φ 21) was sent to Messene to complain of a raid on which Messenians had taken three hundred sheep and their shepherds from Ithaca.

If any one thinks that the father's choice of a husband for his daughter is an indication of the subjection of women, he should remember that in theory the father chose also a wife for his son. Thus Achilles, rejecting scornfully Agamemnon's offer of the hand of one of his daughters, says he would not wed her though she had the beauty of Aphrodite and the accomplishments of Athena, and that if the gods bring him safely home, Peleus himself will seek out a wife for him.[1] So when Telemachus visits Sparta, Menelaus is celebrating the marriage feast for his daughter Hermione, who goes to Thessaly as the bride of Achilles's son Neoptolemus, and for Megapenthes (his son by a slave), for whom he was taking (υἱέι ἤγετο, δ 10) a wife from Sparta.

For the marriage the Homeric Greeks had no formal ceremony of words; the feast and the sacrifice which accompanied every feast were the only formalities of which we learn; very likely the hand of the bride was placed in that of her husband, but the poet has no occasion to mention this. The feast was the *marriage* (γάμος, δ 3) just as the funeral feast was the funeral (τάφος, γ 309). As a rule it was held at the home of the bride's father (α 277, δ 3), and the bride was then conducted to her husband's home. Such a procession is represented on the Shield of Achilles,— "by the light of blazing torches, with a loud wedding hymn, the dance of youths, and the sound of flutes and lyres (for the 'wedding march'), while the women stood in their doorways and looked on" (Σ 491). The bride's family was expected to furnish the wedding garments for the young men who escorted

Marriage.

---

[1] γυναῖκά γε μάσσεται αὐτός, Ι 394. Another reading is γαμέσσεται, *will marry for me*,—but is found nowhere else for a marriage by proxy. For this office of the parents for the son, *cf. Judges* xiv. 2, where Samson says to his father and mother, "I have seen a woman in Timnath of the daughters of the Philistines; now therefore get her for me to wife. . . . Get her for me, for she pleaseth me well," and *Genesis* xxi. 21, where Hagar, acting for Ishmael, "took him a wife out of the land of Egypt." Similarly Abraham feels the responsibility for choosing a wife for his son Isaac (*Genesis* xxiv.).

her, who served as a kind of ushers or "groomsmen" (ζ 28). The gods were all present at the wedding-feast of Achilles's parents, and Apollo had his lyre with him,—evidently to accompany the wedding hymn (Ω 62).   As we have just seen, Odysseus, after killing Penelope's suitors, sought to give to passers-by the impression of a scene of a wedding instead of one of horror, by causing the younger men and the women to dance to the sound of the lyre (ψ 135).   An exception to the rule of having the wedding-feast at the home of the bride's father is made in the case of a double wedding, when both the daughter and the son of Menelaus are married at the same time (δ 4).   Perhaps the fact that the groom's father was the king of the land, made the feast at his palace the more natural, but Telemachus threatens Ctesippus that the latter's father might have to prepare a funeral instead of a marriage feast for his son (υ 307).   Nothing is said of bridesmaids or "maids of honor."   For the prayer at the wedding, we may derive a hint from Odysseus's prayer for Nausicaa, that "the gods may grant to her a husband and home and *union of spirit* (ὁμοφροσύνην, ζ 181), which is the greatest blessing of all,"— a prayer which in itself shows the honorable position of women in the Homeric age.

That marriages were "made in heaven," is indicated by the rather odd combination of expressions of one of Penelope's suitors : "She would wed him who should bring the most gifts and who should be according to fate" (μόρσιμος ἔλθοι, π 392), and perhaps by Aphrodite's making a special petition to Zeus for the marriage of the daughters of Pandareüs (υ 74). But, in those days, everything was determined on Olympus.

For the most part the marriage connexion was formed between young people of the same district and tribe, but this rule had its exceptions.   The Phaeacian nobles would not be pleased if Nausicaa should wed a foreigner (ζ 283), but as has just been seen, Helen's daughter Hermione leaves Sparta for a home in Thessaly.   Odysseus's maternal grandfather lived on the slope of Parnassus (τ 394).   The poet does not tell us what land was the early home of Penelope, but her sister Iphthime was the wife of Eumelus in Pherae of Thessaly (δ 798), and the two sisters were widely separated ; according to the story which appears later, their father Icarius was

brother of Tyndareüs, the putative father of Helen, and
lived in Sparta,—and thus Helen and Penelope were step-
first-cousins,—a story which makes the removal of Penelope
and Iphthime the more notable. That Tydeus of Calydon
married the daughter of the king of Argos (Ξ 121), and
that Bellerophon of Corinth wedded a Lycian princess (Z
192), are only apparent exceptions to the rule, since they
were exiles and each established his home in the country of
his bride. But Hecuba was by birth a Phrygian (Π 718),
and not a Trojan; Laothoë, another wife of Priam, was a
princess from Pedasus, and Castianeira, a third wife, was
from Thrace (Θ 304). And Patroclus promised Briseïs that
she, though a Trojan captive, should be made the lawful
wife of Achilles (T 298).

That Iphidamas married his mother's sister (Λ 226), has
been noticed already. So also, according to the ordinary
interpretation, Diomed's wife Aegialea is the
Marriage between Kindred. daughter of Adrastus (Ἀδρηστίνη, E 412), and so
the sister of his mother. Similarly Alcinoüs weds
his niece (η 66). Aeolus, the master of the
winds, gives his six daughters in marriage to his sons
(κ 7), but he is so far out of the pale of ordinary life that
his case need not be taken as a human precedent, any more
than the act of Zeus in marrying his sister Hera (Δ 58).

Priam of Troy is the only polygamist of the poems.
Hecuba has born him nineteen sons, and Laothoë two. In
all, "when the sons of the Achaeans came" he
Priam the only Polygamist. had fifty sons and twelve daughters (Ω 495,
Z 244). Castianeira was "in form like to the god-
desses," and was "wooed from Aesyme" (Θ 304).
Laothoë was a princess by birth (Φ 85), and had the full
dignity of a wife. Very likely, however, many of his children
were born by concubines, though all his children, with the
exception of Hector and Paris, seem to live with him in
patriarchal fashion, bringing their wives and husbands into the
great household (Z 244, X 62).

As in the Old Testament times, the husband was bound
with a looser tie than the wife. No one seems to have
thought that Agamemnon was in any way unfaithful to
Clytaemestra in keeping Chryseïs as his concubine, though

Aeschylus makes Clytaemestra present this as a palliation for her conduct (*Ag.* 1393) ; nor did Odysseus wrong Penelope by his relations with Circe and Calypso.[1] Naturally Helen could not complain because in her absence a slave bore a son to Menelaus (δ 12). Concubinage was not forbidden by public sentiment, and there were no laws for any offenses ; but Laërtes, in order to. spare his wife's feelings (a 433), did not take Euryclea as his concubine, and the mother of Phoenix violently objected to a similar rival (I 451). Among the gods, Hera is at least accustomed to the wantonness of Zeus with mortal women, but has a clear grudge against Heracles, his son by Alcmene,—a hatred dating from before the hero's birth (T 98). The only instances of adultery on the part of the wife are those of Clytaemestra (γ 272), and of the goddess Aphrodite (θ 267), in addition to that of Helen. The story of Bellerophon and Antea (Z 160) is a close parallel to that of Joseph and Potiphar's wife.

The relations of sons of slave-women (νόθοι) to their half-brothers and fathers were not definite. Teucer, son of Telamon by a captive in war (a Trojan princess, *Relations of* according to the later story, it is true), is the *Half-brothers.* constant companion of Telamon's other son, Ajax, and is one of the bravest of the Achaean warriors. On the second day of battle, when he is shooting his arrows effectively, Agamemnon calls to him, "Shoot on thus, if haply thou mayst prove a light of safety to the Danaans, and a glory to thy father Telamon, who brought thee up in his house, child of a slave (νόθον, Θ 282) though thou art." Antenor's wife Theano, for her husband's sake, brings up as her own child his son by a slave (E 70). The disguised Odysseus, in one of his fictions, says that he is the son of a Cretan by a concubine, and that on his father's death the sons of legitimate[2]

---

[1] The circumstances were peculiar because of his long absence from home, and the poet says not only that Circe commanded Odysseus to share her couch (κ 334), but that the Ithacan (at least near the end of his stay) lay by Calypso unwillingly (παρ' οὐκ ἐθέλων ἐθελούσῃ, ε 155) ; but the principle seems to have been accepted that at least such an act would not introduce an alien element into the family, as the infidelity of a wife might. Gladstone notes that among the Greek chieftains cases of homicide are more frequent than of bastardy.

[2] The terms legitimate and illegitimate do not correspond exactly to the Greek thought which lays stress chiefly on the inequality of station of the parents of the νόθος.

birth had divided the estate among themselves by lot, and had given him only a house and a small property (ξ 202); but because of his personal worth he had married a daughter of a wealthy family. The husband of an illegitimate daughter of Priam "dwelt at Pedaeus before the sons of the Achaeans came," but on tidings of the war, he came to Ilium and lived in the palace of Priam, who "honored him like his own children" (N 173), and an illegitimate son of Priam was Cebriones, the trusted charioteer of his half-brother Hector (Θ 318).

On the other hand, two of the leaders of the Myrmidons are sons of divinities by mortal maidens, who after their connexion with Hermes or the river Spercheüs, married men (Π 174, 185). One of these children was brought up by his mortal grandfather.

The household of Priam is the best Homeric illustration of a patriarchal family. The old king has in his palace apart-*Patriarchal Household.* ments not only for his wives, but for all his fifty sons and their wives, and for his twelve daughters and their husbands, and for all his grand-children (Ζ 244, Χ 63). His older sons, however, have homes of their own near the palace,—so Hector and Paris (Ζ 317), and Deïphobus (θ 517).[1]

Large families were desired. Priam was counted peculiarly happy in his wealth of sons (Ω 546), and the man was pitied *Size of Families.* who had no sons to inherit his possessions (Ε 156). Niobe aroused the ire of Apollo and Artemis by boasting of the number of her own children (Ω 607), while Leto had but one son and one daughter. The Homeric families in general, however, were small. Nestor, indeed, had several sons, but Agamemnon had only one brother, Menelaus, and one son, Orestes. Menelaus had only one son, and him by a slave. Hector had but one son. Telamonian Ajax and his Locrian namesake had each a half-brother, but no brother by the same mother. Achilles and Diomed had no brothers. Telemachus was even more solitary: he himself was the only child of Odysseus and Penelope; Penelope seems to have had no brothers and only one sister (δ 797); Odysseus also had one sister (ο 363) and no brother, and his father Laërtes, too, was an only son (π 117).

[1] Unless Deïphobus inherited the house as well as the widow of Paris.

Like the ancient Hebrews, the Homeric Greeks had a strong desire for the perpetuation of their families. The curse of childlessness is grievous, and is pronounced only in bitter anger (I 455). A father grieves with sorest anguish for the death of a son just married, who has come to man's estate, but leaves no descendants (Ψ 222). No instance of the formal adoption of a son is mentioned. Phoenix says that he adopted Achilles (I 494), but the latter surely did not leave the family of Peleus, and did not exchange fathers (II 15, λ 494).

The marriage state is appointed and natural, for men as well as for women. No unmarried man or woman of mature age is mentioned in the poems, except the old Phoenix, already referred to, on whom the curse *Marriage* of childlessness imprecated by his father had proved *State* *Natural.* effectual (I 456). Somewhat curiously, however, though a woman is expected to marry again on the death of her husband (*cf.* σ 270, and Helen's marriage with Deïphobus on the death of Paris, θ 517), yet no Homeric widower takes a second wife.[1]

To enumerate the Homeric instances of tender family love, would be a long and unnecessary task. In speaking of the cause of the Trojan war, Achilles asks if the sons of Atreus, Agamemnon and Menelaus, alone love *Family* their wives; "every good and sensible man loves *Affection.* and cares for his wife, as I heartily loved Briseïs, captive though she was" (I 341). The land appeared to Odysseus after his shipwreck as welcome as the recovery of a father from a long illness appears to his children (ε 394), and Priam implores Achilles by his love for his father (Ω 486), as having no stronger motive for pity. By the funeral pile of Patroclus, Achilles "mourns as a father in burning the bones of his son, who by his death has brought grief to his wretched parents" (Ψ 222), and Odysseus's mother, after long sorrow for her son, at last hangs herself in her grief (λ 200). Hecuba asks, as we have seen, why she should live, now that Hector is dead (X 431), and to Andromache Hector is all in all

---

[1] An exception has been found in the use of *step-mother* (μητρυιή, E 389),—but this is spoken in regard to the mortal sons of Poseidon, who strove to put Ossa on Olympus and Pelion on Ossa (λ 315), and who had imprisoned Ares. How any one should be their step-mother in the ordinary sense is not clear.

(Z 429). The special duty of the Erinyes, the later Furies, seems to have been to punish breaches of family duty, especially of children to parents. Odysseus's longing to return to his home (α 57), and the readiness of men to fight and to die for wife and children (Θ 57, Ο 497), are sufficient examples and proofs of unselfish devotion and affection. Brothers are often found in close connexion standing by each other in battle, as Ajax and Teucer (Θ 267), or as Hector and Cebriones and Gorgythion (Θ 302, 318). The story of Thetis packing her son's chest as he sets out for the war, and putting into it plenty of woolen garments (II 222), has quite a modern tone.

The Homeric poems contain no instance of a divorce or formal and voluntary separation of man and wife. No stress *No Divorce.* can fairly be laid on the etymology of the words for wife,—meaning simply *woman* (γυνή) or *couch-mate* (ἄλοχος, ἄκοιτις). " I pronounce you man and wife," is sufficiently definite now, though the last words meant originally only man and woman.

The term cousin (ἀνέψιος) is used five times in the poems, but little stress is laid upon this relationship. The poet *"Cousins."* never speaks of such a tie as existing between Telamonian Ajax and Achilles, whose fathers were brothers according to the later story, or between Hector and Aeneas,—but these last would be third cousins.

CHAPTER V

DRESS AND DECORATION [1]

FOR our knowledge of Homeric dress little light has been gained from the study of the monuments of the Mycenaean Age. In the early works of art which have been *Little Light* found at Cnosus, Tiryns, and Mycenae, the men *for Dress* in action, whether in battle with their kind or in *from the* conflict with wild animals, appear either as naked *Mycenaean* or as clad in nothing more than a loin-cloth or *Age.* at most a pair of bathing trunks, while on the other hand the women are elaborately clad in garments which are not only sewed but fitted closely to the person, differing entirely from the Athenian woman's dress of the classical period, and not conforming to the indications of the Homeric poems. In certain respects the garb of the Cretan ladies was surprisingly modern, with entirely separate garments for the upper and the lower part of the body, while the Homeric woman's dress, like the primitive raiment of other branches of the Indo-European family, had no separate skirts or bodice. The dress of a faïence figure about a foot in height, found at Cnosus in 1903, is described by Lady Evans as follows :[2] " This figure appears to be wearing (1) a skirt without gathers, touching the ground evenly all round, decorated with horizontal lines representing either tucks or embroidery or

---

[1] Earlier discussions of this subject were superseded by that of Studniczka, *Beiträge zur Geschichte der altgriechischen Tracht*, 1885. See also Helbig, *Das homerische Epos, etc.*, Percy Gardner, *Grammar of Greek Art*, and Schrader, *Reallexicon der indogermanischen Altertumskunde*, Article *Kleidung*.

[2] *Annual of the British School at Athens*, ix. 80. See also Plate viii. of the same volume.

woven stripes in the material; . . . (2) a double apron or polonaise made without fulness, reaching to the knee at the back and front, and rising to the hips at the sides ; . . . (3) a tight-fitting jacket bodice, of rich stuff decorated apparently in embroidery . . . in front the bodice is cut away in a V-shape from the shoulders to a point at the waist ; . . . (4) a high cap or tiara."

In early Greece, Italy, and Germany alike, the dress of men seems to have differed little from that of women.[1] In *Primitive Dress in Greece.* each of these peoples, the chief garment of both sexes was a quadrangular piece of woolen cloth, not sewed, but fastened by pins. In addition, the men wore loin-cloths (see Fig. 24, page 635), which developed gradually into drawers and trousers, or were discarded and replaced by tunics. The course of development or change of garb, in detail, among the different peoples, was determined naturally not only by caprice and the influence of neighboring fashions, but still more by the climate. The climate of Greece and Asia Minor is mild. The summer there is warm and long, and during this season a man needs but little clothing.

In the making of Homeric dress, little cutting and sewing was required, and probably no fitting. Buttons and hooks *Little Cutting and Sewing.* and eyes were still unknown. The Achaeans had neither tailors nor dressmakers nor milliners. The work of carding, spinning, and weaving was done by the women of the household (X 511); only once in the poems (M 433) does a women spin for pay. Sewing is mentioned but once, when the poet says that the old Laërtes wore a sewed or patched tunic (ῥαπτόν, ω 228). Cloth in general was not woven in long strips from which pieces might be cut according to need ; *i.e.* not cloth, but clothes were woven. Since fashions changed very slowly, and garments were not closely fitted to the person, raiment which was made for one man might serve just as well for another, and in wealthy houses a considerable stock of clothing was

---

[1] See Schrader, *Reallexicon;* *Toga non solum viri sed etiam feminae utebantur,* Nonius *s.v.;* and Varro's statement *ante enim olim toga fuit commune vestimentum et diurnum et nocturnum et muliebre et virile;* Tacitus, *Germ.* 17. On the Harpy Tomb from Lycia, in the British Museum, the sexes are not always distinguished by their garb.

kept on hand.[1]   This might be an important part of a family's wealth, and garments frequently were not only bestowed on men [2] but presented to the gods.   Thus the disguised Athena says that Penelope's suitors, if they should see Odysseus returning to his home, would pray to be light of foot rather than rich in gold and raiment (α 164).   The Trojan women bear a beautiful *peplos* to the temple of Athena as an offering to the goddess (Z 90, 302), and Aegisthus, in gratitude to the gods for his unexpected success in winning the love of Clytaemestra, hangs up at their shrines votive offerings of raiment and of gold (γ 274).

The Homeric man in general wore but two garments,—a tunic or shirt, and a mantle or plaid.   His garb thus was simple in comparison with that of his successor of to-day.   When the king left his palace for the council of his peers, he wore but five articles of *Men wore two Garments.* clothing, including his girdle and his two shoes, instead of the dozen or fifteen articles which are worn by the modern gentleman.   He had no hat, collar, neck-tie, cuffs, or gloves, and carried no handkerchief.   The primitive style of dress was preserved in the main in Homeric Hellas, but the men had added the tunic as an undergarment, while the women, retaining the early form of the *peplos*, had added a thick long veil or wrap as an outer garment.

The shaggy woolen [3] *chlaena* (χλαῖνα)—essentially like the Attic *himatium*, and not very different from the Spartan *tribon* (τρίβων), but not worn in the same manner as the Macedonian *chlamys* (χλαμύς),—was the chief garment of all men, corresponding to the woman's *peplos*, and it *Woolen Chlaena.* served also as a blanket at night.[4]   (See Fig. 4.) It was a large rectangular mantle, plaid, or shawl, and often

---

[1] Z 289, Ω 229, α 165, β 339, γ 348, θ 424, 438.   *Cf.* St. Paul's words to the elders of the church at Ephesus, ἀργυρίου ἢ χρυσίου ἢ ἱματισμοῦ οὐθενὸς ἐπεθύμησα, *Acts* xx. 33.

[2] θ 392, ο 106, π 79, ρ 557.

[3] *Cf.* οὔλη δ' ἐπενήνοθε λάχνη, Κ 134; χλαίνας οὔλας, Ω 646, δ 50, κ 451, ρ 89; χλαῖναν οὔλην, τ 225.

[4] χλαῖναι καὶ ῥήγεα . . . ἐνεύδειν, γ 349; *cf.* δ 299, η 338, λ 189, ξ 520, υ 4.   A goatskin serves the swine-herd as a blanket as well as for a mantle; ξ 51, 530, *Cf.* also Soph. *Trach.* 540, Eur. *Frag.* 603, Theoc. xviii. 19, and *Ruth* iii. 9, *Ezek.* xvi. 8.

was worn folded ;[1] it was thrown over the shoulders and held in place by one or more pins.[2]

That the *chlaena* was originally the chief garment of men is indicated further by the fact that even in later Greece and in Rome to be clad solely in the *himatium* was perfectly respectable, although unusual. Not only Socrates but also Agesilaus king of Sparta appeared in public, and the younger Cato came to the senate, without the tunic, while a man without the *himatium* was called naked.[3] Yet the *chlaena* was not worn ordinarily in the house,—any more than the ancient foot-covering or the modern head-covering,— but was put on only when men went abroad. Thus at night Telemachus, being at home, does not take off his cloak when he goes to bed (α 437),—for he had not worn it for hours ; and Hephaestus, being called to see Thetis in his hall, on leaving his forge, dons a tunic but no cloak (Σ 416). Of course the mantle was not worn commonly on the field of battle,—although Agamemnon holds his in his hand as a signal, at Θ 221,—and it was thrown off in preparing for any exertion. Thus Odysseus casts off his cloak when at the suggestion of Athena he sets out to run through the Achaean camp in order to stop the disorderly flight of the soldiery (B 183) ; Thoas throws off his cloak when he sets out to run from the bivouac to bear a message to the camp (ξ 500) ; and Telemachus lays aside his mantle and sword when he digs the trench for the axes which were to be the mark for the contest in archery (φ 118). Penelope's suitors naturally lay off their mantles when they kill the cattle on which they are to feast (υ 249). That Odysseus at the games of the Phaeacians starts up, cloak and all (αὐτῷ φάρει, θ 186), to hurl the discus, only proves the rule, for the act is noteworthy. Under ordinary circumstances,

Side note: Chlaena *the* Chief Garment.

---

[1] Cf. χλαῖναν διπλῆν, Κ 133, τ 225 ; δίπλακα (sc. χλαῖναν) πορφυρέην, Γ 126, Χ 441, τ 225 ; δίπτυχον ἀμφ' ὤμοισι . . . λώπην, ν 224. Contrast with ἀπλοΐδας χλαίνας, Ω 230, ω 276.

[2] Cf. περονήσατο, Κ 133 ; τ 226. In the latter passage, a single brooch was used. In the shipwreck of Odysseus, his mantle would not have hampered his movements if it had simply been thrown about his shoulders, and not fastened (ε 321, 372).

[3] Xen. *Mem.* i. 6. 2 ; Aelian, *V.H.* vii. 13 ; Plut. *Cato*, 44 ; Xen. *An.* iv. 4. 12 ; Plato, *Laws*, xii. 954 A.

clearly, and if he had not been greatly provoked, he would have laid aside his cloak.

An epithet which is applied seven times to the *chlaena* (πορφυρέη, as δ 115, 154, τ 242) has generally been understood as *purple*, and this interpretation receives support from another epithet of this meaning,— (φοινικόεσσα, Κ 133, ξ 500, φ 118), *purple, crimson,* or *scarlet,*—which also is applied to the cloak. But some scholars understand this epithet when applied to the sea as *seething, foaming,* and when applied to a garment as either *white* as the foam of the sea, or merely *gleaming.* Whether Homeric wool was dyed, has been thought uncertain,—the dark wool which Helen spun (δ 135) possibly being shorn from a black sheep (Γ 103). But twice patterns are interwoven in such cloaks : when Helen was called to the Great Tower of Ilium, she was weaving a large web, a double *chlaena,* and "sprinkled in (ἐνέπασσεν, Γ 126) many contests of the knightly Trojans and the bronze-clad Achaeans"; and, a few days later, when Andromache was startled by the shrieks which betokened the death of Hector, she was weaving a like web, but "sprinkling in many colored flowers" (Χ 441),—*i.e.* so weaving in her web tufts of wool of other colors, as to form a pattern.[1] Such scenes suppose the use of colored, dyed wool. The figures on the plaid might hang symmetrically over the back and thus might be seen fairly.

The ordinary use of the cloak as a protection against cold, is recognized in two similar epithets of *wind-shelter.*[2] Nestor wears his mantle on going by night to the council of the Achaean chieftains (Κ 133), and Agamemnon, Odysseus, and Thersites are reported as wearing this garment to the assembly of the people (Β 43, 183, 262). Agamemnon once holds his cloak in his hand, probably waving it, as a signal to the troops (Θ 221).

The *pharos* (φᾶρος, Β 43) was much like the *chlaena* in form, and probably was only a variety of it. Thus Odysseus wears

Epithets of Chlaena.

---

[1] In view of the fact that flowers seem not to have been used freely in early Greek decoration of garments,—the geometric motives being far more common,— Helbig understands θρόνα here as of ornaments in general, though he acknowledges *rosettes* as a possible translation.—Queen Arete is spinning ἁλιπόρφυρα wool at ς 53,—which seems much like *sea-blue,* though some would understand it as *like the sea-foam.*

[2] ἀνεμοσκεπής, Π 224 ; ἀλεξάνεμος, ξ 529.

a *pharos* in the assembly of the Phaeacians (at θ 84), but
has a *chlaena* a little later on the same day.[1]   It is often
called *great*,—this, however, need not be in contrast
Pharos *a*
Variety of
Chlaena.
with the *chlaena*, but may be a general characteristic
epithet.   But while all men wore the *chlaena*, only
the nobles are represented as wearing the *pharos*.
For this garment no brooches or pins are mentioned, nor any
embroidery or tapestry work upon it, and it is not stated to
have been used as a blanket at night.   It seems to have been
of linen,[2] and to have been used not so much for warmth as
for display.   Thus a fastening to hold it in place was less
necessary than for the woolen *chlaena*.   Flax and linen were
known to the early Greeks (*cf.* λίνον, ν 73, and *linen*), and we
need not suppose this material to have been imported, though
wool was the staple material for clothing in early as well as
in later Greece.

The term *pharos* seems to have meant originally only *web*,
cloth, and later to have received its special application.   It is
Other uses of
Pharos.
applied, as will be seen soon, to the principal
woman's garment, as well as to the cloth given
by Calypso to Odysseus for the making of a sail
(ε 258), and to Penelope's web, which was to serve as a shroud
for the aged Laërtes (β 97, τ 142, ω 147).   With the last use
have been compared the wrapping of the body of Patroclus in
a linen cloth and its covering with a white *pharos* (Σ 352,
cf. Ψ 254), and the shrouding of Hector's body in two of
these mantles (Ω 580).   These details have further been
brought into connexion with indications of the poet's acquaintance with the Egyptian practise of embalming (*cf.* T 39 ; see
page 475), and the use of linen in the wrapping of mummies.
In the New Testament story, also, linen cloths were wrapped
about the dead (*St. John* xi. 44, xx. 6).

Instead of a woven mantle, the skin of some animal was

---

[1] At θ 455. Telemachus has a φᾶρος, γ 467, ο 61, but a χλαῖνα at δ 50, ρ 86,
φ 118.

[2] The epithet *well-washed* (ἐυπλυνές, θ 392, 425, ν 67, π 173) seems better suited
to linen than to a woolen cloak ; conversely, the linen material was less suited than
woolen for tapestry and embroidery.   The etymology of φᾶρος has not been
established, but Studniczka conjectures that the word was borrowed from the
Egyptian, just as *chiton* was borrowed from the Phoenician, and that the garment
was made originally of an Egyptian variety of flax.

sometimes worn. Thus lion-skins are worn by Agamemnon and Diomed (K 23, 177), leopard-skins by Menelaus and Paris (K 29, Γ 17), a wolf's skin by Dolon (K 334), a deer-skin by the disguised Odysseus (ν 436), and a goat-skin by the swine-herd Eumaeus (ξ 530).[1] *Animal's Skin as Mantle.* In the case of the warriors, the uses of the skins for clothing and for light armor, cannot be sharply distinguished. His lion's skin served Heracles as a shield against both cold and enemies. In ancient works of art, he sometimes has the skin bound closely to his body, while in other cases it hangs free (see Fig. 33).

The *chiton* was a tunic or shirt of linen,—not a primitive Greek garment, but borrowed from the Phoenicians and accepted by the Ionians first of all Greeks. It differed from the Athenian *chiton* of later times *Chiton of Linen.* not greatly in shape, but in material,—the later *chiton* being woolen. The name seems to have been borrowed from Phoenicia with the garment, and to be from the same root as our own *cotton*, and possibly even the Latin *tunica*. This gradually took the place of the earlier loin-cloth, which in the Mycenaean period was the sole garb of the man in action. It was assumed on rising (B 42, K 21, o 60), and was doffed on going to bed (a 437),—when clearly the man had no special night gear, but slept naked like the English and the Germans of a few generations ago. Little is said by the poet of its form or material. It never, however, like the *chlaena*, is "pinned on" or "thrown about the shoulders," and no pins or brooches are used for it. Always it is *entered*,[2]—doubtless being drawn on over the head. No slit down the front is mentioned ; without such an opening it must have had large holes for the neck and arms. No indication is given of sleeves, and the ordinary *chiton* may have been as shapeless as a bag or a modern "sweater," which also may have no slit at the neck. The tunic of Odysseus, however, on his leaving home, is compared to a layer of dry onion (τ 232), and is said

[1] In the *Argonautica* of Apollonius of Rhodes (i. 324), Pelias's son Acastus comes to join the expedition, wearing a bull's hide, which reached from his shoulders to his feet, while his companion wore a mantle (δίπλαξ),—evidently for the same purpose.

[2] δῦ δὲ χιτῶνα, Σ 416 ; δύσαντο χιτῶνας, Ψ 739 ; χιτῶνα δῦνεν, o 60 ; ἔνδυνε χιτῶνα, B 42, K 21, 131 ; χιτῶν' ἐνδῦσα, E 736 = Θ 387.

to be as bright as the sun. This description implies a garment which fits snugly and smoothly, as one of linen. A woolen garment of primitive web, does not suggest a layer of onion nor the brightness of the sun.

The *chiton* generally was worn ungirt, and thus on ancient vases, men not in action, old men and men of dignity,—as kings,

Generally Ungirt.

priests, heralds, charioteers,—are represented with *chitons* ungirt and reaching nearly to the ground.

Only once does the poet mention the act of girding the loins ; the swine-herd Eumaeus girds up his tunic as he sets out for his pig-stye to fetch a porker.[1] Not too much, however, must be inferred from this fact. Achilles binds the arms of his captive Trojans with the leathern " straps which they wore over their tunics " (Φ 30), and these straps are best explained as girdles. By Nestor's side at night, in camp before Troy, lay the belt with which he girt himself for battle (ζωστήρ . . . ᾧ ζώννυτο, K 77). At the opening of the third day of battle, Agamemnon with a shout bids his men gird themselves (ζώννυσθαι, Λ 15),[2]—*i.e.* to prepare for the fray.

Not all tunics needed to be of the same length, any more than in later times. The Ionians once are called

Long Tunics.

tunic-trailing (ἑλκεχίτωνες, N 685), but this surely was a general standing epithet for the Ionians, who are supposed to have been the first Greeks to adopt the tunic, rather than an indication that such trailing robes were worn on the field of battle ; that Homeric epithets are sometimes applied without special reference to the circumstances of the case, is a well-known truth. The same epithet is given to the Ionians at a festival, by the poet of the first Homeric Hymn (146). The tunic of Odysseus seems to have reached at least to the knee, else the scar on his leg would have been observed, and his strong thighs earlier noticed by Penelope's suitors

---

[1] ξ 72. *Cf.* "and he [Elijah] girded up his loins and ran before Ahab to the entrance of Jezreel," 1 *Kings* xviii. 46.—The ζωσαμένω of Ψ 685 refers to the boxers assuming the loin-cloth or ζῶμα in place of the *chiton.* They were not girding up their tunics.

[2] While κόλπος in Homer regularly means the bosom or the dress above it, yet at Υ 471, where the dark blood κόλπον ἐνέπλησεν, κόλπον seems to be "the *bosom* or *hollow* of his χιτών, which was belted at the waist."

(ν 434; τ 391, 450, 468; σ 74). From the fact that the thighs of Menelaus, wounded by the arrow of Pandarus, were seen to be stained with blood, the inference is drawn fairly that he wore no chiton, but a loin-cloth (Δ 146; cf. 187). This is supported by the further fact that in order to inspect the wound, the surgeon looses the loin-cloth, while the tunic is not mentioned. That, at the close of the first day of the action of the *Odyssey*, Telemachus is represented as seating himself on his bed before he takes off his tunic (α 437), has been criticised. But perhaps he wore a short tunic, and he may have hitched it up before he sat down. Athena doffs her long robe, and dons her father's tunic (E 734 = Θ 385), in preparation for a descent to the field of battle, and from this the inference has been drawn that the tunic was shorter than the *peplos*. Else why did she make the exchange? But this tunic of Zeus may have been specially fitted for war, by plates of metal fastened upon it; and the natural difference in stature between Zeus and his daughter, may not have been overlooked.

The epithet *twisted* or *twined* (στρεπτός, E 113) seems to be equivalent to *well-spun*, with reference to the linen thread from which the tunic was made. Another epithet of the tunic, also used but once, is *bordered* (τερμιόεις, τ 242),—and this border seems to be the tunic's only ornament,—it having no decoration on any other part. For such ornament, we are reminded again, linen is not so well adapted, as a woolen fabric like the *chlaena*. Laërtes's tunic is called *sewed* (ῥαπτόν, ω 228), which is generally interpreted as *patched*, although in the very next following verse the same epithet is applied to gaiters, where it may mean *well sewed*.

Epithets of the Tunic.

Since the cultivation of flax in Homeric Greece has been unfairly doubted, it is reasonable to note that Queen Arete recognizes the tunic given to Odysseus by Nausicaa as the work of herself and her women (η 234), and that the loom at which these women are busy seems to be for weaving with flaxen thread (η 107).

The girdle or belt[1] of men corresponds to the zone

---

[1] ζωστήρ, Δ 132, E 615, K 77, etc. In Λ 234, κατὰ ζώνην seems to mean *at the waist*, though the ζωστήρ is mentioned just below.

(ζώνη) of women, and was used chiefly to gird up the tunic. It was probably of leather, and may have been adorned, like the reins of chariots, by thin plates of metal, since it is called *gleaming* and *cunningly fashioned* (πανaίολος, Δ 186, δαιδάλεος, Δ 135). The girdle of Menelaus had golden fastenings (ὀχῆες χρύσειοι, Δ 132). Aeneas gave to Bellerophon, and Ajax gave to Hector, girdles bright with purple (φοίνικι φαεινόν, Z 219, H 305).

Girdle of Men.

To the loin-cloth[1] reference has been made already. This garment probably was worn more often than might be inferred from the infrequency of its mention. But for the special description of the treatment of Menelaus's wound, the reader would not know that this warrior wore no tunic. No occasion ordinarily occurs for its mention by the poet. The ancient Greeks disliked to be seen in utter nakedness (Thucydides, i. 6), and even the girt chiton would be a hindrance and a burden in battle on a hot day. The Egyptians of the early dynasties seem to have worn only the loin-cloth in battle. Perhaps the term *zoma* may have been used by the poet at times (as Helbig conjectures for ξ 482) for the short tunic which replaced it.

Loin-cloth.

The *zostra* (ζῶστρα, ζ 38), mentioned but once,—apparently garments of Nausicaa's brothers,—may well have been the short tunics, which replaced the loin-cloth. Since these are the only garments in the list enumerated which could be used by men, and since Nausicaa was undertaking her expedition largely for the sake of her brothers (ζ 62), they are not to be interpreted as women's belts, which further do not deserve precedence over the women's robes in the enumeration.

Under the loin-cloth or the tunic,—if the loin-cloth were not worn,—the warrior might wear about his waist a broad band of metal, or of leather reinforced with metal (μίτρη, Δ 137), for the special protection of his bowels, but this

---

[1] ζῶμα, Δ 187, 216, Ψ 683, ξ 482. See Fig. 26.—For comparison, the following description of the breech-clout of the North American Indian is added. "Originally it was made of skin, a foot wide and three or four long, which was passed between the thighs and then carried up under a belt of sinew, snake skin or some other material, worn around the waist, from which the two ends hung down a foot or more, the one in front with a flap, the other like a tail behind."

was part of his armor rather than of his clothing (see page 658), although it might be worn, as the spear was carried, also in time of peace. This as a rule was hidden by the loin-cloth or tunic, but was some- times visible, so that an Achaean is said to have a bright *mitré* (αἰολομίτρης, E 707). That it was generally, but not always worn in battle, is indicated by an epithet of Sarpedon's comrades who wore chitons without *mitré* (ἀμιτροχίτωνες, Π 419).

Mitré under Loin-cloth.

The *peplos*,[1] the chief garment of women, like the *chlaena*, the principal garment of men, was a quadrangular piece of woolen cloth, which may be represented by *lan.mbo* in I of Fig. 4,[2] in which about a third, along the length of the cloth (*ablm*), has been folded over ; next the whole was folded again, at right angles to the former fold, to form *ab . c . no . d* of II. Then, the person standing between the two folds, at *efgh* of III, the two were pinned together on the breast,[3] a little below the shoulder. The space *fc* would form an abundant arm-hole for the left arm, and the right arm would be left quite free. The edges of the two sides *an* and *bo* may have been sewed together in some cases, at least for part of the way, but the *peplos* which was given to Penelope by one of her suitors, was fastened by twelve pins or brooches (σ 293), and was not sewed at all, but was left open down the side, except as the edges of the garment were held together

The Peplos *of Women.*

---

[1] πέπλος, of uncertain etymology. It is always a woman's garment. So at Ω 229, where Priam takes twelve of these, as a present to Achilles, part of a ransom for Hector's body. Garments were good personal property in general, but Achilles would give these to Brisëis, Diomede, and his other female attendants. The *peplos* is clearly the chief garment also in the Homeric *Hymn to Aphrodite*, 86. The name came to be used in Attic poetry as a general term for *garment, clothing.*—ἑανός or εἱανός (Ξ 178, Π 9, Φ 507, *Hom. Hy.* v. 176) is a synonym for *peplos.* Its relation to the adjective ἑανός (E 734, Θ 385, Σ 352, 613, Ψ 254), *pliant, soft,* is not clear. Apparently it is from the root Fεs, *clothe.*

[2] Borrowed from Professor Percy Gardner's *Grammar of Greek Art*, p. 46.

[3] ἐνέτῃσι κατὰ στῆθος περονᾶτο, Ξ 180. *Cf.* πέπλον· γυναικεῖον ἔνδυμα, τούτεστι χιτῶνα ὃν οὐκ ἐνεδύοντο, ἀλλ' ἐπερονῶντο, scholium on E 734 ; γυναικεῖον ἱμάτιον ... κατὰ τὰ Δωρικά, Eustathius on σ 292.—In later Sparta the like garment of young women was left open at the side, or at least unfastened, as is shown by the epithet applied to them, *thigh-showing* (φαινομηρίδες, Ibycus, 61), as well as by representations on vases,—but these had no girdle.

by pins, and the garment itself was held in place by a
girdle.[1] Very possibly one pin at the shoulder, *e.g.* at *f*,
might ordinarily be left attached to the robe, so that only
the pin at *e* need be fastened or unfastened each time
that the garment was donned or doffed. Aphrodite uses
a fold of her *peplos* for the protection of her son Aeneas
in the battle (E 315), and this act is most easily intelligible
if she is assumed to wear a Dorian robe, not pinned at the
side,—for if this *peplos* were a close-fitting gown sewed down
the side, the act would have been impossible. Preparing

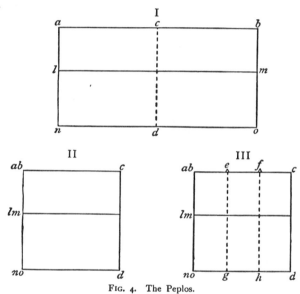

FIG. 4. The Peplos.

to descend from Olympus to the field of battle on the
Trojan plain, Athena lets her *peplos* fall to the floor
(πέπλον μὲν κατέχευεν, E 734 = Θ 385), and instead puts on
the *chiton* of Zeus; and the expression there used, "poured
down her robe," is suited to the gliding of the garment to
her feet when a pin is removed. When Aphrodite is wounded
by Diomed, Athena suggests mockingly to Zeus that the
wound was caused by Aphrodite's caressing some Achaean
woman (E 424), and scratching her wrist on the golden

[1] Doubtless the girdle was considered more important than the pins, and the
suggestion has been offered that not all of these twelve pins were to be used by
Penelope at once, but that an allowance was made for breakage and loss, though
this is not implied in Homer's story.

FIG. 3.—From Herculaneum.

FIG. 5.—Diana of Versailles.

Facing p. 164.

pin of her garment, as she threw her arm affectionately about her neck. Hera's epithet *white-armed*[1] and the mention of the white arms of Aphrodite and Penelope (πήχεε λευκώ, E 314, ψ 240) are in themselves sufficient evidence that the Homeric dress left the women's arms bare.

That the *peplos* was not sewed, is indicated further by its use (or, at least, the use of this term) as a covering for chairs (η 96) and for chariots at rest (E 194) and for the chest in which lay Hector's bones (Ω 796). The *peplos* carried in the Panathenaic **Peplos *not* Sewed.** procession as an offering to Athena, also, seems to have been a rectangular piece of cloth.[2]

The epithet *robe-trailing*,[3] given to Trojan women, bears witness to the length of the garment at the back ; in front it may not have been so long, but in the Homeric *Hymn to Demeter* (176, *cf.* 182), it is held up by maidens when they are running.

The *peplos* ordinarily was of wool. This would be necessary for warmth, and wool clearly was much more plentiful than flax. Further, the epithets *many colored, cunningly wrought*,[4] and the like, imply **Peplos *of* Wool.** colored weaving, and hence probably wool. The Dawn is called *saffron-robed* (κροκόπεπλος, Θ 1, T 1, etc.),— the prototype of Shakespeare's " Morn in russet mantle clad," —but the special color of no woman's robe is mentioned.

The term *pharos* is used twice for the woman's *peplos* (ε 230, κ 543). In the narrative of ε 230, the *pharos* and *kalyptré* of Calypso correspond to the *chiton* and *chlaena* of Odysseus. Since *pharos* seems to mean a linen *chlaena* (see page 158), the supposition is not unreasonable that when it is used of a woman's garment, it means a linen *peplos*.

---

[1] λευκώλενος applied 28 times to Hera, as A 55, and occasionally to Helen, Andromache, and others.

[2] See Michaelis, *der Parthenon*, p. 328.

[3] ἑλκεσίπεπλος, Z 442, H 297, X 105; *cf.* ἑλκεχίτωνες of Ionian men. The similar epithet τανύπεπλος, Γ 228, Σ 385, 424, etc., has been translated *with long stretching robe* or *with large, full robe*.

[4] ποικίλος, E 735, Θ 386, σ 293 ; παμποίκιλος, Z 289, ο 105 ; ποικίλματα, Z 294, ο 107 ; δαίδαλα, Ξ 179.

The *othonae*,[1] likewise, were linen *peploi*. The material is indicated by the description of their weaving by Phaea-

Othonae.

cian women (η 107), where oil drips from the cloth. A like use of oil in the preparation of linen garments is observed (Σ 596) for the tunics of young men, but seems to be unknown for woolen cloth.

The poet mentions no under-garments for women, and Hera, in robing herself after the bath, dons her *heanos* or *peplos* first of all (Ξ 178).

A girdle,[2] which was more necessary for the loose robe, particularly when this was not pinned along the side, than for a tunic, aided to hold the *peplos* in place. Into the hollow between her breasts and her robe,[3] held securely by the girdle, Hera places the *cestus* which she borrows from Aphrodite (Ξ 223), and in the like receptacle the Phoenician nurse of the young Eumaeus places the three golden cups which she steals from the king's table (ο 469),—the articles in both cases being slipped in at the openings left for the arms,—to unfasten the robe at the shoulder being quite unnecessary. The "bosom" was used as a pocket in far more recent times, as when, in *Pilgrim's Progress*, Christian plucks his roll "out of his bosom."

The girdles of Calypso and Circe were adorned with gold (ε 231 = κ 544), as seems to have been also that of

Girdles.

Menelaus (Δ 215); that of Hera had a fringe of fine gold wire or thin strips of gold foil, or tassels, or pendants of some kind (ἑκατὸν θυσάνοις ἀραρυῖαν, Ξ 181). The *cestus* of Aphrodite is not assigned to a definite service, but the fact that Hera does not put it about her waist, but places it into her bosom, cannot prove that Aphrodite herself did not wear it as a girdle. This seems to have been an embroidered or otherwise decorated band

---

[1] ὀθόναι, Γ 141, Σ 595, cf. η 107.—This term as well as ἑανός seems originally to have been a general word for clothing.—In the Septuagint version of the story of Samson (*Judges* xiv. 13), ὀθόνια is used for cambric or muslin under garments with στολὰς ἱματίων for the upper garments.

[2] ζώνη, as Ξ 181, ε 231 = κ 544, λ 245.

[3] κόλπος seems to have meant first the hollow between the breasts, and then the bosom itself,—but not in Homer a fold of the robe, except in Υ 471.

of leather,[1] and might have been recognized as Aphrodite's by Zeus, if it were worn by Hera. The epithet *deep-girdled* (βαθύζωνος, I 594, γ 154) seems to be equivalent to *slender-waisted*, contrasting the outline of the waist with that of the bosom and hips. *Well-girt*[2] refers not so much to the beauty of the girdle as to the trimness of the wearer. The epithet *deep-bosomed*[3] refers to the shapely fulness of the bust.

The Homeric woman had no upper garment which corresponded closely to the *chlaena* or mantle of her husband, but she had a thick and heavy veil which was almost a garment. Certainly it was not a veil in the ordinary modern sense of the word,—used simply as a restraint for the hair from the blowing wind, or as a protection for the complexion from the rays of the sun, or, at most, as it was a generation or more ago, to hide the face of the wearer,—but it was like the long and full bridal veil, in which the old form has best been preserved, and in some uses like the heavy black crape veil of modern mourning. The Homeric veil or *kredemnon* hung from the back part of the head, and covered the back and shoulders, just as many an Irish peasant woman's shawl is thrown over her head and shoulders, as a covering for both head and body,—and it, also, was held in place by the hand, as is shown by its falling from the heads of Hecuba and Andromache when they forget themselves and loose their grasp of it, in grief at the death of Hector (X 406, 470; *cf.* α 334). It could be drawn forward, but generally it did not cover the face. When Penelope appears before her suitors, she wears this veil, but it does not entirely conceal her countenance, for . they are enraptured by her beauty (α 334, π 416, σ 210, φ 65). That Helen, desiring to escape observation as she leaves the Great Tower of

Kredemnon or Woman's Veil.

---

[1] κεστὸς ἱμάς, Ξ 214; *cf.* the πολύκεστος ἱμάς which served as a holder for the helmet of Paris, passing under his chin (Γ 371).

[2] εὔζωνος, A 429, Z 467, I 366, 590, 667, Ψ 261, 760; and its synonym καλλίζωνος, H 139, Ω 698, ψ 147.

[3] βαθύκολπος, Σ 122, 339, Ω 215. Some critics observed that this was applied by our poet only to Trojan women, but modern scholars would attach no importance to this. It is applied to the Muses by Pindar (*P.* i. 12) and by Homer himself according to Zenodotus's recension of B 484.—The poet makes Helen recognize Aphrodite not merely by her neck and eyes, but also by her στήθεα ἱμερόεντα, Γ 397.

Ilium, wraps herself closely in her mantle-like veil (Γ 419), and that in the Homeric *Hymn to Demeter* the goddess in her grief hides her face in her veil (*Hom. Hy.* v. 197), no more indicate this to be the usual office of this garment than the similar act of Odysseus, drawing his mantle over his head (θ 84), shows the ordinary use of his cloak.

This woman's veil, like the man's mantle, is not worn ordinarily at home, and it, too, is thrown off for any special exertion, though Penelope assumes it when she appears to her suitors in her own house, as being part of full dress. Hera puts on her *kredemnon* when she leaves Olympus for Mt. Ida (Ξ 184), and Calypso and Circe do the like when they go to the beach (καλύπτρην, ε 232 = κ 545). Thetis takes a dark "wrap" (κάλυμμα, Ω 93),—the color indicating her sadness of heart, —as she obeys the summons of Zeus to Olympus. Hecuba and Andromache wear their veils when they go to the Great Tower of Ilium to observe the battle (X 406, 470), and, conversely, Nausicaa's maids lay away their veils when they would play ball (ζ 100). That a *kredemnon* was given by Aphrodite as a wedding present to Andromache (X 470), has no special significance ; any garment was an appropriate gift. *Kredemnon* and *kalyptré*[1] seem to be synonymous,— the one name being derived from the office of the veil, and the other from the chief part which it covered.

Kredemnon not worn at Home.

Like the *chlaena* of men, the *kredemnon* of women seems to have been made sometimes of wool, and again of linen,— the material chosen perhaps with reference to the weather, but also, like the *pharos*, according to the wealth of the wearer. Hera's veil is clearly of linen at Ξ 185, where it is "as bright as the sun," and that the *kalyptré* of Hecuba has a sheèn (λιπαρή, X 406), and the epithet *bright-veiled* (λιπαροκρήδεμνος, Σ 382) applied to Charis, would imply the same for them.[2] Doubtless woolen was the usual material.

Sometimes of Linen.

[1] κρήδεμνον, α 334, π 416, etc., from κάρη, *head*, and δέω, *bind*. καλύπτρη, X 406, ε 232 = κ 545, and κάλυμμα, Ω 93, from καλύπτω, *cover, conceal*.—ὀθόναι, Γ 141, and ἐανός, Γ 385, 419, appear to be used of the veil, though both of these words originally seem to have had a general signification.

[2] The epithet ἀργεννal applied to Helen's ὀθόναι at Γ 141 suggests that this was of linen, and we have seen that ὀθόναι was sometimes used for a linen *peplos*.

The poet has little to say of other head-gear for women. But when Andromache, on the last day of the battles of the *Iliad*, hearing the shrieks of the Trojan women, goes to the Great Tower and catches sight of *Head-gear of Women.* the dead body of Hector dragged behind the car of Achilles to the Achaean camp, she faints ; and as she sinks backward *ampyx, kekryphalos, anadesmé*, and *kredemnon*[1] fall from her head.

The *ampyx* is a metal frontlet or diadem, over the forehead,—mentioned in later Greek literature and appearing in works of art, as on the familiar Diana of Versailles. *The* Ampyx. As an ornament, this corresponded in a general way to the high comb of comparatively recent times, but the Homeric lady must wear such an ornament at the front of her head, since if it were at the back it would be hidden by the *kredemnon*. Similar to the *ampyx*, but probably larger, was the *stephané* worn by maidens represented in the dance on the Shield of Achilles, and by Aphrodite in a Homeric Hymn.[2]

The *kekryphalos*[3] was a kerchief of some kind,—perhaps a cap or hood.

What the "woven *anadesmé*" (*cf.* ἀνά, δέω, *bind up*) was, no one knows. It was possibly a ribbon or band to hold the hair or kerchief in place, corresponding to the classical *mitra*.[4] That the *kredemnon* is mentioned last of all in this enumeration can hardly prove that it lay under the *kekryphalos* and the *anadesmé*, but it lay behind the *ampyx*.

No explanation has been offered why Andromache alone should be thus decked. If these articles were for special adornment, Hera might have been expected to wear them when she went to visit Zeus on Mt. Ida (Ξ´184).

Considerable uncertainty as to details of the Homeric

---

[1] ἄμπυκα κεκρύφαλόν τε ἰδὲ πλεκτὴν ἀναδέσμην | κρήδεμνόν τε, Χ 469.

[2] στεφάνη, Σ 597. The χρυσάμπυκες Ὧραι receive χρυσοστέφανον Ἀφροδίτην (*Hom. Hy.* vi. 1, 7), and place a στεφάνη upon her head. *Cf.* ἐυστέφανος, Φ 511, β 120, θ 267, 288, σ 193. These words remind the reader of στέφανος, *crown*, but this word is not used by Homer.

[3] *Cf.* κρύπτω, *conceal*, and the use of καλύπτρη and κάλυμμα for *veil*.

[4] *Cf.* μίτραν κόμας ἄπο ἔρριψεν, Eur. *Bacch.* 1115 ; κεκρυφάλου δεῖ καὶ μίτρας, Arist. *Thesm.* 257, where Euripides is made to supply his night-cap, and 941.

woman's dress would seem natural to a modern man who finds much that is unintelligible in even the latest fashion

Uncertainties of Detail.

magazine. Only the simplicity of ancient dress, and the fixed indisposition of those times to change fashions, render it possible by the aid of later works of art to attain a fairly reasonable and consistent conception of the Homeric garb.

The Homeric poet says nothing of the dress of children.

Dress of Children.

Probably the small boy in summer wore nothing but a loin cloth. Larger children would be dressed like their elders.

Sandals[1] are mentioned nineteen times in the Homeric poems. Like the man's *chlaena* and the woman's *kredemnon*,

Sandals.

they are not worn within the house.[2] Athena binds on her sandals when she sets out on the journey from Olympus to Ithaca, and Hermes dons his when he sets out for Troy or Calypso's island. Agamemnon puts on his sandals as he leaves his tent to go to the council of elders, and Telemachus does the like when he arises from his couch to call an assembly of Ithacans. The swine-herd Eumaeus is making his own shoes (ξ 24) when Odysseus approaches, but the leather-cutter (σκυτοτόμος, H 221) of Hyle may have made for other men sandals as well as shields. Whether the foot-gear were only soles or may have been rude shoes, cannot be said. Hesiod (*Works*, 541) advises felt-lined *pedila* for winter, and the old Laërtes wears gaiters (κνημῖδες, ω 229), which shows a desire for the protection of the ankles. Probably the rank and file of the people through most of the year went barefoot, like Socrates in the Periclean age. Accustomed to this from childhood, their feet were not so tender as those of the modern civilized man. The epithet *sleek* (λιπαροί, β 4, Ξ 241) applied to feet, implies that these were seen more often than those of the present day, and Menelaus even observes that the feet and hands of Telemachus

---

[1] πέδιλα (*cf.* πούς and *pes*) is the ordinary word, as α 96, β 4, δ 309, ε 44, π 154, ρ 2, B 44, K 22, 132, Ξ 186, Ω 340; ὑποδήματα (ὑπό, δέω), ο 369, σ 361.—σάνδαλα is not Homeric, but appears first in the *Hymn to Hermes*, 79, 83, 139, and Sappho, *Frag.* 95.

[2] In the *Prometheus* of Aeschylus (135), that the Ocean nymphs set out from home without sandals, indicates their haste,—comparable to modern young women not waiting to put on their hats.

resemble those of his father Odysseus (δ 149). "Silver-footed" (ἀργυρόπεζα, A 538) applied to the sea-nymph Thetis, is generally explained as comparing the whiteness of her feet with silver, but Milton's translation, "tinsel-slippered Thetis," shows another interpretation.

No woman is said to wear sandals, but this probably is due to mere chance, since these are worn by the goddesses Hera and Athena (Ξ 186, α 96), and the garb of divinities is like in kind to that of human beings.

Leather was made from the skins of kine, goats, weasels, and probably of dogs (as is indicated by the name κυνέη for a cap), but no leather from sheepskin is men- *Leather.* tioned. Which of these skins were used for sandals, the poet does not say. The sandals of the gods are called golden. Perhaps the poet knew sandals adorned with gold foil, but here again he may have yielded to the impulse to represent all the possessions of the gods as of most precious materials.

That the *kredemnon* served as a protection for the head of women, has been observed. But no hat or cap is mentioned for men, except in connexion with war, where the cap might serve as a helmet. In later art, Odysseus was identified by his cap or traveller's hat, but this is not Homeric. In general, men went bareheaded.

The *hormos*[1] was a long chain, passing about the neck and falling over the breast. The suitor Eurymachus *Necklaces.* gives to Penelope one of gold and amber,[2]—the beads alternating.

The *isthmion* (ἴσθμιον, σ 300) was a necklace of ordinary modern length, made to lie near the throat. One such is given to Penelope by a suitor.

Hephaestus, when cast out of Olympus, and living at the home of Thetis, wrought many curious things,—necklaces, brooches, bent *helices*, and *calyces* (Σ 401). The identification of the last two is not certain. The *helices* (ἕλιξ) have

---

[1] ὅρμος, Σ 401, ο 460, σ 295; *Hom. Hy.* i. 103, iv. 88, vi. 11.

[2] ἠλέκτροισιν, σ 296, in itself is ambiguous,—uncertain whether it is from ἤλεκτρον, amber, or ἤλεκτρος, *white gold, i.e.* gold alloyed with silver,—but the latter would not form so good a contrast to gold, and gold and amber are found together in Etruscan breast ornaments.

been interpreted either as spiral, snake-like bands for the arms, or as ear ornaments, or as spiral brooches[1] for the robe,
Ornaments Forged by Hephaestus. or as fastenings for the hair (the τέττιγες of the old Athenians). The interpretation of *calyces* (*bud, rose-bud*) has been thought entirely uncertain, except as the passage quoted in the last note seems to connect it with the robe. A recent plausible suggestion,[2] however, is that both *helices* and *calyces* were pendants, attached to the long necklace, and possibly serving also as brooches to connect this with the robe.

Earrings[3] are mentioned twice, once as worn by Hera, and again as brought by a suitor as a present to Penelope. The same two adjectives are used for both,—apparently indicating ornaments in the shape of a berry, and a group of three, each in form like the apple of the eye.

Pins,[4] safety pins, and brooches have been seen to be of importance both for men and for women, buttons and hooks-
Pins and Brooches. and-eyes being yet unknown. The *peronae* of the robe which was given to Penelope by one of her suitors, had " well-bent locks " (κληῖδες, σ 293), *i.e.* shields or sheaths for the ends of the pins. Helbig compares an ancient Italian brooch with two parts,—the shields for the pins being fastened by hooks to the other part. The brooch on the cloak worn by Odysseus when he set out for Troy was elaborate. It was of gold with a double fastening (αὐλοῖσιν διδύμοισι, τ 227); the front was curiously wrought : a hound with his fore paws held firm a still struggling dappled fawn, which was striving to escape. With this, Pottier has compared an Egyptian painting of a dog holding and killing a gazelle, and analogies have been found also in primitive Greek art.

Peroné is used for the straight pin as well as for the brooch

---

[1] Supported by *Hom. Hy.* iv. 87, ἕεστο. . . εἶχε δ' ἐυγνάμπτας ἕλικας κάλυκάς τε.

[2] Hadaczek in *Oester. Jahreshefte*, vi. 121.

[3] ἕρματα ἦκεν ἐυτρήτοισι λοβοῖσιν | τρίγληνα (*three-eyed*), μορόεντα (*berry-like*, or possibly *gleaming*), Ξ 182, *cf.* σ 297.

[4] περόνη is the general word for *pin*; Ε 425, σ 293, τ 226, 256, *cf.* περονήσατο, Κ 133, Ξ 180; πέρονησε, Η 145, Ν 397. *Cf.* also Soph. *O. T.* 1269. πόρπαι are mentioned at Σ 401 = *Hom. Hy.* iv. 163. *Cf.* Eur. *Hec.* 1170, *Phoen.* 62 (called περόναι at 805). ἐνεταί (ἐνίημι,—apparently at first only an epithet of περόναι) appear only at Ξ 180. See Hadaczek, *Oester. Jahreshefte*, vi. 108.

or safety pin. At the Argive Heraeum,[1] straight pins were far
the more numerous,—in round numbers, 750 of these being
there found, and 150 of the brooches. The straight
pins are represented on the figures of the François *Stick-pins.*
vase (see Fig. 6), which served as a basis for the revised
views of early Greek dress, but on some early terra-cotta
figurines the robe is represented as pinned at the shoulder

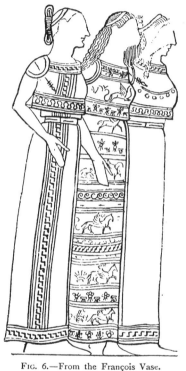

FIG. 6.—From the François Vase.

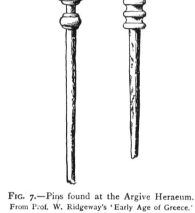

FIG. 7.—Pins found at the Argive Heraeum.
From Prof. W. Ridgeway's 'Early Age of Greece.'

by a large star-like brooch. The assumption of a straight
pin explains most easily the words of Athena to Zeus, suggesting that Aphrodite had scratched her wrist in caressing some
Achaean woman (see p. 164), and its service for the blinding
of Oedipus and of Polymestor, and the stabbing by the
Athenian women of the solitary soldier who returned in safety
from the expedition to Aegina (Herodotus, v. 87). Doubtless
a woman could scratch her arm on a brooch, or even inflict
a bodily injury on another with such a weapon, and with
such an instrument Oedipus could have put out his eyes,

[1] See *The Argive Heraeum*, ii. 207 ff., and Plates lxxvii.-lxxxviii.

but such a purpose would have been served better by a pointed pin, like a stiletto. Some of the Argive pins may have been used as hairpins (*cf.* the Italian and Japanese custom), but such a use is not indicated in the Homeric poems. Possibly some may have been used, like modern hatpins, to hold the *kredemnon* to the head, but many of them are too small for such service, and this use, too, finds no support in the poems. The François vase represents a pin five or six inches in length. The length of the pin may explain why, though the fold of the robe is pinned on the breast just below the shoulder, the pin evidently is thrust upward and not downward ; the hand would need to reach much farther back in order to thrust a long pin downward, and the tension of the garment would hold the pin in place. The pins along the thigh, if not safety pins, would naturally be much shorter than those of the François vase. The frequent use of straight pins only half a century ago on modern garments, where only safety pins would be used at present, may be a partial answer to the doubt whether straight pins could reasonably be used to hold the *chlaena* and the *peplos*, as well as Tacitus's statement that the ancient Germans, in default of a better pin, used a thorn for this purpose. The thickness of many of the straight pins which have been preserved might seem likely to tear a closely woven, delicate fabric, but the Homeric woolen garments ordinarily doubtless were quite as coarse and loosely woven as the Scotch plaid, if indeed they were not like a blanket.

Whether the Homeric robes, like the gowns of the Mycenaeans, were decorated by thin ornaments of gold foil, cannot be stated, but this is not improbable, since thin plates of gold and other metals were used for the adornment of both wood and leather, as for chariots, chairs, and straps.

Of finger-rings, seals, pearls, diamonds, opals, and other precious stones, the Homeric poet shows no knowledge,
Rings, Seals, and Jewels unknown. though seals were much used in Crete as well as in Babylonia. Personal decorations and beauty seem at times to be despised by the poet's characters, but this is only in comparison with prowess in war. Thus Hector mocks at Paris, whose beauty and long hair—the gifts of Aphrodite,—would not avail him in

the conflict with Menelaus, but he would be laid in the dust.[1]

A frequent epithet of the Achaeans is *long-haired* (κάρη κομόωντες, used thirty times).[2] The hair of the contestants in the horse race floats in the air (Ψ 367), Paris is proud of his long hair (Γ 55),[3] and the goat-herd Melanthius is dragged by his hair (χ 188). In general, long hair seems to have been in plaited tresses, or otherwise confined. Achilles's luxuriant hair had been dedicated to the Spercheüs, the river of his Thessalian

" Long-haired " Achaeans.

FIG. 8.—Gold foil ornament for raiment, found at Mycenae.
From Prof. W. Ridgeway's 'Early Age of Greece.'

home, but at the funeral of Patroclus he cuts it off and lays it in the hand of his dead friend (Ψ 141), and the corpse was covered with the hair of his comrades. To "cut the hair and shed tears" were the ordinary tokens of mourning (δ 198).

[1] Γ 44, 54, *cf.* B 673, 872.

[2] Apollo is *unshorn* (ἀκερσεκόμης, Υ 39); *cf. intonsum Cynthium*, Horace, *Odes*, i. 21, and the Apollo Belvedere. The locks of Zeus wave at A 529. *Cf.* also the long hair of Samson and of Absalom, and see Tacitus, *Germania*, 31.

[3] Paris is said to be "splendid with horn" (κέραι ἀγλαέ, Λ 385), and Helbig would understand this not of his bow of horn, but of a stiff spiral braid of hair, standing like a horn by the side of his head.

So on the death of Achilles, the Danaï shed many hot tears and cut their hair.[1]

On archaic works of art the hair of men often reaches to the middle of their shoulder blades. Jason returned to Iolcos, according to Pindar (*P.* iv. 82), with hair gleaming down his back. The Athenian gentlemen of the olden time were wont to fasten up their long locks with golden "grasshoppers" (τέττιγες, Thuc. i. 6), which may have been in form like the Homeric *helices* or spirals, but called grasshoppers from the chirping noise which they made on movement. That the Spartans wore long hair at the opening of the fifth century B.C. is shown by the story of Herodotus (vii. 208) that Leonidas's men before the conflict at Thermopylae were combing their hair in preparation for the battle on the following day.

The locks of Euphorbus, son of Panthoüs, were held in place (ἐσφήκωντο, P 52) by gold and silver ornaments. Such may have been the ornaments of the Carian Nastes who went to war "adorned with gold, like a girl" (ἠΰτε κούρη, B 872).

The Euboean Abantes (ὄπιθεν κομόωντες, B 542) wore their hair cut short, "banged," in front, but suffered it to grow long at the back. The Thracians, on the other *Peculiar Cut of Hair.* hand (ἀκρόκομοι, Δ 533), seem to have had their hair cut short behind, and to have tied their long hair in a knot on the top of their head,—perhaps in a sort of cue, such as appears on monuments of the early fifth century B.C.[2] The poet was familiar with the use of the razor— possibly such a crescent-shaped knife as was commonly used for such purposes in ancient times, of which the form is best preserved in a knife now commonly used only by shoemakers, but possibly also in a form much resembling the modern razor,—since Nestor is made to say that the destruction or safety of the Achaeans stood upon a razor's edge (ἐπὶ ξυροῦ ἵσταται ἀκμῆς, K 173). Probably only the

[1] ω 46. In Euripides's *Alcestis* the question of the chorus whether they shall cut their hair (215), means simply, "Is Alcestis now dead?" Heracles sees that Admetus is in grief by his shorn head (512), and the king orders that his subjects shall cut not only their own hair, but also the manes of their horses (425).

[2] *Athenische Mitteilungen*, viii., Pl. xi. xii.

FIG. 9.—Apollo Belvedere.

Facing p. 176.

moustache was shaved, as at Sparta and on ancient monuments; certainly the beard often was allowed to grow (π 176).

The epithet *fair-tressed*,[1] applied to both goddesses and mortal women, refers to the well-braided tresses rather than to the color, fineness, or abundance of *Fair-tressed.* the hair. Blond hair was assigned to Achilles (ξανθή, Α 197, Ψ 141), Meleager (Β 642), Menelaus (Γ 284), Demeter (Ε 500), Agamede (Λ 740), and Odysseus (ν 399). The hair of Zeus and Poseidon is dark (Α 528, *Color of Hair.* γ 6). Whether light hair was frequent in the Homeric period, or is ascribed to Achilles and Menelaus as a mark of beauty cannot be decided definitely, but the manner of the use of the epithet indicates that it is not intended as a distinction.

---

[1] ἐυπλόκαμος, as Ζ 380, and its synonym καλλιπλόκαμος, as Σ 407, derived from πλέκω, *plecto*. *Cf.* ἐύζωνος and καλλίζωνος.

CHAPTER VI

HOUSE AND FURNITURE

THE Homeric poet describes no house, and so much of the action of the poems takes place in the open air that the

No House Described. certain reconstruction of a typical Homeric house from the incidental indications of its structure, is not easy. Neither the battles of the *Iliad* nor the wanderings of Odysseus could be expected to contribute much to our knowledge of the architecture of the poet's age. But one old error may be excluded at the outset: we need not suppose that every house in the poet's age was built on exactly the same plan. The excavations on the sites of Troy, Mycenae, Tiryns, Cnosus, and Phaestus—not to name the uncovering of less magnificent structures like those at Phylacopi on Melos and at Gournià in Crete,—show the ruins of ancient palaces and private houses of different plans, though with certain resemblances. Doubtless then, as now, the situation of a dwelling had much weight in determining details of form. Nothing indicates that the whole structure regularly formed such a rectangle as is presented in many old books on classical antiquities as the plan of a Homeric dwelling. Sometimes, as seems to be the case at the home

No Absolute Uniformity. of Odysseus on Ithaca, the women's apartment may have been built directly in the rear of the great hall, while again, as apparently at Tiryns, it may have been at the side of the men's apartments. Some houses may have had but two or three rooms, or even only one large hall, like those of the Homeric city of Hissarlik, while others may have had many apartments, like the great Cretan palaces.

The palaces at Tiryns and in Crete certainly were built according to elaborate and complicated plans, and the poet's words with regard to the home of Odysseus make this also appear as an aggregation of structures which have some independence.[1] Telemachus has a bed-chamber of his own, in a sheltered spot of the beautiful courtyard.[2] This room of the young prince clearly had a separate entrance, but it is not at all likely to have been conceived by the poet as an independent and isolated hut or bungalow;[3] it must have been part of the main building. The bed-chamber of Odysseus was built around an olive tree, of which the stump was to serve as a bed-post (ψ 190). He may have made this tree the determining point for his whole structure, but he is more likely to have added this room to the rest of his plan; this chamber was not used in any way during his absence (ψ 227), and it does not seem like part of a regularly built house. To attach additions to the side of the house was the simpler since the great hall had no windows in the modern sense; and the great hall may well have been higher than the rooms on the side, so that such rooms would not prevent the possibility of side openings for light just under the roof. Possibly the structure on the side of the great hall may have had two storeys, the two together equalling the height of the hall, but this is mere surmise. We do not know how much the Greeks of that age cared for exact symmetry in their architecture.

The three essential elements of a Homeric house are an open court (αὐλή), a vestibule or porch (πρόδομος or δῶμα), and an inner room (θάλαμος). In the palaces uncovered

---

[1] ἐξ ἑτέρων ἕτερ' ἐστίν, ἐπήσκηται δέ οἱ αὐλή | τοίχῳ καὶ θριγκοῖσι, θύραι δ' εὐεργέες εἰσίν, ρ 266.

[2] θάλαμος περικαλλέος αὐλῆς . . . περισκέπτῳ ἐνὶ χώρῳ, α 425.—περισκέπτῳ has been translated conspicuous, but this is little suited to such a chamber, and hardly more so to the palace of Circe (κ 211) and the hut of Eumaeus (ξ 6), to which the same epithet is applied.

[3] Protodikos thinks this to have been an isolated structure in the front court, and similarly the bed-chamber of Odysseus to have stood behind not only the main hall but the women's apartments, as an independent building. But this arrangement is neither indicated in the poem, nor reasonable in itself, nor supported by the analogy of ancient buildings uncovered by recent excavations.

at Tiryns and Mycenae, according to Dörpfeld,[1] "this tripartite disposition is present, but it is not so obvious *Essential* since each part is *en suite*. The court is a *Elements of a* double one ; the *doma* is made up of hall, *Homeric* ante-room, and vestibule ; and in place of the *House.* simple *thalamos* we have a special women's quarter with several adjoining rooms." Similar architectural problems were solved differently on Melos and in Crete.

The life of Greek men was spent chiefly in the open air. What had a Homeric warrior to occupy him within the house,—beyond polishing his arms, like Paris *Life of Men* by the side of Helen (Z 321)? Before Troy, the *in the Open* poet says definitely that Nestor and Diomed *Air.* slept in the open air (K 74, 151), and the same is to be assumed for many if not most of the rest of the warriors.[2]   That, on the other hand, Penelope's suitors and the Phaeacian nobles dine in the great halls (α 144, ζ 305, η 136) instead of in the courtyards or porches, is to be explained by the cool season of the year in the action of that poem,—so cool that Arete and Penelope both sit by the fire (ζ 305, ρ 572, τ 55), and the princess Nausicaa has a fire kindled for her in her chamber (η 7).[3]   Probably in summer the suitors would have feasted in the courtyard, in the shade of the porches.

The homes of princes not infrequently stood on heights, being in a sense "hill-fortresses." So Pylus lay on a hill, as well as the homes of Erechtheus at Athens, *Houses of* of Agamemnon at Mycenae, and of Priam at *Princes on* Troy. This was natural in view of the prevail-*Hills.* ing notions with regard to might and right. Marauding expeditions were to be feared by sea and by land, and the home of Odysseus seems to be prepared to

---

[1] Introduction to Tsountas and Manatt, *Mycenaean Age*, xxiv.

[2] The action of the *Iliad*, the poet clearly indicates to have been in warm weather. *Cf.* E 796, K 572, Λ 811, O 241, Π 109, Φ 51, 561, X 2, Ψ 507, 688, 715.

[3] The shipwrecked Odysseus fears that he may be overcome by cold (ε 467, *cf.* 487), and in the hut of Eumaeus the same hero has a warm place to sleep by the fire, with a blanket over him (ξ 518), and he delays his walk to the palace until the sun has warmed the air (ρ 23). *Cf.* α 443, γ 349, λ 373, σ 328, τ 64, 507, υ 3.

meet any such sudden attack (ρ 268). But no indication
is given that the home of Odysseus was situated on a hill,
or that the palace of Menelaus lay in a plain (δ 2).

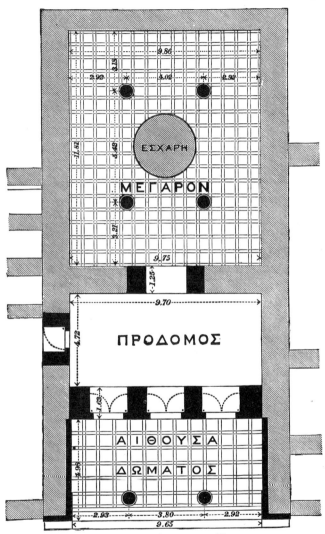

FIG. 10.—Men's Apartment at Tiryns.

The palace at Tiryns had before it an outer as well as
an inner court. Probably most less magnificent *The Court.*
dwellings had only a single court, but this may
have had divisions. The swine which Eumaeus brought for
the feast of Penelope's suitors are suffered to graze in the

enclosure (υ 164), but they may not have been turned loose to wander freely over the whole courtyard, in which the suitors were sitting at ease. The dungheap on which Odysseus's old dog Argos lies, on the hero's return, seems to be within the courtyard, but it may not have been very near the seats of the suitors. Nothing shows the size nor the shape of the court. Doubtless the courts of different houses differed in both respects, being adapted to the lie of the land. The court seems to have lain exclusively before the house ; this house did not stand in the middle of an enclosure, with free grounds all about it. There was no court in the rear, nor any back door. Thus the stalls for horses stood before the house, not behind it, and wagons were left leaning against the front wall. Helen's geese were fed in the court before the house (ο 161, cf. τ 536), and there Penelope's suitors seem to have slaughtered and flayed, as well as cooked, the cattle and swine on which they feasted (β 300). That swine grazed (νέμεσθαι, υ 164) in the enclosure, does not prove that grass grew all over it ; the ground where the suitors amused themselves with "putting the shot" and hurling spears at a mark, seems to have been of hardened clay (ἐν τυκτῷ δαπέδῳ, ρ 169). The court of Tiryns was paved. An olive tree grew in the enclosure of Odysseus (ἕρκεος ἐντός, ψ 190) before it was made a part of his bed-chamber. The courtyard was enclosed by a wall, which at the home of Odysseus had a cornice (θριγκοῖσι, ρ 267,— very likely of the prickly pear, cf. ξ 10) which served the purpose of iron spikes and broken glass in walls about modern gardens and lawns. The ordinary height of such a wall is not indicated, except that Phoenix leaped over his father's wall (I 476), while Odysseus says that no man could easily surmount his (ρ 268). Apparently the herald Medon, while outside of the courtyard (δ 678), hears the plots of Penelope's suitors within the court ; the sound must have come over the wall.

The court was the ordinary gathering place of the men of the family, and it was such an essential part of a home that Achilles had one before his barrack on the field of Troy (Ω 452), the swine-herd Eumaeus had one before his hut (ξ 5), and Polyphemus had one before his cave (ι 184). The clouds seem to form such an enclosure before the dwellings of the gods on Olympus. The Hours have in their charge the "gates of Olympus" (Θ 393),—"both to roll back and to close the thick cloud." In agreement with this is the statement that the Hours unharnessed the steeds of Hera and Athena, on their return from the field of battle to the home of the gods, and tied them to their mangers (Θ 433), for the goddesses naturally would leave their chariots at or near the entrance to the enclosure, where the Hours were stationed.

In the courtyard, but not necessarily at its centre,[1] stood an altar of Zeus Herceius, the guardian of the enclosure.[2] There Peleus is sacrificing to Zeus when he receives the visit of Nestor and Odysseus, there Achilles prays to Zeus when he is about to *Altar in the Court.* send Patroclus into the conflict, there Priam stands to pray to Zeus before going to the tent of Achilles, and there the Ithacan bard takes his place as a suppliant, when Penelope's suitors are slain.

Before the door of Nestor's home stood seats of polished stone, which apparently were covered with a kind of varnish or stucco.[3] There the old Neleus had sat in his time, and there sat his son Nestor and his guests *Stone Seats.* after they arose from their couches in the morning. Similarly, at the general assembly of the gods (Υ 11), the divinities sat in the porch of the hall of Zeus. Within the courtyard of Odysseus, his wife's suitors sat on the hides of the cattle on which they themselves had feasted (α 108). Such an untanned hide Odysseus used as a bed in the porch, on the night after his return to his home, in disguise (υ 2, 96).

Along the sides of the courtyard may have stood storerooms, some of which may have been used as stalls for horses.[4]

---

[1] At Tiryns the altar was near the front gate and on one side of the middle. This left the main space of the court the freer for any activity.

[2] Cf. αὐλῆς ἐν χορτῷ, Λ 774; στὰς μέσῳ ἔρκει, Π 231, Ω 306; Χ 334, 379, Plato, *Rep.* 328 c.

[3] ἐπὶ ξεστοῖσι λίθοισιν . . . λευκοί, ἀποστίλβοντες ἀλείφατος, γ 406 f. Cf. ἰὼ μέλαθρα βασιλέων . . . σεμνοί τε θᾶκοι, Aesch. *Ag.* 518.

[4] The Homeric Greeks had no barns or stables or other special structures for their horses. The number of horses in general was not large, and as a rule these were kept in the open air, in the field (cf. T 281).

Certainly the mills for grinding grain seem to have been in the courtyard, for the disguised Odysseus, on the morning after his return to his home, while in the court and apparently near the porch, hears the prayer of an old woman working at a mill (υ 106). The bed-chamber of Telemachus clearly had an independent entrance from the court (α 425), and the old Phoenix, *paedagogus* of Achilles, who in running away from home as a young man, "broke open the door of his chamber and leaped over the wall of the court" (I 475), cannot have slept in a room which lay behind the great hall. The sons and sons-in-law of Priam had apartments on either side of the court of the palace,[1] all joining with their wives and children in the patriarchal life of the great family. The room of Nausicaa may be assumed to be on the ground floor, for she has a fire in it (η 7), but no material is furnished by the poet for a safe inference as to its position in relation to the great hall, which was the centre of the household life. Nothing shows, either, the place of the apartments of Nestor's sons (γ 396, 413).

Store-rooms and Stalls.

A circular structure, a *tholos* or *rotunda*, of uncertain use, is mentioned, but only in a single connexion as standing in the courtyard of Odysseus (χ 442, 466). Penelope's wanton serving maids, after the slaughter of her suitors, are hung by the neck in nooses of a ship's rope which is stretched for the purpose from a pillar (which may have been part of the front gateway) to this *tholos*. A recent suggestion is that this round structure was an altar, but an altar does not seem well adapted to the hanging of the women.[2]

Rotunda.

---

[1] Z 245 f. The arrangement of these apartments is not made clear by the poet. Nothing indicates that the apartments had two storeys. The rooms of the sons-in-law, twelve in number, are said to be opposite those of the sons, fifty in number, but this would give much greater space to each of the sons-in-law. Possibly, just as the story of the number of Penelope's suitors outgrew the dimensions of Odysseus's dining hall, so also that of Priam's sons outgrew the limits of any reasonable courtyard. But we are not obliged to think of the apartments as palatial according to modern notions. The excavations at Cnosus have shown that inmates of a very splendid ancient palace might be satisfied with very small sleeping-rooms, and the small bed-rooms at Pompeii, the merest closets, are familiar to many readers.

[2] Perrot and Chipiez, vii. 85, incline to believe this to have been a *kiosk* or summer-house.

The gateway which led from the court to the street or road, seems to have been more than a simple opening in the wall. That of Odysseus had double gates *The Gateway.* (ρ 267) and a threshold (α 104), which doubtless was of stone. In order to prevent intrusion and interference from without, when Odysseus slays Penelope's suitors, he has these doors not merely fastened by a great bolt, but also tied by a ship's cable which lies in the corridor close at hand (φ 240, 390). The gate of Achilles's court is fastened by a great bar of pine, which "three of the Achaeans are wont to thrust home or to open" (Ω 453), though Achilles alone can push it home. At Tiryns the gateway resembled the Propylaea of classical times. Telemachus and his companion "drive out of the porch (προθύροιο, ο 191, cf. Ω 323) and resounding corridor" of Menelaus, and the epithet indicates that the corridor[1] was roofed, and echoed to the tread of the horses. The Homeric Greeks were glad to have a shelter from the sun and rain, such as the *stoa* of historical times, which did not check wholly the movement of the air. In this outer porch, goats and kine are tied, waiting to be slaughtered (υ 176, 187), there the corpses of Penelope's suitors are heaped up (χ 449), and there the beggar Irus is set, grievously worsted in his contest with the disguised Odysseus (σ 239). At the opening of the action of the *Odyssey*, Telemachus, seated among his mother's suitors in the court-yard, but taking no part in their games, catches sight of Athena, in the guise of Mentes, standing "at the front gate of Odysseus, on the threshold of the court,"[2] and at the front gate Nestor and Odysseus, on visiting Peleus, stood until Achilles welcomed them (Λ 777). The porch (πρόδομος, ξ 5) in which the swine-herd Eumaeus is sitting, making his sandals, when Odysseus approaches, is probably not that at

---

[1] In this front gateway a fire was built by those who were watching Phoenix, I 472.—The same word πρόθυρον is used, naturally enough, also of the area before the entrance to the main hall. Thus Theoclymenus with prophetic soul sees the *prothyron* and court full of ghosts hurrying to the abode of darkness (υ 355), and the goat-herd Melanthius is dragged through the *prothyron* and court (χ 474),—in both of which passages the porch of the dwelling itself is meant; cf. also σ 385, φ 299.

[2] ἐπὶ προθύροις 'Οδυσῆος, οὐδοῦ ἐπ' αὐλείου, α 103.

the entrance to the court, however, but at the entrance to the hut itself.

Against the front wall of the dwelling, on either side of the entrance, the poles of the two-wheeled chariots were sometimes leaned,—these chariots in this position *Chariots leaned against Front Wall.* requiring a minimum of space,—and similarly spears might be placed thus against the front wall of a barrack. Odysseus here leans his old bow, near the door-post, when he has shot his last arrow at the suitors of Penelope.[1] He shoots his arrows from the doorway, but when these are exhausted (which naturally is unexpected by the suitors), he moves aside quickly behind the wall for protection while he puts on his shield and helmet.

Every house was expected to have a porch or portico[2] at its main entrance. This porch is the ordinary sleeping-*The Porch.* place of guests, as will be seen later. In his porch Eumaeus sits, busy in cobbling, when Odysseus approaches (ξ 5). The columns of the porch doubtless were ordinarily of wood, as at Tiryns, set on stone bases. The entablature between the columns also would be of wood. The columns may not have been very magnificent in every case ; perhaps *posts* would be a better word for most of them. Whether they tapered downward, in Mycenaean fashion, is uncertain. That the court was surrounded by a peristyle, is unlikely.

The word house[3] is a general term, often explained and limited by the context. So, naturally, to "leave the house" *" House " a General Term.* when one is in the *megaron*, is to leave the great hall (φ 188). "In the house" (ο 516) may be contrasted with "in the *hyperoön* or *loggia* on the house top." "Silence throughout the house" may mean only silence in the great hall (η 144,

---

[1] ἐνώπια παμφανόωντα, Θ 435, δ 42 ; Ν 261, χ 121. The epithet *gleaming* implies stucco. The etymology of ἐνώπια, *en face*, seems to refer only to the wall which met the eye of one who entered the court, but perhaps the word was used also of the opposite wall of the enclosure, on either side of the entrance of the court, where according to modern ideas chariots might naturally be left.

[2] πρόδομος and αἴθουσα,—apparently synonymous in δ 297, 302 ; but αἴθουσα was used also of the great entrance to the court, as Ι 472.

[3] δῶμα or δώματα, used without difference of meaning, about 250 times ; δόμος, used a trifle more than 150 times ; οἶκος, nearly 200 times, and οἰκία, 24 times.

cf. Ω 512); and when Odysseus searches "through the house" (κατὰ δόμον, χ 381, *cf.* 291, 440, 455) for any of Penelope's suitors who may have escaped death, he does not leave the *megaron*. Telemachus goes from a store-room "to his house" (ἐς δώματα, β 381), and mingles with the suitors. Conversely, Telemachus on coming to his house (πρὸς δῶμα, β 298) finds the suitors "in the great hall" (ἐν μεγάροισιν) flaying·goats and singeing swine in the court-yard (ἐν αὐλῇ, β 300),—where *hall* must be used loosely.[1]

The material of the house is named only for the palace of Priam (Z 244), which was built of polished stone. The hut of the swine-herd Eumaeus was probably of sun-dried brick, which now is known to have been used not merely for the upper part of the fortifications of the Homeric Ilium, but also for the upper part of the walls of the Heraeum at Olympia and of the palace at Tiryns.[2] For most houses, we may suppose that the walls similarly were of such brick with a footing of stone. The walls of stone and sun-dried brick in the better houses were covered on the interior with stucco, and were painted, and had friezes of colored stones or of blue paste (as at the palace of the Phaeacian king, η 87), with various decorations of metal (δ 73, η 86). Shields and helmets seem to have hung upon the walls or columns (π 284, χ 24), as upon the walls of the poet Alcaeus (*Frag.* 56).

Materials of the House.

Wood must have been used for the door-casings, for the protection of the mud-brick. The roof in most cases was nearly flat,—reeds being laid on cross-timbers and above them a thick layer of clay which was rolled with stone cylinders until it was hard, having only sufficient slope to carry off the rain-water. Such roofs are

Flat Roof.

---

[1] Protodikos gives illustrations of the interchange of the words for house. *E.g.* οἶκος is used (1) of the whole house, as α 375, and often, (2) of the *megaron*, as ο 516, (3) of the women's apartments, as δ 717, (4) of the place where the mills stand, υ 105, and (5) of the other chambers in the court, γ 396.—That οἶκος, α 356, is used of the women's apartments as opposed to the hall, is due to the unskilled adaptation of these verses from Z 490, where οἶκος is contrasted with the street.

[2] Dörpfeld, in *Troja und Ilion*, pp. 109, 118 ; in *Aufsätze Ernst Curtius gewidmet*, p. 139 f. ; and in Schliemann's *Tiryns*, p. 256.

customary in the Troad at present. The poet seems to have been familiar also with gable roofs, for he compares the position of two wrestlers, holding each other in close grasp, to that of the rafters of a high house which a skilled builder fits firmly (Ψ 712). The roof of Achilles's barrack, also, seems to be thatched,—his comrades " roofed it, gathering the shaggy roofing (ὄροφον, Ω 451) from the meadow."

Near the door, but within the great hall, stood a column which served also as a spear-rack. When Athena visits Ithaca in the guise of Mentes, Telemachus takes the spear from her hand, and " leans it against a column, within the well-polished spear-holder (δουροδόκη, α 128) where stood many other spears,—spears of Odysseus." Grooves or flutings in the columns are suggested by this incident ; a single large cut in the column would have weakened it too much, and would have ruined its symmetry. Robert conjectures that such grooves may have given the first hint which led to the fluting of the Ionic columns. On his return to Ithaca, Telemachus leaves his spear at a column before entering the great hall (ρ 29),—depositing it at the entrance, like a modern umbrella, as not needed within the house. But that Eumaeus receives the spear of Telemachus before the latter enters the hut (π 40), does not prove that he left it in the courtyard,—he may have carried it within, as Telemachus carried Athena's. The spears, helmets, and shields which Odysseus removes from the hall on the night before he slays his wife's suitors, clearly are in the hall, and not without the door, for the pretext for their removal is to be that they are defiled by the smoke of the hall (τ 7, 32).

Column as Spear-rack.

The great hall or *megaron* [1] is the centre of the life of the household,—not unlike the baronial halls of the old English castles. Here all classes gather,—the beggar and the retainer as well as the master of the family and the most honored guests. Here, before the advent of the suitors, sat Penelope and her maids, spinning and weaving. Its size naturally

The Great Hall or Megaron.

---

[1] The plural is rather more frequent than the singular, without difference of meaning. *Cf.* δώματα, φ 234 = δῶμα, φ 378, ἅρματα = ἅρμα, and ὄχεα (*chariot*, E 745) with ὄκχον of Pindar, *Ol.* vi. 24.

differed with the circumstances of the owner. Priam would
need a large hall for his patriarchal family,—even without
provision for any guests,—and the suitors of Penelope, if
more than a hundred in number, could not be seated
easily in Homeric fashion in a small room. The Homeric
chairs were heavy, and the tables light, and the chairs were
ranged along the sides of the hall,[1] with room for a small
table between each pair,—the main space of the hall being
left free for weaving and other work. Thus far fewer guests
could sit at dinner than in a modern hall of the same size,
and if we should calculate the size of Odysseus's *megaron*,
according to the number of guests said to be present,
allowing but three feet for the width of each suitor's chair
and table, the dimensions would far exceed all reasonable
limits for the hall of an Ithacan palace. The number of
suitors was multiplied in the story as it appears in the tale
of Telemachus to his father.[2] The hall of Odysseus is not
likely to have been larger than that at Tiryns, or about
forty feet in length.[3]

In addition to the broad front door, the hall of Odysseus
had a door at the rear, leading to the women's apartments,
and a small side door on a higher level.

In the centre of the hall was a fireplace, which at
Tiryns was circular, and about 10 feet in diameter. For
this the middle of the hall was most convenient, since thus
all parts of the room would be heated equally by the
central fire. Still more important, however, was
another consideration, the hall had no chimney *Fireplace in*
and the smoke from the fire must escape as it *Centre of*
Hall.
could,—most of it doubtless being expected to
find its way out through an opening in the roof above the
fire, but the ceiling is called smoky or sooty (αἰθαλόεν,

[1] η 95, Ι 219, Ω 476, 598 ; α 138.

[2] π 247 ff.,—verses which appear to have been rejected by Aristarchus. Nowhere else are such numbers assumed.

[3] The floor-space of three ancient *megara* may be stated in round numbers as
follows : that at Mycenae and the largest found in Homeric Troy, alike about
1420 square feet,—15.30 × 8.40 metres at Troy, and 12.92 × 11.50 metres at Mycenae ;
the *megaron* at Tiryns was somewhat smaller (11.81 × 9.80 metres). An earlier
palace at Troy, perhaps a thousand years before Priam's time, was much larger,
having a *megaron* about 66 feet in length and half as broad.

B 415, χ 239).[1]   About the fire stood four columns in the main hall at Tiryns, and a similar arrangement existed in the palace of Alcinoüs, for the queen Arete there has the seat of honor, near the fire and close by a pillar (ζ 305). So also Penelope sits near the fire (τ 55). These columns about the fire served as supports for the timbers of the roof, and naturally must have been near the middle of the hall. Dörpfeld supposes that no large hole was left in the roof above the fire, for this would have been inconvenient in cold weather, and particularly in rainy or stormy weather, but that the middle part of the roof was raised, leaving vertical openings, a *clerestory*, at the sides of the raised portion. This opening in the roof allowed also the entrance of light, which was important, for at best the Homeric halls were both smoky and dark.[2]   They had no windows in the modern sense.   Possibly, however, there were openings above the cornice, between the ends of the beams which supported the roof,—the *metopes* of Doric architecture.   Homeric life did not require much light for indoor work.   No reading or writing and (apparently) little sewing was done.   Little light was needed for the processes of spinning and ordinary weaving. Those whose occupations called for the best illumination would sit near the door or near the fire.

The hearth[3] at Tiryns was slightly raised above the floor, and at the palace of Alcinoüs, Odysseus sits as a suppliant

The Hearth.   on the hearth in the ashes, by the fire (η 153),— the ashes having spread somewhat from the fire itself.   Cooking was done at this fire as well as in the courtyard (σ 44), and naturally this was the ordinary place for roasting flesh in the swine-herd's hut (ξ 420); no special room in the Homeric house was set apart as a kitchen.   The fire was useful in the evening, also, as giving light (τ 64).

---

[1] At the monastery at Poros in Greece, and doubtless elsewhere in similar structures, still, the smoke from the main fire has no chimney to guide it, but escapes by a hole in the roof.   A conjecture has been suggested that the darkened, mahogany-like color of the beams of the ceiling was admired.

[2] The epithet *shadowy*, σκιόεντα, is applied to the great hall at α 365, δ 768, etc.

[3] ἐσχάρη, ζ 52.   The word ἱστίη (Attic ἑστία) is never applied to this, but is used only in oaths, as ξ 159, ρ 156.

The floor of the great hall at Mycenae was of stone plates, with an alabaster border; that at Tiryns was of concrete. That of the home of Odysseus was *The Floor.* of hardened earth (ψ 46), and Telemachus treats it with so little respect that he digs a trench in it to set up the axes which are to serve as a mark for the archery contest (φ 120). Penelope's maids sweep and sprinkle the floor in the morning (ν 149). After the slaughter of Penelope's suitors, hoes are used to remove the upper layer of blood-stained earth (χ 455). No carpets or floor-rugs are mentioned, and the lack of these explains the importance of the footstools which were attached to the heavy chairs (τ 57).

The ceiling of the hall was the lower part of the roof. If the upper part of the wall was of sun-dried brick, a thick plank or a beam would have been needed over this, to support the cross-timbers.[1] Other beams *The Ceiling.* ran the length of the room, resting on the columns near the fire. Naturally the beams running in one direction passed over or under those which they crossed. Thus an open space was left from which a rope might hang,—as Iocasta hung herself from the ceiling,[2]—or where a bird might perch,—as Athena sat like a swallow on a timber of the ceiling (χ 239). Some of these beams projected so far outwards that a bird could rest on their outer end (τ 544).

The thresholds seem to have been somewhat raised, for he who enters a room is said to "come down" over the threshold (δ 680), and the very frequency of their mention would argue their prominence. They *Thresholds.* appear to have been commonly of stone,[3]—as is true not simply of the palace of Odysseus and the temple at Delphi, but also of the swine-herd's hut. Penelope's store-room had a threshold of oak (φ 43), and the front threshold of Odysseus

---

[1] In τοῖχοι μεγάρων καλαί τε μεσόδμαι | εἰλάτιναί τε δοκοὶ καὶ κίονες ὑψόσ' ἔχοντες, τ 37,—*walls, cross-timbers, pine beams,* and *columns,*—the parts of the structure most obvious to the beholder are enumerated. Some understand the μεσόδμαι to be not the cross-timbers but the beams running the length of the room; but the analogy of μεσόδμη (β 424) as a cross-piece, thwart, of a boat, favors the former interpretation.

[2] ἀψαμένη βρόχον αἰπὺν ἀφ' ὑψηλοῖο μελάθρου, λ 278.

[3] ρ 30, υ 258, ψ 88; θ 80; π 41.

once appears as of ash wood (μέλινος, ρ 339),—doubtless laid over stone, as at the Argive Heraeum. The threshold of the palace of Alcinoüs, as well as those of the palaces of Zeus and Hephaestus, and of the home of Hades, is said to be of bronze,—probably having only a bronze covering over wood.[1] Twice the threshold of Odysseus's hall is said to be polished (σ 33, χ 72), but this epithet is applied both to wood and to stone. As suppliants, the comrades of Odysseus sat on the threshold of Aeolus (κ 62). Odysseus himself, disguised as a needy wanderer, took his place thus in all humility, on his own threshold (ρ 339, 413, 466), and when the Ithacan beggar comes, Odysseus tells him that the threshold will hold them both (σ 17). In the Levant still the threshold is the beggar's seat.

The *megaron* of Odysseus had a third door, which is mentioned only in the story of the death of the suitors.[2]

Side-door of Great Hall. Apparently this is a hanging-door (or possibly a raised door) near the rear of the great hall, opening into a side passage (λαύρη, χ 128), which in turn led in one direction to the courtyard, and in the other direction to the store rooms and other apartments at the back of the house. It was reached by a short ladder or movable steps, though why this side-door should not reach the ground like the rest, is unknown. It cannot have been used ordinarily, or we should hear of it elsewhere; perhaps it may have been raised for light.[3] The ancient scholars and critics of Alexandria and Rome were themselves in doubt and at variance with regard to it. When Odysseus, standing at the main entrance of the hall, has shot with his archery many of Penelope's suitors and is preparing to assail the rest, these propose that some one should go up and out through this door and tell their friends in the city of the action of Odysseus, and thus ask their aid. The goat-herd Melanthius replies that no one could escape in this way. Odysseus, standing at the front door of the *megaron*, com-

[1] η 83, 89, ν 4. χαλκοβατὲς δῶ, Α 426, Ξ 173, Φ 438; θ 321. Θ 15.

[2] ὀρσοθύρη, χ 126, 132, 333. See Schenkl, *Die homerische Palastbeschreibung*, Vienna, 1893, which contains an elaborate statement of the views of old authorities.

[3] Professor Ernest Gardner is quoted as suggesting that it may have been "a species of serving-hatch." *J.H.S.* xxiii. 329.

manded the exit from the narrow passage to the court ; but Melanthius does not raise the objection that the side-door is inaccessible. He thinks he can find the arms which have been conveyed away from the great hall by Odysseus and Telemachus, and apparently slips out by this side-door,[1] and turns to the store-rooms at the rear of the house,— the doors leading to the women's quarters had been fastened by Euryclea according to the injunction of Telemachus (φ 381), but the door to the armory had been left ajar by Telemachus (χ 156),—and fetches twelve shields, spears, and helmets for the suitors. After the suitors have been slain, the bard Phemius, standing near this *orsythyré*, hesitates whether to slip out into the courtyard (evidently by this side-door and the narrow passage) and sit as a suppliant on the altar of Zeus, or to address Odysseus directly (χ 330).

The word for door is generally used in the plural (as θύραι, ζ 19), which indicates that double or folding doors were usual. The singular also is used (as α 441), however, and doubtless some doors were double and others single.[2] The epithet *bright* (φαειναί, ζ 19) implies decorations of metal attached to the wood of the door, and a similar explanation holds for the golden doors, the silver door-post and the silver lintel of Alcinoüs (η 88), the ivory and horn gates of Dreamland (τ 563), and the iron gates of Tartarus (Θ 15). This custom of decoration with plates of metal, was common in Egypt and Mesopotamia also.[3] That the door-casings were of wood, has been seen already ; the front door-post of Odysseus's hall

The Doors.

---

[1] ἀνὰ ῥῶγας μεγάροιο, χ 143 (mentioned only here). What the ῥῶγες are, if not this door, no one knows. The openings between the rafters, under the roof,—or the clerestory,—have been suggested. But how should Melanthius reach these? By swarming up one of the pillars? And the alternative of Odysseus (χ 151), that *either* Melanthius, who knew the house, *or* the women have supplied the arms, would indicate that these arms had been brought by a fairly accessible way. If Melanthius had climbed one of the columns, he would have been more likely to be seen than if he slipped out by a side door.

[2] So in the royal villa at Cnosus. See *Annual of the British School at Athens*, ix. 14.—The leaves of the double door are θύραι, ρ 267, θύρετρα, σ 385, or σανίδες, I 583.

[3] See Helbig, *Homerisches Epos*[2], 433. A solid bronze or iron fire-proof door is not likely to have been known to the poet.

was of cypress.[1] How the doors were hung is not made
clear. At Tiryns the door swung on a pivot which turned
in a hemispherical cavity, the upper end of the beam
turning in a hole in the lintel.[2] These vertical door-beams
were the θαιροί (M 462), broken in the gate of the Achaean
camp before Troy by the force of a mighty stone hurled
by Hector. The door was drawn to, or closed from the
outside, by means of a hook (κορώνη, α 441, η 90, φ 165),
which was of silver for Telemachus's bedroom, but of gold

for the palace of Alcinoüs. By
pulling a strap from the outside
a bolt was shot, which could
readily be pushed back from
within, while from without a key
was needed.[3] The Homeric key
is represented on some ancient
works of art, as borne by
priestesses,—as it were, a badge
of office,—a key between two
and three feet in length, bent
twice at right angles, suggesting vaguely the shape of the
human "collar-bone" (which also
is called κληΐς, E 146). The
opening of a locked door is
briefly described by our poet
in his narration of Penelope's

FIG. 11.—Priestess with key.

going to the store-room in which was kept the old bow
of Odysseus, in addition to many other things (φ 6, 46).
Penelope takes in her strong hand the well-bent key of bronze,
which had an ivory handle ; she unties the strap from the
hook (see above) which had been used to close the door ; she
pushes back the bolts of the door ; as she pressed forward, the
door roared like a bull feeding in the pasture, and the door
opened quickly. This noise, compared to the roaring of a

[1] σταθμῷ κυπαρισσίνῳ, ρ 340. The lintel is ὑπερθύριον, η 90.

[2] See Schliemann's *Tiryns*, 281. For the like arrangement in Crete, see *Annual
of British School*, ix. 290 ; and on Carpathus, *l.c.* 184. Diels, *Parmenides*, 121.

[3] For the Homeric bolts and locks, see Diels, *Parmenides*, 117 ; and for primitive
wooden locks on Carpathus, see Dawkins in *Annual of British School*, ix. 190.

bull, has generally been explained as the door on its hinges grating "harsh thunder," or grating not merely on its hinges but particularly on the threshold ; but Diels holds it to be the noise of the key pushing against the heavy bolts. Whether the bolt was double or single cannot be determined. The best suggested explanation of the knot of the strap of Penelope's lock, since no one was to be fastened within the chamber, is that this served as a seal ; if the knot was cunningly tied,[1] Penelope could be sure that no servant had unlocked the door in her absence ;

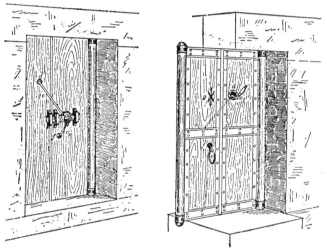

FIGS. 12 and 13.—Door with lock.

the key was too heavy to hang regularly at her girdle. Seals are not mentioned by the poet.[2]

Whether *portières* or curtains were used at the doors of Homeric houses, as is common in the East, as has been conjectured for Tiryns, and as was true at the palace of Menelaus, according to Aeschylus (*Ag.* 691), is uncertain.

---

[1] Odysseus, at the suggestion of the queen, ties about his chest of presents from the Phaeacians (θ 447) a cord in a knot which Circe had taught him, which can be intended only to assure him that the chest had not been opened,—serving as a sealing.

[2] Figures 12 and 13, borrowed from Diels, show the door from the inside and out-side respectively. *a* is a knob on the bolt, against which the key strikes in order to push the bolt back ; *b* is the bolt ; *c* is the strap, by pulling which the bolt may be shot from without ; *d* is the keyhole ; *e* is the key ; *f* is the hole for the strap ; *g* is the hook or κορώνη, by which the door was closed from without.

No such curtain is mentioned by the poet, and with wood casings and sills, the door might have hung from these.

That the great hall or *megaron* is the "living room" of the household, has already been stated.   Indeed, in the Homeric city at Hissarlik no enclosed rooms *Great Hall as Sleeping Room.* existed behind and beside this.   The Homeric poems often seem to reflect the conception of such a simple structure.   For example, the great hall seems at night to be the sleeping apartment of the lord and lady.   Modern notions of the necessity of privacy did not prevail.   At the close of the first book of the *Iliad*, the other gods go to their dwellings, but Zeus to his bed (A 609),— apparently in his great hall.[1]   Similarly, Nestor, Menelaus, and Alcinoüs seem to sleep in their great halls.   This explains why Nestor's bed is not prepared until he is ready to enter it, when his wife prepares it for him (γ 403); it might not stand ready all day in the great hall.   Obviously, Achilles and Briseïs slept in one corner of the big room which in his barrack corresponded to the *megaron* of a palace, and Patroclus with his mate in another corner (I 663, Ω 675). This custom suggests a sufficient reason also for the practice of guests sleeping in the porch.   If the *megaron* was unoccupied, why should not the guests have slept in it, especially on a cold night?   But the Homeric house has no guest-room, and at the homes of Nestor and of Menelaus, Telemachus, though an honored guest, sleeps in the porch (γ 399, δ 302), as did Odysseus in the palace of Alcinoüs (η 336), and Priam

---

[1] See Noack, *Homerische Paläste*.   Hera has a room of her own only at Ξ 166. Noack thinks that Paris has no *megaron* apart from the θάλαμος of Z 321, where the Trojan sits and polishes his armor, while Helen and the maids there spin and weave. Thus θάλαμον καὶ δῶμα καὶ αὐλήν, Z 316, would be equivalent to μέγαρον καὶ δῶμα καὶ αὐλήν of χ 494.   If the house had a *megaron*, we should expect to find the maids there, and not in the θάλαμος, or if the θάλαμος was set apart for women, then Hector might not have entered it so freely.   At Γ 125, Helen is weaving in her *megaron*, but being summoned to the Great Tower of Ilium, she sets out from her θάλαμος, Γ 142. But she may have gone to the θάλαμος in order to put on her sandals and her wrap. At the time of Hector's death, Andromache is weaving "in the recess of the high dwelling" (μυχῷ δόμου ὑψηλοῖο, X 440)—the very expression which is used for the place of the beds of Nestor (γ 402), of Menelaus (δ 304), and of Alcinoüs (η 346, *cf*. Ω 675, ε 226),—but hearing the shrieks from the city wall, she rushes through her *megaron*.   The μυχὸς δόμου, in Noack's view, was not the rear of the house, but the back part of a room.

at the tent of Achilles (Ω 644),—in spite of the cold weather (see note on page 180). Only in the last passage is any explanation thought necessary for the choice of place. The unmarried sons of the household, after emerging from childhood, seem also to have slept in the porch (γ 400), while the married sons naturally had · their own rooms (γ 396, Ζ 244). Telemachus, indeed, has a chamber of his own (α 425), but he is the only son, and his case seems exceptional. That Penelope, in her husband's absence, does not sleep in the great hall should not cause surprise.

Although the *megaron* may serve as the bedroom of Nestor and other princes, yet separate bed-chambers are known. Thus on the visit of Telemachus, Helen comes into the great hall from her chamber (δ 121, *cf.* *Separate Bed-rooms.* τ 53). The most noted bed-chamber of the poems, however, is that of Odysseus and Penelope (ψ 192),—very likely, as has been seen, an addition to the original plan of the house,—which the Ithacan had built around a wild olive tree, using the stump of this tree as a bed-post. Why Penelope should not occupy this room during her husband's absence, is not clear; it cannot have been from loneliness, for as two maids sleep on either side of Nausicaa's door (ζ 18), so Penelope might have had such attendants near her.

The only indication as to the women's quarters is from the house of Odysseus, where they seem to be at the rear of the main hall, and directly connected with this by a door. Nothing is known of the size, lighting, *Women's Quarters.* and heating of this room. Probably it had a hearth, like the *megaron*, and the serving women slept on the floor about the fire, like Laërtes's servants, the family of Dolius (λ 190), and the swine-herd and his comrades (ξ 518); that they had a separate sleeping-room is very unlikely. That the entrance to the women's quarters was from the courtyard, opposite the great hall, according to a recent theory,[1] seems impossible. This theory gives to the women an independent structure, for which the evidence is insufficient, with quite as great publicity as the *megaron* of the men, while the author of it holds that the women were very strictly secluded. For such an arrangement no support appears to be found

[1] See Myres in *J.H.S.* xx. 132.

in the ruins of either earlier or later times.[1]   A less objectionable view gives to the women's apartment an opening on the main court, but at the side of the men's hall,—not unlike the palace at Tiryns.

Behind the women's apartment, and accessible from the narrow side-passage, the *laura*, was the store-room of Odysseus,

Store-rooms in the Rear.

in which were placed the arms which had been conveyed away from the great hall, in order that they might not be accessible to Penelope's suitors (τ 3, χ 143).   In this room was a single column or pillar (χ 176), doubtless in the middle of the room for the support of the roof.[2]   Two other store-rooms are mentioned at the home of Odysseus,—one at the extreme rear, where bronze, gold, and iron are kept (φ 9), and another in which wine and oil were stored, as well as raiment, gold, and silver, and in which Euryclea was continually on guard (β 337).[3]   Menelaus and Helen go to a chamber to fetch a gift for Telemachus (o 99) ; the Phaeacian queen Arete brings a chest from her *thalamos* (θ 439), to hold the presents intended for Odysseus ; Hecuba and Priam go to their chamber for gifts to offer to the goddess Athena (Z 288), and as a ransom for the body of Hector (Ω 191).   This chamber of Priam was finished in cedar-wood, which indicates that the dislike of moths for the odor of cedar was already known.   The store-room of Penelope seems to have had a raised platform (σανίς, φ 51), doubtless designed to keep the iron and the raiment from the dampness of the ground.   Clothes were kept in chests (χηλοί, β 339 ; φωριαμοί, Ω 228) ; wine was stored in large earthen jars (πίθοι, β 340), and was transported either in smaller jars (ἀμφιφορῆες, β 349, ι 164) or in leathern bottles (ἀσκός, ι 196, ζ 78, Γ 247).   Wooden casks or barrels were unknown.   Leathern sacks were used also for the transportation of meal (β 354, ι 213), but grain as well as wine, doubtless, was stored in great earthen jars.[4]

[1] The inference drawn from the remains at Mycenae, is too weak to be called evidence.

[2] Unless this κίων is *a* column, and not *the* column of the room.

[3] Perhaps these two are but one, and the query is raised whether this was not the bedchamber of Odysseus, unused during his absence.

[4] Great jars actually filled with grain were found at Hissarlik, and at Cnosus magazines were found with jars standing in rows, in Homeric fashion.

An upper room (ὑπερώιον, δ 787) is mentioned in the *Odyssey* only for the house of Odysseus, but in it Penelope seems to spend much of her time ; in the *Iliad* it is named twice as the bedroom of young maidens, —of whom one there bears sons to the god Ares

Upper Room (Hyperoön).

(B 513), while another is there visited by the god Hermes (Π 184). Since the palace at Cnosus is found to have had three or four storeys, no prejudice can be felt against the existence of such a room on Ithaca. Clearly, however, this upper apartment cannot have lain immediately over the whole of the main hall or *megaron*, for this would have prevented the entrance of light from above to the *megaron*, as well as the exit of smoke ; but the rooms on either side of the great hall may not have been so high as this, and the *hyperoön* may have lain above the great hall, and yet not have extended over its entire length and breadth. Since the roof of the ordinary Homeric dwelling was flat, or nearly flat, a shelter over this, or over part of this, would form a *loggia*, which would easily develop into a room. One of the comrades of Odysseus, somewhat under the influence of wine, is sleeping on the roof of Circe's dwelling (κ 554) when he hears the noise of his friends' preparations for departure, and, forgetting to go to the staircase, he falls off the roof and breaks his neck. The Ithacan *hyperoön* was reached by a staircase, which apparently was within the house ; it was in no sense a public room, and the maids seem to be there only as attendants of Penelope. From her upper room Penelope hears the song of the bard in the great hall (α 328), and descends the lofty staircase to beg him to choose some other theme than the sad return of the Achaeans from the Trojan expedition. Conversely, the disguised Odysseus, waking early on the morning of the day in which he slays Penelope's suitors, from his sleeping-place in the porch hears his wife's cry of lament over her lot (υ 92),—which proves that her upper room, her *hyperoön*, must have been near the court. Once (ο 517), Penelope is said to be weaving in the upper room, but no ground exists for the supposition that she there wove and unravelled her famous web. She wove this by day in the great hall, and was seen at work,—she unravelled it by night, by torch-light, naturally after callers had departed.

The suitors were not importunate at that time, but when they
virtually took possession of the great hall, then the loom was
removed to the upper room. Only once (δ 787, 802) is this
room represented as a bed-chamber, with closed door. The
standing epithet of the room is *gleaming* (σιγαλόεντα, σ 206),
which may refer to a coating of stucco on the walls.[1]

Every well-appointed Homeric dwelling seems to have had
a bath-room. Baths are offered or taken at the homes of

Bath-room.   Odysseus (α 310), Nestor (γ 464), Menelaus (δ 48),
Alcinoüs (θ 456), Circe (κ 451), and Helen in
Troy (δ 252). Not in every case does a bath imply a bath-
room, however, for Laërtes has a tub in his very primitive
quarters (ω 370), where he slept in winter on the ground near
the fire ; and in the Achaean camp before Troy, Diomed and
Odysseus, after their expedition within the Trojan line, first
bathe in the sea and then enter their bath-tubs (ἔς ῥ' ἀσαμίνθους
βάντες, Κ 576), for which they would hardly have a special
room. No hint is given by the poet of the situation of the
bath-room, except that the princess Nausicaa waits to speak
to Odysseus by the door of the great hall, as he is on his way
from the bath to the *megaron* (θ 456). Thus there seems
to have been no direct opening from the bath to the hall.
The remains of a bath-room were uncovered in the excavations
at Tiryns,[2] with a floor consisting of a single great stone slab,
about nine feet broad by twelve feet long, with a gentle slope
toward one corner, where was an opening into a drain. A
piece of a large terra-cotta bath-tub was found also. Several
ancient bath-tubs have been found in the excavations in
Crete. Our poet says that Menelaus received two silver
bath-tubs as a present from the Egyptian king (δ 128), but
such were not likely to be common. The epithet *well-polished*
(ἐυξέστας, δ 48, ρ 87) is applied not only to the tubs in the
palace of Menelaus but also to those in the home of Odysseus,
and implies a tub of metal or stone rather than of terra-cotta ;
a wooden tub is improbable since the art of the cooper had
not been perfected,—jars, as has been seen, taking the place
of barrels. Not all tubs were of a man's length, as is seen

[1] This upper room appears chiefly in formulaic verses,—Penelope goes thither to
weep, to pray, and the like.

[2] Schliemann, *Tiryns*, 229.

from the account of the bath at Circe's palace, where Odysseus was seated in a tub,[1] and warm water was poured over his head and shoulders. The bath was generally prepared by maid-servants, but Nestor's daughter "bathes" Telemachus (γ 464), and Helén in her Trojan home renders the same service to Odysseus, who had entered the city as a spy (δ 252), as Hebe bathes Ares (E 905) (see page 136. One of Penelope's suitors, hurling an ox's hoof at the disguised Odysseus, says mockingly that this may be used as a gift to the bath-maid (λοετροχόῳ, υ 297), or some other of the servants. A basin was used for the washing of feet, and the bathing of the feet of the disguised Odysseus by his old nurse, affords the opportunity for her recognition of her master by an old scar (τ 386),—but this foot-bath was given in the great hall, where Penelope was sitting by the fire. The foot-bath was naturally more important when sandals were worn out of the house, rather than boots or shoes, and were often if not regularly removed on entering the house. After the bath, the use of ointment is so regular as to seem quite essential. Even when Nausicaa goes to the shore to lave the linen, her mother gives to her oil in a golden flask, that she and her maids may anoint themselves after their bath in the river (ζ 79). Nothing is said about morning ablutions with a wash-bowl ; ablutions are mentioned only as made before eating or after a journey.[2] The use of soap, or fuller's earth, is not mentioned. The bodies of the dead are bathed and anointed before incineration (ω 45, Σ 350).

The furniture of the Homeric house was simple, and consisted of little more than chairs, small tables, and beds. It included no book-cases or library tables, no mirrors, wardrobes, bureaus, or washstands, no sideboards nor large dining tables. Clothes when out of use were kept in chests ; Telemachus's tunic, when

Furniture Simple.

---

[1] ἔs ῥ' ἀσάμινθον ἕσασα, κ 361.

[2] Hesiod is emphatic in his requirement of ablutions (*Works and Days*, 724) before the morning prayer to Zeus, but he seems to think the custom of bathing effeminate (*l.c.* 753). Latrines with intricate drain-system and pipes to supply water for flushing have been found at Cnosus, but are not mentioned in Homer, unless the rotunda (θόλος, χ 442 ; see page 184) in the court served this purpose. The poet nowhere mentions either of the two chief natural human excretions.

For the bath, water is warmed in a kettle (X 443, Σ 346).

he goes to bed, is hung on a peg near him (α 440). The ordinary room in Modern Greece, away from the large towns, is still generally almost empty except for a divan, and the rug which is to serve as seats for the guests, with the low table at which they are to dine, may be brought into the room after their arrival. The only movable decorations of the walls in the Homeric times were shields and helmets. The chairs, for the most part stationary, stood by the wall of the great hall,—often set in pairs,[1] so that two guests might use the same table. The tables were light, and were drawn beside the chairs before each meal (α 138, δ 54, η 174); "the table still stood beside Achilles," as he was concluding his evening meal (Ω 476),

FIG. 14.—Throne of Olympian Zeus.

when Priam entered the room, and this is equivalent to the modern expression, "he was still sitting at the table." The *thrones* (θρόνοι, α 130) were seats of honor, —tall (θ 422) and heavy, probably provided with arms as in later times and with footstools attached (see Fig. 14). As has already been suggested, the footstools were important because the floor had no covering, and often, as on Ithaca, was only hardened earth, while sandals or shoes of any kind were not worn in the house (α 96). Other chairs are mentioned which seem to have been more easily moved, and not less comfortable, but less stately.[2] The easy-chairs of the gods were adorned with thin plates of gold (Θ 436), and that of Telemachus also was richly ornamented ; others were adorned with silver nails or studs (η 162), or were inlaid with silver and ivory (τ 55). These chairs were of wood, and not upholstered, but a linen cloth or a woolen rug or a sheep's fleece was spread over them just before they were to be used ;[3] at the palace of Circe, a linen cloth was thrown over the chair first, and over this

Chairs and Footstools.

---

[1] α 130 f., δ 54; Athenaeus, i. 11 F.

[2] κλισμός, α 132; κλισίη, δ 123, τ 55. At σ 190 Penelope has a nap in a κλιντήρ, which obviously is from the same verb-stem.

[3] λῖτα, α 130; πέπλοι, η 96; τάπητες, υ 150, I 200; δ 124; ῥήγεα, λῖτα, κ 352; κώεα, ρ 32, φ 177.

a woolen rug was laid.   A light stool without back or arms is used as a seat by Helen (Γ 424), and as an easily moved chair in the home of Odysseus (τ 97, υ 259, φ 177). In addition to the footstools attached to the thrones (θρῆνυς, τ 57), others stood free, probably for use with the easy-chairs.[1]   One of these is hurled by a suitor of Penelope at the head of the disguised Odysseus.   In the courtyard were stone benches near the front door, as has been seen (γ 406), but the ordinary seats of Penelope's suitors in the courtyard were the raw hides of the cattle on which they had feasted (a 108, cf. γ 38).

The Homeric tables were small,—large tables being required by no element of their life, neither for reading and writing, nor for books and bric-a-brac.   That the ordinary small table or stand had four legs or feet, is *Tables.* indicated by its name;[2] other stands were three-legged and called *tripods*.   When Thetis visits Hephaestus, to engage him to make arms for her son (Σ 369), the god is engaged in making tripods or small tables, placing wheels or castors under each that they "of their own accord," *i.e.* as *automata*, might go to the assembly of the gods, when they were needed there for any special gathering, and then return to his home.   Hephaestus attaches "ears" to these tables, evidently to serve as handles for convenient transportation, corresponding to the rings seen in representations of later tripods; these were not needed for his automata, but were part of the Homeric conception of a light table.[3]   But when Telemachus had set his seat by that of Athena, a housemaid drew (ἐτάνυσσε, a 138) a table beside them.   The light weight of the tables is indicated by their use as shields by Penelope's suitors when attacked by Odysseus (χ 74), and by their overturning readily when struck by a falling man (χ 19).   The table in Nestor's tent has dark feet

---

[1] σφέλας, ρ 231, σ 394.   The θρῆνυς of ρ 409, also, is attached to no seat.

[2] τράπεζα being for τετρά-πεζα.   Cf. τρυφάλεια, as Γ 376, for the helmet with four φάλοι (cf. Γ 362).

[3] To suppose that these *tripods* were kettles or trivets, is quite impossible.   The poet says that these were to stand "about the wall" of the great hall, *i.e.* along the wall about the room, by the chairs.   The simple fact of their being set on castors should refute the supposition that they might be kettles.

(Λ 629),—probably stained. Table-cloths and napkins were unknown.

To the bed of Paris, the epithet *well-turned* or *rounded* (δινωτός, Γ 391) is applied, as well as to the easy-chair of Penelope and the shield of Idomeneus (τ 56, N 407),—not implying the use of a lathe, but ornamentation.

Beds.

The bed of Odysseus is the most noted in the poems : as has been seen already, the trunk of an olive-tree, which grew in the space enclosed for the chamber, served as one bed-post, on being properly trimmed and cut (ψ 190). Straps (ψ 201) ran from end to end and from side to side of the bedstead, serving as supports for the rugs which were the equivalent of the modern mattress, and affording a slight amount of elasticity.[1] The holes made for the passage of the straps in the bars at the ends and sides of the bed, gave rise to the epithet *perforated*,[2] which is applied to the bedstead six times. Not all bedsteads were stationary, like that of Odysseus, for Achilles bids his maids to place in the porch bedsteads for the sleep of Priam and his herald (Ω 644 = δ 297), which assumes that the beds did not always stand there. The bed of Hephaestus seems to have had tall posts, for he hung about these a cunningly contrived invisible net like a spider's web, dependent from the ceiling (θ 278), as a snare for Aphrodite and Ares, but the poet knows of no bed-curtains or nettings. Above the straps which served as a support for the bedding and the sleeper, were spread sheep's fleeces, rugs, coverlets, and blankets.[3] Of course, nothing like the modern sheet was to be expected. No pillows were used, though Diomed has a rug under his head, and his comrades use their shields thus (Κ 152). The Homeric Greeks had no special night-gear, and doubtless the garment which served as a cloak or mantle by day, was generally used at night as a blanket or coverlet.

At night the Homeric Greeks went to bed early. Thus

---

[1] Ropes, "bed-cords," were thus used on American beds until comparatively recent years.—The use of straps for the chariot-board on which the driver stood (*cf.* εὔπλεκτος, Ψ 335), seems to rest on this quality of elasticity.

[2] τρητός, Γ 448, α 440, γ 399, η 345, κ 12, Ω 720. *Cf.* τέτρηνα τερέτρῳ, ψ 198.

[3] οἰὸς ἀώτῳ, α 443 ; ῥήγεα πορφύρεα, ἐφύπερθε τάπητας, χλαίνας οὔλας, Ω 644.

at the close of the Pylian festival, the remark is made that the sun has gone down, and it is time to return to their homes and go to bed (γ 329); and "when the bright light of the sun set," even the feast of the gods is brought to an end, and each divinity departs to his home (A 605). But the company did not always break up at sun-down. Odysseus comes to the palace of Alcinoüs in the early evening, just as the guests were about to depart (ζ 321, η 137), but finds the great hall bright not only with the light of the fire on the central hearth but also from the blaze of torches, held by golden torch-holders in the forms of youths (ζ 305, η 100). On the next night, the Phaeacians sit late in the hall, listening to the apologue of Odysseus (ι-μ, cf. λ 330),—and ready to listen all night long. Penelope's suitors generally left her home at night-fall (cf. α 423), but at times they remained later. On the night before their slaughter by Odysseus, they thus remained, and the hall was lighted by three *lampters*,[1]—probably braziers on stands, in which dry and small wood was heaped. These required constant tending which was done by the maids, until the disguised Odysseus undertook to do this work. On the departure of the suitors on this evening, when Penelope comes into the hall, the maids throw down upon the ground the fire from the basins and make a fresh blaze (τ 63). These small fires on a cold evening gave the cheer of warmth as well as light (τ 64); that they were sometimes used for cooking, is not stated by the poet, but is altogether probable. In the story of Penelope's web, the poet says that she wove by day, but unravelled her web at night by the light of torches (β 105). In the excavations in Crete several stone lamp-stands have been found about thirty inches in height.[2] Torches were used to conduct Telemachus to his chamber (α 434, τ 48), and by servants in preparing the bed for a guest (δ 300, ψ 290, Ω 647). Oil does not seem to have been used for illumination,

Evening in the Great Hall.

---

[1] $\lambda\alpha\mu\pi\tau\hat{\eta}\rho\alpha\varsigma$, . . . $\pi\epsilon\rho\grave{\iota}$ $\delta\grave{\epsilon}$ $\xi\acute{\upsilon}\lambda\alpha$ . . . $\theta\hat{\eta}\kappa\alpha\nu$ . . . $\kappa\alpha\grave{\iota}$ $\delta\alpha\acute{\iota}\delta\alpha\varsigma$, σ 307.

[2] One of these of lilac gypsum, found on the steps of the tribune in the Royal Villa at Cnosus, is represented in the *Annual of the British School at Athens*, ix. Fig. 89, and part of a pedestal of a similar but more highly ornamented lamp-stand in Fig. 3 of the same volume. Similar stands are said to have been found at Mycenae.

although lamps were used in Crete long before the Homeric time. Since matches had not been invented, nor even the use of flint and steel, fire of course had to be carefully kept, and the poet compares the ship-wrecked Odysseus, reaching land and lying down to sleep covered well with leaves, to coals preserved in the ashes, on a remote farm which has no neighbors near at hand to give fire (ε 488). Wood was still abundant in Homer's time. Shepherds have fires on the mountains (T 376, cf. κ 30), and fire-brands are used to frighten lions and keep them from farmyards (Λ 554 = P 663). Even Polyphemus has a fire (ι 251), though he does not seem to use it for cooking. No means of striking fire are mentioned.

The "divine swine-herd" Eumaeus seems to have absolutely no furniture in his hut. He has no chairs nor tables nor *The Swine-herd's Furniture.* beds nor bedding, and no dishes but a wooden bowl (ξ 78, π 52) and a smaller bowl or cup (σκύφος, ξ 112). His guests sit on a pile of rushes, which is covered for the occasion by a sheepskin or a goatskin (ξ 49, π 47), and he kills a five-year-old hog for supper by a blow with a billet of wood,—and actually in his hut. He must have had an axe for chopping wood (ξ 425), a knife to cut the animal's throat (ξ 426), and spits for roasting the flesh (ξ 430), in addition to his sword (ξ 528). A goatskin serves him as special protection against cold and rain. His hand-mill for grinding grain may have been very primitive, but doubtless furnished the barleymeal with which he dredges his roast-pork (ξ 429). That Polyphemus sleeps on rushes indicates for him no ruder life than the old Laërtes had on his farm, where he slept on the ground near the fire.

That the Homeric house had no kitchen, has been stated already, and that the responsibility for cooking did not rest solely *Kitchen and Table Furniture.* upon the woman. The next chapter, on Homeric viands, shows that little kitchen furniture is necessary, and naturally this is not made prominent in the poems. Rolling pins, chopping knives, and egg-beaters did not exist, but even if these articles had been familiar to him, the poet might not have named them. The hand-mill, consisting of one stone fitted in a way to another beneath it, and perhaps equipped with a handle to facilitate turning, and a mortar and pestle, for the grinding and bruising of grain, may be assumed as present in every household. The roasting of meat required only spits (ὀβελοί) and fire-dogs (κρατευταί, I 214), and the fire-dogs may often have been mere stones on which the end of the spits could rest. A kettle (λέβης, Φ 362 ; cf. μ 237) is named but once,—as used for trying lard. The same name is applied to basins (as α 137), and not always can the two be distinguished,—e.g. not when they are offered as prizes for the games (Ψ 267, 885 ; cf. T 244). Some kettles seem to have three legs and to be called tripods (Σ 344, X 443, θ 435),—thus having the same name as the small tables. Even Polyphemus had vessels which served as pails and pans for his milk (γαυλοί τε σκαφίδες τε, ι 223), wicker crates for his cheese (τάλαροι, ι 247), and a large wooden bowl (κισσύβιον, ι 346). Nestor and Achilles have golden goblets (δέπας, Λ 632, II 225), and the returning Odysseus, though in the guise of a beggar, is served by Telemachus with wine in a golden cup (υ 261). The ordinary cups of the household, however (we may be sure although no word of the poems indicates it), were of earthenware. A large bowl for the mixing of wine with water was one of the most important articles in a luxurious family ; Menelaus gives Telemachus a solid silver mixing-bowl (κρητήρ, ο 115) with gold-plated edges. A silver bowl, with golden cups, was used also at the home of Circe (κ 356). A golden ewer (πρόχοος, α 136) is used by the maid in pouring water on the hands of Telemachus's guest, and a smaller one in dipping the wine from the mixing bowl (σ 397). Spoons are not known, and forks had not been invented. Plates seem not to have been used, but bread was served in baskets, which at Circe's home were of gold and at the tent of Nestor were of bronze (κάνεια, υ 255, κ 355, Λ 630). A meat-tray (κρείον, I 206), probably of wood, was used for the carving of the flesh before it was roasted, and a dresser (ἐλεός, I 215) received the roasted meat from the spits.

CHAPTER VII

HOMERIC FOOD

THE Homeric Greeks, like ourselves, seem to have desired and expected three meals a day,—breakfast, dinner, and supper,[1]—but little regularity was observed. Not infrequently one of the three seems to be omitted. Breakfast is named but twice,—once in the hut of the swine-herd Eumaeus on Ithaca, and once in the tent of Achilles on the plain of Troy. Doubtless it was an informal repast,—as it was in Athens during the historical period, and as it is generally on the continent of Europe at present,—and not an occasion for a family gathering. The Greek countryman of this century does not understand the American's requirement of substantial food before the day's expedition is begun. But at the palace of Menelaus when, early in the morning of the last day of his visit, Telemachus announced his intention to depart for home, the Spartan king asked his neighbor Prince Eteoneus, who happened along (ο 95), to kindle a fire and roast some meat for them. Clearly no definite arrangement had been made for a breakfast for the household. Similarly at the beginning of the second day of the action of the *Odyssey*, Telemachus rises from his couch, dresses, and proceeds to the place of assembly, without any apparent thought of breakfast ; and at the beginning of the day on which Penelope's suitors are slain, a fire is kindled on the hearth it is true, but Telemachus goes to the place of assembly without taking food, and nothing is done in the way of preparation of food until the swine-herd has brought three

Three Meals a Day.

---

[1] ἄριστον, π 2, Ω 124 ; δεῖπνον, Β 381, α 134 ; δόρπον, β 20, H 370.

hogs from his rather distant enclosure, the goat-herd has brought goats, and even the neat-herd has brought a cow and goats across the water from the mainland (v 123, 162, 250).

The dinner is the principal meal of the day, whenever it is taken. It is generally eaten about noon (δεῖπνον, Λ 86),—but no respite could be had from the battle for rest and refreshment when the sun reached the zenith, and on a journey the noon-hour might find the traveller far from hospitable homes. So, on the one hand, the Greeks take "dinner" in the morning before going out to battle,[1] and again Telemachus has dinner at Sparta (δ 61) in the evening, after a long day's drive.

Dinner (Deipnon).

At their feasts, the Homeric Greeks did not recline like the later Athenians and the Romans, but sat, and their chairs were not drawn up before and about a large table in the middle of the room, but were ranged in a single row along the walls of the great hall, with small tables placed beside them (α 138),—in general one small table serving for two guests.[2] The tables were removed at the close of the repast (Ω 476), instead of the guests rising from the table. These tables were not covered with cloths, but as a rule were of polished wood and themselves served as plates, and therefore were carefully wiped with sponges just before each meal (α 111). The guest was provided with no napkin, fork, nor spoon,—nor had he a knife except what he might carry at his own belt;—and so, as his fingers were to serve as fork, water was poured upon his hands immediately before each meal (α 136,

No Plates.

---

[1] As B 381, 399, Θ 53. So Polyphemus "dines" before going out for his day in the pasture, ι 311. At ο 500, the companions of Telemachus, returning from their voyage to Pylus, reach Ithaca and prepare a δεῖπνον,—a "square meal,"—apparently at the very time when Eumaeus and Odysseus were making ready their ἄριστον, π 2.

[2] The Cretans and northern Greeks sat at dinner also in later times, and the guests sat at some of the banquets of Alexander the Great; cf. Xen. An. vii. 3. 22, where Seuthes, too, seems to use no platters. When Orestes came to Athens after slaying Clytaemestra, each guest sat at a separate table (Eur. Iph. Taur. 949), and the same custom is assumed by the story of Thyestes feasted by Atreus on his children's flesh (Aesch. Ag. 1595).

δ 213, I 171), even though he had just taken a bath (as δ 52).[1] The table bore no plate nor other dish, except a cup for wine and a basket or basket-like dish for bread.[2] At times, doubtless, the bread (and perhaps an onion for relish,—Λ 630), as well as the meat, was laid directly on the table. The guests do not seem to have been finical or squeamish about the use of fingers and hands instead of forks and dishes.[3] Platters were not in ordinary use, if, indeed, they were known at all.[4] Menelaus takes up with his fingers the piece of roast meat which had been given to him as the " piece of honor," and places it on the table of his guests Telemachus and Pisistratus (δ 65), for their delectation ; and Odysseus puts into the hands of the Phaeacian herald a fine fat dripping piece of pork to give to the bard Demodocus (θ 476), as a token of appreciation of his lay. At his own home, Telemachus calls to him the swine-herd Eumaeus, and gives to him as much bread and meat as his hands can hold, to convey to the disguised Odysseus, who receives it with both hands (ρ 344, 356) and lays it on the threshold beside him. This is not merely

[1] This custom is familiar from that of the Jews. *Cf.* " Here is Elisha, the son of Shaphat, which *poured water on the hands* of Elijah " (*i.e.* was his attendant), 2 *Kings* iii. 11 ; " For the Pharisees and all the Jews, except they wash their hands oft, eat not, holding the tradition of the elders," *Mark* vii. 3.—No towel or wiping of hands is mentioned by Homer,—nor handkerchief.

[2] The evidence for the absence of plates is from the nature of the case only negative, but it seems entirely sufficient. The only indication of the use of plates has been found in the expression κρειῶν πίνακες, α 141, which has been translated *plates of meat*, but which seems to mean *slices of flesh*. At υ 151, the maids are bidden to wipe off the tables, and wash the cups and bowls,—but no plates. After supper, the maids removed the remains of the food, and the tables and the cups (τ 61),—but no plates. The suitor Eurymachus, when shot by Odysseus, falls over his table and throws the viands and his cup to the floor (χ 85; *cf.* 20),—but no plate. Observe also the argument from the instances which follow in the text.

[3] *Cf.* from Lane's *Modern Egyptians*: "Neither knives nor forks are used. . . . To pick out a delicate morsel and hand it to a friend, is esteemed polite. The manner of eating with the fingers . . . is more delicate than may be imagined by Europeans who have not witnessed it. Every person before he sits down to the table . . . washes his hands . . . or at least has some water poured upon his right hand, . . . a servant brings to him a basin and ewer of tinned copper or of brass."

[4] The ἐλεός of I 215, ξ 432 seems to be a dresser or serving-table.—Aristophanes of Byzantium said that the Homeric Greeks had no platters, but he was "corrected" by Athenaeus (228 D).

treating Odysseus informally, as a beggar, since a little later (σ 121), one of the suitors gives him a golden cup of wine.

Athenaeus (8 F) calls attention to the fact that all men in the Homeric halls share in the same feast,—beggar, swine-herd, goat-herd, neat-herd, and princes. The king's table is spread for all his retainers as well as his subjects of higher rank. All have the same "bill of fare," though the places of honor and the choice pieces of meat are reserved for the most distinguished guests,[1] and indications appear that the common man might be restricted in his supply of wine (Δ 262). No indication is given that one part of the great hall is considered more honorable than another. The hall has no dais, nor a long table at which some might sit "above the salt."

All Share in the Feast.

To some feasts, each guest brought his share of food ($\xi\rho\alpha\nu\sigma$, α 226). The principle was that of the American picnic, but the result was different, not only because these common feasts were held in halls or courtyards, but particularly because of the absence of the feminine element. The poet tells of such a feast at the palace of Menelaus (δ 621-624):[2] some brought sheep and others wine, while their wives sent bread for them. Such may have been the feast to which Andromache imagines the orphaned Astyanax as going (X 492), but as driven away on the ground that he had no rights there, by a boy whose father was at the feast.

Eranos (Picnic?)

Maids in general served as waitresses (α 139, 147, δ 55), but pages assisted at the home of Odysseus (o 331),— apparently free-born youths whom Penelope's suitors had brought with them,—and the herald, who saw to the mixing of the wine, may have had a general oversight of their services. On the last day of the feasting of these suitors, the neat-herd served the bread,

Waiters.

---

[1] H 321, Θ 162, M 311, δ 65, ξ 437. The Celts, too, honored their brave warriors by the best portions of meat (Diod. Sic. v. 28). *Cf.* Plato, *Republic*, 468 D.

[2] These four verses seem not to have been in the edition of Zenodotus and are bracketed in many modern editions. They may be based on an early form of the common feasts of the Spartans.

and the goat-herd acted as cup-bearer (υ 254), so no fixed arrangement need be assumed. At the palace of Menelaus, his son poured the wine (ο 141).

No garlands were worn by the feasters, as was customary in later times in Greece,—flowers were not used then for
Music.					decorations,—but Demodocus or some other bard furnished music, singing to his lyre of the capture of Troy, or the quarrel between Achilles and Odysseus, or the sad return of the Achaeans from Troy, or of other "glorious deeds of men,"[1] and the feast often was followed by the dance. The sound of the lyre or phorminx reaches the ears of Odysseus as he approaches his home after his long absence,[2]—this meant that Penelope's suitors were feasting and making merry. The poet declares song and dance to be the natural accompaniments of a feast (α 152),—this dance naturally being of the men by themselves. After the slaughter of the suitors, Odysseus bids the bard to take his lyre and "lead the playful dance" (ψ 134), in order that any neighbor or passer-by might assume festal joy in the palace. The reader will remember that after the Prodigal's return, the elder brother heard "music and dancing" (*St. Luke* xv. 25), as he approached his home.

The feasts were generally held by day. At Pylus the men are busy with the roasting of meat when the sun
Feasts held by Day.				rises, and at the close of the day the fictitious Mentes reminds Nestor that the sun has gone down, and it is time for them to go home and to bed (γ 332). So at the close of the first book of the *Iliad* (A 605), when the sun sets, even the gods depart for their homes, to go to rest. Women were not present as guests at the feasts,—though Helen and Arete sit with their guests in their own halls,—but fathers were accustomed to bring their boys (X 496). In accordance with Hellenic notions of hospitality, as has been seen already, the door

---

[1] κλέα ἀνδρῶν, I 189; cf. α 325, θ 73, 499.—We read of no music at the feasts of the *Iliad*, except as the youths at Chrysa sang hymns to Apollo (A 472), but the feasts on the plain of Troy were in the midst of war and confusion.

[2] ρ 261. Cf. α 152, θ 63, 499, φ 430. "The gods made the phorminx to be a companion to the feast" (δαιτὸς ἑταίρην, ρ 271).

was not shut against beggars and men of low estate. The beggar Irus came as of full right to the feasts of Penelope's suitors, and while the suitor Antinoüs rebukes Eumaeus for bringing the disguised Odysseus to Ithaca (ρ 375), he does not question his right to presence at the feast.

Feasts were held not simply at the celebration of marriages, but also at funerals.[1] Indeed the feast was the chief part of the wedding and funeral ceremonies.

Plato, in his *Republic* (404 C), calls attention to the simplicity of the diet of the Homeric warriors before Troy. These ate no boiled meats, nor sweets, nor relishes (ἡδύσματα), nor fish, though they were encamped on the shores of the "fishy Hellespont." Bread and roast beef, mutton, goat's flesh, and pork are the only dishes served in the *Iliad*, with the exception of a single onion, served as sauce for a posset (Λ 630). This is indeed a simple diet when compared with that of our own day. Of course we do not expect to find on Agamemnon's table preparations of Indian corn, Irish potatoes, or sweet potatoes, tomatoes, or turkeys, any more than tea or coffee or chocolate, —or tobacco for a last course,—but whole classes of other edibles are lacking which we are wont to regard as almost natural to civilized man, and rice, which is said to be the chief food of more than half the human race at present, is unknown to our poet.

Simplicity of Diet.

Fruits and nuts may have been eaten by Adam and Eve in the Garden of Eden, but they are not reported as abounding in the valley of the Scamander. The poet does not mention oranges, lemons, peaches, plums, cherries, quinces, strawberries, raspberries, blackberries, mulberries, nor melons (in spite of the name μῆλον),—not even medlars. What the so-called apples (μῆλα, I 542, η 120) were, is not known. They are as likely to have been crab apples as anything which we should recognize as an ordinary apple. Pomegranates are named twice in the *Odyssey* (ῥοιαί, η 115, λ 589),—in the garden of King Alcinoüs and as hanging over the head of Tantalus in Hades; figs and pear trees are mentioned in these two places, and also in the orchard of Laërtes on Ithaca (ω 246). These three fruits

Fruits and Nuts?

[1] *Cf.* δ 3, α 226, ψ 135; γ 309, Ω 665, 802.

do not appear in the poems of Hesiod any more than in the *Iliad,* and the passages of the *Odyssey* in which they are mentioned are recognized as of later composition than the bulk of the poems.

Grapes should be mentioned among Homeric fruits, although the poet does not say expressly that they were eaten. The *Grapes.* vintage scene wrought by Hephaestus on the Shield of Achilles (Σ 561) gives a good representation of what may be seen in Modern Greece in any August. The poet tells of the curing of raisins by the Phaeacians (η 123), —also like what may be seen at Corinth in August and September of any year,—and these raisins may have been as great a comfort in winter time to the Homeric Greeks as his were to Robinson Crusoe on an uninhabited island.[1] But we do not hear much of dried grapes in later Greece; Plato in his *Republic* does not mention them as among natural articles of food.

For nuts, Agamemnon was not much better off than for fruits. He had no almonds, pistachio nuts, or walnuts. Whether the Homeric *phegos* tree ($\phi\eta\gamma\acute{o}\varsigma$) bore chestnuts or edible acorns, no one dares say,—but probably the latter.

In the garden of Alcinoüs were flourishing beds of vegetables,[2] and Odysseus remarks to the old Laërtes on *Vegetables.* the care which the latter's vegetable beds (ω 247) had received, but no garden vegetables are mentioned as eaten, and no fresh or green vegetables,—such as squash, spinach, and cucumbers,[3]—are known at all, except an onion[4] in one instance as a relish for wine. The Achaeans seem to have had no "greens" or salads. Even the Hesiodic mallows are not named. Beans and chickpease ($\kappa\acute{v}\alpha\mu\omega\iota$,

---

[1] Among the presents sent by Abigail to David when he was an outcast, were "a hundred clusters of raisins" (1 *Sam.* xxv. 18).—Possibly these grapes of Alcinoüs may merely have been sunned before pressing, as seems to be intended by the direction of Hesiod, *Works,* 611 f.

[2] $\pi\rho\alpha\sigma\iota\alpha\acute{\iota}$, η 127. These may have been only *leek-beds. Cf. $\pi\rho\acute{\alpha}\sigma\sigma\nu$, leek.*

[3] Yet *cf.* the name of the town $\Sigma\iota\kappa\nu\acute{\omega}\nu$ (connected with the word for *cucumber*), B 572, Ψ 299.

[4] $\kappa\rho\acute{o}\mu\nu\sigma\nu$, Λ 630. In later times onions were disdained at symposia, as suited to the taste of sailors rather than of princes (Plut. *Symp. Quaest.* iv. 4).—Cress, mustard, "mint, anise, and cummin," lettuce, and celery, are not mentioned by the poet.

ἐρέβινθοι, N 589) are mentioned together once, in a comparison,—but dried, as is manifest from their mention in connexion with the process of winnowing. Of course these may have been first soaked and then baked, somewhat in American fashion, but more probably they were prepared for food by pounding in a mortar or grinding, *i.e.* they were treated just like grain. Then a porridge or cakes could be made of them.[1]

Of condiments, the Homeric warrior had the best,—hunger ; of artificial spices and relishes, he had few. Salt is mentioned only once in the *Iliad*, being sprinkled upon the meat which Patroclus roasted for the guests *Condiments.* of Achilles (I 214) ; but in the *Odyssey* the Ithacan hero,— apparently as an atonement to the sea-god Poseidon for the blinding of Poseidon's son Polyphemus,—is directed to take his oar and go far into the interior, where men will think his oar to be a winnowing-shovel, and " where they do not eat salt with their food " (λ 123),—which implies not only that the Homeric salt was gained from sea-water, but also that the Greek by the sea-shore was wonted to it with his food. Again in the *Odyssey*, the disguised hero charges the suitor Antinoüs with being so illiberal that he would not give even a grain of salt to a beggar (οὐδ᾽ ἅλα δοίης, ρ 455). Salt-fish (τάριχος) and salt-flesh do not seem to be Homeric, although the poet uses the verb to *pickle* in the sense of to *bury*, *i.e.* to embalm.[2] Pepper, cinnamon, nutmeg, and other spices, and vinegar, are unknown.

Honey served instead of the modern sugar.[3] Comparisons with honey are not unusual,—Nestor's voice flows like honey from his lips (A 249),—but honey itself is mentioned in connexion with food only as *Honey for Sugar.* one of the ingredients of a posset (Λ 624, κ 234, 316), and where Aphrodite is said to have brought up the daughters of Pandareüs " on cheese, honey, and wine "

[1] *Cf.* "let them give us pulse to eat," *Daniel* i. 12.

[2] ταρχύσωσι, H 85. Is this use derived from some custom of embalming, or from an observation of the preservation of the dead in prehistoric graves in Egypt by the natron of the soil ?

[3] At Callatebus in Lydia, according to Herodotus, vii. 31, men manufactured *honey* from the tamarisk and wheat, just as Vermont farmers make " maple-honey " from the sap of the maple tree.

(ν 69), which are the very ingredients of the posset. This honey, of course, was that of wild bees (ν 106). Honey is familiar in legend as the food of the infant Zeus and of others, in un-Homeric accounts, and some see another indication of its use as food, in the jars of honey placed against the bier in the funeral rites in honor of Patroclus (Ψ 170). The corpse of Achilles, too, was burned "in the raiment of the gods (*i.e.* that brought by his mother Thetis), and much oil and sweet honey" (ω 68). Some scholars, however, think that this usage was connected with some process of preserving the corpse in honey. However this may be, no one would call Homeric Greece "a land flowing with milk and honey." Confectionery, sweetmeats, and sweet cakes were unknown.

Just as honey served for sugar, olive oil might be expected to take the place of butter, as it does very largely at present in Greece and Italy. Butter, naturally, was unknown.[1] The climate of Greece is not favorable to the preservation of butter in an attractive condition, and in the classical times at Athens butter was unimportant, being used chiefly as an unguent. Olive oil and the olive berry are so necessary in Greek life to-day that scholars have been slow to recognize the fact that the Homeric poet mentions them neither as food, nor even in connexion with the preparation of food. In Homer, olive oil is always an unguent, and is generally mentioned in connexion with the bath. The princess Nausicaa takes with her a golden flask of oil when she goes to the river (ζ 79, 96), and Aphrodite at Paphos is anointed by the Graces (θ 364). The verse "but when she had bathed and anointed herself richly with oil"[2] occurs a dozen times with slight variations. The epithet *rosy* (ῥοδόεις, Ψ 186) applied to the oil with which Aphrodite anointed the body of the slain Hector, clearly refers to perfume,[3] and we may compare the attar of roses which is now prepared not far away from the Troad. As the last

Olive Oil only an Unguent.

---

[1] Herodotus (iv. 2) and Hippocrates seem to be the earliest authorities for butter.

[2] γ 466, δ 49, 252, ζ 219, θ 364, 454, κ 364, 450, ρ 88, τ 505, ψ 154, ω 366.

[3] *Cf.* ἐνῶδες ἔλαιον, β 339, *fragrant olive oil*, of the oil kept in great jars in the storeroom of the palace of Odysseus.

example shows, even dead bodies were anointed after being washed in preparation for the funeral,—very likely only because anointing was so closely associated with bathing, although the oil may have contained some antiseptic element.[1] The earliest references to the use of oil among the ancient Hebrews also seem to be to its use as an unguent, although these used it also in food and in lamps. Moses received elaborate instructions for compounding the "holy anointing oil" (*Exodus* xxx. 25), and among the gifts for which the Psalmist is grateful (*Psalms* civ. 15), are "wine that maketh glad the heart of man and oil to make his face to shine," with which may be compared "Thou anointest my head with oil, my cup runneth over" of the Twenty-third Psalm.

Pork-fat, suet (ϕ 183), marrow, and the like, served the Homeric Greeks as butter. That these, though in a warm country, did not object to animal fat, is shown by the case of Hector's child, Astyanax, who, according to his mother, had been brought up largely on "the marrow and rich fat of sheep" (X 501), with which we may compare the "fat of lambs," which is mentioned by Moses in his last song (*Deuteronomy* xxxii. 14), together with honey, milk, and butter, as among the good gifts of the Lord. The fat of the tail of the broad-tailed sheep is said to be still much prized in parts of Asia, "entering largely into the preparation of many dishes," and being more easily kept fresh and sweet, it is preferred by many to butter.

Milk does not seem a frequent article of food in the life depicted in the Homeric poems. The warriors perhaps could hardly be expected to drink largely of milk after wine had been introduced. They had passed the nomadic stage of civilization. But a large part of their wealth still consisted in flocks and herds, and what the dairyman calls "milk products" must have been more important in ordinary life than appears in the poems. We remember that the land of Canaan was characterized as a "land flowing with milk and honey,"— not as abounding in roast-beef or roast-turkey, and plum-

Milk Products.

---

[1] Σ 350, Ω 587, ω 73. The body of Sarpedon is bathed by Apollo in the river, and then anointed with ambrosia (Π 680).

pudding,—and milk, curds, and cheese are among the chief
articles of food in Modern Greece, being indefinitely more
important than flesh. But milk is mentioned only four
times in the *Iliad*, and each time in a comparison : the
number of the Achaeans opposed to the Trojans on the
plain of battle, reminds the poet of the flies which gather
about the milk-vessels on a farm in spring-time (B 471),—
which may imply that milk was not ordinarily expected
throughout the year,—the cattle not being kept fresh ; the
confused shout of the Trojans as they advance to battle,
reminds Homer of the bleating of the countless sheep
a-milking in the farmyard of a rich man (Δ 434) ; when pain-
killing herbs are sprinkled on the wound of Ares, the pain
is checked just as white milk is curdled by the sap of the
wild fig tree (E 902) ; and the Greeks gather about
Sarpedon's body as flies swarm about the milk vessels in
spring (Π 641). In the *Odyssey*, Menelaus says in praise
of the country of Libya (δ 89), that there neither master
nor man lacks cheese nor flesh nor white milk, the whole
year round, for the ewes bring forth lambs three times a
year. In the poems, however, Polyphemus alone is represented as drinking milk and making cheese. Cheese, indeed,
seems to be the chief ordinary food of the Cyclops, though
possibly he may have eaten mutton or goat's flesh when he
had no strangers to devour. Euripides in his *Cyclops* (399)
represents the monster as boiling one of the comrades of
Odysseus, and roasting another, but though the Homeric
Polyphemus has a fire, he seems to have no thought of
cookery.[1] Finally, whey is mentioned once (ρ 225), by the
insolent goat-herd Melanthius, as an article of food likely to
give a big thigh to the disguised Odysseus if the latter
would take the place of under-goatherd for his flocks,[2]—

---

[1] Some scholars indeed have supposed cooking to be included in ὡπλίσσατο
δόρπον, ι 291, but the description is detailed in other respects, and the poet would
hardly have omitted mention of the spits. Probably to him as well as to us the
scene of Polyphemus eating "like a mountain lion" was less offensive than that
of a cannibal gourmand like the Cyclops of Euripides ; and that Homer was not
seeking to paint a most harrowing picture is shown by a comparison of the ninth
book of the *Odyssey* with the corresponding passage of Vergil's *Aeneid*.

[2] The use of milk in offerings to the dead (Aesch. *Pers.* 611, Soph. *El.* 895,
Eur. *Iph. Taur.* 162 ; *cf.* λ 27) is thought to point to its early importance as
food,—if any such evidence were needed.

when obviously curds and whey would constitute most of
his food.

Only sheep's milk and goats' milk are used, except by the
Mare-milkers ('Ἱππημολγοί, N 5), whom we may suppose
to be a Scythian tribe. The Mongolian tribes
of the steppes of Central Asia still use the milk   *Cows' Milk
not Used.*
of mares,—not to mention koumiss, which has
become familiar in western countries. Cows' milk is not
mentioned by Homer. Kine are considered to belong to a
more advanced stage of pastoral life than the smaller cattle,
but they are common enough in the poems : they are eaten
freely, and they form the ordinary standard of values. In
classical times cows' milk was not considered wholesome by
many Greeks, and a generation ago only one cow was
reported to be kept for milk in all Attica. Poetic economy,
however, may have been the motive which prevented the
poet from giving kine and a dog to Polyphemus : bulls
would have been less easy for Odysseus to manage than
the rams, while the barking of the dog would have disconcerted Odysseus's best plan.

Cheese (τυρός, ι 219) was a general term which included
everything, from "bonny-clabber" or soft curds to the dry
hard cheese which could be grated (Λ 639). The   *Cheese.*
Cyclops Polyphemus placed his curds in baskets,
which allowed the whey to drain away, and in time the
curds would become hard.

From the absence of fish from the accounts of feasts
in the Homeric poems, not too much must be inferred.
Meleager of Gadara (in Athenaeus, 157 B)   *Fish.*
said that Homer was a Syrian by descent and
therefore represented the Achaeans as abstaining from fish,
and many a commentary says that "fish, afterwards so
prized by Athenian epicures, were eaten by the Homeric
men only to prevent starvation." But, while it is true that
the comrades of Odysseus (μ 331) and of Menelaus (δ 369)
are reported to eat fish only when wind-bound on islands,
and short of provisions, yet, as Athenaeus remarked, they
must have had their fish-hooks with them on the voyage,
since these could not have been found on the desert islands.
Further, abundance of fish is classed with large harvests of

wheat and barley, fruit from trees, and fertility of flocks, among the blessings granted by the gods to the people whose king fears the gods and maintains justice (τ 109). And in his comparisons, the poet shows himself familiar with the practise of fishing not only with hook and line, but also with spear, and with net. The epithet *fishy* (ἰχθυόεις, I 360), applied to the Hellespont, can hardly be due to the number of fish which appeared to the eye and thus attracted attention, but must have been given after experience in catching fish there. Representations of fishes are found on Mycenaean and Cretan works of art. We may believe, then, that the Homeric Greeks were familiar with fish as an article of food.[1]

Oysters (τήθεα, Π 747) are mentioned once: Patroclus hit Hector's brother and charioteer Cebriones with a stone, and *Oysters.* hurled him from his chariot. Then, boasting over him as he fell head-foremost, he said, "How nimble the man is! Even in a stormy sea, he could dive and provide oysters enough for many men." This expression shows incidentally that the Homeric Greeks had not invented the long rakes or dredges which are used by modern oyster-men. Oyster shells and even unopened oysters were found by Dr. Schliemann at Mycenae, and the liking for oysters is not likely to have been lost between the Mycenaean and the Homeric times. In the remains of the Homeric (Sixth) City at Troy are very many cockle shells, but cockles do not seem to be named by Homer.

Eels are mentioned (Φ 203, 353), but only as in the water; they may not have been eaten.

The Homeric warriors are not represented as eating game, any more than fish, when they had beef and pork at hand. *Game.* On Circe's island, Odysseus strikes down a great stag (κ 158), which cheers the hearts of his comrades, but nowhere else is venison mentioned as food. Once, however, a hunter is called a deer-hitter (ἐλαφηβόλος, Σ 319); a lion is said to rejoice greatly in coming upon

---

[1] According to the *Cypria*, Palamedes was fishing when he was murdered by Odysseus (Pausanias, x. 31. 2).—The general statement of Plato in the *Republic*, quoted above, seems to have been the basis of the more detailed remarks of Plutarch, *Morals*, 353 D.

a wounded horned stag or wild goat (Γ 24) ; and again, the Trojans press upon the wounded Odysseus as jackals upon a stag which has been wounded by an arrow (Λ 475),—expressions which clearly imply the chase. On landing at the island opposite the country of the Cyclopes, the comrades of Odysseus found countless wild goats, and took their bows and hunting-spears (αἰγανέας, ι 156) from the boats, and had a " heart-satisfying chase." These warriors had had no flesh-food, and little of anything to eat, for more than ten days, and were prepared to enjoy the game. Wild goats, fawns, and hares were chased by Odysseus with his dog Argos, before he went to the Trojan war (ρ 295). The bow of the Lycian archer Pandarus was made of the horns of a wild goat which he himself had shot (Δ 105, see page 668). The famous hunter Orion continued his chase even in the home of Hades (λ 572). The stories of Artemis (ζ 102) imply that even maidens might pursue wild animals. Of the island near the land of the Cyclopes, the poet says expressly that it had many wild goats, since hunters did not traverse it (ι 120). Wild boars also were hunted, and doubtless not exclusively for their destruction as noxious animals (as I 539) ; Odysseus received the wound of which the scar proved convenient for his identification, on a boar-hunt on the slopes of Mt. Parnassus (τ 429). Of course the very joy of the chase may have been the incitement to it, rather than the desire for the animal's flesh, though those who were accustomed to pork would not have wasted the flesh of the wild boar. The contest after the Calydonian Boar Hunt, however, arose not over the animal's carcase, but over the disposition of his head and shaggy hide (I 548), i.e. the trophies of victory. Thrushes and wild pigeons were taken in snares (χ 468), which would imply distinctly their use as food.

That in later times game and fish were not ordinarily sacrificed to the gods, argues nothing against the earlier use of these creatures for food. According to one view, it was the life of the animal,—its blood,—which was offered to the gods, and as a rule little life or blood was left in fish or deer when these were brought to the fire of the hearth, and therefore they could not be offered in sacrifice.

As for fowls, our familiar cocks and hens seem to have been not common in Greece until shortly before the Persian

Fowls. Wars, about five hundred years B.C., so their absence from Homeric life can cause no surprise.[1] An eagle bears a goose from the courtyard of Menelaus (o 161), and Penelope has a flock of twenty geese (τ 536), which eat wheat soaked in water in a trough. Penelope delights in watching her geese, but this does not prove that she is unwilling to eat them and their eggs. Homer, however, nowhere mentions eggs of any kind.

As for ordinary flesh, Plato observed that Homer did not feed his warriors on boiled meat.[2] The Homeric Greeks

No boiled Meat. knew no soup, although the poet was acquainted with the phenomenon of fat pork boiling in a kettle (Φ 362),—apparently the process of "trying" lard ; and in the *Odyssey*, the suitors call for a "wheel" (τροχός, φ 178) or large cake of tallow (στέαρ), that they may rub this as an emollient upon the unyielding horn of the bow of Odysseus.

Beef clearly is the favorite meat of the Homeric warriors, and the flesh of full-grown animals is preferred to that of the young,—five-year-old beef (B 403, H 315, ξ 419, τ 420)

Beef the Favorite Meat. to veal, which indeed does not seem to be eaten by them. But pork, too, was always in good repute among the Greeks, and later was even thought to be more digestible than beef. The meat of hogs, also, was preferred to that of young pigs.

---

[1] But a cock appears on a monument of much earlier date in the Museum at Sparta, and on Greek vases of the sixth century B.C. Homer has the proper names Ἀλέκτωρ (δ 10) and Ἀλεκτρυών (P 602),—but these seem to be elder brothers of the later word for cock, rather than derived from it,—or even may be derived from λέχος, and ἀλέκτωρ may be the masculine of ἄλοχος.—No hen, cock, chickens, or hen's eggs are mentioned in the Old Testament either.

[2] Hesiod, however, knows the use of a kettle for cooking food (*Works*, 748), and Vergil, though he doubtless desires to follow his Greek model, makes the sea-tossed companions of Aeneas, on reaching land and obtaining venison, at once set in order their kettles on the shore and build fires under them.—That the Children of Israel at the passover service ate the flesh of the lamb "roast with fire," not "sodden at all with water" (*Exodus* xii. 8), indicates that the Hebrews considered this the ancient approved method of cooking ; but part of the trouble with the sons of Eli arose because of their preference for roast meat to the sodden flesh of the ordinary sacrifice (1 *Samuel* ii. 13). Cf. *Exodus* xxix. 31, *Lev.* vii. 31, *Judges* vi. 19, *Ezekiel* xlvi. 20, 24.

Eumaeus apologizes to Odysseus for offering to him a young porker (ξ 80), although he supposes his guest to be only a common tramp; Penelope's suitors, he says, want all the grown hogs.

The animal is killed only just before his flesh is to be eaten; the Greeks did not care to have their meat gamey. This custom doubtless was due largely to the exigencies of the climate, in which meat soon *Meat eaten* becomes uneatable, and the custom is maintained *as soon as Killed.* in Modern Greece, where Easter lambs, for instance, are always sold alive. Only once[1] in the Homeric poems do we read of meat as being on hand uncooked (I 207): on the arrival of the embassadors from Agamemnon, Achilles produces the chines of a sheep and a fat goat, and the spare-rib of a well-fed hog, all ready to cook. In general, the animal has to be killed after the guest arrives. Thus on the visit of king Priam to the tent of Achilles, the latter springs up and cuts the throat of a sheep (which seems to be conveniently close at hand), and his comrades dress and cook the flesh (Ω 621). We may compare with this the visit of the three angels to Abraham on the plain of Mamre: " And Abraham ran unto the herd and fetcht a calf, tender and good, and gave it unto a young man; and he hasted to dress it. And he took butter and milk, and the calf which he had dressed, and set it before them " (*Genesis* xviii. 7).[2] Homer knew ice (X 152, ξ 477) and snow (as Γ 222, K 7, δ 566), but his friends made no use of these for the preservation of food, and only once (π 49) does he speak of the use of meat which remained from the previous evening's repast.[3]

The fullest account of the cooking of meat is found in the narrative of the visit of Agamemnon's embassadors to

[1] On the departure of Telemachus from the palace of Menelaus, the latter bids his neighbor Eteoneus to kindle a fire and to roast meat (o 97); whether the animal must be killed first, is not stated.

[2] See also *Judges* vi. 19, for Gideon's dressing a kid for an angel of the Lord.

[3] In like manner among the Jews, "that which remaineth" until the morning of the passover ieast, the Israelites were directed to "burn with fire" (*Exodus* xii. 10); and the same rule held for every "sacrifice of thanksgiving" (*Leviticus* xxxii. 30); apparently no meat was to be kept until the third day (*Leviticus* xix. 6).

Achilles (I 206). Patroclus places the great meat-tray near the blaze of the fire, and puts in it the chine of a sheep and that of a goat, and the loin of a hog, drip-ping with fat. Achilles cuts these skilfully and spits them. A fine fire is kindled, and when the flame has died away, the coals are spread, and the spits are stretched over them, rested upon the stone fire-dogs, and salt is sprinkled on the meat. When the meat is roasted, it is drawn from the spits and is put into a tray (ἐλεοί). In the hut of Eumaeus, Odysseus dredges his roast-pig with barley meal.[1] At formal feasts, the nobler vitals, the heart and liver (and lungs?) are cooked, and a portion is given to each guest, before the outer flesh is roasted (κρέα ὑπέρτερα, γ 9, 65). In general, as in the tent of Achilles, the carving is done before the cooking, but the *divider* (δαιτρός, α 141, *cf.* ξ 433) may have cut as well as distri-buted the meat. The cooking of a large roast, weighing ten or fifteen pounds, not to speak of a whole leg of beef, would have occupied so much time as to be inconvenient on such an occasion as the visit of the embassadors to Achilles, while the roasting of small portions would entail but little delay. At times, the meat was given to the guest, spit and all, fresh from the coals.[2] Meat thus cooked over coals, in large mouthfuls (*kebabs*), on a skewer not larger than a big knitting-needle, is familiar to every traveller in Asia Minor and is sometimes seen in rural districts of Greece,—doubtless a direct inheritance from Homeric times ; but the French *en brochette* refers to what is essentially the same custom, and nature suggests this for the cooking of salt pork in a logging camp or in a camp of explorers.

Long bronze pins which seem to have served as such spits for the cooking of meat, were found in the excavations on the site of the Argive Heraeum.

The Homeric Greeks knew no professional cooks and had no servants set apart for this office. In fact, in no case in the poems is the cooking of meat entrusted to menials or even to women. Just as Achilles and Patroclus, on the

Cooking of Meat.

---

[1] ξ 77. Unless indeed this ἄλφιτα λευκὰ πάλυνεν means that the meat was wrapped in a barley cake.

[2] πάντα φέρων παρέθηκ' 'Οδυσῆι | θέρμ' αὐτοῖς ὀβελοῖσιν, ξ 76.

occasion to which reference has been made, themselves prepare the food for their honored guests, so the suitors of
Penelope do their own cooking (ρ 178),—at least
of meat; the bread may well have been made *No Professional Cooks.*
by the women.[1] This cooking is simple; no
ragouts or "made dishes" of any kind are known.
The dinners are hearty, but consist of a single course only.
But one exception has to be made to the last remarks:
mention is made of a sort of "black pudding" or haggis
or *blutwurst,*—the intestine of a goat (γαστὴρ αἰγός, σ 44,
cf. υ 26) filled with fat and blood,—which is toasted rather
than roasted before the fire. One such is given by the
suitors as a prize of combat to the disguised Odysseus, when
in a pugilistic contest he overcomes the beggar Irus. This
is a "made dish," but the ingredients are simple.

How much meat was thought to be a fair allowance for
a Homeric warrior, is not easily determined. The swine-
herd Eumaeus thinks that Odysseus and he need
a small roast-pig apiece for luncheon (ξ 72); and *How much Meat allowed?*
then at the close of the day they are ready to
kill a five-year-old hog, which they divide into
seven parts,—one for Hermes and the nymphs, and one for
each of the six feasters,—an ample meal, as it would seem.[2]
It is only fair to say, however, that so much of this pork
remains after dinner that Odysseus and his host have enough
for luncheon the next day (ξ 419, π 49), but the like would
now be expected if six or seven men had dined on a single
"sparerib." For Penelope's suitors on the last day of their
feasting, the goat-herd Melanthius, accompanied by two helpers,
brings the best of his flocks (ρ 212),—from Ithaca alone eleven
goats each day, the swine-herd says (ξ 105); but in addition,
Philoetius brings other goats and a cow from the mainland
(υ 185), while Eumaeus brings three fat swine (υ 162). This
seems to be about the ordinary daily supply from the flocks
and herds of Odysseus. The household of the Ithacan prince

---

[1] So on the Shield of Achilles, Σ 560, while the heralds are dressing the carcase
of a great bull, women are making barley cakes or porridge for the reapers.

[2] "For the entire establishment [of Napoleon on St. Helena], the Governor
set down one hundred pounds of meat *per diem,* besides eighteen fowls, game-birds,
etc., and a ham."

was always large, and was increased by more than a hundred suitors with their attendants, but the supply of meat seems abundant. At a public feast at Pylus (γ 5), nine companies of five hundred men each, had eighty-one bulls to eat, or one bull for fifty-six men. This would seem to be at least nine or ten times as much as was necessary. The Homeric heroes were "valiant trenchermen," to use Shake-speare's phrase, or "able eaters," to use an old New England expression. Critics have been amused by the warriors' readiness to take food at all times. For instance, early in the ninth book of the *Iliad*, the Achaean chieftains eat a "heart-satisfying meal" (μενοεικέα δαῖτα, I 90) in the tent of Agamemnon ; thence Odysseus and Ajax go as embassadors to the tent of Achilles, who at once roasts three kinds of meat for his guests, before the reason for their coming is mentioned (I 206); while on their return to Agamemnon's tent, they are invited again to cheer their hearts with food and wine before going to rest (I 705). Similarly, when Priam visits the tent of Achilles, to ransom the body of his son Hector, he finds the son of Thetis just finishing his evening meal (Ω 475), but a sheep is soon killed, and the host and guest together partake of the meat (Ω 621). Achilles cannot have been hungry in the latter instance, and in the former, Odysseus says plainly to Achilles (I 225), though after a formulaic verse with regard to driving out the desire for eating and drinking, that they have no need of a well-ordered feast,—this they have had in the tent of Agamemnon,—but they desire his help in battle. Clearly the offer of food was the first duty of hospitality,[1] and hospitality was one of heaven's highest laws. Thus no Homeric host but the Cyclops Polyphemus inquires of his guest's errand before he has given him food.[2] The king of Lycia feasted Bellerophon for nine days (Z 174),

"Able Eaters."

---

[1] *Cf.* ξείνοις ἄτ' ἐλθόντεσσιν εὐεργέται | δεῖπν' ἐπαγγέλλοντι πρῶτον, Pindar, *Pyth.* iv. 30.

[2] α 123, γ 69, δ 60, ι 252, ξ 46. At ε 87 ff., the nymph Calypso asks Hermes the reason of his coming when he appears, but he gives no reply until he has eaten and drunk. When Thetis is summoned to the council of the gods, Hera puts a golden cup in her hand, and she drinks, before Zeus tells her why she has been summoned (Ω 101).—In Modern Greece, a cigarette is often offered as a like indication of hospitality.

killing an ox each day, before he asked to see his letter of
introduction. Such a repast as that provided by Achilles
for Ajax and Odysseus was purely formal and honorific,—
an act of courteous welcome. Gluttony was never one of
the crying sins of the Greeks, and certainly did not belong
to the Homeric age,—being seldom found, indeed, together
with Homeric simplicity of fare.

But if the Greeks of Homer's time were hearty eaters,
they certainly were not hard drinkers. Only three instances
of drunkenness occur in the action of the Homeric
story, and a heavy punishment follows each. One *Not Hard Drinkers.*
of these instances is immediately after the capture
of Troy,—in celebration of the victory at the conclusion of
a ten years' siege : an assembly is called at evening, the
Achaeans come heavy with wine (γ 139), and a sad quarrel
between the leaders follows. The second instance is that
of the Cyclops Polyphemus, which really was accidental,
but cost the monster his sight (ι 345),—he did not expect
the wine to prove so strong, he being like a countryman who supposes champagne to be only very excellent
cider. The third instance of drunkenness in the action of
the poems is that of Odysseus's comrade Elpenor,—"the
youngest of the company, and neither very brave in battle
nor well-balanced in mind" (κ 552),—who paid for his
indulgence with his life, falling from the roof of Circe's
palace, where he had been sleeping, on being roused
before he had quite recovered himself. The poet refers
also to the drunkenness of the centaur Eurytion in the
home of Peirithoüs (ϕ 295),—but he, like Polyphemus, was
not a Greek, and he, too, was miserably punished. Not even
Penelope's insolent suitors, nor the luxurious Phaeacians,
incline to drink too much wine. Homer knows no drinking-
bouts (although this used to be a favorite class-room translation for εἰλαπίνη, α 226). "Heavy with wine" (οἰνοβαρές,
A 225), addressed in anger by Achilles to Agamemnon, is a
grievous reproach and nothing in the poems indicates that it
was justified.[1] Telemachus, as a mere pretext for removing
the arms from his great hall, is to say that he feared lest

---

[1] Athenaeus (i. 11 A) adds to I 119 a verse which represents Agamemnon as
ascribing his folly either to wine or to the gods.

the suitors heated with wine (οἰνωθέντες, τ 11) might misuse them ; and the disguised Odysseus begs not to be reminded of his sorrows, that no one may suspect him of maudlin tears (τ 122). Penelope's suitor Antinoüs charges the disguised Odysseus with being either drunk or crazy, because of his desire to make trial with Penelope's suitors of his ability to string the bow (φ 293), but this does not imply that any one actually had been drinking wine too freely. On Hector's return from the field on the first day of battle to urge the Trojan matrons to offer vows to Athena, Queen Hecuba bids her son wait until she shall bring him a cup of wine, which "increases the strength of a weary man,"—but he replies, "Lift not for me the wine, revered mother, lest you weaken my limbs, and I forget my might and valor" (Z 258).

Greek wine, in Homer's time as well as in our own, was mixed with water before drinking. The usual proportion of water to wine is unknown. Hesiod (*Works*, 596) *Wine mixed with Water.* recommends for the dog-days three parts of water to one of wine, but the later Greeks thought that this was a draught suited to fishes rather than proper for men. That the wine which intoxicated Polyphemus was commonly mixed with twenty parts of water (ι 209), shows nothing for ordinary wine ; it was necessarily of extraordinary strength, for its special purpose. That the proportion of water to wine was not always the same, is seen from Achilles's direction to Patroclus on the visit of Ajax and Odysseus, to mix the wine stronger for the honored guests.[1] The poet is so accustomed to the weakening of wine with water that he represents the nymph Calypso as thus mixing her nectar before she offers it to Hermes (ε 93), and the gods, like men, dip their draughts from a mixing-bowl (ἀπὸ κρητῆρος, Α 598). The meaning of the epithet (ἄκρητον, ι 297) applied to the milk which Polyphemus drinks, has been considered obscure,— scholars hesitating to translate it *unmixed*, as if men were in the habit of weakening their milk,—but the commentator seems to be right who translates it thus, with the remark, "half humorous, from the custom of diluting wine."

The mixing-bowl stood opposite the main entrance to

[1] ζωρότερον δὲ κέραιε, Ι 203.

the great hall (φ 145), and the wine was served from left to right (ἐνδέξια, Α 597, cf. φ 141).

Since the wine was weakened with water, it was given even to small children, (as to Achilles, Ι 485). Eurymachus, one of the suitors, tells Penelope that in former times, in his childhood, Odysseus often seated him on his knee, placed the roast-meat in his hands, and held *Wine given to Children.* the cup of wine to his lips (π 442),—which shows incidentally that very small boys were brought to feasts. Andromache, picturing the wretched life of a boy in orphanage, thinks of him as going to the companions of his father at a feast ; one of those who pity him holds a cup of wine for a moment to his lips,—" it wets his lips, but it does not wet his palate " (Χ 494) ; but the grudging gift of wine was not represented as due to the thought that wine was unsuitable for boys. Nausicaa takes a leathern bottle of wine with her when she goes to the shore with her attendant maidens (ζ 77). Aphrodite brought up the daughters of Pandareüs on cheese, honey, and wine (υ 68),—which seems to mean a posset rather than three separate articles of food *Possets.* and drink. Such a posset (κυκειών, Λ 624, κ 234) is described as given to the wounded Machaon in the tent of Nestor, where it is called a draught, and as given by Circe to the comrades of Odysseus, where it is called food (σῖτος, κ 235), and thus may be supposed to be of thicker consistency.[1] In both instances cheese, barley meal, and honey are mixed with Pramnian wine, which, in later times, had the reputation of being rather heavy. No other special sort of wine is named, except that from Thracian Ismarus (ι 196) which Odysseus gave to the Cyclops.

Several towns or countries are called *vine-clad* (ἀμπελόεις), as Epidaurus (Β 561), Phrygia (Γ 184), Pedasus (Ι 152) ; or *rich-in-grapes* (πολυστάφυλος), as Arne (Β 507) and Histiaea (Β 537). Some names are derived from wine, as Oenops (φ 144, cf. Ε 707) and that of Diomed's grandfather, Oeneus (Ζ 216), if not Oenomaus (Ε 706).

Wine is brought to the Achaeans before Troy, from Thrace " daily " (Ι 72), and from Lemnos (Η 467), and exchanged

---

[1] At the symposium of Xenophanes (i. 9), after the feast, golden loaves are at hand and a table laden with cheese and rich honey in addition to the wine.

for copper, iron, cattle, hides, and slaves, and other objects which the Achaeans have plundered from the neighbors of the Trojans.

The Homeric Greeks knew no intoxicating liquor obtained from grain or from honey,—no whiskey or beer or mead ; but

No Beer or Mead.

they were familiar with the improvement in wine when carefully kept. Nestor orders wine eleven years old to be taken from its jar, in honor of his guest Telemachus (γ 390), and Odysseus's old housekeeper is guarding certain wine of unusual quality against the time of her lord's return (β 340). In the house, wine is kept in jars (I 469); it is transported either in leathern bottles (ε 265, ι 196), or in smaller jars (β 290, ι 204).

Water is not directly mentioned as drunk without wine, but Calypso puts a leathern bottle of water as well as one

Water for Drinking.

of wine on the craft of Odysseus (ε 266), and, as we should expect, a supply of fresh water is one of the most important characteristics of a good landing-place for voyagers (δ 359, ι 85, 140, μ 306, ν 109).

Barley meal, wine, and beeves (in this order) are enumerated as the constituents of a long and hearty feast (τ 197), and

Bread.

though meat was eaten freely, bread[1] was, if not the "staff of life," at least the "marrow of men" (μυελὸς ἀνδρῶν, β 290, υ 108), but this bread would hardly be recognized as such by modern occidental bakers and housewives.

Of one of the earliest stages in the use of cereals, the Homeric Greeks possessed a survival in the use of barley-

Parched Barleycorns.

corns[2] in sacrifices to the gods. In nothing are men more conservative than in their ritual of worship, and these barleycorns offered in sacrifice seem to have represented the food of the early worshipper, corresponding to the parched grain which in primitive times

---

[1] It this name may be used for ἄρτος (*wheat bread*,—only ρ 343 and σ 120) and σῖτος,—so unlike our own. πυρνόν is given to beggars (ο 312, ρ 12, 362); probably it was made ot coarse meal.

[2] οὐλαί or οὐλοχύται, γ 441, 445. *Cf.* ταύταις (*sc.* κριθαῖς,—in contrast to ground grain) ἀπ' ἀρχῆς μὲν οὐλοχυτεῖτο κατὰ τὰς πρῶτας θυσίας τὸ ἀνθρώπων γένος, Porphyry, *de Abstinentia*, ii. 6.—Another theory is that these barleycorns were a sort of preliminary offering, a sacrifice to Earth before the main sacrifice to the higher divinities.

was eaten without being beaten or ground.[1] Many American
boys have eaten maize parched after the manner of their
Iroquois and Delaware predecessors, and "Robinson Crusoe"
teaches us that the English were familiar with a similar usage
three hundred years ago. This custom of eating parched
corn probably lasted in Greece until after Homer's time, but
the barleycorns are mentioned by the poet only in connexion
with sacrifices.

A natural step of advance upon the earliest parched-corn
stage of culture was the bruising of the grain (after parching)
in a mortar with a pestle, or between two stones,
the lower of which would be somewhat hollowed *Mortar and Pestle.*
in order to keep the grain and meal from scatter-
ing.[2] The mortar of Hesiod (ὅλμος, *Works*, 423) was three
feet in height; his pestle was to be three cubits, or about
four and a half feet, in length. Such a mortar is mentioned
by Homer once, in a comparison (Λ 147),—a simile for
Peisander's body after his head and arms have been cut off,
but on early Cretan sites and at Hissarlik pounding-stones
have been found, only a few inches in length. Scenes on
old vases show that the use of the mortar and pestle for
pounding grain was long continued in Greece. In Africa,
on the Isthmus of Panama, and in other countries on the
same level of civilization, this use is familiar at present.[3]

[1] The separation of the kernel from the husk must have been troublesome to the
primitive man until he discovered that the removal of the chaff by fire left the grain
more palatable, more readily broken, and more easily digested. In classical times
in Greece, grain seems to have been at least somewhat parched before it was
ground. *Cf.* the oracle quoted by Herodotus with regard to Salamis ("the
women of Colias shall parch their grain with oars," Hdt. viii. 96), and Thucydides's
statement that the Athenian expedition against Syracuse took with them large
quantities of parched corn (Thuc. vi. 22). For the usage of the Israelites, *cf. Lev.*
xxiii. 14, I *Sam.* xvii. 17, 2 *Sam.* xvii. 28 ; *Ruth* ii. 14 "and he reached her parched
corn, and she did eat and was sufficed, and left." *Cf.* also *Nunc torrete igni fruges,
nunc frangite saxo*, Verg. *Georg.* i. 267, and *fruges . . . torrere parant flammis et
frangere saxo*, Verg. *Aen.* i. 179. The Romans ascribed to Numa Pompilius the
introduction of the custom of parching corn.

[2] Apparently the Greeks did not roll their grain on a slab like the Mexicans,
but their grinding-stones may have resembled the stones used for rolling, as much
as they resembled the Scotch *quern*.

[3] *Cf.* "Though thou shouldest bray a fool in a mortar among wheat with a
pestle, yet will not his foolishness depart from him," *Proverbs* xxvii. 22 ; "ears of
corn dried by the fire, even corn beaten out of full ears," *Lev.* ii. 14.

The bruising of grain between two loose stones was followed
by the hand-mill.   Such family mills, as well as larger grist-
Hand-mills.   mills to be turned by horse power, have been
found in the ruins of Pompeii.   These hand-mills
are used in Palestine still, and the Scottish *quern* has been
discarded only within the last century.   In Homer, mills are
mentioned twice,—in the palace of Alcinoüs (η 104), where
fifty maids are occupied with spinning and grinding, and in
the home of Odysseus (υ 106, 111), where twelve women
grind.   That grinding is the work of women in Greece as
well as in Palestine ("Two women grinding at the mill"),
is what we should expect.   Under Penelope's management,
the meal or flour for each day's use in general was ground
each morning early, but yet some must have been ground in
advance, for, on his journey to Pylus, Telemachus takes
with him twenty measures of barley meal (β 354).[1]   A stone
which Ajax hurls at Hector (H 270), is likened to a mill-
stone, and on the third day of battle the defenders of the
Achaean wall are said to hurl mill-stones (μύλακες, M 161)
upon their assailants.   No sieve is mentioned,[2] and the meal
must have been coarse, with a considerable admixture of sand
and other dirt.[3]   The mill-stones were not always chosen for
their hardness, nor were they always fitted to each other.
Dr. Schliemann says that the saddle-querns found by him
on the site of Troy could have produced nothing like flour.

The earliest use of the meal from the mortar or the mill,
would be for porridge,—being mixed with water or possibly
Porridge.   with milk.[4]   The clearest Homeric example of
this use is in a harvest scene on the Shield
of Achilles, in which "women are sprinkling much white
barley meal as a dinner for the workmen,"[5]—which has been

---

[1] Herodotus thinks it worthy of notice that grain *already ground* (ἀληλεσμένος,
vii. 23) was sent from Asia to those who were engaged in digging the canal across
the isthmus of Athos.

[2] The Danaïd story is not Homeric.

[3] Skulls of North American Indians sometimes show teeth in excellent condition
except in that they are worn off nearly to the gums, a circumstance due not only
to the mastication of imperfectly ground grain, but also to the presence of sand in
the meal.

[4] *Cf.* μᾶζά τ' ἀμολγαίη, Hesiod, *Works*, 590.

[5] Σ 560, λεύκ' ἄλφιτα πολλὰ πάλυνον.

interpreted often as meaning simply that the women sprinkled barley meal on the flesh of the ox which had been roasted, but which is more naturally interpreted as referring to the preparation of thick porridge or barley cakes. These cakes or porridge would be the ordinary food of the working man. The warriors before Troy and Penelope's suitors might have beef and pork to eat every day, but the ordinary Greek was doubtless as frugal then as now, and seldom tasted flesh.[1] With this porridge have been compared the posset which has been mentioned and the sacrificial mass which is spoken of in Attic tragedy.[2]

From the oatmeal porridge, as thick as it is used in Scotland, to the Scotch cakes or bannocks, is but a short and easy step. The *maza* (μᾶζα) of the classical period seems to have been such a barley cake,— *Barley Cakes.* perhaps not always baked,—corresponding to the Italian *polenta*.[3] According to Athenaeus (iv. 137 E), these barley cakes were served to the guests in the Prytaneum at Athens on ordinary days, and wheat bread only on festal occasions.

Leavened bread is a product of later development,— appearing in Greek literature first in Xenophon's *Anabasis* (vii. 3. 21). The Jews had leaven long before that time, having learned its use in Egypt, but their *No Leavened Bread.* avoidance of leaven in the celebration of the pass- over, is a clear proof of their memory of the time when it was unknown to their ancestors. Why the Greeks did not learn of leaven early, no one knows. No arrangements for the baking of bread have been found at Hissarlik, Mycenae, or Tiryns, nor in Crete, further than earthenware vessels,

---

[1] Wellhausen says that to the Semites "flesh was an uncommon luxury, and they ate it with quite different feelings from those with which they partook of fruits or of milk. . . . The pouring out of blood was ventured upon only in such a way as to give it back to the deity, the source of life." So in Aeschylus (*Ag.* 1592) a day of festivity is κρεουργὸν ἦμαρ, a day on which flesh is eaten.

[2] πέλανος, as Aeschylus, *Persians*, 204. This seems to designate food of the porridge or "mush" variety, whether as thin as gruel or as thick as dough.— Roscher (*J.J.* 1888, 523) calls attention to the fact that barley meal is the most important ingredient of the κυκεών or posset which has been mentioned above.

[3] Plato in his *Republic* (ii. 372) plays upon the word,—μάξαντες μάζας and πέψαντες ἄρτους.—The word μᾶζα is not Homeric.

which seem to have been used as bread pans, and Homer says nothing of the baking of bread.[1] The poet seems to have known no loaves of bread in the modern sense. Homer's bread[2] probably was like that still ordinarily used in Asia Minor,—cakes in form like the Jewish Passover-bread, or even more like the Mexican *tortillas*,—about a foot in diameter[3] and a fifth of an inch in thickness, made daily, baked on a plate of iron or a hot stone, and rolled up to look something like a ribbon.[4] Of these cakes, men eat four to six a day, with cheese, curds, leeks, etc., as a relish. They serve also as plates, to receive the portion of other food assigned.[5] Such cakes are represented on ancient vases. On his journey to Pylus, Telemachus took with him wine and twenty measures of meal, but no bread. From the meal, the cakes were readily made, and porridge was easily mixed.

No Loaves.

[1] The γρηὺς καμινώ, *oven*-woman, of σ 27, according to Aristarchus and Herodian, was not a baker of bread, but a woman who parched the barley as a preliminary to grinding,—τῇ φρυττούσῃ τὰς κριθὰς πρὸς τὸ ποιῆσαι ἄλευρα.

[2] See Benndorf, *Altgriechisches Brot*, in *Eranos Vindobonensis*.

[3] Earthenware pans for baking bread, a foot to fifteen inches in diameter, with small holes in the bottom which may have made an imprint on the cake (like *waffles*), have been found at Tiryns (Schliemann, *Tiryns* 116) and in Crete (*Annual of the British School*, ix. 325).

[4] So the ἄρτος οὖλος of ρ 343 would be a *rolled* or *curly* cake. *Cf.* οὔλη as an epithet of λάχνη, *wool*, Κ 134.

[5] *Cf.* the oracle in Vergil's *Aeneid* (iii. 256, vii. 107), that the Trojan refugees should *eat their tables*. Their tables were their plates; their bread, at the fulfilment of the oracle, served as both tables and plates.

CHAPTER VIII

HOMERIC PROPERTY

IN Homeric times much of the land, if not most of it, was held as common property, not in severalty. In the earliest period of the Hellenic occupancy, land in itself had little value,—its chief worth was due to the *Much Land held in* labors of the men who cleared away the trees *Common.* and underbrush and stones, and first tilled it. Plenty of ground remained to be improved in this way, all of which belonged to the community. The inhabitants who remained in the country from a conquered tribe which had formerly been in possession, if such inhabitants there were, having no civil rights, were obliged to till the soil and to tend flocks and herds, in return for their maintenance and the privilege of existence ; their lives had been spared when the right of the conqueror might have been exercised to the uttermost, and they had no claim to a share in the possessions of the community. The first division of land would be among families and clans ; the individual's claim would be but temporary,—he had only a life interest. The land of a family was under a strict entail, and could not be sold nor otherwise alienated. Even when alienation of real estate became legal, it did not become at once respectable, and we may fairly compare the words of Naboth to Ahab in Palestine (I *Kings* xxi. 3), " The Lord forbid it me that I should give the inheritance of my fathers unto thee."

Within the limits of the family domain, and under the control of the head of the clan, a house would be built. A field cultivated for a crop of grain need not be in the permanent possession of a single man or family, for it was,

and is, the custom of the Greeks to allow their land to lie
fallow, often, if not between every two crops, and the man
Grain-land who had cultivated a field two years ago, might
and Fruit- have no special right or claim to it for this year.
land held in His services to the land had been as temporary
Severalty. as his occupancy of it ; the land might have a
rotation of possessors as well as of crops.[1]   But although
this temporary possession is not in itself improbable, not
a word in the Homeric poems implies that the tilled land
of Greece at the poet's time was not held like any other
property.   The contention that then land in Greece was
not held in severalty by common men, does not seem to
have been proved.[2]   In the scene described on the Shield of
Achilles (Σ 541), the ploughmen must be working for one
master, for as each comes to the end of his furrow, he
receives a cup of wine from an attendant, and the situation
is similar to that of Λ 67, where several reapers are busy in
harvesting a rich man's grain.   Certainly the chief men, and
not the princes only, had homes of their own, and the ownership of a house in primitive times almost necessarily implied
ownership of ground.   As the stage of culture in which grain
is planted, is an advance on nomadic life, and assumes that
the ground is in possession of the individual for at least a
year, so the cultivation of vines and fruit trees obviously
assumes permanent occupancy of the land.   A man will
plant pears and vines that his children may eat of the fruit,
although he may not expect to enjoy this himself ; no man,
however, under such conditions as existed in Homeric Greece,

---

[1] *Cf.* Caesar, *Gallic War*, vi. 22.   The statement of Tacitus, *Germania*, xxvi.,
is less certain : *agri pro numero cultorum ab universis in vices occupantur.*   "Tacitus
appears to describe a condition of things somewhat further advanced than Caesar's,"
with assignments made for longer periods.

[2] See especially Ridgeway, *The Homeric Land System*, in the *Journal of Hellenic
Studies*, vi. 319, and Pöhlmann, *Feldgemeinschaft bei Homer*, in *Altertum und
Gegenwart*, p. 105.   Ridgeway holds that land in the early epic age was the
property of the community in general, and that "the idea of property in land
is foreign certainly to the *Iliad*," but that in the *Odyssey* are to be found "evidences
of a state of society later in time and more advanced in institutions than that
portrayed in the *Iliad*." "πολύκληρος (ξ 211) indicates most clearly an age when
property in land is recognized as an important item of wealth, and when many
κλῆροι had come to be accumulated in the hands of one individual, and when
consequently landed property was held perpetually in severalty."

would plant an orchard in which he and his children had no special rights, but which should belong to the community in general. The importance of the Homeric vineyard is shown by the fact that wine is the ordinary drink of the people,—not merely that of the princes but also that of the swine-herds (ξ 78, π 14). As a matter of fact, all such orchards and vineyards in Homeric Greece are in private ownership. In these poems we have to do chiefly with kings and nobles, and it is true that the two orchards which are described in detail are those of Alcinoüs, king of the Phaeacians (η 112 ff.), and of Laërtes, the old king of Ithaca (ω 221 ff.), but nothing indicates that the possession of land was a royal prerogative. Laërtes had "acquired" (κτεάτισσεν, ω 207) his farm,—which does not seem like a peculiarly royal act. Royal domains and sacred groves for the gods (both called by the same name,—τέμενος, cf. τέμνω, templum) very probably were set apart from common use before ordinary men held land in severalty. Thus Sarpedon and Glaucus had corn-land and fruit-land in Lycia (M 314), and Tydeus received the like with the hand of Adrastus's daughter at Argos (Ξ 122), but without any pasture land. But the mention of fruit and grapes (Σ 561), and of the care of an olive tree (P 53), of itself indicates that private men might have fields of their own. Odysseus comments on the promised fertility of the island near the home of the Cyclopes (ι 131 ff.), —"if it were well tilled, it would bear all things in their season." This expression, "if it received proper care," has been thought to show that the poet was accustomed to see all good land occupied,—but this inference is rather more than the premisses warrant,—the Ithacan was simply filled with admiration of the island. Cultivated fields need not always have been in close connexion with the habitation of their owner. The name given to them corresponds exactly to the name ordinarily given to the fields of the early settlers in New England (κλῆροι, lots); they were lots since they were allotted (ζ 10). A poor man was "one without a lot" (ἄκληρος, λ 490), while a rich man had many lots (πολύκληρος, ξ 211). For the assignment of lots in a new settlement, we may compare the Athenian cleruchi (κληροῦχοι), who received lots, or allotted portions, of land in conquered territory. On the third day of the battles of the *Iliad*, Hector, urging the Trojan to fight bravely, tells them that even if one falls, his "wife and children, house and lot" will be safe, if only the Achaeans are driven from Troy (O 497 ff.). *Lot* here naturally means neither inheritance in general nor the citizen's right to a temporary use of the public lands, but property in land, and this weighs much against the view of those who hold that the portion of land was called a lot on the assumption that the portions of inherited property were allotted to the heirs (as ξ 209). Still more clear is the expression at ξ 63, where Eumaeus expresses his confidence that Odysseus, if he had returned in safety, would have given to him "house and lot and wife."

While no land is sold in the Homeric poems, clearly it could be sold in Hesiod's time, for, according to him, one of the rewards of the gods' favor is that "no one shall buy your lot, but you shall buy another's" (*Works and Days*, 341). Restrictions on the sale of land were well known in early Attica, among the Locrians, and in Sparta, and are advocated by Plato in his *Republic*, but do not mean that the possessor has a weak title as against another claimant ; he may hold it as the representative of his family, in which case it is virtually entailed.

No Land Sold.

Private ownership might be secured in more than one way. Some land would be allotted for homes, grain fields, and orchards when the tribe first took possession of its newly won territory.[1] Other land would be given as the reward of a tribe to a benefactor.

How was Ownership Secured?

So at I 574 ff., a field is promised to Meleager if he will drive the enemy from Calydon, and at Υ 184 ff., a field is suggested as an offer of a reward to Aeneas if he shall kill Achilles. In neither of these cases is the land strictly part of a royal domain, and when Bellerophon, at Z 193 ff., receives half of the kingdom and a domain, we are not to suppose that the previous domain of the Lycian king is divided, but that an additional portion of the public

---

[1] *Cf. Numbers* xxxiii. 53: "And ye shall dispossess the inhabitants of the land, and dwell therein. . . . And ye shall divide the land by lot for an inheritance among your families." See Athenaeus, iv. 167 D, for the allotment of land by the colonists of Syracuse.

lands is set apart for Bellerophon's use. Other land would become the property of him who reclaimed it from forest or marsh. Plenty remained to be thus reclaimed. The country was not so thickly settled as to make wild land valuable except in large quantities. In telling of the removal of the Phaeacians from their earlier homes, where the Cyclopes troubled them, the poet says, "Nausithoüs settled his people in Scheria, ran a wall about the city, built houses, erected temples for the gods, and divided the grain fields" (ἐδάσσατ᾽ ἀρούρας, ζ 10). This must have meant more than the assignment of fields for the tillage of the next year; it was such an allotment as was made by the early settlers of some of the New England towns, where each head of a family received the assignment of a village lot and a farm lot,[1]—one for his home, and the other for his plough,—without exhausting the land of the community. The reader observes that the Phaeacians seem to have dispossessed no previous occupants. They clearly came to an uninhabited region and took possession of the land for their use. They lived in fairyland, it is true, but the poet is wont to ascribe to all peoples the customs of those with which he is familiar. In the so-called Homeric *Hymn to Aphrodite*, the cultivated land (ἔργα ἀνθρώπων, 122) is contrasted with the unallotted and untilled land (ἄκληρόν τε καὶ ἄκτιτον, 123), over which wild beasts wander. To attempt to determine even approximately the ordinary size of the Homeric "lots" of land, would be futile. But since garden vegetables were an insignificant part of their diet, the home lot may have been small.

"Squatter's rights" seem to have been acquired easily in the Homeric age, and indeed are secured without much difficulty in the Greece of to-day, as they were for more than the first half of the nineteenth century in the United States.

In Lacedaemon during historical times, vast tracts of land which were used as pastures, were "commons,"

---

[1] For a field at a distance from the village, *cf.* ἀγροῦ ἐπ᾽ ἐσχατιῆς, δ 517, ε 489. So Euryclea comforts Penelope, by assuring her that the gods care for the house of Laërtes, and that some one will remain to keep the "lofty dwellings and the rich fields far away" (ἀπόπροθι πίονας ἀγρούς, δ 757).

where all citizens might pasture their cattle. The Spartans
retained the traditions of the Homeric age in many particulars, and the only wealth really honorable
among them was property in flocks and herds.
Commons in Later Greece. among them was property in flocks and herds.
This was a natural survival from the customs
and rights of an earlier period, when all mechanical labor
was considered menial, and trade was despised, but the care
of cattle was compatible with royal dignity. In Boeotian
Orchomenos (*C.I.G.* 1569 *a*), the right to pasture on public
lands a hundred and twenty kine or horses and a thousand
sheep or goats, was granted to a former creditor of the
state in return for his favors and concessions. Extant
records show that several times as a recognition and partial
compensation for important services, a Greek state in the
classical period granted to a foreigner, together with certain
other privileges of citizenship, the right to own a house and
to pasture herds and flocks.[1] Clearly Odysseus had rights
of pasturage on the mainland, and Noëmon who lends his
boat to Telemachus for his voyage to the home of Nestor,
two or three days later desires it that he may cross to Elis,
where he has brood mares, and fetch a young mule to break
(δ 635). So in Modern Greece, much of the wilder land
belongs to the government (just as the land on the mountain
slopes of New Hampshire in some cases still belongs to
the town in which it lies), and flocks are taken by their
shepherd to the mountains for weeks or months, just as
the Swiss cattle are driven to the mountain pastures for
the four months of summer. The Messenger in Sophocles's
Oedipus Tyrannus (1134) says that for three summers,
"from spring to Arcturus," his flocks on Mount Cithaeron
had grazed next those of Laius, while, for the winter, one
flock was driven to Thebes and the other to Corinth, *i.e.* the
flocks of Thebans and of Corinthians, during the summer,
were herded together on the same mountain slopes.

Odysseus's swine were kept on the hills, at a little distance
from the town,—hardly less than an hour's walk from the

---

[1] ἔπασιν γᾶς καὶ οἰκίας, ἐπινομίαν καὶ ἀσυλίαν, *C.I.G.* 1724 *b*. *Cf.* *C.I.G.* 1335.—
According to *C.I.G.* 2556, a treaty was made between two neighboring states in
Crete, which among other things allowed the people of one state to pasture their
flocks on the land of the other.—Mares with foal are still sent from Arcadia to
Elis because of the good pasture there.

palace,—and were taken from their pens every day to be fed in the fields.[1] Melanthius, the goat-herd, overtook Odysseus on his way from his herds to the palace (ρ 212), and so we may assume that he kept his goats nearly as far away from the town *Odysseus's Pastures.* as the swine. The swine had no provender provided for them in their pens; all their food came from the fields, and nothing indicates that these were private property. Eumaeus enumerates twelve flocks of sheep, twelve herds of goats, and twelve droves of swine,—all belonging to Odysseus and feeding on the mainland opposite Ithaca,—while the Ithacan king has 960 swine and eleven herds of goats on the island itself; but the "divine swine-herd" says not a word about his master's broad acres and luxuriant crops of grain. Nor are these fields mentioned elsewhere in the poems, although opportunities for such mention are not lacking. Though the fields existed, they were less important than the cattle. Eumaeus's reticence is not due solely to his being a swine-herd, and thus less interested in fields of grain than in living creatures. Wealth in cornland is predicated of no one in the poems,[2] but this should not be understood as implying lack of private ownership. The absence of the mention of the pastures, on the other hand, is characteristic. Probably the greater part of the island was still available for such use. It certainly was not occupied with grain fields, and there were no meadows in the modern sense of the term.[3] In this connexion we may note that while grain-fields and fruit-land are promised and given in return for public services, according to Homer, no pasture-land is so bestowed. Why should it be? Its use was free, with only indefinite restrictions. Pastures were not counted as part of a man's estate. They were often on land which was

---

[1] ξ 25, 372, π 3, ω 150. So in Theocritus, *Idyls*, xiii. 25, the sheep are taken in the spring to the "remote pastures" (ἐσχατιαί). *Cf.* Euripides, *Cyclops*, 27.

[2] πολυλήιος, E 613, is pretty near this, but strictly is *rich in standing grain*, "with abundant harvests."

[3] λειμών (as B 461) is a *grassy place*, and grass was sometimes cut for the use of the flocks (σ 366 ff.), but no hay seems to have been cured and stored for winter use, and the meadow was a mere adjunct to the pasture. The grass was cut with the sickle (δρέπανον, σ 368). Such meadows were naturally often well watered (ὑδρηλοί, ι 133).

not fit for the plough, especially on the mountain side. Thus Priam's brother and his son tended their flocks and herds on the foot-hills of Mount Ida (Z 25, Λ 105), where Aeneas was watching his cattle when Achilles came upon him (Υ 188), and there Apollo attended the kine of Laomedon (Φ 449). The prominence of wild beasts in the life of the poet's age, shows that much land was left unoccupied and was ranged by wild boars and lions, with wolves and jackals not unknown.

As long as the land and other property belonged to the family as such, and not to the individual who happened to be its head, of course no will or testament was possible. On the death of the head of the family, his sons divided the estate by lot (ξ 209). The son of a concubine apparently could demand no definite portion ; but he might receive a house and a smaller share of flocks and herds than his brothers (ξ 210). As in later Athenian law, women do not seem to inherit. They go with the estate, and the brother would be expected to have a father's care for them, and to plan for their marriage. Of course the normal state of woman in such a civilization is in the marriage relation. No arrangement is made for her except as part of a family, and on her marriage she becomes a member of her husband's family. She has no property of her own, because she needs none. The poet knows that at times, in default of descendants, the estate goes to more remote relatives (χηρωσταί, E 158, cf. Hesiod, *Theogony*, 607). If the family of Odysseus had not been so small,—neither he himself, nor his wife, nor his father, nor his son had any brother,—we might have learned more about the rights of succession in that early age, but the poet has no occasion to give detailed information on this point. Andromache (X 488) implies that her son would inherit lands, but fears that, being fatherless, he may be deprived of them ; the question clearly was not so much whether he would receive, as whether he could keep them.

Land Entailed.

We remember that Solon was accounted the first law-giver to allow the right of making a will, and that at no time in Greece could a man bequeath his property if he had legitimate sons. Thus in a true sense, not only land but all property continued to belong to the family through the classical period.

While grain-fields and orchards are carefully enclosed, the very practise of herding cattle assumes the absence of fences and clearly marked boundaries. The herd is taken now to one region, and again to another,—wherever it is likely to find the best pasturage,—just as the youthful Joseph found his brothers not in Shechem but in Dothan (*Genesis* xxxvii. 17). So even much later, in the poems of Theocritus (*Id.* iv. 17), when Battus mockingly inquires whether a certain slender heifer is fed on dew like the cicada, the herdsman replies : " No, indeed ! At one time I pasture her on the banks of the Aesarus, and again she skips about shady Latymnum." And again (Theocritus, *Id.* viii. 37), Daphnis sings : " Fountains and pastures, if Daphnis sings like the nightingale, fatten this herd ; and if Menalcas lead any cattle hither, let him, too, have abundance,"—assuming that the pastures did not belong to a particular owner, but that any herdsman might bring his cattle to them, Menalcas as well as Daphnis. That flocks might mingle in the pasture, is seen from a comparison of the leaders of the Achaeans, arranging their forces before going into battle, with goat-herds separating their broad flocks when these have become confused in the fields (B 474).

Bread was the "marrow of men" ($\mu\nu\epsilon\lambda\grave{o}\varsigma$ $\mathring{a}\nu\delta\rho\hat{\omega}\nu$, β 290), as we have seen already, yet the poet tells us little of grain-fields and their cultivation. The movement of the *Grain-fields.* assembly of the Achaeans before Troy is likened to that of a field of tall grain before a strong west wind (B 147); Ajax, stubbornly resisting the onsets of the Trojan warriors is compared to a stubborn ass which small boys are unable to drive from a field of grain until his hunger is satisfied (Λ 559); the glad heart of Menelaus on receiving a prize in the chariot-race in honor of Patroclus, is bright like the dew on the ears of growing grain (Ψ 598). On the Shield of Achilles, Hephaestus forges scenes which appear to stand for the three seasons of spring, summer, and autumn :—(1) a rich thrice-ploughed corn-field, on which many ploughmen are driving their teams to and fro, while an attendant stands, ready to give to each a glass of wine, as he reaches the end of his furrow ; (2) a royal harvest-field, on which reapers are busy with sickles, while three binders are tying in sheaves the grain which boys bring to them in their arms; the prince is looking on, well-pleased, and dinner is preparing under an oak; (3) a vintage scene, with young men and maidens merrily bringing baskets of grapes, with feet keeping time to the music of a lyre and the vintage song of a boy (Σ 541 ff.). But these scenes afford us but a scant basis for a detailed account of the farm-life of the Homeric period. The three ploughings of the fields perhaps refer not to work done on three separate occasions, at different times of the year (as in accordance with later usage), but to the earnest efforts to "ear" the ground thoroughly before the sowing. The primitive Greek plough did not turn the soil up and over, like its modern successor in western lands; it only tickled the earth, and a single ploughing did not suffice to loosen the soil and bring its chemical elements into relation with the grain which was to be planted. In Modern Greece, the traveller may see the husbandman give his newly ploughed field a second tilth, with furrows at right angles to those which were run at first, in order to prepare the soil more perfectly for the seed.

That Homer's spring scene represents the activity of many ploughmen, must not be understood as a strong indication that the poet knew no small fields ploughed and sown. The number of ploughmen, like the presence of the attendant with cups of wine, is simply for the greater animation of the scene. The poet as a rule chooses to depict that which is on a large scale, and somewhat magnificent according to the standards of the time, rather than to paint the life of the farmer of Hesiod, who gains scanty returns for hard labor. Not only is the song addressed to princes and warriors rather than to peasants and petty farmers, but he does not choose to describe in realistic fashion the sufferings of the poor. The difference of tone between the Homeric poet and Hesiod, however, we have learned elsewhere, is due not so much to the difference of audience as to the different spirits of the poets themselves. The later poet's experiences had embittered his life, and he found only weariness and vexation of spirit, where the Homeric poet would have something to enjoy or to praise.

To determine the size of the Homeric grain-fields, is not easy. A field of fifty *gyae*,[1]—half for orchard and half for grain,—is offered to Meleager as an inducement to render military service for the Calydonians (I 577). *Size of the Fields.* The disguised Odysseus proposes as a trial of strength with Eurymachus, that they mow together a field of four *gyae* (σ 374), and this is the size of the garden of Alcinoüs (η 113). Odysseus evidently proposes what would be a full day's work, but we must remember that the work was to be done with the sickle, and not with the scythe or modern mowing machine. According to Eustathius, the garden of Alcinoüs was a hundred feet square,[2] but this has been thought inadequate, and other authorities would multiply this by twelve,—making a field four hundred feet long by three hundred feet broad.[3] This might seem to agree with Eustathius's view that the field was as large as a strong man with good oxen could plough in a single day, for a plot one hundred feet square would seem too small for such a stint; this was exactly the definition of an English *acre*, which was much larger, and naturally the standard was not entirely fixed,—in some districts a day's ploughing amounted to more than in others. An ordinary standard of an acre seems to have been thirty-two furrows, each a furrow (furlong) long. But here again we may receive light from modern usage in oriental lands. According to Van Lennep (*Bible Lands*, p. 74), "the standard measure of land throughout the Turkish empire is called a *dunum*,[4] and is the area which one pair of oxen can plough in a single day; it is equal to a quarter of an acre, or a square of forty *arshuns* (nearly

---

[1] Ridgeway derives the use of γύη for a division of land, from γύης, the curved part of the plough, which was used for the plough itself.

[2] The πέλεθρον of Φ 407, λ 577, is naturally brought into connexion with the Attic πλέθρον, *one hundred feet*; as a measure of surface then it would be 10,000 square feet,—though this makes the overthrown Ares to cover a space 700 feet by 100, which presents him as a monster. What place would such a creature have on the battlefield? How could he be wounded by Diomed (E 855)? But the epic poet did not shrink from telling of scenes which could not be represented on the stage.

[3] See Hultsch, *Metrologie*,[2] 41.

[4] "Derived," says President Washburn, of Robert College, "from *dunmek, to turn.* The Bulgarian and Slavic words for about this measure also come from the verb meaning to turn, and therefore they probably have some relation to ploughing."

one hundred feet)."[1]   The modern Turkish plough so closely resembles that of the old Greeks, that an inference from the work done by the present implement, to the Homeric measures of land, would be reasonable enough in itself, but the garden of Alcinoüs and the domain offered to Meleager would be much less magnificent than we are wont to think them. The more abundant we suppose the supply of land to have been at that time, in comparison with the demand, and the smaller the measure of the *gya*, the less valuable was the inducement which was offered to Meleager for his defence of Calydon.

Grain-fields are carefully limited,[2] and fruit-fields are enclosed by dykes or stone walls or hedges.[3]   The poet once compares the contest between the Achaeans and the Lycians over the wall of the Greek camp (M 421) to that of two men with regard to the bounds that should fix their rights in a grain-field which had been held in common,—but here clearly was no enclosure ; possibly the ground in question may have been the space left untilled between two allotments.

Boundaries of Fields.

[1] Pöhlmann, *Aus dem hellenischen Mittelalter*, in *Altertum und Gegenwart*, p. 178, believes the square *plethron* to be what a man could plough in half a day, and the γύη to be a double *plethron*, or 100 by 200 feet. Thus a πεντηκοντήγυον field would contain twenty-five or thirty acres. But he thinks that not all γύαι were of the same size, and accepts the view of the Scholiast on η 113 for the garden of Alcinoüs, that the side was of two stadia, or a trifle more than 1200 feet, and then the πεντηκοντήγυον field would cover about 140 acres. The question is complicated, since, at some times and in some places, the standard was set by the work done by a team of eight oxen, and in others by a team of two oxen. That the work done in half a day should form a standard, results from the fact that with the fodder available in some places, oxen could draw the plough but half a day, needing the afternoon for rest and food. Hence some would understand the Homeric time of "loosing cattle from the plough" (βουλυτόνδε, ι 58) as noon rather than late afternoon (see page 48).—One hundred feet seems to us very short for a furrow. The very name *furlong* is a reminder that the old English furrow was more than 650 feet in length.

[2] *Cf.* a stone as *boundary of the field* (οὖρος ἀρούρης, Φ 405, where Athena overthrows Ares, by hitting him with such a stone) and ἀπουρήσουσιν ἀρούρας, Χ 489, *remove the boundary of his fields*. Compare with the latter the Hebrew injunction, "Thou shalt not remove thy neighbor's landmark, which they of old time have set in thy inheritance" (*Deut.* xix. 14), and the very first of Plato's *Laws*, μὴ κινείτω γῆς ὅρια μηδείς (*Laws*, 842 E).

[3] γέφυραι, ἕρκεα ἀλωάων, E 88 f., *cf.* Σ 564, η 113, ω 224.

For ploughing either oxen or mules were used (K 351, N 703, θ 124). Mules were preferred to oxen for this work : the poet takes as a measure of distance *Oxen or* the length of the furrow of mules, " for these are *Mules for* better than oxen to draw the well-made plough *Ploughing.* on the deep fallow ground." [1] That horses should not be used, is as we should expect ; horses were never set to menial tasks in ancient Greece, being the " delight of proud luxury," according to Aeschylus, and not to be *Horses.* humiliated by service as common draught animals. Horses were to be used [2] in war, in the games, for display, and for occasional journeys, but not for hard labor. When Priam goes to the Achaean camp in order to ransom Hector's body, the king drives in a chariot drawn by horses, while his old herald follows him in a cart drawn by mules, for the taking of the ransom and the bringing of the dead body (Ω 263 ff.). No horse pulls a plough or common wagon, but a chariot drawn by horses conveys the young Telemachus and his friend Pisistratus from Pylus to Sparta (γ 496). Nausicaa takes a vehicle drawn by mules when she goes with her maids to the sea-shore to wash the family linen (ζ 73). Oxen and mules are used to bring the dead bodies from the field of battle to the camp (H 333), and mules draw and carry from the mountain to the plain the wood for the funeral pyre of Patroclus (Ψ 111, 121). So in P 742, the weariness of the Achaeans in bringing the body of Patroclus to the camp, is likened to that of mules in drawing a ship-timber from the mountain.

" Mules of the field " are said to come from the Eneti in Paphlagonia (B 852), and at Ω 277 the Mysians are said

---

[1] Others would understand this measure to be of the breadth, not of the length of the patch ploughed,—supposing that the length of the furrow was uniform, but that the mules moved faster, and thus ploughed more furrows in a day.

[2] The Greek feeling is well illustrated by that of the Arabs : " Abd-el-Kader . . . declares that many of the horses of the Arab race have fallen from their nobility because employed in tillage, in carrying burdens, and doing useful rather than ornamental work. He declares that if the true horse even treads upon the ploughed land, he diminishes in value." " There has been no blessing upon our country since we have changed our coursers into beasts of burden and of tillage. Has not God made the ox for the plough, the camel to transport merchandise, and the horse alone for the race ? "

to have given a pair to king Priam. The Homeric mule seems a more dignified animal than the mule of the Occi-
Mules. dent, but less so than his cousin of the Orient.
The ordinary word for mule is *half-ass* (ἡμίονος); *mountain-beast* (οὐρεύς, from οὖρος, *mountain*) is used four or possibly five times. No distinction has been made clear between the use of the two, and we may suppose them to have been synonymous. So far as appears, the mare is the mother of the half-ass (at Ψ 266 a mare is big with a mule colt, and at φ 23 and δ 636 mares have mule colts), and some one has conjectured that the οὐρεύς had a horse for sire,—but this is uncertain. Manure of oxen and mules lies in the courtyard of Odysseus's palace on Ithaca (ρ 298), but the poet tells of no horses on the island, and makes Telemachus say expressly that this is better fitted for goats than for horses, and decline Menelaus's offer of a gift of three horses and a chariot (δ 589 ff.). Mules are bestowed as gifts and as prizes for excellence in games (ο 85 and Ψ 662). The patience of this animal is recognized, but also the fact that he is not easily trained to labor (Ψ 662, 665). The ass (ὄνος, Λ 558) is mentioned but once, and that in a comparison, as a symbol of stubborn obstinacy.

Homer gives no description of the plough, but this unquestionably was much like that of Hesiod, for such
The Plough. implements are still used in Greece and in the Orient generally. The plough which Echetlæus wielded effectively as a weapon of offense on the battlefield of Marathon (Pausanias, i. 32. 5) cannot have been such an implement as is used in the great grain-fields of the North-west, and even in Modern Greece a woman sometimes carries home her plough on her shoulder, while she drives her oxen (or, more exactly, her kine, since as in old times cows are used for draught and not as milch cows) before her.[1]

Of orchards we read little in Homer except in three passages which critics incline to think of later composition than most of the poems: (1) the orchard of the old king

---

[1] Homer gives to the plough the epithet well-joined (πηκτόν, K 353), and does not mention the αὐτόγυον of Hesiod, in which the share and the pole seem to have been of the same piece of timber. See page 331.

Laërtes on Ithaca (ω 222 ff., 340 ff.), (2) that of Alcinoüs, king of the Phaeacians (η 112 ff.), and (3) the representation of a vintage scene on the Shield of Achilles *Orchards.* (Σ 561 ff.), where the vines are stayed on props. The extent of Laërtes's orchard is indicated by his gift to his son Odysseus, when a boy, of ten apple trees, thirteen pear-trees, forty fig-trees, and fifty rows of grape-vines, bearing all manner of varieties of grapes. Alcinoüs had "pears, pomegranates, bright gleaming apples, sweet figs, and luxuriant olives." His succession of grapes, too, was long,—at the same time, some being ready to be picked, and others just changing color, while others were only shedding their flowers. These grapes of Alcinoüs were not only for wine but were also to be dried for raisins (η 123), unless the exposure of the gathered grapes to the sun in this passage was simply to prepare them for the wine press. This Phaeacian garden may have been arranged in terraces, but these are indicated for no other garden or vineyard of the poems. The grotto of Calypso is overhung with a domestic vine laden with clusters of grapes (ἡμερίς, ε 69). The two verses which enumerate the fruit trees of Alcinoüs, recur in the description of the punishment of Tantalus in Hades (λ 589 f.): Tantalus is surrounded with fruit, but can reach none. The fall of Euphorbus when he is struck by Menelaus, is compared by the poet to the overthrow by the wind of a young olive tree, which a man had planted in a trench, well supplied with water (P 53). It was an olive tree, too, of which Odysseus fashioned the stump into a post for his bed (ψ 190), allowing it to stand firm where it had grown, and building the wall of his bed-chamber about it.

Wealth in the Homeric age consisted largely in flocks and herds, as has been already intimated. Indeed, cattle were the natural and usual standard of value, and *Flocks and* the most convenient medium of exchange. Kine *Herds.* were valued then for their flesh and hides on their death, and for their services as draught animals during life. They also served incidentally in other ways, as for threshing grain (Υ 495),—"treading out the corn," as among the ancient Hebrews. The milk of cows was not used.

No difference in breed of cattle is noticed, and probably all were much alike.[1]

One female slave costs the worth of twenty cattle (a 431), while another is worth only four (Ψ 705): a suit of gold armor is worth a hundred cattle, while one of bronze is worth but nine (Z 236); a tripod may be worth twelve cattle (Ψ 703); a captured son of Priam is sold by Achilles to a Lemnian prince, who evidently bought him on speculation, for the equivalent of a hundred cattle (Φ 79). Not that cattle served as money, but that they formed the basis and standard of values,—one evidently not differing much in worth from another. Thyestes was "rich in lambs" (πολύαρνι, B 106), Iphiclus was "rich in flocks" (πολυμήλου, B 705); Agamemnon offers to Achilles as part atonement for his wrong to him, cities in which are men "rich in sheep and kine" (πολύρρηνες, πολυβοῦται, I 154); Mentor was "rich in horses" (πολυίππου, N 171); Pelias was "rich in sheep" (πολύρρηνος, λ 257). Tydeus (Ξ 122) "had abundance of corn-fields and orchards and flocks, and was best of the Achaeans with the spear." Treasures and flocks are coördinated in β 75. The confused voices of the Trojans as they go into battle are compared to the bleating of countless sheep in the folds of a rich man (πολυπάμονος, Δ 433). The Trojan king Erichthonius had three thousand mares feeding on the lowlands (Υ 221). Antenor's son Iphidamas gave for his bride (although she was his mother's sister, and his grandfather would not be expected to be exorbitant in his demands for wedding presents) one hundred cattle, and he promised to give in addition one thousand sheep and goats (Λ 244). With this dowry we may compare the epithet which is given to maidens, (ἀλφεσίβοιαι, Σ 593) "bringing cattle" to their fathers. The general expression "rich in possessions" (πολυκτήμων, E 613) seems to refer to flocks and herds,—κτήματα. Hesiod (*Fragment*, 80) as well as Homer recognizes flocks and herds as meaning wealth.

---

[1] Ridgeway, however, would distinguish in Homer cattle with crumpled horns, such as are represented on Mycenaean monuments, and a breed with short straight horns, which he believes to have been introduced after the Mycenaean period, from the north.

Less frequently than cattle are harvests[1] or gold or bronze (as πολύχρυσος, πολύχαλκος, Κ 315) used as indications of wealth. Only once is wealth in slaves mentioned (ρ 422). The suitors of Penelope are declared likely to wish for themselves speed of foot rather than wealth of gold and raiment, if they should see Odysseus returning to his home (α 165). This may be intended to show what was precious in their eyes, but in that age clothing was a much more permanent possession than now, not merely because fashions were less fickle, but also because garments were not "fitted" to the person, but could be worn by one as well as by another. *Wealth in Other Possessions.*

The Homeric flocks and herds in general seem to have been brought home from the pasture at evening, though the practise was not uniform. Very likely the usage differed in different seasons of the year, but the protection at home was not more from the cold than from wild beasts and thieves. At Λ 548, Ajax, withdrawing before the enemy, is likened to a lion reluctantly leaving a cattle-yard,—driven away by men and boys who keep watch all night; and similarly, Menelaus (P 109, 657) leaves the body of Patroclus, before the advancing Hector and the Trojans, like a lion driven unwillingly from a farm-yard. At Δ 433, the voices of the Trojans are likened to the bleating of countless sheep in the farm-yard of a wealthy man,—a-milking and hearing the voices of their young, from which manifestly they have been separated during the day. When Odysseus returned to his companions from the palace of Circe, these ran to meet him as calves run to meet their mothers on their return to the yard, "and the pens no longer hold them" (κ 410 ff.). Diomed is roused by a wound, as a lion is roused when wounded by a shepherd, as he leaps over the wall of the sheepfold (E 137). After the third day of battle, the Achaean guards sit watchful, as dogs keep guard over their flocks in a farm-yard when they hear a wild beast coming through the forest over the mountain (K 183). At M 300, Sarpedon is compared to a lion which is driven by hunger to assail the flocks even within the fold, and in spite of *Flocks and Herds at Night.*

[1] So πολυλήιος, E 613; cf. ἀλήιος, I 125, βαθυλήιος, Σ 550.

shepherds with dogs and spears. The warriors about
Sarpedon's dead body are likened to flies gathering about
the pails of milk in a farm-yard in spring-time (Π 641).
On the Shield of Achilles, Hephaestus forges a representation
of a great sheep-pasture in a glen, with stalls, well-roofed
lean-to's, and pens (Σ 588), and of a herd of cattle going
with lowing from the farm-yard to the pasture, attended by
four shepherds and nine dogs, but attacked by two fierce
lions (Σ 575). In the *Odyssey*, we see not only the droves
of Odysseus's swine taken out to pasture in the morning and
brought back at evening (ξ 25, 410, π 3), but also the
herds and flocks of the Cyclops Polyphemus, who left only
the kids and lambs in their pens, during the day (ι 217
ff., 237 ff., 315, 336, 449 ff.), and was wont to leave the
rams and the he-goats in the courtyard, without the cave,
at night. On the eve of the night when the Cyclops was
blinded, having a presentiment of ill, he drove all the flocks
into the cave,—evidently expecting an attack upon his sheep
and goats by wild beasts or marauders. Polyphemus, we
may remark incidentally, had no dogs to aid him in the
care of his flocks. This was well managed by the poet,
for a single dog would have frustrated Odysseus's wisest
schemes for escape; but while the swine-herd Eumaeus has
dogs (ξ 22), we read of no sheep-dogs in the fields.
Another instance of the herding of cattle in the *Odyssey*,
is in connexion with the short nights of the Laestrygonians,—
where the shepherd as he drove home his flocks at night-
fall was hailed by the herd who was then driving out his
cattle for the next day!—and the poet adds that in that
land a man who needed no sleep could earn double wages,
one by herding kine, and the other by tending sheep,—
evidently each for twelve hours (κ 82 ff.). But when
Odysseus by the aid of Aeolus so nearly reaches his home
that he sees men tending fires (πυρπολέοντας ἐλεύσσομεν,
κ 30), these must be shepherds bivouacking on the mountain,
" keeping watch over their flocks by night." The flight of
the Trojans over the plain at the beginning of the third
day of battle is compared to that of a herd of cattle
attacked by a lion in the darkness of the night (Λ 172);
if these fled, they cannot have been in an enclosure, but

must have been in their pasture, in a field or on a mountain. So the poet speaks of a thick mist as "not at all dear to the shepherd, but better than night for the thief" (Γ 11), which does not imply, as some commentators have believed, that the flocks were in folds at night, but rather only that the thief was as secure against detection in the mist as by night, and yet could see better for the conveyance of his booty. A principal duty of the herdsman was, as we have seen, to protect his cattle against wild beasts, and at O 632, the poet compares the Achaeans put to flight by Hector and Zeus, to cattle under the care of a herdsman who was not yet skilled in fighting with beasts, attacked by a lion.

The farm-yard and farm-buildings were often primitive, and no more of a protection than the cave into which the herdsman is represented as driving his flocks for *The Farm-Yard.* shelter on the approach of a storm, at Δ 279. The goat-herds of Homer's Greece as well as those of Theocritus's Sicily may have regarded a cave as affording a reasonable amount of shelter. The yard of Odysseus's swine-herd, Eumaeus, was made with palisades of oak, but the hut contained no furniture of any kind. A goatskin was thrown over a heap of rushes as a seat for Odysseus (ξ 49), and a similar provision was made for Telemachus on his arrival (π 47). Odysseus (in disguise) was honored by a place to sleep on goatskins and sheepskins near the fire (ξ 518), while the swine-herd himself threw a thick cloak about him, took a big goatskin, and went out to sleep near the swine under shelter of a rock. So far as Eumaeus is concerned, then, the swine and their herd might as well have been at any sheltered spot on the mountain side: but this was on a winter night, and perhaps the swine were not driven to their pens at all on the ordinary summer night. No table is mentioned in the hut of Eumaeus, and we can hardly believe that he had this article of furniture when he had neither bed nor chair. That the Cyclops Polyphemus has no table, bed, or chair, then, does not prove his barbarism ; he has as much furniture as ordinary shepherds. So the old Laërtes, when he lays down the cares of state, such as they are, and goes to dwell upon his farm, lives like the rest, the servants : in winter he sleeps on the ashes by the fire, while in the summer he finds his bed on the leaves, wherever he happens to be, in the fields (λ 190); he has no bedstead and mattress.

Of the domestication of wild animals, the poet says nothing. Wild goats feed in great numbers on the island which lies opposite the land of the Cyclopes (ι 224), and Odysseus and his companions in a brief chase kill more than one hundred for food. The swine-herd Eumaeus had the skin of a wild goat as his blanket (ξ 50). Odysseus's dog Argos in his prime was taken out to hunt wild goats, hares, and fawns (ρ 295), and comparisons with the hunt for wild goats are found at Γ 24 and O 271. The bow of the Lycian archer Pandarus (Δ 105) was made from the horns of a wild goat which the archer himself had shot on the hills. The exact species of these animals can only be conjectured ; we need not believe that the domesticated was of the same species as the wild goat. No wild horses or asses are mentioned by the poet, but he seems to refer to wild bulls at N 571, where Adamas, pierced through the bowels by the spear of Meriones, struggled as a bull which herdsmen bind with thongs upon the mountains, and lead by force against his will. This might be a bull which had strayed from his herd, and had become enamored of a free life, but the representations of a bull-chase on the beautiful gold cups which were found at Vaphio near Sparta (see Fig. 15), and on the frescoed wall of the palace at Tiryns, confirm the interpretation of the Homeric passage as referring to wild cattle. Wild boars are frequently mentioned by Homer. Their fierce courage was as proverbial to the Greeks as that of lions, with which they were often pitted. The hunt of the Calydonian boar, which laid waste the field of Oeneus, and the conflict which ensued over the trophy, was one of the best known of the early Greek stories of adventure, and is referred to by Homer at I 529 ff. The scar by which the returning Odysseus was recognized by his faithful nurse, was from a wound received on a wild-boar hunt in his youth (τ 392 ff.).

Wild Cattle.

Metals naturally were stored as treasures (κειμήλια, β 75).
Three times we read: "Many treasures lie in the home of

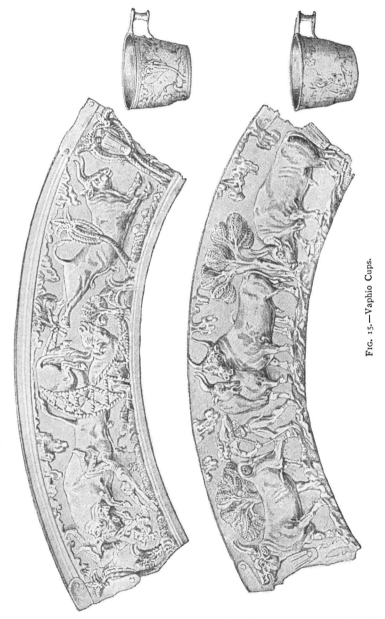

Fɪɢ. 15.—Vaphio Cups.

my father,—copper and gold and the well-wrought iron.
From these he would give thee gladly a boundless ransom,

if he should learn that I was alive at the ships of the
Achaeans" (Z 47, K 379, Λ 133).

Whence came the Homeric gold and silver? No one can
say definitely. No mines are mentioned by the poet, and
thus the provenience of the metals is but a matter
of conjecture, although this is based on some
facts. Did the Greeks of that age know of the
veins of silver in Attica, or of the silver and copper on
Euboea (Strabo, x. 447)? Did they bring their copper from
Cyprus, or from Magna Graecia, or did they find it near
Argos? At Athena's visit to Ithaca in the guise of Mentes,
in the first book of the *Odyssey*, she says that she is on
her way to Temesa for copper, taking a cargo of iron for
exchange. The story is fictitious, but it was devised
to seem probable to the listener. The situation of this
Temesa from which the copper was to be brought, has been
much discussed, but it seems to be on the west coast of
Bruttium.[1] The poet does not indicate, either, where the
Taphian king Mentes could most easily have procured his
load of iron which he was to give for copper, but iron is
said to be found in the island near Acarnania which Dr.
Dörpfeld is disposed to identify with the Homeric Taphos.

Gold and Silver.

The uses of the metals in Homer's time are discussed in
Chapter X.

The life of the Greeks of Homer's time was in the country.
Indeed they knew no city life as it is understood in modern
times,—opposed to country life. Their towns were
small. Manufactures were domestic. Every man
was a farmer. Princes thought the tending of
cattle not beneath their dignity.[2] Anchises was keeping his
herds when he was visited by the goddess Aphrodite (E 313),
and the three goddesses in their contest for the prize of
beauty sought the judgment of the herdsman Paris on his
farm (Ω 29). When Telemachus's absence from the palace
is noted, it causes no surprise; he is thought to be somewhere on the farm (δ 640). The old Laërtes, having yielded
his throne to his son, retires to his farm, and spends the

No City Life.

[1] α 184. See Wilamowitz-Moellendorff, *Homerische Untersuchungen*, 24; Strabo,
vi. 255. But for the Cyprian site, see *Jahrbuch*, xxii. 41.

[2] Z 25, 423, Λ 105, Υ 188, ν 222, ο 386.

close of his life in patched garb, cultivating trees, with gloves and gaiters as protection against thorns (ω 227). On the Shield of Achilles a king is represented as watching with glad heart the harvesters in his field (Σ 556). The disguised Odysseus vaunts against Penelope's suitors his strength and skill in mowing and ploughing (σ 366), as though these young suitors, too, with all their insolence, prided themselves on such accomplishments. Men were in close connexion with the soil. The use of plough and sickle was as familiar as that of sword and spear.

No such painful poverty is pictured by Homer as by Hesiod, who is a prophet,—with a clear eye and ringing voice to see and to denounce the sordid character of the peasant's life. In Homer's time, land was *" Neither Poverty nor Riches."* abundant, and the tiller of the soil in that climate was able to secure a subsistence without excessive labor. But doubtless some of that generation felt the burdens of life, though the poet does not tell about them. The swine-herd and neat-herd of Odysseus were not aware of their privations, and enjoyed what goods they had. A sharp contrast between the life of the rich and the poor, we should not expect to find at a time when wealth could secure so few advantages. The occupations of the wealthy were about the same as those of the poor, and the wealthy were not indolent,—although of course the rich man was not obliged to work when he did not want to do so,—and their possessions were, for the most part, such as were liable to be removed by a marauding expedition or other hostile incursion. To increase one's herds was to increase the temptation for an invasion of his neighbor over the border. The rich man had no opportunity to buy government bonds, or make other safe investments. The natural disposition to save and increase wealth was thus checked by other considerations. The wealthy man had few of the amusements of the rich man of to-day. He had no pictures, no library, no scientific collections. His chariot and horses did not differ greatly from those of his neighbors. He had no excitement from the promotion of great industrial enterprises.

CHAPTER IX

SLAVERY AND SERVITUDE

THE term slavery implies to the modern reader much that did not exist in Homeric Greece. Nowhere in the civilized world at present is to be found just such a relation *No Slavery in Modern Sense.* between the superior and the inferior as prevailed in Greece a thousand years before Christ. During no period in ancient Greece was slavery a dominant economic factor, as it became in the southern states of America. And in Homer's time manufactures and mines had not yet given importance to this institution, as in later Athens the father of the orator Demosthenes had thirty-two slaves working as cutlers and twenty as cabinet-makers ; the orator Lysias and his brother had one hundred and twenty slaves employed in their arms factory ; the general Nicias had a thousand slaves engaged in the silver mines at Laurium, Hipponicus had six hundred slaves at work there, and a certain Philemonides had three hundred slaves there. The Bedouin chieftain may have many devoted followers, who would do his bidding and would render any service demanded by their leader, but these are not his *slaves.* Loyal submission does not make slavery. The ordinary Homeric man and woman did not shrink from physical exertion. Toil was not considered a curse upon the race then, and no contempt was felt for either labor or the laborer.

Shall we call the dependents of the Homeric age followers, retainers, vassals, henchmen, servants, bondmen, serfs, thralls, or slaves ? They were their master's *men*, but were they *slaves* ? For convenience we may call them slaves, but we must remember that they possessed considerable independence and comfort, and that they lacked the two distinguishing marks of a slave according to modern writers,—being allowed to possess wife and property of their own, and thus having the rights of *connubium* and *commercium*, and not being sold. *Followers? Henchmen?* Eumaeus had the *commercium* and Dolius the *connubium*, and both apparently lacked the third mark of a slave,—the danger of being sold away from their homes. If they had been sent away for sale, this would have been an act of violence, not in harmony with the sentiment of the people, unless unusual provocation had been given. The ordinary Greek word for slave (δοῦλος) is not found in the Homeric poems in its masculine form,[1] and its nearest equivalent is cognate to the word which Priam uses of the freemen,—the soldiers,—who are subject to Agamemnon on the plain of Troy.[2] The subjects were bound to perform certain services for their feudal lord,—to labor on his fields, or to give tribute from the fruits of their land and flocks in time of peace, and to follow him to battle in time of war. But these services were determined and regulated by no law, and in most instances must have been entirely indefinite. Some lords would require more than others, just as in other matters, too, the constitution of society left much to the will or caprice of the stronger. Since the state as such afforded no protection to life and property, the comfortable existence of an isolated peasant was impossible. The peasants were obliged to seek or accept the patronage of some leader who should care for their interests in peace, and who would defend them and their families in the troublous times of war,—and most of those times were troublous. They needed a master of some sort as much as ever the Children of Israel needed a king. The economic situation, if not war, was almost sure to bring them into a dependent relation ; and if a peasant of independent spirit did not make himself the vassal of a stronger man, he was likely to be reduced to this position by the strong man himself, without any one's interference in his behalf. Thus, just as in

---

[1] But *cf.* δούλη, δ 12, Γ 409 ; δουλοσύνη, χ 423 ; δούλιον ἦμαρ, Ζ 463 ; δούλειον εἶδος, ω 252.

[2] *Cf.* δμώς, ω 257, δμωαί, a 147, with δεδμήατο, Γ 183.

Attica in early times, many of the poor tilled the soil and herded the cattle of the rich and powerful, and were paid in the products of the soil and the herds, and in the use of ground for themselves, as well as by the security which association with a mighty man afforded. Then the peasants who failed to bring their tribute to their lord, being in debt to him, were much in the position of serfs : they were not truly free, though they could not be sold from the land. Any attempt at resistance might accelerate the process, and make the subjects slaves at once. Similar conditions in Attica, after coined money had been introduced, brought about the selling of many of the people into foreign lands.[1] The state of the Homeric bondman ($\delta\mu\omega\varsigma$) in certain respects corresponded to that of the Spartan Helots and the Thessalian Penestae of the historical period, but was not identical with it. Nothing in Homer points to a class of slaves whose fathers had been the owners of the land, but had been reduced to servitude by a conquering tribe, as seems to be true of the Helots and Penestae, though the evidence for this is not perfect.

The Homeric family is patriarchal and independent ; it is sufficient in itself. The servants are strictly members of

Servants Members of the Family. their master's family, but naturally not all have the same office,—some are subordinate to others. The Homeric bondman is less of a " living tool," however, than his successor in Attica. The name of slave is applied to him no more justly than to the retainers of Abraham, of Lot, and of Laban, who followed and did the bidding of their tribal chief, without considering themselves his slaves. The servants of the Greeks as well as those of the Israelites, took part in the sacrifices and feasts of the family.[2] The fact that they had no rights before the law, does not indicate that they were treated with cruelty. No one at that time

---

[1] " The people were in debt to the rich," Plutarch, *Solon*, xiii.

[2] For the Israelites, note that the family servants, but no foreigner or hired servant, took part in the celebration of the Passover. *Cf. Exodus* xii. 45, *Deut.* xvi. 11. Abraham's steward Eliezer was so distinctly a member of his family that if Abraham had died without issue, Eliezer would have succeeded him (*Gen.* xv. 2). And Sheshan, having no son, gave his daughter to his Egyptian servant to wife (1 *Chron.* ii. 34 f.).

possessed rights before the law. The head of the family punished his child on the same principles, and with the same lack of legal limitations, as he punished his servant.[1] Odysseus put to death the faithless maid-servants of Penelope, as well as her insolent suitors, and the goat-herd Melanthius who had sided with them (χ 458 ff.), and severe punishment is threatened to men for disorderly conduct in another passage of the *Odyssey* (o 444), but these are exceptional acts of violence,—the hanging of the women no less than the slaying of the men.[2] When Euryclea, acknowledging her fault, says to Penelope, "Kill me if you like, dear lady, but I will tell the truth" (δ 743), she certainly does not expect to be taken at her word. Nor does Odysseus, when he threatens to kill the same old woman, who had been his nurse in his childhood, if she shall make known his identity, expect to be obliged to kill her; he really does not doubt her fidelity (τ 488).

In general, the interests of master and servants are held to be identical. The latter are heartily devoted and loyal to the family, in the Homeric poems as well as in the representations of the same age in Attic tragedy.[3] Agamemnon believed that his return would be "welcome to his children and his servants" (λ 431), and Andromache's maids weep with her over the approaching death of Hector (Z 500) as well as over his actual death (Ω 746). Penelope's women mourn

Servants and Masters Friendly.

---

[1] *Cf.* St. Paul's words, "The heir as long as he is a child differeth nothing from a servant" (οὐδὲν διαφέρει δούλου), *Galatians* iv. 1.

[2] Summary procedure is not unusual in primitive times, and the situation of Odysseus would justify almost any measures in the judgment of Homer's hearers. We are reminded of the informal order which Shakespeare makes Henry V. give for the execution of the Earl of Cambridge, Lord Scroop of Masham, and Grey of Northumberland (*Henry V.* ii. 2. 177),—"Get you therefore hence, Poor miserable wretches, to your death." This was a summary process, in truth.

[3] *Cf.* in Aeschylus the loyal attachment to his master of Agamemnon's old servant (*Ag.* 32 f.), the sympathy of the Choëphori for Electra and Orestes (*Cho.* 152, and *passim*), and in Euripides the fidelity of Medea's women (*e.g. Medea*, 54, "to good servants the misfortunes of the master are a source of grief," and Medea's appeal to another to tell nothing of Medea's plans, "if indeed you are a friend to your mistress," *Medea*, 823), and the grief of the old attendant in the *Alcestis* for his mistress's death. So in the *Helena* (1640) the leader of the chorus says that to die for their mistress is a noble death.

in sympathy with her loneliness (δ 719). The captive women of Achilles and Patroclus grieve on learning of the latter's death (Σ 29). Odysseus's servants shed tears of joy at his safe return (ϕ 223; *cf.* χ 498, ω 397), and at that of Telemachus (ρ 33). The trusted Eumaeus is full of affectionate regard for his young master (π 15), and says that servants delight to talk with their lord, and to eat and drink in the great hall, and Telemachus on his part calls Eumaeus "daddy" ($\check{a}\tau\tau a$, π 31),—just as both Telemachus and his father call Euryclea "mammy" ($\mu a\hat{\imath}a$). The daughter of old Dolius, who was given to Penelope by her father on her marriage, was brought up as her own child (σ 322), and Eumaeus, purchased as a child from traders by Laërtes, was brought up with Odysseus's sister Ctimene (o 365). Certainly the relation between master and man was not thought of as one of natural hostility. That a servant or slave might have a certain dignity and a right to an honorable title, is shown by the case of the swine-herd Eumaeus, to which we shall recur: he is called "god-like" twelve times ($\delta\hat{\imath}os$, ξ 48), and "leader of men" ($\check{o}\rho\chi a\mu os$ $\grave{a}\nu\delta\rho\hat{\omega}\nu$, ξ 121), and he has a slave of his own,—yet he is one of the few servants noted in the Homeric poems as purchased.

To distinguish accurately and sharply between the different classes of servants and the different degrees of servitude in the Homeric age, is obviously impossible. Doubtless
Classes of Servants. the lines between them were not broad and clear even to men of that time. The three main classes of servants exist: (1) slaves by descent, born in the household, (2) captives in war, and (3) bought slaves; but one class does not seem inferior to another either in privileges or in social estimation. Captives in war or purchased slaves might be of princely birth, but this past history is not shown to affect in any way the present or future condition of the servant. Eumaeus, the swine-herd, was the kidnapped son of a king, but in the establishment of Odysseus he was of no higher rank and had no greater privileges than the goat-herd who was born in slavery. Hector thinks of his wife Andromache, a king's daughter as well as a prince's wife, as enslaved after the fall of Troy,

and fetching water from the spring in some Greek land, or as plying the loom under the direction of an Achaean mistress (Z 746). So in the *Trojan Women* of Euripides (192), old Hecuba looked forward to her lot as changed from that of the queen of Troy to that of a keeper of the door, or a nurse of children in Greece ; and in the *Hecuba* (367), the princess Polyxena accepts her lot of death more readily because of the alternative,—to sweep, to weave, and make bread, and be wedded to a slave. The attendants whom the suitors of Penelope bring with them to their feasts seem to be free men, though the word (θεράποντες) which is applied to most of them is as indefinite as the English word attendant ; in the *Iliad* it is used freely of the esquire, who might be the social peer of his knight, and in Sparta it ever retained this meaning, being used of a comrade in arms. The term *oikeus* designates merely a member of the household or family (οἶκος), and Hector uses it of his wife Andromache and his son Astyanax (Z 366),[1]—though in later times it came to mean a *domestic*. The *thetes* appear to be " hired men," " day laborers"; but the time for which they are hired may be indefinite in duration,[2] and the terms of their payment uncertain. The cognate verb is used of the service which Apollo and Poseidon were sent to render to Laomedon of Troy for a year, in tending herds and in building a wall about the city (Φ 444) ; also of the position which the ghost of Achilles declares that he would prefer,—" to labor on the field of a poor man rather than to rule over all the dead in the realm of Hades " (λ 489) ; and of the place offered in jest to the disguised Odysseus by one of Penelope's insolent suitors (σ 357). Poseidon and Apollo, we are told by the poet, were dismissed from this service to Laomedon at the expiration of their year of humiliation, and without their wages in spite of their protests ; Laomedon even threatened to sell them into slavery (Φ 453). What their wages should have been, we do not learn. The incident

---

[1] *Cf.* also E 413. οἰκέτης has the same meaning in Herodotus, as viii. 44, 106, and οἰκέτις in Theocritus, *Idyls*, xviii. 38.

[2] But the term of service of Apollo and Poseidon to Laomedon of Troy, of Apollo to Admetus, and of Heracles to the Phrygian Omphale (Sophocles, *Trachiniae*, 253), is a year in each case.

reminds the reader of the injunction of the poet Hesiod, not many generations later, that wages should be duly paid (*Works*, 370). That hired workmen were familiar to the poet's hearers, is shown by his remark on the short night of the Laestrygonians: a man without need of sleep could there earn double wages (δοιοὺς ἐξήρατο μισθούς, κ 84),— clearly by serving as shepherd for twelve hours, and as neat-herd for the remaining hours of the long day. Odysseus's herds on the mainland, too, are under the care of "strangers and his own herdsmen" (ξ 102), and clearly these "strangers" must have been hired men.[1] Nothing indicates that any fixed rate of compensation was known,—for example, any relation between the worth of a sheep and a day's labor. What they received often might be called gifts as well as pay, though, naturally, at times an agreement might be made for a fixed number of kine or sheep, or measures of grain or wine. These *thetes* had no land of their own; they held that which they occupied on condition of rendering services to their lord in peace as well as in war. They were bound to serve him in reaping the grain of his fields as well as in fighting his battles, and such service could not always be defined in terms of days' work. That a *thes* might be the servant of a poor man, is made clear by the expression of Achilles's ghost which is quoted above.

The ordinary word for bond-servant is *dmōs* (δμώς, fem. δμωή), which means strictly only *subject*, as we have seen.

Bond-servant. Once the epithet *compulsory* (ἀναγκαῖοι, ω 210) is added, and once a compound, *underling* (ὑποδμώς, δ 386), is applied to the sea-god Proteus in his relation to Poseidon.

The word ἔριθοι, *workmen*, is used twice (Σ 550, 560) of the reapers on a royal domain. It has been thought to mean *slaves* simply. Commentators were averse to admitting that the king might not have enough slaves to do all his work. But it may refer quite as well to free retainers who were performing part of their quota of work for their lord. The latter view is supported by the use of the compound συνέριθος (ζ 32), where Athena in the guise of a maiden friend of Nausicaa offers to accompany and aid

Workman.

---

[1] So at δ 644, Odysseus is said to have both δμῶες and θῆτες.

her in her expedition to the river to wash the clothes of the family. These *erithi* were called in for a special piece of work, while the *thetes* (see page 263) were hired for a year, or at least for a term of months.—δρηστήρ and its feminine δρήστειρα, serving-man or woman (from δράω,—cf. ὑποδρώωσιν, ο 333), are used five times : of the nymphs who serve in the house of Circe (κ 349), of the six attendants of the fifty-two suitors for the hand of Penelope who come from Dulichium (π 248, cf. σ 76, υ 160), and of the serving women in Odysseus's house (τ 345).—δούλη (δ 12, Γ 409) is not distinguished from δμωή, though in both passages it is used of a concubine.—ἀμφίπολος may be the feminine counterpart of θεράπων, being used to designate a female *attendant* in a general sense.—ἀνδράποδον is used but once (Η 475), and that of the captives whom the Achaeans before Troy exchange with the Lemnian traders for wine.—The χερνῆτις of Μ 433 is clearly a free woman, since she is striving by working with wool to earn a miserable pittance for the support of her children. But her wool may be for sale, and she may not be working for hire, but independently, and then she does not concern us in this connexion.

Male slaves seem unknown to the ordinary household life of the Homeric time. Thus the Achaean chieftains took no body-servants with them to Troy.[1] They needed none. They were themselves accustomed not only to other forms of physical exercise, but also to hard work. The Achaeans rowed their own boats, built their own barracks, cared for their own arms and armor, and for their horses ; they killed, dressed, and cooked the cattle for their repasts, and they would have been puzzled to find occupation for valets. When the embassy for reconciliation comes from the Achaean chieftains to Achilles, the latter himself, with the aid of his comrades Patroclus and Automedon, cooks mutton and pork for his guests (Ι 207).

Male Slaves in the Household ?

[1] Philo Judaeus makes a similar remark (ii. 467, M.) with regard to the heroes of the Argonautic Expedition for the Golden Fleece, who took no slaves with them, but supplied their own needs. These primitive customs endured long in the parts of Greece which were remote from the new culture, especially in Phocis and Locris according to Timaeus (Athenaeus, 244 C), and in Euboea, where it continued customary for the younger to wait upon the elder, and where the page might become the lord.

His comrades, not servants, place the water over the fire to prepare the bath for the body of Patroclus (Σ 343). On receiving a visit from the old king Priam, who would ransom Hector's body, the same proud warrior, Achilles, kills a sheep, which his comrades cook (Ω 621); and in his lament over the body of Patroclus (Τ 316), he recalls how this friend often had placed food before him. The preparation of food, then, is not assigned to the captive Trojan women in the Achaean camp, unless, as we may suppose, they had charge of the grinding of grain and the making of the so-called bread. In the household of Odysseus on Ithaca, although fifty women are engaged in various labors, no man-servant is mentioned.[1] The "heralds and ready attendants" (θεράποντες, α 109) who prepare the feasts for Penelope's suitors, seem to have accompanied these from their homes (six δρηστῆρες, π 248; two θεράποντες, π 253), and we may safely agree with the Alexandrian scholars in thinking them to be freemen. Nothing contradicts this view. But these wipe the tables with sponges (α 111), assist in mixing the wine and the water, and split wood for the fire (υ 160). Even in the palace of Menelaus at Sparta, with all its splendor of gold, silver, and ivory, were no male household servants, with the exception of Asphalion, the "ready attendant" (θεράπων, δ 216) who once pours water on the hands of the king and his guests. On the arrival there of Telemachus and Pisistratus, "prince Eteoneus" (κρείων 'Ετεωνεύς, δ 22) with his comrades unharnesses their horses, and ties these to the manger; and at the close of their visit, when Telemachus makes known his desire to depart, the same Eteoneus, who "dwelt not far away," happens along and is bidden by Menelaus to light a fire and cook meat for breakfast (ο 95 f.). Would Menelaus have done this work himself, if Eteoneus had not come? At this same breakfast at which Eteoneus cooks and carves the meat, Menelaus's son acts as butler, and serves the wine (ο 141). No servant is mentioned in connexion with the departure: the cooking and serving, as we have seen, are done by two princes; Helen and Menelaus

---

[1] One such has been found by some in the "wine pourer" or butler (οἰνοχόος, σ 396, cf. 416); but we can hardly suppose him to be a servant of Odysseus, when all his associates are attached to the persons of the suitors.

themselves fetch the gifts for the departing guests, and Telemachus and Pisistratus themselves harness the horses to the chariot (o 145). In Troy, king Priam bids his sons to harness his horses and his mules, when he would visit the Achaean camp (Ω 253). In Phaeacia, the king, Alcinoüs, orders his men-servants, it is true, to harness the mules for Nausicaa's use (ζ 71), but on the princess's return from the river, her brothers unharness these mules (η 6). We may assume that Hector had no man-servant at his house, if, as he says, Andromache often fed his horses on his return from the battle-field (Θ 186). Nestor bids his sons, not his servants, to fetch the goldsmith, the comrades of Telemachus, and a heifer for sacrifice, and to harness the horses for the journey of his Ithacan guest (γ 418, 475). The account of Nestor's sacrifice to Athena (γ 430 ff.) contains no mention of any servant. Possibly, for religious reasons, only members of the family in the strictest sense were to take part in these rites, though in general slaves shared in the sacrifices and feasts of the family (Aeschylus, *Ag.* 990), but the poet gives to his hearer the impression that the establishment of Nestor was modest. A housemaid there brings wine for the guests (γ 392), but the daughter of the family arranges the bath for the chief visitor (γ 464), and Nestor's couch is prepared for him by his wife, not by a maid (γ 403),—yet Nestor led ninety ships of the Achaeans to the siege of Troy.

That Nausicaa joins with her attendants in "laving the family linen," and then in the bath, the luncheon, and the game of ball, shows that she regards them rather as companions than slaves, and does not think *Dignity of Labor.* of the work as servile,—no more than are the spinning and weaving at which Circe, Helen, Andromache, and Penelope work with their women. No young lady of the southern United States, before the Civil War, would (or could be imagined to) have gone with slave women on such an excursion. So, too, the "wives and fair daughters of the Trojans" were wont to wash their gleaming raiment in the stone washing-troughs near the city, before the war (X 153 f.). If slavery in the modern sense had existed at that time, high-born dames would not have demeaned themselves to the toil which was ordinarily done by drudges. The dignity of labor was upheld, since this occupation was shared by the high as well as by the low. To perform manual labor involved no loss of self-respect. The work of the laundry by the river-side was not drudgery ; Nausicaa evidently took it as a pleasant day's excursion, though as a duty,—and not as an exceptional task ; and she and her attendants made a contest (ἔριδα προφέρουσαι, ζ 92) or game of the employment. No young woman of modern life takes a golden jar of cosmetics with her, as Nausicaa did, when she goes out for a day's washing ! If she has the golden jar, she does not go out to wash linen. A partial illustration of the disposition toward labor in Homeric times may be found in the different feeling on this subject in New England at the middle of the last century from that which prevailed at the same period in the southern states. A lady of New England then might do with her own hands, and without hesitation, services which one of her culture, wealth, and tastes at the south would certainly leave to the slaves. Slave labor in Homeric Greece had not driven out free labor. Fair Helen of Troy sat with her attendants, spinning and weaving (Z 323),—taking part in the ordinary occupations of women, just as her husband Paris did in the work of the men, when he took an active part in the building of his house (Z 314), and tended his flocks on the mountains (Ω 29), and as old Laërtes tended the trees of his orchard (ω 227).[1] On Odysseus's return to Ithaca, Athena meets him in the guise of a delicate youth, a shepherd of flocks, " such as are the sons of kings " (ν 223).

We might expect at least to find a porter on duty at every palace gate ; but none is mentioned,—neither on Ithaca,

No Porter. where Telemachus is the first to notice the approaching guest (α 113), nor in Sparta, where a neighbor, Eteoneus, reports the guests' arrival to the host, Menelaus (δ 22).

The divinities on Mount Olympus are as independent of male servants as are mortals. When on the first day of battle, Hera and Athena descend to the Trojan plain, Hera herself, assisted by Hebe, harnesses her steeds (E 721) ; on

---

[1] So among the Israelites, Saul, after he was anointed king, continued his life as a common farmer, and drove his cattle home at night (1 *Sam.* xi. 5).

the same day Iris unharnesses the horses of Ares (E 368);
on the next day of battle, Zeus himself makes ready his
chariot (Θ 41) for a drive to Mount Ida, while on
his return, Poseidon looses for him his horses, *No Servants on Olympus.*
and puts the chariot in its place (Θ 440). Such
service was not menial. Indeed no service was menial
except perhaps the grinding of grain in the hand-mill,
which the gods did not need; of the preparation of
their nectar and ambrosia we learn nothing, but at least
they are never represented as cooking. Athena was not
reduced in social rank by fashioning a robe for Hera
(Ξ 178), as well as her own garment (E 735); she did not
stand to Hera in the relation of dressmaker to customer.
Circe was at work at her loom, singing as she wove, when
the comrades of Odysseus came to her palace (κ 221 f.).
Every lady of the age not only spun and wove, but was
proud of her skill in these accomplishments. Nor did
Hephaestus on Mt. Olympus lose social position by making
tables and other articles for the use of his associates. This
work did not make of him a blacksmith, although the most
realistic picture in the poems of the work of a smith is in
the account of Hephaestus's smithy (Σ 372 ff., 470 ff.).
Clearly labor was no disgrace on Olympus, and affected
social standing there no more than it did on earth; and
conversely, we may be sure that the blacksmith on Ithaca
was conscious of no sort of humiliation or degradation in his
calling. The two pictures of life, on earth and on Olympus,
as usual agree with and illustrate each other. The nymph
Calypso serves Odysseus with food and drink, before she
seats herself to be served in turn with ambrosia and nectar
by her attendant nymphs (ε 196 f.). Doubtless the mortal
wife often or regularly rendered such service to her husband.
Nausicaa did not become a " laundress " by taking the
family linen to the river, and laving it, any more than Hebe
was a " waitress " because she served the gods with nectar
and ambrosia (Δ 3), and prepared the bath for Ares (E 905),
as Polycaste did for Telemachus (γ 465); nor was Poseidon
a " groom " because he cared for the horses of Zeus (Θ 440).
Apollo and Poseidon were punished by being made subject to
the mortal king Laomedon (Φ 446), but the labor which they

performed for him did not humiliate them ; to tend herds and to build a wall were honorable employments even for divinities, and Poseidon takes pride and pleasure in the wall which he built (H 452). This last myth was offensive to Lucian in the century after Christ, but not to the poet's hearers.

Perhaps we may compare fairly the life of a modern party camping in the woods of Maine or the Adirondacks, when each person, no matter what his distinction, takes his part in the work which is necessary for the common comfort. Something of the same spirit is seen at a " picnic," where each expects to serve as well as to be served.

Clearly the men-servants, the bondmen, of the Homeric age, in general were employed in the fields, and not about *Men-servants* the house, nor in the arts, except for their own *in the Fields.* masters : they were ploughing, planting, reaping, threshing and winnowing, curing grapes and making wine, laying stone walls, arranging hedges, building sheds, chopping and splitting wood, tanning hides, making shoes for themselves or other members of the family, doing smith's and carpenter's work on the farm, and tending the flocks and herds. Thus Melanthius was the chief goat-herd on the estate of Odysseus (ρ 212 ff.), while his sister Melantho was one of the women of Penelope's household (σ 321), and their father Dolius had charge of the farm on which the old Laërtes lived (ω 387).[1] The simple, primitive character of life in the Homeric age is always to be remembered. All the ordinary wants of the family,—food, clothing, house, and furniture,—were met by home production, but without trained artisans as slaves.

In war, the men of the defeated army were generally slain, while the women and children were led into captivity. *Captives in* This was the custom among the early Jews, too, *War* and these suffered from it as late as the Maccabean *Enslaved.* times (1 *Macc.* i. 32). " To the victor belong the spoils." Mercy or the desire for gain might lead a conqueror to spare the life of the man whom he

---

[1] We are not concerned here with the problem why on Odysseus's visit to this farm (ω 387 ff.), no reference is made to the killing of Melanthius and Melantho on the preceding day by order of Odysseus. Possibly, of course, this Dolius may not be the same as the father of the unfaithful servants,—but the present principle is unchanged.

had overcome. Sons of rich fathers might be ransomed ; other captives would be sold, while others still might be kept as slaves (Φ 40, Ω 751). Thus Agamemnon has not only the daughter of the old priest Chryses, but also at least seven Lesbian women as his captive attendants, for he offers these to Achilles (I 128), and Achilles has not only Briseïs and Diomede (I 665) as his female slaves, but a considerable company of others (Σ 28, 339, T 301). These female captives often were taken as concubines ; such was the fate of war. The old priest Chryses finds no fault with Agamemnon for making Chryseïs his concubine, but only for his refusing to give her up in exchange for an abundant ransom. Andromache's mother was brought in captivity to the Achaean camp on the capture of her city, but was ransomed by her father (Z 426). Hector looks forward to the time when Troy shall be taken and his wife Andromache shall weave at the bidding of another, and shall fetch for her mistress water from the springs of Argos or of Thessaly (Z 456); while Andromache herself anticipates a life of toil under a pitiless master as the lot of her son Astyanax (Ω 734). No rank in life secured against slavery a captive in war, although of course powerful friends might provide a ransom. But in itself, as we have seen, to fetch water from the spring, or to weave, was not always the work of slaves,—though the Old Testament expression, "hewers of wood and drawers of water," reminds us that such service in oriental countries was generally imposed on the meaner members of the household. The Laestrygonian princess was fetching water from the public spring when she met the companions of Odysseus (κ 105), and according to Herodotus (vi. 137), the free-born Athenian maidens were wont in early times to go to the Enneacrunus to fetch water, "for neither they nor the other Greeks of that time had slaves." But though all the captives became, like Cassandra (Aeschylus, *Ag.* 1038), truly members of the great household into which they were conveyed, yet the aliens, brought from a hostile city, would naturally be called to perform the hardest labor, and would receive the fewest privileges. They had no legal rights, as we have seen. That their lives had been spared, was in itself an act of mercy, and they could not justly complain if their associates treated them with contumely.

Greece naturally had more female than male slaves,— this was true in all periods of its history, and necessarily, since the females were saved when the males *More Female than Male Slaves.* were slain in battle. Trojan warriors, if their lives were spared, were sent on their capture to a neighboring island for sale (H 475, Φ 102, Ψ 766, Ω 75), but the poet tells of no such Trojan male slaves in Greece, nor do any such appear in the stories of the Attic tragedians. The men in Greece who have been reduced to slavery according to the Homeric poems, were kidnapped in childhood, like Eumaeus.

The purchased slaves of whom we hear in Homeric Greece are but three in number : Euryclea, the old nurse of Odysseus, *Purchased Slaves.* who was bought by Laërtes in her prime for the worth of twenty cattle (a 430),—who may have been free or even a princess by birth, for the poet names her father and grandfather ; the swine-herd Eumaeus, who as a small child was bought by Laërtes from Phoenician traders who had stolen him from his home (o 483) ; and this same swine-herd's own servant, Mesaulius (ξ 449). The positions of the two former seem very comfortable. The one was the most trusted of all Penelope's women, and had the oversight over them ; while Eumaeus had been brought up with Odysseus's younger sister Ctimene (o 363), and he is called the " divine swine-herd " and " leader of men " (o 301, 351). Eumaeus has a certain right to be called a leader, since he not only has three subordinates, but also owns the servant just referred to, Mesaulius, whom he had purchased from the Taphians on his own account (ξ 449), and who waits on him and his companions at dinner.[1] Eumaeus had some independence, surely. He is the faithful retainer to whom both Odysseus and Telemachus come first

---

[1] For the money or property of Eumaeus, with which he bought a slave, compare 1 *Samuel* ix. 8, where Saul's servant offers to lend to his master a quarter of a shekel of silver, when he wishes to consult the seer Samuel. At o 461 f., Eumaeus tells of the visit of a Phoenician trader to his parents' home, and the offer of a golden necklace which his mother *and the maidservants* admired and chaffered for. The maids themselves, then, had their *peculium*, which made the purchase of a gold necklace not absolutely out of the question for them.

(at the suggestion of Athena, it is true), on their return to Ithaca; and Telemachus treats him as a freeman when he tells him that he will send from the palace food and clothing for the disguised Odysseus, that the latter may not be a burden to the swine-herd and his comrades (π 83 f.). Perhaps the secluded position of the swine-herd's hut, was the reason for Athena's sending Odysseus thither, rather than to his old friend Mentor, to whose care he had left his estate on embarking for Troy (β 226).

In the absence of Odysseus, Eumaeus thinks of seeking another master, and so cannot have been bound to the soil. His spirit is far from that of an ordinary slave, both in relation to his master, and in particular *Not bound to the Soil.* with regard to his work : although the night is cold and stormy, he leaves the other swine-herds and Odysseus to sleep about the fire, while he takes his goatskin cloak and his javelin, and goes from his cabin to sleep near his swine,—evidently to protect them from robbers or wild animals (ξ 524 ff.). In speaking of Odysseus, Eumaeus says that he will never find another master so kindly, wherever he may go (ὁππόσ᾽ ἐπέλθω, ξ 139),—which surely does not mean wherever he may be sold as a slave. The neat-herd Philoetius, too, says that he has often thought of leaving Odysseus's cattle, but has been restrained by loyalty to his absent master, nor will he go while Telemachus lives (v 218). This story is told as of a simple change of home and employment,—not as of escape from bondage. Philoetius would be no freer nor better off elsewhere, except for the relief from the annoyances of the insolent suitors. His duties are not degrading ; king's sons have performed the like.

To Eumaeus and Philoetius, for their help against the suitors, Odysseus promises that each shall have a wife, a house, and possessions (φ 214),—they shall be as brothers to Telemachus ;—but nothing is said of *Favors to Servants.* their manumission, which cannot be necessary in any formal way. Old Dolius and his sons on Laërtes's farm sit with their lords at dinner without the feeling of any incongruity (ω 411). They are not treated as slaves nor even as servants, but as faithful and esteemed retainers ;

Odysseus, as he greets them, says that dinner has been waiting for them. Dolius's daughter, we have noticed, had been brought up by the daughterless Penelope as her own child (σ 322 f.).

We have seen that Dolius had a family of his own,—seven sons and a daughter,—and nothing indicates that this was an unusual privilege, though we learn that he was given to Penelope by her father on her marriage (δ 736), as was also her maid Actoris, of whom we hear only once (ψ 228). Eumaeus has no doubt that if Odysseus had returned to his home at the close of the Trojan war, the slave would have received from his master "house, and lot, and comely wife" (ξ 63); these, indeed, are to be expected by faithful servants of a kindly master.

Servants had Families.

If a slave woman bore a son to her master, this son might have not only freedom, but also an honorable civil position (ξ 202). Teucer, the half-brother of Telamonian Ajax, was the son of a captive, though his case is not normal, since his mother (at least according to the later story) was a Trojan princess, and he is not on the ordinary footing of sons of captives in war. But he is an honored leader, and only once is reference made to his special duty to be brave and to honor his father, who cared for him in his house "though he was the son of a captive" (νόθον ἐόντα, Θ 284). The captive might become the wife of her master, as Patroclus promised Briseïs that Achilles would marry her (Τ 297).

Sons of Slave Women.

The disguised Odysseus suggests to his host, the swineherd Eumaeus, that the wanderer might secure a situation as servant to Penelope's suitors (ο 317),—he is skilled in chopping wood, in carving and in roasting meat, and in serving wine,—"such services as inferiors render to their betters,"—which shows that some houses had butlers, or at least men-of-all-work. He receives the reply that the suitors' servants are better clad and kempt than he; but his proposal is significant,—it is not that he should become a slave, nor of course would he receive money as pay; he would be a hired servant, he would receive food, clothing, shelter, and occasional gifts such as

Hired Servants.

slaves also received. A definite proposition (though very likely spoken in irony) is made to the disguised Odysseus by one of the suitors, Eurymachus (σ 358), of work as hedger and ditcher. Nowhere do we read of definite wages being paid, and we are reminded that smiths and other public servants seem to have had no regular rates of compensation. No tariff of charges had been introduced, and indeed this was difficult before the introduction of money. The goldsmith who adorns for Nestor the horns of a heifer for sacrifice to Athena, presents no bill for his services (γ 432 ff.). Probably he was expected to do such work whenever it was required, in return for privileges granted by Nestor, the lord of the land. The system of giving fees instead of pay for minor services, which still endures in Europe, may be a survival of such a state of society. The custom of a guest's bestowing presents on his host's servants is assumed by Penelope's suitor, Ctesippus, who says that he will present the disguised Odysseus with a gift which he may give to the bath-maid or to some other of the servants (v 297),—and then he hurls at him the hoof of an ox.

To estimate the number of serving-men on the estate of Odysseus, of which we know more than of any other, would be mere conjecture. He possessed on Ithaca nearly a thousand swine in twelve herds, normally *Number of* of one hundred each, but the demands of the *Odysseus's* suitors had reduced the number of the hogs *Servants.* (ξ 13 ff.), and eleven herds of goats; and on the mainland he had twelve herds of kine, twelve flocks of sheep, twelve droves of swine, and twelve herds of goats (ξ 100 ff.). Five men seem to have cared for his Ithacan swine,—and the task must have kept them busy: but in general, each herd or flock would appear to require the services of at least one man. These had to be guarded as well as tended. To keep them together and feed them was not enough. Cattle must be defended against thieves (Γ 11), marauders (Λ 677 ff., ϕ 18), and wild beasts (K 183 ff., P 657 ff.),—particularly against lions. An unskilful herdsman might allow the destruction of his cattle (O 632, Π 352). The defense of the flocks required both skill and courage which were worthy of princes. The lion sometimes even entered the farm-yard in which the flocks and herds were gathered (E 136, 556), and at night he had to be kept away with firebrands. Further, the cultivated fields and orchards of Odysseus required care, and at least Dolius and his six sons were employed in such work (ω 223 f.). Dolius, himself, we are told, had charge of Penelope's garden (δ 735).

Women-Servants. The men-servants of Odysseus, then, including the hired men who cared for his flocks on the mainland, must have been at least as numerous as the maid-servants of Penelope, who numbered fifty (χ 421), although his men on Ithaca itself may have been far fewer. The Phaeacian queen, as well as Penelope, had fifty women in her household (η 103). But Circe had only four nymphs for her service (κ 348),—born from fountains, springs, and groves. Her family was a small one, and more attendants do not seem to have been needed. As we have seen, nothing is said of the preparation of nectar and ambrosia for her use, or for that of any other of the divinities, whether lesser or greater. Living on an island, she had no need of horses and grooms, and seems to have had no boats. Her life was nearly as retired as that of Calypso, who, we are told, received few visits.

Occupations of Women-Servants. The women-servants card wool, spin, and weave (η 103, χ 422, Z 456); they wash clothes (ζ 25), fetch water from the spring (Z 457, υ 153), wait on table, which includes the pouring of water on the guests' hands (α 136 ff.), they clear the table (τ 61), wash dishes (υ 151), prepare the baths for guests (δ 49, κ 361), throw rugs over the chairs (δ 124), see to the lights in the hall (σ 311), make the beds and show the way to the chamber with torches (δ 296, ψ 294), and grind the grain for the daily use of the family (υ 108). Naturally the care of the children devolved upon the women (Z 372). Euryclea gives in the morning her directions for the day's work (υ 149). Euryclea (α 429) and Eurynome[1] (ψ 293) on Ithaca, and Eurymedusa in

---

[1] One is tempted, indeed, to think that Euryclea and Eurynome were originally identical. Certainly at ψ 293, Eurynome does not only what Euryclea had done for Telemachus at α 429, but what we should expect of Euryclea from τ 344 ff.,

Scheria (η 8) are chambermaids ($\theta\alpha\lambda\alpha\mu\eta\pi\acute{o}\lambda o\iota$),—an office which on Ithaca includes the care of the store-rooms (β 345). Of Penelope's fifty maids, twelve worked at the hand-mills (υ 107), but these were obliged to prepare flour and meal for the suitors of Penelope as well as for the family proper. No women seem to work in the fields. Twenty women, which appears a large number for the purpose, went to the spring for water (υ 158). One served as housekeeper ($\tau\alpha\mu\acute{\iota}\eta$, α 139, γ 392, δ 55).

Two maids served as personal attendants of the mistress, but this certainly was incidental, not their chief work. Penelope never appears before the suitors in her great hall except so attended (α 331, π 413, σ 211). Helen and Andromache are each accompanied by two maids as they go to the Great Tower by the Scaean Gate of Troy (Γ 143, X 461), and Helen as she enters her own hall (δ 121). Yet when Andromache goes with her child to the Scaean Gate, she seems to be attended only by the nursemaid (Z 399). Two maids appear to be assigned also to the personal service of the princess Nausicaa, and sleep on either side of her door, probably within her chamber (ζ 18).

Of all the occupations of the household, the labor of grinding grain seems to have been considered most menial. This was sedentary and laborious, and required little but brute force, and yet was performed *Grinding Grain.* by women. So in Palestine: that the blinded Samson should be set to grind at the mill was a manifest degradation; it would have humiliated any man. The hand-mills were doubtless essentially like those which have been in use in the Orient from immemorial times, and the Scottish *querns*. In the New Testament, we read of "two women grinding at the mill," but in the only Homeric passage which is specific on this point (υ 111), one old woman was at work alone. The mills in the palace of Alcinoüs are mentioned at η 104. In the Trojan attack

and she conducts Odysseus and Penelope to their chamber on the first night after the hero's recognition by his wife. We may compare the pairs of names to designate one person,—Epicaste and Iocasta, Perimede and Agamede, Iphianassa and Iphigenia. But at ψ 289 "Eurynome *and* the nurse" prepare the couch.

on the Greek camp, the assailed defend themselves with millstones (μυλάκεσσι, M 161), which would indicate that the mills were not very carefully prepared, but that almost any stone approximately circular and nearly flat might be used for the purpose, and that some which had been so used were not regarded as of special value. In his single combat, Ajax hurls at Hector a stone "like a millstone" (μυλοειδέϊ πέτρῳ, H 270), which roughly indicates the size.[1] The use of mortar and pestle for pounding grain, is indicated by only one expression: in Λ 147 the armless and headless trunk of Pisander's body is rolled like a mortar (ὅλμον ὥς). In Hesiod (*Works and Days*, 423), directions are given that the mortar (ὅλμος) is to be three feet in height, and the pestle (ὕπερος) three ells in length. The grain used in sacrifices seems to have been bruised rather than ground (οὐλόχυται, οὐλαί), maintaining the early customs,—possibly being pounded with such stones as have been found in Crete, which were the precursors of primitive mills. The sieve is not mentioned by the Homeric poet, nor does its name appear in other early Greek literature.

In addition to the grinding of grain, which was always considered as the proper work of woman, occasionally other tasks requiring physical strength were imposed *Women carry Loads.* on women. Thus at ν 68, one of the women of Arete, the Phaeacian queen, is sent to carry to the boat Odysseus's chest, which must have been heavy since it contained twelve or thirteen suits of clothes. The faithless women of Penelope are made to carry from the great hall, into the courtyard, the dead bodies of the queen's suitors (χ 446).

Of separate servants' quarters, we have no hint. Nausicaa's two maids slept on either side of her door. The old Laërtes, whose wife was dead and whose son's return was not expected, living on the farm, slept with the servants "near the fire" (λ 190), as Odysseus and the swine-herds lay in the hut of Eumaeus (ξ 518).

The slave trade, so far as it exists in the Homeric period,

[1] *Cf.* "It were better for him that a millstone were hanged about his neck," *S. Matthew* xviii. 6.

is in the hands of Phoenicians[1] and Taphians,—the chief
traders and the most notorious pirates of the Homeric
poems. Kidnapping is a natural associate of *Slave Trade.*
piracy, which was then tolerated, as we have
seen, if it were not actually respectable. The disguised
Odysseus asks Eumaeus how he came to his life of servitude,—whether his city was sacked, or he was captured
alone while tending sheep or cattle (*o* 384). Eumaeus
was the son of a king, and was stolen by Phoenician
traders and his Phoenician nurse, who in turn had been
captured by Taphian pirates (*o* 427). Eumaeus had purchased his own attendant, Mesaulius, from the Taphians
(ξ 452). According to a fictitious story of the disguised
Odysseus, a Phoenician trader induced him to come upon
his ship, with the plan of selling him into slavery (ξ 297),
but the boat was wrecked on the Thesprotian coast. The
king of the Thesprotians received Odysseus kindly, according to the story, but the Thesprotian sailors who were
ordered to convey him home, planned to enslave him
(ξ 340). Of course the fictitious character of the story
does not impair its value as evidence of the customs of
the poet's times; such a story seemed plausible to him.
That the Sicels were ready to buy slaves, we learn from
v 382, and the wife of Penelope's slave Dolius, who cared
for the aged Laërtes, seems to have come from them
(*ω* 211). No family servants are sold. As we have
seen, the army before Troy sells its captives to Lemnos,
Samothrace, and Imbros (Ω 753), *i.e.* to the neighboring
islands, in exchange for wine and probably for other
provisions (H 475), but this does not constitute a regular
slave trade,—it is a mere incident of the war. The tribes
of Greece doubtless seldom had an abiding peace, but
Homer nowhere tells us of slaves as part of the booty of
such wars. The Greeks, however, who had no scruples
about killing inoffensive men and enslaving their wives and
children, in Thrace or Egypt, and who seem to have had
so slight a consciousness of the difference between " Greeks

---

[1] *Cf.* the prophet *Joel* iii. 4 f.: "What have ye to do with me, O Tyre and
Zidon, and all the coasts of Palestine? . . . The children also of Judah and the
children of Jerusalem have ye sold unto the Grecians."

and barbarians," could not be expected to be very scrupulous in their treatment of the children of Greeks of another tribe, whose cattle they were driving away. Those who were "fighting in behalf of their city and their wives" (λ 403), were not at war solely with non-Greeks.

The question whether Achaeans were kept as slaves by Achaeans, cannot be answered categorically. Euryclea at least "had a grandfather," as we have seen, and he may have been a Greek for all that we know. And Eumaeus was kidnapped in early childhood from his home on the island of Syrie (ο 403), but where this island was, and of what race were its inhabitants, we do not know.

For only two slaves is the price mentioned : Laërtes paid the worth of twenty cattle for Euryclea (α 430); and a
Price of Slaves. slave woman, skilled in various accomplishments, who is offered as a prize in the funeral games in honor of Patroclus, is estimated to be worth four cattle (Ψ 705). The market for slaves before Troy evidently was glutted by the war, just as in later times, after the victory of Lucullus in Pontus, a slave could be bought for four drachmae.[1] Lycaon, Priam's son, was sold by Achilles to Jason's son, Euneüs of Lemnos, for the worth of one hundred cattle (Φ 79, Ψ 746), but this clearly was not the price of a slave,—it was a prince's ransom, offered on speculation by Euneüs who required the payment of thrice as heavy a price from the young man's father.

A tradition that the early Greeks had no slaves, is mentioned by Herodotus (vi. 137), and Athenaeus quotes Timaeus
Early Greeks had no Slaves. and Theopompus as holding that it was not the custom of the ancients to own purchased slaves, but to do their own work, to practise *autodiakonia*.[2]
The Locrians and Phocians in particular had no men-servants nor maid-servants (οὔτε θεραπαίνας οὔτε οἰκέτας), and the Chians were the first to have slaves from foreign lands, after the Spartans had reduced to subjection the Helots, the old Achaean holders of the land, and the Thessalians had made Penestae of the Perrhaebians whose

[1] Plutarch, *Lucullus*, 14.—Procopius (*de Bello Vandalico*, ii. 12. 27) says that after Solomon's victory, Moor boys were sold for the price of sheep.

[2] Athenaeus, 18 B, 264 C, 272 B.

land they took in a similar way. Whether Hesiod considered a slave to be an essential part of a well-to-do household, is uncertain. He has been thought to name him in his *Works and Days*, 602, but the expression for the workman is *thes* (θής),[1] which in Homer is applied to the free peasant or "hired man," while the work-woman is an *erithos* (ἔριθος, who seems to be free in Homer), and we must note also the fact that the five verses in which this line occurs interrupt the connexion of thought in the passage, and very likely are not original.[2] But the Greeks of the historical period had no doubt that slavery was natural : some men were born to be slaves and others to be masters, though there was no difference of color between them. Plato would have no Greek reduced to slavery (*Republic*, 469 C), and makes the slave no part of his ideal state (*cf. Rep.* 371 E for the hirelings), but he takes no position on principle against the institution of slavery, while Aristotle (*Politics*, i. 2) defends it.

The demoralizing influence of compulsory service, is expressed by Eumaeus in a noted speech : "Servants (δμῶες) are not inclined to do their duty when their master is not in control. A man loses half his manhood (ἀρετή) when he falls into slavery" (δούλιον ἦμαρ ἕλῃσιν, ρ 323).

Demoralization of Slavery.

[1] Philo (ii. 285 M.), too, contrasts the slaves and the *thetes*, saying that because of the Jewish Year of Jubilee δούλους μὲν ὀνομάζεσθαι συμβέβηκε, θῆτας δὲ τῷ ὄντι εἶναι.

[2] In *Works and Days*, 459, 502, 573, 597, 608, 766, Hesiod uses the word δμώς, assuming that the farmer has a *man*, but this δμώς may be no *slave*, in the modern sense. Hesiod, as well as Homer, does not use the word δοῦλος.

CHAPTER X

TRADE AND THE CRAFTS

EACH household for the most part supplied its own wants, whether of shelter, clothing, or food. Odysseus built his own bed-chamber, and constructed his own bed (ψ 189 ff.). That he built his own house, with the assistance of his men, we may readily believe, since he skilfully (ἐπισταμένως, ε 245) made the craft which bore him from Calypso's grotto to the land of the Phaeacians,—a voyage of seventeen days,—and even the effeminate Paris built his own house, with the assistance of the best workmen of the Trojan city (Z 314). The chairs and the tables, as well as the bed, were doubtless of domestic manufacture, though possibly the aid of a specially skilled worker in wood sometimes was called in. Of course the meat eaten in Odysseus's halls was the flesh of his own flocks and herds, which furnished also milk to drink and cheese both as a relish and as food, hides for leathern bottles, shoes, and belts, helmets and shields, and wool which Penelope and her maidens carded, spun, and wove into garments. The Homeric swine-herd as well as the Hesiodic farmer makes his own shoes. Then as later, in Greece, the cutting and sewing of cloth were unimportant. If the lord and lady wore raiment of linen, this was woven probably from the flax of their own fields,—though of this we cannot be so certain, linen being little used. Their fields produced the grain which the women of the family ground into flour or meal, from which their bread was baked and their porridge stirred. In general the grain was ground on the day when it was to be used for bread,—never apparently in

Each Household Independent.

large quantities, though Telemachus, setting off unexpectedly on a journey, bids the old housekeeper to provide him with twenty measures of barley meal in well-sewed leathern bags (β 354). The poet knew no large grist-mills which served a community. The animal of which the flesh was to be eaten, also, was slaughtered only when and where its flesh was desired. Vines, too, grew on the island of Ithaca (ν 244, ω 341), and fruit to supply all the needs of the family in that respect. Pottery surely could be made on the island, and this would include the great jars which served for the storage of grain and wine, and perhaps also of oil, in place of modern barrels and casks. Chariots had no place on Ithaca (δ 601 ff.), but if they had been wanted they could have been made at home: Priam's son, Lycaon, was taken captive by Achilles one night as he was cutting the young shoots of a wild-fig tree for the rim of a chariot (Φ 37), and we have no reason to suppose that he had more skill in wagon-making than was possessed by other princes. Of all necessaries, metals alone seem to be lacking among the products of Ithaca, but these were far less important then than they have come to be in modern life. Possibly olive oil and other perfumeries, and fine embroideries and rugs, also were imported. Ivory and amber were brought from the south and the north, but only as rare luxuries. The purple dye, which was highly esteemed, was gained from a little shellfish that seems to have drawn the Phoenicians to Greece in early times, and we need not suppose that the Achaeans bought this dye back from the Phoenicians instead of preparing it themselves, though Maeonian and Carian women were particularly skilful in staining ivory with purple (φοίνικι, *Phoenician color*, Δ 141). If most of the iron and copper was imported, yet doubtless some one on the farm could fashion them into the needed articles. So one of the prizes which Achilles offers in the funeral games in honor of Patroclus, is a mass of iron to be used in "putting the shot,"—a mass so large that with it at hand "neither shepherd nor ploughman would go to town in need of iron, but this would supply it" (Ψ 834). Clearly, the shepherd was expected himself to fashion the metal into the tools and appliances which he needed. So Hesiod's farmer makes his own plough and farming implements (*Works and Days,* 423 ff.). But the poet tells of a bronzesmith at Pylus (γ 432), and one of the impudent maids of Penelope suggests that the disguised Odysseus should go to the smithy to sleep (σ 328). Metals were far less important than in the present century, since the home had no stove or furnace, few and small kettles, no pails, few pans, and no forks or metal spoons. Not only was life much simpler than at present, but pottery and wood were much used for articles in which they now are replaced by metals.

The Homeric community thus had no place for grocers, butchers, millers, or bakers, nor for tailors, haberdashers, milliners, or shoemakers. We read of no shop-keepers or peddlers. Each house as well as each hamlet was independent. Homer knows no word for *trader*. Phoenician traders appear now and then, it is true. The fictitious Mentes says that he is taking a boat-load of iron to Temesa, to exchange for a cargo of copper (α 184). But he is not a professional trader,—he is a king,—and his cargo may not be very heavy, since he is seeking copper only for himself and his subjects. Ships from Lemnos, sent by Euneüs, the king of that island, brought wine to the Achaean army before Troy, to be exchanged for captives or other booty of the army; but this was a temporary arrangement, and the wine may have been brought by the very men who produced it.

No Butchers or Bakers.

From Φ 40, Achilles seems to have taken in person some of his captives to Lemnos for sale, or he sent them in the care of one of his lieutenants. So Hesiod's farmer will take his own boat and carry his produce to those who will receive it (*Works*, 641),—perhaps for exchange with those who have less grain or more wool or wine than he. The question which is put to Telemachus by Nestor and to Odysseus by Polyphemus[1] is better translated, "Do you come on an errand?" than "Do you come for trade?" In a noted passage, however, Odysseus is taunted by a young Phaeacian as resembling a "commander of sailors, who is watchful of the cargo and of greedy gains," rather than an athlete (θ 162). Trade and manufactures, then, had but a

[1] γ 72, ι 253, κατὰ πρῆξιν . . . πλεῖθ' ὑγρὰ κέλευθα;

small place in the Greece of the Homeric age. Thebes, for instance, could furnish little that Athens lacked, and what did Mycenae produce which Sparta could not provide for itself?

The expedition of the Achaeans with 1186 ships against Troy is in itself the best evidence for the free use of the sea by the Greeks of the Homeric age (but see page 39). Of these ships one hundred were manned by the forces of Agamemnon, who in *Trade by Sea.* addition (according to the Catalogue of Ships, B 612) furnished sixty ships to the Arcadians, who had no boats of their own, since their territory alone of the states of Hellas did not touch the sea at any point. At Ithaca were many boats, "both old and new" (β 293),—of which some probably were used for fishing. The poet makes Odysseus note that the Cyclopes have no vessels which would accomplish their errands, "as men often traverse the sea to each other" (ι 128), as implying a lack of civilization. The Phaeacians were given to a maritime life,—they were not warlike, but seamen (ζ 270), though it is a Phaeacian who speaks contemptuously of trade and traders (θ 161; see p. 60). We learn of a number of short voyages. Odysseus went to Ephyra and Taphos (α 258 f.), and his son Telemachus went to Pylos in quest of tidings of his father (β *fin.*). Helen says that Idomeneus often came from Crete to visit Menelaus at Sparta (Γ 232), and Telemachus tells Athena in the guise of Mentes (α 176) that many visitors used to come to Ithaca in his father's time, and that Odysseus himself was fond of visiting men (ἐπίστροφος ἦν ἀνθρώπων). King Proetus of Tiryns married a Lycian princess, and Bellerophon on his banishment went to Lycia (Z 168 ff.). The suitors of Penelope propose to send a boat to the Sicels (υ 383), and the old woman who cares for the wants of Laërtes, seems to have been brought thence (γυνὴ Σικελή, ω 211). The Phaeacians, however, mariners though they were, thought the island of Euboea to be very remote (τηλοτάτω, η 322), and the Greeks' notion of Egypt was inexact,—Pharos being counted a full day's sail from the mainland, and Egypt being thought a four or five days' sail from Crete (ξ 257). But after all, coast trade in Greece was easier than traversing the mountain paths, a thousand years before Christ, as it was even during the first two-thirds of the nineteenth century of our era. Corinth was rich (ἀφνειός, B 570), and the wealth of Mycenae and Troy also would indicate trade, for how else was their gold obtained? But whether this trade was by land as well as by sea, is not indicated, nor how much of the gold was secured simply by yielding the products of the neighboring country to the Phoenicians, who long had controlled the "carrying trade" of the Mediterranean.

The great trade routes of the Homeric times are in no way referred to by the poet. He gives no hint as to the *Trade Routes.* source of the supply of metals, except that silver came from Alybe of the Halizonians (ὅθεν ἀργύρου ἐστὶ γενέθλη, B 857), between the Paphlagonians and the Mysians, and that a load of copper was expected from Temesa (α 184), a place which used to be sought in Cyprus, but now is found by scholars on the western coast of Italy, in Bruttium. That these were the main sources of supply of these metals, is very improbable. No word is uttered about ivory as coming from the south, or of amber as brought from the north. In so far as such objects were supplied by Phoenician traders, we should expect no emphasis to be laid on their provenience; the Phoenicians did not desire to give information which would aid others in breaking their monopoly, and the purchasers, on the other hand, cared little to learn the source of the articles which the Phoenicians brought. Hence many even of the people who possessed objects of ivory, amber, and gold, may have had only very vague notions of the countries from which these came. That the amber found by Dr. Schliemann at Mycenae was brought from the Baltic, has been ascertained by chemical analysis, and the discovery of similar beads in ancient tombs in Switzerland and other inland countries has done much to prove the existence of great through trade routes from the north to the head of the Adriatic.[1] Along such routes, rather than from the wanderings of adventurous sailors, seem to have come the stories of a land where the nights were very brief (of the Laestrygonians.

[1] See Ridgeway, *Origin of Metallic Currency*, 105 ff. ; *Early Age of Greece,* i. 359 ff.

κ 86), and of another which was perpetually shrouded in darkness and mist, where the sun never shone (of the Cimmerians, λ 14 ff.),—stories which indicate some knowledge of the short summer nights and the long winter nights of northern regions. The difference between the length of the day in summer and that in winter naturally is less marked in Greece than in New England, not to speak of North Britain and Germany.

No man in Homeric Greece produced ordinary commodities for sale, but primarily for the use of his own family ; any surplus naturally he was glad to exchange for what he could not make, or cause to grow, for himself.

The Homeric Greeks were used to the sea, but clearly did not like long voyages, and were not adventurous mariners. They did not like to spend the night upon the water, and preferred to take a much longer course than one which would carry them far from land. *Long Voyages Disliked.* To skirt the western coast of Asia Minor, and then the shores of Crete, and then come north to Argos or Sparta, seemed as natural as from Lesbos to strike boldly to the west, across the Aegean Sea, although this is studded with islands ; time was of little importance to them. So we cannot be surprised that trade is still largely in the hands of the Phoenicians. Indeed the poet tells us of no Greek professional merchant or trader. As the first prize for the foot-race in honor of Patroclus (Ψ 744), Achilles offers a silver mixing-bowl, holding six measures, which Sidonians had wrought, and which Phoenicians brought to Lemnos, where they gave it to the king of the island as a sort of harbor dues, clearly for the privilege of trade.[1] Odysseus, returning in disguise to Ithaca (ν 272), tells Athena, whom he does not recognize but supposes to be a young shepherd, that he had been obliged to flee from Crete because of a murder which he had committed, and that Phoenicians had brought him on his way, but had been unable to land him at Pylus or Elis. A little later on the same day (ξ 288), the disguised Odysseus tells to the faithful swine-herd

---

[1] So the Lemnian king, in sending wine for sale in the Achaean camp, sent a thousand measures of wine as a special gift to the two chief leaders of the expedition, Agamemnon and Menelaus (H 470),—a sort of customs duty.

Eumaeus a fictitious story of his wanderings, which includes an adventure with a Phoenician who (according to his story), fell in with him in Crete, took him to his Phoenician home for a year, and then took him to Libya as an assistant supercargo, but with the intention of selling him there. On the following day, Eumaeus tells the disguised Odysseus the story of his boyhood : he was the son of a prince on the island of Syrie, but Phoenician traders spent a year in trade there, and beguiled his Phoenician nurse who ran away with them and took the boy, who was purchased from the traders by Laërtes (o 415 ff.). So the Homeric story agrees with our other information of the fame of Phoenician traders, though it tells of no Phoenician trading station or settlement in Greece. That the tales told by Odysseus are fictitious, does not injure their value as evidence in this matter ; they were designed to have the fullest verisimilitude.

Although cattle formed the chief Homeric standard of value, and trade was still for the most part barter (see
Trade was Barter. page 36), and gold, silver, and copper were articles of merchandize rather than a medium of exchange, yet a foundation seems to have been laid for a gold standard of values. A "talent" (τάλαντον, *weight*) of gold appears to have been a piece of metal of definite weight, and it may have had conventional value, though it is not named as the price of a commodity. Ten talents were part of the recompense which Agamemnon gave to Achilles for the wrong he had done him (T 247), and a like amount was part of the ransom paid to Achilles by Priam for Hector's body (Ω 232), and among the presents received by Menelaus in Egypt (δ 129). The priest of Apollo at Ismarus gave to Odysseus, for sparing his life, seven talents of gold (ι 202), a mixing-bowl, and wine. Each of the Phaeacian nobles contributes a talent of gold, a cloak, and a tunic, for the wanderer Odysseus (θ 393). Two talents were given by Aegisthus as a year's pay to the lookout whom he set to watch for the returning Achaeans (δ 526). To the contestants in the foot-race in honor of Patroclus (Ψ 751), an ox is offered as the second prize, and half a talent in gold as the third (or "consolation")

prize ; while in the chariot race, a mare is the second prize, a bronze basin the third, and two talents of gold the fourth (Ψ 269). Finally, in the court scene depicted on the Shield of Achilles, two talents lie before the judges to be given to him who shall "state justice most straightly" (ὃς μετὰ τοῖσι δίκην ἰθύντατα εἴποι, Σ 507 f.; see page 91).

Evidently, the Homeric talent, being worth less than a mare, and half a talent being the third prize where an ox is the second, must have been very different in value from the Attic talent, which as a round sum was equivalent to about $1,000 in modern silver, but had five or ten times as great *The Talent not the Attic Talent.* purchasing power. That a half-talent is mentioned, is perhaps the clearest indication of a definite weight or value : if *talents* were mere pieces of gold of indefinite size, then a half-talent would mean nothing,—it might be as large as another whole talent.

To ascertain definitely the value of the Homeric talent, however, is impossible. Hultsch (*Metrologie*[2], 128) believes it to have been the *heavy* shekel of 16.8 grams, while Ridgeway (*Origin of Currency and Weight* *A Shekel?* *Standards*, 7) believes it to have been the light shekel, 8.4 grams or 130 grains Troy weight, the *Daric* of later times, the didrachm of the Attic-Euboic standard, not very far from the American eagle and the British sovereign.[1] Ridgeway holds, moreover, that the Homeric gold talent had the value of an ox, and that in practise these gold pieces may have been in more common use than one would infer from the language of the poems,—the old standards being preserved in speech after metal was used in ordinary commercial transactions. But the Draconian code, in the seventh century B.C., still imposed fines on the standard of cattle, and Solon, in the next century, assumed a definite relation between the value of a drachma and that of a sheep or a goat.[2]

---

[1] In *Journal of Hellenic Studies*, xiii. 225, Arthur Evans, from the weight of Mycenaean rings, concludes "that the Mycenaeans possessed a weight standard the unit of which was a stater of 135 grains." *Cf.* also Ridgeway in *J.H.S.* x. 90 ff.

[2] κἀν τοῖς Δράκοντος νόμοις ἐστὶν ἀποτίνειν δεκάβοιον· καὶ ἐν τῇ παρὰ Δηλίοις θεωρίᾳ τὸν κήρυκα κηρύττειν φασὶν ὅτι δοθήσονται αὐτῷ τοσοῦτοι βόες· καὶ δίδοσθαι καθ' ἕκαστον βοῦν δύο δραχμὰς Ἀττικάς, Pollux, ix. 61 ; Plutarch, *Solon*, xxiii.

Since trade was barter, the craftsmen can have had no fixed prices for their labor and the products of their craft. *Prices for Service.* Each sale or piece of work was the subject of a special bargain, except in so far as a general arrangement was made with particular persons. Often, doubtless, an act of service was as unlimited as one of friendship,—" I will do this for you now ; you will do as much for me at another time." The later introduction of money and the consequent haggling over details, degraded the relation between the buyer and the seller, the employer and the employed, just as it made definite debts possible. Nestor himself furnishes to the smith the gold which he desires to have moulded about the horns of the heifer for sacrifice (γ 436), and no special payment is named for the smith's services. Pandarus himself shot the wild goat whose horns were used by a skilful craftsman in the manufacture of his bow (Δ 106). Just so in New England, in the eighteenth century, the cloth which was made at home, of wool from the domestic flocks, carded, spun, and woven in the home, often was given for making into garments to a tailor who came to his customer's house to do the work.

As has been observed in connexion with servants, the work which was to be done indoors was done by women : *Work of Men and Women.* the carding, weaving, and spinning of wool and flax, the grinding of corn, and the baking of bread are all left exclusively to them, and in the higher of these employments all women take part. Thus not only do Helen and Andromache weave and spin, but Athena makes a robe for Hera (Ξ 178). The women, too, lave the linen (X 155, ζ 31),—even Nausicaa, the fair daughter of the luxurious Phaeacian king, taking part in such work. Maid-servants bring water for the household from the spring (γ 429, κ 107, Z 457), and the Laestrygonian princess does her part in this service. Women, also, have charge of the fires in the house (γ 429, η 7, σ 307), and of the lights (torches) in the great hall. Man's place is in the fields, and in doing the heavy work of carpenter, mason, or smith. Since the people lived for the most part in small hamlets or in scattered dwellings, not in towns or cities, each man as well as each family was more independent than in the ordinary cultured life of to-day. He was a Jack-of-all-trades, a "handy" man, who could do almost any required work,—just as many a New Hampshire farmer even now can shoe a horse, or make a wagon, or lay a stone wall, or build a house, or run a saw-mill, or bind up a wound with considerable skill, while his wife is equal to a physician for many ailments, and can make a gown, or cook, or cultivate flowers. The Homeric Greeks knew no refined division of labor. The pastoral stage of civilization has no division of labor in the strict sense, and in the early agricultural stage each household is fairly independent. Eumaeus made his own shoes (ξ 23), and built the stone wall of his court-yard (ξ 7). One servant of Odysseus is set to care for his swine, as Eumaeus, another to care for his goats, as Melanthius, and a third for his kine, as Philoetius,—but ordinary men have no division of labor, and these three probably could have exchanged work with little inconvenience. The disguised Odysseus, suggesting that he might secure employment from the suitors of Penelope, says that he can not only chop wood and tend the fire, but also roast and carve meat, and serve wine (o 322); he is ready to be a "man of all work,"—butler as well as drudge.

In such a primitive community as existed in Homeric Greece, a trained artisan would find little to do. Not only is no need felt there for plumbers, gas-fitters, furnace-men, engineers, and electricians,—no more *No trained Artisans.* than for lawyers, editors, civil-engineers, and college professors,—but even carpenters, masons, and black-smiths have no regular occupation in the exercise of their craft, and rely chiefly on their farms for the support of their families. They cannot afford to lie idle in the intervals between their technical engagements. The *Iliad* and the *Odyssey* know no Cabiri, Telchines, or Cyclopes at the forge ; Polyphemus's brothers seem to bear no relation to Hesiod's Cyclopes who forged the thunderbolt of Zeus.

But the chief crafts already existed in a rudimentary stage in Homer's day, and although the leader of the people would prefer to care for his flocks or herds, or to oversee the work on his fields, rather than to have part in any handicraft, yet no such stigma rested on the work of the artisan in early times as at Athens in the sixth and fifth centuries before our era. Hephaestus, as we *Chief* see elsewhere, did not lose social standing on *Crafts in a* Olympus because he was a Tubal Cain. We read *Rudimentary* *Stage.* of a shield-maker Tychius, "best of all workers in leather" (H 220), who, though he lived in Boeotia, made the great "shield like a tower," of seven bulls' hides, for Telamonian Ajax of Salamis. His fame as a workman must have been considerable in order to bring him a commission from Salamis. Though a worker in leather, Tychius hammered (ἤλασε) upon the shield its outermost layer of bronze. A worker in horn is not above attaching metal tips to the bow which he has made (Δ 111), a wagon-maker cuts his own poplar (Δ 485), and ship-carpenters fell their own trees.

What crafts existed in Homer's time? The general name for a skilled workman is *wright* (τέκτων—not yet specialized to the meaning of carpenter,—connected with *What* τέχνη, *art*), who builds ships or houses, and makes *Crafts* furniture and adorns it with silver and ivory (τ 56, *existed?* of Icmalius), or who joins and smooths horns to form a bow (Δ 110). We read also of smiths (χαλκεύς, γ 432, σ 328, etc.), a worker in gold (χρυσοχόος, γ 425), a potter and his wheel (κεραμεύς, Σ 601), a wagon maker (ἁρματοπηγός, Δ 485), a worker in leather (σκυτοτόμος, H 221), and seamen or sailors (ἁλιεύς, μ 251, ω 419, πορθμεύς, υ 187) who doubtless often served as fishermen. The tanning or curing of leather (P 389), by stretching it repeatedly in many directions, may have been done on the farm. In Hesiod's time (*Works and Days*, 25), the potter's craft was so firmly established that the jealousy of potter for potter was taken as an illustration of the rivalries in life. The "workers for the people" (δημιοεργοί, ρ 383) who may be called from one place to another, are enumerated as "a seer, a healer of ills, a worker in wood, and an inspired bard who cheers men by his song." These might receive inducements to make their homes here or there, just as in early colonial days in America, a clergyman, a teacher, or a physician often received a homestead or other privileges, and as at present manufacturers are drawn by promoters to one growing town or another. Long after Homer, the Spartans gave special prerogatives to a seer, according to Herodotus (ix. 33). Whether the herald should be included in the list of craftsmen, may be questioned ; he seems to be attached closely to the person and service of the king. The bard was a daily guest in the palaces of Odysseus and of Alcinoüs ; but he does not seem to have been one of the household.

What recompense did these craftsmen receive ? Probably in many cases none which we should recognize as definite pay. They were "clients," and received from their chief what they needed from the products *Recompense.* of his fields or from his herds,—a relationship which has not entirely died away even in modern life, in the midst of the commercial spirit. But, of course, a shield-maker or a chariot-maker might stipulate for a certain number of kine or sheep in return for his skilled labor.

That the craftsman's whole time in general was not devoted to his craft, has been intimated. The two surgeons in the army before Troy were primarily warriors, and actually only once in the *Iliad* is either one *Craftsmen also Farmers and Fighters.* of them called to exercise his art. Amphiaraus, according to the poet of the *Thebaid*, was both a good seer and a good spearman, Priam's fatidic son Helenus is a warrior (Z 76, H 44), as well as a seer, and of the Trojan allies the Mysian Ennomus was both seer and warrior (B 858, P 218). Whether the seer Calchas (A 69, B 322) had other duties than those of seer, is not plain, but that Poseidon takes his form (N 45) when he would rouse the Greek warriors in battle to more vigorous action, may imply that he was an active fighter. That a herald might be a rich man, we see from the wealth of Dolon's father (K 315, 380). Epeus, the builder of the wooden horse, which was a great undertaking for those times, is nowhere called a carpenter ; he was one of the warriors before Troy, though he himself says that he is a better boxer than spearman (Ψ 670). The difference between man and man as craftsman was rather in the degree than in the kind of their knowledge. Paris could build his own house, but some of the Trojans had special skill in building (Z 314).

The skilled workman or wright (τέκτων) had as tools an axe (πέλεκυς, ε 234), an adze (σκέπαρνον, ε 237), an augur (τρύπανον, ι 385, τέρετρα, ε 246), and a plumbline or rule (σταφύλη, B 765), as well as a hammer (σφῦρα, only mentioned as one of the smith's tools, γ 434) and doubtless also a saw, which is not named, but which was used on stone in the earlier period at Tiryns and Mycenae. The file and chisel, too, are not named, and metal nails and screws were lacking. The smith had an anvil and bellows, as well as smelting pots and hammer and tongs (Σ 372, 470, 476). Wooden pegs (γόμφοι, ε 248) are used by Odysseus in the construction of his barge. Odysseus's axe had a helve of olive wood (ε 236). A test of skill in archery was to shoot an arrow through twelve axes (φ 76, 120) which were fixed in a trench in the earth. The arrow can hardly have passed through twelve helve-holes, and perhaps we must suppose that the helves of the axes were crossed and that the arrow was shot between them. In the games in honor of Patroclus, ten axes are offered as the first prize of archery, and ten hatchets (*half-axes*, ἡμιπέλεκκα, Ψ 851) as the second prize.

Tools.

From the comparison in which a chariot-maker (ἁρματο-πηγός, Δ 485) is mentioned, we might infer a craft for that service, but, as we have seen, Priam's son Lycaon went out of Troy by night to cut young shoots of a wild-fig tree for the rim of a chariot (Φ 36). This young prince doubtless had received no special training in the making of chariots, and many another Trojan warrior could have made as good a wagon, but this was part of a man's work. The prince did not become a chariot-maker, in the modern sense, by making a chariot.

Chariot-makers.

Architects we might expect to come nearest to forming a profession, when we think of the noble and elaborate structures of the Mycenaean age. That Greece had known sculptors not very long before Homer's day, the Lions' Gate at Mycenae still testifies. But architects, painters, and sculptors are not mentioned, and only one reference (and that indirect, Z 303; see page 492) to

Architects.

a statue is found in the poems. Doubtless no broad line was drawn between the artisan and the artist, but even the artisan painter seems to be lacking, except so far as the ships are painted black, with vermillion bows, for which work no special skill was needed.

The smith was strictly a *worker in bronze* (χαλκεύς, Δ 187), but this name is applied to the goldsmith (χρυσοχόος, γ 425) Laërces, as well as to the blacksmith, in the passage in which the eye of Polyphemus is said *Smiths.* to hiss when Odysseus thrust the heated stake into it, just as hot iron hisses when a smith dips this into water to temper it (ι 392). The smithy (σ 328, *cf.* Hesiod, *Works*, 493) is a semi-public place where a vagrant would be likely to seek warmth and shelter. The workshop of Hephaestus is described with some detail (Σ 468 f., *cf.* θ 273),—near his dwelling on Olympus, not on Lemnos nor in Mt. Aetna. Hephaestus keeps his tools in a silver chest (λάρναξ, Σ 413), and has hammer and tongs (ῥαιστήρ, πυράγρη, Σ 477). His anvil is placed on the anvil-block (ἄκμων, ἀκμόθετον) only when it is to be used. He has smelting pots (χόανοι) for his metals, and when these are placed on the fire, a score of self-acting bellows blow in among them. When busy at his work, he wears no tunic (Σ 416), and when summoned to receive the visit of Thetis, he sponges off his face, arms, neck, and breast.

Hephaestus appears to us as a typical smith, and we may fairly take the works of his craft as examples of what his follower on earth would try to make. At the time of Thetis's visit he is engaged in making *Hephaestus* small tables, which could be used at the feasts of *a Typical* the gods. These are automata, being mounted *Smith.* on wheels or castors in order that at the god's bidding they may go to and return from the great hall of Zeus. Hephaestus has wonderful crutches, also,—golden maidens, endowed with thought and speech (Σ 418), and instructed by the immortals in various accomplishments. By the coming of Thetis, Hephaestus is reminded of the time when in her grotto he had made brooches and necklaces. He made also a silver bowl with gilded edges which Menelaus received as a gift from the king of Sidon and bestowed in

turn on Telemachus (o 115). He makes armor for Achilles
(Σ 478 ff.). He made the aegis for Zeus (O 308), and the
sceptre of Agamemnon (B 101) which had descended to the
Greek leader through Zeus and Pelops. Hera promises Sleep
that Hephaestus shall make a fine throne for him (Ξ 239).
Hephaestus also built the homes for the gods (A 607 f.,
Y 10 ff.), and thus seems to be a worker in stone and
wood as well as in metals. The moulding of gold about
silver is ascribed (ζ 232) to one whom Hephaestus and
Athena have taught. That simple apparatus may suffice for
an iron furnace and for delicate work in gold, is shown by
the rude forges of the interior of Africa and the delicate
filigree work of the goldsmiths in India and Mexico.

Metals were used not only for arms and for tools, for
cups, pitchers, and basins, but also for the ornamentation of
staves, of chariots and furniture, and of leather
belts and straps, and for the covering of doors
and thresholds. Chairs and beds were inlaid with
plates of metal, and Telemachus, coming from the island of
Ithaca, wondered at the gleam of copper, gold, electrum,
silver, and ivory in the great hall of Menelaus at Sparta
(δ 72). The latter passage may refer to plates of metal
fastened as decorations upon the wall, as rosettes of bronze
were attached to the wall of the so-called Treasury of
Atreus at Mycenae. Possibly, however, the reference is
chiefly to the shields and helmets, and even basins received
as prizes, hung upon the walls,—for which we may compare a
fragment of the poet Alcaeus (*Frag.* 56), who says that his
great hall gleams with bronze, and goes on to explain that
his whole house is adorned for Ares: helmets, greaves,
shields, and cuirasses are hanging on the pegs (doubtless, of
the walls). In the fairyland of Phaeacia, dogs of gold and
of silver stood on either side of the entrance to the palace,
and golden figures of youths served as torch-holders in the
great hall (η 91 ff.). An elaborate (presumably silver) cup
of Nestor (Λ 632) is adorned with golden studs; it has
two supports, and four handles, with two doves at each
handle (*cf.* Fig. 16). The cuirass of Agamemnon is described
in a passage (Λ 19 ff.) which bears marks of comparatively
late composition; it has ten circles of dark *lapis lazuli*,

*Use of
Metals.*

twelve of gold, and twenty of tin, and three dark serpents on either shoulder stretch up toward the neck. Another Homeric work of art was the golden brooch of Odysseus (τ 226): a hound held with his forepaws a dappled fawn which struggled and endeavored to escape. On the golden baldric of Heracles in Hades were wrought figures of bears, wild boars, and lions, as well as representations of battles

FIG. 16.—"Nestor's Cup," from Mycenae.

(λ 610). The golden maidens of Hephaestus, who served him as crutches, have been mentioned already (p. 295). Apollo had a silver bow (ἀργυρότοξος, A 37), and Hera had a chariot of metal, with a silver pole and a yoke of gold (E 722),—but these, like Apollo's "golden lyre" in Pindar, were drawn from the imagination for the adornment of the scene. The lyre of Achilles, taken from the spoils of Cilician Thebes, had a bridge (ζυγόν, I 187) of silver; but perhaps this was only adorned with silver, as the "golden staff" of the priest Chryses was doubtless of wood, adorned with golden handle and studs

(A 15, *cf.* 246), and the "iron mace" of Areïthoüs (H 141) seems to have been a wooden club with knobs of iron. The arms (*i.e.* the great shield?) of the Lycian Glaucus are said to be of gold, worth one hundred cattle, while the arms of Diomed were of bronze, and worth nine cattle (Z 236); but the gold or bronze in these was chiefly external, and largely for ornament. The shield of Nestor, too, is said to be of gold (Θ 193), "both the rods and the shield itself"; but even here the gold probably was thought of as forming the outermost layer, with one or more layers of oxhide beneath it (*cf.* H 223). So a belt which the "smiths wrought" (χαλκῆες κάμον, Δ 216) may have been so lined with cloth or skins that we should not be sure whether the metal was of primary or secondary importance.

Six metals are named by the Homeric poet : copper or bronze, iron, lead, tin, silver, and gold. Naturally the last *Six Metals.* two were precious. The poet has no one word for metal. No mines are mentioned. Only for copper and silver does he seem to know the source or a source of supply.

The poet seems to be living near the close of the Bronze Age of Greece.[1] In the poems bronze is mentioned *Close of the Bronze Age.* far more frequently than iron,—more than 320 times, including derivatives, in the *Iliad*, and more than 90 times in the *Odyssey*, while iron is named only 23 times in the *Iliad* and 25 times in the *Odyssey.* That bronze is mentioned so much more frequently in the *Iliad* than in the *Odyssey* was understood for a time as an indication of the earlier date of the composition of the *Iliad*, but now it is explained more reasonably by the observation that the weapons of the *Iliad* were of bronze. Since the name of this metal is often used by the poet as a synonym for spear or other weapon, just as steel is used in modern times,[2] bronze naturally appears often in

---

[1] Hesiod, *Works*, 151, puts the Bronze before the Iron Age. *Cf. Et prior aeris erat quam ferri cognitus usus,|quo facilis magis est natura et copia maior*, Lucretius, v. 1287; χαλκὸν δὲ τὸν σίδηρον λέγει διὰ τὴν πάλαι ποτὲ χρῆσιν τοῦ χαλκοῦ, Eustathius on A 236.—Copper was naturally the first metal to be used by man, since it occurs in a comparatively pure state, easily malleable.

[2] *Cf.* "foeman worthy of his steel." See *Iron in Homer*, by F. B. Jevons in *Journal of Hellenic Studies*, xiii. 25, and Cauer, *Homerkritik*, 179.—Of the 23

the books which treat of battles. Doubtless, too, just as the name copper-smith is given to the worker in iron and in gold (χαλκεύς, ι 391, γ 432), so also the word for copper was used often where the actual implement or article was of iron.

The Homeric instances of the use of iron have been subjected to various unsuccessful analyses, in the endeavor to gain from them an indication of different strata in the poems. Iron still remains firm in *Iron in Homer.* what is acknowledged to be the older parts of the poems, unless unjustifiably bold excisions are made of otherwise inoffensive verses. The following articles are of iron: in the *Iliad*, a club, probably of wood with iron knobs, such as Heracles in later works of art is often represented as bearing (H 141), knives (Σ 34, Ψ 30), an arrow-head (Δ 123), axes (Δ 485, Ψ 851), the axle of Hera's chariot (E 723), and the gates of Tartarus (Θ 15); in the *Odyssey*, axes or adzes (ι 393) and bonds or chains (α 204). Cauer observes that in nine instances iron is mentioned only as a possession, with no indication of its use; fifteen times it is used to express firmness of body or soul (as a "heart of steel," in English), with figurative use, as "the iron might of fire" (Ψ 177), and the epithet of iron applied to the firmament (ο 329); and thrice objects of iron are mentioned which had no real existence,—the gates of Tartarus, the axle of Hera's chariot, and the bonds which were imagined to hold Odysseus. In most of the other instances iron is used for tools; only half a dozen times is iron used for weapons of war, as for the club of Areïthoüs, the arrow-point of Pandarus, and the knife or sword with which the throats of kine were cut. From his examination of the passages, Cauer infers that this metal was not familiar to the people, but that its reputation for hardness was fixed. An epithet used four times, "much-worked" (πολύκμητος, as Z 48), implies that it was known to be less malleable than copper. But a great mass of unwrought iron is used in the contest of "putting the shot," in the

---

examples in the *Iliad*, according to Cauer, three are in Δ, three in H, five in Ψ, and two in Ω; ten books have no mention of iron. Eleven books of the *Odyssey* contain no mention of iron. See also Lang, *Homer and his Age*, 176 ff.

games in honor of Patroclus (Ψ 826), and is itself the
prize. If a man had this, Achilles assured the Achaeans,
his shepherd or ploughman would not need to go to the
town for iron, since this mass would supply it.   This
implies, as we have seen, that some one on the farm was
expected to have skill in working in iron, and the Achaeans
may well have had primitive but efficient forges.   The
comparison for the noise caused by the burning of the
Cyclops's eye,—that this hissed about the red-hot stake
"as when a smith dips an axe or adze in cold water,
tempering it, for this is the strength of the iron" (ι 391),
shows that this process was well known.   The fictitious
king of the Taphians is said to be taking a cargo of iron
to Temesa to exchange for copper (α 184).   Where he
obtained this iron, the poet does not intimate.   Since the
Taphians were noted pirates, the iron may have been gained
by unlawful means, but iron is reported to have been found
in very recent times near or on the island of the Taphians.
If the Achaeans had iron to give in barter for copper, they
may be supposed to have learned how to prepare it for
their own use.

That bronze or copper was the ordinary metal of the
arts of the Homeric age, has been stated already.   Assays
Bronze or Copper. have shown the admixture of tin to have been
in general so slight at Mycenae and Hissarlik,
that the question is fair whether bronze or
copper is the better translation for the Homeric χαλκός.
The poet shows no knowledge of its being an alloy.
Apparently the Achaeans were able to make this metal
harder than the copper of modern commerce, since they
used it not only for spear-points but also for knives and
razors, but once (Λ 237) the bronze point of a spear is
"turned back like lead" on meeting the silver plate which
adorned and strengthened a warrior's belt.   Copper is to
be procured at Temesa (α 184), which probably was in
Bruttium.   Sidon is called "rich in bronze" (ο 425), but
this may be a general expression for wealth.   Doubtless
Phoenician traders brought articles of copper as well as of
silver, but the poet may not have thought of these metals
as derived originally from Sidon.   Bronze was used for all

weapons and armor (including a battle-axe, N 612), for basins and cups, as a covering for thresholds (as η 83), and as a decoration for chariots, furniture, and even walls (as η 87). Ares receives the epithet of bronze (χάλκεος, E 704),—probably from his equipment of arms, though possibly also from his unyielding firmness. The horses of Zeus are *bronze-footed* (χαλκόποδες, Θ 41),—certainly not as shod with bronze, but as strong-hoofed. The loud-voiced Stentor is *bronze-voiced* (χαλκεόφωνος, E 785), as "trumpet-tongued" or unwearied in the battle-cry. Similarly, at the introduction to the Catalogue of Ships, the poet says he could not name all the warriors though he had a heart of bronze (B 490).[1]

Lead is mentioned but twice in the Homeric poems,—as a sinker on a fish line (μολυβδαίνη, Ω 80), and as a standard for what is pliant and yielding (μόλιβος ὥς, Λ 237).

Lead.

Tin[2] appears more frequently than lead, being mentioned ten times, but of these, six are in connexion with the arms of Achilles (Σ 474, 565, 574, 613, Υ 271, Φ 592), and two of the remaining instances are in connexion with the armor of Agamemnon (Λ 25, 34), and one with the cuirass of Asteropaeus (Ψ 561). In the remaining instance, tin is used with gold in the decoration of the chariot of Diomed (Ψ 503). This metal has too little power of resistance to be useful for armor; it must have been used for ornament rather than for strength, and a difficulty arises since, in a scene on the Shield of Achilles (Σ 565), tin is used with gold, silver, and blue enamel, where the difference in appearance between the silver and the tin must have been only slight. Hephaestus makes the greaves of Achilles of tin, which would awaken little surprise, except for the resistance which these greaves show to the spear of Agenor (Φ 593). The suggestion has been made that tin formed only an outer layer, over some harder substance, but the poet does not appear to be well acquainted with the properties of this metal, though it is named ten times,

Tin.

---

[1] With this one may compare the epithet χαλκέντερος (*bronze-bowelled*) applied to the indefatigable Homeric scholar Didymus.

[2] See Ridgeway, *Early Age of Greece*, i. 608.

and no indication is given as to the source of its supply. Of course it may have been brought from Cornwall, but pure tin is said to have been found among the lake-dwellings of Switzerland.

Little gold was found in Greece proper in historical times, and the source of supply of the Homeric gold,—

Gold. whether the shores of Thrace or Lydia,—is entirely conjectural. Its brilliancy and freedom from oxidation made it to be highly prized, and thus it was said to be used by the gods even for purposes for which it is ill fitted. That the pavement of the hall of Zeus is of gold (Δ 2), reminds the reader of the picture of the New Jerusalem.[1] The house of Poseidon was of gold (N 22), as well as the thrones of Zeus and other gods (Θ 436, 442), the aegis of Zeus (Ω 21), the wand of Hermes (ε 87), the yoke and fellies of Hera's chariot (E 724, 730), the hobbles of Poseidon's horses (N 36), and many other possessions of the gods. Aphrodite is called *golden* (as Χ 470),—with reference to her gold ornaments more probably than because of the color of her hair. Men as well as gods had an abundance of gold. The palace of Menelaus fairly gleamed with gold (δ 72). Wine was served in golden cups at the home of Odysseus (α 142), and water for the hands was brought in a golden ewer (α 136). Helen had a golden distaff (δ 131). The shield of Nestor is said to have been of gold (Θ 193), but this seems to refer only to the framework and the outer layer. Hector's spear had a gold ferule about the bronze point (Z 320). Agamemnon's sword had golden knobs or studs on the hilt (Λ 29). Antimachus went to battle with gold ornaments, very likely for his hair, " like a girl " (B 872). Nausicaa on going to the river took olive oil as an unguent in a gold flask (ζ 79). Goldfoil was moulded about the horns of a victim for sacrifice (γ 437). Hundreds of thin gold laminae were found in the tombs excavated at Mycenae which clearly were used for decorative purposes (Fig. 8, p. 175), and the Homeric Achaeans also had thin gold plates as decorations for straps and furniture. The edges of silver bowls were sometimes covered with a gold plate ;

---

[1] ἡ πλατεῖα τῆς πόλεως χρυσίον καθαρόν, *Rev.* xxi. 21.

thus being literally *plated* (as δ 616). In the manufacture of Achilles's shield (Σ 468 ff.), Hephaestus seems to have inlaid the precious metals in the manner of swords found by Schliemann at Mycenae (see Fig. 24).

Silver is not mentioned in the Homeric poems so frequently as gold. It is said to be derived from Alybe (B 857), whence came allies of the Trojans. *Silver.* The relation of this place to the later Chalybians (assumed by Strabo, 549), is not clear. The silver mines at Laurium in Attica do not seem to have been opened so early. Apollo's bow is of silver (A 37), since this was a precious metal,—perhaps with a thought also of the gleam of the silver, as like the rays of the sun-god,—and the poet had no thought of its lack of elasticity. Achilles's mother Thetis is *silver-footed* (ἀργυρόπεζα, A 556),—the epithet which Milton translated by *tinsel-slippered.* The pole of Hera's chariot is of silver (E 729), as well as Circe's tables (κ 355), the tool-chest of Hephaestus (Σ 413), the mixing-bowls and basins (as δ 616, α 137) of several mortals, the bridge of Achilles's lyre (I 187), and the door-posts and lintel of Alcinoüs (η 89). Menelaus even received two silver bath-tubs as a present from an Egyptian king (δ 128). Silver as well as gold was used for the decoration of furniture, belts, hilts of swords, sceptres, and the like.

White gold, a mixture of silver and gold, is assumed for the decoration of the palace of Menelaus (ἠλέκτρου, δ 73),—named with gold, silver, and ivory. The word for *Electrum.* amber would have the same form, but amber seems less fitted for such a use. On the other hand, *electron* seems to mean *amber* when it appears in two necklaces (ο 460, σ 296).

Amber appears in the Homeric poems only in the two instances which are cited in the last preceding sentence, and the poet shows no knowledge of the source from *Amber.* which it is derived. The excavations at Mycenae have shown that it was highly esteemed there, and the route has been traced by which it was brought down from the Baltic.[1]

---

[1] See Ridgeway, *Early Age of Greece*, i. 359 ff.

The Achaeans before Troy had no ivory, but the poet was familiar with it, though he nowhere mentions the elephant, and may not have known whence the ivory was derived. Of course it was imported and foreign to Greece. Penelope is made by Athena fairer than ivory (σ 196). The white thighs of Menelaus, stained with his blood, are compared by the poet to ivory stained purple by a Maeonian or Carian woman, to serve as a cheek-piece (παρήιον, Δ 142) for horses. The leader of the Paphlagonians had for his steeds reins white with ivory (λεύκ᾽ ἐλέφαντι, E 583),—thin plates of ivory being used just as metals were employed with leather. Ivory is used also for the decoration of a bedstead (ψ 200) and an easy chair (τ 56), for the handle of a key (φ 7), for the scabbard of a sword (θ 404, cf. Alcaeus, *Frag.* 36), and even with gold, silver, and electron for the adornment of the great hall of Menelaus's palace (δ 73 ; cf. I *Kings* xxii. 39, *Amos* iii. 15). Finally, the gates through which deceitful dreams pass are said to be of ivory (τ 563, with a play on ἐλέφας, *ivory*, and ἐλεφαίρομαι, *deceive*), while the truthful dreams come through the gates of horn (with a play on κέρας, *horn*, and κραίνω, *accomplish*).

Cyanus (κύανος, η 87) was an imitation of *lapis lazuli*, a kind of blue paste. It was used for a cornice-decoration in the great hall of Alcinoüs,[1] and for the adornment of Agamemnon's cuirass and shield (Λ 24, 35), and of the shield of Achilles (Σ 564). The adjective formed from this word is used freely for *dark*, being applied not only to clouds and ships but also to the brows of Zeus (A 528) and to the hair of Poseidon (κυανοχαίτης, γ 6),— which gave the suggestion for Neptune's " blue-haired deities," in Milton's *Comus*, 29.

Ivory.

Cyanus.

---

[1] *Cf.* the frieze of the great hall at Tiryns ; Tsountas and Manatt, *Mycenaean Age*, p. 47, fig. 11.

CHAPTER XI

SEA LIFE AND SHIPS

THE Greeks of the Homeric age were not hardy and adventurous mariners, and the shield which Hephaestus fashioned for Achilles (Σ 483 f.), although it is adorned with representations of actions of war *Not Bold* *Mariners.* and of peace, of ploughing, of reaping, of the vintage, of the herding of cattle, of contentions before judges, of the marriage procession, and of the choral dance —including most of the experiences of human life,—yet has no scene taken from sea-life.[1] On their return from the siege of Troy, Menelaus, Nestor, and Diomed at Lesbos (γ 169) "pondered over the long voyage,"—whether to sail across the open Aegean Sea to the southern end of the island Euboea, about 110 miles, with the island of Psyria for their encouragement, about mid-way,—or to follow the coast of Asia Minor,. to the south, and then to skirt the shore of Crete, and thus come up to Peloponnesus from the south,—a route more than twice as long for Diomed, but keeping close to the land all the way. Indeed they did not dare "cleave the open sea" until they received a guiding omen from the gods. Then they sailed directly from Lesbos to Euboea,—a long day's sail,—and arrived after nightfall (γ 177). Agamemnon, the leader of the expedition, took the other course and sailed past Cape Malea (δ 514) on his way to Mycenae. Later on his

---

[1] None of Homer's characters sail for recreation, just as none of them seem to fish for sport. They are too near the primitive life to care for this.—On the other hand, only once is a possible reference made to (freedom from) seasickness (ἄνουσοι, ξ 255).

wanderings, Odysseus is thought cruel by his companions because, though they are "overcome by weariness and sleep,"

Sleep on Shore.

he bids them not to land at evening on the island of the Sun (μ 274). "Let us obey black night," say they, "and remain and prepare our supper by the side of the swift ship." The ships were only open boats, with no hold and no cabin, with no berths or hammocks, and thus with no arrangements of any sort for cooking or for sleeping. No one can wonder then that Odysseus's comrades, in spite of his warnings of danger from the landing, desired to spend the night as usual on shore. The element of time was not so important for them as it is at present; a Phoenician trading ship was content to remain for a whole year in one port (ο 455). At times, indeed, the crew were obliged to spend one or more nights on board their boat, as when for more than nine days the fleet of Odysseus was driven by north winds, from Thrace to the land of the Lotus Eaters (ι 82), but the men were very wretched meanwhile. The only night-voyages which are willingly undertaken are those of Telemachus to Pylus and return (β 434, ο 296), in which he desires to escape notice, and the convoy of Odysseus by the Phaea-cians (ν 29 f.), where again it was of the highest importance that his arrival should be unobserved. Since, when the mariners were out of sight of land, the stars and the sun were their only guides for the course, men at sea on a stormy night must suffer themselves to be driven aimlessly by the wind. On his way home from Calypso's island (ε 270), Odysseus took no sleep by night, constantly "observing the Pleiades, the late-setting Boötes, and the Bear which men call also the Wain,[1] which turns in one spot and watches Orion, and alone has no part in the baths of Oceanus" (*i.e.* does not set). Not that Odysseus had no sleep for more than a fortnight, but he could sleep most securely by day, when, before lying down to rest, his watchful eye could reach a distance of many miles before him. Naturally, during the winter months a journey by sea would be avoided, and Hesiod (*Works and Days*, 620)

[1] According to Strabo, i. 3, the Phoenicians taught the Greeks to use this constellation as a guide in their voyages.

advises his friends at the setting of the Pleiades to draw up their boats and make these secure on land, and to bring into the house all the tackle, including oars and rudder. The boats would take no large store of provisions, but would carry parched grain or meal in leathern bags (β 354, ε 266), and water and wine in jars or leathern bottles (ε 266, β 349, ι 165). The sailors were particularly glad to find a spring of fresh water at their landing place (δ 359, ι 85, 140, κ 56, ν 109).

The boats were for transport, not for naval warfare, with no beak or ram for hostile purposes, as in later times,—low, with a small deck at either end, with high bow and stern. They were blackened (μέλαιναι, B 524), probably with pitch, but often had red or blue prows.[1] The use of the word *cheek*, in the note below, would imply that the bow was not sharp, and the early Egyptian boats, too, seem to have been designed to slip over the water rather than to cleave the waves. The most frequent Homeric epithet of ships is *swift*, though they can hardly have deserved this adjective on modern standards ; the epithet next in frequency is *hollow* or *curved*, then *black*. Ships are *straight-horned* (ὀρθόκραιραι, Σ 3),—which was long understood of the raised stem and stern, but has been interpreted recently as a reference to the two ends of the yard.[2] They were *hooked* (κορωνίδες, τ 182), and this has been explained as referring to the curved ends.[3] The stern apparently had some carved ornament.[4] The ships were called *well-decked*, though the deck covered but a small part of the boat.[5]

Ships not for Warfare.

The trees named as used for ship-building are oak, white poplar, and pine (N 389 = Π 482).

Timber.

The Achaean sailors were prepared to use sails if the

---

[1] μιλτοπάρῃοι, B 637, *vermillion-cheeked*; φοινικοπάρῃοι, λ 124, *purple-cheeked*; κυανόπρῳρος, ι 482, *blue-prowed*,—but this blue may be very dark. *Cf.* κυανώπιδες νᾶες, Aesch. *Pers.* 559.

[2] *Cf. cornua antemnarum*, Verg. *Aen.* iii. 549.

[3] *Cf.* ἀμφιέλισσαι, ζ 264, *curved at both ends*. Also ἐΐσαι, ζ 271, *equal, well-balanced*.

[4] ἄφλαστον, O 717, *cf.* Hdt. vi. 114; and ἄκρα κόρυμβα, I 241.

[5] ἐΰσσελμος, B 170; the noun σέλμα is not Homeric.

wind was fair, but every man on board, except the com-
Every Man Rows. mander (and perhaps also a steersman), was
expected to ply an oar in a calm, and the oar
was so personal a possession that Odysseus's
comrade Elpenor desired to have his oar planted as a
monument on his grave (λ 77).[1]

Merchant ships have twenty oarsmen (ι 322), and a boat
of this size is used to convey Chryseïs to her father (Α 309),
Size of Boat. Telemachus to Pylus (α 280), and the suitors of
Penelope on their expedition of hostility to
Telemachus (δ 669). If we suppose that two
men sat on each thwart, and allow an interval of three feet
between the thole-pins on the same side, and leave a little
space for the deck at bow and stern, such a boat would
be about forty feet in length. Its breadth cannot have
been less than eight feet, and is not likely to have exceeded
ten feet. These are about the dimensions of the Gloucester
seine-boat, which is built of cedar, with special reference to
lightness, and weighs about a ton before it is put into the
water. The Homeric boat for twenty men is not likely to
have weighed less than two or three tons. But the ordinary
ships used by the Achaean expedition against Troy were
much larger. The ships of Achilles and of Protesilaus had
each fifty oarsmen (Π 170, Β 719); the Phaeacian ship which
brought Odysseus to his home had 52 men (θ 48); Odysseus's
own boat had 46 men (κ 208), after six had perished in
battle with the Ciconians (ι 60), and six had been devoured
by Polyphemus (ι 289, 311, 344); the ships of the Boeotian
contingent bore each 120 men (Β 510, *cf.* Thuc. i. 10).
Unless we are to suppose that not more than half of the
Boeotians rowed at once, their boats would have been inconveniently and insecurely long, for no hint is given that
two or more men toiled at a single oar, nor that the

---

[1] In the *Argonautica* of Apollonius of Rhodes, each hero, except Jason the leader
and Tiphys the helmsman, plies an oar and often all night long, and in Pindar's
account of the same expedition, though with a favorable breeze, the "rowing went
on unwearied" (*Pyth.* iv. 202). According to Theocritus (xiii. 37), who probably
follows some older poet, Heracles and Telamon shared the same table,—which is
simply another way of saying that they rowed on the same bench and were comrades.
—*Cf.* αὐτερέται δὲ ὅτι ἦσαν καὶ μάχιμοι πάντες, ἐν ταῖς Φιλοκτήτου ναυσὶ δεδήλωκεν
(*sc.* Ὅμηρος), Thuc. i. 10.

oarsmen were then arranged in banks or tiers as became common in later times. Aeneas's comparison of a boat with a hundred thwarts [1] is a clear hyperbole.

The importance of the oars, as not simply resorted to in an emergency but used almost constantly on the voyage, is shown by the prominence given in the story to the number of oarsmen. The oars, not the sails, were the "wings of the ship" ($\pi\tau\epsilon\rho\grave{a}$ $\nu\eta\upsilon\sigma\acute{\iota}$, λ 125).[2] *Oars the Wings of the Ship.* The joy of the Trojan warriors on the return of Hector and Paris to the field of battle (H 4) is likened to that of sailors, weary with beating the sea with their oars of fir, on some god's granting them a favorable breeze. On their second voyage homeward from the isle of Aeolus, the souls of Odysseus's comrades are wearied by the grievous rowing, since no breeze aids them (κ 78). The Achaean sailors prayed for favorable winds, but did not always wait for them.[3] Only when on the island of Pharos, near Egypt, Menelaus was detained by a calm (δ 360), but to their minds Egypt was at an almost immeasurable distance from Greece ; and Odysseus with his comrades was detained by contrary winds on the island of the Sun (μ 325),—but how far he thought this to lie from Ithaca, we cannot guess, since it was in fairyland. In particular, oars were commonly used on entering or leaving a harbor.[4]

The small decks or platforms ($\emph{ἴκρια}$) at bow and stern afford a resting-place for two or three passengers. Here ($\emph{ἐνὶ πρυμνῇ}$, β 417, cf. o 285) sit Athena, in the *Small Decks.* guise of Mentor, and Telemachus, for the voyage from Ithaca to Pylus, and Odysseus lies sleeping on the deck at the stern ($\emph{ἐπ' ἰκριόφιν πρυμνῆς}$, ν 74) when he is conveyed by the Phaeacians to his home. Under these decks must have been some storage room, but when Odysseus

---

[1] $\nu\eta\hat{\upsilon}s$ $\epsilon\kappa\alpha\tau\acute{o}\zeta\upsilon\gamma$os, Υ 247. $\pi o\lambda\upsilon\kappa\lambda\hat{\eta}\iota$s, θ 161, *with many rowlocks*, is used eleven times as an epithet of ships.

[2] *Cf.* $\tau\alpha\rho\sigma\hat{\wp}$ $\kappa\alpha\tau\acute{\eta}\rho\epsilon\iota$ $\pi\acute{\iota}\tau\upsilon\lambda o\nu$ $\emph{ἐπτερωμένον}$, Eur. *Iph. Taur.* 1346. But in Aeschylus (*Prom.* 468), the sails are the wings of ships.

[3] The story of the detention of the fleet at Aulis by contrary winds (Aesch. *Ag.* 187) is not Homeric.

[4] A 435, o 497.—To row was to drive ($\emph{ἐλαύνειν}$, *sc.* $\nu\hat{\eta}\alpha$) ; *cf.* η 109, μ 276, γ 157. At H 6, however, it is "beating the sea" ($\pi\acute{o}\nu\tau o\nu$ $\emph{ἐλαύνοντες}$), and at η 319, "beating the calm" ($\emph{ἐλόωσι γαλήνην}$, *sc.* $\theta\acute{a}\lambda\alpha\sigma\sigma\alpha\nu$?).

takes his three reluctant companions from the land of the
Lotus Eaters, he binds them under the thwarts (ὑπὸ ζυγά,
ι 99), showing that he had no free room for them at the
end of the boat ; and king Alcinoüs in person "goes through
the boat" and sees to it that the Phaeacian gifts for Odysseus
shall be so stowed under the thwarts (ν 21) as not to be
in the way of the rowers, while he would have used the
hold for storage if it had existed.   If the bow and stern
rose as rapidly as in the Egyptian boats, little space would
be left under the decks.   When Odysseus fears that if he
should tell his comrades about the monster Scylla they in
fear would hide themselves " within " (ἐντός, μ 225), he must
have in mind their crawling under the benches.   But the
Phoenician nurse of Eumaeus falls from the deck into the
bilge-water (ἄντλῳ δ' ἐνδούπησε, ο 479), which indicates an
open space between the rowers and the deck or the station
of the steersman, and such a place must have been needed
for the hecatomb which Odysseus took to Chrysa (A 309),
though not for the sheep which he took to the land of Hades
(λ 4).   The thwarts served both as seats and as bonds
(ζυγά) between the sides of the boats ; whether any of them
could easily be removed, is not stated.   A gangway ran
from stem to stern, and thus the commander could pass
" through the ship encouraging his comrades " (διὰ νηὸς ἰών,
μ, 206) but whether this was a plank between the oarsmen,
or by the side of the gunwale, is not clear.   From the
bow to the mast, it might well have lain between the rowers,
but towards the stern, the lowered mast seems to have
required this place.

The oars [1] were of pine or fir (H 5, μ 172), as in modern
times they are often of spruce.   They were well-polished
The Oars.   (ἐυξέστης, H 5) and sharpened at the blade
(προήκεα, μ 205).   That the oar-blades were
broader than in modern times, is indicated by the direction
of Teiresias : in order to appease the wrath of Poseidon,
Odysseus is to take his oar on his shoulder and journey

---

[1] The oar is ἐρετμός, pl. ἐρετμά (ζ 271) ; *cf.* Lat. *remus* and English *oar*.
The blade is πηδόν (η 328).   The handle is κώπη (ι 489), which is used also for
the hilt of a sword (A 219) or the handle of a key (φ 7), and at times this seems
to be used for the oar itself (as ι 489, μ 214).

inland until he shall come to men who know not the sea nor eat salt with their food, and who will think his oar to be a winnowing shovel (λ 128). As in modern times, the oarsmen faced toward the stern, where the commander had his place (β 417). Thus (as at ι 490) the captain could direct his men by a nod, without words. The oars were fastened to thole-pins (*keys*, κληῖδες, θ 37, 53, *cf.* μ 203) by leathern thongs (τροποί, δ 782) as also in modern times in Greek lands, so that when the oar-handle was dropped, the oar was not lost, but its blade clattered along the side of the boat (μ 204). The oars might thus be made ready hours before the departure of the boat (θ 53, δ 782).[1]

The rudder (πηδάλιον, γ 281, ε 255) was a steering paddle, perhaps with a broader blade than the ordinary oar. Whether it was attached to the side, or passed through the stern of the boat, is uncertain. It was removed *The Rudder.* when the boat was drawn up on shore, and Hesiod would have it hung above the fire (ὑπὲρ κάπνου, *Works* 45, 629),— *i.e.* under the roof, in a dry place and out of the way, —during the winter.[2]

A sort of ladder or landing-plank is referred to once [3] as depending from the stern. Some such device must have been generally convenient, and at times almost necessary, and is observed on vase-paintings of a *Landing-Plank.* later age. The steersman had a bench or platform seven feet in length (θρῆνυς ἑπταπόδης, O 729); on such a platform Ajax took his stand while defending the Achaean fleet drawn up on the Trojan shore.

The mast of Telemachus's ship is of fir (εἰλάτινον, β 424). The wild-olive trunk which Polyphemus had cut to serve as a staff (ι 322), is likened in length and thickness *The Mast.* to the mast of a twenty-oared ship, and this comparison has been used for the basis of determining the

---

[1] *Cf.* Aesch. *Pers.* 376, τροποῦτο κώπην σκαλμὸν ἀμφ' εὐήρετμον, as one of the early preparations for naval service just before the battle of Salamis.

[2] The use of the plural οἰήια (as μ 218) is explained as referring to the parts of a rudder with T-form handle.

[3] ἐφόλκαιον, ξ 350,—evidently from ἐφέλκω, *drag after.* The epithet *polished* (ξεστόν) indicates that it is of wood, as we should expect, for it is not likely to have been of metal. This has been explained by some as a rudder, but with little probability.

height of such a mast,—hardly more than twenty or twenty-
five feet,—but who knows how long a staff Polyphemus
needed? Obviously, if the twenty-oared boat was forty feet
in length, the height of such a mast would be about half
the boat's length, and if it were placed in the middle of
the boat, it would, when lowered, just reach to the stern.
This mast was set on the keel in a mast-step.[1] When the
boat was drawn upon shore, the mast was lowered toward
the stern, and was held in a mast-crutch (ἱστοδόκη, A 434),
which may have been the top of the stern-post. When set
up (ἱστάναι, β 425), the mast leaned against the principal
thwart or cross-timber of the boat (μεσόδμη, β 424 = ο 289),
which had a deep notch[2] in which to receive it.

The mast was held in place by two fore-stays (πρότονοι,
β 425),—ropes which reached from near the top of the
Fore-stays. mast to either side of the bow. The loosening
of these allowed the mast to sink toward the
stern, where its top rested in a crutch. In a storm (μ 409),
the fore-stays of Odysseus's boat break, and the mast falls
backward suddenly and kills the steersman. How Odysseus
fastened the mast in the craft which he himself constructed
on Calypso's island, is not stated: it was securely stepped,
for it was broken in the middle, not torn from its fastenings,
by a fierce blast (ε 316). The yard to which the sail was
fastened, was drawn up the mast by a back-stay (ἐπίτονος,
μ 423) of ox-hide, which must have passed through a ring
attached to the mast-head, or through a hole in the mast
itself, which served as a pulley. Where it was made fast
below, is not stated, but this was probably near the stern.

[1] ἱστοπέδη, μ 51. This may have been held sometimes by a pivot at the
bottom, in order to facilitate its lowering and raising; but this device would have
little practical value. Certainly the mast was easily removed from the boat. Probably
the foot of the mast was held firm on three sides by the frame of the mast-step.

[2] The Homeric expression is literally "within the hollow cross-timber," which
implies that the mast passed through the main thwart of the boat used by
Telemachus. This is entirely practicable for a mast of the length supposed, though
it would be difficult in a large ship; when freed from the weight of the sail and
yard, it could be lifted without difficulty. Such lifting of the mast seems to be
implied further in ἀείραντες, β 425, but is inconsistent with the lowering of the
mast simply by loosening the fore-stays. The mast of Odysseus's craft was broken
(ε 316) because he either forgot or was not able to lower his sail on the sudden
approach of a storm.

Since the yard with the sail hung in front of the mast, the back-stay not only held up the sail but also steadied the mast, and relieved the strain on the mast in a high wind. Without it, the mast would be kept from falling forward only by the fastenings at its step and by the thwart. The strain and friction on this back-stay, used in hauling up the yard and sail without a block, were unusually great, and of this rope alone does the poet say that it was of ox-hide; and it was a back-stay with which the ship-wrecked Odysseus bound together mast and keel to serve him as a kind of raft (μ 423).

Braces (ὑπέραι, ε 260) were fastened to either end of the yard to set and hold this in the right position as regards the wind, and at the stern. These corresponded to the sheets (πόδες, ε 260, the *feet* of the sail) which were fastened to the lower corners of the sail, and then to either side of the ship, probably not much aft of the mast.[1] The sail was a square-sail, and cannot have been much broader than the boat,—thus spreading only about 200 square feet of canvas for a boat forty feet in length. For a sail thus set, a "fair" breeze, from directly astern, would be better than one on the quarter.

Braces and Sheets.

[1] The "foot of the ship" (πόδα νηός, κ 32), which Odysseus held continuously during the nine days' voyage from the island of Aeolus to Ithaca, can hardly have been the *sheet*, or the feet of the sail, but must have been the rudder; so in Pindar (*Nem.* vi. 55) the wave dashes πὰρ ποδὶ ναός, and the scholiast interprets this as *rudder*, πηδάλιον, and in Timotheus, *Persians* 102, the πόδας ναός are the *oars* (*cf.* the πτερὰ νηυσί of λ 125). Sailing, as they were, with a fair wind, the adjustment of the sheet was of less importance than the management of the rudder, and the same man could hardly have held both. Further, if the sheet, without a block near the mast, had been drawn tight by the helmsman, the lower part of the sail would have been drawn too much toward the stern, and this would have given to the whole sail an unprofitable slant.—Once (ε 260) the word κάλοι (*ropes*) is used in connexion with sheets and braces; perhaps referring to the stays, though others interpret it as *buntlines*, "used to haul up to the yard the body of the sail when taking it in."—ὅπλον (ξ 346, φ 390) is a strong ship's rope or cable. At φ 391, it is βύβλινον, which should mean *of papyrus* (*cf.* Hdt. vii. 34, 36), and it has been thought to be *of rushes*, simply in order to escape the inference of close connexion between Ithaca and Egypt. That most of the ropes were not of leather, is shown by Agamemnon's words before Troy (Β 135): "their ship-timbers have rotted and their ropes (σπάρτα,—of rushes or hemp) are loosed," *i.e.* untwisted.—The *implements* (ὅπλα) of β 390 seems to refer to mast, sail, and oars, as well as ropes.

To "loose the sail" (λύον ἰστία, ο 496) is to loose the halyard or back-stay which held up the yard.[1] The word for sail is generally used in the plural,[2] but means only one sail, and the plural marks the consciousness of the strips of cloth of which it is made.[3] Certainly Odysseus's craft had but a single yard (ἐπίκριον, ε 254), and so only a single sail, but for this sail the plural form is used. This sail of Odysseus was made of linen cloth furnished by Calypso (φάρεα, ε 258 ; see page 158).

The Sail.

In addition to the implements already mentioned, a ship might have a long pole (κοντός, ι 487), to aid in pushing off and in coming to land,—in particular when the sailors were to land against resistance. Such pikes the Achaeans use in defending their ships from the attack of the Trojans (ξυστόν, Ο 388). That wielded by Ajax (Ο 677) was twenty-two ells in length, and was made of several pieces of wood bound together. This is called "made for a ship-fight" (ναύμαχον), but this does not imply naval engagements in the modern sense, but only contests waged from the boats against men on land, who resisted the landing of the assailants, a manner of strife much like that in which Ajax actually used this pike.

Boarding Pike.

When the stay on land was to be very brief, a boat might be moored, with stern-ropes (πρυμνήσια, Α 436) fastened to a tree or a rock on shore, and, if the wind was from the sea, fastened with anchor-stones (εὐναί, Α 436) cast from the bow. No anchors of modern form, with flukes, were known until much later. The habit of mooring the ship with the stern by the land, was a natural precaution of early ages, making ready for a speedy departure if this should prove necessary. At some landing places, holes were made in large stones or rocks

Stern Ropes.

---

[1] To *lower* the sail is καθέμεν, ι 72, or καθελεῖν, ι 149 ; to *furl* is μηρύσασθαι, μ 170. To *take down* the sail, in a general sense, is στεῖλαι, γ 11. It is hard to see how the sail was shortened ; perhaps the Achaeans were acquainted with some species of brailing. To *hoist* sail is ἀνὰ ... ἐρύσαι, ι 77 ; to *spread* it, is ἀνὰ ... πετάσαι, Α 480.

[2] ἰστία, ε 259,—the singular but three times.

[3] *Cf.* ὄχεα (Ε 794) of a single chariot, δώματα (Ζ 313) of a house, and βασίλεια (Xen. *An.* i. 2. 7) of a palace. Another suggestion of the use of the plural is that the ropes are included,—"all that belongs to the mast."

near the water for the convenience of fastening the stern-ropes (κ 96).[1] The length of a stern-cable is inferred only from the use of one to hang at once the twelve unfaithful maids of Penelope,—one end being fastened to a column of the palace or the gateway, and the other to a building in the courtyard (χ 465), and nooses being made to receive the women's heads. For this purpose a rope sixty feet in length would not have been too long, and such a length would be suitable for a boat's cable.

For a stay of a night or two, the boat was generally run up on shore, stern foremost. With the tools of the Homeric age, the ships could not easily be made water-tight. The joints cannot have been close. That *Boats on Shore.* these were caulked and pitched in some way, is probable, but no clear statement is made to this effect.[2] Naturally then the boat was not left in the water longer than was necessary.

When the stay was to be of weeks' or months' duration, the boat was drawn upon land, stern foremost as before, entirely out of the water, and props,—sometimes stones, as Ξ 410,—were put under the sides to keep them from resting and rotting on the ground (Α 486, Β 154). The keels were probably of little depth. Deep keels would be inconvenient in drawing the boats upon shore, and they were unnecessary, since the Homeric Greeks had not learned to sail close to the wind ; but the boats were not absolutely flat-bottomed,—they had keels.[3] The ships of the Achaeans when they were encamped before Troy were so completely out of the water that when the Greeks started to depart for home they not only removed the props but also cleared out the trenches (οὐροί, Β 153) along which the ships had been dragged. No rollers are mentioned as used in drawing the boats up and down, though Apollonius of Rhodes makes much of them (φάλαγγες, *Arg.* i. 388). Hesiod (*Works*, 624)

---

[1] Others less reasonably understand this stone to be perforated for convenient use as an anchor.

[2] The suggestion has been made that σπάρτα, Β 135, means not *ropes* (see above), but hemp used for caulking. But this is improbable.

[3] Odysseus represents himself as hugging the keel (τρόπις, η 252) of his wrecked ship, and thus borne to the isle of Calypso, though at μ 424 he says (as we have seen above) that he bound keel and mast together by the back-stay.

recommends his hearers when they draw up their boats for the winter to weight them with stones, and to take out the plug in the bottom, that water may not gather in them, —but of this Homer says nothing.

The preparations for a voyage are stated in detail at δ 780, θ 51 : the ship is drawn to the sea, the mast and *Preparations for Voyage.* sails are placed in it, and the oars are made fast to the thole-pins. When most of the crew are in their places (*cf.* A 480, o 552, β 418), the stern-ropes are loosed from the shore, then the mast is raised, the sail is spread, the wind fills the belly of the sail, the dark wave roars about the cutwater, and the sailors, having made all fast, sit in their order while the ship accomplishes her course.[1]

On their return from the voyage, conversely, the sailors furl the sail,—probably still attached to the yard, for a yard *Return from Voyage.* only ten or twelve feet long, with sail furled upon it or gathered up against it, would be easily handled,—and lay it in the ship, lower the mast to its support, row to the mooring-place, and then bind the stern-cables to the shore (A 433, γ 10, o 496). In general, as we have seen, the crew expected to row into and out of the harbor (*cf.* also λ 640).

The winds most dreaded are the north and west,— "Boreas and Zephyrus, which blow from Thrace" (I 5), *Dreaded Winds.* though the comrades of Odysseus fear "lest a blast of wind may come suddenly, either of Notus (the south wind) or of harsh-blowing Zephyrus, which especially tear a ship in pieces, even against the will of the guardian gods" (μ 288). Two winds are needed to make a storm (I 4, ε 331 ; *cf.* Aesch. *Prometheus* 1087), though of course a single wind may drive a mariner from his course (ι 67).

The longest voyage of which the poet speaks, with a definite course and time-limit, is from Crete to Egypt,—a *Length of Voyages.* voyage of four days (ξ 257),—though Odysseus was seventeen days on his craft, sailing from Calypso's island to the land of the Phaeacians (ε 278). For nine days the Ithacans were driven by Boreas

[1] For the description of a ship in a storm, see ε 313, ι 67, μ 405, O 625.

from Cape Malea to the land of the Lotus-Eaters (ι 82), and for nine days they were borne by the west wind from the island of Aeolus to Ithaca (κ 28). From Circe's island to the stream of Oceanus and the land of shades, was a sail of but a single day with a favorable breeze (λ 11). The voyage from Ithaca to Pylus occupied a single night (β 434, ο 296, 495). The voyage from the Achaean camp before Troy to Chrysa seems to occupy but a few hours ; at least Odysseus sets out with Chryseïs after the assembly of the Achaeans had been held, and at Chrysa they offer sacrifice and sing hymns to Apollo "all day long" (A 472). On his return from Troy, Nestor spent the first night at Tenedos (about fifteen miles from Troy), the second at Lesbos (about fifty miles from Tenedos), the third at Geraestus, at the southern end of Euboea (110 miles.) ; then his associate Diomed reached Argos on the fourth day, but Nestor, with a favorable wind, kept on his way to Pylus (γ 159 ff.). The Phaeacians in a single night bring Odysseus from Scheria to Ithaca (ν 33, 95), but their ship is "as swift as a thought" (ὡς εἰ νόημα, η 36), and since the Phaeacians dwell in fairyland, the length of the voyage is unknown.

Cape Malea, at the south-eastern corner of Peloponnesus, has justly been called the "Cape Horn of ancient navigation." There Menelaus met with a storm which ended in the destruction of most of his ships (γ 287). *Cape Malea.* There Agamemnon himself was caught by a blast which bore him out of his course (δ 514). There the current and the north wind drove Odysseus far to the south (ι 80), and from that cape the disguised Odysseus represents his real self as driven to Crete, when he desired to proceed to Troy (τ 187).[1]

The indications, found by some scholars, of primitive beacons to warn sailors by night from dangerous coasts, refer, when rightly interpreted, only to the camp-fires of shepherds on the mountains (κ 30, Τ 375). *Lighthouses.* Only a bright moonlight night would tempt a Homeric mariner willingly to continue his voyage.

[1] Strabo (378) attributes the prosperity of Corinth largely to the trader's fear of Malea, and quotes the proverb, "On rounding Malea forget your friends at home."

The poet has little to say of professional sailors, though he notes the Cyclopes' lack of ships, "which would accom-

Professional plish each errand, visiting the cities of men, as
Sailors. men often traverse the sea to visit one another"
(ι 125). He represents no Greeks as traders, except the Taphians; the Phoenicians and the Taphians are traders (α 184, ξ 452; ο 415 ff.), and with trade then, piracy[1] and kidnapping were often connected (ο 427, 449). The Aegean Sea was safe for the Homeric boat during only a few months of the year. Hesiod (*Works*, 663) considers the fifty days after the summer solstice the only really secure period for a voyage, though he allows that men may sail also in the spring, when the fig-leaf is as large as a crow's foot. No man, then, would be a sailor without other occupation; through most of the year he would be a farmer, or busy with some handicraft. Conversely, most Greeks, living by the sea as they did, could manage a boat. "Ferrymen"[2] brought Odysseus's cattle from the mainland to Ithaca (υ 187), as they "bring other men, too, on their way, whoever may come to them." Similarly, the bodies of Penelope's slain suitors from other lands were given to "men of the sea" (ἁλιεῦσι, ω 419) to convey to their homes. Telemachus has no boat of his own, and clearly the state has none; that he may make his voyage to Pylus, Athena borrows for him a boat of Noëmon (δ 634), who four days later himself desires it in order to bring from Elis some young mules which he is pasturing there.

The Phaeacians[3] are the typical race of seamen, but they live in fairyland. Almost all of their names are derived

Phaeacian from the sea or seamanship. Their place of
Sailors. assembly is by the sacred precinct of Poseidon (ζ 266), and there they make their ropes and sails, and

---

[1] In a well-known passage (i. 5. 4) Thucydides asserts that piracy was no disgrace in Homer's time, but this was disputed by Aristarchus. *Cf.* γ 73=ι 254, ι 40, ξ 85, 262.

[2] πορθμῆες, υ 187; the Attic prose meaning of the word is not to be pressed, since Herodotus (i. 24) uses it of the sailors who undertook to convey Arion from Tarentum to Corinth, and Euripides (*Iph. Taur.* 355) uses πορθμίς of a ship which should bring Helen from Greece to Thrace; yet no man would keep his cattle many hours' sail from his home. See page 71.

[3] These have often been thought to be Phoenicians, but see page 60.

fashion their oars. They do not care for war, but delight in ships. In one passage the Phaeacian boats are said to need no rudders,—"they are possessed of intelligence and themselves know the thoughts and minds of men, and the cities and fields of all men, and most swiftly traverse the sea" (θ 557),—but this is inconsistent with the more prosaic account of the shipyards, and of the oarsmen tossing up the sea with their oars (ν 78), and the force of the rowing which ran the boat half its length on land (ν 115, cf. 22).

The most detailed account of ship-building presented by the poet is in his story of the craft built by Odysseus for his return from Calypso's island. This cannot have been a ship in the ordinary sense of the term. It is not called a ship, but a *frame* (σχεδίη), and nothing even hints that it has the shape of a ship. Odysseus shrinks from risking his life in it for a voyage across the sea (ε 174). If it were a ship, then Calypso's excuse would have been very paltry : she tells Hermes that she cannot send Odysseus home, for she has no ships (ε 141). It was built in four days (ε 262) by a single man, with no tools but axe,[1] hewing axe, and augurs,—thus without either saw or nails. Furthermore, the timber was not previously prepared : Odysseus's work included even the felling of the trees, the making of the wooden pegs or treenails, and the sewing of the sail. Homer often represents his heroes as doing acts which require extraordinary power,—as where Hector hurls a stone which no two men of the poet's age could lift,—but nowhere else is Odysseus made to have such magic force as to do in four days what would require more than as many weeks of another man's work, and the poet had little to gain by hurrying the achievement of his plan,—Odysseus might have

Odysseus's Ship-building.

---

[1] The axe (πέλεκυς, ε 234) has a helve of olive-wood, and is "sharpened on both sides,"—not both front and back, for the back must have been needed as a hammer or mallet,—which would give a wedge-like cut ; while the hewing-axe (σκέπαρνον), being sharpened only on the inner side of the edge, would leave a smooth surface below. The augurs (τέρετρα, ε 246) were to bore holes of different diameters for dowels and treenails. These clearly could be used by a single person ; a larger auger or drill for ship-timbers, to be worked by three or four men, is used as an object of comparison for the hot pointed stick turned in the eye of Polyphemus (τρύπανον, ι 385).

been employed (like Robinson Crusoe) four months upon his craft, if necessary. Even with the trees felled and sawed into beams and boards, and with the best of modern tools, a skilled carpenter would need more than four weeks to build such a boat as some modern scholars have imagined that of Odysseus to .have been.[1] Without a saw the making of boards so straight that they could be fitted together with water-tight joints was very laborious and slow work. Further, the poet's expression with regard to the wreck of the craft, —"the waves scattered it as the wind scatters a heap of chaff" (ϵ 368),—seems to indicate a raft rather than what would deserve the name of a boat.

The only hint of the size of Odysseus's raft is given by a comparison with the bottom of a merchant ship (ϵ 249), but
Odysseus's Raft. this should not be pressed.[2] Odysseus fells twenty dead, well-seasoned trees,—alder, black poplar, and fir,—choosing these because they "would float lightly" (ϵ 240). The alder is heavy, but it may have been used for pegs. Of the size of the trees the poet says nothing, but they need not have been more than six or eight inches in diameter. One of these would have been needed for the mast, and part of another for a yard ; another would have to be split into boards or slabs to be used as binders. If a conjecture is to be risked, perhaps we may fairly suppose the raft to have been twenty or twenty-five feet in length and ten or twelve feet in breadth,—it was as broad as a "broad merchantman" (ϵ 249). The felled trees were laid side by side, after they had been trimmed and cut so as to lie close together (ϵ 245) ; at either end, and probably near the middle, a bed would have to be prepared for the slabs which were laid across the trimmed trunks of trees to serve as binders (ἁρμονίαι, ϵ 248), being fastened to the timber below by wooden pegs (γόμφοι). After this frame was

---

[1] And as for size, Buchholz imagines the craft to have been about 50 × 20 feet. But how could Odysseus have brought this into the sea? Would he have succeeded better than Robinson Crusoe in launching such a heavy, clumsy structure? The very fact that Odysseus had but twenty trees, and these all felled in a short time, if not in a single morning, should have kept scholars from assuming a large and complicated craft.

[2] The term may be used here of a barge rather than of a ship built to ply between different countries.

completed, Odysseus made a sort of a deck (ἴκρια, ε 252) or platform, supported by props (σταμίνες) which allowed the waves to wash over the raft without wetting the voyager. Then he made a mast and a yard, and a steering oar, and a railing with wicker bulwarks to keep off the spray, and finally heaped upon the platform boughs of trees, to be his seat[1] and his couch for the long voyage,—a couch over which were thrown cloaks and rugs. This work, with the sewing of the sail, would seem sufficient occupation for four days.[2] Whether the distance from Calypso's island to the land of the Phaeacians was too great to be traversed by a raft in seventeen days, depends on the situation of Circe's island and the strength of the wind provided by Circe,—both of which are unknown. That Odysseus's craft was not a mere raft has been argued chiefly from the care taken to trim the timber " straight to a line " (ε 244), but this would be convenient also for a good raft. The eighty or a hundred treenails necessary for such a raft would amply justify the epithet " with many fastenings " (πολύδεσμος, ε 338).[3]

[1] Cf. the boughs or shrubs which serve for seats in the hut of Eumaeus, ξ 49, π 47.

[2] Others, less reasonably, have thought the σχεδίη to have been conceived as not flat-bottomed, but as composed of a series of combinations of four timbers ; of these, the lower two of each set were joined at about a right angle, and this angle served as a keel, while the upper two were morticed to the others as uprights, as \/ . The number of pegs necessary for such a boat would abundantly justify the epithet πολύδεσμος. But the labor of building such a craft would be indefinitely greater than that of making a few such frames, and covering them with planks. The chief objection to the supposition of such a craft is that Odysseus could not possibly have made it in four days or in four weeks. Another difficulty is to understand the use of the wattles "as a defense from the wave," if the gunwales were as high as they are depicted in some modern books, and yet Odysseus by this scheme is left *in* the trough, and not high above the water, as in ε 163 f.

[3] The best statement with regard to the craft of Odysseus is : Assman, *Das Floss der Odyssee*, Berlin, 1905,—published after this chapter was written. The views of scholars differ widely with regard to Odysseus's craft. When technical terms are used but once their exact meaning may be quite ambiguous, and thus the poet's story may be obscure to those who have an uncertain view of these technical terms. Even as early as the time of Aristophanes (*Dait.* 15), the Athenian boy must learn at school the meaning of words like κόρυμβα, *stern ornaments.*—ἐπηγκενίδεσσι, ε 253, has been interpreted as *planks*, but better as long *binders* to form the gunwale ; and σταμίνεσσι, ε 252, as *ribs*, *braces* for the sides, but better as *uprights* let into the floor of the raft, as supports for the platform or " hurricane " deck.—A scholiast supposed the boughs of trees to be intended for

The ships which bore Paris to Greece in quest of Helen were made by Tecton (*Carpenter*, E 60), the son of Harmon

Ship Builders.

(*Joiner*), who was taught his art by Athena herself. Perhaps this indicates a sort of guild of builders in which the skill might descend from father to son,[1] but more probably the names were simply invented by the poet as appropriate to the story.

Penelope calls ships "the chariots of the sea" (ἁλὸς ἵπποι,

"Chariots of the Sea."

δ 708), and the quick motions of the Phaeacian ship are compared to a chariot drawn by four stallions quickly accomplishing their course over the plain (ν 81).

The early Greeks doubtless learned much with regard to navigation from the Phoenicians, but none of the Homeric

Influence of Phoenicians.

nautical terms have been traced to a Phoenician source, as might be expected in view of the large number of such terms which the English language has borrowed from the Dutch, as *ahoy*, *avast*, *belay*, *boom*, *skipper*, *sloop*, etc., and those which the French have borrowed from the English, as *beaupré*, *cabine*, *paquebot*, *touer*.

ballast, which is quite absurd.—δρύοχοι, τ 574, is another word of uncertain meaning, used but once, in a comparison for the setting up of axes as a mark for bowmen in the hall of Odysseus. It has been understood as *ribs*, but now is interpreted as the pieces of timber which supported the keel while the ship was building.

[1] The untiring strength of Hector is likened by Paris to that of an axe which cleaves a ship-timber (Γ 61). *Cf.* N 391 = Π 484, O 410, P 744, ι 384, 498. But many men then knew how to build ships.

CHAPTER XII

AGRICULTURE, PLANTS, AND TREES

THE ownership and the limitation of fields have been discussed already, and the reader has been reminded that the life of the men in Homeric Greece was in the fields,—not in houses, counting-rooms, or factories. *No Ornamental Gardening.* These fields were for use rather than for ornament. We find no indications of avenues of trees, not to speak of more elaborate landscape-gardening, and few hints of care for flowers. The grove in which the nymph Calypso lived (ϵ 63 f) most nearly resembled a park, but it was a natural park. The only shade trees which seem to have been planted are the elms which the mountain nymphs planted about the grave of Andromache's father (Z 419). Gardens ($\kappa\hat{\eta}\pi o\iota$), which included fruit trees and vines, are mentioned six times and are nearly equivalent to *orchards* ($\ddot{o}\rho\chi a\tau o\varsigma$, ω 222, Ξ 123). The vineyard which was depicted on the Shield of Achilles was enclosed by a trench and a hedge (Σ 564), and entered by a single path. The garlands in which the companions of Alcaeus and the Athenians of the fifth century B.C. delighted, were not worn at the feasts of Homer's heroes. Flowers were not used for the adornment of either the house or the person. The poet nowhere alludes to the fragrance of either flowers or fruit.

The rose is not mentioned in Homer except in the epithets *rosy-fingered* ($\dot{\rho}o\delta o\delta\acute{a}\kappa\tau\upsilon\lambda o\varsigma$, β 1 and oft), which is applied to the Dawn, and *rosy* ($\dot{\rho}o\delta\acute{o}\epsilon\iota\varsigma$, Ψ 186), which is given to Aphrodite's perfumed unguent, that very probably came from the Orient, and is used on the body of Hector to keep it from corruption.   The violet is named once ($\stackrel{''}{\iota}o\nu$, ε 72) as growing with parsley on the meadow of Calypso ;

The Rose, it may have been the pansy.   It does not seem
Violet, and to have been of a bright blue color, for the
Crocus. sheep of Polyphemus are said to have " dark violet wool" ($\iota o\delta\nu\epsilon\phi\grave{\epsilon}s$ $\epsilon\hat{\iota}\rho os$, ι 426), which seems to mean   simply   that   they   were   " black   sheep."   The crocus also appears once ($\kappa\rho\acute{o}\kappa os$, Ξ 348) as joining with the hyacinth and the lotus to form a couch for Zeus and Hera, and four times the epithet *saffron-robed* ($\kappa\rho o\kappa\acute{o}\pi\epsilon\pi\lambda os$, Θ 1) is applied to the Dawn.   No mortal woman or other goddess wears a robe of this color, though in Pindar's time this was thought to have been a royal color in the heroic age.   This saffron dye, too, may have been imported from the Phoenicians, but the crocus as well as the lily is found in works of art in the palace at Cnosus in Crete.   Very possibly the poet had only a slight acquaintance with the rose, the lily, and the hyacinth,—his ignorance being due either to their general neglect at that time, or to their being comparative strangers to Greece.   Both the lily and the rose are thought to have been brought from Media

Hyacinth and and Persia.   The hyacinth appears on two other
Lily. occasions, furnishing a comparison for the hair of Odysseus ($\acute{\upsilon}\alpha\kappa\iota\nu\theta\acute{\iota}\nu\omega$ $\mathring{\alpha}\nu\theta\epsilon\iota$ $\acute{o}\mu o\acute{\iota}as$, ζ 231),—in which we may believe the likeness to lie not in the color, but in the thick curl of the flower.   The lily appears in the so-called Homeric Hymn to Demeter (427), which is assigned to the seventh century B.C., but in the *Iliad* and *Odyssey* it serves only for a rather remarkable comparison with the soft voices of the Trojan elders ($\mathring{o}\pi\alpha$ $\lambda\epsilon\iota\rho\iota\acute{o}\epsilon\sigma\sigma\alpha\nu$, Γ 152), and in a mocking speech of Hector, with the soft skin of Telamonian Ajax ($\chi\rho\acute{o}\alpha$ $\lambda\epsilon\iota\rho\iota\acute{o}\epsilon\nu\tau\alpha$, Ν 830).   The

Asphodel and asphodel   is   named   only   as   growing   on   the
Poppy. " Asphodel Plain " of Hades (λ 539, 573, ω 13), until the Homeric Hymn to Hermes (221).   In the early spring this flower has grace and beauty, but later in the year its tall, dry stalk is barren and dreary, and we cannot be quite sure whether the poet thought of the Asphodel Plain as cheerful or as dismal.   This plant still grows   in   neglected   cemeteries   as   in   other   desolate   and

waste fields of Greece, and is thought to have been planted over graves by the ancients. The bulb, according to Hesiod (*Works and Days*, 41), formed part of a very frugal diet, but is not mentioned by the Homeric poet. The poppy grew in gardens (μήκων . . . ἐνὶ κήπῳ, Θ 306), but it may have been cultivated for its oil or for its soporific qualities, rather than for the beauty of its flower. Some would hold that the

> "Nepenthes which the wife of Thone
> In Egypt gave to Jove-born Helena"

(δ 221), was a kind of opium, or at least that the story was based upon the effects of opium. Parsley (σέλινον, B 776) is named as food for the horses of Achilles, together with the *lotus*, which is recognized as a kind of clover,—of course entirely distinct from the plant of the "Lotus Eaters" (Λωτοφάγοι, ι 92), which is thought to be the *jujube*, found in Libya, with cherry-like fruit. The Egyptian lotus is not mentioned.

The flowers which have been enumerated were doubtless for the most part wild flowers. Nowhere in the world, perhaps, are the fields brighter with spring flowers than in Greece. The "flowery mead" (λειμῶν' ἀνθεμόεντα, μ 159) is mentioned by Homer, *No Flower Beds.* however, only in connexion with the Sirens (μ 159), and the plain of the Scamander (B 467), where an allusion is made to the leaves and flowers of spring-time ; Pyrasus is also called *flowery* in the Catalogue of the Ships (B 695). But, as has been observed by others, the absence of expressions of enthusiastic love for flowers, does not prove the absence of feeling for them, any more than indifference on the part of the Greeks of the Periclean age to the sculptures of the Parthenon may justly be inferred from the neglect of these in classical literature. Odysseus, however, seems to have had at his home no front lawn nor flower beds, since we learn that before the Ithacan palace lay a heap of manure (ρ 297), and that swine wandered through the courtyard (σ 105, υ 164), while goats and kine for slaughter were tethered in the front porch (υ 176, 189), and probably were killed in the front yard.

The Homeric Greeks knew no meadows in the modern

sense, since they cut and cured no grass for hay,[1] and
grass does not readily form turf in Greek soil and climate.
Other herbs there are more important for cattle than our
grass. But cyper grass grew on the banks of the
Scamander (κύπειρον, Φ 351) and served as fodder for
horses (δ 603). In addition to this, horses were fed on
lotus (B 776), white barley (κρῖ λευκόν, E 196), wheat (πυρός,
Θ 188), and spelt (ὄλυραι, E 196, ζειαί, δ 604).

Herds and flocks have been seen to be the chief source
and element of wealth in the Homeric time, and doubtless

Country Life the Natural Life.

were the chief care of the prosperous man. Princes
are "shepherds of the people" (ποιμένες λαῶν,
B 85), and tend their flocks with a dignity
which would not comport well with active labor
in the harvest field or in the smithy. Farming was the
occupation of the old Romans, too, and Cato preferred the
pastoral to the strictly agricultural stage. Comparatively
little land was devoted to agriculture,—whether to grain
land or to fruit land. But a country life was the natural
life of all, and no manual labor (except grinding at the mill)
was noted as menial, while grain had become an important
part of subsistence. It is significant that the word *works*
(ἔργα, π 140) is used for *farm* in Homer, while in Attic Greek
it is used for a mine or a factory. On the Shield of Achilles
(Σ 541-572) are represented three scenes of agricultural life,
for the three Greek seasons,—ploughing, reaping, and the
vintage, for spring, summer, and autumn. Fields had to be
tilled, sown, and reaped. The Cyclopes alone are so blest
by the gods, and their land is so fertile, that wheat, barley,
and vines grow for them unplanted and unsown, but
Polyphemus makes no use of grain, and has but an inferior
sort of wine; Ismaric wine is as nectar to his taste. The
Cyclopes clearly had not advanced beyond the pastoral or
nomadic stage,—tending their flocks and enjoying wild fruits.
Grass was not cultivated; the expression "clovery plains"
(πεδία λωτεῦντα, M 283) does not require the assumption of
cultivation. The clover (λωτός) is mentioned four times; it
served as fodder for horses, and clearly was not abundant

---

[1] The herbage which is mentioned once as cut (σ 368) was taken probably at once
to the animals which were to eat it.

on Ithaca (δ 603), which was a "land for goats rather than for horses." No special fodder was prepared for the winter season.

Beans (κύαμοι) and chick pease (ἐρέβινθοι) are the two kinds of legumes mentioned by Homer, and that only in a comparison : an arrow bounded from the armor of Menelaus like pease and beans from a *Beans and Pease.* winnowing shovel (ἀπὸ πτυόφιν, N 588). This shows that these vegetables were allowed to ripen fully, and were dried. Probably they were treated like grain, and were bruised or ground before being prepared directly for use as food. They were vegetables of the field rather than of the garden.

Garden vegetables, in modern American variety and profusion, were unknown to the Homeric Greeks, as they were to their remote descendants until very recent years. Garden beds are mentioned in connexion *Leeks and Onions.* with the palace of Alcinoüs (η 112 ff.) and the farm of Laërtes (ω 247), but no specification is given of the variety of plants, and the name for the bed (πρασίη,—cf. πράσον) implies that these vegetables were of some species of leek or garlic,—of which the pungent flavor has always been enjoyed in Southern Europe,—and we remember that an onion was served as a relish with a posset, in Nestor's tent (κρόμυον ποτῷ ὄψον, Λ 630). The conjecture that the leeks served only as a border for the beds in which other vegetables were planted, is unsupported. The layers of the dried onion are referred to by Penelope (τ 233) as a comparison for the smoothly finished and fitting cloak of Odysseus.

Of the grains, barley and wheat were the chief; rice, rye, oats, and buck-wheat were unknown. Barley has always been more common in Greece than wheat. In 328 B.C., according to an Eleusinian inscription *Barley and Wheat.* (*Bulletin Corr. Hell.* viii. 194 ff.), about ten times as many bushels of barley as of wheat were raised in Attica. Probably since it was recognized as the oldest of the grains, it was used chiefly in sacrifice, only partially bruised or ground. Of the words for bearded barley, ἄλφιτον (only three times) or ἄλφιτα (plural, with reference to the meal or groats) occurs fifteen times in the Homeric poems;

κρῖ (three times) or κριθή occurs nine times. Barley is called *white* (κρῖ λευκόν, Ε 196) and *broad-growing* (εὐρυφυές, δ 604), which is interpreted as indicating the variety with six rows of kernels on the ear; the two-rowed variety is said to be ἀκοστή, which appears in the poems only in the participial form (ἀκοστήσας, Ζ 506 = Ο 263),—used of the high feeding of a horse. Spelt (ζειά, δ 41, 604) is named but twice, and both times as fodder; but it occurs twelve times in an epithet of the earth, *grain-giving* (ζείδωρος, Β 548). Some would interpret this as *sesame*; the exact determination of the species of Homeric plants and animals is difficult when it is not impossible. One-grained barley, *i.e.* with but one row of grains on the ear (ὄλυραι, Ε 196, Θ 564) also is named twice, and as fodder for horses. Wheat (πυρός, δ 604) is mentioned nine times, six times in the *Odyssey* and three times in the *Iliad*, and four times a plain or fields are called *wheat-bearing* (πυροφόρος or πυρηφόρος, γ 495). The name Pyrasus (Πύρασος, Β 695) of a Thessalian village which is called the sacred field of Demeter (Δημητρὸς τέμενος), indicates the cultivation of wheat in that region. Wheat is said to grow for the Cyclopes, as well as barley and grapes, without sowing and planting (ι 110). It is called *honey-sweet* (μελιηδής, Κ 569) and *sweet-hearted* (μελίφρων, Θ 188), as well as *apple-faced* (μῆλοψ, η 104), which we have interpreted as *golden*. Twice in the *Odyssey* wheat is the food of geese, and twice in the *Iliad* it is fodder for horses. Rich harvests of wheat and barley are among the blessings which the gods bestow on a land where the king maintains justice (τ 112). "Eating bread"[1] is characteristic of men, in contrast both to the gods who eat ambrosia and drink nectar, and to raw-flesh-eating (ὠμοφάγοι λύκοι, Π 157, οἰωνοὶ ὠμησταί, Λ 454) wild beasts and birds of prey.

Flax was of less importance in the Homeric period since not only the ordinary outer garments of men, and the rugs

Flax.   which were thrown over chairs as upholstery, but also the ordinary bedding, was of wool. The poet does not mention the flax plant. But since the Homeric

---

[1] ἐπὶ χθονὶ σῖτον ἔδοντες, ι 89; σιτοφάγοι, ι 191; οἳ ἀρούρης καρπὸν ἔδουσιν, Ζ 142, cf. Φ 465; ὃς ἔδοι Δημήτερος ἀκτήν, Ν 322.

Greeks used linen for garments of both men and women, for bed-clothing (ν 73, 118), for burial shrouds (Ψ 254), for tunics in war (B 529), and for fish lines (Π 408) and nets (E 487), to doubt their cultivation of the plant would be unnecessary. The word for *tunic* (χιτών, English *cotton*) is supposed to have been borrowed from the Phoenician *kitonet, linen,* and indicates that the Greeks received their knowledge of linen, or of its best preparation, from the Phoenicians, who in turn are thought to have learned this from the Egyptians, through the Jews. Possibly the Achaeans may still have imported their finest linen from the East, but this is mere conjecture. If the Achaeans procured their linen from the Phoenicians, Homer certainly does not tell of this. The Homeric word for linen (λίνον) is cognate with the English *linen* and *lin-seed* (possibly with *line*), and the German *Leinen*. The φᾶρος of Circe and of Calypso was of linen, probably identical in form with the πέπλος, and of linen were the ὀθόναι of the maidens represented in the dance on the Shield of Achilles (Σ 595),—possibly under oriental influence. At times a linen cloth, as well as a rug, was thrown over a chair before this was occupied (ὑπὸ λῖτα πετάσσας, α 130), and over a god's chariot when this was set away (Θ 441), and a similar cloth was used as a covering for the body of Patroclus (Σ 352). Of linen was the thread spun by the Fates (Υ 128, Ω 210, η 198), and the Phaeacian women wove and spun linen (η 107). In weaving linen, oil was used in its finish (η 107, Σ 595). The ropes of the ships (σπάρτα, B 135) were ordinarily of tow, or some kind of hemp,—though possibly they were of rushes at times. A ship's rope at the palace of Odysseus is said to be of papyrus (βύβλινον, φ 391 ; see pages 313, 315). Cotton seems to have been unknown.

In poems of war and adventure, we do not expect to find detailed accounts of agricultural processes such as Hesiod gives, but Homer's view of life is so *Irrigation.* broad that many indications of rural employ· ments are given. That the Homeric Greeks knew the advantages of irrigation, we see from a comparison of the river Xanthus, overtaking Achilles as he fled from it, with the stream which a gardener guides among his vines

and plants, removing the obstructions with his mattock
(Φ 257 f.); and, again, a few verses later, where the Trojan
plain was dried "as a newly watered field" is dried by
the north wind in late summer (Φ 346 f.). In his description
of the garden of Alcinoüs, too, the poet says that one
spring scatters its water in different directions through
the whole garden, while another flows to the threshold
of the courtyard, for the use of the palace and the
people generally (η 129). Before the grotto of the
nymph Calypso were four springs flowing with clear water
in different directions (τετραμμέναι ἄλλυδις ἄλλῃ, ε 71),
evidently for the refreshment of the vine and the trees
which have been mentioned in the text. The story of
the daughters of Danaüs (unknown to Homer), carrying
water in sieves in the lower world, has been interpreted as
based upon such irrigation as now makes parts of the Argive
plain to "blossom as the rose."[1]

The use of manure as a fertilizer is shown by the notice
of a heap lying near the palace of Odysseus (ρ 297), waiting

Manure.

to be taken by the servants to enrich the king's
great domain. Hesiod does not mention it, and
king Augeas, according to the later myth, does not seem
to have known its value, since he allowed it to accumulate
in his stalls until Heracles turned the stream of the Alpheüs
through these, and cleansed them.

The cultivated fields were allowed to lie fallow,[2] as in
modern Greece, for their refreshment; how long they rested,

*Fallow
Fields.*

we are not told. Pindar (N. vi. 9 f.) says that
fields in alternate years render their fruits and
regain their strength. Rotation of crops is
nowhere indicated. The legumes may have alternated with
the grains,—but this is only conjecture. Such fallow ground
was ploughed thrice.[3]

---

[1] Professor Bassett suggests that the expression, "the rain of Zeus gives it increase"
(καί σφιν Διὸς ὄμβρος ἀέξει, ι 111 = 358) of the fruits of the Cyclopes, implies that
elsewhere artificial irrigation was employed.

[2] νειός,—cf. νέος. K 353, N 703. But this etymology is uncertain, and νειός
may mean simply *field*.

[3] Σ 541, ε 127. Whether this triple ploughing was, once each, in spring, summer,
and autumn, or all at one season, cannot be absolutely determined. The former

Agricultural methods and implements were primitive, no doubt, in the Homeric age, but they differed little from those now employed in Asia Minor.   The plough *Agricultural Implements.* was the most important tool, and its name[1] is cognate with those for grainfield (ἄρουρα, Γ 246) and for tilth (ἄροσις, I 580).   The mattock (μάκελλα, Φ 259) is mentioned but once.[2]   Laërtes uses a hoe in loosening the ground around a vine (λιστρεύοντα, ω 227), and a like tool is used in removing from the floor of the great hall of Odysseus, the earth which was stained with the blood of Penelope's slain suitors (λίστροισιν, χ 455).

To the plough Homer gives the epithet *well-joined* (πηκτὸν ἄροτρον, K 353).   Hesiod knows not only this manufactured plough but also one made of a single *The Plough.* piece of wood (αὐτόγυον, *Works and Days*, 433), and recommends the farmer to have both, that if he should break one, he may have the other ready for use.   Of the implement used in the Cyclades, Bent writes (*Cyclades*, p. 97) : " The chief ingredient in a plough is a tree ,with a trunk and two branches ; one branch serves as a tail, and the other has a bit of iron fixed to it, and penetrates the ground ; the trunk is the pole."   Such a plough has no great weight, and at times a ploughman in Greece may be seen returning from his work at night, driving his kine before him, and carrying his plough upon his shoulder.   Homer does not name ploughshare, beam, nor head.   The share may not have been tipped with metal, as it does not seem to have been even in the classical period ; but the use of iron by a ploughman is assumed in one passage (Ψ 835 ; see page 300). The primitive plough did not turn the clod, but only tore it ; it simply " tickled " the ground.   Two names are used for the furrow,—ὦλξ (N 707, σ 375) and ὄγμος (Σ 546). The latter of these is used also for the swath of the reaper (Σ 552), and may indicate that the grain was planted rather than sown ; but it seems to be connected with ἄγω, *lead*,

---

has been thought probable, but has no Homeric support, and the other is certainly reasonable. *Cf.* Columella, ii. 4 ; Xenophon, *Oec.* xiii. 11 ; Theocritus, xxv. 25 ; Vergil, *Georgics*, ii. 399.

[1] ἄροτρον, ν 32, Lat. *aratrum*, *cf*. Eng. *ear* in " ear the ground."

[2] The δίκελλα is not named.

and thus may mean only *line drawn*, whether ploughed or reaped. Care was taken to make the furrow straight.

For ploughing, cattle (cows as well as oxen, *cf.* Z 309), and by preference (K 352) mules, were used,—not horses, which never in Greece were subjected to menial tasks except in emergencies, they being a "delight of proud luxury." The ass is mentioned not at all by Hesiod, and by Homer only once (Λ 558), where the animal's stubbornness is taken as an illustration for that of Ajax. Hesiod counts an ox for ploughing (βοῦν ἀροτῆρα, *Works and Days*, 405) as the most important part of a farmer's establishment, next to his wife. A like estimate of the ox is indicated by a fragment (25) of Archilochus. The question has been raised whether the cattle may not have pulled by a band about the forehead,—as at present in parts of Germany and Nova Scotia,—instead of by a yoke about the neck, since the poet speaks of sweat as gushing forth at the roots of their horns, as they plough (N 705), and seven times applies to cattle the epithet "with broad forehead" (εὐρυμέτωπον, γ 382); but in the first of these passages the yoke is mentioned as holding the oxen apart, and no good reason exists for thinking of this yoke as essentially different from that of their horses.

Animals for Ploughing.

The weary toil of the ploughman is indicated in a comparison: Odysseus on the night before his return to Ithaca, though in the hospitable palace of the Phaeacians, longs for the sun to set (which is the time appointed for the beginning of his voyage), as does a ploughman "for whom all day the two dark-faced kine have drawn the well-made plough over the fallow field . . . and his knees shake as he goes" (βλάβεται δέ τε γούνατ' ἰόντι, ν 31 f.).

The furrow naturally would be as long as the animals could draw the plough to advantage without resting. We have learned (see page 245) that in Asia Minor this distance is one hundred feet, which is very much less than that of Occidental fields. Of course the furlong (*furrow-long*) has been from Anglo-Saxon times an important measure in England. In the spring scene repre-sented on the Shield of Achilles (Σ 541), each ploughman receives a cup of wine from a youthful attendant as he

The Furrow.

reaches the end of his furrow. This refreshment would hardly be needed for every two hundred feet of ploughing, but it might at least be offered. The comparison with old Teutonic customs has suggested that this provision of wine was in accordance with the law, written or unwritten, that when the retainer was performing labor for his liege lord he

FIG. 17.—Egyptian Plough.

should be well furnished with both food and drink, and that a great feast for the retainers was part of their recompense for the toil. Professor Ridgeway [1] holds that the length of the furrow was fixed, and much greater than one hundred feet, but that in Greece the *breadth* of a day's ploughing was one hundred feet.[2]

[1] In *Journal of Hellenic Studies*, vi. 319.

[2] With a single exception (ἐκατόμπεδον, of the pyre of Patroclus, Ψ 164), the *foot* is not used by the Homeric poet as a measure of distance,—but the hand-

The time of harvest is not specified by Homer, but must have been very nearly the same as at present. Hesiod (*Works*, 383 ff.) directs that the harvest should begin at the heliacal rising of the Pleiades, or just before the first of June, and that the ploughing should begin with the setting of the same constellation. Barley naturally is harvested somewhat earlier than wheat.

Seasons for Ploughing and Reaping.

Grain was reaped with a sickle (δρεπάνη, Σ 551, δρέπανον, σ 368). The reapers are called *mowers* (ἀμητῆρες, Λ 67), and worked in rivalry with each other; the harvest was the *math* (ἄμητος, T 223). We have seen that the swath received the same name as the furrow (ὄγμος, Λ 68). Armsful of grain are δράγματα (Σ 552), which were gathered by boys, and furnished by them to the binders (ἀμαλλοδετῆρες, Σ 554).

Reaping.

No mention is made of music in the harvest-fields, such as is found at the vintage and such as was customary in the time of Theocritus (*Idyls*, x. 16). But once we read of a harvest-home festival (θαλύσια, I 534, *cf.* Theocritus, vii.), or Feast of First Fruits, as celebrated apparently in thanksgiving for the harvest.

The treading out of the wheat by a yoke of oxen in a carefully prepared threshing floor (εὐκτιμένῃ ἐν ἀλωῇ, Y 496) is used as a comparison for the horses of Achilles's chariot trampling under foot shields and corpses, as the warrior pursued the Trojans to their city. The reader will remember the Mosaic injunction, "Thou shalt not muzzle the ox when he treadeth out the corn," in *Deuteronomy* xxv. 4. Flails and other threshing machines are unknown.

Treading out the Grain.

The process of winnowing is referred to in E 499 (λικμώντων), where the dust which arose in the conflict and

breadth (Δ 109), fore-arm or ell (κ 517), the distance of a horse from the wheel of his chariot, or that of the weaving-rod from the breast of a woman at the loom (Ψ 517, 760), a fathom or the distance between the fingers of a man's hands, extended in opposite directions (Ψ 327); the cast of a spear (K 357, O 358), or of a discus (Ψ 431), or of a shepherd's crook (Ψ 845); or a bow-shot (μ 83), or the reach of the voice (ι 473). If the *pelethron* of Φ 407, λ 577, (a square measure), is the square of the Attic *plethron* (100 feet), it would imply other examples of the exception already made.

fell upon the Achaeans, is likened to the chaff (ἄχναι) of the winnowing floor ; the winnowing of beans and pease is mentioned in a comparison in N 590, where the winnower is λικμητήρ, and the winnowing tool *Winnowing.* is named in the direction of Teiresias to Odysseus, that with his oar on his shoulder he shall proceed far inland until he comes to a country where men do not know salt, and where the oar is mistaken for a winnowing-shovel (ἀθηρηλοιγόν, λ 128),—which indicates both the shape and the size of the implement.[1] A heap of chaff was ἀχυρμιή (E 502). Not only in primitive but also in later times the grain was parched, which facilitated the removal of the husk and chaff, before it was pounded or bruised in a mortar, or ground in a mill, but of this parching the only Homeric indication is in καμινώ, *oven-woman* (σ 27,—see pages 230, 234).

That the soul of the farmer was not free from the trial of weeds, is indicated by the mention of thistle-down (ἀκάνθας, ε 328) as borne by the north *Thistles.* wind in late summer.

For fruit, grapes, olives, figs, pears, apples, and pomegranates were known and cultivated.

The fall of Euphorbus, slain by Menelaus (P 53 f.), is likened to that of a young olive tree which had been planted carefully by itself where it would have sufficient water, and which was luxuriant with white blossoms, *The Olive.* but was suddenly overturned by a blast of wind, and stretched upon the ground. Olive trees are mentioned also in the gardens of Alcinoüs and of Laërtes, but are not enumerated in the scenes of life depicted on the Shield of Achilles, with the vine and the corn field. That the Homeric Greeks were familiar with the wild olive, has been inferred from their possessing for it a name of their own. But since the Homeric and Hesiodic poems show no use of the olive berry as food, nor of the oil except as an unguent, some scholars have thought that the cultivated olive was hardly known in Greece a thousand years B.C.,—holding that the climate of Greece was not favorable for the development

---

[1] The λίκνον or *vannus*, *winnowing-fan* of later times (see Miss Harrison in *Journal of Hellenic Studies*, xxiii. 292, xxiv. 241) is not Homeric.

from the wild to the cultivated variety, and remembering
the myth that the olive was established in Greece as the
special gift of Athena to Athens.   The olive tree, however,
seems to be represented on a fragment of a silver vase
found at Mycenae (see page 630), and appears as a "motive
for decoration both for frescoes and vase paintings" at
Cnosus, and olive stones were found at Mycenae in the
rubbish of ancient houses, as well as in Crete, and a jar
of olive stones was found at Tiryns, while remains of prehistoric oil-presses are discovered on the island of Thera,
at the palace of Cnosus, and elsewhere.   The use of oil
in funeral ceremonies (Ψ 170) also indicates its early close
connexion with human life.   Hesiod may not have known
or mentioned the tree simply because his verses were for
Boeotians, and their climate was not suited to the olive.
Neither the fig nor the vine is mentioned by him, either,
though he knows wine well.   The olive in Homer is not
associated with Athena, any more than the laurel with Apollo
or the vine with Dionysus.   The olive club which Polyphemus
cut as a walking stick, but which Odysseus thrust in the
Cyclops's eye, was as long as the mast of a "twenty-oared
black ship, a broad merchantman" (ι 322).

That the Homeric poet does not mention the olive berry
or oil as food, or mingled with food, has been noted.   As
Olive Oil. an unguent, the oil seems to have been, at least
frequently, perfumed.   Thus the oil with which
Aphrodite anointed the body of Patroclus, is called *rosy*
(ῥοδόεντι, Ψ 186), and that which was stored up in the
palace of Odysseus, is called *fragrant* (εὐῶδες, β 339),[1]—
epithets which would not be applied to the modern olive
oil of commerce.   This use of perfumed oil seems to have
been learned by the Greeks from the Phoenicians, from
whom also the Children of Israel appear to have taken it.
Compare *Exodus* xxx. 23 f., where the recipe is given, of
pure myrrh, cinnamon, sweet calamus, and "oil olive": "and
thou shalt make it an oil of holy ointment, an ointment
compound after the art of the apothecary [perfumer]; it
shall be an holy anointing oil."   Possibly the perfumed oil
itself was imported to Greece in the Homeric time.   Olive

---

[1] *Cf.* ἐλάας καρπὸς εὐώδης, Aesch. *Pers.* 617.   See page 216.

oil was used also in dressing cloth.[1]   Lamps are not mentioned.

The olive tree (ἐλαίη, ε 477), under which Odysseus crept when he escaped from his shipwreck, may have been an oleaster, or wild olive.   The bar with which *Wild Olive.* Odysseus blinded the eye of Polyphemus was of "green olive" (ι 320), and the post of the same hero's *lectus genialis* was an olive stump (ψ 190).   Olive wood was used also for axe-helves (ε 236, N 612).

Grape-vines grew wild on the land of the Cyclopes (ι 110), and the cultivated vine twined luxuriantly about the entrance to Calypso's grotto (ε 69).   On the Shield of *Grape-vines.* Achilles is represented a vintage scene (Σ 561 ff.), with young men and maidens merrily bearing baskets of the ripe fruit, keeping time with their feet, while a boy sings a harvest song to the accompaniment of a lyre.[2]   The vines in this scene are supported on props (κάμαξι),—not on a trellis,—each by itself, as in Modern Greece.   So they were trimmed close, and did not stretch over much ground nor climb trees.   In the vineyard of Alcinoüs, king of the Phaeacians, Odysseus found grapes in all stages of advancement (η 121 ff.),—some just shedding their flowers and others just changing their color, while others fully ripe were sunning or drying for raisins, and others were picking for the wine-press.

Nothing in Homer hints at a tradition of the introduction of the grape vine to Greece from another land.   If the Greeks originally learned from the Semites how to stop the fermentation of the juice of the grape at the vinous stage, long before Homer's time they had forgotten that they ever needed such a lesson, though the Italians seem to have received their wine from Greece, and Pliny (*N. H.* xiv. 88) tells of ancient rites, instituted by Romulus, in which milk, and not wine, was poured as a libation.   In

---

[1] *Cf.* χιτῶνας . . . στίλβοντας ἐλαίῳ, Σ 596, and ἀπολείβεται . . . ἔλαιον, η 107. Helbig[2], 168, Studnička, 48 f.

[2] For the merry-making at the vintage festival, compare *Judges* ix. 27 : "And they went out into the fields and gathered their vineyards and trod the grapes, and made merry."—This Homeric festival is not in honor of Dionysus, but seems a natural precursor of the Dionysiac festivals of later centuries.

Homeric Greece wine was the ordinary drink of all classes,. —from beggars and swine-herds to kings ; of all ages,— from children in arms (I 489, π 444) to old Nestor ; and of both sexes,—the fair and youthful princess Nausicaa taking a flask of wine with her luncheon when she went to the river bank to "lave the linen" (ζ 76). Andromache in lamenting the fate of her infant Astyanax on Hector's death, pictures the life of an orphan : the boy goes to his father's comrades at their feast, and one gives him a draught of wine which wets his lips but does not wet his palate (X 494). In the two poems no one is represented as thirsting for or drinking water. Even the horses of Hector are refreshed with wine after their day's labor (Θ 189, if the text is right), as modern race horses are said to be treated at times after a sharp contest.

Homer calls Epidaurus " rich in vines " (ἀμπελόεντα, Β 561), while Arne in Boeotia and Histiaea in Euboea are " rich in *Epithets from the Vine.* clusters" (πολυστάφυλον, Β 507, 537). Tydeus was the son of Oeneus, the *wine-man* (Οἰνεύς, Ζ 216) of Calydon in Aetolia, and the early name of the island Aegina was *Vineyard* (Οἰνώνη, Herodotus, viii. 46). Wine is brought to the Achaean camp before Troy *Wine.* from Thrace (I 72) and from the island of Lemnos (H 467). Thracian wine from Ismarus (ι 196) is used by Odysseus to intoxicate the Cyclops Polyphemus. This last was the gift of the priest Maron, and was so strong that it was ordinarily diluted with twenty parts of water to one of wine. Ismaric wine was noted later, and is named by the poet Archilochus (*Frag.* 3), whose home was at Thasos, not very far away. Pramnian wine (probably so called from Pramne, a mountain on the island Icaria) is mentioned twice (Λ 639, κ 235) as the important part of a posset. No other special varieties of grapes or wine are named by Homer, and none by Hesiod.

The poet makes no allusion to the fermentation of the juice of the grape nor to any process of its care. The wine was stored ordinarily in large earthen jars (πίθοι, β 340), and carried in smaller earthen *amphorae* (ἀμφιφορῆες, ι 204), or in goatskin bottles (ἀσκοί, ι 212). Only once is allusion made to the pressing of the grapes (τραπέουσι, η 125), and the word does not indicate clearly the treading of the grapes in a vat, though this is probable. Grapes as such are not reported to be eaten, but no more are any other kinds of fruit, and it is highly improbable that, with grapes so abundant, none were used for eating.

Figs, apples, pears, and pomegranates are mentioned only in connexion with orchards, not with repasts, nor as food. Cherries, plums, and peaches are not mentioned at all. Fig-trees were in the garden of Alcinoüs *Figs, etc.* (η 116, 121) and in that of Laërtes (ω 246, 341), and grew in Hades for the aggravation of Tantalus (λ 590); —in two instances the fruit is called sweet. Clearly the fig was not so important in Greece as among the Semites, where to live under one's " own vine and fig-tree" was an ideal state of comfort. Neither the *Iliad* nor Hesiod mentions the cultivated fig, and the wild fig (ἐρινεός, Φ 37) was useful, so far as we see, only as furnishing wood for the rim of a chariot. The Roman Horace expresses clearly enough the ancient low estimate of the value of its wood. Scholars have observed the small number of Greek geographical names derived from the fig (σῦκον), in comparison with those drawn from the vine and the olive. Thus the passages of the *Odyssey* which mention the fig are reasonably suspected of not being of early composition. But the fig may have been known and cultivated in Asia Minor, where it still is at its best, long before it reached Greece and could be known to a Boeotian poet like Hesiod, who moreover had to do rather with the necessaries than with the luxuries of life. That the fruit of the fig-tree ripens at different times of the year, is recognized in the description of Alcinoüs's garden (η 121).

Apples are mentioned by Homer in the three passages which name the fig, and also in the ninth book of the *Iliad* among the trees destroyed by the Calydonian *Apples.* Boar (I 542). These passages are all supposed to be of comparatively late composition. No one dares say how closely the so-called apple (μῆλον) of Homeric times (any more than that of Milton's Garden of Eden) resembled the apple of to-day, and much less whether it was a russet, a greening, or a pippin. Some have thought it was a quince, and the epithet apple-faced (μῆλοψ, η 104), as applied to wheat, is thought to refer to the golden color of the fruit of the quince. The climate of Greece in general is too warm for apples and pears. The name of apples, with a qualifying epithet which later became the distinctive name, was applied in after times to quinces (Κυδώνικα μῆλα), plums (Δαμασκηνὰ μῆλα), and peaches (Περσικὰ μῆλα), and gave to the Romans the name *melon* which has come to our own day, and thus seems originally to have included a large variety of fruit.

Pears (ὄγχναι), again, appear only in the gardens of Alcinoüs and of Laërtes, and near Tantalus in Hades.

Pears. The reader may compare what is said of the fig. The branches of the prickly wild pear (ἄχερδος, ξ 10) were used to form a hedge.

The pomegranate (ῥοιή) is not in the orchard of Laërtes, but like the pear, apple, and fig is in the garden of Alcinoüs, *Pomegranates.* and near Tantalus. It appears in later Greek first in the Hymn to Demeter (372, 412), where Persephone's marriage tie to Pluto was confirmed by her swallowing a pomegranate seed as his gift. It seems to have been brought from Persia, and to have reached Greece through Syria.

The Homeric mention of the mulberry rests upon the interpretation of an adjective which twice is applied to ear- *Mulberry.* rings (μορόεντα, Ξ 183, σ 298). Are these to be thought of as *gleaming*, or as *mulberry-like*? Scholars are not agreed, but incline to the latter view.

The *chestnut* has been found in the Homeric φηγός (*cf.* the Latin *fagus*), though this seems to be an oak with *Chestnut.* edible acorns. One notable tree of this variety, sacred to Zeus, was the most frequently mentioned land-mark on the Trojan plain, not far from the Scaean Gate of the city.[1]

The laurel (δάφνη, ι 183) is mentioned as decking the entrance to the cave of Polyphemus. In the Hymn to *Laurel.* Pythian Apollo (215), it is brought first into connexion with that divinity.

The word for oak (δρῦς) is used seventeen times in the

[1] E 693, Z 237, H 22, 60, I 354, Φ 549.

Homeric poems,—almost for *tree* in general,[1] according to the observation of the great critic Aristarchus (as X 126, Ψ 118), just as *oak-cutter* (δρυτόμος, Λ 86, Π 633, Ψ 315) stands for *wood-cutter*, and an *oak-grove* (δρυμά, Λ 118) for *thicket*.   The oak is the favorite tree in comparisons, as " He fell as an oak or a poplar or a slender pine, which carpenters cut on the mountains for ship-timber" (N 389), and "These two stood before the high gates as high-crowned oaks on the mountains, which await wind and rain through all days, fixed firm with their great long roots " (M 132).   The oak of Zeus at Dodona was the seat of the Thesprotian oracle (ξ 328).

Oak.

The fragrant cypress (εὐώδης κυπάρισσος, ε 64) was among the trees near Calypso's grotto, and of this wood was a door-post in the palace of Odysseus (ρ 340). Two names of places also, in the Catalogue of Ships, are derived from this (B 519, 593).

Cypress.

The cluster pine or pinaster (πεύκη, Λ 494, Ψ 328) is named twice with the oak.   It is said by specialists to be the most important conifer of Greece.   The dark pine (πίτυς, N 390, Π 483, ι 186) stood with the oak about the cave of Polyphemus, and was cut on the mountains for ship-timbers.   Pitch is mentioned once in a comparison for a black cloud (πίσσα, Δ 277) ; the suggestion that this was crude petroleum, is gratuitous.   The stone pine is said to have been introduced into Greece after the Homeric period.

Pines.

The juniper (κέδρος, ε 60) was burned upon the hearth of Calypso, and furnished the wood-work for the treasure chamber of Priam (Ω 192).

Juniper.

The fir (ἐλάτη) is mentioned six times.   It is called *tall*, " reaching to heaven " (οὐρανομήκης, ε 239), and it furnished material for oars (μ 172, H 5) and for the barrack of Achilles (Ω 450).

Fir.

The ash (μελίη, used sixteen times) was the ordinary wood for the spear-shaft, which is often called by the name of the tree.   Thus the spear of Achilles was the " Pelian ash (Πηλιάδα μελίην, Π 143) which Chiron gave

Ash.

---

[1] The reader will remember the etymological connexion apparent between δρῦς, *Druid*, and *tree*.

his dear father from the summit of Pelion, to be the death of warriors,"—but the ash is said not to be found on Mt. Pelion in modern times. We may compare the epithet " with good ashen spear " (εὐμμελίης), which is used eight times,—applied chiefly to Priam. The front threshold of the palace of Odysseus was covered with ash (ρ 339).

Elm. The elm (πτελέη, Ζ 419, Φ 242, 350) was planted by mountain nymphs about the grave of Andromache's father, but nowhere else appears in connexion with tombs or mourning ; probably these trees were only to make a pleasant grove. One grew also on the bank of the Scamander, was undermined by the waters, and fell across the stream,—thus forming a dyke which checked the current. Elms are named also, together with willows and tamarisks, on the Trojan plain, not far from the river.

Tamarisk. The tamarisk (μυρίκη, Κ 466 f., Φ 18, 350) grew on the Trojan plain as a shrub or small tree. On one of these Odysseus hung the armor of the scout Dolon, whom he killed on a night-expedition, that this might await his own return from the Trojan camp. Achilles leaned his spear on a clump of them, when he leaped into the Scamander with his sword, to slay the Trojans who were struggling in the eddies of the river. Others are mentioned in connexion with elm and willow, and in one a chariot of the Trojans, hurrying to flight, was caught and broken (Ζ 39).

Alder. The alder (κλήθρη, ε 64, 239) stood by the grotto of Calypso, and was one of the trees on the shore of her island which Odysseus felled for the construction of his barge or raft.

Poplars. The black poplar (αἴγειρος, Δ 482, and in eight other places) grew on a moist lowland. It is named both times with the alder on the island of Calypso. A grove of poplars sacred to Athena stood near the city of the Phaeacians (ζ 292). Poplars grew also about the cave to which Odysseus came on the island opposite the country of the Cyclopes (ι 141), on the shore of the land of Hades (κ 510), and by the fountain of Ithaca, where they are called *water-fed* (ὑδατοτρεφέων, ρ 208). Fellies for a chariot-wheel are made of this wood (Δ 485).

The silver poplar (ἀχερωΐς, N 389, Π 482) is named twice in an identical verse, in which its fall illustrates that of a warrior.

The box (πύξος, πύξινον, Ω 269) is mentioned only as furnishing the wood for the yoke of Priam's mules. This tree is said not to ·grow in Greece, and the conjecture has been offered that Priam may have received his yoke as well as his mules from Mysia.

Box.

The myrtle is named only as it is contained in the proper name Μύρσινος in the Catalogue of Ships (B 616).

Myrtle.

A plane tree (πλατάνιστος, B 307, 310) stood over the spring at Aulis, where the Achaeans gathered for their expedition against Troy. The devouring of sparrows in their nest on this tree by a serpent was the portent which showed the length of the Trojan war.

Plane Tree.

The palm tree (φοῖνιξ, ζ 163) is mentioned once: Odysseus compared the slender Nausicaa to a young palm which he had seen growing by the altar of Apollo on the island of Delos.

Palm.

The cornel tree (κράνεια, Π 767, κ 242) once is named among the trees of a forest beaten by the wind, and once its fruit is thrown with acorns before the comrades of Odysseus who had been transformed into swine by Circe.

Cornel.

The willow (ἰτέη, κ 510, Φ 350) grew on the Trojan plain near the Scamander, and on the shore of the land of Hades. With *withes* (ῥίπεσσι οἰσυΐνῃσιν, ε 256), Odysseus formed a woven bulwark for his barge, and bound his comrades to the sheep which were to convey them out of the cave of the Cyclops (λύγοισιν, ι 427), and tied together the feet of the great deer which he killed on Calypso's island (κ 166).

Willow.

The ivy (κισσός) is not named by the Homeric poet. The etymology of the name of the great bowl (κισσύβιον, ι 346, π 52) which rustics used for milk and wine, is uncertain. Certainly ivy-wood would seem particularly ill-suited for such a purpose.

Ivy.

CHAPTER XIII

ANIMALS, FISHES, BIRDS, AND INSECTS

THE Homeric poet has no word for *animal*, either as a living thing, the later ζῷον, distinguished from vegetable or mineral matter, or as distinguished from bird or fish.[1] The ordinary word for beast (θήρ, θηρίον) connotes *wild beast*, especially a fierce wild beast, as a lion. Thus Mt. Ida above Troy is the "mother of wild beasts" (μητέρα θηρῶν, Ξ 283). The Aeolic form of this word (φήρ, A 268, B 743) is used of the centaurs, who receive the epithets *shaggy* (λαχνήεντες, B 743) and *with homes on the mountain* (ὀρεσκῷοι, A 268), but are not indicated otherwise as having the form familiar from later myths and works of art, of a combination of man and horse.[2]

The poet had no occasion to name many living creatures with which he may have been acquainted, and mentions most but once or twice, and this in comparisons.

Living Creatures not Mentioned. He may have known the fox, the rat, the cuckoo, the butterfly, the lizard, the frog, the ant, and the musquito,—but he does not mention them; and no lions make their appearance actually in the course

---

[1] κνώδαλον is used in ρ 317, of a wild beast of the forest. πέλωρ and πέλωρον seem nearly the equivalent of the English *monster*,—thus being applied to the Gorgon (Ε 741, λ 634), Scylla (μ 87), a serpent seized by an eagle (Μ 202), the portent of a transformed serpent (Β 321), the lame Hephaestus (Σ 410), the Cyclops Polyphemus (ι 428), a goose seized by an eagle (ο 161), a great stag (κ 168), and beasts transformed by Circe (κ 219).

[2] In literature this form of a quadruped appears first in Pindar's *Second Pythian Ode*. The centaurs are mentioned by their ordinary name in Λ 832, where Chiron is called "most just of the centaurs," and in φ 295 f., where reference is made to the conflict between the centaurs and the Lapithae, because of the drunken insolence of the centaur Eurytion.

of the story, though they are mentioned often in comparisons. We are not surprised at his ignorance of the ape and the camel, the tiger and the kangaroo, though the Phoenicians in his time were bringing apes and peacocks to Tyre, and so naturally to their customers on the shores of the Aegean Sea. The cat and the hen had not been introduced into Greece in the poet's time. The elephant is not named, but ivory is known (ἐλέφας,—see page 304); the spider, too, is not named, but a spider's web is mentioned twice (ἀράχνια, θ 280, π 35). Purple is named as a hue, but not the little mollusk from which the dye was gained. The mouse is not named, but Apollo seems to have received his appellation *Smintheus* (A 39) as the destroyer of field-mice. Similarly the weasel is not named as an animal, but the Trojan Dolon, when he was preparing for an expedition by night as a spy on the Achaean camp, took for the protection of his head a weasel-skin cap.[1]

From Homer we expect no scientific distinctions, and at this remove of time, and with so slight indications, in many instances we dare not be dogmatic in the assignment of different species. His verses were composed for those to whom both the creatures and their names were familiar. Chance had much to do with the mention of many of these animals, which appear but once in the poems, and that in a comparison. No significance is to be attached to such a fact as that swine are not mentioned in Troy. The poet tells his hearer little about the details of life in the Trojan city, and speaks of no eating there except in a bare reference to the funeral feast in honor of Hector. Little weight is to be attached to negative evidence in such a field.

The domesticated animals and fowl of which Homer speaks are the horse, the ass (once), mules, the dog, kine, sheep, goats, swine, and geese. The horse is mentioned more than 450 times, cattle about 175 times, dogs about 115 times, lions 62 times. Of wild animals, Homer mentions lions, leopards, wolves, jackals, wild boars, wild goats, deer, and hares.

Varieties of Living Creatures.

---

[1] κτιδέην κυνέην, K 335. A scholiast on this verse says the ἰκτίς is an animal which eats birds and is knavish (πανοῦργος); it is larger and shaggier than a γαλῆ (*cat?*), but similar, and some call it a wild γαλῆ.

The bear is named once (ἄρκτοι, λ 611) as part of the decoration for the baldric of Heracles, and twice (Σ 487, ε 273) as the appellation of the well-known constellation of the northern heavens. Of sea animals, the seal and the sea-calf (κύνες, μ 96) are mentioned with dolphins and other creatures of the sea. Of fishes, no species is named but eels and dolphins ; of other sea creatures, the poet knows the oyster, the polyp, and the sponge. Of birds, the poet names the eagle, the osprey, the falcon, the goshawk, the vulture, the gull, the crane, the swan, the heron, the diver, the halcyon, the wild goose, the crow, the jackdaw, the starling, the nightingale, the thrush, the sparrow, the swallow, and the pigeon. The *chalcis*, as it was called by gods, or *cymindis*, as it was called by men (Ξ 291), cannot be identified. Of other flying things, Homer knows the bat, the bee, the wasp, the fly (which may include the gnat), the gadfly, the cicada, and the locust. No varieties of serpent are named except the water-snake (ὕδρος, B 723) which bit Philoctetes. Of worms Homer knows the earth worm (σκώληξ, N 654, to which a warrior stretched on the ground is compared), the *borers* (ἶπες, φ 395, the larvae of a beetle which eat wood and horn, and thus might have injured the bow of Odysseus), and maggots (εὐλαί, T 26, X 509, Ω 414) which feed upon the bodies of the slain. For completeness the insect,—probably some kind of a flea,—which annoyed the old dog Argos as he lay upon the dung-heap (κυνοραιστής, ρ 300) may be added to the list, though it cannot be identified.

Living creatures are not associated with special divinities, as under their patronage, except in so far as the eagle was

Sacred Animals. beginning to be the messenger of Zeus (Ω 292), and Poseidon perhaps appears once as the patron of horses (Ψ 307), where Zeus and Poseidon taught Antilochus horsemanship,—but Poseidon was an ancestor of Antilochus, and may have taught him out of pure friendship. The owl is not yet sacred to Athena, nor the dove to Aphrodite, nor the peacock to Hera. Artemis was indeed the goddess of the chase, but she was not the special patroness of young animals as she is in the *Agamemnon* of Aeschylus. That the Sun has flocks and herds is not important in this connexion ; these are his like any other possession.

Attention has been called by Miss Clerke[1] to the fact that the poet pays slight heed to the noises of animals. " Homer's horses neither whinny nor neigh,[2] his pigs refrain from grunting, his jackals do not howl, the roar of the lion nowhere resounds through his forests."

Noises of Animals.

In the *Iliad*, as the story of war, the horse is naturally the most prominent and important animal. In the Old Testament, too, the horse is recognized as adapted to battle : " Hast thou given the horse strength ? Hast thou clothed his neck with thunder ? . . . The glory of his nostrils is terrible. He paweth in the valley, and rejoiceth in his strength : he goeth on to meet the armed men. . . . He saith among the trumpets ' Ha, ha !' and he smelleth the battle afar off, the thunder of the captains, and the shouting " (*Job* xxxix. 19-25). The Hebrews thought of the horse as the animal of war, while the ass and the mule were used in peace, and in Greece never was the horse used as a beast of burden, nor for menial work of any kind. Thus Priam takes a wagon drawn by mules to the Greek camp, bearing to Achilles the ransom for Hector's body, and to bring back the corpse, while the old king himself drives on a chariot drawn by horses (Ω 279). The longest journey by chariot and horses described in the Homeric poems, is the two-days' drive of Telemachus and Pisistratus from " sandy Pylus " to Sparta (γ 475-δ 2), but Menelaus sends his newly married daughter from Sparta to Thessaly with horses and chariot (δ 8 f.), and Aegisthus

The Horse.

---

[1] *Familiar Studies in Homer.*

[2] χρεμέτιζον, M 51, must mean *snorted*, rather than *neighed*, for the beasts were in a state of excited terror. So ὑψηχέες, E 772, Ψ 27, must mean *snorting*. *Cf.* the expression of the book of *Job*, quoted in the text.—Perhaps we may infer the roar of a lion from K 183 where dogs are wakeful, hearing a mighty beast [lion] coming through the forest. Certainly the sheep bleat ; the clamor of the Trojan army is compared to the incessant bleating of innumerable sheep, a-milking and hearing the voices of their lambs (Δ 435); cattle low and sheep bleat at μ 265 ; and on the morning after the blinding of Polyphemus, his ewes bleat unmilked about the pens (ι 439). At the opening of the third book of the *Iliad* the din of the Trojan army is compared to that of cranes on their way to the streams of Oceanus.

comes to the shore with horses and chariot to meet his cousin Agamemnon on his return from the siege of Troy, and to invite him to be his guest (δ 533). The divinities also use chariots and horses. Zeus harnesses his "bronze-hoofed horses, swift of flight," for the journey from Olympus to Mt. Ida (Θ 41); Hera and Athena once drive from the home of the gods to the Trojan plain (E 720), and again begin this drive, but are stopped by the command of Zeus (Θ 382 ff.); Ares has his chariot with him on the Trojan plain, but lends it to Aphrodite when she is wounded by Diomed (E 355 ff.), and himself, when wounded, rises "to the broad heaven with the clouds" (E 866); Poseidon (at N 20) on seeing that Zeus is not attending to the conflicts between the Greeks and the Trojans, goes from Samothrace to his home at Aegae, harnesses his steeds, and drives to a grotto between Tenedos and Imbros, where he leaves his horses hobbled by golden fetters, while he goes to the plain of Troy. Poseidon seems to have used his horses and chariot also on his journey to the Aethiopians (ε 380). Near the close of the *Odyssey* the horses of the Dawn are named as Lampus and Phaëthon (ψ 246). Elsewhere the divinities traverse space without a vehicle, as Athena comes to the Achaean army in each of the first two books of the *Iliad*, and the need of the chariot is not apparent. In particular, Poseidon, we should say, might more easily have taken the usual course from Samothrace to the Troad.

The chapters on Homeric War show that riding was not customary, and give a sufficient reason for the preference of the chariot over the saddle-horse in the Homeric battle,—the chariot was used not as a platform, from which to fight, but as a vehicle for quick and easy transportation of the warrior and his heavy shield from one part of the field to another. The horse may have been smaller than his successor of to-day, but the evidence for this is slight. We remember that in the wars of the Old Testament, also, and in those depicted on the monuments of Egypt and Assyria, chariots were used rather than cavalry, but these were used as points of vantage by the warrior. That riding on horseback was not wholly unknown, might be supposed. Returning from a midnight expedition into the

Riding.

Trojan camp, Odysseus and Diomed ride the horses of Rhesus which they have captured (K 513), just as a boy rides a horse bareback from the pasture. Ajax, leaping from stern to stern of the Greek ships drawn up on shore, in his defense of the fleet against the Trojans who are bringing fire to destroy it, is likened to a man well skilled in riding (κελητίζειν), who drives four horses to town, leaping from the back of one to another (O 679). This circus-rider perhaps finds his best ancient counterpart in the acrobat above a bull on a fresco at Tiryns, and in women, who seem to be exhibiting in an arena, in a fresco painting recently found at Cnosus in Crete. After the wreck of his barge, Odysseus bestrode a timber as he would ride on the back of a horse (κέληθ' ὡς ἵππον ἐλαύνων, ε 371). But these examples are insufficient to prove the custom of riding on horseback against the weight of negative evidence.

Horses were for the enjoyment of chieftains, not the possession of ordinary men. The figure of a horse and chariot on a Mycenaean tombstone (fig. 18) seems intended primarily to indicate equestrian rank.[1] *Horses for Chieftains.* Telamonian Ajax, from the island of Salamis, and Odysseus, from the island of Ithaca, use no chariots in the conflicts before Troy. They had none at their homes, naturally, for they could not use them on these rugged islands. Telemachus declines to accept Menelaus's offer of horses and chariot as a gift; he could not use them on Ithaca, which has no broad roads nor meadow (δ 601). The Ithacan Noëmon had twelve mares, but he kept them across the strait, on the mainland, in Elis, and bred mules, which would be useful in rocky Ithaca (δ 635). In a long story of the achievements of his youth, Nestor tells of a foray in which the Pylians carried off 150 mares of the Eleans, with many colts (Λ 680). Achilles in emphasizing the fact that he had come before Troy for the sake of Menelaus, not

---

[1] For this we may compare the terms ἱππόδαμος (H 38), ἱππότα (B 336) or ἱππηλάτα (Δ 387), ἱπποκέλευθος (Π 584), ἱππιοχάρμης (Ω 257), πλήξιππος (B 104), and perhaps ἱπποκορυστής (B 1), which correspond in a general way to our terms *knight, chevalier, cavalier* (from the French *cheval* and the Latin *caballus*), associated with *chivalry*. Horsemanship (ἱπποσύνη, Δ 303) sometimes is much like *knighthood*. Fifteen Homeric proper names are formed from ἵππος, as Hippodamia, Hippolochus, Hippotades, Pheidippus.

because of any personal grievance, says that the Trojans never had driven off his cattle or his horses (A 154). Erichthonius, son of Dardanus, is declared to have been the richest of men, and to have had 3000 mares with frisking colts feeding on the lowlands of the Troad (Υ 219). Priam seems to have had a stock farm for horses at Abydus, on the Hellespont, for his son Democoön comes thence "from the horses" (παρ' ἵππων, Δ 500). The Danaäns were called *men of swift steeds* (ταχύπωλοι, Θ 161), and the epithet *with good steeds* (εὔπωλος, Ε 551) was applied to Ilium. The epithet *horse-feeding* (ἱππόβοτον, γ 263, Τ 329) seems to have been transferred to southern Argos, the Argolid, from northern Argos, Thessaly, which during all its history was noted for its horses. The application of the adjective *with renowned steeds* (κλυτόπωλος, Ε 654) which is given to Hades, has not been satisfactorily explained ; according to a familiar later myth he carried Persephone on his chariot from earth to the realms below.

Horses generally were pastured in herds (Λ 680, Τ 281, Υ 221), but some were fed in stalls (Ζ 506, Κ 568). *The Care of Horses.* For fodder, the Homeric horse had white barley (κρῖ λευκόν, Ε 196), spelt (ὄλυραι, Ε 196), sesame, wheat, clover, cyper-grass (ζειαί, πυροί, λωτός, κύπειρον, δ 603 f.), and some species of parsley (σέλινον, Β 776). They had no oats. According to Θ 189, wine was given on occasion ; this line is of doubtful authenticity, but is followed at least by Matthew Arnold in his *Sohrab and Rustum*. The steeds of gods naturally fed on ambrosial fodder (Ε 369). Andromache herself feeds Hector's horses on his return from the field of battle (Θ 186), and Patroclus bathes the steeds of Achilles and oils their manes (Ψ 281). According to the usual text of Ψ 266, a mule might not be set to work until his sixth or seventh year ; how early colts were used, is not stated. The milk of mares was not used by the Trojans or Achaeans, but the poet knows of the *Mare-milkers* (Ἱππημολγοί, Ν 5), who lived on this milk, and who were at least the neighbors of the "most just of men." The tail or flowing mane (ἔθειραι) of horses was used as crest for the warrior's helmet (λόφος ἱππιοχαίτης, Ζ 469). The Homeric horses must have been well trained, for they drew the chariot by a yoke, without traces, and so were much freer than the horse harnessed to a modern carriage. But this discipline needs not to have been so strict as that for a modern fire-engine horse,—perhaps not more than that for a polo pony,—and in modern battles

Fig. 18.—A Mycenaean Tombstone.
From Prof. W. Ridgeway's 'Early Age of Greece.'

a riderless horse has been known to keep his place in the familiar troop. The book of *Job* has been quoted already as witness to the steed's joy in the conflict. Since Poseidon used metal "hobbles" for his horses (N 36), this was probably the custom of men also. That the driver made much use of his voice is shown by Pandarus's choice to wield the spear by Aeneas's side rather than to drive the horses of Aeneas, lest "missing thy voice" they should delay (E 234), and by the shouts in the horse-race (Ψ 452). The whip was a goad with a lash (ἱμάντες, Ψ 363), and that it was important, is shown in the horse-race, where Apollo thought to take the prize from Diomed by making him drop his whip (κέντρον, Ψ 387). The chariot race was the first and most important of the games in honor of the dead Patroclus, and is described at greatest length (Ψ 262-615). A good horse is eager for the race as well as for the battle (Ψ 300). Old Nestor tells (Ψ 638) of his own part in the chariot race in honor of the dead king of the Epeans, and of his father's sending a chariot and four horses to race for a tripod in Elis, when king Augeas (of the famous stables) detained chariot and horses, but let the charioteer go (Λ 699). Clearly the horse-race was a common event, and the epithet *prize-bearing* (ἀεθλοφόροι, X 22) is given to horses five times. In the race the ordinary chariot was used.

The horses of Aeneas were descended from steeds which Zeus had given to king Tros (for whom Troy was named) *Breeds of* as a consolatory return for Ganymede, whom *Horses.* Zeus had taken as his cup-bearer (E 265). The horses of Achilles were immortal, sired by the wind Zephyrus and born by the Harpy Podargé (*Fleetfoot*, Π 150), and were the gift of the god Poseidon to Peleus (Ψ 277); naturally enough they "flew with the winds" (ἅμα πνοιῇσι πετέσθην, Π 149). One of these steeds, Xanthus, is endowed with the power of speech for a moment by Hera, that he may explain to Achilles the death of Patroclus, and may predict the great warrior's own death (T 407). With the mares of Erichthonius, the north wind Boreas generates twelve colts of wonderful lightness of foot, which run over the grain without breaking it, and over the foam of the sea (Y 223). The horses of the Thracian Rhesus are "whiter than snow, and as swift as the winds" (K 437). One of the horses of Diomed was a sorrel (φοῖνιξ, Ψ 454) with a round white spot on the forehead. The "tawny heads of horses" (I 407) are supposed to have been bays, but the Homeric definitions of color are not very exact, and the adjective is that which Pindar applies to cattle. The two immortal horses of Achilles are Xanthus and Balius (Π 149),—probably *Bay* and *Dapple*. A third horse of Achilles is called Pedasus, perhaps from the place where it was bred ; he captured it at Thebes (Π 153). Agamemnon had a mare Aethé (*Bright*), and Menelaus a horse Podargus (*Fleetfoot*, Ψ 295). In a line which has been thought a late interpolation, because it assumes four horses as attached to a single chariot, Hector addresses his steeds as Xanthus, Podargus, Aethon, and Lampus (*Shining*, Θ 185). The swiftest horse of previous generations is declared to have been Areion (*Horse of Ares?* Ψ 346), the property of Adrastus. The steeds of the Dawn are Lampus and Phaëthon (*Gleaming*, ψ 246). The chariot in general is drawn by two horses, but according to the reference just given, Hector had four, Neleus sent four to contend for a prize at Elis (Λ 699), and the Phaeacian ship conveying Odysseus to his home is compared to four stallions rushing over the plain under the blows of the whip (ν 81). A side-horse (παρήορος, Π 474, *cf.* Θ 87) is twice referred to, which is attached to the chariot only by straps, and apparently is to be used only in case of an accident to one of the other horses ; but curiously enough, in both of these instances the side-horse himself is wounded and is a hindrance, while in the second instance he could not have been needed since the other two horses were immortal.

At least a score of epithets are applied to horses by the poet, of which six refer to speed.[1] The epithet *high-stepping* (ἀερσίποδες, Γ 327) is evidently contrasted with that of *winding-gaited* (εἱλίποδες, Ζ 424) applied to the clumsy kine. *Bronze-hoofed* (χαλκόπους, Θ 41) of the horses of Zeus does not imply that these were shod by the smith, but refers only to the strength of their feet, like *strong-hoofed* (κρατερώνυξ, Ε 329). An epithet which is applied more frequently than any other except *fleet*, is of uncertain derivation and meaning (μώνυχες, Ι 127),—it being understood by some as *solid-hoofed*, while others would interpret it as *eager-*

Epithets of Horses.

---

[1] ὠκύς, Δ 500 ; ὠκύποδες, Ε 296 ; ποδώκεας, Ρ 614 ; πόδας αἰόλος, Τ 404 ; ταχύς, Χ 464 ; εὐσκάρθμοι, Ν 31,—no two of which are of the same metrical value.

hoofed.[1]   The horses of the gods are *swift-in-flight* (ὠκυπέτα,[2] Θ 42), as the horses of men are fleet of foot (ὠκύποδες).

The word for horse, when used without reference to sex, is generally feminine in Homer. This has been understood by some as indicating that mares were preferred for service in war, but this interpretation is unnecessary, and in the chariot race (Ψ 409) Antilochus urges his steeds to hasten lest Aethé, a *mare*, should put them to shame.

The most notable comparison in which the horse appears, is that in which Paris in the pride of his heart, in armor gleaming like the sun, laughing aloud, borne on *Horses in Comparisons.* by his swift feet as he descends from the Trojan city to the battle on the plain, is compared to a horse well-fed at the manger, who has broken his halter and is galloping with clattering hoofs over the plain, proudly holding his head high, and with mane floating on his shoulders, as he seeks the haunts and pasture of the horses (Z 504).[3] Just before the death of Hector, Achilles in pursuit of the Trojans is likened to a horse, which has received prizes, running over the plain. The poet did not fail to notice the frisking of colts (Υ 222).

The reader is told elsewhere that the chariots were low and light; and that the occupants commonly stood, not sat,—as indeed might be most comfortable, since the vehicle had no springs. The charioteer was called the *rein-holder* (ἡνίοχος, E 231). No more than two persons occupy a single chariot.

Only once does the poet refer to the offering of horses as a sacrifice to divinities. On the last day of battle, *Horses in Sacrifice.* Achilles, throwing the corpse of a son of Priam into the river Scamander, says that the Trojans shall not be saved even by the silver-eddying river to which they sacrifice many bulls, and into whose

---

[1] The former taking μώνυξ for μον-ονυξ, corresponding to μονόχαλα of Eur. *I.A.* 225; the latter associating it with the root of μέμαα, *am eager*. The Greeks did not make sharply the Hebrew distinction between cloven-footed animals and those "which part not the hoof,"—Homer never speaks of cattle as cloven-hoofed,—and in Homer μόνος is never found for μοῦνος.

[2] Mortal horses, indeed, at times are said to fly over the plain (πετέσθην, Ψ 381), but this is clearly figurative and not a good basis for an epithet.

[3] This passage was borrowed by Vergil and applied to Turnus (*Aen.* xi. 492).

eddies they sink living horses (Φ 131). This sacrifice of horses is called un-Hellenic.[1] Perhaps in this connexion, however, the slaughter of four horses at the burial of Patroclus (Ψ 171) should be noted, although these horses, like the two dogs who were then killed, were not a sacrifice in the ordinary sense.

The ass (ὄνος, Λ 558) appears but once in Homer, and that in a comparison. The mighty Ajax unwillingly with- *The Ass.* drawing, when overpowered by the Trojans, is likened to a stubborn ass, on whose back many clubs have been broken, who has entered a field of tall grain, and is driven out by boys only after he has satisfied his hunger. The comparison contained nothing undignified for the warrior. The ass and the mule in oriental countries have a higher reputation than in the west.

The mule was the ordinary beast of burden and draught animal for menial service. He has two names, one designating him as a *half-ass* (ἡμίονος, B 852) and the other *The Mule.* as a *mountain-beast* (οὐρεύς, A 50).[2] His sure step and small foot make him important also in modern times on mountains, while his strong digestion makes him valuable in war. In general, mules seem to have been bred from mares (Ψ 265, δ 635, φ 22). The breed of the Eneti in Paphlagonia appears to have been approved (B 852), and Priam received mules as a present from the Mysians (Ω 278). One is offered as the second prize in the chariot race (Ψ 266), and another as the first prize for boxing (Ψ 654). Mules draw the car on which lies Hector's body (Ω 150), and that with which Nausicaa goes with her washing to the river side (ζ 37). They draw the cars which bring the dead bodies from the field of battle to the Achaean camp (H 333, 426), and bring wood, apparently fastened directly to the animal (Ψ 121), from Mt. Ida for the funeral pile of Patroclus. As mules draw from the

---

[1] Stengel, *Kultusaltertümer*,[2] 120, refers to the sacrifice of a span of white horses by Mithridates before the war with the Romans (Appian, *Mith. Bell.* 70), and a similar sacrifice by Sextus Pompeius (Dio Cassius, xlviii. 48).

[2] The two words are synonyms. See Ψ 111, 115, 121. οὐρεύς was originally an adjective, and became a noun, like πτώξ (P 676, *cowering*) for the hare and τρήρων (*timid*, in πολυτρήρων, B 502) for the dove.

mountain along a rugged path a beam or great ship-timber, and are distressed "by weariness and sweat," so the two Ajaxes bear away the body of Patroclus, hard pressed by the Trojans (P 742). They are counted better than oxen for the plough (K 352). The difficulty of breaking them to labor is recognized (Ψ 655).[1] They are called *strong-hoofed* (κρατερώνυχες, ζ 253), *patient in labor* (ταλαεργός, Ψ 654), *working in harness* (ἐντεσιεργός, Ω 277), and *of the field* (ἀγρότερος, B 852, with reference to the herd).

The dog was not needed in the ordinary occupations of the *Iliad*, and in that poem generally appears in an *The Dog.* unpleasant way, as a scavenger and a wild beast of prey, while it was more important in the peaceful and pastoral life of the *Odyssey*. We need to assume no "reversal of sympathies" for the horse and the dog in the two poems, although, as Mahaffy and Geddes[2] have pointed out, the horse has greater prominence in the *Iliad*, and the dog has a pleasanter character, though it is not mentioned so often, in the *Odyssey* than in the *Iliad*. Only once in the *Iliad*, and that in one of the books which Geddes considered Odyssean, are dogs in the Achaean camp before Troy mentioned as having an individual master (Ψ 173); these are the nine dogs of Patroclus, of whom two are slain and thrown upon the funeral pile of their master. King Priam, too, has dogs, but he fears lest these dogs which he has "fed with food from his table, to guard his doors," after he has been slain, and when they have been maddened by the taste of his blood, will themselves tear his body (X 66). This shows that their wolfish nature was only hidden, and indeed many dogs of Constantinople and even of Athens in recent times have been essentially wild beasts.[3] No variety of species is mentioned by Homer.

[1] Ordinary texts read ἐξετέ' ἀδμήτην κτλ., but the conjecture that the words should be divided differently, ἐξετέα δμητήν, (so that the meaning should be *six years old, well broken*, instead of *six years old, unbroken*) is reasonable. That a mule of such an age was unused to labor, would not increase its value, as seems to be intended in the expression.

[2] *Problem of the Homeric Poems.* See also Miss Clerke, *Familiar Studies in Homer*.

[3] Geddes refers to Byron's *Siege of Corinth* for the fierceness of Greek dogs under Turkish rule.

Dogs appear in Homer as shepherd-dogs to guard flocks, as watch-dogs for the house and as companions, as hunting-dogs in the chase, and as scavengers.   Their *Uses of Dogs.* watchfulness is pictured at K 183, where the Achaean guards are likened to dogs in a sheep-fold hearing a lion coming through the forest on the mountains, and "sleep has perished from their eyes."   Again, at M 303, a hungry lion seeks to enter the sheep-fold, though he finds "the herdsmen keeping guard with dogs and spears."   On the Shield of Achilles is wrought a scene in which four herdsmen and nine dogs are accompanying a herd of cattle to the pasture ; two lions hold a bellowing bull, and the men urge on the dogs in vain,—the dogs bark but keep out of the lions' way (Σ 578).   At E 476, also, dogs cower before a lion.   Eumaeus, the swine-herd, has four dogs "like to wild beasts" (ξ 21) which guard his farm-building in his absence (ρ 200).   These nearly tear Odysseus in pieces, but he on their approach sits down and throws away his staff, which act stops them for a moment, until Eumaeus appears and drives them off with stones.   Two days later, however, on the approach of Telemachus the dogs welcome him (π 4), and thus assure Odysseus that the newcomer is an acquaintance of Eumaeus.   A little later, on the same day, the same dogs are filled with awe, whine, and slink away at the coming of the goddess Athena (π 162).

Mention has been made of the dogs which Priam reared "to guard his door" (θυραωρούς, X 69).   On either side of the door of the palace of King Alcinoüs *Watch-dogs.* on Scheria stood gold and silver dogs which Hephaestus had made to "guard the house" (δῶμα φυλασ-σέμεναι, η 93).   Before the palace of Circe were wolves and lions into which she had changed men, who fawned upon the companions of Odysseus "as dogs fawn upon their master when he comes from the feast, for he always brings some tid-bits for them" (κ 216).   The watch-dog of Hades is referred to twice (Θ 368, λ 623), but is not named as Cerberus. Thrice Telemachus is accompanied by two dogs as he goes to the "place of assembly" (β 11, ρ 62, υ 145).   The dis-guised Odysseus, inquiring about the dog Argos, suggests that he may have been one of the pet dogs which men

feed with food from their table because of their beauty
(ρ 309).

In the chase, the hunter is often accompanied by dogs.
Indeed the term *dog-leader* (κυνηγέτης, ι 120) is used once
for *hunter*, and the same notion is the basis of
Dogs in the a similar name (ἐπακτῆρες, P 135). For a lion
Chase. or wild-boar hunt, dogs were quite indispensable
(I 545, P 725, Θ 338). The youthful Odysseus was hunting
a wild boar with dogs on Mt. Parnassus when he received
the wound of which the scar remained for his identification
(τ 436). At the close of the last day of battle of the
Iliad, Achilles pursues Hector as a dog pursues a fawn
which it has started from its couch upon the mountains
(X 189); though the fawn hides under a bush, the dog
scents it out and finds it. Two days earlier, Diomed and
Odysseus follow the Trojan scout Dolon, as two sharp-toothed
dogs, well skilled in the chase, press upon a fawn or hare
(K 360). Odysseus, when he left home for Troy, had a
golden brooch ornamented by the figure of a dog holding
a dappled fawn by his fore paws (see p. 172). Of course the
most noted dog of antiquity, and the only animal to receive
a proper name in the *Odyssey*, is Argos, the only creature to
recognize Odysseus on his return from his absence of a score
of years,—who, seeing his master, wagged his tail and died
(ρ 291 ff.). This Argos had been a famous hunter in his
day: no wild goat, fawn, or hare could escape him by
flight, and he was distinguished for his keen scent.

But in the *Iliad*, as has been said, the dog in general is
a scavenger, a wild beast, no better than a jackal. Thus
at the very opening of the poem, the prooemium
Dogs as says that the Wrath of Achilles made the bodies
Scavengers. of many brave warriors to be the prey of dogs
and a feast to the birds, with which we may compare the
prophecy sent from Elisha, "The dogs shall eat Jezebel in
the portion of Jezreel" (2 *Kings* ix. 10). Hector was eager
to secure the body of Patroclus, that he might give it to
the Trojan dogs (P 127); but when himself at the point
of death, he begged Achilles not to allow the dogs to devour
him by the ships of the Achaeans (X 339). When Priam
is on his way to the Achaean camp to ransom the body

of his son, one of his first questions to Hermes, who represents himself as a companion of Achilles, is whether Achilles has cut Hector limb from limb and given him to the dogs (Ω 409); and Hermes's reply is: "The dogs and the birds have not devoured him."

The general reputation of the dog being what is implied and contained in the preceding paragraph, no one can be surprised that the dog was to the Homeric Greeks the personification of shamelessness. So Achilles *Dogs as Shameless.* addresses Agamemnon, "O thou with the eyes of a dog and the heart of a deer" (A 225); and he says of Agamemnon, to those who had come to beg him to return to the battle, "Doggish though he is, he would not dare to look me in the face" (I 373). The name *dog* is applied contemptuously, as in modern times. Helen applies it to herself (Z 344, 356), Iris applies it to Athena (according to our text of Θ 423), and Penelope applies it to her unfaithful serving-maids (τ 91, 154). The shade of Agamemnon in Hades, in telling of his death and Clytae-mestra's behavior, says that nothing is more doggish than such a woman (κύντερον, λ 427); and Odysseus, rousing his heart for endurance, says, "Be patient now, my soul; thou hast endured what is more doggish still" (υ 18). *Dog-eyed* becomes thus equivalent to *shameless* (κυνῶπις, δ 145, λ 424). The sublimation of persistent insolence is found in the term *dog-fly* (κυνάμυια, Φ 421), which need not be understood as indicating a special variety of fly.

The epithets applied to Homeric dogs refer to their sharp white teeth, to their fleetness of foot, and (seldom) to their barking.[1] The term *raging, raving, mad* (λυσσητῆρα, Θ 299, cf. λυσσώδης· N 53) *Epithets of Dogs.* refers to violent anger, not to the disease *rabies.* The dog-star, as the Dog of Orion, is named at X 29. That caps were often made of dogskin, seems to be indicated by their name; though the derivation is forgotten at times, and Dolon has a *weasel-skin dogskin* (κτιδέην κυνέην, K 335, where dogskin must mean simply *cap*). The dog Argos is distressed by some parasitic insect (κυνοραιστέων, ρ 300,

---

[1] ἀργιόδοντας, Λ 292, καρχαρόδοντε, K 360; πόδας ἀργοί, Σ 578, ἀργούς, A 50, ἀργίποδας, Ω 211, ταχέες, Γ 26; ὑλακόμωροι, ξ 29, *barking.*

dog destroyers,—formed on the analogy of θυμοραϊστέων, Σ 220, *life destroying*), which need not be identified. The whelp, puppy, is mentioned three times: at μ 86 the voice of Scylla is said to be like that of a young whelp (σκύλαξ,— with an evident play upon her name); at ι 289, Polyphemus seizes two of the companions of Odysseus, and dashes them like puppies on the ground; and at υ 14, the heart of Odysseus is compared to a mother-dog, standing over her tender young, and barking at the approach of a stranger.

Geddes calls attention to the curious circumstances that the dog, often appearing in the similes for combat, generally represents the Trojans,[1] and that the term *dog* is applied to Hector more frequently than to any other warrior.

The importance of cattle in Homeric life is indicated by their being the standard of value. They formed the chief item of personal property. The worth of a slave, a shield, or a basin is estimated in terms of cattle (see page 250). The poet Hesiod's first advice to his brother is to buy cattle for the plough (*Works and Days*, 405). Cow's milk was not used,[2] but in addition to their value on the farm, cattle were the most honored sacrifice to the gods, their flesh was the favorite food of the warriors, and their hides were useful in many ways. The herding of cattle was an honorable occupation, followed by kings' sons. Anchises was tending his cattle when he was visited by the goddess Aphrodite (E 313), and Phoebus Apollo himself tended the herds of Laomedon in the glens of Mt. Ida (Φ 448). Cattle were the ordinary present to the father of a bride (Λ 244), and maidens thus receive an epithet as *bringing cattle* (ἀλφεσίβοιαι, Σ 593) to their fathers. They were the booty most frequently sought and gained on forays, and thus were a usual occasion of war. Thus Achilles, reminding Agamemnon that he had come against Troy only on the latter's account, says that the Trojans have done him no wrong: they have never driven away his cattle or horses (Α 154); and Nestor tells how he and his friends drove away from the

Cattle.

---

[1] As Θ 338, Λ 292, 325, 414, M 147, N 198, P 65, 110, 282, 658, 725.

[2] In Epirus, in much later times, after the classical period at Athens, great cows were kept which yielded ten gallons of milk a day. Aristotle, *H.A.* iii. 21, Aelian, *N.H.* iii. 33.

Eleans fifty herds of cattle and other spoil (Λ 678). On his visit to Hades, Odysseus inquires of the shade of Agamemnon the occasion of his death, whether he perished in the sea, or enemies slew him on land as he was cutting off their cattle or fair flocks of sheep (λ 399). Naturally, then, importance is attached to the possession of large herds of cattle, and they seem to be found in every land, although the Cyclops Polyphemus has none. Ithaca was called a good pasture for cattle (βούβοτος, ν 246); Odysseus, however, had his kine, twelve herds, tended on the adjoining mainland (ξ 100), and from these Philoetius brought a cow for the last feast of Penelope's suitors (υ 185). On the island of Thrinacia, the sun-god had seven herds of cattle and as many flocks of sheep, with fifty in each herd and flock (μ 129); the numbers seem to indicate that the cattle represented the days of the Homeric year, but that does not concern us here. Whether Homer knew different breeds of cattle has not clearly been made out.[1] The neat-herd had not a *crook*, but a club, which he threw for the guidance of his herd (καλαύροπα, Ψ 845).

The two Ajaxes, standing together in defense of the Achaean ships, are likened to two wine-faced oxen with like spirit, drawing a well-joined plough, while the abundant sweat gushes forth at the roots of their horns as they press along the furrow (N 703). *Cattle and the Plough.*
The longing of Odysseus for the sun to set, on the evening before his return to Ithaca, is compared to that of the farmer whose oxen all day long have been drawing the plough (ν 31). The disguised Odysseus, when Penelope's suitors speak contemptuously of his strength, tells them that if they had an acre-field, and two well-fed oxen of like draught, and the clod should yield to the plough, they would see whether he could cut a straight long furrow (σ 371). But at K 352 the poet says that mules are better than oxen to draw the plough in the deep fallowland.

The hour for loosing the cattle from the plough defines the time of day (βουλυτόνδε, II 779). See page 48. That

---

[1] Ridgeway (*Early Age of Greece*, i. 332) holds that there were two species,—the straight-horned Mycenaean variety, and another with longer, curved horns, which had recently come down with immigrants from the north.

the cattle were used for the plough only during the morning, is a mere hypothesis, and is opposed to the information in the comparison quoted in the preceding paragraph.

Less frequently, doubtless, were cattle used for drawing wagons; roads were few, and pack-animals and men's shoulders carried most burdens. But oxen were of service in bringing the dead bodies to the camp for burial (H 333), and in bringing wood from Mt. Ida for the funeral pile of Hector (Ω 782). They also "trod out the corn" on the threshing floor (Υ 495), with which may be compared the Hebrew custom which is indicated by the injunction, "Thou shalt not muzzle the ox when he treadeth out the corn," *Deut.* xxv. 4. They were kept in herds and watched on the pasture, but often were driven to the farmyard at night. The comrades of Odysseus rejoice at his return from Circe's palace as calves rejoice in the return of their mothers from the pasture (κ 410). In the pasture they are at times driven madly by the gadfly (χ 299). On the Shield of Achilles (Σ 573) was wrought by Hephaestus a representation of a herd of cattle on its way to the pasture, with herdsmen and dogs, and attacked by two lions. Comparisons are drawn from cattle attacked by lions, at E 162 and Λ 172; clearly lions were the chief danger of the herd.[1] As the Achaeans first go out to meet the Trojans in battle, Agamemnon, conspicuous among the warriors, is likened to a bull, preëminent in the herd of cattle (B 480). That the ox was sometimes fed at a manger, is shown by the comparison of the death of Agamemnon, at the feast to which Aegisthus had invited him, to the killing of an ox at the crib (ἐπὶ φάτνῃ, δ 535).

Cattle for Draught.

Cattle were offered in sacrifice to Zeus (B 410, H 314, Θ 240), to Apollo (A 41, 316), to Athena (Z 308, K 292, Λ 729, γ 443; *cf.* B 550), to Poseidon (Λ 728, α 25, γ 6, 178, λ 131), to the Alpheüs (Λ 728), and to the river Xanthus (Φ 131). The term *hecatomb* (ἑκατόμβη, A 315) may have been applied originally to an offering of one hundred cattle, but it came to be used of sacrifices in general, as B 306. The largest offering which is mentioned is that of eighty-one bulls in a great feast of

Cattle in Sacrifice.

[1] *Cf.* E 556, Λ 548, Π 487, P 61, 542, 657.

the Pylians in honor of Poseidon (γ 7). The ox was killed by striking him with a sharp axe behind the horns, and severing the mass of sinews there ; then the creature ran forward and fell (P 520). When Nestor sacrifices a heifer to Athena (γ 430 ff.), after the animal is stunned, Nestor's sons raise her, and one cuts the throat so that the blood pours out.

The hides of cattle were useful for many purposes. Untanned, they were made into shields of various forms (H 222), so that *dry ox hide* is used without other limitation for *shield* (as H 238, M 425). The hide was *Uses of Hides.* "tanned" or cured by giving it a liberal covering of oil or grease, and then by pulling it and stretching it vigorously in every direction, so that the oil should enter the pores (P 389). Ox leather was used for large sacks (κ 19), greaves or gaiters (ω 228), helmets (K 258), sandals (ξ 24), ship-ropes (β 426, μ 423), reins for horses (Ψ 324), straps for helmets (Γ 375), a cestus for the boxer (Ψ 684), and straps for beds (to be stretched from side to side and from end to end of the bedstead, serving as springs, ψ 201), and the body of Hector was fastened behind the chariot of Achilles by thongs of ox hide (X 397). The sinews of the ox served as bowstrings (Δ 122, O 469). A hide served as a bed for Diomed in camp (K 155), and for the disguised Odysseus on the night before the slaying of Penelope's suitors (υ 142), and the suitors sat on such hides as they played draughts in the courtyard of the palace (α 108).

When Penelope's suitors are striving to string the bow of Odysseus, a great cake of tallow (στέατος τροχόν, φ 178) is brought out, in the hope that the bow when well greased would be more pliable. Whether the jars of ointment (ἀλείφατος, Ψ 170) which were placed on the pyre of Patroclus, were of animal or vegetable fat is uncertain.[1]

Epithets in large variety are applied to cattle. They are *fat* (πίονα, B 403), *well-fed* (ζατρεφέων, H 223), *spirited* (μεγάθυμον, Π 488), *straight-horned* (ὀρθο- *Epithets of Cattle.* κραιράων, Θ 231), "of broad forehead" (εὐρυμέτωπον, K 292), *bellowing* (ἐριμύκων, Y 497, ἐρύγμηλον, Σ 580),

---

[1] To say that ἀλοιφή is used always of animal fat, and ἄλειφαρ of vegetable oils, is arbitrary. The connexion decides.

wine-faced (οἴνοπε, N 703), *all black* (παμμέλανας, γ 6). Several epithets are of uncertain meaning : ἦνις, Z 94, seems to mean *sleek*, but other scholars understand it as *one year old* ; ἀργοί, Ψ 30, may mean *white* or *sleek* ; αἴθωνα, Π 488, may mean either *spirited* or *tawny*. The most frequent epithet (ἕλικας, α 92, used fourteen times) is thought by some to mean *crumpled-horned*, by others to mean *winding-gaited*, and by others to mean *sleek*. It is applied at μ 355 to the cattle of the Sun, which at μ 348 are straight-horned, and so there should not mean *with crumpled horn* ; but six times it accompanies the next epithet to be considered, which certainly refers to the gait, so the two cannot be synonymous. εἰλίποδας (α 92), used ten times, is interpreted as *winding-gaited* from the curious motion of the hind feet of the cow, contrasted with the epithet *high-stepping* (ἀερσίποδες) applied to horses. The cow does not pick up her feet neatly and move them directly forward, but swings them loosely outward, in a manner which may be illustrated roughly by the following diagram, in which *B* represents the horizontal motion of the left foot, and *A* that of the right :

Only three or four times, as has been noted, is the color of the kine specified, and it may be of interest to remember that Pindar calls the Thracian bulls red (ξανθός, *Pythian*, iv. 205).

Color of Kine.

The large, calm eye of the cow is recognized in the epithet *ox-eyed* (βοῶπις, A 551), which is applied fifteen times to the goddess Hera, and once each to two mortal women. The care of a young cow for her offspring, standing over it in its defense, forms a simile for Menelaus, bestriding the body of Patroclus and warding off the Trojans (P 4). The bellowing of a bull serves as a comparison for the roaring of the river Xanthus (Φ 237), the grating of the gate of the Achaean camp forced open by a stone thrown by Hector (M 460), and the creaking of the long unused door which opened from the treasure-chamber of Odysseus (φ 48).

Ox-eyed.

The chase of wild bulls may be referred to at N 571, where the struggle of a wounded man is likened to that of a bull on the mountains which herdsmen have bound with ropes and are leading away. Such a contest is repre- sented on beautiful golden cups of the Mycenaean period found at Vaphio, near Sparta (see p. 255). *Chase of Wild Bulls.* But the use of the term *herdsmen* instead of *hunters*, allowed the hearer to think of the capture of a bull which had escaped from the herd and was loath to be deprived of his new freedom.

Small cattle, sheep and goats (μῆλ', ὄιές τε καὶ αἶγες), like kine, are an important element of wealth in the time of Homer. They are well adapted to the moun- *Small Cattle.* tainous districts of Greece, more easily than kine climbing over the rocks and providing themselves with food. Ithaca in particular is said by Telemachus to be a land for goats rather than for horses (δ 606). Arcadian Orchomenus is called "rich in flocks" (πολύμηλον, B 605), Pelias is said to have been "rich in lambs" (πολύρρηνος, λ 257), and Agamemnon promises to give to Achilles, if he will but desist from his wrath, seven cities in which men dwell "rich in sheep and rich in kine" (πολύρρηνες πολυβοῦται, I 154). In Libya, ewes and she-goats bear young thrice yearly (δ 86), and there the young are born with horns.

The keeping of no other herd is described by the poet so fully as that of the Cyclops Polyphemus. The sheep and the goats were brought for the night into his cave,—the males being left as a rule in the outer *Flocks of Polyphemus.* yard. By day the older flocks were driven out on the mountain, while the young were left in pens, separated in three companies according to age. Early in the morning and at evening the ewes and the she-goats were milked first by Polyphemus and then by their young (ι 217 ff.). The flocks of the Laestrygonians, also, were driven forth to pasture by day (κ 82).

The flesh of both sheep and goats was eaten, and the milk of both was used for drinking and for cheese. Sheepsgut was used for the strings of the phorminx (φ 408). The clothing of the ordinary man and *Uses of Sheep and Goats.* woman was of wool. Telemachus slept "wrapped in the down of the sheep" (α 443), which is better under- stood of the woolen bedding than of sheepskins. But sheepskins were thrown over the chairs, as upholstery (ρ 32), and upon the pile of green boughs or rushes on which Telemachus sat when he visited the hut of the swine-herd (π 47). Hector bore a great stone to hurl against the gate of the Achaean camp, as a shepherd "easily bears in one hand the fleece of a ram" (M 451). Black sheep[1] are known as well as white (ἀργεννάων, Γ 198 ; ἄργυφα, κ 85). The epithet ἁλιπόρφυρα, ζ 53, applied to wool on the distaff, seems to mean *sea-blue*, though some would understand it as *gleaming white*.

The general epithets for both sheep and goats are *goodly* (ἴφια, μ 263), *fat* (πίονα, M 319), *fair-haired* (καλλίτριχα, ι 469), *long-legged* (ταναύποδα, ι 464). Sheep are *Epithets of Sheep and Goats.* *huddling* (ἀδινά, α 92) as contrasted with goats which feed scattered in "broad herds" (αἰπόλια πλατέα, B 474). The special epithets of sheep are borrowed naturally from their wool,—*close-fleeced* (πηγεσιμάλλῳ, Γ 197), *thick-fleeced* (δασύμαλλοι, ι 425), *woolly-fleeced* (εἰροπόκοις, E 137), and *shaggy* (λάσιος, Ω 125).

At Γ 196, Priam compares Odysseus to a ram stalking through a flock of sheep. Aeneas is followed by the Trojan soldiery as a ram is followed by sheep (N 492). *Comparisons with Small Cattle.* The Danaans attack the Trojans as ravening wolves attack lambs or kids (Π 352). As we have seen already, the noise of Trojan troops advancing is likened to the bleating of innumerable sheep (Δ 433). Between wolves and lambs there can be no friendship, Achilles tells Hector (X 263). Lions, also, are enemies of sheep (E 136, ζ 130), and an eagle swoops upon a tender lamb (ἄρν' ἀμαλήν, X 310). The shepherd needs to protect his sheep against thieves and robbers as well as against wild beasts (Γ 11).

Rams and lambs are sacrificed to Apollo (Δ 120, Ψ 873), and rams to Erechtheus at Athens (B 550). For the sacrifice which preceded the truce on the first *Sheep in Sacrifice.* day of battle, the Trojans furnish a white male lamb to be offered to the Sun, and a black ewe lamb to be offered to the Earth, while the Achaeans bring another male lamb for sacrifice to Zeus (Γ 103). For Teiresias in Hades, Circe bids Odysseus kill a black ram

---

[1] μέλαιναν, K 215 ; παμμέλανα, κ 527 ; ἰοδνεφὲς εἶρος ἔχοντες, ι 426.

(κ 524),—the color clearly being chosen as suited to the inhabitants of the realm of night.

That goats were counted as less valuable and honorable than sheep, is nowhere expressly stated, as it is in the idyls of Theocritus, but may easily be understood, since *Goats.* the wool of the sheep was so important. That goats were sometimes kept with sheep, has been seen above, in the case of the Cyclops Polyphemus. They feed scattered, and different flocks sometimes mingle in the pasture (B 474); they are driven into a cave at the approach of a storm (Δ 275); they are kept in pens at night, and green fodder is brought for the kids (ρ 224). Ithaca, as a hilly island, is well suited for goats (αἰγίβοτος, δ 606, ν 246). Odysseus has twelve flocks of goats on the mainland near Ithaca, and eleven on Ithaca itself (ξ 101). In the *Iliad*, goat's flesh is eaten but twice,—in the tent of Achilles (I 207) and at the funeral feast of Patroclus (Ψ 31). In the *Odyssey*, the goat-herd brings daily the best of his flock for the feasts of Penelope's suitors (ρ 213, υ 173, *cf.* β 56, 300). A sort of blood-pudding, haggis, or *Blutwurst*, was made by filling a goat's intestine with fat and blood, and roasting or toasting it before the fire,—a viand which was eaten apparently after the more solid meats (σ 44), and appears but once in the poems. This was given by Penelope's suitors to the disguised Odysseus as a sort of prize for his beating the beggar Irus. Goat's cheese was grated for a posset which was prepared for the wounded Machaon (Λ 639). From goatskin were made leathern bottles for wine (ἀσκῷ ἐν αἰγείῳ, Γ 247, ζ 78, *cf.* ι 196) and the cap of old Laërtes (ω 231). A goatskin served as a mantle for the swine-herd Eumaeus, being thrown over his ordinary cloak, when he slept in the open air near his swine (ξ 530),—which may be compared with the deerskin of the disguised Odysseus (ν 436).

Goats are called *bleating* (μηκάδες, Λ 383), *fat* (πίονος, I 207), *well-fed* (ζατρεφέων, ξ 106; εὐτρεφέος, ξ 530).

Offerings of goats are made to Apollo (A 66), to Hermes (τ 398), and to Ithacan fountain nymphs (ρ 242).

Wild goats are found by Odysseus in large numbers on the woody island opposite the land of the Cyclopes (ι 118). The skin of a wild goat is spread by Eumaeus over a heap of rushes (ξ 50) as a seat for the disguised Odysseus. The archer Pandarus himself shot the wild goat of which

Wild Goats. the horns were used in making a bow used at Troy (Δ 105, see page 668). The epithets applied to the wild goat are of uncertain meaning,—$\overset{"}{\iota}\xi\alpha\lambda\circ\varsigma$ (Δ 105,— possibly *agile*) and $\iota\circ\nu\theta\acute{\alpha}\varsigma$ (ξ 50,—probably *shaggy* or *bearded*).

The Chimaera ($X\acute{\iota}\mu\alpha\iota\rho\alpha$, Z 179) is strictly a *kid* in name, but it is a fabulous monster with a lion's head, the head

Chimaera. of a kid projecting from its back, and a serpent for its tail,—" breathing forth the might of blazing fire." [1] (See Fig. 19.)

The importance of swine in the life of the Homeric age is indicated by the fact that Odysseus has twelve droves

Swine. ($\sigma\nu\beta\acute{\circ}\sigma\iota\alpha$) on the mainland in addition to the 960 swine under the care of Eumaeus and his three assistants on Ithaca itself (ξ 13 ff., 101). That boys were used in driving swine, is shown by Achilles's comparison of himself, when in danger from the river Scamander, with a " boy swine-tender " ($\pi\alpha\hat{\iota}\delta\alpha$ $\sigma\nu\phi\circ\rho\beta\acute{\circ}\nu$, Φ 282) swept away by the water as he crosses a ditch in winter. Fifty droves of swine are among the booty gained by Nestor and his friends from Elis (Λ 679). Pork is next to beef as the favorite food of the Homeric warrior, and apparently each day three fat swine are brought for the feasts of Penelope's suitors (υ 163); roast pig, however, is not highly valued (ξ 81). At the funeral feast of Patroclus, " many white tusked swine, abounding in fat, were stretched singeing through the flame of Hephaestus " (Ψ 32),—which teaches that the bristles were removed not by scalding but by the direct use of flame. The shade of Agamemnon in Hades compares the slaughter of his comrades in the home of Aegisthus with that of swine in the house of a rich man, for a marriage feast or a banquet (λ 413). Lard is nowhere mentioned as used, but hog's fat is " tried " in a kettle (Φ 363). Boar's teeth are strung about a helmet (K 263), probably both for ornament and as a protection for the head (see Fig. 31); teeth which had been so used have been found at Mycenae.

---

[1] The foundation for the story is unknown. Bérard would derive the name from the Semitic languages. He understands it to mean *seething*, and compares Sicilian Himera and its hot springs.

The most frequent epithet of swine is *white-tusked* (ἀργιόδοντα, I 539). The adjective *sleeping-upon-the-ground* (χαμαιευνάδες, κ 243, ξ 15) is used twice. The swine were taken from their sties (συφεούς, ξ 13) *Epithets of Swine.* by day to feed upon the hills (ξ 410, π 3), but as in the case of the sheep and goats the young ones were left at home (ξ 73). The males of Odysseus's droves were kept apart from the females, and were far less numerous since they were preferred for food by Penelope's suitors (ξ 17). The favorite food of swine was acorns, chestnuts, and the

FIG. 19.—The Chimaera.

fruit of the cornel tree (κ 242, *cf.* ν 409), and these are cast by Circe before the comrades of Odysseus whom she has transformed into swine.

The hog, when domesticated, was not an animal to arouse the poet's enthusiasm or imagination, but in spite of this a distinguished position was given to the " divine swine-herd " (δῖος ὑφορβός, ο 301) Eumaeus, at *" Divine Swine-herd."* whose hut, by the plan of Athena, Odysseus on his return to Ithaca met his son Telemachus, and determined the death of Penelope's suitors (π 1 ff.) He was a " leader of men " (ὄρχαμος ἀνδρῶν, ξ 22).[1]

A hog is offered to Zeus and other divinities at the

[1] For his position as a servant, see the chapter on Slavery (p. 272).

sacrifice in confirmation of the reconciliation between Agamemnon and Achilles (T 250), and Teiresias directs
Swine in Sacrifice. Odysseus to offer to Poseidon a hog with a bull
and a ram (the *su-ove-taurilia* of the Romans), in
order to appease the god's anger (λ 131).

Wild boars appear frequently in comparisons and are
counted next to lions[1] in courage and might. Odysseus and
Wild Boars. Diomed fall upon the Trojans as two wild boars
with proud hearts fall upon hunting dogs (Λ 324).
Hector attacks the retreating Achaeans as a dog fastens
upon a wild boar or a lion, pursuing him with swift feet,
and watching him as he turns (Θ 338); and a little later
he sets the Trojans upon the Achaeans as a hunter sets
his white-toothed dogs upon a boar or a lion (Λ 292).
Idomeneus awaits Aeneas as a boar on the mountains,
trusting to his strength, with bristling back and gleaming
eyes, and whetting his tusks, awaits a throng of men and
dogs (N 471). Hector and Patroclus fight as a lion and a
tireless boar fight on the summit of a mountain, for the
water of a little spring (Π 823). As the body of Patroclus
is borne from the field of battle, the Trojans press on the
retreating Achaeans as dogs upon a wounded wild boar
(P 725). At P 20, Menelaus says that the spirit of
Euphorbus surpasses that of leopard, lion, or wild boar, whose
heart rages most mightily. When the youthful Odysseus
visits his grandfather on the slopes of Parnassus, on the very
day after his arrival he is taken out to a boar hunt, evidently
held in his honor, and he receives a wound of which the scar
serves as a means of identification many years later (τ 429).
Wild boars were hunted not merely for the excitement of
the sport, but also as being harmful to crops and to trees.
Sometimes the men of a whole district gathered for such a
hunt, with which we may compare the similar forces raised
against lions; and we may remember that such gatherings
have been necessary in modern times, as for example even
in the winter of 1830, an army of wolves descended from
the mountains in Tamworth, New Hampshire, and farmers,
six hundred in number, from all the neighboring towns, came
against them, and formed a sort of military organization

[1] *Cf.* Plato, *Laches,* 196 E.

under a former army officer.   Thus the hunters and dogs from many cities (I 544) were collected by Meleager to hunt the Calydonian boar, which Artemis had sent in anger at Meleager's father's neglect to honor her at his harvest-home festival (θαλύσια, I 534).   This boar, we are told, "put many men upon the grievous funeral pile" (I 546), after wasting the fields and even uprooting fruit trees.[1]   The sea-god Proteus took the form of a wild boar in his efforts to escape from Menelaus (δ 457).

The epithets applied to the wild boar are *tireless* (ἀκά-μαντα, II 823), *white-tusked* (ἀργιόδοντα, I 539), *of the field* (ἀγροτέρῳ, Λ 293), and *destructive-minded* (ὀλοόφρονος, P 21).

The poet does not mention the wild boar as an article of food, but we remember that venison appears in the poems only once, though undoubtedly it was eaten freely.

The only domesticated fowl which appears in the Homeric poems is the goose (χήν, o 161, τ 536).   Whether it is kept for diversion or for eating, is not clear.   An eagle *Geese.* seizes a white goose from the courtyard of Menelaus, just as Telemachus is setting out to return to his home ; and Helen interprets the omen to mean that Odysseus will return to Ithaca and take vengeance on Penelope's suitors.   On the evening before the slaying of the suitors, Penelope tells to the disguised Odysseus her dream : she has twenty geese which eat wheat soaked in water, and she delights in watching them ; she dreamed that a mighty eagle came from the mountain and killed them all, but then with human voice he declared that he was her husband and would slay the suitors ; on waking she sees the geese eating wheat by the trough as before.

The wild goose is mentioned twice (B 460, O 692) in an identical line, with cranes and swans.   Upon these an eagle pounces at O 692, and at P 460 Automedon pursues the Trojans as a falcon pursues geese.

The lion (λέων, λίς) is eminently the wild beast most dreaded by herds and herdsmen.   It is named sixty-two

---

[1] *Cf.* Heracles's "labor" of killing the Erymanthian boar, and the killing of the Crommyonian sow by Theseus.

times in the poems, appearing in comparisons about thirty times in the *Iliad*. This animal must have been familiar to the poet and his hearers, and zoölogists praise the accuracy of Homeric expressions.[1] Naturally it is not introduced directly into the narrative.

Lion.

A lion's skin was used by Agamemnon and by Nestor as a mantle for protection against cold, and as light armor to ward off missiles (K 23, 177), just as Heracles wore the skin of the Nemean lion.

The principal epithets applied to the lion are *mighty* (κρατεροῖο, δ 335), *ravening* (σίντης, Υ 165), *gleaming-eyed* (χαροποί, λ 611), *raw-flesh eating* (ὠμοφάγοισιν, Ε 782), *terrible* (σμερδαλέω, Σ 579), *mountain-nurtured* (ὀρεσίτροφος, Μ 299), *bearded* (ἠυγένειος, Ο 275), and *tawny* (δαφοινόν, Κ 23). Whether αἴθων (K 24) means *fiery* in spirit or *tawny*, is not certain. As in all times, the lion is the incarnation of fierce courage, and the epithet *lion-hearted* (θυμολέοντα, Ε 639, Η 228, δ 724) is applied to Heracles, Achilles, and Odysseus. Since the lion is associated with death and destruction, Hera says that Artemis is "a lion to women," because she sends quiet death to them (Φ 483 ; see p. 432).

Epithets of Lion.

The Homeric comparisons represent the lion as brought up in a thicket on a mountain summit (Ε 554). Ajax stands over the body of Patroclus as a lion stands over his young when met by hunters (P 133); Achilles grieves for Patroclus as a bearded lion for his whelps (Σ 318). The lion goes out at night, with a roar, for his prey (K 184). The Trojans fled before Agamemnon on the third day of battle like cows which a lion puts to flight in the darkness of the night,—he breaks

Comparisons with Lion.

[1] Lions are not found in Greece and Asia Minor now, but we are told that in Palaeolithic times the lion ranged over a great part of Europe, the remains of bones showing that there were European as well as African and Asiatic lions. The story of Heracles and the Nemean lion indicates that the Greeks had heard of lions in Peloponnesus. Herodotus (vii. 125) says that lions came down from the mountains of Thrace and attacked the camels in Xerxes's army, 480 B.C., and his story is confirmed by Aristotle, *Hist. An.* vi. 31, viii. 28; Xenophon, *Cyn.* xi. ; and Pausanias, vi. 5. Lions were known to the writers of the Old Testament, but now have disappeared from that part of Asia; *cf. Isaiah* xxxviii. 13; "The lion hath roared, who will not fear?" *Amos* iii. 8.

the neck of one, and gulps down her blood and inward parts (Λ 173). Menelaus is driven against his will from the body of Patroclus as a lion is kept from a farmyard by the spears and voices of men (P 109), and he sets out to seek for Antilochus, like a lion who, though hungry for flesh, has been kept from the farmyard in the night by dogs and men with javelins and firebrands, and departs unwillingly at dawn (P 657). Odysseus, after the wreck of his barge, emerging from the thicket to meet the princess Nausicaa, is like a lion going in wind and rain to seek cattle or sheep or deer (ζ 130). Menelaus declares that Odysseus will return to his home and slay Penelope's suitors, just as a lion returns and kills suckling fawns which the doe unwittingly has left in his thicket, while she seeks pasture in the neighboring grassy glens (δ 335). At Γ 23, Menelaus in meeting Paris rejoices as a hungry lion rejoices on finding a horned stag or a wild goat which hunters have just wounded or killed ; Hector and Patroclus contend together for the body of Hector's brother and charioteer Cebriones, just as two lions fight for a slain doe (Π 756), and a little later Hector overcomes Patroclus as a lion overcomes a wild boar, in conflict for the water of a small spring on a mountain (Π 823). Like the wild boar, the lion is sometimes hunted by the men of a district : Achilles advances against Aeneas like a ravening lion which men assembling from a whole district are eager to kill ; the lion comes on at first with little heed for them, but when one of the youths has hit him with a spear, he gathers himself together, his mouth is wide open, foam collects about his teeth, he lashes his side and flanks with his tail, and with gleaming eyes he is borne by his fury straight onward, if haply he may slay one of the men (Υ 164 ; cf. δ 791, M 41). Achilles tells Hector that there is no truce between lions and men, and there shall be none between these warriors (X 262). Naturally the poet refers to the lion less frequently in the *Odyssey* than in the *Iliad*, but the Cyclops Polyphemus devours the companions of Odysseus like a mountain-bred lion, " vitals, and flesh, and marrowy bones " (ι 293).

The leopard (πάρδαλις) appears three times in Homeric comparisons, and is among the forms which the sea-god

Proteus assumes (δ 457), between the lion and serpent and the wild boar. On the last day of battle, Achilles advances

Leopard. to meet Agenor, "as a leopard goes from a deep thicket to meet a hunter, nor does it fear in soul nor flee when it hears the barking of the dogs; for even though the hunter shall be first to wound, by blow or throw, yet though pierced by the spear it does not cease from its defense until it come into close quarters or be slain" (Φ 573). At P 20 its fury is compared with that of a lion or wild boar, and at N 103 it is classed with jackals and wolves as an enemy of deer. As a lion's skin is used by Agamemnon and a wolf-skin by Dolon, so leopards' skins (παρδαλέη, Γ 17, Κ 29) are worn by Paris and by Menelaus as a mantle or aegis.

Every reader will remember the reference to the leopard in the Old Testament, as a familiar animal: "Can the Ethiopian change his skin or a leopard his spots?" (*Jeremiah* xiii. 23.)

The bear (ἄρκτος) does not appear in the Homeric poems in person or in a comparison. On the baldric which the

Bear. ghost of Heracles wore in Hades, however, were represented bears, with boars and lions and conflicts of all sorts (λ 611). Twice the constellation of the Great Bear is named;—once as represented on the Shield of Achilles, with the sun, the moon, "and all the constellations with which the heaven is crowned, the Pleiades, the Hyades, and the strength of Orion" (Σ 487); and again as guiding the course of Odysseus on his way from the island of Calypso, who bade him "watch the Pleiades and the late-setting Boötes, and the bear which men call also the wain, which turns on the same spot and watches Orion" (ε 273).[1]

The wolf (λύκος) is named by the poet ten times, as a bold and cruel animal, and an enemy of the small flocks.

Wolf. At Δ 471 and Λ 72, the warriors rush upon each other like wolves. Ravening (σίνται, Π 352) wolves attack lambs and kids, and timid deer are a prey

---

[1] Strabo, i. 3, says that the Phoenicians taught the Greeks to use this constellation in their navigation. Bérard thinks that the *wain* was the Phoenician name for the constellation, and the *bear* the Greek name. *Bear* (*rikshas* = ἄρκτος) was also the name of the Great Bear in India in the Vedic age.

to them as well as to jackals and leopards (N 103).   Just as wolf and, lamb cannot agree, neither can Achilles and Hector live at peace with each other (X 263).   The Myrmidons, going forth to battle with Patroclus, are compared in spirit to "raw-flesh eating wolves" which have devoured a great horned stag on the mountains, and with cheeks crimson with blood go in a pack to lap with their thin tongues the top of the dark water from a spring, belching out the gore of blood (Π 156).   Circe transformed men into "wolves of the mountain" (ὀρέστεροι, κ 212, cf. κ 433), but these retained their kindly human spirit.

Epithets, other than those which have been mentioned, applied to wolves, are *gray* (πολιοῖο, Κ 334), and of *mighty claw* (κρατερώνυχες, κ 218).

The Trojan scout Dolon wore a wolf-skin (ῥινὸν λύκοιο, Κ 334) over his shoulders, just as Agamemnon wore a lion's skin.

The jackal (θώς) appears in two Homeric comparisons.   At Λ 474 the Trojans follow the wounded Odysseus as tawny (δαφοινοί) jackals on the mountain press upon a stag, wounded by an arrow, which has escaped the *Jackal.* hunter but at last sinks from loss of blood.   The jackals are devouring this deer in a shady grove when a lion appears, and they scatter.   So flee the Trojans in different directions when Ajax appears to the defense of Odysseus.   In the other passage (N 103), the jackal is simply classed with leopards and wolves as the enemy of deer.

The deer (ἔλαφος), strongly contrasted with the lion, the leopard, and the wolf, is the symbol of cowardice (X 1). The Trojans are likened to timid does (φυζακινῆς *Deer.* ἐλάφοισιν, N 102); Agamemnon cries to the Argives, " Why stand ye thus, dazed like fawns? " (ἠΰτε νεβροί, Δ 243); and Achilles, as his most bitter insult to Agamemnon, says that he has the " eye of a dog and the heart of a deer " (A 225).   At Λ 113 the helplessness of the Trojans to defend a comrade slain by Agamemnon is likened to that of a doe whose fawn is killed by a lion, while she is near at hand but is forced to flee.   Naturally deer are the prey of all carnivorous wild beasts, of lions (δ 335), of wolves (Π 158), of leopards, and of jackals (N 103, Λ 474).   A fawn carried away by an eagle, but let fall by the altar in the Achaean camp, is an omen sent by Zeus (Θ 248). The only deer which appears in its own person and not merely in a comparison, in the Homeric poems, is killed by Odysseus on Circe's island, when oppressed by the heat it comes from the forest to drink at the river (κ 158,—*cf.* " As the hart panteth after the water brooks," *Psalm* xlii. 1). This is the only occasion when the poet speaks of venison as an article of human food, but the deer was often hunted, and naturally for its flesh. Artemis goes over Mt. Taÿgetus or Mt. Erymanthus, delighting in the wild boars and swift deer (ζ 104), which seems like the chase, since she is the archer-goddess, and at Φ 486 Hera tells Artemis that the killing of wild beasts and deer on the mountain is her proper work. The Achaeans, pressing on their enemies, but stopping short at the sight of Hector, are compared to countrymen in hot pursuit of a horned stag or wild goat, but suddenly met by a bearded lion who is roused by their voices (O 271); and, a few verses later, Antilochus rushes upon the wounded Melanippus as a dog rushes upon a fawn which a hunter has wounded (O 579). Odysseus and Diomed pursue Dolon as two sharp-toothed dogs well skilled in the chase pursue a deer or a hare (K 361). A fawn in the clutches of a dog is the device for the brooch of Odysseus (τ 228), and Achilles pursues Hector as a dog pursues a fawn on the mountain (X 189). Odysseus's old dog Argos in his prime was taken to hunt wild goats, roes, and hares (ρ 295). Once a hunter is called a *deer-hitter* (ἐλαφηβόλος, Σ 319).

The epithets of deer are *horned* (κεραόν, Γ 24), *with high horns* (ὑψίκερων, κ 158), *swift* (ταχείης, Θ 248), *of the field* (ἀγροτέρας, ζ 133), and *fugitive, cowardly* (φυζακινῆς,

Epithets of Deer. N 102). The fawn is *new-born, suckling* (νεβροὺς νεηγενέας γαλαθηνούς, δ 336), or *dappled* (ποικίλον ἑλλόν, τ 228). The κεμάς of K 361 has not been well identified; it may be a two-year old deer, or it may be an antelope. So the πρόκες of ρ 295, pursued by the dog Argos, may be roes, but the meaning of the term is uncertain.

A deerskin (δέρμα ἐλάφοιο, ν 436) is given by Athena to

the disguised Odysseus on his arrival at Ithaca, to serve as a beggar's cloak. This corresponds pretty nearly to the skins of lions and leopards worn by warriors, and the goatskin worn by the swine-herd Eumaeus.

Deerskin.

The hare (λαγωός, πτώξ, P 676) appears in the poems four times in comparisons; twice as espied and killed by an eagle (P 676, X 310), and twice as pursued by dogs (K 361, ρ 295). It is *swift of foot* (πόδας ταχύς, P 676) and *cowering* (πτῶκα, X 310). The latter epithet is used as a noun at P 676, with which may be compared the use of *mountain beast* (οὐρεύς) for mule, and *circler* (κίρκος) for hawk.

The Hare.

As for creatures of the sea, fish (ἰχθύες) were caught by hook and line, by net, and by spear, but they are not often mentioned as eaten. The sea is called *fishy* (ἰχθυόεντα, T 378) twelve times, however, and the poet was more likely to be impressed by the fish that were drawn out of the deep than by those which remained there. This epithet is applied also to the Hellespont (I 360) and to the river Hyllus (Υ 392). Iris, bearing a message from Zeus to Thetis, sinks into the sea like the lead fixed upon the horn of an ox, which bears death to fishes (Ω 80). The use of the lead as sinker is familiar to modern readers; probably the horn was intended to prevent the fish from biting off the line. Odysseus, in the story of his adventures, says that Scylla raised to her cave in the rock his struggling companions, as a fisherman on a projecting rock, with long rod, casting bait as a deceit to small fishes, throws into the sea the horn of an ox and then draws out the struggling fish (μ 251); here the horn clearly implies the hook, as in the foregoing passage; but probably it is not to be understood as the hook itself. Patroclus strikes in the jaw a Trojan in his chariot, and draws him over the chariot-rim as a man sitting on a projecting rock draws a big fish forth from the water by line and bright bronze (λίνῳ καὶ ἤνοπι χαλκῷ, Π 408). Here, of course, the bronze must be the hook; the lead and the horn have no occasion to be mentioned. So also on the island of Pharos near Egypt, the comrades of Menelaus fished with bent hooks (γναμπτοῖς ἀγκίστροισιν, δ 369), and, according to ordinary texts, the

Fishes.

comrades of Odysseus did the like on the island of the Sun
(μ 332). When the ships of Odysseus (all at least but his
own) incautiously entered the harbor of the Laestrygonians,
the people of the land, " not like to men but to giants," sunk
the ships by hurling great rocks upon them, and speared
the men as fishes (ἰχθῦς δ' ὣς πείροντες, κ 124). The slain
suitors in the palace of Odysseus are like fishes which men
of the sea have drawn with the many-meshed net (δικτύῳ
πολυωπῷ, χ 386) upon the curving shore from the grey
deep. Sarpedon reproaches Hector with the indifference of
the Trojans, who do not seem ready to fight, " that ye may
not be caught in the meshes of the all-embracing net (ἀψῖσι
λίνου πανάγρου, E 487) and become the prey and spoil of
the enemy." It is true that the poet mentions fish as eaten
only by the comrades of Menelaus and those of Odysseus
when wind-bound on islands, and after their stores of
provisions were exhausted ; but, as Athenaeus remarks, they
must have had their fish hooks with them on the voyage, since
these could not have been found on the islands. Further,
abundance of fish is named with large harvests of wheat and
barley, fruit from trees, and prosperity of flocks, among the
blessings granted by the gods to the people whose king " fears
the gods and maintains justice " (τ 113). And we must not
forget that only once, too, is venison mentioned as eaten, and
yet we have seen that men often hunted deer. That men
at that stage of civilization seldom hunted and fished for
mere pleasure, we may surmise ; they were not very remote
from the period when these occupations were not pastime
but were counted as hard labor ; and we must believe that
the hunting, fishing, and laying snares for birds were, as
both before Homer and in the classical period, chiefly for
food. The poet explicitly mentions the griefs (ἄλγεα, ι 121)
of hunters traversing the forest and mountains, and gives
nowhere any indication of " sport " in hunting and fishing,
except, perhaps, in the case of the wild boar, and in the
delight of Artemis in the wild beasts. To chase the wild
boar then required much more skill and courage than
modern " pig-sticking " in India.

No special variety of fishes is mentioned except eels and
dolphins ; and the poet does not seem to have considered

eels to be fish in a strict sense, but says " both eels and
fishes " (ἐγχέλυές τε καὶ ἰχθύες, Φ 203, 353).[1] Before a huge
dolphin (δελφῖνος μεγακήτεος, Φ 22) the other fish
flee into the recesses of the harbor, " for eagerly *Eels and Dolphins.*
does it devour whatever one it takes," and so
the Trojans fled before Achilles.   The dolphin itself, in turn,
is associated with the sea-dog or sea-calf (κύνας, μ 96) and
other creatures,[2] for which Scylla fishes (ἰχθυάᾳ) about her
rock.   Seals (φῶκαι, δ 404) are noted in particular, because of
one of the experiences of Menelaus : detained on *Seals.*
the island of Pharos near Egypt, by the advice
and with the aid of a daughter of Proteus, he hides himself
and three comrades under newly flayed seal-skins, in the
group of seals lying on the seashore, that he may take the
sea-god off his guard, and compel him to give advice for
the return to Greece.   The seals come forth from the water
to sun themselves, a little before noon, and lie in a line on
the shore.   The most noticeable characteristic of the seal, to
the mind of Menelaus, seems to be its disagreeable odor,—
an " ancient and fish-like smell " ; but they are called also
well-fed (ζατρεφέας, δ 451), *sea-bred* (ἁλιοτρεφέων, δ 442), and
offspring of the daughter of the sea (νέποδες ἁλοσύδνης, δ 404,—
unless indeed νέποδες means *swim-footed*).   Seals are named
also among the creatures which would devour a corpse thrown
into the sea (ο 480).   Ordinary fishes, too, are thought of
as tearing the flesh of corpses in the water.   Achilles drags
the body of Priam's son Lycaon to the bank of the Scamander
and throws him into the river with the words : " There lie
now among the fishes who shall lick the blood from thy
wound. . . . The eddying Scamander shall bear thee within the
broad bosom of the sea.   Many a fish shall leap up under
the dark ripple to eat the white fat of Lycaon " (Φ 122).
Achilles left the body of Asteropaeus in the bed of the
Scamander, " lying on the sand, and the dark water wet
him, and both the eels and the fishes were busy about him,
tearing the fat above the kidneys " (Φ 201).   The old Laërtes,
despairing of the return of Odysseus, says, " Doubtless far

---

[1] With ἐγχέλυς *cf.* ἔχις, *serpent,* and the Latin *anguilla.*

[2] κῆτος, *cf. cetaceous,* and μεγακήτης of the dolphin in Φ 22.   At N 27 the κήτεα
sport about Poseidon as he drives over the sea in his chariot.

from his friends and his native land, either fishes devoured him in the sea, or on the land he became a prey to beasts and birds" (ω 291). And the epithet *raw-flesh eating, cruel,* is applied to fishes (ὠμηστῆσιν ἰχθύσι, Ω 82), as it is elsewhere to beasts and birds of prey and to Achilles.[1] To Homer the fishes are not "dumb" as in Aeschylus.

Oysters. The oyster (τήθεα, Π 747) appears in one comparison. The charioteer and half-brother of Hector, Cebriones, is hit by Patroclus in the forehead with a stone, and falls head foremost from his chariot like a diver (ἀρνευτῆρι ἐοικώς, Π 742). Patroclus mockingly says, in his exultation: "Truly the man is agile; how easily he turns a somersault! If he were on the fishy sea, he would provide oysters for many by diving from the ship, though the weather were stormy."

Octopus. The octopus or polyp (πουλύποδος, ε 432, *many-footed*) is mentioned once. The skin of Odysseus's fingers, as he clung to a rough rock after his shipwreck, striving to save himself from the sea, stuck to the rock as pebbles remain fixed to the tentacles (κοτυληδονόφιν, *cups*) of a polyp drawn out of its chamber.

Sponge. The sponge (σπόγγῳ, Σ 414) is used exactly as in modern times. Hephaestus, after his work at his forge, sponges his face and arms, his neck and shaggy breast, before he dons clean linen and leaves his smithy to receive the visit of Thetis (Σ 414). And the tables in the great hall of Odysseus were wiped with the "porous sponges" (σπόγγοισι πολυτρήτοισι, α 111, *cf.* υ 151, χ 439, 453) before each repast.

The sea monster (κῆτος, Υ 147) which came against Troy in the time of Laomedon (demanding the king's daughter, according to the later story), and from which Heracles freed the land, was fabulous and needs no identification.

The general name for birds is *ornīthes* (ὄρνιθες, *cf.* ornithology),—whether large or small, from an eagle or a crane

---

[1] The epithet ἱερός as applied to a fish at Π 407 has not been satisfactorily explained from ordinary Greek usage; instead of meaning *sacred*, it seems to mean *active, vigorous,* or *strong*. *Cf.* the same epithet applied to the picket-guard of the Achaeans at Κ 56.—"The corresponding Sanskrit *ishirá* = ἱερός, is *active, agile, strong,* and is applied to horses, spies, gods, mind, women, and cows."

to a pigeon or a sparrow.[1] The term *oiōnos* (οἰωνός)[2] is limited to large birds of prey, as the eagle and the vulture, and since oracles were drawn particularly from the flight of these great birds, this term often means omen. *Birds.* Thus when Pulydamas urges Hector to yield to the will of the gods for their retreat, as shown in particular by an eagle skirting their host to the left, Hector replies, "One omen (οἰωνός, *bird*, M 243) is best,— to fight for one's native land." In the Catalogue of Trojan forces, of Ennomus who led the Mysians the poet says, that he was a *seer of birds* (οἰωνιστής, B 858), "but not by birds (οἰωνοῖσιν, *omens, i.e.* by the interpretation of omens) did he ward off black fate." Priam, when Hecuba strives to discourage him as he is about to go to the Achaean camp to ransom Hector's body, says to her, "Be not thyself to me a bird of ill-omen" (ὄρνις κακός, Ω 219), and a few verses later she urges him to ask from Zeus a favorable bird of omen (οἰωνὸν δεξιόν, Ω 292).[3]

Birds of prey are mentioned often as feeding on the corpses of the slain. At the very opening of the *Iliad*, the poet says that the wrath of Achilles made the bodies of many brave warriors "the booty of dogs and a *Birds of Prey.* feast to the birds of prey" (οἰωνοῖσί τε δαῖτα, A 5). Addressing his men as they are setting out for the first battle of the *Iliad*, Agamemnon declares that any man whom he shall see desiring to remain in the camp, away from the battle, shall not "escape the dogs and birds" (B 393). Achilles reiterates to the dying Hector the threat that the "dogs and birds" shall devour him (X 335, 354); but Priam on his way to the Achaean camp to ransom Hector's body is cheered by learning from Hermes that the "dogs and birds" have not devoured his son's corpse (Ω 411). Nestor, in telling Telemachus of the death of Agamemnon, says that if the

---

[1] The cognate ὄρνεον is found only at N 64. πετεηνά (πέτομαι), *flying* things, is used by the poet three times as an adjective, as π 218, and seven times as a noun, as Θ 247.

[2] This has often been connected with the adjective οἶος, *alone*, since these birds do not gather in flocks; but it is better associated with the Latin *avis*, *bird*. Cf. *ōmen* (**ovismen*).

[3] See the chapter on Divination (page 521).

hero's brother Menelaus had found the murderer alive when he returned to Achaea, the "dogs and birds" would have devoured Aegisthus on the plain (γ 259). Diomed says of him whosoever is hit by his spear,—"his wife's cheeks are torn in grief, his children are orphans, and there are more birds than women about him," *i.e.* his body is not composed for burial but is torn by birds of prey (Λ 395).[1]

The eagle, as we should expect, is recognized as the king of birds. It is the strongest, swiftest, and most perfect of

Eagle.

flying things.[2] It has the keenest sight of all birds, and espies a hare even when this is crouching under a leafy bush (P 676). Its home is on the mountain (ο 175), and it flies high in the air (ὑψιπέτης, M 201, ὑψιπετήεις, ω 538); it has a hooked beak (ἀγκυλο-χείλης, τ 538); and it is a hunter (θηρητῆρα, Ω 316),—attacking wild geese, cranes, and swans (Ο 690). Three similar epithets meaning *black, dark,* or *dusky* are applied to the eagle, once each (μέλανος, Φ 252; μόρφνον, περκνόν, Ω 316). The epithet αἴθων (Ο 690) probably means *tawny,* but may mean *fiery.* The eagle is the dearest of birds to Zeus (Ω 311), and preëminently the bird for omens. Thus Zeus sends an eagle to encourage Priam (Ω 315), as he had sent another to cheer the Achaeans (Θ 247), and he sends two for Telemachus (β 146). On other occasions, what divinity sends the eagle as an omen is not known (M 201, N 821, ο 160, υ 242).

Near the close of the conflict between Achilles and Hector, Achilles swoops upon his adversary as an eagle which descends to the plain, through the dark clouds, to seize a tender lamb or a timid hare (Χ 308). As the river Scamander arose in wrath against Achilles who was in its stream, Achilles sprang a spear's cast away, with the rush of a dark eagle

---

[1] *Cf.* "Our monuments shall be the maws of kites," *Macbeth,* iii. 3. 72; "The eye that mocketh at his father and despiseth to obey his mother,—the ravens of the valley shall pick it out and the young eagles shall eat it," *Proverbs* xxx. 17, *i.e.* this man's body shall be eaten by birds of prey; and Goliath's words to David, "Come to me and I will give thy flesh unto the fowls of the air and to the beasts of the field," and David's reply, "I will give the carcases of the hosts of the Philistines this day unto the fowls of the air, and to the wild beasts of the earth," 1 *Samuel* xvii. 44 ff.; *cf.* also Sophocles, *Antigone,* 205, where Creon declares that the body of Polynices shall be eaten by dogs and vultures, and Aeschylus, *Sept.* 1021.

[2] κάρτιστός τε καὶ ὤκιστος πετεηνῶν, Φ 253, τελειότατον, Ω 315.

(Φ 252). The gaze of Menelaus seeking Antilochus as a messenger to Achilles of the death of Patroclus, is like that of an eagle (P 674). Homer does not represent an eagle as bearing Ganymede to Mt. Olympus to be the cup-bearer of Zeus. The reader has seen that the eagle assailed geese, cranes, swans, lambs, and fawns (Θ 248). An eagle is carrying to its nest for its young a serpent, when the serpent bites it in the neck and is dropped into the midst of the Trojan throng (M 201).

The sea eagle or osprey (φήνη,—perhaps named from the whitish color of breast and belly) is named twice. In leaving Nestor and the Pylians, the goddess *Osprey.* Athena departs like this bird,—apparently taking its form (φήνη εἰδομένη, γ 372), though some would interpret the expression merely "as swiftly as an osprey." At π 217, the loud sobbing of Odysseus and Telemachus is compared to the cries of these birds or falcons when deprived of their young.

The falcon (αἰγύπιος, N 531,—connected with γύψ ?) is named six times. Athena and Apollo sit like falcons[1] on an oak tree to watch the proceedings of the *Falcon.* Achaeans and the Trojans, "delighting in the men" (H 59). At N 531, Meriones leaped forward like a falcon to recover the spear which he had thrown. Sarpedon and Patroclus rush upon each other with a mighty shout, as falcons fight with loud cries, on a high crag (Π 428). Automedon on the chariot of Achilles, driving upon the Trojans, is compared to a falcon pursuing geese (P 460). At χ 302, Odysseus and his companions rage against the suitors of Penelope, like falcons of hooked beaks and crooked talons, coming from the mountains and assailing small birds, which flee the clouds (*i.e.* the falcons descending from the clouds), while men delight in the chase. Are these falcons trained as in modern times to aid men in the chase? As is observed in the preceding paragraph, Odysseus and Telemachus weep for joy more vehemently than ospreys or crooked-taloned falcons for their young (π 217).

---

[1] *Cf.* "Thence up he [Satan] flew, and on the Tree of Life,
The middle tree and highest there that grew,
Sat like a cormorant."
Milton, *Paradise Lost*, iv. 194.

The goshawk[1] is the *lightest, swiftest of flying things* (ἐλαφρότατος πετεηνῶν, Χ 139, ν 86 ; ὤκιστος πετεηνῶν,

Goshawk. Ο 238), *swift-winged* (ὠκύπτερος, Ν 62), and *swift pigeon-killer* (φασσοφόνῳ, Ο 238). It is found with the sea-crow nesting in the trees of Calypso's island (ε 65). This also is a bird of omen,—appearing to Telemachus as a "swift messenger of Apollo," with a dove in its talons, and scattering the dove's feathers on the ground (ο 526). Its speed is the quality most noted in comparisons. Poseidon left the Ajaxes, as swift as a hawk (Ν 62). Thetis, having achieved her purpose, darts from the smithy of Hephaestus on Olympus, as a hawk (ἴρηξ ὥς, Σ 616). Ajax, threatening, says that Hector will pray to have horses swifter than hawks in flight (Ν 819). Achilles pursues Hector as a hawk on the mountain swoops after a timid pigeon (Χ 139). At ν 86, the Phaeacian ship, conveying Odysseus to Ithaca, cleft the waves so swiftly that not even a hawk could keep pace with it. Patroclus pressed through the foremost fighters of the Achaeans upon the Lycians and Trojans, like a hawk which puts to flight jackdaws and starlings (Π 582), and, on the other hand, after the death of Patroclus, the Achaeans flee before Aeneas and Hector as a cloud (νέφος) of starlings or jackdaws flee before a hawk "which bears death to small birds" (Ρ 757).

The *harpé* (ἅρπη, Τ 350,—connected with ἁρπάζω?) is a

Harpé. long-winged clear-voiced (τανυπτέρυγι λιγυφώνῳ) bird to which Athena is likened as she leaps down from Olympus through the aether. It is thought to be a bird of prey.

Vultures (γῦπες, Δ 237) are mentioned by Homer seven times, but receive from him no epithets. They feed upon

Vultures. the bodies of the slain (as Λ 162, Π 836), in which they are associated with dogs (as Σ 271, Χ 42), except at λ 578, where two vultures, one on either hand, tear the liver of Tityus in Hades,—the liver being to the Greeks the seat of the passions, and he being punished for an assault upon Leto.

---

[1] ἴρηξ, Ν 62 ; κίρκος, Χ 139,—probably originally an epithet from its flight in a circle.—The κίρκος possibly may be a species of ἴρηξ, appearing in apposition with it in ν 87 ; ἴρηξ seems like a general term for hawk.

The *scōps* (σκῶπες, ε 66) is not identified. It nests in the alders and black poplars of Calypso's island, with the hawk and sea-crow.[1]

Scōps.

The *chalcis* (χαλκίδα, Ξ 291), as it is called by gods, or *cymindis* (κύμινδιν, Ξ 291), as it is called by men, is also unidentified. Sleep, *Hypnos*, hides like to this clear-voiced (λιγυρῇ) bird of the mountains in the branches of a fir tree, to await the result of Hera's interview with Zeus.[2]

Chalcis.

The crane (γέρανος, B 460, Γ 3, O 692) appears three times in the poems,—with geese and long-necked swans, on the banks of the Caÿster, or attacked by an eagle as they feed by the side of a river; and the clamor of the advancing Trojan army is compared with that of cranes as these flee from winter and ineffable storm to the streams of Oceanus, bearing death and fate to the Pygmies. This is said to be the earliest notice in literature of birds of passage, and the Plain of the Caÿster is declared to be one of their natural stations on their route. Some have thought the stork (which is not named by Homer) to be included in the designation of cranes.

Crane.

The swan (κύκνος, B 460, O 692) is mentioned twice, in an identical line,—only with geese and cranes, as detailed in the foregoing paragraph. Its epithet is *long-necked* (δουλιχοδείρων).

Swan.

Athena sends a heron (ἐρωδιός, K 274) as an omen on their right to Odysseus and Diomed as they set out by night as scouts into the Trojan camp. They do not see it, but hear its croak.[3]

Heron.

The sea-gull (λάρῳ, ε 51) is mentioned once. Hermes on his journey to the island of Calypso moves over the waves like a gull which in seeking fish dips its thick plumage into the briny flood.

Sea-gull.

---

[1] Aristotle thought this to be a night-bird, *H.A.* ix. 592 b; Pliny, *N.H.* x. 49. 70, did not know the bird. Scholars have commonly called it an owl,—a screech owl or a horned owl. Bérard derives the name from the Semitic, and thinks it a vulture.

[2] Aristotle, *H.A.* ix. 615 b, thinks it to be a mountain bird as large as a hawk, but says it is not often seen. He says that the Ionians call it *cymindis*, but may refer only to the Ionian Epic. Others have thought it a species of owl.

[3] Sir Charles Fellowes saw herons on the Trojan plain (*Asia Minor*, 56).

The sea-crow (κορῶναι) appears in the poems thrice. It nests in alders, black poplars, and cypresses on Calypso's island (ε 66),—being called *of the sea* (εἰνάλιαι, ε 67) and *tongue-stretching* (τανύγλωσσοι). Twice, but in an identical line (μ 418, ξ 308), the comrades of Odysseus on their shipwreck, as they are borne on the waves, are likened to sea-crows.

Sea-crow.

The *aethyia* (αἴθυια, ε [337], 353) is clearly some kind of a diver. After advising Odysseus on his raft in the midst of the storm, the sea-nymph Ino, like this bird, sinks beneath the wave.[1]

Aethyia.

The *cēx* (κήξ, ο 479) is another undefined sea bird. The nurse of the child Eumaeus falls into the hold of the ship, as the *cēx* of the sea. Some have thought this to be a sea-hen, others a gull; while others have brought it into connexion with the halcyon, since the κηΰξ was thought to be the male halcyon; and others think it originally not a "specific bird-name, but a mystical term connected with the halcyon-myth."

Cēx.

The *halcyon* (ἀλκυόνος, I 563) is mentioned but once by Homer. According to the story of the old Phoenix, Alcyone received this name because her mother suffered the grief of a halcyon in the loss of her husband. The poet does not show knowledge of the "halcyon days" at the winter solstice.

Halcyon.

The sparrow (στρουθοῖο, B 311) is said to be the most common bird in Greece, as well as in other countries, but it is mentioned by the Homeric poet in only one passage. On their way against Troy, while the Achaeans were sacrificing at Aulis, a serpent devoured the eight young of a sparrow and the mother-bird herself, as they were resting on the branch of a great plane-tree, and the seer Calchas interpreted the portent to mean that they should fight for nine years and should capture Troy on the tenth. Surely the poet did not expect his hearer to be disturbed by the unusually large number of the sparrow's young. This must have been part of the portent. Aristotle was quoted by Athenaeus (391 F) as saying that the sparrow might have eight young.

Sparrow.

[1] Aristotle, *H.A.* v. 9, says that the αἴθυια lays her eggs in early spring, while the λάρος lays eggs in summer.

The jackdaw (κολοιούς, Π 583, Ρ 755,—*brawler?*) and
starling (ψῆρας, Π 583, Ρ 755) are named together
without epithets as fleeing before a swift hawk. *Jackdaw.*
So fled both the Trojans before Patroclus, and the Achaeans
before Aeneas and Hector.

The nightingale (ἀηδών, τ 518,—connected with ἀείδω, *sing?*)
sings in the thick foliage of the trees at the opening of
spring, pouring forth an ever-varying strain in
lamentation for her dear child Itylus, whom she *Nightingale.*
has unwittingly slain. The epithet χλωρηΐς seems best
interpreted as *yellow-throated, brownish-throated.*

The swallow (χελιδών) is named twice. The sound of the
bowstring as Odysseus twanged it, to try if his old bow
were still whole, is likened to the note of a swallow
(φ 411). And after encouraging Odysseus in his *Swallow.*
slaughter of Penelope's suitors, Athena "like to a swallow"
(χελιδόνι εἰκέλη, χ 240) rose and sat on the cross-timbers of
the ceiling.

The thrush (κίχλαι, χ 468) is caught in snares. The bird
struggling to escape serves as a comparison for the unfaithful
serving-women of Penelope, hanging by the neck *Thrush.*
in punishment for their misdeeds. It is called
wing-stretching (τανυσίπτεροι). That it is snared in nets,
implies its use for food, and in later times it certainly was
considered a dainty.

The dove or pigeon (πέλεια, Φ 493 ; πελειάδες, Λ 634,—
probably named from its ash color) is *timid* (τρήρωνες,[1] μ 63,
cf. τρέω and *tremble*).[2] Like the thrush, it is *Dove.*
caught in snares. No domesticated pigeons are
mentioned. The gait of the goddesses Athena and Hera
as they come upon the field of battle,—Athena wearing the
martial dress of Zeus,—is likened to that of doves, their
feminine mincing steps probably being contrasted with the
long strides of the warriors (E 778). The chief enemy of
the pigeon naturally is the hawk. Thus Achilles rushes upon
Hector as a hawk upon a pigeon ; the pigeon seeks to

---

[1] This epithet becomes a noun in the compound πολυτρήρων, *rich in doves,*
applied to Thisbé (B 502) and to Messé (B 582).

[2] The word φάσσα, *wood-pigeon,* appears in O 238 in the epithet of the hawk,
φασσοφόνῳ, *pigeon-killer.*

flee, but the hawk with a shrill shriek darts upon it again and again (X 139). In the conflict of the divinities on the Trojan plain, Artemis flees from Hera as a pigeon flees from a hawk into a hole in the rock, and escapes (Φ 493). The eagle, too, is an enemy to be feared ; as an omen of warning to the suitors of Penelope an eagle appears to them on their left, bearing a timid dove (υ 243). Nestor's golden cup was adorned by figures of doves (*cf.* page 297). In Homeric times a live pigeon was used as a mark for sportsmen with the bow (Ψ 853).

The bat (νυκτερίς, μ 433, ω 6) is named manifestly from its nocturnal habits. Odysseus, after his shipwreck, holds
Bat. to the tree which overhangs Charybdis, like a bat, being unable to rest his foot on any support, from one tide to the next. The souls of Penelope's suitors go to Hades squeaking [1] like bats which in a great cave hang together, when one of the number loses its hold on the rock.

The serpent (δράκοντα, M 202 = ὄφιν, M 208) is *blood red* (φοινήεντα, M 202 ; δαφοινός, B 308) and *wriggling* (αἰόλον,
Serpent. M 208). The epithet *dark blue, dark* (κυάνεος, Λ 39), applied to the serpent represented on the baldric of Agamemnon, may refer either to the material of the representation or to the living creature represented. The portent which predicted the length of the siege of Troy was a serpent at Aulis which devoured eight young sparrows and the mother bird, and then was turned to stone (B 308). At the opening of the first day of battle of the *Iliad*, Paris is striding before the ranks as a champion of the Trojans when he catches sight of Menelaus, whose wife he has carried from Sparta, and he starts back as a man at sight of a serpent, in the glens of a mountain, starts back,—trembling seizes his limbs and paleness comes over his cheeks (Γ 33). Near the close of the last day of battle, Hector awaits Achilles as a serpent on the mountain, having eaten poisonous herbs, filled with dire wrath, awaits a man, coiling about

---

[1] For the squeaking of ghosts, *cf.* "The sheeted dead did squeak and gibber in the Roman streets," *Ham.* i. 1. 115; "ghosts did shriek and squeal about the street," *Julius Caesar*, ii. 2. 24. Herodotus, iv. 183, says that the Troglodytes do not have a language like other men, *but squeak as bats* (τετρίγασιν κατάπερ αἱ νυκτερίδες).

its hole (X 93),—in which incident the herbs seem both to have maddened the serpent and to have provided its venom. At M 202, an eagle bearing to its young a serpent (its hereditary foe), is bitten by this serpent in the neck, and forced to let it fall into the midst of the Trojan throng, to whom it comes as an omen of Zeus. The sea-god Proteus takes the form of a serpent, among other shapes, in his endeavor to escape from the arms of Menelaus (δ 457). The Chimaera had a serpent for a tail (Z 181). No species of serpent is named except the destructive-minded water-snake (ὀλοόφρονος ὕδρου, B 723), of which the bite caused the wound of Philoctetes.

The bee (μέλισσαι, M 167) is mentioned three times by Homer; honey (μέλι, Λ 631) is named seven times, and enters into several compounds. The Achaean soldiers, coming to the place of assembly, are *Bee.* likened to swarms of huddling (ἀδινάων, B 87) bees ever coming afresh from a hollow rock, and flying in clusters to the spring flowers. The spirit of the Lapithae in defense of the gate of the Achaean camp, is compared to that of wasps or bees who have their nests by a rocky road, and do not desert their homes but fight with hunters in defense of their young (M 167). In a cave by the seashore of Ithaca, bees store their honey in jars of the nymphs (ν 106). Honey served the ancient Greeks as sugar. It was an ingredient of a posset mixed for Nestor (Λ 631) and another prepared by Circe (κ 234), and Aphrodite brought up the daughters of Pandareüs on cheese, honey, and wine (ν 69). Nestor's "voice flowed sweeter than honey from his tongue" (A 249). Achilles wishes an end to anger, "which urges even a wise man to rage," and "which is sweeter than dripping honey" (Σ 109). Honey was among the offerings at the funeral piles of Patroclus (Ψ 170) and of Achilles (ω 68), and mixed (with milk) is poured as a libation to the dead (μελικρήτῳ, κ 519). Sleep is *honey-hearted* (μελίφρων, B 34), and the same epithet is applied to wine at Z 264. Beeswax (κηρός, *cf. cera*) is mentioned in only one connexion: in accordance with Circe's injunction, Odysseus stops the ears of his comrades with wax, that they may not hear and be charmed by the song of the Sirens (μ 173). Hives of bees are familiar to Hesiod

(*Theogony*, 598), but in Homer's time the bees seem to have stored their honey in crevices of the rock.

The term fly (μυῖα) seems to be general, including gnats, common house flies, and carrion flies. As the Achaean forces

Fly.

advance to meet the Trojans on the first day of battle, their number is compared to that of flies about the farm buildings in spring time when the milk fills the pans (B 469). When the Trojan Pandarus treacherously shoots at Menelaus during the truce, Athena keeps the arrow from Menelaus as a mother keeps a fly from her child lying in sweet slumber (Δ 131). At P 570, Athena puts in Menelaus the spirit of a fly which though often driven away seeks to bite a man, for "sweet to it is human blood." Achilles expresses to his mother the fear that flies may enter the wounds of the dead Patroclus and beget maggots (εὐλάς, T 25); and as she beholds Hector's corpse dragged away behind the chariot of Achilles, to the tents of the Achaeans, Andromache closes her lament by saying, "but now will the wriggling worms devour thee, when the dogs shall have sated themselves on thee" (X 509).

Ares applies the term *dog-fly* (κυνάμυια) to Athena,— apparently as combining the impudence of a dog with the

Dog-fly.

bold pertinacity of a fly (Φ 394), and a few verses later Hera uses it of Aphrodite (Φ 421). This word (in the form κυνόμυια) was used by the Septuagint translators of the Old Testament for the flies which formed one of the plagues of Egypt; but it seems to have been the name of no insect in Homer's time.

The gadfly (οἶστρος, χ 300) appears once in a comparison. When Athena raises her aegis in the palace of Odysseus,

Gadfly.

during the conflict between Odysseus and Penelope's suitors, the suitors flee as cows flee before the "quick-moving (αἰόλος) gadfly in the spring time, when the days grow long."

The wasp (σφῆκες, M 167, Π 259), as we might expect, is a symbol of irritability. It is *slender-waisted*, or more

Wasp.

literally *quick moving at the middle* (μέσον αἰόλος, M 167). Wasps, like bees, build their nests by the wayside in rocky places, and defend their young against hunters. Boys are wont to tease them, and so they consider every wayfarer to be an enemy, even if he disturbs them unwillingly.

The borers (ἶπες, φ 395) are larvae of a beetle which eat wood and horn, and so might have injured the *Borers.* bow of Odysseus during his absence of twenty years.

The cicada (τεττίγεσσιν, Γ 151) was appreciated through classical antiquity more highly than in modern times. The Trojan elders on the tower by the Scaean Gate *Cicadae.* of their city, watching the armies on the plain below, are compared to cicadae " which in the forest sit upon a tree and utter their lily-like voice."

Locusts (ἀκρίδες, Φ 12) are represented as fleeing to a river in order to escape fire. Apparently the farmers have been burning the grass and herbage in order to *Locusts.* destroy the locusts, which have been driven along until they came to a stream, and have fallen into that.

The flea may have been the undetermined insect (κυνοραιστής, *dog-destroyer* or *dog-plague*) which distresses the old dog Argos as he lies neglected on a dunghill (ρ 300).

The only worm mentioned by the Homeric poet is the common earth-worm (σκώληξ, N 654), to which a fallen warrior, stretched upon the ground, is likened.

CHAPTER XIV

OLYMPUS AND THE GODS

In several respects this is the most difficult and perplexing chapter of Homeric antiquities.[1] With regard to religion as in other matters, scholars have sought to find in the Homeric poems the earliest condition of society to be known in Hellas, or at least a stage which should be recognized as intermediate between the earliest and the later stages. Yet, while the poems give a fairly consistent account of a system of divinities and a body of beliefs with regard to the state of the dead, they offer no intimation of certain other beliefs and associated practises which existed not only among other Indo-European peoples in very early times but also among the Greeks themselves in later ages. For example, the poems contain no trace of a belief in fetishes and of the worship of natural objects,—sticks or unwrought stones,—yet these were worshipped and dreaded as the embodiment or seat of supernatural powers in Hellas a thousand years later, and no one believes that these primitive superstitions had their rise between the age of Homer and that of Augustus. At Cnosus Mr. Evans has found[2] a shrine with fetish images of natural formation which he thinks present in most primitive guise " the traditional Cretan cult of Mother Rhea and the infant Zeus,"—of an age far earlier than the Homeric poems or the Trojan war. The only trees which are in any way sacred in Homer are an

A Difficult Chapter.

No Fetishes.

---

[1] Nägelsbach, *Homerische Theologie*, 3te Ausgabe, 1884, is antiquated but not superseded.

[2] *Annual of British School at Athens*, xi. 11.

"oak of Zeus"[1] which served as a land-mark on the plain of Troy (Z 237), and the "oak of Zeus" at Dodona (ξ 328), but nothing indicates that either was thought to be the dwelling place of the god. Hesiod's thirty thousand guardian angels (*Works*, 252), also, find no place in the Homeric poems.

Further, long after the Homeric age indications remain that in the early period the Greeks worshipped local divinities, and that no one god had secured preëminence over all the rest ; whereas in Homer, Zeus is absolute in his authority, and secure on *No Local Divinities.* his throne. No one doubts his supreme power, except the savage Cyclopes, and even the Cyclops Polyphemus claims to be Poseidon's son, and thus belongs to this dynasty. In later times Athena was more important at Athens than Zeus, who had no shrine within the wall of the Acropolis, and Poseidon was chief in Ionia, Apollo was preëminent at Delphi if not in Sparta, and the Graces were queens at Minyan Orchomenos, but these all were far from being local deities. That the Homeric Hera is particularly fond of Sparta, Argos, and Mycenae (Δ 52), and that Ares has special connexions with Thrace (N 301, θ 361), and Aphrodite with Cyprus (θ 362, E 422), does not constitute them local divinities in the ordinary sense of the word. Hephaestus is said to have been cared for by the Lemnians, when Zeus hurled him from heaven (A 593), and Lemnos was to him the "dearest of all lands" (θ 284), but, though he is comparatively unimportant, his worship is not restricted to that island, and his workshop is not yet established there. The chief hint of local deities in Homer is found in the statement that before the first battle of the *Iliad*, "one of the Greeks offered sacrifices to one, and another to another of the ever-living gods" (B 400), while Agamemnon sacrificed to Zeus. But this may indicate only a system of individual patron saints, rather than that all the Greeks from a single district offered sacrifice to the same divinity. If the latter were true, Agamemnon as coming from Mycenae would be expected to sacrifice to Argive Hera. Odysseus and Diomed, for instance, though one from Ithaca and the other from Argos, both worship Athena, and Nestor offers sacrifices to

[1] Or chestnut. See page 340.

Poseidon, but Athena was certainly not a local divinity of Ithaca or of Argos, any more than Poseidon was the local god of Pylus.   On the other hand, the river-gods,—as the Scamander (Φ 212), the Spercheüs (Ψ 142), and the Enipeus (λ 238),—and the mountain-nymphs (ὀρεστιάδες Ζ 420), which may fairly be called local deities, have too little influence on the action of men to be called divinities in the strict sense.

Again, the scholar finds in Homer slight indication of apotheosis or any worship of the dead or of sacrifices at *No Worship of the Dead.* their tombs,—although the graves at Mycenae, with openings to convey the offerings as directly as possible to the corpse, bear witness to the existence of such worship there long before Homer's day, and similar customs continued through the classical period.[1]

Finally, no monstrous deities are worshipped by the *No Monstrous Deities.* Homeric Greeks or Trojans, such as the horse-headed Demeter of Phigalia, and the ass-headed Mycenaean divinities, and the stag-headed or boar-headed Cretan figures.[2]   No indications of any sort of totemism are found in the Homeric poems.

Of the origin of the Homeric system of gods, the poems give little information.   Whether these gods were originally *Origin of the Gods.* personifications of the forces of nature, or were developed from fetish-worship, or were introduced from other peoples, the poems assume and report them as simply existing, without any question as to the past.   The poems show little interest in the origin or even the early history of either men or gods.   Of few families

---

[1] The Sirens, as we shall see, have no apparent connexion with the souls of the dead.

[2] Paus. viii. 42. 4 ; *Journal of Hellenic Studies*, xiv. 81 ; *Annual of British School at Athens*, xi. 18.   Scylla (μ 85) cannot be ‘cited as an exception, nor the Chimaera (Ζ 181).   Both were composite monsters, but neither was worshipped.—To the four particulars mentioned above in which the Homeric religion differs from what is expected on the basis of modern investigations with regard to primitive religion, some scholars would add two : (1) the absence of human sacrifices, such as that of Iphigenia at Aulis by Agamemnon, according to the Cyprian epic ; and (2) the absence of mysteries, like those at Eleusis or Samothrace, or of the Cabiri at Thebes.   But the former of these has to do primarily with worship, and as to the latter we know too little of their origin and their prevalence, to wonder that Homer does not mention them, though our poet reasonably might be expected to know some of them.

does the poet give any " family tree." If Cronus ever reigned before the Homeric Zeus, no details of his sway are noted. Homer presents no such theogony or cosmogony as that of Hesiod, and troubles himself with no theodicy. He is no prophet, like Hesiod, with a burdened soul. Hera seldom appears in Homer with the traits of the special guardian of women, which connect her with the Roman Juno. If Hermes ever was a wind-god, our poet shows no consciousness of this. If Aphrodite and Heracles were imported from Phoenicia, or if their cults were even deeply influenced by Oriental beliefs and worship, the poet considers them fully naturalized and no foreigners, and nothing Oriental appears in his mention of them. However much the early Greeks may have been affected by the religious beliefs and customs of the Phoenicians and Egyptians and other nations, they so assimilated all these foreign elements that these can no longer be separated clearly from what was native.

The difficulty of the study of Homeric religion is greatly increased since the agreement of facts in this field is not nearly so complete as appears at first sight and has been thought. Here are great inconsistencies, *Incon-sistencies.* though not such as to aid as yet in the analysis of the poems into earlier and later elements, while the philological discussion of the composition of the poems has been unfruitful for religion and mythology. For example: in general the realm of Hades lies beneath the earth (Θ 16). On the last day of battle, Aïdoneus seems to be immediately beneath the Trojan plain, and fears that the earth may be torn open and expose his murky realms to the light of day (Υ 61 ; see page 457). But in the eleventh book of the *Odyssey*, the Ithacan hero reaches Hades not by descending through a cavern, like Heracles at Taenarus and elsewhere, on his expedition to bring up the dog Cerberus, but by a voyage to the far west (λ *init.* ; see page 46). Olympus, in general, is a lofty mountain, on the summit of which the gods dwell, but again it seems nearly equivalent to heaven (Θ *init.*).[1] Hephaestus in the *Odyssey* has Aphrodite to wife (θ 268), but in the *Iliad* his

---

[1] Aristarchus held that the poet was faithful to the former usage ; but clearly he did not persuade all his contemporaries. Lehrs, *Arist.*[3] 163. See note on p. 418.

wife is one of the Graces (Σ 382). Poseidon claims equal
rights with Zeus on earth, and superiority to him on the
sea (O 189), but he is sent by Zeus to serve the Trojan
king Laomedon for a year (Φ 444), in which time of
service he builds the city-wall of which he later boasts
(H 452), and he, as a younger brother, unharnesses the
horses of Zeus on the latter's return to Olympus (Θ 440).
The winds are in the keeping of Aeolus (κ 21), but each
divinity can command a favorable breeze,—as Apollo for the
Greeks on their return from Chrysa (Λ 479), Athena for
Telemachus on his voyage to Pylus (β 420), and even lesser
divinities, as Calypso and Circe for Odysseus (ε 268, λ 6);
while Hera causes a storm for the discomfiture of Heracles
(Ξ 254), and Poseidon rouses all the winds to wreck the
craft of Odysseus (ε 292). Near the close of the action of
the *Iliad*, again, the winds are feasting in the home of
Zephyrus,—apparently in Thrace (Ψ 200, *cf.* 230),—and
each seems to have independence; Iris tells Zephyrus and
Boreas that Achilles desires their services, and will give
them beautiful sacrifices, and they set out at once to fan
the flames of Patroclus's pyre.

The Greeks never had a generally accepted body of dogmatic theology. Their priests had no office of instruction
or exhortation, and were in no sense teachers of
No Dogmatic the people. They were bound only to maintain
Theology. and perform the appointed traditional ritual service
at the altars which they served. No Greek was liable to
be " cast out of the synagogue " or punished in any way for
holding views different from those of the rest of his tribe or
nation, though he must not *teach* what might interfere with
the standing order of the state. Naturally, then, the views
of the people were not settled with regard to the gods, and
the expressions of the poet Pindar with regard to the future
life are not altogether consistent with each other, but we
expect in the verses of no single poet such differences as
have been pointed out in the Homeric poems. That both
Greeks and Trojans worship the same divinities, is part of
a general question which is touched elsewhere.

The Homeric divinities, however, in spite of all inconsistencies, form a fairly well-defined company of clearly drawn

characters.   Men made their gods in their own image, and the society on the Homeric *Olympus* is the counterpart of that on earth.[1]   The life of the gods is a reflec- *Men made* tion of that of men.   The most realistic picture *Gods in their* of an Homeric smithy is that of Hephaestus, *own Image.* who on being summoned to meet Thetis, gathers up his tools and puts them away in a chest, sponges off his face, arms, and neck, and dons his tunic (Σ 412),—just as any human blacksmith would do.   Homeric gods are not free from human frailties,—their subjects have no conception of a Being "infinite in power, knowledge, wisdom, holiness, justice, goodness, and truth."   Though kindly, the gods are not always patient and reasonable.   In their needs, appetites, and passions, they are not far removed from human beings ; indeed the morality of the Olympian gods is on a lower plane than that of the best families on earth, and we cannot wonder that Plato would not have the Homeric gods presented as models for imitation in his ideal State.   Hermes appears as a sort of patron saint of thievery (τ 396), and in general the motives of the gods are no loftier or more unselfish than those of men.   The duties of men to the gods are ritualistic rather than ethical.   A man has a fairly free conscience as regards the divinities if he offers sacrifices at proper times, and does not abuse the god's name by perjury (Γ 279).   Zeus warns Aegisthus (α 37) that he will be punished for his adultery and murder,—*i.e.* vengeance will come upon him from Orestes, the son of the murdered Agamemnon,—but the propriety of punishment being inflicted by the gods for such crimes, does not occur to him.   Orestes is not held to be the "instrument" of Apollo, but simply

[1] The criticisms of Xenophanes in the sixth century B.C. are familiar (*Frag.* 11, Diels) : that Homer and Hesiod ascribed to the gods all actions which are a blame and reproach among men, as theft, adultery, and deceit.   Xenophanes declared that there was but one god,—and he not in human form,—saying that if cattle and horses could paint pictures they would represent the gods as in their own image ; and just so, and with no more reason, men had represented the gods in human form (*Frag.* 15).   In Plato's time and later, these Homeric stories of the gods were explained as allegorical.   A third of a century ago, they were explained as nature-myths, which made moral character for them impossible.   For the relation of the religion to the morality of the Greeks, see Packard, *Studies in Greek Thought* ; L. Schmidt, *Ethik der Griechen.*

avenges his own wrong. But though "commandments" are few and the gods lack holiness, yet, after all, "evil deeds do not prosper" (θ 329), "the blessed gods do not love wicked deeds" (ξ 83), and the good are rewarded (τ 109).[1] Penelope is assured that her "son will return, since he is not an offender in the eyes of the gods" (δ 807). Gods visit men in disguise, like the good Haroun al Raschid, that they may observe their lawlessness or righteous spirit (ρ 485). Zeus even sends storms and floods in his anger at men who give "crooked judgments" ($\sigma\kappa o\lambda\iota\grave{a}\varsigma$ $\theta\acute{\epsilon}\mu\iota\sigma\tau a\varsigma$, II 387) in the assembly. Penelope, at first disbelieving the message of the return of Odysseus, thinks some one of the immortals has slain her suitors, angry at their insolence and evil deeds (ψ 64).[2] The gods are wont to support the right, but, no more than mortal kings, are they bound to have wrong punished and to make right prevail. They are influenced by caprice, personal preference, and by gratitude for services performed. Hera gives no reason for her hatred of Troy and her love for Sparta and Argos (Δ 26, 51). If we follow the later story, and suppose her to be incensed by the preference of Paris for the beauty of Aphrodite, certainly the desire for ideal justice was not uppermost in her mind. Nothing in the poems supports the modern suggestion that she was moved simply by her sense of wrong. If she was so keen for right, why did she leave the punishment of Aegisthus to the mortal Orestes? The punishment, when rendered, might be out of all proportion to the offense.[3] When the Achaean army suffers from the

---

[1] For a brief discussion of the ethics of the Homeric Greeks, see the close of this chapter. The moral standard of the *Odyssey* has been thought to mark an advance on that of the *Iliad*, but perhaps this apparent difference is due to the circumstances of the two actions.

[2] *Cf.* χ 414, ω 352, a 46, β 66, 143.

[3] Even in the book of *Job* (ii. 10) we read, "Shall we receive good at the hand of God and shall we not receive evil?"—"The idea of God [among the rude tribes of Syria] is very vague, but he seems to be mainly an enlarged edition of a Bedouin sheik; that is of a beneficent but capricious despot, . . . somewhat more powerful, of course, than their own head-man, but in other respects of much the same style and character" (Curtiss, *Primitive Semitic Religion*, p. 67). "In the belief of the ruder Semitic peoples of to-day, God may mislead man" (*l.c.* p. 69). "Misfortune comes not because a man or woman is guilty of some sin, but because God is arbitrarily angry" (*l.c.* p. 220).

plague, and Achilles calls an assembly to consider what shall be done, the question is not what drug can be found as a specific for the pestilence, but how the god is to be appeased ; and not what sin has been committed, but whether some vow has been left unperformed or some sacrifice unoffered (A 64). The plague was sent, not because of a common act of all the people (like the plague which destroyed 14,700 of the people of Israel, because of their murmuring, *Numbers* xvi. 49), but because Agamemnon had refused to give up for ransom the captive daughter of a priest of Apollo, in spite of the fact that this priest had presented reverence for his god, in addition to boundless gifts, as a motive for granting his request. The offense was a lack of respect,— not a moral crime. The god would not have been offended if Chryseïs had not happened to be the daughter of his priest. The act of Apollo must have been opposed to the will of Hera and Athena, and Zeus does not seem to have been consulted in the matter. Perhaps he might not have been interested in it. The chief motive urged by the old priest, in his desire for vengeance, is the services which he had rendered to Apollo, in offering sacrifices and making shrines,—not the cruelty of Agamemnon in keeping a girl captive.

The Homeric divinities are all anthropomorphic, and each has his own physical characteristics, though they are able to change their forms at pleasure. Agamemnon is said to have the head and eyes of Zeus, the *Anthropomorphic.* girth of Ares, and the chest of Poseidon (B 478). The gods are of what corresponds very nearly to human flesh and blood ; and Athena's helmet is said, with remarkable hyperbole, to be fitted to the infantry of a hundred towns (E 744). Diomed wounds both Aphrodite and Ares (E 339, 858). From Aphrodite flows immortal blood,—*ichor*, " such blood as flows in the veins of the blessed gods, for they do not eat bread nor drink wine." Ares, when wounded by Diomed, shouts " as nine thousand or ten thousand men shout in battle " (E 860,—Poseidon gives a similar shout at Ξ 148) ; and when overthrown by Athena he sprawls over seven *pelethra* of land (nearly two acres, Φ 407).[1]

_____
[1] See page 245.

His wound is soothed by a pain-killing herb. Clearly the gods are not removed from physical pains and indignities. Ares complains that if he had not fled swiftly he would have been left among the dead, helpless (E 885). He had had similar experiences before, having been imprisoned by mortals in a bronze jar for a full year (E 387). Hera and Hades himself had been wounded by arrows from the bow of Heracles (E 392). The clothing of the gods corresponds to that of men, and Athena changes her ordinary raiment for the armor of Zeus when she goes to the field of battle (E 734), and takes a helmet and a light shield. She is not so incorporeal that she cannot feel pain, nor is her divine body proof against human spears. The gods slip off their sandals on reaching Olympus, and put them on when they go on a journey (Ω 340). In a passage which more nearly resembles a burlesque than any other in the poems,—the conflict of the gods on the plain of Troy (Φ 385-513),— Athena hits Ares in the neck with a large stone, and overthrows him ; Aphrodite then leads him from the battle, but Athena follows the two and with a blow of her "thick hand" casts both upon the ground. A few verses later, Hera boxes the ears of Artemis, and sends her in tears from the field of battle. In the same episode, Poseidon reminds Apollo that they two were sent down by Zeus to serve Priam's father Laomedon for a year,—that the one built a wall for the city and the other tended flocks, but that at the expiration of their term of service, Laomedon had dismissed them without the pay which had been stipulated, and with the threat to bind them hand and foot, and send them to distant lands to be sold as slaves, or he would lop off their ears for them (Φ 444). Apollo had rendered a similar service to Admetus of Pherae, tending his flocks and herds (B 766, cf. Ψ 383). Hera declares that she herself *sweat*, and that her horses were wearied in arousing the Achaeans against the Trojans (Δ 27). The test which Zeus proposes for the comparative strength of himself and the rest of the gods is purely physical,—it is a "tug of war." They are to take hold of one end of a golden chain, and he of the other, to make trial whether they can draw him from heaven to the plain, or he shall lift them together with earth and sea (Θ 19). Of course the gods were far mightier than men. Apollo easily with his feet breaks down the Achaean ramparts (O 362), just as a child destroys the walls of sand which he has built in play on the seashore. Olympus trembles when Zeus nods (A· 530), or when Hera moves uneasily on her throne (Θ 199).

The gods need sleep and food as truly as any mortal. After his promise to Thetis that he would honor Achilles, Zeus lies awake, in anxious care, when all the rest, both gods and men, are asleep (B 1); *Gods need Sleep.* and while Hera sleeps by his side he commissions a delusive Dream to go to Agamemnon. Once during his slumber, long before the action of the *Iliad* (Ξ 252), Hera raised a storm, and drove Heracles from his course, and again, while he slept, Poseidon drove the Trojans in confusion from the Achaean camp (Ξ 359). Zeus and his court are sorely troubled by the threat of the sun-god to descend to Hades (μ 383), and they bid him still to "give light among immortals and for mortal men." The Dawn (*Eos*, T 1), "in russet mantle clad" "arises from the streams of Oceanus to bear light to immortals and to mortals." The divinities have separate homes (A 606, Ξ 166, Σ 369, 376, θ 268), but gather frequently,—apparently each day,—in the great hall of Zeus, just as earthly nobles assemble to feast in the palace of their king (A 533, Δ 1, O 84, α 27). They have no family life in the modern sense, —there are no children among them,—yet their community life is distinctly patriarchal. Zeus is *Patriarchal Life.* eminently "father of both gods and men" (πατὴρ ἀνδρῶν τε θεῶν τε, A 544), though not in a literal sense; he is the head of the family, the clan. The relationships of the gods to each other are not always clear. Zeus is both husband and brother of Hera at Δ 58, but here alone specifically. Both are children of Cronus, but Cronus is a very indistinct personality. Aphrodite is not yet born of the sea; she is the daughter of Zeus (θ 308) and Dione (E 370). Hermes has no father, and is the son of Maea only at ξ 435; apparently he is not yet the Argus-slayer (in spite of his epithet *Argeïphontes*), and few myths are known with regard to him. The myth of Athena as having sprung fully armed from the head of Zeus, is not Homeric, but she is the daughter of Zeus (E 875), and no mother is mentioned for her. Hephaestus is son of Hera (A 572). Ares is son of Zeus and Hera (E 892). Apollo is the son of Zeus and Leto (A 9).

The gods desire food and drink, and Hebe serves as waitress (Δ 2), though she loses no dignity by this service.

Ambrosia and Nectar. Ambrosia as food appears only in the *Odyssey*,— as served at Calypso's table (ε 93, 199), as brought by the Pleiades to Zeus (μ 63), and as a simile in words of Polyphemus (ι 359).[1] The relation between ambrosia and immortality is not made clear,—whether, for instance, a man would live as long as the gods if he too had such a diet, which seems to be Pindar's view (*Ol.* i. 62). When Calypso remarks that Hermes does not often visit her home, he, having satisfied his appetite (ἤραρε θυμὸν ἐδωδῇ, ε 95), replies with a question,—"Who of his own accord would make such a journey far from the cities of mortals who offer sacrifices to the gods?" The savor of the sacrifices rises to heaven (A 317) and is pleasing to the gods,[2] though it is not represented as their food. Evidently the poet was far from thinking of the gods as incorporeal, and his position is only a trifle less materialistic than the view burlesqued by Aristophanes (*Birds*, 183) in the suggestion that by interposing a barrier between gods and men the birds could starve the divinities.[3] The gods go to feast with the Aethio-

---

[1] In the *Iliad*, ambrosia is used as fodder for the horses of Ares (E 777), or is an unguent (Ξ 170, Π 670). Leaf (on B 19) follows Verrall in understanding this as *ambergris*, ἀμβρόσιος, *fragrant*, from a Semitic word, and having no connexion with ἄμβροτοι in the sense *immortal*. Roscher held that ambrosia and nectar were preparations of honey (*Lex.* i. 280).—The hair of Zeus, the sandals of Athena, the fodder of Ares's horses, and the robes of Aphrodite and Hera are "ambrosial" (A 529, α 97, E 369, 338, Ξ 178), and Helen's gown is "nectarean" (Γ 385). Aphrodite anoints the corpse of Patroclus with ambrosial oil (Ψ 187), and Athena cleanses Penelope's face with "ambrosial beauty, such as Aphrodite anoints herself withal" (σ 193).

[2] A 66; and ἡδεῖαν, Θ 550, if that which is quoted as Homeric in the Pseudo-Platonic *Alcibiades* is good evidence. Not improbably the meat of sacrifice was burnt as the most effective means of conveying it to the gods. Similarly clothing was to be burned for the ghost of Hector (X 512), and part of Hector's ransom was to be conveyed to the shade of Patroclus (Ω 595). The Chinese burn prayers written on paper, in order to convey them most effectually to their gods.

[3] Jehovah also "smelled a sweet savor," according to *Genesis* viii. 21. Is this only that he is gratified by the honor paid him?

pians (A 423, Ψ 207, α 22), and Alcinoüs says that the gods feast with the Phaeacians, seated by their side (η 203), and appear before their eyes as they offer hecatombs. Apparently at these feasts gods and men partook of the same food. That a member of the Trojan royal family, Ganymede, should be a cupbearer for the gods, does not seem unreasonable.[1] Athena, in human guise, eats and drinks human food and wine (α 139, γ 40). No food is cooked or otherwise prepared by the gods, however.

Children are born to the gods by mortal women,[2]—Heracles and Dionysus may serve as examples,—and Aphrodite is enamoured of the Trojan Anchises and bears to him Aeneas (E 313). Sarpedon is a son of Zeus *Children born to the Gods.* (Z 198),—the only own son of this god in the generation of the Trojan War. Nestor is grandson of Poseidon; Ares has two sons in the Achaean army (B 512, O 112). Many of the warriors, like Achilles, Agamemnon, and Hector trace their lineage to Zeus in the third or a more remote generation. Achilles of course is the son of the sea-nymph Thetis; and of the other lesser divinities, both Circe and Calypso desire to retain Odysseus as husband (ι 29),—Calypso definitely offering to him immortality if he will remain with her (ε 209). The Dawn has as her consort (Λ 1) Tithonus, a brother of Priam (Υ 237), to whom she bore a son Memnon (δ 188, λ 522), and an earlier husband had been Orion (ε 121). The Dawn had "snatched up" another mortal to dwell with the gods, because of his beauty,—Cleitus, ο 250,—but the poet does not say whether she took him as her spouse. The only mention in the *Iliad* of fountain or stream nymphs is as the mothers of sons by mortal lovers (Z 22, Ξ 444, Υ 384). Achilles's sister Polydora bears a son to the river Spercheüs (Π 174), and a son of the river Axius fights as an ally of the Trojans (Φ 141). One of the three instances of adultery in the Homeric poems (the other two being of Helen with Paris,

---

[1] Ganymede is mentioned but twice, E 266, Υ 232, and does not appear on Olympus. The poet does not say how he was taken to Olympus, but says that Zeus gave to Tros horses in exchange.

[2] So according to Bedouin belief a spirit may be the physical father of a child (Curtiss, *l.c.*); and this is a frequent notion in all mythologies.

and of Clytaemestra with Aegisthus) is that of Aphrodite with Ares (θ 268).

The divinities have chariots and horses "swift of flight" (ὠκυπέτα, Θ 42). Each stride of the steeds of Hera carries them as great a distance as a man can see through the mist (E 769). Zeus harnesses his horses in order to journey from Olympus to Mt. Ida (Θ 41), and there releases them from the chariot and covers them with mist, as he takes his place to view the battles of the Trojans and Achaeans ; when Hera visits him there, he assumes that she has driven (Ξ 299), although she appears to him without a chariot. Hera and Athena take a chariot to go to the Trojan plain (E 720, Θ 374), but more frequently, Athena descends without special equipment (A 194, B 167, Δ 74, H 19, X 187). At α 97, if the text is right, Athena has winged sandals like those of Hermes. At Θ 455, Zeus says that if Hera and Athena had disobeyed him they would not have returned to Olympus on their chariots,—i.e. their chariots would have been broken and they themselves would have been utterly disabled,—not in ten years would their wounds have been healed. Ares goes with his car to the field of battle, and allows the wounded Aphrodite to use it for her return to Olympus (E 363); when he himself is wounded, a little later, he rises to the heavens like a thick mist (E 864), but again (at O 119) he orders his horses to be made ready for a like journey to the Trojan plain. Poseidon takes his horses to go to this Trojan plain, and leaves them hobbled in a grotto between Tenedos and Imbros (N 23), though apparently he could have gone comfortably without them, since he makes but four strides for the distance between Samothrace and Aegae,—wherever this may be (N 20). The divinities are so corporeal that when Athena enters the chariot of Diomed, the oaken axle creaks loudly (E 838) from the unaccustomed weight. Hermes, on being sent to Calypso's island, takes no chariot, but ties on his winged sandals for the flight. When Calypso remarks that she has not seen him of late, he replies (ε 100), as we have seen already, "Who of his own will would journey over so vast a sea?"—implying that distance was thought to be a barrier for gods as well as for men. The only divinity

Divinities have Chariots.

represented as winged, and she but twice (Θ 398 = Λ 185), is "golden-winged Iris."

Homer knows no divine providence, in the sense of a definite purpose and guidance for the life of a man or for the development of a city or nation. When Zeus goes from Olympus to feast with the Aethiopians (A 424), he has not even an inkling of the storm *No "Divine Providence."* of trouble which is to break upon the Achaean camp before his return. Nor does he know what Hera will say in regard to his promise given to Thetis to aid the Trojans, except that his past experience has taught him that she will be highly displeased (A 518). Thoughts come to Athena just as they do to mortals (β 382, 393). The gods discuss a plan just as men would (a 76),—by no means seeing the end from the beginning. At the opening of the second day of battle (Θ 5), Zeus forbids the divinities to take part in the conflict, while two days later he commands them to do so (Υ 24). No sufficient reason is given for the change, which appears to be the result of mere caprice. So on the second day of battle, Zeus weighs the fates of the Achaeans and the Trojans, and the latter rise, *i.e.* have the advantage. He then hurls a thunderbolt into the midst of the Achaean host to terrify them, and again to stop the advance of Diomed and Nestor, and thunders thrice again from Mt. Ida (Θ 69, 76, 133, 170); but a little later he pities the Greeks, and sends his eagle carrying in its talons a fawn, which it drops by the side of his altar in the Achaean camp, in order to encourage the Greeks (Θ 247); again, however, when the Trojans are hard pressed he encourages and strengthens them. All this, in the course of a single day, is vacillating caprice,—not the result of a plan.

The gods, and Zeus in particular, are said to "know all things" (δ 468, v 75), but they are far from omniscient in the modern theological sense. Zeus looks off at the Thracians (N 4), and fails to observe what is *Gods not Omniscient.* doing on the Trojan plain at his very feet. Poseidon is surprised and vexed at the action of the gods taken in his absence, with regard to the return of Odysseus (ϵ 286). If Poseidon had tarried only a few hours longer with the Aethiopians, Odysseus would have been saved a shipwreck. Iris is sent by Hera to Achilles secretly, without the knowledge of the other gods (Σ 168); and Hephaestus, when thrown from heaven by his mother, is concealed for nine years in the home of Thetis (Σ 398),—the din of the surging waves covering the noise of his hammer and anvil, as he works in the grotto; apparently no one but Thetis knows where he is. A god is able to hear a prayer, however, although far away. So Glaucus prays to Apollo, "Whether thou art in Lycia or in the land of Troy,"— Apollo can hear wherever he is.[1] In general, however, the gods help only when near at hand. Hera's sweat and the weariness of her horses (Δ 27) show that she was not satisfied with inspiring interest in the expedition from afar, but herself went about to gather the military forces to proceed against Troy.

When Telemachus speaks in a despairing tone of the return of Odysseus, Athena, in the guise of Mentor, rebukes *Gods' Powers* him: a god could bring home a man in safety *are Limited.* even from a distant land (γ 231). But practically the gods' powers are limited either by the plans and desires of their associates or by an indefinite fate. They may strive to thwart each other, and in the Trojan War some zealously favor the Achaeans, while others as earnestly aid the Trojans. Near the close of the first day of battle, Athena descends to the Trojan plain, evidently to aid her friends; but Apollo catches sight of her and hurries to meet her with the suggestion of a single-combat between Hector and some Achaean (H 17). Athena accepts the suggestion, saying that she herself had come with that very desire,—a statement which the connexion forbids our believing. On the night after the second day of battle, again Apollo observing Athena accompanying Odysseus and Diomed, suspects some ill for the Trojans, and sets out to follow them, but arrives on the scene of action just too late to save the life of the Thracian Rhesus (K 515). A few days later, in the chariot-race held in honor of the dead Patroclus,

---

[1] δύνασαι δὲ σὺ πάντοσ᾽ ἀκούειν, Π 515. But that, while the gods are feasting with the Aethiopians (A 424), Apollo hears the prayer of his old priest Chryses (A 457), and Hera sends Athena to the Trojan plain (A 195), is an inconsistency in the poems.

Apollo knocks the whip from the hand of Diomed that the advantage may be given to his chief competitor Eumelus, whose horses Apollo himself had tended during his year of service to Admetus ; but Athena sees the trick, restores the whip to Diomed, and breaks the yoke of the chariot of Eumelus,—thus causing him to lose the race (Ψ 384). To such pettiness do these great gods descend. But Athena shrinks from helping Odysseus, on the wanderings of his return, as she tells him, because she desires to avoid a quarrel with Poseidon (ν 341).

Quarrels. Their several human favorites, and their plans for them, cause the greater part of the quarrels and jealousies of the gods, as they are presented in the Homeric story. These quarrel, however, as a rule, not for long. Zeus and Hera sleep peacefully side by side after their sharp words at the close of the first book of the *Iliad*. Poseidon is on perfectly good terms with Zeus on the last day of battle (Υ 13), though he was very angry at him on the day preceding (O 185).

Gods in Human Form. The gods appear in their proper form only to a single mortal at once,—never to a group or a large number (π 161, A 198, E 123).[1] Generally they appear in the guise of men. Thus Athena takes the form of a son of Antenor when she enters the Trojan army seeking to effect a breach of the truce (Δ 86); that of Priam's son Deïphobus, to deceive Hector (X 227); that of Mentes, king of the Taphians, when she first visits Telemachus (α 105); that of Mentor, an Ithacan friend of Odysseus, in order to accompany Telemachus to Pylus, and to encourage Odysseus in his slaughter of Penelope's suitors (β 268 ff., χ 206, ω 503, 548); that of a Phaeacian maiden, in order to guide Odysseus to the home of Alcinoüs (η 20); that of a Phaeacian man (yet recognized by Odysseus) in the games at Scheria (θ 194); that of a young Ithacan shepherd, at the return of Odysseus (ν 222);[2] when she

---

[1] With this, perhaps reasonably, may be compared the fact that in modern superstitions ghosts appear only to one person ; a small boy will see no ghost if he is not alone.

[2] Whether Athena ever actually takes the form of a bird, is not entirely clear. She flies upward "as a bird" (α 320), departs "like to a sea-hen" or osprey

visits Odysseus at the hut of Eumaeus (π 158), she perhaps appears in her own form, "as a woman, beautiful and tall, and skilled in goodly accomplishments." No other of the gods takes such a personal part as Athena in the affairs of men. Apollo takes the form of Asius, Hector's uncle (Π 717), that of Priam's son Lycaon (Υ 81), and that of Antenor's son Agenor (Φ 600). Poseidon likens himself to the seer Calchas (N 45), and a little later to the Aetolian Thoas (N 216) or possibly to another (N 357). Hermes in the guise of a princely youth conducts Priam to Achilles's quarters (Ω 347); when he appears to Odysseus on Circe's island as a young man, he may be in his own form (κ 278),—but this conception of him does not seem to be the earliest. Aphrodite appears as an old woman servant of Helen (Γ 386),—apparently changing only her garb and face, for Helen recognizes her by her neck and breast,—and Iris takes the form of Priam's most beautiful daughter, Laodice, to call Helen to the tower by the Scaean Gate (Γ 124). None of the stories of Zeus in disguise as a lover are Homeric. Penelope's suitor Antinoüs is warned by his companions not to ill-treat the disguised Odysseus, for "the gods in all forms visit the cities of men, observing their insolence and their law-abiding spirit" (ρ 485). Athena removes the mist from the eyes of Diomed (E 127), that he may distinguish god from man, and thus he recognizes Aphrodite and Ares, though the rest do not. When the gods feast with the Aethiopians or with the Phaeacians doubtless each appears *in propria persona*,—but these dwelt in fairyland. Curiously Athena is not only seen by Odysseus but also recognized by the swine-herd's dogs,[1] which whine

---

(φήνῃ εἰδομένη, γ 372), sits "like a swallow" (χελιδόνι εἰκέλη, χ 240) on a rafter of Odysseus's hall, and sits with Apollo "like vultures" (ὄρνισιν ἐοικότες αἰγυπιοῖσιν, H 59) on the high oak of Zeus, to watch the single-combat of Hector and Ajax.

[1] In Theocritus, *Idyls*, ii. 35, the howling of the dogs shows that Hecate is at the cross-roads. In Maeterlinck's *Intruder*, the old blind grandfather, alone of persons, recognizes the coming of the ghostly messenger, but the dog slinks into his kennel, and the birds are still. So in the ordinary superstitions, the howling of the dog means affliction to the family. *Cf.* also Longfellow's *Golden Legend*, *The Nativity*, viii. : "In the Rabbinical Book it saith | The dogs howl when with icy breath | Great Sammael, the Angel of Death, | Takes through the town his flight."

and flee, though she is unseen by Telemachus (π 162). The sea-god Proteus is seized by Menelaus (δ 456), and in striving to escape becomes in turn a bearded lion, a serpent, a leopard, a wild boar, flowing water, and a high-branched tree.[1] Once, in attacking Ares (E 845), Athena puts on a "cap of Hades," which makes her invisible even to her fellow-divinities. No token is given, like ·unwinking eyes or the lack of shadows, by which gods can be recognized.

Proteus in many forms.

Every human action of any importance is ascribed to the suggestion or coöperation of some divinity. Nothing could be more characteristic than the first question of the *Iliad* (A 8),—"Which one of the gods brought Agamemnon and Achilles together in strife?"— which assumes that some god is responsible for the quarrel. Apollo sends the pestilence upon the Greeks (A 50). Only a few verses later, Achilles calls the Achaeans to an assembly, "for Hera put it into his heart" (A 55). In the midst of the quarrel of Achilles and Agamemnon, Athena, at the suggestion of Hera, comes down from Olympus and, stepping up behind Achilles, takes him by his tawny hair (A 195). He is astonished to be thus approached, but does not seem in the least surprised to find that it is a divinity. He recognizes Athena at once by her flashing eyes,—he must have seen her before. At the opening of the second book of the *Iliad*, Zeus sends a delusive Dream to Agamemnon, in order to influence his action. A little later, on the same day, Athena, again at the suggestion of Hera, descends to the Trojan plain and rouses Odysseus to stop the departure of the Achaeans (B 166). Near the close of the same book, the goddess Iris is sent by Zeus as a messenger to Hector, to tell him that the Achaean forces are advancing (B 786). In the third book, Iris brings Helen to the Great Tower to watch the conflict (Γ 121), and Aphrodite, after saving Paris from death at the hands of Menelaus (Γ 374), fetches Helen home again (Γ 389).

Constant Interference of Divinities.

---

[1] Proteus's readiness to change his form may be due to his being a divinity of the changing sea. *Cf.* the familiar similar stories about Thetis.—That the poet received the story of Proteus in a settled form, is indicated by the shapes taken by the sea-god, including *flowing water*, which Menelaus could not have held.

Early in the fourth book, Athena is sent down to secure a breach of the truce between Achaeans and Trojans (Δ 74), but so guides the arrow of Pandarus that it brings no great harm to Menelaus (Δ 129), she turning it aside "as a mother keeps a fly from her sleeping babe." In the first verses of the fifth book of the *Iliad*, she "gives might and courage to the son of Tydeus," and so on. Thus also at the opening of the action of the *Odyssey*, Athena is sent (but on her own motion) to Ithaca with directions for Telemachus (α 88), and at the close of the last book (ω 529) she makes peace between the Ithacan parties. Hermes is the "affable spirit" (Ω 334), but Athena,—partly as being goddess of war, and partly as the special patron of Odysseus,— interferes actively in the affairs of men more often than any other divinity. She even gives Telemachus confidence to approach Nestor (γ 77), sets a mark for Odysseus in the Phaeacian games (θ 193), and cleanses the face of Penelope with "ambrosial beauty" such as Aphrodite uses (σ 192), in order to secure for her the increased admiration of her suitors. The Locrian Ajax says that Athena cares "like a mother" for Odysseus (Ψ 783),—she had caused Ajax to slip in the foot-race, in order that Odysseus might win the prize; Nestor declares that he never saw gods displaying such care for other men (γ 222); and Athena herself says that she stands by him and guards him in all toils (ν 301), being charmed by his ever-ready wit. Odysseus is so accustomed to indications of her presence and care that he wonders at not seeing her from the time of the capture of Troy, until he reaches the land of the Phaeacians (ν 316).

Every mortal who possesses distinction has received this from some god. Zeus grants the sceptre to kings (Β 205). *Every Distinction comes from a God.* Apollo gives skill in divination (Α 87), and bestows a bow and skill to use it (Β 827). A skilled hunter is taught by Artemis (Ε 51), and a smith or carpenter is taught by Athena or Hephaestus (Ε 61, ζ 233), and Paris has the "gifts of Aphrodite" (Γ 54).

A *deus ex machina* appears to save several Trojans in the battle, removing them bodily from danger. Thus Aphrodite carries Paris from the single combat to his home (Γ 380), and starts to carry Aeneas away from Diomed (E 318). When she is wounded, and drops her son, Apollo bears Aeneas to his temple in Troy (E 445). Near the close of the battles of the *Iliad*, Poseidon saves Aeneas from Achilles, causing him to leap over "many ranks of men and of chariots" (Υ 325), while Apollo snatches up (ἐξήρπαξεν, Υ 443) first Hector and then Agenor (Φ 597). For Apollo at that time to have placed Hector within the walls of the city, however, would have interfered too much with the progress of the action.

Similarly, if a mortal suffers ill, he assumes that some god is angry. Menelaus, detained on an island by unfavorable weather, desires to know whom he has offended, —what god fetters him (δ 378). Artemis sends *Every Ill comes from a God.* a fierce wild boar upon the fields of Calydon because Oeneus failed to remember her at his harvest-home festival (θαλύσια, Ι 534), when he offered sacrifices to the other gods. Athena causes an evil return from Troy for the Achaeans, whose cause she had been aiding for ten years, because of the offense of one of their number (α 327, γ 145, δ 502), for which Agamemnon had striven by sacrifices to atone. Poseidon retains for nearly ten years his wrath at Odysseus for blinding Poseidon's son Polyphemus (α 68, ν 341), and finally prepares destruction for the Phaeacians on account of their kindness to Odysseus (ν 149). The lesser Ajax, though shipwrecked, might have been saved but for his insolent word,—that he was safe in spite of the gods,—which offended Poseidon (δ 503). The sun-god Helius is so enraged at the slaughter of some of his cattle by the comrades of Odysseus, that he threatens to descend to Hades, and to give no more light to gods and men, if he is not well avenged (μ 382), and at his instance Zeus wrecks the Ithacan ship and brings death to all but Odysseus, who is free from blame in this matter. The "mindful wrath" of Hera and Athena because of their slighted beauty, is familiar from the later story, and is mentioned in one passage of the present text of the Homeric poems (Ω 29).

Naturally in these poems the divinities seem most concerned with the Trojan war; all show a deep interest in the conflicts on the Trojan plain, and have taken sides definitely. They are divided into parties on this issue. Only

Gods' Interest in Trojan War.

Ares is charged with being fickle (ἀλλοπρόσαλλος, E 831),—having changed from a helper of the Achaeans to a defender of the Trojans. No reason for this change is given. The poet, as we have just seen, alludes but once to the cause of the desire of Hera and Athena for the overthrow of Troy (Ω 29), and but once to the reason for Poseidon's position on the same side (Φ 442),—the treatment which he had received from Priam's father, Laomedon.

The wrong to the laws of hospitality done by Paris in bringing Helen to Troy has been suggested seriously as a ground for the course of Hera and Athena. In that case, however, Zeus, preëminently the god of hospitality, should be more angry even than they, but he never hints at such a reason for the destruction of Ilium, and cannot understand why Hera is so bitter (Δ 31) in her hatred of the Trojans.

No reason is stated why on the last day of the action of the *Iliad*, Artemis supports the Trojans and Hermes opposes them (Υ 35, 39); in general these take no part in the fray. Athena, Hera, and Poseidon alone of the gods are active on the side of the Achaeans, and Apollo, Ares, and Aphrodite on the side of the Trojans,—and Aphrodite is a " cowardly goddess," not fit for war, and is advised by her father, Zeus, to keep away from the battlefield (E 331, 428).

Under ordinary circumstances, the divinities are very well disposed toward men, their subjects. They are kindly rulers

Gods kindly toward Men.

and patrons, with abundant sympathy in human joys and sorrows. No one of the gods is malicious and delights in causing suffering. They have no mischievous attendant spirits, or hobgoblins, to frighten the children of men. Homer was very far from believing in any devils,—or at least he considered them beneath his notice.[1]

---

[1] Professor Hopkins calls attention to the facts that the "Vedic Hymns ignore the host of disease-devils, etc., which a special Veda, the Atharva (Witchcraft) Veda, shows to have been feared and worshipped, and from the Babylonian Epic we should not know much of the Babylonian Devil worship."

The language of the gods is said to differ somewhat from that of men. The river Scamander is called *Xanthus* by the divinities (Υ 74), and these call Aegaeon, *Briareüs* (Α 404), Batieia, *Myrina* (Β 814), and the bird cymindis, *chalcis* (Ξ 291), while they give the name *Planctae* (μ 61) to "the justling rocks," and *moly* to a plant which men cannot easily dig (κ 305). Of these six words all but *moly* have an obvious Greek derivation, and the reason for assigning them to the gods' special vocabulary is hidden.

Language of the Gods.

As for the occupations of the divinities, Hephaestus is the only one who has a clear profession, a definite vocation. For the most part, like earthly rulers, the gods spend their time in watching their subjects and in feasting. They seem to have no games, however, like the draughts of Penelope's suitors and the quoits of the young Phaeacians. They have music at their feasts (Α 603), but no dancing. Artemis is a huntress (Ε 51, ζ 102). Apollo is an archer (Ψ 872, φ 258), but probably as a warrior rather than as a hunter of wild beasts. Athena has skill in weaving and spinning (Ε 735, Ξ 179,—but perhaps as a female rather than as a patron goddess of the art), and she also teaches skill in working wood and metal (ζ 233, Ε 61). Hermes and Iris are sent to bear messages (Ω 143, 334),—but Hermes is not a messenger-boy. He is dispatched as a member of the family,—not as an underling; this service was not his regular occupation.

Occupations of the Gods.

Monarchy prevails in heaven as on earth. Zeus,—the typical monarch of the poems,—is at least as absolute a ruler as Agamemnon. Once, indeed, Hera says to Poseidon (Θ 205) that if those gods who were on the side of the Achaeans would unite, they could constrain Zeus, and drive back the Trojans. At once, however, she is rebuked by Poseidon, who acknowledges Zeus's superior power, and an hour or so later, when she and Athena have started for the Trojan plain and are stopped by a stern threat from Zeus, brought by Iris, she says to her companion that she does not favor a contest with Zeus for the sake of mortals (Θ 427). Achilles refers to one attempt at insurrection (Α 399), when Hera, Poseidon,

Monarchy on Olympus.

and Athena (as it chances, the very three who aid the Achaeans, but this seems to have no importance for our story), desired to bind Zeus, but Thetis called to Olympus the hundred-handed Briareüs, who sat by Zeus, "exulting in his glory," and the gods desisted from their attempt. How Zeus secured his throne is not told,—further than that he had divided their new kingdom with his two brothers, Hades and Poseidon (O 187). No account is given of the rule or the overthrow of the preceding dynasty, if Cronus had ever ruled, as seems unlikely. Cronus is invented, since Zeus must have a father, but he is hardly a personality in the poems ; he does indeed receive the epithet " crooked-minded " (ἀγκυλομήτης, Δ 59), but no explanation is offered for the use of this adjective.

Four sharp distinctions are made between men and the higher gods : (1) these are mortal, while those are immortal and ever young ; (2) these toil and labor, while *Four Distinc-* the gods "live at ease " ; (3) these eat bread and *tions between* drink wine, while those feast on ambrosia and *Gods and* nectar ; and lastly (4) these dwell on earth, while *Men.* the gods inhabit heaven and Olympus. Of course the power and wisdom of the gods are far greater than those of men, but, after all, they are of the same kind, differing chiefly in degree, while in their needs, appetites, and passions we have seen that the gods are not far removed from men.

The gulf between mortals and immortals, though distinct, is not impassable. Leucothea had been a mortal with human voice (βροτὸς αὐδήεσσα, ε 334), but later received *Gulf between* the honors of the gods in the depths of the sea. *Gods and* Calypso offered immortality to Odysseus (ε 209), *Men not* though she was only one of the lesser divinities. *Impassable.* Heracles had a peculiar lot: his ghost was in Hades, but he himself had Hebe to wife and feasted with the immortal gods (λ 603).[1] Ganymede, of the Trojan royal

---

[1] Menelaus was not to die, but to go to the Elysian Plain (δ 563). According to the ruder Semitic beliefs, also, no impassable gulf lies between God and man.— The chasm between divine and mortal horses, too, is not broad. The steeds of Aeneas are descended from those which Zeus gave to Tros to comfort him for the loss of his son Ganymede (who was taken to heaven as cup-bearer, E 266), but

family, because of his beauty, is carried to Olympus to serve as cup-bearer for the gods (E 266, Υ 234). He needs no change of physical constitution, but how can Leucothea, a daughter of Cadmus, become a divinity of the sea?

The poet uses no word to distinguish different orders and ranks of divinities,[1] but not all gods are equal in power and wisdom, even of the Olympian divinities, and Proteus is an underling of Poseidon (δ 386). Aphrodite is advised by Zeus not to meddle with war (E 428), but to leave that to Ares and Athena. The most important gods are Zeus, Hera, Athena, Apollo, Artemis, Hephaestus, Aphrodite, Hermes, Ares, and Poseidon. Iris serves as a messenger. Dionysus, Hebe, Dione, Leto, and Demeter have little or no part in the action of the poems.

The Muses are daughters of Zeus (B 598, α 10), without names and special offices. Their number is stated but once (ω 60,—a passage of late composition), where the nine sing the funeral dirge for Achilles; their *The Muses.* earlier number may have been three, but neither have the Fates, the Graces, or the Furies any number in the Homeric poems. The Muse of the first verse of the *Odyssey* is clearly the same as the Goddess of the first verse of the *Iliad* (*cf.* α 10). The poet regards his story as that of the Muses and appeals to them at times at the beginning of a new narrative.[2] They sing on Olympus at the feast of the gods (A 604),—"responsively," whether to the song of Apollo, or in turn among themselves, is not clear.

The Hours are gatekeepers of Olympus (E 749 = Θ 393, 433). Até is not a real divinity,—though Agamemnon says

mixed with a strain from Anchises's stables. Two of the horses of Achilles are offspring of the west wind Zephyrus by the "harpy" Podargé (Ιl 150, P 444), and were given by Poseidon to Peleus (Ψ 277), while the Trojan king Erichthonius had twelve mares which bore colts to the north wind Boreas (Υ 223). Nestor speaks of a swift horse of Adrastus of the preceding generation, "the divine Arion, of the race of the gods" (Ψ 346).

[1] The word δαίμων is often equivalent to θεός, and has no shade of the meaning of *demon*; but δαιμόνιος is sometimes applied to one who is under the influence of a divinity for ill, while θεῖος is always used in a good sense. So far as a distinction is drawn, δαίμων seems to be applied especially to a divinity in relation to men. See Jörgensen in *Hermes*, xxxix.

[2] B 484, Λ 218, Ξ 508, Π 112.

that Zeus seized her by her fair-tressed head and threw her from the starry heaven (T 126),—but rather an abstraction like the Supplications (Λιταί, I 502), who are themselves also daughters of Zeus, but wrinkled, lame, and cross-eyed, seeking to repair the harm done by Até.   Other personifications are Rumor,[1] Night, who is "mistress of gods and men" (δμήτειρα, Ξ 259), the twin brothers Sleep (who is "lord of all," πανδαμάτωρ, Ω 5) and Death (Π 682, Ξ 231), and Ares's sons Terror and Flight (O 119).   With these may be named Strife ("Ερις, Δ 440, Λ 3, 73), who is the "sister and comrade of Ares," and Right (Θέμις, Υ 4, O 87, β 68), who calls the gods to an assembly on Olympus and presides over the gatherings of men.

The Hours and Personifications.

Asclepius (Aesculapius) is not yet deified; his sons are warriors as well as surgeons.   Pan, Silenus, and the Satyrs are not mentioned, and no Eros or Persuasion follows Aphrodite.   The Dioscuri (Castor and Pollux) are still mortals when Helen refers to them (Γ 237), but when Odysseus visits the realm of Hades (λ 303), they have life and death on alternate days, and enjoy honor equal to the gods.

No demi-gods are known; the sons of mortals by divinities are mortals, and do not form a class by themselves,—as Aeneas, Achilles, and Sarpedon.   Aeneas enjoys the special care of his mother Aphrodite and other divinities, but he has inherited no supernatural traits or powers.

The sun (Helius) is more distinctly personified than any other natural object, but here again the line is not clearly drawn between the heavenly body and the divinity of the same name.   He is invoked in an oath, since "he sees all things and hears all things" (Γ 277, *cf.* Τ 259),—but even here he is associated with the "rivers and earth," which are not personified.   He informs Hephaestus of the improprieties which he has seen in the conduct of Ares and Aphrodite (θ 271, 302).   On the island Thrinacia he has 350 kine and 350 sheep grazing (μ 127), tended by fair-tressed nymphs, Phaëthusa and Lampetié, whom Neaera bore to him.   These sheep and kine may represent (as Aristotle thought) the nights and days of a year of

The Sun.

[1] Ὄσσα, B 93, ω 413; *cf.* α 282.

fifty weeks. A young white ram is sacrificed to the sun (Γ 103), while a dark ewe lamb is sacrificed to the earth, which can hardly be called a personality. The moon is not personified in Homer, and to the moon, Artemis bears no special relation.

The preceding list of principal gods does not agree with that of the Twelve Gods at Athens or at Olympia, nor with that of the *deorum consentium* at Rome. The largest company on Olympus is gathered at the beginning of the twentieth book of the *Iliad*, at the opening of the fourth day of battle, when, *Not the Twelve Gods of Athens.* at the command of Zeus, Themis summons an assembly of the gods, to discuss the Trojan War. At this meeting all the nymphs are present, and every river but Oceanus.

The Titans are not prominent in the poems,—this name being used but once (Ξ 279); they are in Tartarus, and none are named but Cronus and Iapetus (Θ 479). *The Titans.* The existence of Uranus is inferred only from a once-used epithet.[1] The wife of Uranus, Gaea, is not named at all as a person, except possibly in a late passage of the *Odyssey*, where she is the mother of Tityus (λ 576). Oceanus is once called the source of all the gods (Ξ 201, *cf.* 246,—the one bit of theogony in the poems), but again he is called the source of every sea and river (Φ 195), without a word about the still higher dignity.

The home of the gods is on Mt. Olympus, of Thessaly,—the summits of which tower above the clouds into the clear aether, above the region of wind, rain, snow, and storm (ζ 42). Zeus dwells in the aether (αἰθέρι ναίων, Β 412),—the *aether* being the stratum above *The Home of the Gods.* and purer than the air (see page 50). The epithet snowy (ἀγάννιφος, Α 420) applied to Olympus refers to the high peaks still within man's vision ; the home of the gods itself was unseen. That Ares, seated on the summit of Olympus, is " under golden clouds " (Ν 523) does not indicate a different authorship for that passage. Such inconsistency would trouble none of Homer's hearers. The clouds form a wall about

---

[1] In general the Οὐρανίωνες are simply "the gods of heaven," as Α 570; but ἐνέρτερος Οὐρανιώνων, Ε 898, can hardly mean anything but "lower than the sons of Uranus," *i.e.* the Titans.

Olympus, and are gates which are opened and shut by the Hours.[1] The home of Zeus is on the highest summit (Θ 3).[2] The other gods dwell round about (A 606, Λ 76, Σ 369, 376). Perhaps at times the poet thinks of them as having their homes on other peaks, but in general their dwellings seem near at hand.

In later literature, heaven and Olympus were absolutely identified, and the Olympian deities were the heavenly gods as opposed to the lesser gods or the divinities of Hades, but in Homer, as a rule, Olympus is still a mountain,[3] though often the terms are synonymous : Athena comes from heaven, but returns to Olympus (A 195, 221). Ares mounts to heaven, and "comes to the seat of the gods, lofty Olympus" (E 867 f.). Thetis ascends to heaven, and is greeted by Zeus with the words, "Thou art come to Olympus" (Ω 97, 104). Apparently, when Otus and his brother strove to place Ossa on Olympus, and Pelion on Ossa, that they might scale heaven (λ 315), they were eager to attack the gods who, on their approach, withdrew from Olympus to heaven.

The Homeric Fate (Αἶσα, Μοῖρα) is a vague, impersonal influence, often not to be distinguished from the will of the gods. The expressions used about it are not consistent with each other. At times it seems superior to the divinities of Olympus, but at other times it is subject to them. Clear and consistent expressions on such

Fate.

---

[1] Θ 393. That the gate is a cloud is made perfectly clear, and yet as a gate, it grates on its hinges (μῦκον).

[2] The early Semites, too, believed their gods to dwell on the heights. *Cf.* "I will lift up mine eyes unto the hills," *Ps.* cxxi. 1 ; *Micah* iv. 1. "It is on Carmel that the Prophet Elijah repairs the altar of Jehovah that was thrown down (1 *Kings* xviii. 30). It is upon a mountain that Abraham is directed to offer up his son (*Gen.* xxii. 2). It was on a mountain that Jacob offered up a sacrifice before parting from Laban (*Gen.* xxxi. 54). . . . It is Mount Sinai or Horeb, which is called repeatedly the Mount of God, upon whose summit God revealed himself to Moses (*Ex.* iii. 5, xxiv. 12), and long afterwards to Elijah (2 *Sam.* xv. 30, 32; the imperfect indicates customary action)." Curtiss, *Primitive Semitic Religion*, p. 134.

[3] According to Seiler-Capelle's *Wörterbuch*, the frequency of the use varies as follows:
in the *Iliad*, Οὔλυμπος : οὐρανός :: 77 : 61 ;
,, Odyssey, ,, ,, :: 15 : 41.
In the *Odyssey* Olympus is not called *lofty* (αἰπύς), *snowy* (ἀγάννιφος or νιφόεις), or *with many-ridges* (πολύπτυχος) ; its only epithet applicable to a mountain is μακρός (*great*), for *gleaming* (αἰγλήεις, υ 103) would be given as appropriately to the sky.

a matter are not to be expected in our poems. Sometimes it is said to belong to Zeus (Διὸς αἶσα, P 321), or to an indefinite divinity (δαίμονος αἶσα, λ 61, θεοῦ μοῖρα, λ 292). Its impersonality is shown by the fact that no word of prayer is ever addressed to Fate.[1] Yet the conception of Fate as spinning a thread which represents a mortal life is indicated in several passages, of which the most important are quoted just below.

Athena in the guise of Mentor says that not even the gods are able to ward off death from a friend, when the fate of death seizes him (μοῖρα θανάτοιο, γ 238), but again Euryclea is sure that Athena can save Tele- *Gods subject* machus even from death (δ 753). Alcinoüs *to Fate?* promises that he will convey Odysseus to his home, but "then at Ithaca he will suffer what Fate and the stern spinsters spun for him at his birth";[2] but again it is Zeus who appointed sorrow and trouble for Menelaus at his birth (K 71). Old Hecuba, bewailing the fate of her son Hector, says, "Thus, as it seems, mighty fate (μοῖρα κραταιή, Ω 209) spun for him." The ghost of Patroclus says to Achilles, "But hated fate swallowed me (κὴρ ἀμφέχανε, *yawned*),—the fate which received me at my birth" (Ψ 78). Achilles says that not even Heracles "escaped fate" (φύγε κῆρα . . . μοῖρ' ἐδάμασσε, Σ 117), but "destiny mastered him." Zeus himself laments that it is the lot of his son Sarpedon (μοῖρα, Π 434) to be slain by Patroclus; he yields, however, not since fate is irresistible by him, but on being reminded by Hera that if he saves Sarpedon, the other gods will wish to save their sons as well (Π 445). But the "thought of Zeus" (Διὸς νόημα, P 409) is "ordained" (πέπρωται, Σ 329). Several times the poet speaks of deeds as "beyond fate,"[3] but most of these are more or less

---

[1] μοῖρα (used 109 times), κήρ (79 times), αἶσα (42 times), and πότμος (35 times) in general are used only of death; to fulfil one's destiny or to meet one's destiny, is to die. μοῖρα (cf. μέρος) and αἶσα originally designated *share, portion, fitting share*, but came to be used of the allotment or the allotting power. πότμος seems to be that which falls to one (πίπτω). κήρ is used something like δαίμων, and at least once is nearly equivalent to *guardian genius* (X 210).—"Fate covered him" (μοῖρά μιν ἀμφεκάλυψε, M 116) is spoken of a dying man, very much like "night covered him" (νὺξ ἐκάλυψε, E 310).

[2] αἶσα, κλῶθές τε βαρεῖαι νήσαντο, η 197, cf. Υ 127.

[3] ὑπέρμορα νόστος ἐτύχθη, B 155; ὑπὲρ αἶσαν, Π 780; ὑπὲρ Διὸς αἶσαν, P 321; ὑπὲρ θεὸν, P 327; ὑπὲρ μόρον, Υ 30, Φ 517, ε 436.

hypothetical, except where Zeus says that "mortals have
woes beyond fate" (α 34), and gives as an illustration the
vengeance which overtook Aegisthus, who "beyond fate" wooed
the wife of Agamemnon, and "slew the king himself on his
return." This seems to imply that each man is bound to
have a certain amount of suffering, but that he can bring more
upon himself if he chooses; and that Aegisthus was free not
to woo Clytaemestra, yet in spite of the gods' warning he
had persisted in his plan. When Poseidon says it is fated
(μόριμον, Υ 302) that Aeneas should escape death by the
hands of Achilles, this does not relieve the god from the
responsibility of immediate interference to save him,—rather
it devolves this duty upon him. The most distinct expression
of fatalism uttered in the poems is put into the mouth of
Hector, who, comforting Andromache as he returns to the
field of battle, says, "My poor wife, grieve not overmuch for
me, for no man shall send me to Hades beyond my fate
(ὑπὲρ αἶσαν, Ζ 487),—and no man, brave or coward, ever
escaped his lot" (μοῖραν, Ζ 488). But Odysseus encourages
his comrades on Circe's island by saying, "We shall not go
down to the home of Hades until the fated day shall come"
(μόρσιμον ἦμαρ ἐπέλθῃ, κ 175). "Destructive fate bound
Hector" to remain outside of the Scaean Gate, when the
other Trojan warriors sought safety within the walls (Χ 5),
but a little later (Χ 174) Zeus asks the gods what is to be
done with Hector; is he to be slain by Achilles, or may
his life be spared? Not infrequently the blame for an evil
act is thrown upon fate or the gods,—a custom to which Zeus
is represented as objecting (α 33). Thus Helen throws on
Aphrodite the responsibility for her desertion of her home
(δ 261), and Priam blames not Helen, but the gods who
brought upon Troy the war of the Achaeans (Γ 164).
Menelaus, too, courteously ascribes to the influence of some
unkindly divinity, the ingenious device of Helen in Troy for
discovering the trick of the Wooden Horse (δ 275). The
disguised Odysseus says that some divinity had deceived
him (ξ 488,—apparently with regard to the weather), and
made him leave his cloak in his tent when he went off for
service in an ambuscade on a cold night. Odysseus's comrade
Elpenor says that "the evil fate of a divinity" *and* too much

wine had been his ruin (λ 61). Such excuses are hardly to be taken seriously. The influence of the gods in these cases differs entirely from the direct deception of Agamemnon by a delusive Dream sent by Zeus (B *init.*). Helen and Elpenor had erred as human beings.

Zeus is so distinctly the chief of the Olympian state that at times the religion seems almost monotheistic. " The will of Zeus is accomplished " (A 5). He is " father *Zeus.* of both gods and men " (A 544,—an epithet which Aristotle, in his *Politics*, 1259 *b*, explains as based on his patriarchal rule), he is " most exalted of rulers " (ὕπατε κρειόντων, a 45,—*king of kings*), he is " most glorious and most great " (Ζεῦ πάτερ κύδιστε μέγιστε, Γ 276 ; *cf. Jupiter Optimus Maximus*), he is the " lord of both gods and men " (B 669); he is wisest of all (N 631), and has all power (δ 237); neither god nor mortal can elude his notice nor thwart his plans (ε 104); and he destroys the citadels of many towns (B 116). The councils of the gods are held in his great hall (A 533, Δ 1, Θ 2, Υ 6), just as mortal chieftains gather at the palace of their feudal lord. At these gatherings Zeus presides. All rise on his approach (A 533). At the opening of the twentieth book of the *Iliad*, he bids Themis to summon to his hall all the divinities, —even the river-gods and the fountain-nymphs,—for a general assembly. He dispenses the joys and ills of men (Ω 527), and determines the issues of war (ταμίης πολέμοιο, Δ 84). To him oaths are addressed (ὅρκια, H 411, *cf.* T 258), and he is chief giver of omens (πανόμφαιος, Θ 250 ; *cf.* υ 98). He is the guardian of strangers and suppliants (ι 270). One of his most frequent epithets, " aegis-bearer " (αἰγίοχος, B 275) refers to him as a mighty warrior, the aegis being a primitive form of shield (see p. 649). This aegis, made for him by Hephaestus, he once lends to Apollo (O 308). He is the mighty Thunderer, and directs the elements,—sending clouds and storm (II 364, ε 303, 175), rain (M 25, II 385, ι 111), snow (T 357), thunder and lightning (B 781, η 249), and setting the rainbow in the heavens (Λ 27).[1] When he nods his dark brows, great Olympus trembles (A 530).

---

[1] *Cf.* the epithets : νεφεληγερέτα, a 63 ; τερπικέραυνῳ, η 164 ; ἐρίγδουπος, θ 465 ; ὑψιβρεμέτης, ε 4 ; ἀστεροπητής, A 580 ; στεροπηγερέτα, II 298. Poseidon, too, caused

Zeus is eminently "the Olympian,"[1] but he has a sacred grove and altar on Gargarus, one of the peaks of Ida (Θ 47 ; cf. X 171), and his subjects on the plain *"The Olympian."* of Troy often address him as at the nearest seat of his worship.[2] Achilles prays to "Pelasgian Zeus of Dodona" (Π 233), and uses for his libation a goblet which he employs for no other service. The Achaean hero naturally turns to the god of his home, and Dodona in Epirus seems to have been the earliest important seat of the worship of Zeus in Greece. There the Selli, who apparently had taken the vows of poverty (having "unwashen feet" and "sleeping upon the ground"), are the prophets, the spokesmen of Zeus. The oracle at Dodona, which retained its importance for a thousand years, is mentioned in but one connexion in the Homeric poems (ξ 327 = τ 296): Odysseus is reported to have gone thither, to inquire of the tree of Zeus, with regard to his return to Ithaca. The poet betrays no consciousness of any belief that this tree was the habitation of the god, and gives no indication of the character of the oracle. On the plain of Troy, not far from the Scaean Gate stood an "oak of Zeus"[3] which serves as a land-mark, but the poet knows of no other sacred trees,—not even the laurel as sacred to Apollo, or the olive to Athena.

In the conflicts of the Greeks and the Trojans, Zeus takes no immediate part, but he is not entirely inactive. He never reveals himself directly to men, however. *Zeus in the Iliad.* Urged by Thetis, to whom he is under obligations, he sends a delusive and destructive Dream to Agamemnon, inciting him to a battle in which he is not to be successful (B 1). Under the influence of Hera, who desires not peace but the destruction of Ilium, he directs

a storm (ε 291), and almost any divinity could send a favorable breeze (as A 479 ; see page 396). Athena lengthens the night after Odysseus slays the suitors (ψ 241, cf. Joshua x. 12, "Sun, stand thou still upon Gibeon, and thou, Moon, in the valley of Ajalon"), while Hera sends the sun unwillingly to the west (Σ 239),—but natural phenomena are preëminently under the direction of Zeus.

[1] Cf. A 580, 583, 589. Ὀλύμπιος without other qualification always refers to Zeus.

[2] Ἰδηθεν μεδέων, Γ 276, X 171, Ω 308.

[3] Διὸς φηγός,—with edible acorns,—or a chestnut. Cf. E 693, Z 237, H 22, 60, I 354, Λ 170, Φ 549 (?).

Athena to secure a breach of the truce between Trojans and Achaeans (Δ 68). He allows Athena and Hera to descend to the field of action on the first day of battle, though he stoutly forbids this on the second day (E 765, Θ 397). He rebukes Ares as a lover of strife (E 890), and Poseidon for fearing that the Achaean wall may become more famous than that which Poseidon and Apollo built for Laomedon (H 455). He thunders all through the next night, planning ills for both armies (H *fin.*). On the second day of battle, he takes his station on Mt. Ida, overlooking the battle (Θ 47). Three times on this day he thunders, encouraging now the one and again the other party; once he sends an eagle with a fawn as an omen to cheer the Achaeans (Θ 247), while again he rouses the might of the Trojans with no special omen (Θ 335). On the third day of battle, he is at first less watchful, and after he has sent Strife to the ships of the Achaeans (Λ 3), he looks away from the battle to the land of the Mare-Milkers (Ἱππημολγοί, N 5), and thus gives Poseidon his opportunity to aid the Achaeans. Later, his attention is more completely distracted by an amorous episode with Hera, and he sleeps (Ξ 352). On waking, and finding the Trojans in a rout, and Hector wounded (O 4), he is very angry, and sends Apollo to aid Hector (O 221), and Iris to bid Poseidon to withdraw from the fight (O 158). Then he fixes his eyes on the conflict. At the death of Sarpedon he grieves, and sends the twin brothers Death and Sleep to convey the body to Lycia (Π 433, 667). He pities the immortal steeds of Achilles (P 443), in view of their master's approaching death, and strengthens them to save their charioteer Automedon. In a passage of uncertain age of composition, he reproves Hera for her untiring hatred for the Trojans (Σ 357). At the beginning of the fourth day of battle, Zeus calls an assembly of all the gods, and sends them to the Trojan plain, to aid either Greeks or Trojans, according to the pleasure of each (Υ 4), while he himself remains on a ridge of Olympus. He pities Hector (X 168), but weighs the fates of Hector and of Achilles in his golden scales, and assents to the death of the Trojan. At the opening of the last book of the *Iliad*, the gods are at strife with one another,—some being eager to steal the body of Hector from the tent of Achilles, while others oppose this as a wrong to the Greek, and Zeus orders a compromise (Ω 64),—that Achilles shall give up the body of Hector for a great ransom,—and in order to prepare the way for this, he sends Thetis as his messenger to Achilles (Ω 106) and Iris to Priam (Ω 144), and a little later dispatches Hermes, "the affable archangel" (Ω 334), to conduct Priam in safety to and from the Achaean camp.

In the action of the *Odyssey*, Zeus has less frequent occasion to interfere than in that of the *Iliad*. He assents *Zeus in the* to Athena's journey to Ithaca (α 76), and sends *Odyssey.* Hermes to Calypso's island to direct the return of Odysseus (ε 29). By his thunder he gives a favorable omen to Odysseus on the morning before the slaughter of Penelope's suitors (φ 413), and at the close of the action he orders harmony and peace for the Ithacans (ω 481). From the recitals of Nestor and Odysseus, we learn that he had sent a storm upon the Greeks soon after their departure from Troy (γ 288, ι 67), and wrecked the ship of Odysseus because the Ithacans had killed the kine of the sun (μ 415).

On the second day of battle, Zeus draws his golden scales, placing in one the fates of the Trojans, and in the *The Scales* other those of the Achaeans (Θ 69), and similarly *of Zeus.* he weighs the fates of Achilles and Hector (X 209,—perhaps the model for the other passage). This may be merely a metaphor for his "weighing" the matter in his mind.[1] At all events these scales do not imply that the destiny of the armies or men was settled by the change in the balance, uninfluenced by the will of Zeus.

To Zeus, Ares and Hephaestus are born by Hera, *Children of* Aphrodite by Dione, Apollo and Artemis by *Zeus.* Leto, and Persephone (probably) by Demeter (λ 217).

Hera is a daughter of Cronus and Rhea, but was nurtured

---

[1] See also Π 658, T 223. *Cf.* " Th' Eternal . . . hung forth in heaven his golden scales . . . | Wherein all things created first he weighed . . . now ponders all events, | Battles and realms," Milton, *Paradise Lost*, iv. *fin.*, where the English poet plays on the word *ponders*.

by Oceanus and Tethys, who received her from Rhea when Zeus put Cronus beneath the earth and the sea (Ξ 201).[1] She is both sister and wife of Zeus (Δ 58, Σ 365). The assembled gods rise at her approach *Hera.* (Ο 85), and she and Athena wield the thunderbolt (Λ 45). She is a violent partisan of the Achaeans (Δ 24, Σ 357, Ω 25) against the Trojans, whom she hates. She herself had sweat, and she had wearied her horses, in rousing the Greeks for the destruction of Troy. Yet she does not take so active a part as Athena in the action of the *Iliad*, and takes no part at all in the action of the *Odyssey*.[2] She sends Athena twice to the Trojan plain, however (A 195, B 156), and accompanies her thither once (E 713); again the two set out together for the battlefield (Θ 381), but are checked by a stern message from Zeus. On the field of battle she accomplishes nothing, but she distracts the attention of Zeus, and affords an opportunity for Poseidon unrestrained to aid the Achaeans (Ξ 153). She dispatches Iris secretly to counsel Achilles (Σ 168), and sends the sun unwilling to the west (Σ 239, T 407). She gives human voice to a horse of Achilles (T 407). She spreads a mist before the fleeing Trojans to detain them (Φ 6), and interferes to save Achilles from the angry Scamander (Φ 328). She is " Argive Hera " (Δ 8), and Argos, Sparta, and Mycenae are her favorite cities (Δ 51). According to the later story, the Greek leaders swore fealty to Agamemnon at the Argive Heraeum.[3] She is the mother of Hephaestus (A 586) and of Ares (E 892). She and Zeus are the only married pair on Olympus,—for Hephaestus's rather uncertain relations to a Grace (Σ 382) or Aphrodite (θ 268) are hardly to be considered in this connexion. But they are not always affectionate: the first book of the *Iliad* closes with unpleasant language used by each to the other. Zeus

---

[1] This is clearly inconsistent, however, with Ξ 296, which implies that the intimacy of Zeus and Hera began before the overthrow of Cronus. Both passages seem to be of rather late composition.

[2] The name of Hera seems to be used 128 times in the Homeric poems; Athena's, 320 times; Apollo's, 155 times; and Ares's, 129 times. In the *Odyssey* her name occurs seven times, and Athena's 160 times.

[3] See *The Argive Heraeum*, by Waldstein, vol. i. 35.

dislikes to grant Thetis's request for the honor of Achilles, simply because Hera will be angry at it, and he begs Thetis to leave him at once, that Hera may not see them together (Λ 522). When Hera sets out for the field of battle on the second day of the conflicts of the *Iliad*, Zeus says that she is wont to thwart his plans (Θ 422), and he explains the waywardness of Ares by the impetuous spirit of Ares's mother, Hera, who is with difficulty controlled (E 892). After she has tricked him by amorous dalliance on the next day of battle, he reminds her of an occasion when in the previous generation of men, during his slumber, she had driven Heracles far from his course, and in punishment had been hung up by the wrists with anvils attached to her feet (O 18)! On a like occasion of Zeus's rage, Hephaestus came to the aid of his mother as she was beaten, and was himself hurled out of heaven,—the occasion on which "from morn To noon he fell, from noon to dewy eve" (A 590).

The goddesses who preside over child-birth, Eileithyae, are daughters of Zeus and Hera (Λ 270), and she directs them in the case of the birth of Heracles (T 119), but elsewhere Hera has no functions like those of Juno Lucina.

The most frequent epithets of Hera are "white-armed" (λευκώλενος, A 55), "ox-eyed" (βοῶπις, A 551), and "golden-throned" (χρυσόθρονος, A 611). Of these the

Epithets of Hera. first is only a general epithet to imply beauty. The divinities dressed as human beings, and their arms were bare.

Athena[1] is the deity most immediately active in the story of both poems,—being the chief divinity of war (E 333,

Athena. Δ 541), and the special patroness of Odysseus. So her name occurs more frequently than that of any god but Zeus (see note on page 425). In the *Odyssey*, from first to last she is aiding Odysseus,—not, however, because of his warlike qualities, but rather on account of his ready wit (ν 297, 331),—she declares that he is first of men, as she is first of divinities, in all manner of devices.

---

[1] Athena's surname Pallas is generally interpreted as connected with πάλλω, *brandish*, as the *spear-wielder* (*cf.* ἀμπεπαλών, Γ 355); but some scholars would take it as *maiden* (see Strabo, 816).

A temple of Athena stands on the acropolis of Ilium (Z 297), to which the Trojan matrons go in solemn procession to ask her help against the might of Diomed. At Athens, according to η 81, she makes her home in the palace of king Erechtheus, *i.e.* she has a shrine there; but in the Catalogue of Ships (B 549), Erechtheus is her nursling, to whom she gives a place in her own rich temple, where offerings are brought to him. She seems to have a shrine also at Marathon (η 80).

Athena is not only, of all the immortals, the most skilled in devices: she also presides over handicrafts. That she weaves a gown for Hera (Ξ 178), as well as one for herself (E 735), does not imply special skill *Patroness of Handicrafts.* in the arts; every woman was expected to weave, and Penelope and Helen had great skill in this art. But in a twice-used verse (ζ 233 = ψ 160) she is classed with Hephaestus as teaching a goldsmith. Her suggestions are the source of the skill of an accomplished ship-builder (O 412), and she is said to love exceedingly the Tecton (*Carpenter*, E 61) who built the ships which carried Paris to Sparta. The Wooden Horse was made by Epeüs under her direction (θ 493). She, too, gave to Penelope unusual skill in beautiful works, as well as many shrewd devices (β 116; *cf.* η 110). To the daughters of Pandareüs, Hera gave beauty of face and understanding, and Artemis gave stature, while Athena taught them goodly accomplishments (υ 72), *i.e.* to spin, to weave, and perhaps to sew or embroider. Achilles, declining the offer of Agamemnon on the condition of his returning to the field of battle, says that he would not wed Agamemnon's daughter though she vied with Aphrodite in beauty and with Athena in accomplishments (ἔργα, Τ 390).

Preëminently, however, Athena was a goddess of war,—far mightier than Ares. Her most frequent epithet is "gleaming-eyed,"[1] and Achilles recognizes her at once by the fierce flash of her eyes (A 200). She is also the *Goddess of War.* "rouser of the soldiery" (λαοσσόος, N 128) and the "giver of booty" (ἀγελείη, Δ 128). Two of her epithets are not of certain interpretation,—*Triton-born* (Τριτογένεια,

---

[1] γλαυκῶπις, A 206, and more than fifty times.—This epithet was applied to the moon by Empedocles and Euripides. *Cf.* χαροπός as applied to lions and to Ares.

Δ 515) and *Alalcomenean* ('Ἀλαλκομενηις, Δ 8), but both are thought to refer to some story of her birth at Alalcomenae in Boeotia ; a third epithet (ἀτρυτώνη, Β 157) is entirely unexplained,—unless perchance it is *unwearied*. She is daughter of Zeus (Ε 880), and stands in particularly close relations to him, as his loved daughter, but the poet does not refer to the (later) story of her birth from the head of Zeus. As goddess of war, she, as well as Zeus, wears an aegis (a skin thrown over the left arm to serve as a light shield, Β 447, Ε 738),—which had a hundred well-pleated golden tufts or tassels, each worth a hundred cattle, and on which is represented the Gorgon's head. She throws this aegis about the shoulders of Achilles as he stands unarmed by the trench of the Achaean camp, to face the Trojans, after the death of Patroclus (Σ 204) ; and at the climax of the attack of Odysseus upon Penelope's suitors she displays her aegis from the ceiling, and the suitors make no further defense (χ 297).[1]

A wish earnestly desired, but still entirely unlikely of fulfilment, is addressed to Zeus, Athena, and Apollo,[2]—and these three divinities have been thought by some, notably by Mr. Gladstone, to form a sort of Homeric trinity. The relations between Athena and Apollo, however, are not particularly close.

"Zeus, Athena, and Apollo."

As the last paragraph has shown, Apollo,[3] son of Zeus and Leto (Α 9), is one of the three mightiest divinities in the eyes of the Homeric poet. At the close of the second day of battle, in the excitement of his victory, Hector wishes that he were as sure of being honored as Athena and Apollo are honored, as he is that the next day will bring calamity to the Greeks (Θ 540).

Apollo.

In the *Iliad*, Apollo appears as a violent partisan of the Trojans and Lycians and consequently an enemy of the Achaeans.[4] Of all the gods, he is the most effective on

---

[1] For such use of the aegis to dismay men, *cf.* Δ 167, Ο 230. See p. 650.

[2] Β 371, Δ 288, Η 132, Π 97, δ 341, η 311, ρ 132, 235, ω 376.

[3] His epithet λυκηγενής (Δ 101) seems to be connected with the name of the country Lycia.

[4] Von Wilamowitz-Moellendorff (in a very interesting article in *Hermes*, xxxviii. 575), emphasizing such facts, argues that Apollo was a pre-Hellenic god, found

the Trojan side (II 94). His sanctuaries which are named in the poems are near Troy (A 37), with the exception of the temple at Delphi and the sacred groves on Ithaca, with a festival at the new moon (υ 278), *Patron of Trojans.* and at Ismarus in Thrace (ι 200). His temple in Troy is named but once (E 446); there Artemis and Leto tend and heal the wound of Aeneas. He inspires the seers Calchas (A 72), Amphiaraüs, and Polypheides with the power of prophecy (ο 245, 252). He holds the lyre in the feast of the gods (A 603), when the Muses sing, and Odysseus compliments the Phaeacian bard, Demodocus, by saying that he must have been taught by a Muse or by Apollo (θ 488). The poet gives no hint of any connexion between Apollo and the sun-god Helius,—unless this be found in some of his epithets,—nor between him and the god of healing, Paeeon (E 401, 900), except that a paean is sung to him (A 473).

Apollo is an archer,[1] and as an archer 'he is a god of war. Elsewhere in this book we are reminded that in early times the bow was not held in such contempt in Homeric Greece as in the age of Aeschylus. *Apollo as Archer.* Apollo gave a bow to Pandarus (B 827) and another to Teucer (O 441); this might mean only that these were skilled archers, but his gift of a helmet to Hector (Λ 353) clearly indicates personal good will. Vows are offered to him by Pandarus before shooting at Menelaus (Δ 119), and by Meriones before shooting at a mark in the games (Ψ 872); Teucer offers no vow in this latter contest, and Apollo grudges him the victory (Ψ 865). Penelope's suitors explain their inability to string the bow of

in Asia Minor, and perhaps on the islands subdued by the Greeks. These learned to appease his anger, and he was Hellenized, and took the lyre. According to this view, his religion was re-formed at Delphi after the Homeric time, and his worship spread thence. Wilamowitz calls attention to the facts that Apollo's sole Greek sanctuary, according to the *Iliad*, is at Pytho (I 405 ; *cf.* θ 79), and that the *Odyssey* adds only the grove of Apollo on Ithaca (υ 278); and that the only Achaean favored by him in the *Iliad* is Calchas, whose home is not mentioned in these poems, but who was from Claros in Asia Minor, and was brought into the Epic by the Colophonians. [The Achaean Teucer received his bow from Apollo (O 441),—but this may mean only that he was a skilled archer.]

[1] Note the epithets : ἐκατηβελέτης (A 75), *The Far-darter*, and its short form, ἕκατος (A 385) ; ἐκηβόλος (A 14), and ἐκάεργος (A 479). He does not appear as a hunter, but his sister Artemis, famed for her long shots (ἐκηβολίαι), is a huntress.

Odysseus by the fact that the trial is made on the festival of Apollo (φ 258),—when it would seem that the god was jealous of their success.

At the opening of the action of the *Iliad*, Apollo's old priest, Chryses, being slighted by Agamemnon, prays to him for vengeance, and he sends a pestilence which rages for ten days in the Achaean camp. Then atonement is made, and the god is satisfied. The sending of the plague does not in itself prove him to be a god of sickness and health ; perhaps some other divinity might take vengeance in the same way. But the pestilence is said to be caused by the arrows of the angry god, and all sudden, otherwise unexplained, deaths of men are ascribed to his agency,[1] just as similar deaths of women are attributed to the arrows of Artemis.[2]

Apollo and the Plague.

Early on the first day of battle (Δ 507), Apollo appears in the action : he is watching the conflict from the citadel of Troy, and rouses the spirit of the weakening Trojans. A little later, he saves the wounded Aeneas (E 344), and bears him to his temple in Troy, where Leto and Artemis so much refresh the Trojan that he soon reappears on the field of battle (E 513). Again Apollo comes forth from the Trojan citadel on seeing Athena descend from Olympus (H 20), and the two plan a single-combat between Hector and Ajax, which they watch, sitting like vultures on the branch of a tree. When Hector is overthrown by Ajax, Apollo sets him on his feet again (H 272), and in the next day of battle he turns away an arrow from him (Θ 311). On the third day of battle, as Hector assails the Achaean camp, Apollo goes before him, with a cloud wrapped about his shoulders, and an aegis (O 307), and smooths the way for him, breaking down the banks of the moat (O 355). With his own hand he thrusts Patroclus back from the Trojan wall (Π 700), and, a little later, even strikes him such a blow that he is easily slain by Hector (Π 793). He urges Hector to go against Menelaus (P 72, 582), but advises him not to fight with Achilles (Υ 375), and a few verses later he snatches him up and

Apollo in the Iliad.

---

[1] Ω 758, γ 279, η 64, ο 410, ρ 251, 494.
[2] Z 205, 428, T 59, Φ 483, ε 123, λ 172, 199, 324, ο 410, 478, σ 202, υ 80.

saves him from the son of Thetis (Υ 443). He leaves Hector only after the golden scales of Zeus have determined his fate (Χ 213). After Hector's death, he draws a dark cloud over the body, and wraps this about with the aegis (Ψ 188, Ω 18), and urges that this body be stolen from Achilles (Ω 32). At the close of the second day of battle, on seeing Athena follow Diomed, he suspects mischief (Κ 515), but reaches the Trojan camp just after the Thracian Rhesus and his comrades are slain. At the command of Zeus, he saves the corpse of Sarpedon, and sends it by the brothers Death and Sleep to the land of Lycia (Π 667),— a peculiarly fitting service for a divinity who was to be so closely associated by the Greeks with Lycia,—and he heals the wound of Sarpedon's cousin, Glaucus (Π 527). On the third day of battle he causes confusion among the Achaeans (Π 729, Ρ 118) and rouses Aeneas to fight boldly (Ρ 323, Υ 79, 118). He takes the form of Agenor, at the close of the fourth day of battle, in order to lead Achilles away from the city gate that the Trojans may enter the town unmolested. He thus gives Hector the opportunity to go within the gates ; he does not actually take him up and put him in the town, for the appearance of the *deus ex machina* must not be too obvious and frequent. In his active part in the contests on the field, he takes the form of other mortals : of Hecuba's brother Asius (Π 716), of Mentes, the leader of the Cicones (Ρ 73), of the herald Periphas (Ρ 323), and of Hector's cousin Phaenops (Ρ 583).

Why Apollo should be patron of the boxing-match (Ψ 660), is not clear. The story of his servitude to Admetus (Β 766) explains his interest in the success of Admetus's mares in the chariot-race (Ψ 383). His year of service to Laomedon is referred to twice (Η 452, Φ 444), but no reason for it is given. He is unshorn (ἀκερσεκόμης, Υ 39), but this need not be an indication of his youth, since the Achaeans in general were long-haired (Β 11).

Artemis, the maiden sister of Apollo, takes little part in the action of the poems ; in general she is a mere counterpart of her brother (Υ 71, Ω 606). In obedience to the command of Zeus, she goes to share in the conflict of the gods on the Trojan plain, but Hera

Artemis.

boxes her ears with her own archery, and sends her away in flight like a timid dove (Υ 39, Φ 470).

Artemis is a huntress,[1] and taught the Trojan Scamandrius to hunt all wild animals which the forest nourishes on the mountains. She herself "wanders over the long range of Taÿgetus or Erymanthus, delighting in the boars and swift deer" (ζ 102). She sends a devastating wild boar upon the fields of Calydon, because she had been neglected at the harvest-home festival of Oeneus (I 533). She is a head taller than her companions in the chase (ζ 107), and gives slender stature to the daughters of Pandareüs (υ 71).

Artemis as Huntress.

As has been seen in connexion with a similar office of Apollo (see p. 430), if any woman has a peaceful, sudden death, this is thought to come from the arrows of Artemis. Calypso says that Artemis slew Orion (ε 124), since the gods were unwilling that the Dawn should have a mortal husband. She kills the daughter of Bellerophon (Z 205), apparently in punishment for her yielding her virginity to Zeus, and her arrows kill the daughters of Niobe because of the latter's boast in her many children, in comparison with Leto, who had but two children, Apollo and Artemis (Ω 606).

Artemis sends Peaceful Death.

The lame Hephaestus, the god of fire, the Greek Tubal Cain, is the only deformed god, and the only craftsman on Olympus. He is son of Hera (A 572, Ξ 239) and Zeus (A 578), and at the close of the first book of the *Iliad* he does his best to reconcile his parents and to restore good cheer to the feast. Two explanations are offered for his lameness: he was hurled from heaven by Zeus (A 591), and after an all-day fall was picked up by Sintians on the island of Lemnos, with little life in him; or, he was born deformed, and Hera, ashamed of him and desirous to be rid of him, hurled him to earth, where Thetis received him and concealed him for nine years in her grotto (Σ 395), in which he forged all manner of trinkets. In the *Iliad* he has as his wife one of the Graces (Χάρις, Σ 382). According to the song of the Phaeacian bard, in the *Odyssey* (θ 266), his wife was Aphrodite, but she was unfaithful to him,

Hephaestus.

---

[1] ἰοχέαιρα, E 53.—Though Apollo is Ἕκατος, Artemis is not Hecate.

preferring Ares.   In the conclusion of the bard's lay, Hephaestus expected to sue for a divorce and the return of the presents which he had made to her father (θ 318),—but of this we hear nothing further.

Hephaestus is the builder of the houses of the gods (A 608, Ξ 167, 339, Υ 12).   He made for Zeus the aegis (O 310), and the sceptre which, by way of Pelops, descended to Agamemnon (B 101).   The armor *Hephaestus as* *Craftsman.* of Diomed is ascribed to him (Θ 195), as well as a silver mixing-bowl given by the Sidonian king to Menelaus, and later bestowed on Telemachus (o 117), the gold and silver dogs which watch the palace of Alcinoüs (η 91), and a golden jar in which the bones of Achilles are laid (ω 75).   At the request of Thetis he makes armor for her son Achilles, and he adorns the shield with scenes from all departments of human life, which are described with considerable detail (Σ 478 ff.).   When Thetis visits him (Σ 369), he is engaged in making twenty golden "tripods," evidently small three-legged tables,—fitted with castors, so that they should "of their own accord" go to the great hall of Zeus, when they might be needed, and return again to the home of Hephaestus.   Still more remarkable "automata" are the golden maidens, endowed with speech and reason, and with many accomplishments (Σ 417), which serve him as crutches, supporting him on either side as he walks from his smithy to his great hall.   He is associated with Athena in teaching technical skill (ζ 233 = ψ 160). His name is used by "metonymy" for fire (B 426; *cf.* P 88).

In the battles on the plain of Troy, Hephaestus takes little part.   He interferes to save a son of his Trojan priest Dares (E 23).   In the battle of the gods, he is opposed to the river Scamander (Υ 73), and when that *Hephaestus in* *the* Iliad. stream endeavors to drown Achilles, he burns its waters (Φ 330).   In this conflict, fire and water are seen to be at strife.   This brings Hephaestus back to his elemental nature, and indeed of all the Homeric divinities he has most of the elemental character.

Aphrodite is the goddess of love and of beauty,—not fitted for war but for the "works of marriage" (E 428).   She is

the daughter of Zeus and Dione (E 348, 370).[1]   In the lay
of the Phaeacian bard (θ 266), she is the unfaithful wife of
Aphrodite.   Hephaestus, in close relations with Ares. Her relation to Hephaestus is not elsewhere mentioned, but
in the conflict of the gods on the Trojan plain, she is associated
with Ares, and helps him away from the field when he has
been overthrown by a stone hurled by Athena ; but Athena
follows them, and by a blow of her hand casts both upon
the ground (Φ 416).

The standard of beauty is found in Aphrodite.   Achilles
would not wed the daughter of Agamemnon though she were
Aphrodite as   as accomplished as Athena and as beautiful as
Standard of   Aphrodite (I 389).   Briseïs, Cassandra, and
Beauty.   Penelope are " like to golden Aphrodite " (T 282,
Ω 699, ρ 37), and Helen's daughter Hermione
" has the beauty of Aphrodite " (δ 14).   The goddess, though
in the guise of an old woman, is recognized at once by Helen,
from her " beautiful neck and bosom and bright eyes " (Γ 396).
She is the giver of beauty to Paris (Γ 54).   Once her
embroidered girdle or " cestus " is said to be the seat of
her magic power (Ξ 214), and it is borrowed by Hera when
the latter wishes to make herself most attractive to Zeus.
She is attended and served by the Graces (σ 194, θ 364,
E 338), who make her gowns as well as assist in her toilet.
She is the mother of Aeneas by Anchises (B 820, E 248,
Υ 209).   Once she is said to have a sanctuary and altar at
Paphos on Cyprus (θ 363), and in the fifth book of the *Iliad*
she is called *Cypris* (E 330, 422, 458, 760, 883).   Twice she
is called *Cytherea* (θ 288, σ 193).   She goes to Zeus to ask
a fitting marriage for the daughters of Pandareüs (υ 73).

Since Aphrodite persuaded Helen to leave Menelaus and
go to Troy with Paris (Ω 30, δ 261), naturally she favors the
Aphrodite in   Trojans in their conflicts with the Achaeans.
the Iliad.   Her part in the battles is not great, however.
In the single-combat between Paris and Mene-
laus on the first day of battle, she saves Paris from
death, conveys him to his home, and then fetches Helen

---

[1] The story of her birth from the foam of the sea is not referred to by the poet. *Cf.*
Hesiod, *Theogony*, 195.—Homer mentions Dione only in this passage, but she is well
known later as the consort of Zeus at Dodona.

to him (Γ 374). A little later on the same day, in striving to save her son Aeneas from the spear of Diomed, she herself is wounded, and letting fall her son (who then is rescued by Apollo), she borrows the chariot of Ares in order to return to Olympus (E 312). Her last appearance on the plain, in connexion with Ares, has been mentioned above. She protects the body of Hector, keeping off the dogs and anointing it with ambrosial oil (Ψ 185). She gave a veil to Andromache on her marriage with Hector (X 470).

The principal epithets of Aphrodite are *smile-loving* (φιλομμειδής, Γ 424), "daughter of Zeus" (Διὸς θυγάτηρ, Γ 374), *divine* (δῖα, Γ 389), and *golden* (χρυσέη, Γ 64). The poet does not attempt any descrip- *Epithets of Aphrodite.* tion of her beauty. The epithet golden perhaps implies that she was a blonde, or it may be interpreted as referring to her golden ornaments. Once "Aphrodite" is used by metonymy for "love" (χ 444), just as "Hephaestus" is used for fire.

Hermes serves as messenger of the gods, perhaps with somewhat more authority than Iris, who also is often thus employed. The only mention of his parentage *Hermes.* calls him son of *Maeas* (Maea,—ξ 435). His father is not named.[1] He is the father of Eudorus, who leads one division of the Myrmidons (Π 185). As a "sociable spirit," he is sent by Zeus to conduct Priam to and from the tent of Achilles (Ω 334 ff.), and to Calypso's isle to carry the order for the release and return of Odysseus (ε 28). On Circe's isle he gives Odysseus the plant *moly,* and thus saves him from Circe's charms (κ 277). He carried from Zeus to Pelops the sceptre which was to descend to Agamemnon (B 104), he stole away Ares from the bronze jar in which the sons of Aloeus kept him prisoner (E 390), and he helped Heracles to return from Hades (λ 626). In return for many thigh-pieces of lambs and kids, he gives to Autolycus, the maternal grandfather of Odysseus, pre-eminent skill in "thievery and swearing."[2] The last libation

---

[1] Cyllene seems to be referred to as his birthplace in the epithet *Cyllenian* (Κυλλήνιος, ω 1).

[2] τ 396.—Apparently Autolycus could keep the letter of his oath while breaking its spirit. His namesake of *The Winter's Tale* was not his superior in roguery.—The

is made to him before men go to rest (η 137), and Eumaeus sets aside a portion of his evening meal for the nymphs and Hermes (ξ 435). He is a patron of servants, apparently (ο 319), and the giver of wealth (Ξ 491). He favors ·the Greeks in their conflicts with the Trojans (Ο 214), and in the battle of the gods is opposed to Leto, but courteously declines to assail her, saying that she may boast of a victory if she pleases (Υ 35, Φ 497). Doubtless because of his cleverness in such matters, although he favors the Greeks, he is urged by the gods to steal the body of Hector from Achilles (Ω 24). At the beginning of the last book of the *Odyssey* (long ago recognized as of later composition than most of the poem), he conducts to the realm of Hades the souls of Penelope's suitors, just slain by Odysseus, but nowhere else in the poems has he this office of *psychopompus*,— his assistance to Heracles in the matter of Cerberus was just such as Athena rendered in the same undertaking. In conducting the shades of the dead, he bears a golden wand, and this he carries when he escorts Priam to the Greek camp, apparently that he may put to sleep the warders of the gates (Ω 343, 445),—his "opiate rod." This wand suggests his epithet "of the golden wand" (χρυσόρραπις, κ 277); with it may be compared the magic wand of Circe (κ 238, 319). The most frequent epithet of Hermes is *Argeïphontes*,[1] but the meaning of this word is uncertain.

Epithets of Hermes.

Ares, son of Zeus and Hera (Ε 893 f.), who was later the chief Greek god of war, naturally has a prominent part in the action of the *Iliad*, though he appears among the men on the field of battle only during part of the first day, when he withdraws, being wounded

Ares.

only burglary of the poems is committed by Autolycus, who carried off a helmet which was given first to a man of Cythera, then to a Cretan, and later was lent to Odysseus (Κ 267). When this latter passage was composed, possibly Autolycus was not yet recognized as the grandfather of Odysseus.

[1] This for a long time was translated "Argus-slayer," but the Argus-myth is not referred to otherwise in the poems, and the word is best taken as a proper name, with its original meaning lost. The second stem may be that of φαίνω, not of φόνος, and the first stem may be that of ἀργός, *white, clear.* See Roscher, *Hermes, der Windgott.* The meaning of three other epithets of Hermes is somewhat uncertain: ἐριούνης (*helper?* θ 322), διάκτορος (*guide?* ε 43), and ἀκάκητα (Π 185).

by Diomed and Athena (E 868). His home seems to be in Thrace (N 301, θ 361), and of all Olympian gods he appears to be the most of a foreigner to Hellas. Strife ("Ἔρις, Δ 440) is called his sister and companion, and he is attended also by Terror and Flight (Δεῖμος and Φόβος,— who *inspires* flight, not who flees), whom he bids to yoke his horses (O 119), and of whom Flight is called his son (N 299). The Theban myth which made him the husband of Aphrodite, opposing another (perhaps Lemnian) myth which counted her as the wife of Hephaestus, led to the story of an adulterous relation between the two (θ 267); he is associated with her also in the conflict of the gods (Φ 416), and lends to her his chariot on the first day of battle, but there she calls him brother (E 359). A mortal maiden bears him twin sons, of whom one falls in battle (B 512, N 518). He had favored the Greeks, but now for some reason aids the Trojans, and is chided as fickle (ἀλλοπρόσαλλος, E 831). He rouses the Trojans (Δ 439, E 461), covers the battle with night for their advantage, and leads their advance (E 592). As god of war he is often associated or contrasted with Athena (E 766, P 398, Σ 516, Υ 69, 358), but she is mightier than he. They are opposed to each other in the conflict of the gods (Φ 391), but he comes off ignominiously,—being overthrown by a stone hurled by her, and then when Aphrodite tries to help him depart from the field, Athena with her thick hand (Φ 424) knocks both of them down. On the first day of battle, Athena leads him away from the active fight (E 30), and on the third day of battle, when he learns of his son's death and desires to return to the field, she takes the helmet from his head and the shield from his shoulders, and bids him be seated (O 125). Apollo induces him to return to the fight on the first day, and he slays mortals with his own hand, which no other god condescends to do, if indeed he does not strip them of their arms (E 847). He journeys to the plain in his chariot, but allows the wounded Aphrodite to use this, and himself returns among the clouds (E 867). When he is overthrown by Athena, he covers about two acres of land (Φ 407), and when wounded by her and Diomed, he yells as nine thousand or ten thousand men shout in battle (E 860). Reference is made to a former occasion on which he had been imprisoned by mortals in a bronze jar, but had been stolen away by Hermes (E 385).

Very often the name Ares is used for war or the spirit of battle, as Hephaestus stands for fire, and Aphrodite for love. Thus, that "Ares slew Isander in battle with the Solymi" (Z 204), means simply that Isander fell in the fight. Compare "Many are fallen whose dark blood Ares shed on the banks of the Scamander" (H 329), "that we may rouse keen Ares" (B 440), "that we may bring together Ares" (B 381), "bear Ares upon each other" (Γ 132), "Ares subdued" Sarpedon by the spear of Patroclus (Π 543); Achilles will fight with Hector "until one or other fall, and with his blood sate Ares, the shield-bearing warrior" (X 266). Warriors are "servants of Ares" (θεράποντες Ἄρηος, B 110), or "scions of Ares" (ὄζος Ἄρηος, B 540), or Martial (ἀρήιοι, Δ 114), or are "like to Ares" (ἀτάλαντος Ἄρηι, Θ 215, ἴσος Ἄρηι, Λ 295). Menelaus in particular is "dear to Ares" ('Αρηίφιλος, Γ 21). Like Athena, Ares has fierce eyes: on the second day of battle, Hector "has the eyes of the Gorgon or of man-slaying Ares" (Θ 349). Like Achilles, he is swift of foot (θ 331).

"Ares" for "War."

The principal epithets of Ares are *mighty, bloody, dreadful, destructive*. Enyalius[1] is a surname for him.

Poseidon, god of the sea, is son of Cronus and Rhea (O 187); his relation to Amphitrite is not mentioned. With his brothers Zeus and Hades, he had divided their new kingdom,—he receiving the Sea while the Earth and Olympus were to be common territory. He recognizes Zeus as the elder and mightier brother, however (O 204, O 211, Υ 16, ν 148; *cf*. N 355), and once on the latter's return to Olympus, he unharnesses for him his horses (Θ 440). His dwelling is in the depths of the sea, near Aegae (N 21, ε 381), but he appears on Olympus at the councils of the gods (H 445, Θ 440, Υ 13). He is the father of the Cyclops Polyphemus (α 73, ι 412),

Poseidon.

---

[1] ὄβριμος, E 845; μιαιφόνος, E 844; οὖλος, E 461.—*Cf*. N 519, H 166, etc. Enyalius appears once ('Ἐννεύς, I 668) in the form Enyeus, which is the masculine of *Enyo*, who is an impersonal Bellona, mentioned twice (E 333, 592).

and ancestor of Alcinoüs, king of the Phaeacians (η 61), and of Nestor (λ 241),—and he cares well for his descendants (a 69, ϵ 290, N 554, Ψ 307). Like his elder brother, Poseidon has dark hair ($\kappa\upsilon\alpha\nu o\chi\alpha\acute{\iota}\tau\eta s$, γ 6).

In the *Iliad*, Poseidon is a strong partisan of the Achaeans. He had been sent by Zeus[1] in the previous generation of men, with Apollo, to serve Priam's father, the Trojan king, Laomedon, who at the close of their service dismissed them with contumely and without their stipulated pay, although Poseidon had built the wall about his city (*cf.* H 453). He is particularly active on the third day of battle, when he rouses the Achaeans again and again.[2] Seeing him engaged in this work, in order that he may not be interrupted, Hera distracts the attention of Zeus, but when Zeus observes what is doing, he sends Poseidon back to the sea, whither he goes in high dudgeon (O 208). In the battle of the gods, Poseidon is opposed to Apollo, but the latter is unwilling to fight against his uncle (Φ 468). Although a friend of the Greeks, he is very angry at them for building a wall about their ships, since he fears it may obscure the glory of that which he built for Laomedon (H 446, *cf.* M 17), and he saves Aeneas from death at the hands of Achilles, since it is fated that the descendants of Aeneas shall reign over the Trojans (Y 302).

Poseidon in the Iliad.

In the *Odyssey*, Poseidon is so full of wrath at Odysseus for blinding his son, the Cyclops Polyphemus, that the other gods hesitate to insist on the Ithacan's return (a 20, 68) to his home.

In the Odyssey.

As lord of the sea, Poseidon rouses storms,[3] or gives a favorable voyage (I 362, δ 500). Angry because the Phaeacians convey too many ship wrecked mariners to their homes, thus interfering with his province, he turns into stone the Phaeacian ship which

Lord of the Sea.

---

[1] Φ 442. The poet gives no reason for this humiliation. Poseidon's part in the conspiracy against Zeus (A 400) cannot have been the cause, for in that he was not associated with Apollo.

[2] N 44, 94, 351, 435, Ξ 135 (where he takes the form of an old man), 384. He is enraged at the death in battle of a grandson, N 206.

[3] ϵ 291, *cf.* ι 283, λ 399, ψ 234, ω 109.

has just carried Odysseus to Ithaca (ν 163), although the Phaeacian king is his grandson. He brings death to Locrian Ajax in return for his impious boast that he had escaped the perils of the sea, even against the will of the gods (δ 505). Odysseus and Telamonian Ajax pray to him as they pass along the shore of the sea to the tent of Achilles (I 183),—probably since he was thought to be peculiarly near, in his element. The trident is the symbol and instrument of his power (M 27, δ 506). His most frequent epithets are *earth-shaker* and *earth-supporter*,[1]—earthquakes being caused, according to the Homeric view, by the movement of the water on which the earth was borne. He is also already the patron of horsemanship (*cf.* Ψ 584),—possibly because of the natural comparison between boats and chariots (δ 708, ν 81),—and he taught Antilochus to drive skilfully (Ψ 307). His wedding present to Peleus was a pair of immortal horses (Ψ 277), which Achilles later used in the battles on the plain of Troy. He himself has chariot and horses, which he leaves hobbled in a cave of the sea while he takes part in the battle (N 23).

Poseidon has sanctuaries at Onchestus (B 506), Helicé, and Aegae (Θ 203). Bulls are offered in sacrifice to him at

Worship of Poseidon.

Pylus (γ 6), and by the Phaeacians (ν 181), and a bull is dragged by youths in honor of the "Heliconian king" (Υ 404).[2] A bull, a ram, and a boar are to be sacrificed to him as an expiatory offering by Odysseus, in a land where the people know not the sea and eat food without salt (λ 131 = ψ 278,—*suovetaurilia*).

Of the lesser sea-divinities, Proteus is called distinctly an

---

[1] ἐνοσίχθων, H 445; ἐννοσίγαιος, N 43; γαιήοχος, α 68; *cf.* Υ 63. The Israelites, too, thought of the earth as resting upon the water. *Cf.* "Thou shalt not make unto thee any graven image of anything . . . that is in the water under the earth," *Exodus* xx. 4; "The earth is the Lord's and the fulness thereof . . . for he hath founded it upon the seas, and established it upon the floods," *Psalms* xxiv. 1.—The form ΓαιαϜόχῳ in a Spartan inscription (Cauer, 17), shows this word to be connected with the Latin *veho*, English *wagon*, rather than with the root of ἔχω, and thus to mean *carry*, not *hold*.

[2] The aim of this dragging is not stated, and the suggestion is made (Dörpfeld, *Troja und Ilion*, p. 565), that for this sacrifice the bull was drawn up the trunk of a tree or up a large post, until his body and legs were removed from the ground, as is represented on some ancient gems. See page 515.

underling of Poseidon. By the connivance of his daughter (Eidothea, δ 365), he is caught by Menelaus, on Pharos near Egypt, and tells him what has happened at home during the Spartan king's absence, and what he must do in order to return. Another sea-god, Nereus, is known only as the father of his daughter Thetis, who from the Trojan plain sends back to him her sister Nereids, who have accompanied her to the tent of Achilles, while she goes to the home of Hephaestus (Σ 141). After the death of Achilles, the sisters go to the Troad again to mourn with her (ω 55). Atlas, too, seems to be a sea-god, from his epithet, "who knows the depths of all the sea" (α 52). He does not appear to be a mountain ; the columns which support both earth and heaven appear to be the sea itself. Of Phorcys, the poet tells even less : he is the father of Thoösa, Polyphemus's mother (α 72), and a harbor of Ithaca is named for him (ν 96). Ino, Leucothea, was daughter of Cadmus, but became a divinity of the sea (ε 333), and saves Odysseus when his raft is wrecked. The question how a mortal maiden could be transformed into a sea-nymph, does not seem to have troubled the poet ; he simply accepts the story.

Lesser Sea-Deities.

The hundred-handed Aegaeon, called by the gods Briareüs (Α 403), whom Thetis summoned to Olympus to the aid of Zeus against the conspiracy of the mightiest of the gods, seems to be a sea-monster, and son of Poseidon, but he is mentioned only once, and that incidentally.

Aegaeon.

The relation of the river-gods to Poseidon, is not clear. He takes the form of one, the Enipeus (λ 241), to gratify his desire for Tyro. The Acheloüs is personified as one of the mightiest of rivers (Φ 194) ; the Alpheüs is father of Orsilochus (Ε 546) ; the Asopus is father of Antiope, who bore to Zeus two sons, Amphion and Zethus (λ 260) ; the Axius is the father of Pelegon (Φ 141) ; the Spercheüs has a son by Peleus's daughter (Π 176). To the Spercheüs, Peleus vows the hair of Achilles as a thank-offering, if he should return to Greece ; but sure that he is to fall before Troy, Achilles cuts off his hair and places it in the hand of his dead comrade

River-Gods.

Patroclus (Ψ 144). Near the close of the last day of battle, the Trojan river Scamander makes a vigorous effort to help the Trojans, by drowning Achilles, but he is opposed by the god of fire, Hephaestus, who proves the mightier (Υ 73, Φ 212, 356). This Scamander has a priest (E 77), and the Spercheüs has a sanctuary and altar (Ψ 148). As rivers have mortal children, so the Gygaean Lake is the mother of two Mysian chieftains in the Trojan army (B 865); here the Gygaean Lake is clearly a brief expression for the nymph of that lake (cf. Υ 384, 391).

Iris serves only as a messenger, taking no part in any discussion or action, except that she asks Poseidon, when *Iris.* he demurs at following the command of Zeus to depart from the conflict, whether he really means the answer which he first gives, and thus she recalls him to his sober mind (O 201). In addition to this errand she is sent by Zeus to warn the Trojans of the Achaean approach (B 786); without special instructions, she calls Helen to the Great Tower of Ilium to watch the single-combat (Γ 121), and aids the wounded Aphrodite to return from the field of battle (E 353, 365); she is sent by Zeus to stop Hera and Athena from descending to the plain (Θ 399) and to instruct Hector not to fight with Agamemnon (Λ 186); she is sent by Hera to rouse Achilles after the death of Patroclus, and to bid him appear before the Trojan warriors (Σ 167), and by Zeus to bid Priam go to the tent of Achilles to ransom Hector's body (Ω 144).[1]

Dionysus takes no part in the action, and does not appear on the Homeric Olympus. Indeed, the four passages in *Dionysus.* which he is named are suspected, with reason, of being of later composition than the bulk of the poems. He is the son of Zeus and Semele (Ξ 325), his nurses are attacked by Lycurgus on the Nyseian hill and he seeks shelter with Thetis (Z 132); he bears witness to Ariadne's elopement with Theseus from Crete (λ 325), and he gives to Thetis the golden jar, a work of Hephaestus, in which the bones of Achilles are buried (ω 74).

---

[1] Iris is not mentioned in the *Odyssey*, but the fact that the Ithacan beggar was nicknamed Irus because he ran errands (σ 6), shows that her office was familiar to the Odyssean poet.

Hebe is the cup-bearer for the gods on Olympus (Δ 2), and aids Hera in preparing her chariot for a drive to the Trojan plain (E 722). On the return of Ares *Hebe.* from the battlefield, she makes ready the bath for him (E 905). In the eleventh book of the *Odyssey*, she is the wife of Heracles (λ 603).

Dione appears as the wife of Zeus and mother of Aphrodite only in one brief passage (E 370-417).

Leto, the mother of Apollo and Artemis by Zeus (A 9, Ω 607 ; *cf.* Ξ 327), is associated with Artemis in caring for the wounded Aeneas (E 447). In the conflict *Leto.* of the gods on the plain of Troy, she is opposed to Hermes, but he courteously declines to contend with her, and she gathers the scattered archery of Artemis, and leaves the field (Φ 498).

Demeter is the goddess of the grain, and separates the chaff from the kernel (E 501). Pyrasus in Thessaly is called her sacred field (τέμενος, B 696), doubtless as being *Demeter.* peculiarly productive of grain. In a passage of late composition (Ξ 326), she is one of the numerous loves of Zeus, and Calypso cites her as a goddess who had passionate love for a mortal, Iasion (ε 125). She is not named in connexion with Olympus nor with the action of either of the two Homeric poems.

As master of the winds, Aeolus appears in a single passage (κ 1-76). He dwells on an island not far from the land of the Cyclopes, with six sons and six *Aeolus.* daughters, and receives hospitably . Odysseus and his comrades on their leaving the cave of Polyphemus. He not only directs a west wind to convey these to Ithaca, but gives to Odysseus the other winds, tied up in a leathern bag, to make sure that none of them blows so much as a little to interfere with their return. Unfortunately, however, the comrades of Odysseus suspect that this bag contains treasures of gold and silver, and as sleep overpowers their leader on coming in sight of home, after he has held the rudder continuously for nine days and nights, they untie the bag, and the winds burst forth, and hurry back to their home, the island of Aeolus, carrying the boat of Odysseus with them. The master of the winds infers that Odysseus must be hated by the gods and so refuses to help him further.

Of nymphs, the most noted are Calypso (a 14, ϵ 57) and Circe (κ 136, 543). Polyphemus is son of the nymph
Nymphs. Thoösa (a 71). The daughters of Helius, who tend his kine, are nymphs (μ 132). Nymphs, daughters of Zeus, sport with Artemis over the mountains of Taÿgetus and Erymanthus (ζ 103). On Ithaca was a cave near the sea by the harbor of Phorcys, sacred to the naiad nymphs (ν 104), in which were not only stone jars but a stone loom where the nymphs wove their mantles,[1] while on a higher part of the island was an altar of fountain-nymphs (νύμφαι κρηναῖαι, ρ 240), by a spring. In the *Iliad*, three naiad nymphs are mentioned as mothers of mortal sons (Z 21, Ξ 444, Υ 384),—all dwelling in north-western Asia Minor,—and others who dance on the banks of the Acheloüs (Ω 616). Mountain-nymphs (ὀρεστιάδες, Z 420) plant elms about the tomb of Andromache's father. The nymphs appear on Olympus but once (Υ 8),—the nymphs "who inhabit the groves, and sources of rivers, and grassy meadows."

The poet gives no intimation as to the form of the two Sirens (μ 182), who charm men by their song. Odysseus
Sirens. is able to hear them by stopping the ears of his comrades with wax, that these may not be beguiled to desert him, and by suffering himself to be bound securely to the mast, that he may not be able to follow the enticements of the Sirens. They promise him both pleasure and profit from their song, addressing him as "highly praised Odysseus, great glory of the Achaeans," and saying that they know all things which are done upon the earth. Around them lies a heap of "bones of rotting men" (μ 45), but how these men have perished is not told. The Sirens are not represented as having relations to the gods.

The misshapen Scylla—a sea-monster, with the voice of a whelp (μ 85), with twelve feet, and six long necks,

---

[1] Of course, nymphs wove, as well as Athena and Helen, but stone looms, from the analogy of modern "Devil's punch bowls," suggest the possibility that the stone formation supplied the name, without any belief in their actual use

on each of which is a terrible head, with triple rows of teeth,—is not worshipped, and can hardly be called a divinity in any reasonable sense, but *Scylla.* her mother is an abstraction, *Mighty Strength* (Κράταιϛ, μ 124).

The Chimaera is said to be of "divine race and not of men" (θεῖον γένος οὐδ' ἀνθρώπων, Z 180), but this is very nearly what is said of the Calydonian Boar sent by Artemis against the fields of Oeneus (δῖον γένος, *Chimaera.* I 538),—both are monsters sent by the gods,—and she has been mentioned in the category of animals, page 368.

The Harpies are apparently merely "snatching winds" (ἅρπυιαι ἀνηρείψαντο, a 241, ξ 371, υ 77). No notion whatever of their form is given, except that the "harpy Podargé (*Swift Foot*), feeding on the *Harpies.* meadow by the stream of Oceanus, bore to the West Wind" (Π 150) two horses, which Poseidon gave to Peleus, apparently as a wedding present.

That the duties of men to the gods were ritualistic rather than ethical, has been stated already. The Homeric Greeks had no Ten Commandments with divine sanction, and their gods were not in duty bound to *No " Ten* punish evil deeds, and to reward righteousness, *Command-ments."* although they were likely to do so. Men had received no prohibition against honoring as many gods as they liked, or against making and worshipping graven images, or against laboring whenever they chose, or against coveting the possessions of their neighbors, or indeed against committing theft, murder or adultery,—though circumstances might make one of these last acts exceedingly offensive to the gods as well as to men. As Plato points out (*Euthyphro*, 8), according to the Homeric theology, an act that was pleasing to one god, might be hateful to another. Of the Ten Commandments of the Israelites, the Achaeans in strictness had but two,—" Thou shalt not take the name of a god in vain," and " Honor thy father and thy mother." With respect to Zeus, a third commandment may be formulated, as " Thou shalt have respect unto the stranger and the suppliant, to pity them" (*cf.* ε 447, ι 270, ξ 404). Zeus was the special avenger of suppliants and strangers.[1]　Another offense against the gods, and perhaps the only sin of thought known to the early Greeks, is an overweening pride; they were to "walk humbly" with their gods. This pride, as in the time of Aeschylus and Herodotus, arouses the "envy" of the gods,—hardly the god's jealousy, in the ordinary sense of the term, but a strong disapproval of one man's exaltation high above all his fellows, and thus an unwillingness that any particular life should be perfectly happy (ψ 211).　Even in battle the combatants indulge in comparatively little proud boasting.　Achilles's words to the dead Hector are characteristic: "Lie there, dead,—but my fate I will receive when Zeus is pleased to send it" (X 365). Akin to the principle of distributive justice is the principle of compensation,—if Achilles is to be shortlived he should be happy while he lives (A 352, 415).

In the Homeric times, custom is not only law but also equity.　A man who follows the ways of the community is just and righteous.　The later word for virtue ($\mathring{a}\rho\epsilon\tau\acute{\eta}$)[2] means excellence, of any kind; occasionally (as ν 45; cf. θ 329, τ 114) it seems to mean no more than prosperity.　Under the circumstances of the life depicted in the poems, excellence in war is most important, and *virtue* (like the Latin *virtus*) often means *bravery*. Similarly a good man ($\mathring{a}\gamma a\theta\grave{o}s$ $\mathring{a}\nu\acute{\eta}\rho$) is one who is of value to the community.　In general, then, in the Homeric poems, a "good man" is not one who is pious and honest and pays his debts, and never is angry or drunken, but one who is a "mighty man of valor."　And a "bad man" ($\kappa a\kappa\grave{o}s$ $\mathring{a}\nu\acute{\eta}\rho$) is not a man who steals, or tells lies, or gets drunk, or stabs his fellow, but a coward and a weakling; and baseness ($\kappa a\kappa\acute{o}\tau\eta s$) may be nothing but cowardice or poltroonery.　The later word for character, from which our *ethics* is derived, is used but three times ($\mathring{\eta}\theta\epsilon a$, Z 511 = O 268, ξ 411),—twice of the wonted pastures of horses, and once of the pens of swine.　The later word for justice ($\delta\acute{\iota}\kappa\eta$) generally means *custom, manner*, but then naturally comes

"Custom" is Right.

---

[1] Achilles's fear to "offend the behests of Zeus" ($\Delta\iota\grave{o}s$ δ' $\mathring{a}\lambda\acute{\iota}\tau\omega\mu a\iota$ $\mathring{\epsilon}\phi\epsilon\tau\mu\acute{a}s$, Ω 570) may refer to the special command to spare Priam's life; but Zeus assures Priam that Achilles is "not wicked but will spare a suppliant" (Ω 157).

[2] $\mathring{a}\rho\epsilon\tau\acute{\eta}$ seems to be connected with $\mathring{a}\rho a\rho\acute{\iota}\sigma\kappa\omega$, and thus originally meant *fitness*.

to mean *the approved way.* So what in later Greek would be translated the *just man,* means little more than the courteous, well-mannered man (γ 52). Evidently the reflective ethical sense was not yet highly developed.

Of Plato's four cardinal virtues,—bravery, wisdom, temperance, and justice,—bravery naturally was the most important in the Homeric times, indeed we have just seen that it is often virtue itself. The Homeric noble's chief ambition was for distinction in war. If this were gained, the other requirements for his happiness —satisfactory marriage, wealth, power—were likely to follow *Cardinal Virtues: Bravery.* readily. Bravery, according to the Greek idea, is manliness,[1] and Hector's injunction to the Trojans is identical with that of St. Paul to the Corinthians,[2]—"Quit you like men, be strong,"—though the poet and the apostle had very different standards of manhood. Homeric life has little place for the quiet virtues,—it is a life of action.

The second cardinal virtue also, wisdom, is highly appreciated, and is considered as the proper complement of bravery. The highest praise to be conferred on men is that they are first both in the council and in *Wisdom.* battle (*cf.* A 258, B 202, 273, I 53),—"first in war and first in peace,"—men of thought as well as of action. So Helen says of Agamemnon that he is "both a good king and a mighty warrior" (Γ 179),—a verse which was the favorite of Alexander the Great. The boy Achilles was put in charge of the affectionate and trusty Phoenix that he might become "a speaker of words and a doer of deeds" (I 443). Odysseus preëminently is ever ready with devices (πολύμητις and πολυμήχανος), and the goddess who is distinguished for wisdom on Olympus, not only "cares for him as a mother" (Υ 783), but says plainly that she is fascinated by him, and cannot leave him,—he is so quick-witted and ready of mind (ν 331).

Of Plato's third virtue, temperance or self-control, perhaps again the best Homeric example is Odysseus. Plato reports

---

[1] Attic ἀνδρεία, Homeric ἠνορέη,—both formed from the stem of ἀνήρ, *man,* as the Latin *virtus* is derived from *vir.* Perhaps in these cases, as often, the derivative retains the primitive meaning.

[2] ἀνέρες ἔστε, φίλοι, Ζ 112: ἀνδρίζεσθε, κραταιοῦσθε, I *Cor.* xvi. 13.

Socrates as quoting more than once the words of Odysseus, "Be patient, now, my soul; thou hast endured still worse than this."[1] As regards anger, this self-control was warmly commended to Achilles by his father (I 255). As for the bodily appetites, the Homeric warriors do not seem to have been inclined to go to great excess. Their life in the open air, with simple food, appears to have been wholesome in this respect as well as in others, and the principle of excess in nothing (μηδὲν ἄγαν) is approved by the Greeks of Homer's age, as well as by their successors in the days of Sophocles.

Self-control.

As for the fourth Platonic virtue, justice,—the absence of the name does not prove the lack of the quality. In the chapter on the Homeric state (page 80), the reader may see evidence that the general sentiment of the community was so reasonable that little governmental interference was expected or necessary. The number of what we should call minor lawless acts, recorded or referred to in the poems, is very small. The single act of burglary was committed by Odysseus's maternal grandfather Autolycus (K 267, *cf.* τ 396), whose reputation in both the poems we have seen to be about as unsavory as it is in Shakespeare's *Winter's Tale.* Old Priam, in the bitterness of his grief for Hector, calls his surviving sons thieves of lambs and kids (Ω 262),—but this cannot be understood literally, and perhaps it implies chiefly that they lacked the courage to go on forays. Odysseus cheats the Trojan scout Dolon, whom he and Diomed take captive : these clearly give Dolon to believe that, if he will furnish them the information which they require, his life shall be spared (K 383), but after he in his cowardice has told them eagerly what they want to know, they kill him. Hera takes for Zeus an oath which is true according to the letter, but not in spirit (O 41). The most despicable and abominable act reported in the poems, as it would appear, is that of a goddess : Athena takes the form of Hector's brother, in order to deceive him and, by the false promise of her help, to persuade him to withstand Achilles (X 226). The only justification for this

Justice.

---

[1] τέτλαθι δὴ κραδίη. καὶ κύντερον ἄλλο ποτ' ἔτλης, υ 18. *Cf.* Plato, *Republic,* 390; *Phaedo,* 94 E.

is rather far-sought,—that the golden scales of Zeus have determined the issue of the conflict, and the speediest death for Hector is the most merciful.[1]

Human life is held in light esteem. Murder in itself is no very serious crime. Elsewhere we have seen that every man is obliged to avenge his own wrongs. No guardians of the law are watching to see that *Vengeance* his rights are maintained. Thus the gods clearly *belongs to the* approve of Orestes's act in killing his father's *Wronged.* murderer Aegisthus (a 46), just as in modern times the best men approve the action of a court in convicting and sentencing a murderer. Orestes himself is recognized as the proper executioner,—indeed he or Menelaus was the only possible executioner.

The public sentiment with regard to family relations is wholesome and good. Children are expected to love and honor their parents. The delight of the ship- *Family* wrecked Odysseus on sighting land, after he has *Affection.* been in the water for two days and nights, is compared to the joy of children on their father's recovery from a long illness (ε 394). So, on the other hand, Odysseus speaks of himself as the " father of Telemachus " (B 260), and a man's deepest sorrow is in burying his son who dies in early manhood (Ψ 222). The position of women in the family is far more modern and occidental in Homeric than it was in Periclean Greece. Helen and Areté are the mistresses of their households. The princess Nausicaa clearly expects to accept no husband on the mere choice of her parents ; she (not her father !) already has declined some offers of marriage (ζ 283). The Trojan warriors' chief motive for fighting is the defense of their children and their wives (θ 57, II 833). The servants were treated as members of the family rather than as slaves in the modern sense (see p. 258 f.).

The motive of patriotism is strong, as well as the love of kindred. When Hector is warned by a comrade to retreat,

---

[1] Very likely the poet's hearers regarded the justification of this act to lie in its being in a sense a return for that of Apollo, who struck Patroclus, and thus allowed Hector to kill him (II 791) ; but that, too, seems a rather dastardly act on the part of a divinity.

since the omens are unfavorable, he replies: "One omen is best of all,—to fight for the fatherland."[1] A little later on the same day, urging his men to fight, *Patriotism.* he calls to them that it is not unseemly to die in the defense of the fatherland,[2] and that, though a man dies, yet his wife and children will be safe, and his house and lot unharmed, if the Achaeans are driven away. And after Hector's death his mother proudly mourns for him as slain in the defense of Trojan men and Trojan women (X 435).

Unselfish generosity appears most distinctly in connexion with hospitality, but it is conspicuous in the readiness of one *Generosity.* people to aid another in war. This readiness is not explained solely by the love of conflict, and eagerness for the spoils of war, and the desire to secure allies who themselves may bring safety in the future,—it springs largely out of a generous spirit. Achilles had little to gain by the expedition against Troy; he reminds Agamemnon that the Trojans had not plundered his lands, nor were they likely to do so (A 153). With such a chivalrous spirit the Mycenaeans were about to aid the Theban Polyneices against his usurping brother, but were dissuaded by unfavorable omens (Δ 380). Neither Achilles nor these Mycenaeans seem to have been under any political obligations to render such service.

Truthfulness was never a highly developed virtue of the Greek race. Odysseus in disguise is ready with as many *Truth.* new and false stories of his life and adventures as any hearer could desire (ν 256, ξ 192, τ 172). One of these he tells to his own patron goddess Athena, with such verisimilitude as to win her hearty admiration. Zeus sends a Delusive Dream to Agamemnon (B *init.*), and Hera tells a direct falsehood to Zeus (Ξ 307). Near the close of the first day of battle, Athena seems to lie to Apollo without compunction: seeing the Greeks hard pressed in battle by the Trojans, she comes down from Olympus, evidently intending to aid them, but Apollo is watching

---

[1] εἶς οἰωνὸς ἄριστος, ἀμύνεσθαι περὶ πάτρης, M 243.

[2] οὐ οἱ ἀεικὲς ἀμυνομένῳ περὶ πάτρης | τεθνάμεν, O 496. This seems to be the earliest form of the Horatian *dulce et decorum est pro patria mori.*

and comes to meet her from the citadel of Troy, with the proposition that they arrange a single-combat between Hector and the bravest of the Greeks; to this Athena replies that she had come from Olympus for this very end (H 17). But Achilles in a well-known passage counts as hateful as the gates of Hades the man who conceals one thought in his breast and utters another (I 312). Odysseus, in words very similar to those of Achilles, expresses his hatred of the man who lies for the sake of gain (ξ 157), but only a few verses later he reports with commendation a frank lie (ξ 495).

Achilles, perhaps, and largely on account of the word just quoted, would satisfy the requirements of Aristotle's "magnanimous man" better than any other of the Homeric heroes, though he might not receive *Magnanimity.* this epithet in the modern sense of the term; but in the vehemence of his anger he is far from Aristotle's model. Menelaus in his Spartan home and Alcinoüs at Scheria approach the standard of Aristotle's "magnificent man.' Referring to Aristotle's other virtues, we may note that the Homeric poems have a buffoon (Thersites, B 212), but no prodigal and no flatterer.

In the discussion of the morals of the life depicted in the Trojan poems, the reader must always *Iliad* remember that the *Iliad* represents an army *Depicts a* near the close of a long war, with all the *Demoralized* demoralization that war brings. This considera- *Life.* tion must serve as a palliation for the treatment of Hector's body. On his death, the Achaeans stand around him, and look with wonder on his form and beauty,—but then each stabs him with his spear, and says: "Dear me! Hector is easier to handle now than when he burned our ships with blazing fire" (X 370). The mutilation of the faithless servant Melanthius, after the slaughter of Penelope's suitors (χ 475), was under very extraordinary provocation.

Great courtesy and tact, in general, are shown by the Homeric characters. Old Nestor will not refer to the troubles caused by Penelope's suitors on Ithaca until Telemachus himself broaches the subject (γ 211). At the home of Menelaus in Sparta, after Helen's return, one would say that the topic of her abandonment of her husband in order to go to Troy with Paris, was so delicate that it might well be tabooed, and that at least she would not refer to it. But she speaks of it with such regret, and so clearly throwing upon the gods the blame for her infatuation in leaving a husband, "inferior to no one either in mind or in body" (δ 261), that the result is a compliment to her husband, and no reproach to herself. To Helen's tact and grace, perhaps as much as to her beauty, seems to be due the fact that she is little blamed for her fault (see page 117). In the guise of an Achaean youth, Hermes meets King Priam on his way to the tent of Achilles, in order to ransom Hector's body,—addresses him as "Father," and cheers, and encourages him (Ω 362). This courtesy on the part of an Achaean pleases, but does not seem to surprise, the old king. Respect to elders is expected. The cup for a libation is offered to Athena in the guise of Mentor (γ 49), before it is given to Telemachus, because of Mentor's age. "It is well" to listen to a speaker, and not interrupt him (T 79). "It is an evil thing" to speak false (lit. *windy*, ἀνεμώλια, δ 837) words. "It is not well" for a Phaeacian to say that Odysseus, a stranger, does not look like an athlete (θ 166). "It is not well" that the guests of Telemachus should be slighted (υ 294 = φ 312). "It is not holy" to boast over the slain (χ 412), nor to contrive ill for the son of a benefactor (π 423).

A somewhat more detailed discussion of Homeric hospitality [1] is in place here, since this has not been considered, like most of the other virtues, in other relations.

Hospitality is one of the cardinal virtues of the Homeric Greeks, and an oath is taken "by Zeus, the table of hos-

Hospitality. pitality, and the hearth of Odysseus to which I am come" (ξ 158). Axylus of Arisbe was "dear to men" (Z 14), since "he dwelt by the wayside and was hospitable to all." Public houses of entertainment were unknown. No special guest-room, however, was furnished ; the guest was expected to sleep in the porch (as γ 399, δ 302, η 345). Telemachus, sitting in his courtyard among Penelope's suitors, observes Athena, disguised as a Taphian prince, at

[1] See Trumbull, *Studies in Oriental Social Life*, for parallels in the Orient.

the entrance to the courtyard, and is "troubled in soul that a stranger should stand long at the gate" (α 119). He grasps her hand, relieves her of her spear, and assures her of food first, and then an opportunity to tell her errand. Telemachus and Nestor's son Pisistratus arrive unexpectedly at the palace of Menelaus on the evening of the day of a double marriage there, but the king is offended by the suggestion of an attendant that the two young strangers should be allowed to seek some other host (δ 3 ff.). The shipwrecked Odysseus appears suddenly in the palace of the Phaeacians, and before telling who he is, he receives thirteen suits of clothes, a dozen pieces of gold, tripods and basins, and other gifts, and is feasted; and later he is conveyed to his home (θ 389, 439, ν 12),—and all this in spite of the fact that the Phaeacians in general did not favor strangers, and desired not to be visited by men of other lands. The great hall of Menelaus is full of gifts which he had received from his hosts on his wanderings : the king of Aegyptian Thebes had given to him two silver bath tubs, two tripods (probably three-legged tables), and ten pieces of gold, while the Aegyptian queen gave to Helen a golden distaff, and a silver basket on castors, with edges plated with gold, for her wool,—a "work-basket" (δ 128). On his departure from the home of Menelaus, Telemachus receives from his host a silver bowl with two handles,—solid silver, with gold-plated edges,—which Menelaus himself had received as a present from the king of Sidon; and Helen gives to the young Ithacan a robe which she herself had woven,—with the suggestion that this should be a present for his future bride, to be cared for meanwhile by his mother (ο 115). The obligation to "welcome the coming, speed the parting guest," is recognized in this very form (ο 74). A friend is said to be almost as good as a brother (θ 546, cf. ο 54).

The episode of Glaucus and Diomed (Ζ 119-236) affords excellent illustrations of the strength of the tie formed between guest and host. The grandfather of Diomed had entertained at his home Bellerophon, the grandfather of Glaucus, and on parting they had exchanged gifts; Diomed still had at home the golden cup which his grandfather received from Bellerophon. This

Guest-Friendship.

tie of friendship was transmitted to the descendants, though these were in ignorance of each other, so that when the two grandsons of the two friends meet as enemies, on the field of battle, on learning of the connexion of their ancestors, they not only separate in peace, saying that each has plenty of others to slay, but even exchange arms,—though this leads Glaucus to give " gold arms for bronze arms, arms worth a hundred cattle for arms worth nine."

A Potiphar's-wife charge was brought falsely by the wife of Proetus of Tiryns against Bellerophon, grandfather of Glaucus (Z 160). Proetus might not slay one who *Bellerophon's* had been his guest, but he sends Bellerophon to *Experience.* his father-in-law in Lycia, with a tablet in which were cut deadly tokens, requesting him to put Bellerophon out of the way. But the Lycian king, before asking to see the letter of introduction, entertains his guest royally, slaughtering a bullock every day for nine days. On reading the letter from his son-in-law, the king is in a quandary, having no right to kill one who has been his guest, and yet desiring to comply with the wishes of Proetus. So he sends him first to slay the Chimaera, and next against the Solymi, and then against the Amazons,—expecting him to perish in each expedition ; finally, he sets an ambuscade for him, but Bellerophon kills all his men. Then the king recognizes his guest as under the care of the gods, and gives him his daughter in marriage, and half his kingdom.

The inheritance of the tie of friendship is emphasized also *Tie of* by Telemachus, son of Odysseus, in bidding *Friendship* farewell to Nestor's son, Pisistratus, who had *Inherited.* accompanied him to Sparta.[1]

In the cave of Polyphemus, Odysseus appeals to the Cyclops to spare him and his comrades, as strangers in the Cyclops's dwelling (ι 268), and after he has blinded *Appeals on* the monster he exults over him as punished by *Basis of* Zeus and the other gods (ι 478). Similarly, *Hospitality.* Ajax, coming with the embassy to Achilles, begging him to return to the fray, reminds him that they are under his roof (I 640),—they are his guests. Near the close of the battles of the *Iliad*, Achilles comes upon

---

[1] ξεῖνοι δὲ διαμπερὲς εὐχόμεθ' εἶναι | ἐκ πατέρων φιλότητος, ο 196.

Priam's son Lycaon, whom on a former occasion he had taken captive, and had sent to Lemnos for sale, but who had been ransomed, and had returned to the war (Φ 54). Lycaon pleads vainly that though he had not been exactly a guest of Achilles, at least he had eaten bread at his tent, when a captive, and that therefore Achilles should not kill him now. The evil deed of Paris, in stealing from Menelaus Helen and many treasures, was greatly magnified by the fact that Paris was a guest in the home of Menelaus (N 625), and the murder by Heracles of Iphitus, his own guest, was a horrible act (φ 28).

CHAPTER XV

HADES AND HIS REALM[1]

HADES in Homer is the name of a person,[2] not of a place. He is son of Cronus, and brother of Zeus and Poseidon, who divided among the three their new kingdom,—
Hades a Person the realm of murky darkness (ζόφον ἠερόεντα) falling to Hades (O 191).[3] In the action of the story, he does not appear on Olympus, but the poet says that he went thither for healing, when wounded by Heracles (E 398). His personality is not prominent in the poems, nor does he possess any marked characteristics. He is "Nether Zeus" (Ζεὺς καταχθόνιος, I 457). His name is so connected with Persephone's that she seems to be his wife (I 457, κ 491), but in another passage she is daughter of Zeus (λ 217); perhaps, however, if Zeus is the brother of his wife Hera, Hades may be the uncle of his wife Persephone. Persephone is not known as the daughter of Demeter. Her relation to Hades's rule, also, is not clear, either; it is she who

---

[1] The eleventh book of the *Odyssey* (the *Nekyia*), which tells of the visit of Odysseus to the home of Hades, contains much that is without parallel in the rest of the poems,—partly from the nature of the case; the scene in that realm at the opening of the last book of the *Odyssey* (the so-called *Second Nekyia*) has been recognized by most scholars as of late composition, and the ninth book of the *Iliad*, to which reference is made below, cannot be one of the earliest parts of the poem. So our conclusions on this subject must contain much that is doubtful.

[2] The name *Pluto* is not Homeric.—The occasion for Hades's epithet "with famous steeds" (κλυτόπωλος, E 654=Λ 445) is not explained.

[3] Erebus is used as the name of the place of darkness. Thus comrades of Sarpedon "go to Erebus" (II 327), and Heracles was sent to "fetch the dog of Hades from Erebus" (Θ 368). *Cf.* I 572. Elsewhere ἔρεβος may be simply darkness, or even the west (as μ 81; *cf.* κ 528, λ 564).

gives wisdom to the ghost of the old seer Teiresias (κ 494), and she seems to have more immediate direction of the shades than Hades himself (λ 213, 217, 226). Neither is the relation to him of Minos distinct, who "gives judgments" to the dead (λ 569),—apparently serving as ruler, but whether in an executive or judicial capacity, is uncertain. Only once in the poems does Hades act as a person: when the gods are assembled for conflict on the Trojan plain, and Poseidon shakes the earth and the mountains (Υ 61), Hades leaps from his throne, with a cry, in fear that the earth may be torn open and expose his "dolorous mansions to the peering day." He is "implacable and unyielding" (ἀμείλιχος ἠδ' ἀδάμαστος, Ι 158), and so the most hateful of all gods to mortal men. In the former generation he had been wounded by an arrow of Heracles (Ε 395),— possibly when Heracles brought up his watch-dog (Θ 368, λ 625), but this is not stated. He is a mighty gate-keeper (πυλάρτης, Θ 367, Ν 415, λ 277). In a prayer to Hades and Persephone, invoking a curse upon her son, the mother of Meleager sits upon the ground and beats the earth with her hands, evidently to attract the attention of the nether divinities (Ι 569), just as the hands were raised to the sky in addressing the Olympian gods. In making the truce for the single combat of Menelaus and Paris, Agamemnon prays to Zeus, the sun, rivers, earth, and *the two* who beneath the earth punish the breach of oaths (τίνυσθον, Γ 279), and these two may be supposed to be Hades and Persephone.

In general the realm of Hades lies beneath the earth, like the mediaeval hell,[1] yet Odysseus, on his visit to the home of the dead, descends through no cavern,[2] but sails to the land of shades in a single day from Circe's island (λ 11). It lies on the borders of Oceanus, near the country of the Cimmerians, who are wrapt in mist and cloud, and on

Realm of Hades beneath the Earth.

---

[1] ψυχὴ κατὰ χθονὸς ᾤχετο, Ψ 100 ; κατελθόντ' Ἄιδος εἴσω, Ζ 284 ; Η 330, Θ 16, Ξ 457, Υ 61, Χ 425, κ 174, 560, λ 65, 164, 475, 625, ψ 252.—That the realm of the dead should be thought to lie beneath the earth, perhaps implies the practise of inhumation. The expression "the earth held them down" (Γ 243) may refer rather to the burial of the bodies than to the situation of the souls.

[2] How Heracles visited Hades in the Homeric story, is not made clear.

whom the sun never looks. The river which the soul of the unburied Patroclus is not allowed to cross, can hardly be Oceanus (Ψ 73), but is rather the Styx, which in an oath seems to be in a way a symbol of Hades, being associated with Heaven and Earth (O 37). The geographical course of the Styx, however, is not indicated in any way, nor that it appears at any place upon the earth. The rivers Acheron, Pyriphlegethon, and Cocytus (which last is a branch of the Styx) are merely named, and that only once (κ 513). None of these rivers is seen by Odysseus on his visit to that realm. The ferryman Charon has no place in the Homeric story, and the river Lethe and the Acherusian Lake are not mentioned at all. Though Hades is a gate-keeper (Θ 367), and Heracles was sent to fetch his dog, yet Odysseus on his visit thither sees neither gate nor dog, nor even Hades himself. Clearly Elpenor and the ghosts of Penelope's suitors have to cross no river Styx,—but why this river could not be crossed as easily as Oceanus itself, is not easy to imagine ; both were running waters. At the opening of the last book of the *Odyssey*, Hermes leads the souls of Penelope's slain suitors " along the murky ways, past the gates of the sun and the country of dreams, to the Asphodel Plain, where dwell the souls, the images of the dead " (ω 10). The opposition between these views of the situation of the realm of Hades seems clear, and scholars generally hold to a different authorship of these different parts of the poems,[1] although some would believe that, by sailing to the far west, Odysseus was thought to find a horizontal entrance to the inner part of the earth.

How this realm of Hades is lighted, the poet does not tell his hearers. In the *Iliad*, as we have seen, it is a gloomy land (Υ 65); but on his visit to it, *How is it Lighted?* Odysseus recognizes without difficulty his former acquaintances, and the element of gloom is not even indicated. Odysseus indeed does not penetrate into

---

[1] See p. 45.—Another view suggested is that Hades is still beneath the ground when Odysseus reaches the entrance to it, and that the ghosts come up out of the earth, as appears in some ancient vase-paintings ; and that in turning the heads of the victims to Erebus (εἰς ἔρεβος, κ 528), he turned the heads not to the west or north but down towards the ground.

the inmost recesses, but even the neighboring Cimmerians have no sun. Angry because his kine have been killed by the companions of Odysseus, the Sun-god threatens to leave heaven and earth, and to descend and give light to the dead, but this threat is not fulfilled (μ 382).[1]

Tartarus is mentioned only in the eighth and fourteenth books of the *Iliad* (Θ 13, 481, Ξ 279). At the beginning of the second day of battle, Zeus threatens the divinities that he will "hurl into murky Tartarus,— *Tartarus.* far away, where is the deepest pit beneath the earth, where are the iron gates and the bronze threshold, as far beneath Hades as heaven is high above the earth,"—any of the gods whom he shall see aiding either Greeks or Trojans. Again, near the close of the same day, in wrath at Hera's disobedience, he says that he heeds not her anger, "though she should go to the extreme bounds of earth and sea, where Iapetus and Cronus sit, cheered neither by the rays of the sun nor by breezes, but lofty (*deep*) Tartarus is about them." And, again, Hera swears by all "the gods beneath, in Tartarus ($\dot{v}\pi o\tau a\rho\tau a\rho\iota ov\varsigma$, Ξ 279), who are called Titans." Here appears the same inconsistency as in regard to the position of the realm of Hades; in the second of these passages, Tartarus does not seem to be beneath the earth, while in the other two passages it is subterranean.

That Tartarus was thought of as a place of suffering,— an ancient hell,—is nowhere intimated in Homer. The Titans are not in chains, and the lack of breezes can hardly of itself prove the temperature to be uncomfortable; the Cimmerians, too, are beyond the reach of the sun's rays, and probably are not visited by breezes, but the poet does not indicate that they are suffering punishment. When Zeus says to Hera that he cares not for her anger, even if she should go to Tartarus, he certainly cannot be thinking of this as a place of intense suffering. To say that she may go there is very different from bidding her go thither. Homer did not think of Tartarus as a mediaeval *hell*; it certainly contained no devils. Perhaps Tartarus was a place

---

[1] Pindar's supposition (*Frag.* 129) that the sun shines for the dead during our night, finds no support in Homer unless President Warren's theory be adopted (*Paradise Found*, pp. 467 ff.).

to which undesirable gods were transported, just as men were transported a century ago from England to New Zealand or Australia.

The Elysian Plain is mentioned but once (δ 563): the sea-god Proteus predicts that Menelaus is not to die, but is

Elysian Plain.

to be sent to the Elysian Plain at the bounds of the earth, where dwells the tawny-haired Rhadamanthys and where life is easiest for men,— without snow or storm or rain, but with the breezes of Zephyrus sent by Oceanus for the refreshment of men. This lot of Menelaus has been compared with the translation of Enoch (*Genesis* v. 24), who " was not, for God took him." But why is Menelaus to be thus favored? Because of his upright moral character or martial renown? Not at all,—he was but a weak warrior (μαλθακὸς αἰχμητής, P 588), and not distinguished in the council. He has this distinction simply because he is the husband of Zeus's daughter Helen. Rhadamanthys is mentioned casually in two other passages of the Homeric poems (Ξ 322, η 323), but why he should be sent to Elysium is not indicated, either, nor why his brother Minos should be made a judge or ruler in the realm of Hades, except that he was a mighty ruler while he lived on earth. Why should not Sarpedon or Hector, both so dear to Zeus, and one of them his own son, have been so favored, as well as Menelaus? Who else dwells there, in addition to Rhadamanthys? The poet does not tell his hearers. The passage seems of late composition, and strongly resembles a description of Olympus itself (ζ 42).

The Islands of the Blest are not mentioned in the Homeric poems.

According to a familiar later view, the soul of the dead was not admitted immediately to the realm of Hades, but

Burial Required.

wandered in loneliness on the confines of that land, until the body was either burned or buried. In only one Homeric passage, however, is this belief clearly expressed, while in one other it may be assumed, if the reader chooses. The soul of Patroclus appears by night to Achilles, with the stature, eyes, and voice, and in the raiment, of the dead friend, and says: " Bury me at once. Let me pass the gates of Hades. The

souls of the dead keep me far away, nor do they suffer me
to join them on the other side of the river" (Ψ 71). And
when Odysseus reaches the land of Hades, the first to greet
him is the soul of his comrade Elpenor, who had fallen
from the roof of Circe's dwelling on the preceding night,
and whose body was still unburied (λ 51).[1] A euphemism or
periphrasis for death, is to depart to the home of Hades (as
E 646, X 482). No guide seems to be needed for this
journey,[2] just as no ferryman is required for the Styx, nor
are any rites of burial absolutely necessary. Hector, it is
true, is eager and anxious that his body may be returned
to his home for burial (H 77, X 339),—but he makes no
allusion to this as necessary for the future peace of his soul,—
and this motive appears to be used by the poet chiefly in
order to excite the hearer's interest in the fate of Hector's
body as it is dragged to the Achaean camp, and around the
tomb of Patroclus, behind the chariot of Achilles, and as
Priam visits the tent of Achilles in order to ransom it. Priam
does not urge upon Hecuba (Ω 194) this motive for attempting
to ransom their son's body. Hector himself had been eager
to cut off the head of Patroclus and fix it on a stake above
the Trojan walls (Σ 176), and to give the body to the
Trojan dogs (P 127). That men did not wish to have the
bodies of their friends or of themselves torn by wild beasts
and vultures, does not even begin to show that they had
inherited old beliefs with regard to the connexion between
the soul of the dead and the body which this soul had once
inhabited, leading to a certain treatment of the corpse.[3] The

[1] One of the old scholars asked why Odysseus did not meet on the threshold of
Hades his other comrades, who had been devoured by the Cyclops or the Laestrygonians. The rather gruesome answer to the problem was that these had been
buried, although ἀθέσμως, in the maws of the cannibals (Scholia on λ 51). But if
this were a satisfactory burial, then their "monuments" well might be "the maws of
kites." Not a hint is given that the souls whose bodies were made the "prey of the
dogs and a feast to the birds" (A 4) on the Trojan plain, were at a disadvantage when
sent to Hades.—That Elpenor's soul should be seen by Odysseus before any other's, is
quite intelligible, since he was the very latest arrival, having died only the preceding
night.

[2] Once only Hermes is represented as ψυχοπομπός, conducting to Hades the souls
of Penelope's slain suitors (ω 1).

[3] That in earlier times, and perhaps by many Greeks of Homer's age, the soul was
thought to maintain a species of connexion with the body and to care for it, cannot

ordinary modern care of a friend's dead body, and the laying of flowers upon his grave, are prompted by no conscious thought that the friend is pleased by the adorned coffin or by the smell or the sight of the flowers. Epicurus required the usual funeral honors for himself and his friends (Cicero, *de Fin.* ii. 102), although he denied the existence of the soul after death, and many a successor of Epicurus desires religious rites at his funeral, and a handsome monument. Nowhere in our poems is the ill-treatment of a body after death brought into connexion with the misery or discomfort of the soul, nor is this effect upon the soul mentioned in connexion with the negotiations for a truce for the burial of the dead (H 327, 375, 409). That a man, instead of a man's soul, is said to go to Hades, or to be in Hades,[1] is no greater inaccuracy than the ordinary ancient and modern expression, to bury a man, instead of to bury his body (*cf.* Plato's *Phaedo*, 115 C), and proves nothing even as to the popular belief.

In the belief that the soul at the point of death, when half in the body and half out of the body, had a disembodied spirit's freedom, and could foretell the future, the *Soul at Point of Death may Prophesy.* Homeric Greeks agreed with many others. Thus Hector at the point of death predicts the killing of Achilles by Paris and Phoebus Apollo (X 359), as Patroclus had predicted the death of Hector himself (II 852). See page 520.

Many synonymous expressions are used for death: " These two were stretched in the dust " (Δ 536), " bite the earth " *Synonyms for Death.* (B 418), " darkness covered his eyes " (Δ 461), " his limbs were loosed " (Δ 469), " hated darkness seized him " (E 47), " death covered him " (E 68), " dark night covered his eyes " (E 659), " the end of death covered these " (E 553), " the dark cloud of death encompassed them " (δ 180), " the two entered the earth " (Z 19), " his soul descended to Hades " (κ 560), " sent many mighty souls to Hades " (A 3), " enter the home of Hades "

be doubted. But caution is necessary that the reader may not assume the Greeks who maintained certain customs to have inherited also the beliefs on which those customs were originally based.

[1] As Λ 262, Φ 48, X 52.

(H 131), "fell in the dust and seized the earth with his hand" (Λ 425), "Fate enveloped him" (M 116), "life-destroying death was poured about him" (N 544), "his soul left him" (Π 410), "to leave the light of the sun" (Σ 11), "met death and destruction" (T 294), "meet death and fate" (Υ 337), "fell asleep" (Λ 241). As darkness is associated with death, so to live is "to see the light of the sun" (E 120, *cf.* A 88).

The existence, the "life" if it may be so called, of the souls after death is a shadowy reflection or imitation of man's life on earth,[1]—almost as neutral as the Hebrew *Sheol*. *Life in Hades.* Even the voices of the dead are but echoes of their former selves. The ghosts, like Shakespeare's "sheeted dead," "do squeak and gibber"; the voices of the shades of Penelope's suitors, "trooping to their infernal jail," are compared to the squeaking of bats in a great cave (ω 9; *cf.* Ψ 101). The souls are as unsubstantial as dreams,—and we have seen that Death and Sleep are twin brothers, and the entrance to the land of shades lies hard by that to the country of dreams,—but the ghosts in the main pursue the very occupations in which they were employed while upon the earth, kings remaining kings, and hunters following their old game,—though others have the outward form of their last appearance upon earth. Thus that the later myth makes the daughters of Danaüs carry water in Hades, may not have meant originally that they were punished; they may have been merely continuing in Hades the processes of irrigation or fetching water which had occupied them on earth. That Odysseus sees at the entrance to Hades "men slain in battle, with bloody armor" (λ 40), is in harmony with the doctrine of modern ghost-stories in which the apparition of a murdered man is wont to show the wound which caused his death. So Banquo's ghost shook "gory locks" at Macbeth. On the other hand, the ghost of Patroclus, on its visit to Achilles, seems to be clad in the clothing which Patroclus himself was wont to wear (Ψ 67), just as the elder Hamlet's ghost seemed to wear "the very armour he had on | When he the ambitious Norway

---

[1] *Cf.* Pindar's account (*Frag.* 129) of the dead as entertaining themselves, some with horse-races and gymnastic contests, others with draughts, and others with the lyre,— but in Pindar's time the ghosts had gained much additional vigor.

combated " (*Hamlet* i. 1. 60), and Agamemnon's ghost cannot have borne the marks of Aegisthus's blows, or Odysseus would have known that the " king of men " did not meet his death by drowning (λ 399). Odysseus in Hades recognizes at once his mother and his other friends ; their faces and forms are not greatly changed,—nothing is said even of pallid cheeks. The shade of Heracles (though " he himself," curiously enough, is " feasting with the immortal gods," λ 602) carries a bow and appears ready to shoot ; and the ghost of the mighty hunter Orion, with a bronze club,—doubtless only the shade of his former club,—is chasing the ghosts of the wild beasts which long before he had hunted and slain upon the mountains.[1] Minos acts as governor or judge (λ 568), apparently doing after death just what he had done while alive,—ruling and judging.

Circe tells Odysseus that Persephone grants prudence (πεπνῦσθαι, κ 495) to the ghost of the seer Teiresias only, while the rest of the dead flit as shades. Thus

Teiresias alone has Wit in Hades. the mother of Odysseus, though preserving her former appearance, and recognized immediately

by her son, does not recognize him until she has partaken of the offering of blood (λ 152), which clearly is not intended merely to please the shades, and still less to appease any anger which they may cherish, but at least chiefly to give them strength for a brief period of consciousness,—*i.e.* it is not a sacrifice in the ordinary sense.[2] Each of the Famous Women who come up to Odysseus, one after another, and relate to him the stories of their lives and families, requires the draught of blood before she speaks (λ 228) ; and thus also the soul of Agamemnon drinks of this offering (λ 390), but after him the blood is not mentioned in the narration, possibly only because the frequent repetition of the act would be monotonous in the story, although movement on the part of Odysseus is assumed when he sees Minos, Tityus, and others.[3]

---

[1] λ 572. A club would seem an unsatisfactory weapon for a hunter, but according to Pindar (*Nem.* iii. 51) Achilles killed deer without dogs and nets, for he was swifter of foot than they,—ποσσὶ γὰρ κράτεσκε.

[2] This seems at least not to be identical with the later offerings which are expected to maintain the shades in good condition, as by regular daily food.

[3] Odysseus certainly does not penetrate into the inmost recesses of the realm of Hades. The souls come to him, he does not go to them (λ 37). This supports the

Though the souls are as unsubstantial as dreams, yet they not only have the human form,[1] but also may feel anger, like Ajax (λ 565), or joy, like Achilles (λ 540), or may weep, like Agamemnon (λ 391); they are kept from the offering of blood by the drawn sword of Odysseus (λ 48, 147), and they partake eagerly of the blood and wine and honey which are provided. *Capacities of Souls.* If the ghosts of Tantalus, Sisyphus, and Tityus are included, we see dead men suffering not only hunger and thirst, but also physical pain, and performing physical labor. Agamemnon's ghost is eager to learn about his son Orestes, and Achilles inquires concerning his son Neoptolemus, but they have not heard of them from any of the new-comers before the arrival of Odysseus,—though this may be simply the poet's device not to forestall his hero's story. That the ghosts of Patroclus (Ψ 65) and Elpenor (λ 51), and the shades of Penelope's suitors (ω 120), have no need of the strengthening draught of blood before speaking, is perfectly reasonable,— they have been dead but a few hours. How long the effects of a draught would continue, would be a useless question.[2] That the companions of Odysseus, on retreating from the land of the Ciconians (ι 65), called thrice on the souls of their fallen comrades, implies at least that these souls were thought to possess intelligence and the power to hear, as well as that they desired a resting-place at home, and did not want to be left in the land of the Ciconians.

Even this shadowy existence of the souls of the dead, is not conceived as lasting for ever,—it is not immortality in the modern sense, though no hint is given that they endured only as long as their memory was kept alive on earth. *Immortality not clear.* Odysseus sees in Hades no ghost older than the second or third generation before

comparison of his visit to Hades with the evocation of the spirit of the prophet Samuel by the Witch of Endor, for King Saul (1 *Sam.* xxviii. 7).

[1] The diminutive size of the ghost as depicted on old Greek vases, seems to be a device to indicate the invisibility of the soul to mortal eyes. Odysseus marks no difference of stature in his friends, when he sees them in the realm of Hades.

[2] But Agamemnon's ghost in the *Second Nekyia* (ω 20 f.) talks with his comrades without any strengthening potion.

him.[1]   But the so-called heroic period of Greece had very few generations.   Homer's Hades naturally is an Achaean Hades, and the poet knows no un-Hellenic customs there any more than elsewhere in the world.

In these matters, least of all, is strict consistency to be expected or demanded.   Dante's spirits are incorporeal, and

Not perfect Consistency.
yet suffer from cold and heat and other pains; their voices, too, are but a shadow or echo of themselves, yet Casella can sing.   Pindar's pictures of the future life are not entirely consistent.   That Achilles in one book of the *Iliad* is assured that Patroclus is beyond his reach, never to return (Ψ 75), and yet in the next book hopes that his friend will not be angry with him, if, though in Hades, he shall learn that the body of Hector has been given to Priam (Ω 592), and that Achilles thus promises to him a portion of the ransom,—this does not prove that the first scene was by an Aeolic and the second by an Ionian poet.   No more does the less elaborate description of the funeral rites of Hector than of those of Patroclus, justify the inference that the rites were simplified as the belief became common that the consciousness of the dead continued after the funeral rites,—for the poet may not have desired so soon to repeat so long an account.[2]

The word *idol* (εἴδωλον, λ 83) which is used of the ghosts of the dead, is used also of a wraith of the living Aeneas,

Idol.
over which the Achaeans fought (E 449) while Aeneas himself was healed in Apollo's temple, and of a representation of Penelope's sister,—virtually a dream,—which is sent by Athena (δ 796) to Penelope for

---

[1] Ghosts in India are said to be individual for only three generations.   Thus a man needs to pay no special worship to the shade of his great-great-grandfather.

[2] We have no Hellenic evidence to show that the funeral ceremonies were more elaborate at the time when the soul was believed never to return after these rites were completed, than they were when the soul was thought to hover long about its body's resting-place.   The soul of Patroclus was not hovering about its body, but came on a special errand, when it visited Achilles.   To say that this ghost had no good reason for visiting Achilles, who was already intending to burn his body the next day, is as otiose as to say that Odysseus had no good reason for going to Hades, since Circe told him more than Teiresias, and that Telemachus had no good reason for going to Pylus and Sparta, since Athena could have told him all that was necessary.

her comfort.   Such an *idol* of Helen, according to Stesichorus, accompanied Paris to Troy (*cf.* Plato, *Republic*, 586 C).

Whether the Asphodel Plain (λ 539, ω 13) was thought of as a cheerful or a dreary place, cannot be made out with certainty.[1]   That the existence in Hades was not satisfactory to Achilles, is shown by his reply to Odysseus, who congratulates him on his honors in Hades as a worthy sequence to his glorious *Asphodel Plain cheerful?* life on earth : " Speak not comfortably to me of death, O glorious Odysseus.   I should rather be upon the field as the servant of another, of one who had no land and little property, than be the king of all the dead " (λ 488).   And if the proud Achilles would rather serve on earth than reign in Hades, doubtless the ordinary man expected to gain nothing by death.   A recently published view that, in the oldest parts of the poems, men, weary of the struggle for existence, looked upon death as a relief from toil (*cf.* εἴδωλα καμόντων, λ 476) cannot seriously be maintained.   In general, the Homeric heroes enjoyed life and strongly desired its continuance.   According to the poems, *Death not Welcomed.* Epicasta (λ 277), mother and wife of Oedipus, Anticlea (λ 202, ο 359), mother of Odysseus, and apparently Clytaemestra (γ 310), unfaithful wife of Agamemnon, commit suicide ; but two of these were driven to the act by shame and remorse, and Anticlea by her longing for her absent son.   Odysseus himself meditates suicide when, on nearing his native land, he awakes to find that his companions during his slumber have untied the bag of winds (see page 443), and that he is borne with them again away from his home (κ 51), but he endures patiently.   The suicide of Telamonian Ajax is not stated distinctly, but is implied in saying that the arms of Achilles brought death to him (λ 555).   These are the only instances of suicide in the poems.   The Homeric Greeks take a wholesome, cheerful view of life.   The famous saying, " As is the race of leaves,

[1] That the asphodel in Greece often grows in modern graveyards, as in other deserted places, proves nothing for ancient associations.   That the Homeric Greeks thought of the dead as receiving physical nourishment or other advantage from the bulbs of the asphodel growing above their bodies, as is sometimes suggested, is very improbable.—Unprejudiced visitors to Greece in early April generally think the asphodel a cheerful flower, but a little later it is unquestionably cheerless.

such also is that of men" (Z 146), is not uttered in a pessimistic tone, and the words of the disguised Odysseus, " Of all creatures that move and breathe upon the earth, man is the most helpless " (σ 131), must be understood in connexion with his warning to the man whom he addresses,— one of Penelope's suitors, whose father he well remembered, but who soon is to fall by the speaker's hand. Similarly, in the conflict of the gods on the field of battle (Φ 464), Apollo says to Poseidon that they should not fight together for the sake of wretched mortals who are like to the leaves (cf. " as a flower of the field, so he flourisheth," *Psalms* ciii. 15), which are now luxuriant, and again wither,—but the contrast between gods and men is particularly marked at this moment.

Men are neither punished in Hades, in general, for their evil deeds done upon earth, nor rewarded there for the good deeds done in this life. Three notable apparent exceptions stand by themselves, seen by Odysseus on his visit to the realm of Hades,—Tityus, Tantalus, and Sisyphus.[1] Tityus lies stretched over more than two acres of land, with his liver torn by two vultures, paying the penalty for an assault on Leto (λ 576). Tantalus stands hungry and thirsty, with water and fruit just out of his reach (λ 582). Sisyphus continually and unavailingly urges a great stone up a hill (λ 593). But, curiously enough, why Tantalus and Sisyphus suffer and toil, the poet does not say ; it can hardly be, as has been suggested, because of gluttony and an undue spirit of enterprise ! Sisyphus[2] did not have a bad name everywhere in Greece : not only does the Lycian Glaucus boast his descent from him (Z 153), but Pindar counts him one of the glories of Corinth (*Ol.* xiii. 52), and in his address to his

Neither Rewards nor Punishments.

---

[1] The punishment in Hades of Ixion and the Danaids is un-Homeric.—This passage (λ 576-600) has no organic connexion with the story of Odysseus's visit to Hades, and cannot have been an original part of it. He was sent thither by the poet not only to consult the seer, but also for the sake of his meeting with his mother and his former comrades on the plain of Troy. But the sufferings of Tantalus and his associates have nothing to do with Odysseus, and are not even made out to be characteristic of the place.

[2] The name seems to be formed by reduplication from σοφός, *wise*. The epithet κέρδιστος (Z 153), *shrewdest*, applied to him, seems to be used in a complimentary sense.

judges, Socrates thinks with pleasure of the possibility of interviewing Odysseus and Sisyphus in Hades (Plato, *Apology*, 41 C). Strictly speaking, then, Homer knows of no instance of rewards, and of only one case of punishment, after death. Sisyphus and Tantalus suffer, but for no stated crime. Mr. S. Reinach ingeniously explains the stories of the three sufferers as really based on misinterpreted paintings : Tityus was a man slain in battle, with body torn by birds of prey,—just as Odysseus saw in Hades men who had been slain in battle, with gory armor. Sisyphus, the old ruler of Corinth and builder of the Sisypheion on Acrocorinthus, was doing in Hades just what he had been doing in life, heaving great stones up a hill,—just as Orion continues his occupation of hunting. Finally, according to Reinach, Tantalus with a stone over his head (Pindar, *Ol.* i. 57) and standing in a marsh, personifies his city, which was overthrown by an earthquake and became a marsh, with high rocks on the hill above.

The question how unsubstantial spirits can be plagued by physical pain, does not disturb Homer any more than it did his great successor, Dante ; and not only the *Physical Pain.* neo-Platonist Plutarch (*de Sera*, 567) but even Plato himself (*Phaedo*, 113 D) uses language which implies the possession of bodies in describing the sufferings of the souls in their *Infernos*. The Christian Father, Justin Martyr, has no doubt that the souls and bodies of men are to be reunited for eternal suffering.

In making the truce for the single-combat between Menelaus and Paris, Agamemnon invokes the two divinities who beneath the earth punish perjurers (Γ 278),[1] but this has its only Homeric parallel in the *Punishment beneath the Earth.* similar invocation of the gods by Agamemnon, at his reconciliation with Achilles, when he swears by "the Erinyes who beneath the earth" punish perjury (Τ 259),—where "beneath the earth" cannot be equivalent to "after death," as is indicated clearly by the order of words as well as by the other offices of these divinities.

---

[1] In Γ 278, the use of καμόντας declares that the punishment follows death, but this odd use for θανόντας is found only here, and thrice in εἴδωλα καμόντων (as λ 476).

The Erinyes are not to be understood as ministers of
suffering to the souls of the dead. No imps or devils are
Erinyes. employed in torturing, or even in guarding and
overseeing the suffering of Tantalus, Tityus, and
Sisyphus. The Erinyes do not correspond to the modern
notion of Furies,—the Homeric Greeks knew of no evil-
minded or unkindly divinities. In no case are they represented by the Homeric poet as punishing murder, and the
only instance in which they are connected with perjury is
the one just named. Their principal duty seems to be the
maintenance of proper family relations. Meleager's mother,
cursing her son for killing her brother, prayed to Hades
and Persephone (I 569),—clearly not for his future punishment, but for his immediate death (which was granted,
according to Bacchylides),—and "the Erinys that walks in
darkness" heard her in Erebus, and brought the enemy
against the city; and conversely, the father of Phoenix
invoked the Erinyes to curse his son, and the nether Zeus
and Persephone granted his prayer (I 454),—not for the
punishment of Phoenix after death but simply for his
childlessness, and so his desolation, in this life. Telemachus
fears woes in this life from the Erinyes, if he shall send his
mother away from his home,[1] and Oedipus, while still
living, suffered woes from the Erinyes of his mother (λ 280).
When Poseidon hesitates to obey the command of Zeus,
Iris reminds him that the Erinyes always accompany the
elder brother,—which surely was not intended to be a threat
to the god of his punishment after death (O 204). Once the
Erinyes appear as guardians of the rights of hospitality (ρ 475),
and once they seem to be used like Nemesis to humble the
proud (υ 78), but still without reference to the dead. The
reader will remember that Odysseus sees no one in Hades
suffering punishment for perjury. So the prayer of Agamemnon
stands alone, and this warrior himself, in referring to the breach
of the truce which is confirmed by this prayer, does not say that
the Trojans will be punished after death for this act of perjury,
but that Zeus will take vengeance upon them by the destruction
of their city, and the death of Priam and his people (Δ 160).
The Erinyes certainly are not ministers of suffering after death.

---

[1] μήτηρ ἀρήσετ' ἐρινῦς, β 135; cf. Φ 412, O 204.

While the spirits of men after death were thought to lead such a shadowy existence as is indicated for them in the Homeric poems, no need was felt for cheering or propitiating them in any way. They had passed *No Need of Propitiation.* from the region of earth never more to return ; they were helpless and powerless. The shade of Patroclus appears as a dream to Achilles, but says expressly that it can never again return when once it has received due rites of fire, *i.e.* of burial (Ψ 75). Thenceforth, when once admitted to the realm of Hades, it is beyond the reach of friends and enemies on earth ; it can receive no satisfaction, and it can work neither weal nor woe.[1] Odysseus's mother tells him that the might of the funeral fire has destroyed the flesh and sinews (λ 219) of the dead.

No satisfactory explanation has been found for the inconsistency between the views of the Epic poets,—for Hesiod, too, says nothing of the worship of the dead,— and the practise of the later Greeks in paying *Why no Worship of the Dead?* sacrifices and making libations to the dead, customs which we must suppose them to have inherited from very early times, and which archaeological excavations show to have prevailed at Mycenae long before the Homeric age. The most plausible suggestion offered in explanation of this inconsistency, is that on leaving their old homes and the graves of their ancestors, on the mainland of Greece, and in particular on adopting the custom of burning the bodies of the dead, which would remove the possibility of the soul's return to its former habitation, the Greeks who migrated to Asia Minor left behind them also their belief in the influence over them of the spirits of their ancestors. But this is not wholly satisfactory, for even if they left their old ghosts behind them, they could have gained new ones in the next generation.[2] Certain rites in

[1] Elpenor's threat (λ 73) that he may be the cause of the gods' wrath to Odysseus, if his body is left unburied, does not refer to any visitation or other vengeance which the ghost itself can bring, nor to any future punishment of Odysseus in Hades, but only indicates the displeasure of the gods. *Cf.* X 358.

[2] Helbig calls attention to the large number of haunted houses and rooms in England, and the fewness of these in America,—but the New England colonists did not abandon their belief in ghosts, as the German scholar seems to have been informed, and many an American garret is still full of ghosts,—which even cremation

the funeral of Patroclus may be understood as the survival
of customs from an earlier worship of the dead, but here,
too, the tokens of reverence end when the corpse is consumed
by the fire, and the funeral mound is raised.

Twice in the poems, offerings are made which bear a close
resemblance to sacrifices to the souls of the dead,[1] although
they may be distinguished from them. At the
*Offerings to
the Dead.* funeral-pyre of Patroclus, Achilles leans jars of
honey and of oil against the bier on which the
corpse lies (Ψ 170). The jars of oil can hardly have been
intended primarily to encourage the burning of the body,
which was already wrapt in the fat of sheep and kine,—and,
in that case, the oil would have been poured upon the wood,
and the jars would have been carried away or broken. And
when Odysseus goes to the realm of Hades to consult the
seer Teiresias, following the directions of Circe, he digs
a small pit in the ground, a cubit square, and "pours about
it a libation for all the dead, first mixed-honey [*i.e.* milk and
honey], then sweet wine, and thirdly water" (λ 25). Then
after a prayer to the dead, including a vow that on his
return to Ithaca he will sacrifice a farrow cow and burn a
pyre full of treasures, and in particular that he will sacrifice
a black ram to Teiresias, Odysseus cuts the throats of a
ram and of a black ewe in such a manner that their blood
flows into the pit.[2] As we have seen, the distinct immediate
purpose of the sacrifice by Odysseus is to give to the souls
of the dead sufficient physical strength to answer his
questions, and the promised sacrifices were not to be made at
the graves of the dead, as for example at Thebes for Teiresias,

would not banish. Even in California are haunted houses, for which no mortal
tenant can be found. Rohde gives as the *cause* of the adoption of cremation by the
ancestors of the Homeric Greeks, a desire to rid themselves of the souls of the
dead; and as a *result* of the change, the abandonment of the old ritual and
sacrifices.

[1] In the Catalogue of Ships, B 550, Erechtheus at Athens receives annual offerings
of bulls and rams, but this part of the poems stands by itself in many ways, and
Erechtheus is there son of the grain-giving land and nursling of Athena,—*i.e.* virtually
deified, the only instance in the poems of such deification.

[2] *Cf.* the offerings to the dead: milk, honey, water, wine, olive oil, and flowers to
the shade of Darius (Aesch. *Persians*, 610); milk, wine, honey, oil (Eur. *Iph.
Taur.* 159, 633).

but to be made on Ithaca, actually in the court or the
hall of Odysseus, to which we may not conceive the ghosts
to be personally invited,—*i.e.* no connexion is assumed between
the soul and the place where its body (or its body's ashes)
was laid.   But that the ghosts were attracted by the scent
of the blood, indicates familiarity with such offerings of
blood as were made at the tomb of Pelops in Olympia in
Pindar's time (αἱμακουρίαις, *Ol.* i. 90).   These vowed offerings,
to be paid on Ithaca, have been thought by some to be
of merely sentimental value, though the choice of a black
ram and a farrow cow is not so explained; thus Andromache,
seeing the naked body of Hector dragged behind the chariot
of Achilles to the ships of the Achaeans, wishes that she
might wrap it in the raiment which lies in her halls,—this
raiment she will burn, she says, "of no advantage to thee,
Hector, since thou wilt not lie therein,[1] but to be an honor
in the eyes of the Trojans" (X 513).   These seem like
survivals of old, not fully understood customs.   That, at the
funeral feast in honor of Patroclus, cattle were slaughtered
so freely that the blood flowed in streams,[2] may indicate not
so much the shedding of blood for the advantage of the
corpse, as the abundance of the provision for the feast, as
is shown by the two previous verses, which are devoted
to the singeing of swine, which can have had no immediate
relation to the dead.

The nearest relation or friend was expected to close the
eyes of the dead.   Thus Agamemnon is particularly grieved
and wroth, that after his murder by Aegisthus,
his wife Clytaemestra would not even close his   *Closing the*
eyes and mouth (λ 426), and Odysseus threatens   *Eyes of*
a Trojan antagonist on the field of battle that   *the Dead.*
his father and mother shall not close his eyes, but the
vultures shall tear his flesh (Λ 452).   This closing of the
eyes and mouth seems to have been a symbolic rite, indicating
that the work of the body was done.

---

[1] The inference that these garments would be of advantage to Hector if his
body were wrapped in them at the time of his burial, is not clear.   Why should
they not profit him as well if they were burned separately, as Achilles seems to
propose for Patroclus at Ω 595?

[2] κοτυλήρυτον, Ψ 34, literally, *so that it could be taken up in cups.*

When the body of Patroclus is brought to the tent of Achilles, it is bathed with warm water, and anointed,[1]—the wounds in particular being filled with ointment (Σ 350), which may have had antiseptic properties to delay corruption. Then, covered with a soft linen cloth,[2] and a mantle above this, it is laid upon a couch which serves as a bier, with the feet toward the door (T 212),[3] and, all night long, Achilles leads the lament of the Achaeans, with his hands laid upon his friend's breast. Achilles will not bury the body of Patroclus until he has slain Hector, but meanwhile captive Trojan women shall wail about the bier (Σ 339). He also stoutly refuses to taste food until he has avenged his friend's death.[4]

Treatment of the Dead.

The body of Hector, though at the tent of Achilles, is anointed with ambrosial oil by Aphrodite (Ψ 187), and on its ransom it is bathed and anointed by the serving-women of Achilles, and is wrapped in a tunic and covered with a mantle,[5] and laid upon a bier (Ω 587). On its return to Troy, it is met by the Trojans before the city gates, and Hector's wife and mother hasten to the wagon and embrace his head. When the body is brought to the palace, minstrels are set beside it who sing

Hector's Funeral.

---

[1] Similarly the body of Sarpedon is bathed by Apollo, and anointed with ambrosia (II 670).

[2] Helbig thinks the soft linen cloth may have been in the form of bandages, like the mummy-wrappings of Egypt; but the same expression ($\dot{\epsilon}\alpha\nu\hat{\omega}$ $\lambda\iota\tau\dot{\iota}$, Ψ 254) is used of the cloth in which the urn itself is wrapped a little later. (See page 158.)

[3] This is thought to indicate a desire that the ghost shall not return, but if this was the origin of the practise, it may have been forgotten long before Homer's time.

[4] T 209. *Cf.* "And when all the people came to cause David to eat meat while it was still day, David sware, saying, 'God do so to me and more also if I taste bread, or aught else, till the sun be down,'" 2 *Sam.* iii. 35.

[5] Helbig compares a Cean inscription of the fifth century B.C. (Dittenberger, *Sylloge*, ii². n. 877), which ordered that only three garments be laid with the dead,—one under the body ($\sigma\tau\rho\hat{\omega}\mu\alpha$) and one over the body ($\dot{\epsilon}\pi\dot{\iota}\beta\lambda\eta\mu\alpha$), in addition to the tunic. *Cf.* Plutarch, *Solon*, 21. Penelope's famous "web" was announced as a funeral robe for the old Laërtes,—perhaps, as Helbig suggests, the one which was to be laid over the corpse. Thetis furnished these robes for her son's funeral (ω 67).

a dirge, while the women of the palace groan and shriek in response,[1]—this corresponding to the lamentation of the captive women about the body of Patroclus in the tent of Achilles. Then, in succession, Andromache, Hecuba, and Helen sing brief lyric laments, to which the women of the palace respond as before (Ω 709). "For nine days," Priam tells Achilles, "we would mourn for Hector in our halls; on the tenth we would bury him, and the people would feast; on the eleventh we would build a mound over him, while on the twelfth we will fight, if indeed we must" (Ω 664).

Some process of preserving the dead body from decay seems to have been known and used,[2] for the body of Achilles is committed to the flames on the eighteenth day *Embalming.* after his death (ω 65), and that of Hector is treated with despite by Achilles for eleven or twelve days (Ω 31), and then is bewailed by the Trojans for nine days before his burial (Ω 664). The body of Patroclus is kept from decay by Thetis, who drops "ambrosia and red nectar" through his nostrils (T 38), and the body of Hector is anointed with ambrosial oil by Aphrodite (Ψ 185), but something must have suggested to the poet such a preservation. We have seen that the dead body after bathing was anointed, but this may have been simply because, in ordinary life, ointment was always used after a bath. Possibly honey was used as a balsam.

The Homeric warriors were much freer than westerners of modern times, in the expression of their emotions. For example, Agamemnon sheds abundant tears in his council of Achaean elders (I 14) and Telemachus weeps in the assembly of Ithacans (β 81). So no one should be surprised at the violence of their expressions of grief. On learning of the death of Patroclus, Achilles stretches himself on the ground, and heaps dust and ashes on his head, while the captive women run out of the tent with loud shrieks, and

[1] For the modern Oriental custom, see H. C. Trumbull, *Oriental Social Life,* but the Irish *keen* shows that the usage was not limited to the East.

[2] ταρχύω, H 85, strictly cannot mean to *bury,* but to *embalm.* The connexion with τάριχος, *dry salt fish,* would seem to show that the Greeks were familiar with the preservative effect of the nitre in the soil, on bodies buried in Egypt.

beat their breasts (Σ 23). In grief for Hector, King Priam sits upon the ground in the court-yard, wrapt close in his mantle, and heaps dust upon his head; his sons sit about him weeping, and his daughters and his sons' wives mourn within the palace (Ω 161). The death of Protesilaus left his wife "with both cheeks torn" (ἀμφιδρυφής, B 700) in her grief. So Diomed boasts that of the man hit by his spear, "his wife's cheeks are torn, and his children are orphans" (Λ 393). And Briseïs, on returning to the tent of Achilles and seeing the dead Patroclus, "shrieks loudly, and with her hands tears her breast and neck and face" (T 284). No instance occurs of rending one's garment in grief.[1]

Expressions of Grief.

The use of black in mourning appears but once. When, near the close of the action of the *Iliad*, Thetis, with heart full of grief for the approaching death of her son Achilles, is summoned to Olympus, she takes a dark wrap (κάλυμμα κυάνεον, Ω 93), "than which is no blacker garment,"—clearly as a sign of deep mourning.

Black in Mourning.

One princely, military funeral is described in detail,— that of Patroclus (Ψ 110 f.). Agamemnon sends men and mules to the foot-hills of Mt. Ida to bring wood to the shore for the funeral pile. Achilles bids his Myrmidons gird themselves as for battle, and to prepare their chariots. The chariots,—bearing the knights, the nobles,—lead the way, the infantry follow. In the midst, his comrades bear the body of Patroclus, covered with the locks of hair which they had cut off as a sign of mourning.[2] Achilles follows the corpse as chief mourner,[3] bearing his friend's head. When they reach the place appointed for the pyre, Achilles cuts off his long tawny

Funeral of Patroclus.

---

[1] This is recognised as an oriental custom by Aeschylus in his *Persians*, 124, 199, 468, 537, 835, 1060; *Choëphoroe* 29.

[2] Nestor's son Pisistratus classes cutting the hair with weeping, as a mark of respect and mourning for the dead (δ 198). *Cf.* ω 46; Euripides, *Alcestis*, 427; Plato, *Phaedo*, 89 B; Xenophon, *Hell.* i. 7. 8.—Apparently already here the lock of hair stands as a symbol for the person; as to give a lock of hair is symbolically to give the whole person, to cut the hair may be a survival of the mutilation of the body.

[3] King David himself also "followed the bier" of Abner (2 *Sam.* iii. 31).

hair and places it in the hand of Patroclus. The pyre is built, a hundred feet square, and the body is laid upon it at the centre, wrapt from head to foot in the fat of many sheep and kine (doubtless to facilitate the cremation), while the carcases of the beasts are laid on the outer part of the pyre. Jars of honey and oil are leaned against the bier. Four horses, two pet dogs,[1] and twelve young Trojans, taken captive on the last day of battle, are then slain, and their bodies laid on the outer part of the pyre, and finally fire is applied. Since the pyre does not burn freely, Achilles calls upon the winds, Boreas and Zephyrus, and promises them goodly sacrifices in return for their aid. Being notified by Iris, these winds come and fan the flames all night, while all night long, Achilles moves slowly by the side of the pyre, pouring wine upon the ground and calling upon the soul of his comrade. In the morning, the coals are quenched with wine (with which water may have been mixed), the bones of Patroclus are collected, and, placed between a double layer of fat to preserve them from disintegration, are laid in a golden[2] basin or urn (φιάλη, Ψ 253). This urn is wrapt in a soft cloth and set in the barrack of Achilles, apparently to await the death of that hero, that the bones of the two friends may be buried together. But on the site of the pyre a temporary mound is reared, which for the present is a cenotaph. This mound will be made higher and broader on the death of Achilles (Ψ 247). After these services are completed, Achilles prepares for an elaborate series of athletic contests in honor of his friend,—a chariot-race, a boxing-match, a wrestling-bout, a foot-race, a contest with spears, another in hurling the discus, another in shooting at a mark, and finally one in hurling the spear.[3] (See page 143.)

---

[1] Dogs' teeth were found in the bee-hive tomb at Vaphio. Tsountas and Manatt, *Mycenaean Age*, 152.

[2] The material of the urn is naturally chosen for merely sentimental reasons, just as a magnificent coffin or tomb is prepared for a prince in modern times.

[3] Ψ 258 ff. With these funeral games, *cf.* those of Achilles (ω 85), of Oedipus at Thebes (Ψ 679), and of Amarynceus (Ψ 631); also X 163; Hesiod, *Works and Days*, 654. Many of the great stated athletic contests of Greece were thought to be funeral in origin, and such funeral games were instituted in later, historical times.

The funeral ceremonies of Achilles (ω 63) are not reported
with such fulness of detail as those of his friend, but he was
Funeral of Achilles. mourned for seventeen nights and days,—the Muses
themselves acting as the singing women (ω 60),—
and his body was covered with oil and honey, and
wrapt in raiment brought by his goddess-mother. While the
pyre burned, the Greeks moved about it,—both infantry and
chariots,—and in the morning the white bones were collected
and placed in a golden urn, the gift of Thetis, presented to
her by Dionysus, and the work of Hephaestus,—with oil and
unmixed wine, and with the remains of Patroclus. Over this
urn a high mound was reared on a promontory projecting into
the broad Hellespont. Games followed, as at the funeral of
Patroclus,—the prizes being offered by Achilles's mother,
Thetis.

The funeral ceremonies of Hector seem to have been similar
to those of Patroclus (Ω 784), though the narration is brief,
Funeral of Hector. but no funeral games followed. His bones are
gathered from the pyre, wrapt in soft purple
robes, and laid in a golden chest (λάρναξ, Ω 795),
—which must have been a kind of coffin,—and this is placed
in a trench or grave (κάπετος, Ω 797). Apparently the
customs of inhumation are here combined with the usages of
incineration.[1] Nothing is said of burying arms or other
treasures with the bones of Hector or Achilles ; although the
argument *ex silentio* is dangerous, apparently no such tribute
is paid. The ceremonies of the funeral of Hector close with a
feast in the palace of Priam,—a rite which is familiar enough
not only in the orient but also in the west, and of which

These games were in honor of the dead (Ψ 274, 646), but nothing in the Homeric
poems indicates that the dead were believed to find any delectation in them, or
that they were usually held before and not after the burial (see page 143).

[1] Similarly the shade of Patroclus begs Achilles that one *coffin* (σορός, Ψ 91) may
contain their bones. The use of honey on the pyre of Patroclus is explained by Helbig
as derived from its use in the preservation of bodies,—a sort of embalming process ;
while others more reasonably see in it a survival of an offering of food. In either case
a custom of burial is followed in the act of cremation. Euripides (*Iph. Taur.* 634)
knows a custom of pouring honey on the pyre.—At the Archaeological Congress in
Athens in 1905, Dr. Dörpfeld maintained that in ancient Greece the general custom
was to burn the body before burial, but that the bodies seldom were actually consumed by the fire. Mr. Evans thought that the indications of fire in the tombs might
be the ashes of the family hearth transferred from the home.

survivals remain in Great Britain and America as well as in Ireland.[1] The funeral feast ($\tau \acute{a} \phi o s$, Ψ 29) for Patroclus is held before the funeral pyre is lighted. That for Hector, in Priam's palace, is held after the burial mound is reared (Ω 802); but that the Trojans had another feast, before the mound was built, is indicated by words of Priam to Achilles already quoted: "on the tenth day we would bury him and the people would feast, and on the eleventh day we would raise a mound over him" (Ω 665). No hint intimates that the shade of Patroclus cared whether the feast was held before or after the burial or the erection of the mound.

In Mycenae, at the time of its prosperity and power, inhumation of the dead was practised, though perhaps in combination with cremation, and men seem to have believed that the happiness of the soul could *Gifts to the Dead.* be increased by gifts placed with the body, and by later sacrifices and libations at the tomb, while in the Homeric poems cremation is the rule, as indeed it seems to have been in still earlier times in Greece. That the Greeks before Troy are in a foreign land, and might not want to bury their dead in hostile soil (*cf.* Aeschylus, *Agamemnon*, 455), of course, does not explain the burning of Hector's body. This difference of custom has not been explained, but it must not be considered very important since the customs of cremation and inhumation have subsisted side by side in many places and times, just as they did in Athens at the time of Socrates.[2] Inhumation was common in Asia Minor in early historical times, and scholars have called attention to Agamemnon's expression with regard to the possibility of Menelaus's bones rotting in the land of Troy (Δ 174), which would be used more naturally of a buried than of an incinerated body, and to the statement of the

---

[1] See Trumbull, *Oriental Social Life.* Dean Stanley wrote of wine and cake as handed round between the Scripture lessons and prayers at a Scotch funeral in 1860: "It seems that this is a relic . . . of a feast given to the friends, which for many years was the only service at a Scotch funeral, the clergyman being asked only to say grace before and after, and in the grace introducing appropriate remarks." Stanley, *Life and Letters*, ii. 95. Hamlet's "funeral baked meats" are familiar. Dr. Trumbull says that such feasts were "an expensive accompaniment of funerals in the rural communities of New England" at the middle of the nineteenth century.

[2] Crito asks Socrates in effect whether he prefers to be cremated or to be buried. Plato, *Phaedo*, 115 C.

Little Iliad (Kinkel, *Epici*, 40, 3) that the body of Ajax was not burned but was placed in a coffin (σορός).

The killing of captives, horses, and dogs by the pyre of Patroclus, is like to the usages of some of the North American Indian tribes, but the analogies should not be pressed. The Trojan captives seem to have been killed in a spirit of vengeance,—not to furnish attendants for the next world. On the third day of battle, angry because of the death of Asius, Deïphobus kills a Greek and says that Asius even in going to the home of Hades will be glad in soul, since Deïphobus has supplied him with an escort (πομπόν, N 416), but this need not be interpreted literally any more than Romeo's words to Tybalt, "Mercutio's soul | Is but a little· way above our heads; | Either thou or I or both must go with him" (*Romeo and Juliet*, iii. 1. 131). That two dogs are killed at the pyre of Patroclus, just as two dogs attend Telemachus when he goes to the Ithacan place of assembly, may not be significant.

Killing of Captives at the Pyre.

The word used four times for funeral honors (κτέρεα, α 291) originally meant *possessions* (as Ω 235), and indicates that in earlier times all a man's personal possessions,—his arms and his clothing,—were burned or buried with him. These were indeed all his property, for the real estate, and probably the cattle, belonged to the family or clan. The arms of Patroclus and of Achilles are not said to be buried with these warriors, but Eëtion's were burned with him (Z 418; *cf.* μ 13), and Andromache speaks of this as a fitting honor for a brave man,—not, however, as though it were necessary for the comfort of his soul. To bury him without these, would be to treat him as a captive or slave who owned no arms. Odysseus's comrade Elpenor not only begs to be buried but also that his oar may be set up on his tomb (λ 77), but he makes no request to have anything buried with him.

Arms buried with the Dead.

The high mound which was raised over the ashes of the dead, itself served as a monument. In challenging the bravest of the Achaeans to single-combat, Hector imagines his antagonist to be slain by him, and a mound to be raised over this Achaean on the banks of the Hellespont, so that men even of future generations should

Mound for Monument.

say as they sailed over the sea, "That is the tomb of one
who died long ago, slain, fighting bravely, by glorious Hector"
(H 89). So also the mound of Achilles is raised upon a
promontory, that it may be seen by men far away upon the
sea (ω 82). The mound would lead the younger generation
to ask their fathers who was buried there, and thus would
keep alive the memory of the dead.[1] Before the days of
writing, such monuments were the best reminder to the
parents to transmit to their children the memories of the
past. Every boy on seeing the mound of Ajax by the shore,
would ask his father who was buried there, and then "Who
was Ajax?"[2] Similarly, the passover service was intended to
remind the Israelites to tell to their children the story of the
release from captivity in Egypt (*Exodus* xii. 26). Menelaus
raises a mound in Egypt in memory of his brother Agamemnon (δ 584), and Telemachus would have erected such a
mound on Ithaca for his father, if Odysseus had not returned
(α 291). Clearly in the case of Agamemnon, the mound in
Egypt was not intended to secure rest for his perturbed
spirit,—his body had been buried at home,—but simply to
maintain his name and fame. In addition to the mound, a
column or slab (*stele*) was sometimes used, for women as well
as for men (P 434); it is even counted as almost a right of
the dead (γέρας, Η 675). Nothing indicates that this monument was carved,—much less that it bore any inscription,—
but some Mycenaean grave monuments are extant, on which
the figured chariot is thought to be intended chiefly to
declare the dead man's rank (see p. 351). Over the grave
of Odysseus's comrade Elpenor, who died at the palace of
Circe, his oar was fixed, in addition to a tombstone (μ 15), to
mark this as the grave of a sailor. That for such a monument wood might be used as well as stone, is shown by
Nestor's uncertainty whether the wooden beam which Achilles
set as the turning-post for the chariot-race, had been originally

---

[1] *Cf.* the command to the Israelites to set up twelve stones "out of the midst of
Jordan," "that this may be a sign among you, that when children ask their fathers
in time to come, saying, 'What mean ye by these stones?' then ye shall answer
them . . . and these stones shall be for a memorial unto the children of Israel
forever," *Joshua* iv. 6.

[2] "Such mounds are raised to-day as memorials of chiefs in north-eastern India."

a monument (σῆμα, Ψ 331) for a grave, or a goal in an earlier race.

Elms were planted by mountain-nymphs about the grave of Andromache's father, Eëtion (Z 419). No other tree

Elms Planted by Tomb. seems to be associated in any way with the dead, except that black poplars and willows grow in the groves of Persephone near the entrance to Hades (κ 510). Perhaps Eëtion's elms were only intended to make the spot more cheerful.

No grave-yards or cemeteries are mentioned by the poet, and no necropolis has been found on the mainland of

No Grave-yards. Greece of so early an age as the Homeric period, though much earlier grave-yards have been discovered in Crete. High mounds were heaped up in the Troad both earlier and later than Homer's time, but no tombs have been found there of the age of Laomedon and Priam.[1] The poems mention as landmarks not only the tomb of Ilus, son of Dardanus and founder of Ilium, in the middle of the plain (Λ 166), but also the high mound of the old Aesyetes, on which a Trojan scout sits in order to watch the movements of the Achaean forces (B 793), and a hill on the plain "which the immortals call the tomb of the agile Myrina" (B 814), who may have been one of the Amazons to whose invasion of Phrygia old Priam refers (Γ 189).

In the Homeric poems no exact analysis of the powers of the soul is expected, such as would have satisfied Plato

Psychology. or Aristotle.[2] The study of the Homeric realm of Hades has shown us that the distinction was not sharply drawn even between spirit and matter. The gods as a rule are corporeal and material, but still they are not ordinarily subject to the laws which bind matter,— though Ares could not escape from the chains with which Hephaestus bound him (θ 298), nor from the bronze jar in which he was kept imprisoned by mortals (E 387), and

---

[1] The Turkish officials now refuse to allow the scientific examination of these mounds, fearing that from these heights observations might be made of the neighboring fortifications at the mouth of the Hellespont.

[2] See W. Schrader, *Die Psychologie des ältern griechischen Epos*, in *JJ.* 1885, pp. 145 ff.

where he was as helpless, and as powerless to escape, as the *jinn* of the *Arabian Nights*. On the other hand, the ghosts in Hades, as a rule immaterial, yet have some characteristics of corporeal beings,—shedding tears (λ 466), drinking a libation (λ 390), and being kept from their draught by a drawn sword (λ 95). So the terms which correspond roughly to soul (ψυχή), heart (θυμός, κραδίη, κῆρ, or ἦτορ), and spirit or mind (φρένες) are not used with precision, and no one English word represents accurately any of these, except heart for κραδίη and κῆρ.[1]

The soul[2] (ψυχή) is not the principle of life, as in the works of Aristotle, and it has its seat in no particular part of the human body, but is rather the man's second self (*alter ego*),—an image, the invisible *The Soul.* counterpart, of his body (an *idol*, εἴδωλον, λ 602); it has no intelligence, no *nous*, and no emotions, and is never represented as perceiving, thinking, willing, or feeling, at least as long as it is in the body. The proëm to the *Iliad* says that the wrath of Achilles sent the souls of many mighty warriors to the home of Hades, while it made themselves (αὐτούς, A 4) the prey of dogs and the feast of birds.[3] On its separation from the body,—leaving it either through the mouth or through the opening of a wound (I 409; Ξ 518, Π 504),—the soul flits away to the realm of Hades,[4] from which it has no return. So not all the treasures of the temple at Delphi are a man's recompense for it (I 401, 408). Sarpedon threatens that Tlepolemus "shall give glory to him, and his soul to Hades" (E 654 = Λ 445); but a little later, Patroclus strikes Sarpedon "where the midriff supports the thickly beating heart," and, setting his

---

[1] ψυχή is used about 80 times in the poems,—more frequently in the *Odyssey* than in the *Iliad*, because of the *Nekyia* in λ. θυμός is used about 750 times, about 325 occurrences being in the *Odyssey*. κραδίη occurs about 60 times, κῆρ 80 times, and ἦτορ nearly 100 times. φρένες is used nearly 350 times, and νόος a trifle more than a hundred times.

[2] See E. Rohde, *Psyche*. Its etymology indicates that it is the breath of life; *cf.* Latin *anima* and *spiritus*, and Sanskrit *ātman*, *breath*, *soul*.

[3] According to a passage of the *Odyssey* which seems to have been added after the story was essentially in its present form (λ 602), the soul of Heracles is in Hades, but "he himself is with the immortal gods."

[4] ψυχὴ δ' ἐκ ῥεθέων πταμένη Ἀιδόσδε βεβήκειν, X 362, Π 856.

foot upon the fallen man, he "draws out at the same time Sarpedon's soul and the point of his spear" (II 505). Naturally *soul* comes to be used as a synonym of *life*.[1] Thus Odysseus suffers in "striving for his own life (ψυχήν, α 5) and the return of his comrades"; and in the cave of the Cyclops, he plans "as for his life" (περὶ ψυχῆς, ι 423), *i.e.* he knows that his soul or life is at stake. Similarly, when Achilles pursues Hector about the walls of Troy, both run swiftly since they are running for no ordinary prize, but "for the life (ψυχῆς, X 161) of the knight Hector." And Hector begs Achilles "by his life (ὑπὲρ ψυχῆς, X 338) and his parents" not to allow the Achaean dogs to devour him. Shortly before this, Agenor, awaiting the attack of Achilles, encourages himself with the thought that Achilles, too, may be wounded with the sharp steel, and has but one life (ψυχή, Φ 569).

In syncope the soul may leave the body for a time, *i.e.* fainting is thought to be a temporary death. On seeing the
Fainting. corpse of Hector dragged to the Greek camp behind the chariot of Achilles, Andromache "breathes forth her soul" (ἀπὸ δὲ ψυχὴν ἐκάπυσσεν X 467), but her spirit (θυμός) returns to her breast a little later. So, when the spear is drawn from the wound of Sarpedon, "his soul leaves him" (τὸν δ' ἔλιπε ψυχή, E 696), but the breath of Boreas soon revives him.

Heart, spirit, mind, and the like, are connected only with the body, not with the soul. The heart, *thymos* (θυμός,—*cf.*
The Heart (Thymos). κραδίη or κῆρ, ἦτορ) includes some of the functions of the mind, and is often used for *spirit* as in later Greek, though never in contrast with matter. This word is never used in the anatomical sense. The heart urges (B 276), bids (K 534), desires (Θ 301), hopes (P 395), is restrained (N 280), grieves (Θ 202), is distressed (P 744), is torn (I 8), is eager (A 173), is glad (N 494), is god-fearing (τ 364), is proud (B 196), is insolent (O 94), is mad (P 22), is of iron (X 357), dares (P 68), is fearless (II 163), is cowardly (E 643), lacks nothing (A 468), is

---

[1] *Cf.* γ 74, ι 255, 523, χ 245, I 322, 401.—In the Authorised Version of the New Testament, ψυχή is translated *life* in some places where the Revised Version uses *soul*.

satisfied (ε 95). Achilles is lion-hearted (θυμολέων, H 228). "In heart" (ἐνὶ θυμῷ or κατὰ θυμόν) a man not only suffers (α 4), mourns (ν 379), is rebuked (Γ 438), prays (ε 444), and hopes (ψ 345), but also suspects (τ 390), wonders (α 323), remembers (α 29), considers (α 294 and often), plans (ι 299), and is persuaded (η 258). His heart speaks to him (X 122, 385), and conversely he speaks to his heart (ε 285),—this being used as a substitute for the reflexive pronoun, *himself.* So also one consumes his heart (his soul, Z 202, ι 75), in grief. One "takes heart" (κ 461), and Telemachus assures his father that he will show him his heart (*i.e.* his courage, spirit, π 309). Agamemnon wishes that such a heart (*i.e.* spirit) as that of Ajax were in the breast of every Achaean (Δ 289). Poseidon shuns the heart (*i.e.* the anger, ν 148) of Zeus. But several times, as the source of energy, this heart is equivalent to life.[1]

The second word for heart (κραδίη, Attic καρδία, Latin *cor*), which in later Greek is used most frequently of the bodily organ, is in general equivalent to *thymos,* but is used not a tenth so often. The heart of *κραδίη.* Hector is unyielding (κραδίη, Γ 60), Achilles charges Agamemnon with having the heart of a deer (A 223), Thetis has cheered the heart of Zeus (A 395), and grief comes to the heart.[2] When Agamemnon's "heart leaps from his breast and his knees tremble beneath him" (K 94), one may ask whether the action of the heart is not as physical as that of the

---

[1] θυμὸν ἀπούρας, ν 270, *taking away his life,* cf. P 236 ; ἀπὸ θυμὸν ὀλέσσαι, μ 350, *to lose one's life*; ὀλίγος θυμὸς ἐνῆεν, A 593, *little life was in me*; ἐπεί κε λίπῃ ὀστέα θυμός, ψυχὴ πεπότηται, λ 221, *when the life leaves the bones, and the soul has flown away*; θυμὸν ἀποπνείων, Δ 524, *breathing forth his life* (cf. Andromache's "breathing forth her soul," considered above) ; even θυμὸς ᾤχετ' ἀπὸ μελέων, II 606, *his life departed from his limbs.* ἐκ μελέων θυμὸς πτάτο, Ψ 880, may reasonably be translated as *his soul flew away from his body,*—θυμός being here the synonym of ψυχή,— and in θυμὸν ἀπὸ μελέων δῦναι δόμον Ἄιδος εἴσω, H 131, the θυμός is supposed not simply to leave the body but even to enter the home of Hades,—but this is inaccurate. The ψυχή has a place in Hades, but not the θυμός. "Etymologically, θυμός expresses agitation, feeling."—For the use of θυμός as a reflexive pronoun, cf. εἰ δ' ἄεθλα γαρύεν ἔλδεαι, φίλον ἦτορ, Pindar, *Ol.* i. 3 ; "Bless the Lord, O my soul" (εὐλόγει ἡ ψυχή μου τὸν κύριον), *Psalms* ciii. I.

[2] κραδίην καὶ θυμόν, Θ 147,—where a distinction between the pair is not easily drawn. For *gnawing, consuming the heart* in grief, ἔδεαι κραδίην, Ω 129, forms a perfect parallel to θυμὸν κατέδων, translated *cor edens* by Cicero, Z 202.

knees, though the expression cannot be so literally true ; but when a coward's " heart beats hard in his breast " (κραδίη στέρνοισι πατάσσει, N 282), the expression is exactly paralleled by the use of the other word which is never used in a physical sense.[1] So, though the sensation is physical, when Andromache " quivers in heart " (X 461), the heart need not be the organ of the body, any more than a few moments before, when " her heart leaps into her mouth " (ἦτορ ἀνὰ στόμα, X 452). The only two passages in the poems in which by *heart* the physical organ is clearly meant are, first, where Idomeneus fixes his spear in the heart (κραδίη, N 442) of a brother-in-law of Aeneas, and the palpitation of the heart shakes even the butt-end of the spear ; and, again, of the wound of Sarpedon (κῆρ, Π 482).[2] The cognate κῆρ is in general synonymous with κραδίη, but has a somewhat narrower range of use. More than half of its occurrences are as datives or as accusatives of specification, as, for example, grieving or rejoicing *in heart* (cf. ἦτορ, below). This, too, rejoices (Ξ 139), fears (M 45), and grieves (Z 523). It even remains without food (T 319), here clearly standing for the man himself.[3] A curious idiom is " the shaggy heart of Patroclus (Πατροκλῆος λάσιον κῆρ, Π 554, cf. B 851) roused the Achaeans,"—manifestly equivalent to " the shaggy-breasted Patroclus ; "—Achilles's breast was shaggy (A 189).

The third word for heart (ἦτορ) differs in use little from the other two, but, like the first, is never employed of the physical organ. This also bids (a 316), rejoices (Ψ 647), mourns (Π 450), is roused (Ω 585), is of iron (Ω 205), is brave (E 529), is confident (T 169), dreads (O 166), is dismayed (Γ 31), is eager (E 670), is chilled (P 111), is loosed (*i.e.* loses its strength, Φ 114), regards (O 554), and ponders (A 188). It may be taken

ἦτορ.

---

[1] θυμὸς ἐνὶ στήθεσσι πάτασσεν, H 216. This however seems to be an extension of the earlier use, following the analogy of κραδίη. Compare the approximation of θυμός to ψυχή.

[2] Possibly a third instance should be added,—ἐν κραδίῃ στένει ἦτορ, T 169,—though κραδίη may be used here for *breast*. Sanskrit *hrd*=κῆρ, and *hrdaya*=καρδία=*breast*.

[3] " My soul fasts from food " can hardly be a poetical way of saying " My soul will not allow me to eat."

away,[1] and then is equivalent to the soul. Nearly half of its occurrences are as accusatives of specification,—sad *at heart* (α 114), grieving *in heart* (ι 62), etc. In the proëm to the Catalogue of Ships, it has been thought to mean lungs,—" The multitude of the men I could not tell, though I had ten tongues, and ten mouths, and an unbroken voice, and a *heart* (ἦτορ, B 490) of bronze,"—but heart here seems to mean strength or spirit in a general sense.

The word [2] which in an anatomical use means *midriff* or *diaphragm*, which " separates the cavity of the chest from that of the abdomen," is used nearly a hundred and fifty times for mind or intellect, occasion- *" Midriff," Intellect.* ally including the whole soul, but generally forming the complement to the θυμός (as in κατὰ φρένα καὶ κατὰ θυμόν, α 294). It is generally used in an oblique case, being thought of as acted upon rather than as acting, while θυμός is used almost as often in the nominative as in the accusative case. Thus Hera puts it in the mind (ἐπὶ φρεσί, A 55) of Achilles to call the Achaeans to an assembly. Achilles recognizes in his mind (ἐνὶ φρεσί, A 333) the heralds of Agamemnon, and knows why they are come. Zeus takes away the mind (φρένας, Z 234) of Glaucus, in leading him to exchange golden armor for arms of bronze. And Paris says that Antenor's mind has been ruined by the gods, if he is serious in his proposition to surrender Helen to the Greeks (H 360). Similarly " the mind of Zeus (φρήν, K 45) is turned, and he regards the sacrifices of Hector rather " than those of Agamemnon. Wine " comes about the mind " (*i.e.* " goes to the head,"— περὶ φρένας, ι 362) of the Cyclops. The mind of Odysseus is well-balanced (φρένας ἔνδον ἐίσας, λ 337), and Hermes excels in mind (ἐπὶ φρεσί, Y 35).[3] Occasionally the word

---

[1] ἦτορ ἀπηύρα, Φ 201, seems to differ only metrically from θυμὸν ἀπηύρα, Φ 179, of the same persons. Here again the use of ἦτορ seems to be an extension of the original use, under the influence of similar words.—What distinction is to be drawn between the two nouns in ἐν κραδίῃ στένει ἦτορ, Υ 169, is not clear. If ἦτορ = Sanskrit *vāta(r)*, *wind*, *breath*, this would be *the spirit groans in his breast.* See note above.

[2] φρήν, generally plural φρένες. *Cf.* the verbs φρονέω, *think*, and εὐφραίνω, *cheer*, and the adjectives ἄφρων, *fool*, and πολύφρων, *very wise.*

[3] That this expression is used for the "good heart" of Clytaemestra (φρεσὶ γὰρ κέχρητ' ἀγαθῇσιν, γ 266) is paralleled by the expressions κεδνὰ ἰδυῖα, α 428 (lit.

is used for the whole soul or person. Thus desire for food seizes a woodman's mind (φρένας, Λ 89), and passionate love for Helen envelops the mind of Paris (Γ 442). The anatomical use of this word is rare. That the diaphragm of Agamemnon shakes in his grief (Κ 10), may be no more physical than the quivering of the heart of Andromache (see above). But in the cave of the Cyclops, Odysseus plans to "wound Polyphemus on the breast, where the diaphragm holds the liver" (ι 301), and Patroclus hits Sarpedon "where the diaphragm encloses the heart" (Π 481). Four times the epithet "black on both sides"[1] is applied to this word, but this is best understood of the "heart" as darkened with anger, grief, or even courage. In one passage the interpretation is doubtful: setting his foot on the breast of the dying Sarpedon, Patroclus draws forth his spear, and the midriff (φρένες) follows it; he draws forth at once his spear-point and the soul (ψυχήν, Π 504) of Sarpedon. The second statement seems to be a repetition of the former, in varied form; but Sarpedon had been wounded in the diaphragm, and this word may be used in its anatomical sense. Not infrequently the heart rages or mourns or is encouraged in one's breast (lit. *diaphragm*; Θ 413, 202, Π 242).

Little need be said here of the mind or reason (νόος), which at times becomes thought, plan, purpose. Occasionally this approaches the use of heart,—as men "are hospitable and have a god-fearing mind";[2] "the mind of the Ithacan bard is roused"[3] to sing of the woes of the Achaeans. Hector has an "undismayed mind" (Γ 63), and the "mind of Ajax is harsh" (Ψ 484).

Reason.

The seat of the mind, as of the emotions, is the breast (μετὰ φρεσίν, Σ 419); the head is never the seat of intelligence in the Homeric poems.

Only one indication appears of the later belief that the liver is the seat of the passions: in the realm of Hades,

---

knowing faithful (thoughts) faithful hearted, trusty; ἀθεμίστια ᾔδη, ι 189, *had a lawless heart*; ἄγρια οἶδεν, Ω 41, *has a fierce heart*; but ἄκοσμα ᾔδη, Β 213, *had a disordered mind*. See the second following note.

[1] ἀμφιμέλαιναι, Λ 103, Ρ 83, 499, 573.

[2] νόος ἐστὶ θεουδής, ζ 121; cf. θεουδέα θυμὸν ἔχοντα, τ 364. See the second preceding note.

[3] νόος ὄρνυται, α 347; cf. ἀνήσει θυμὸς ἀγήνωρ, Β 276.

the liver of Tityus ($\hat{\eta}\pi\alpha\rho$, λ 578) is torn by vultures because of his assault on Leto,—but the similar suffering of Prometheus, according to the later story, does not strongly support the inference that the liver of Tityus was thought to be particularly criminal. *Liver the Seat of the Passions.* In her uncontrollable grief, Queen Hecuba wishes that she could cling to the very liver of Achilles and devour it (Ω 212) in vengeance for Hector's death,—but this may indicate only that the liver was thought to be the chief vital organ, as Odysseus thinks of striking Polyphemus, not to the heart, but to the liver (ι 301). Elsewhere in the poems, the liver is mentioned only in connexion with wounds.

That the Homeric Greeks were frank in the expression of their emotions, has been seen. Achilles weeps for Briseïs, for Patroclus, and for Peleus (Α 349, Ω 511), and on learning of the death of Patroclus he *Expression of Emotions.* heaps dust and ashes on his head (Σ 23), and lies stretched out in the dust. In the Council at the close of the second day of battle (Ι 14), Agamemnon, the commander-in-chief, sheds tears so abundant that they remind the poet of a stream pouring over a rock. Patroclus on seeing the danger and defeat of the Achaeans weeps like a little girl at her mother's side (Π 3 ff.). That Penelope should weep herself to sleep, we cannot wonder (τ 603).—Assent was expressed by a nod of the head (κατανεύω, Α 527); refusal was expressed by throwing the head back (ἀνανεύω, Χ 205, φ 129). To slap one's thighs indicated distress (Ο 113, ν 198). Biting the lips indicated vexation (α 381, σ 410). To tear the hair and to beat the breast are natural expressions of grief (Κ 15, Σ 27, 31, Ω 711). To give the right hand is a natural pledge (Β 341), and to take the hand at the wrist (ἐπὶ καρπῷ, Ω 671, σ 258),—so that one's hand should lie in the other's,—gave the fullest confidence. To rise at the approach of a superior, is only respectful (Α 533, Ο 86). Similarly, prostration of body, in clasping the knees of one to whom supplication is made (Α 500), indicates prostration of spirit. That kissing was not very common, has been seen (p. 139),—but Odysseus kisses even the soil of the Phaeacians,—so glad is he to reach land (ε 463).

CHAPTER XVI

TEMPLES, WORSHIP, AND DIVINATION

TEMPLES of the gods were not numerous in the Homeric age.[1] The "groves were God's first temples," and a field or grove was set apart for the divinity's worship before any building was erected for him there. The earliest Greek temples were mere shrines,—sometimes no more than a hollow tree,—for the protection of the god's image or representative.[2] Perhaps some men

Temples Few and Small.

---

[1] No remains of temples of the earliest age have been found at Mycenae or Troy. The later temple at Mycenae was built over the ruins of the earlier palace, as well as on its model. So in η 81, Athena goes to the home of Erechtheus at Athens, which seems to have been in accord with the earlier stage of belief and usage,—the goddess visiting her shrine in the king's palace, and not having a separate house of her own. At Cnosus in Crete, Mr. Evans found in 1902 a "shrine belonging to the late Mycenaean period, with the cult-objects and idols in place," and later came upon another shrine. But these were in the palace and not without it, and no such cult-objects are mentioned in the Homeric poems. In Gournià of Crete, however, Miss Boyd found the remains of a Mycenaean village-shrine, "a small rectangular building." On the island of Delos the earliest known temple was both small and rude ; and the first temple at Delphi, according to tradition, was built of laurel boughs (Paus. x. 5, 9 ; Philost. *Apoll.* vi. 10, 110),—a mere booth or cabin, probably much like those built by Chryses (A 39). Similarly an old temple of Poseidon near Mantinea was said to have been built of oak logs (Paus. viii. 10, 4). The earliest temple of Demeter at Eleusis seems to have been built in a day, from the Homeric *Hymn to Demeter*, 297, and the temple which Xenophon built at Scillus in Elis (*Anabasis* v. 3, 13), though on the model of the great temple at Ephesus, is not likely to have been more than a small "chapel." See Perrot et Chipiez, *Histoire de l'Art*, vi. 656, vii. 112.

[2] The "oak-tree of aegis-bearing Zeus" (E 693, Z 237, H 22, etc.) has been thought by some to have been counted sacred as sheltering the divinity,—but no one would guess this from the *Iliad*. According to Apollonius of Rhodes, the Argonauts erected a wooden image of the Dindymian Mother under tall oak trees (φηγοῖσιν, *Arg.* i. 1121), which clearly were to serve as a shrine.

were moved to erect a more substantial temple by a thought like that of King David, who said to Nathan the prophet, " See now, I dwell in an house of cedar, but the ark of the Lord dwelleth within curtains" (2 *Sam.* vii. 2). That the temples were often small, temporary shrines is indicated by the prayer of Apollo's old priest, Chryses, that if he had ever roofed a temple pleasing to the god, or had burned for him the fat thigh-pieces of bulls and of goats, Apollo would listen to his prayer and avenge him on the Achaeans (A 39). The temples roofed by the old priest must have been simple shrines ; he had made these with his own hands, and this service is compared with that of offering sacrifices. That he had assistance in building his shrines as well as in offering his sacrifices, is probable and may be assumed. The Greek temples of classical times were built on the model of the Homeric *megaron*,[1]—the great hall of the palace,—and possibly the temple of Athena at Troy may have had already the type of the *megaron* of Priam ; but some scholars would insist that the mention of a temple in Troy belongs to a comparatively late period in the development of the Trojan story.

The passage just quoted shows that Apollo had a temple at Chrysa. The same god had a temple with a stone threshold at Pytho, the later Delphi (θ 80, I 405), to which rich gifts were brought, and another temple on the citadel of Troy (E 446, H 83), where Leto and Artemis tended the wounded Aeneas. *Five Temples Mentioned.* Athena also had a temple in Troy (Z 297), to which the matrons of the city went in procession with vows and gifts, and another in Athens (B 549) into which she received Erechtheus, and which must have been the predecessor of the Erechtheum built in the fifth century B.C. No other temples are directly mentioned,—not even a temple of Zeus,—but the poet names the building of temples and the division of the grain fields, immediately after the building of the wall about the city and the erection of houses, when the Phaeacians settled at Scheria (ζ 10). The comrades of Odysseus, too, propose to erect on Ithaca a temple for the sun-god Helius to atone for their slaughter of his cattle (μ 346).

[1] See Lechat, *Le Temple grec.*

No more than in the classical period were the temples used as places of worship, like the churches in Roman Catholic countries, or for the religious instruction of the people, like the churches in Protestant countries. Altars stood before or by the side of the temples,—not within them,—just as the Children of Israel in the Wilderness came to the "altar of the Lord at the door of the tabernacle of the congregation" (*Lev.* xvii. 6). No indication is given by the poet of the size, shape, or material of any temple. The Trojan matrons appear to have entered Athena's temple when they made their vow to the goddess (Z 298), but this is not certain,—if the shrine were small, the opening of the door would have sufficed to bring them into the presence of the divinity,—and the poet does not say how many matrons were present That vow promised "twelve kine in the temple" (ἐνὶ νηῷ, Z 308), but this must not be understood literally, since the altar unquestionably stood without the temple, and there the victims were slain.[1] The temple at Chrysa is not mentioned in the account of the sacrifice there in honor of Apollo (A 440), but on the other hand Odysseus proceeds immediately from his ship to the altar. The divinity was not thought to dwell continually in his temple, but only to sojourn there occasionally, as Athena visited the palace of Erechtheus at Athens (η 81), and as Aphrodite went to Paphos (θ 362).[2] Men thought the god more ready to visit them if he had a "place to stay" in the midst of them. The temple at Pytho was rich because of the votive offerings there (I 404). Hector proposes to hang up the armor of Ajax, if he kills him, on the front of the temple of Apollo in Ilium (H 83), just as, many centuries later, shields captured from the enemy were hung upon the Parthenon at Athens.

Only once in the Homeric poems is a statue of a divinity mentioned or assumed to be in a temple (Z 303): the

[1] " Perhaps νηός, *dwelling*, = τέμενος ἱερόν, including the ground where the altar is." But this cannot be made out from the poems.

[2] So at Delphi the god was present to give oracles only on stated occasions (*cf.* Pindar, *Pyth.* iv. 5). At other times he might be present at other shrines or feasts, or he might be on Olympus with his peers.

Trojan matrons "lay a robe on the knees of the fair-haired Athena." This figure seems to have been in a sitting posture, and, if so, Homer shows no knowledge of the very primitive *Xoana*, or wooden standing images, which were held peculiarly sacred in later *Statue of a Divinity.* times, nor of such a "figure of a goddess, cylindrical below," as has been found at Cnosus. The so-called *Palladia*, as they appear on ancient vases, are all standing. Five times the expression "this lies on the knees of the gods " $(\theta\epsilon\hat{\omega}\nu$ $\dot{\epsilon}\nu$ $\gamma o\acute{v}\nu a\sigma\iota$ $\kappa\epsilon\hat{\iota}\tau a\iota$, a 267) is used by Homer to mean "the decision rests with the gods "; and this indicates a conception of the divinities as sitting in council, but does not necessarily imply familiarity with such statues. Of course no possible objection exists to the supposition that the poet knew statues; but he has no special occasion to mention them.

Altars are mentioned in the Homeric poems more frequently than temples. Probably every temple had an altar, though many public altars were not associated with temples. The Achaeans before setting sail *Altars.* for Troy offered sacrifices on the altars of Aulis (B 305), they "passed by no altar" on the islands without paying due homage thereon (Θ 238), and they had altars in their camp (Θ 249, Λ 808). Zeus had an altar and sacred field ($\tau\acute{\epsilon}\mu\epsilon\nu os$) on one of the summits of Mt. Ida (Θ 48, X 171), and Apollo had altars on Delos (Ζ 162) and, as has been already noted, at Chrysa (A 440). The river Spercheüs had an altar in Phthia (Ψ 148), and the nymphs had an altar on Ithaca (ρ 210), on which "all way-faring men offered sacrifices." Aegisthus offered sacrifices on the altars of Argos or Mycenae in gratitude to the gods for his success in winning the love of Clytaemestra (γ 273), and hung up votive offerings of gold and raiment, probably in the sacred grove about the altar. A private altar is mentioned in the home of Odysseus (χ 334). Peleus and Priam are represented as offering sacrifices (Λ 774) or libations (Ω 306) in the courtyards of their dwellings,[1] and we may believe that

---

[1] If the offerings were to be conveyed to the gods by the smoke, the altar would naturally be in the open air, just as King Solomon "offered burnt offerings in the middle of the court that was before the house of the Lord" (1 *Kings* viii. 64).

an altar stood in the enclosure of every large house, before the great hall.

Apollo had a sacred grove[1] at Ismarus in Thrace, and another on Ithaca (v 278). Athena had a grove of alders at Scheria (ζ 291). Aphrodite had a sacred field[2] on Paphos. In each of these doubtless stood an altar. In similar sacred places stood the altar of Zeus on Mt. Ida, and that of the river Spercheüs. Poseidon had not only an altar at Scheria (v 187) but also sanctuaries at Helicé and Aegae (Θ 203), but these may have included temples as well as altars.

Sacred Groves.

The form of the altar is not specified in any case. Sometimes it may have been a single large stone or a mere heap of stones. Sometimes it may have been a pit-altar, such as was found in the ruins at Tiryns, or a mere hearth, such as have been found in Troy and Mycenae.[3] The raised altar may have been thought of as a table on which were placed gifts for the divinities. The altar at Chrysa would seem to have had considerable size, since a number of cattle were sacrificed at it (A 447).[4]

Form of Altar.

The ordinary informal offerings at each meal were burned in the fire on the hearth (ξ 429, I 220). The indications of a special sanctity of the hearth are slight. Odysseus, coming as a suppliant to the palace of Alcinoüs, does not at once take his place on the hearth, like Jason and Medea at the home of Circe, according to Apollonius (*Arg.* iv. 691), or like Themistocles at the home of the Molossian king (Thuc. i. 136), but turns directly to supplicate the

---

[1] ἐν ἄλσεϊ, ι 200. For the word ἄλσος, *cf.* the *Altis* at Olympia.

[2] τέμενος, θ 363. For the word, *cf.* τέμνω and the Latin *templum*. The word was used also for a royal domain, see page 83.

[3] In Theocritus, xxvi. 5, "altars" are made by the bacchantes of leaves of oak, ivy, and asphodel. *Cf.* the *aras gramineas* of Vergil, *Aen.* xii. 119. This indicates that even in later times the form of an altar was not so fixed as is often popularly supposed.

[4] See Reisch in Pauly-Wissowa, *Real-Encyclopädie*, i. 1640. βωμός is the ordinary word for *altar*. The word ἐσχάρα, which in later tim• is often a designation of an altar with an opening to convey the blood of the victim to the dead or to the nether gods, or of an altar simply as a hearth of a divinity, is a *hearth* of a home in Homer (η 153).

queen, Areté, and then sits "on the hearth in the ashes, by the fire" (η 153). The disguised Odysseus swears four times by the hearth ($i\sigma\tau i\eta$, ξ 159) of the home to which he has come.

Priests[1] formed no caste or hierarchy. Those of one temple had no relation to those of another. Each was attached to a shrine,—a temple, or an altar,—and his chief official duty was to care for the temple or altar and for *Priests.* the sacrifices offered there. Thus no priests are mentioned in the Achaean army before Troy. Priests may have ordinary vocations, and Theano the Trojan priestess of Athena is the wife of Antenor and the mother of many brave warriors. If any priest had come to the war before Troy, he would have come simply as a fighter, without any priestly offices. So far as appears, no special restrictions were laid upon the conduct and life of the priests,—they were not required to be peculiarly holy men, and they wore no special garb, except perhaps a fillet for the head when they were engaged in the duties of their office. Chryses came to the Achaean camp as a suppliant with "the fillet[2] of the god upon a golden staff" (A 14, *cf.* 28); the staff was hardly a badge of office, though it implied dignity. The priests needed no special education, and but little training, and had no religious instruction to give. Nothing is said of their perquisites, which were carefully defined in later times, as they were among the Hebrews for Phinehas and Hophni (1 *Sam.* ii. 13). No "tithes" were paid to the priests by the people, but they naturally shared with the god the meat offered at the altar. But the priest of Apollo at Ismarus (the only priest mentioned in the *Odyssey*,—ι 200) "dwelt in the grove of Apollo," and doubtless had a right to the use of the sacred field. "Of the modern theory that kings and priests were originally identical, kings being later evolved from priests, Homer has no trace."

In addition to Maron at Ismarus, to whom reference has just been made (ι 198), and Chryses, whose treatment by

---

[1] The ordinary word is $\iota\epsilon\rho\epsilon\upsilon\varsigma$. Chryses is called $\dot{\alpha}\rho\eta\tau\dot{\eta}\rho$ (*praying man*, A 11), and Dolopion was $\Sigma\kappa\alpha\mu\dot{\alpha}\nu\delta\rho\upsilon\upsilon$ $\dot{\alpha}\rho\eta\tau\dot{\eta}\rho$, E 78. "Similar is the Sanskrit *Brahman, prayer-man.*"

[2] The fillet ($\sigma\tau\epsilon\mu\mu\alpha$, *cf.* $\sigma\tau\epsilon\phi\omega$ and $\sigma\tau\epsilon\phi\alpha\nu\sigma\varsigma$) does not appear elsewhere in the poems,—neither for priests or suppliants, nor for sacrificial victims or athletes.

Agamemnon is the occasion of the "wrath of Achilles" (A 11), Panthoüs, father of Pulydamas in the Trojan army *Priests Mentioned.* (O 522), seems to be a priest of Apollo, as Vergil distinctly declares him to be (*Aen.* ii. 319). Onetor is the priest of Idaean Zeus (Π 604), Dares is a priest of Hephaestus in Troy (E 10), Dolopion the priest of the Scamander (E 77); and the "priests of the gods" are mentioned as sent by the Aetolians as embassadors to the angry Meleager (I 575). The last incident indicates the respect paid to the office of priests, and twice the poet says that a priest was "honored as a god" by the people (E 78, Π 605). Odysseus spares Maron "since he dwelt in the grove of Apollo" (ι 200), *i.e.* since he was the priest of Apollo. Having to do with sacrifices and temples, the priests were dear to the gods, as their faithful servants, and were more likely than other men to know the divine will. Achilles suggests that some "seer or priest" might tell the cause of the plague (A 62), and Priam implies a like office of the priest in Ω 221. Hephaestus saves the son of his priest (E 23), and Apollo rescues Panthoüs's son (O 521), and avenges the slight offered to the priest Chryses (A 43). The only priestess mentioned in the poems is Theano, wife of Antenor and mother of many brave warriors, who has charge of the temple of Athena in Troy, and opens the door for the offering of a present and vows by the Trojan matrons (Z 298). She was chosen by the people, and this is the only reference to the manner of priestly appointment. Other priests may have been appointed by the men who built the temple. Doubtless at times a private family cult was adopted by the tribe or clan, and the head of the family might choose his own priest.[1] Among Penelope's suitors on Ithaca was one who had charge of sacrifices (θυοσκόος, φ 145, χ 318),[2] but no temple is mentioned there.

---

[1] *Cf.* "And the man Micah had an house of gods, . . . and consecrated one of his sons, who became his priest," *Judges* xvii. 5. This Micah afterwards hired a Levite to be his priest for "ten shekels of silver by the year, and a suit of apparel, and [his] victuals," *ib.* 10.

[2] The duties of the θυοσκόος are not specified. Probably if Odysseus, the head of the family, had been at home, this Leodes would have been equally unnecessary both as θυοσκόος and as suitor. Priam names θυοσκόοι in connexion with priests (Ω 221). The name does not imply, as was long believed, an inspection of the entrails for omens.

Priests were not necessary, as they were among the Jews,[1] for the proper performance of a sacrifice. Another man might do as well as they; and the king regularly performs the sacrifices for his people (B 411, Γ 275).[2] The only sacrifice conducted by a priest in the Homeric *Priests not Necessary.* poems is one in which this priest is the chief person, apart from his priestly office (Chryses, Λ 450), and which is on his own account. Evidently no complicated system of ritual was to be observed with precision, any more than by the Bedouins of to-day, and the ordinary rites were familiar to all men. In general, each master of a family was the priest of his household, *i.e.* he was the representative of his family before the gods as well as before men. This made the worship at the temple or the public altar far less important than if the intervention of the priest had been essential. The temples had no regular service with ritual to be performed daily or several times daily,—no morning and evening sacrifice to be maintained,—and no special days were set apart for worship, as "holy unto the Lord." In later times, as life became more complicated, the priests were supposed to have peculiar knowledge of what was pleasing to the gods ; but the priestly families of classical times had for the most part inherited their rights to the sacrifices over which they presided, their shrine originally having been a family shrine, and they had inherited also special directions for worship.

The worship paid to their gods by the Homeric Greeks was joyous. In general, men then did not stand in dread of their divinities. They could fulfil their duties to them in simple and easy fashion, and when *Worship Joyous.* they had paid their sacrifices, they owed them no debt ; they were in the position of a debtor who has paid his debt in full. They had no ceremonies of purification,[3]

---

[1] According to the Levitical code, every sacrifice must be performed before "the door of the tabernacle of the congregation" (*Lev.* xvii. 8), and thus apparently by the priest. So also the Celts offered no sacrifice apart from the Druids (Strabo, 198 c), and the Persians required the presence of a *magus* (Hdt. i. 132).

[2] "The king in the heroic age had charge of the sacrifices, except the hieratic," Aristotle, *Politics* 1285, b 10. So at Athens, the King Archon had the care of almost all the public sacrifices ; see Arist. *Pol. Ath.* lvii.

[3] According to the *Aethiopis* of Arctinus, Achilles slew Thersites in a burst of anger, and then went to Lesbos to be purified, but not even the Homeric Orestes seems to

such as were important in the time of Aeschylus, nor of atonement for sin, such as were required of the Jews. They knew no fasting in sackcloth and ashes, no flagellation, humiliation, or mourning, in connexion with their religious rites. Their religious festivals are joyous feasts in which the gods are invited to share. When the Achaeans desire to appease the wrath of Apollo, who has sent a pestilence upon them in return for the slight offered to his priest, they make sacrifices of bulls and goats in their camp (A 315), and also send to Chrysa, the priest's home, animals for sacrifice. At Chrysa, after a brief prayer by the priest, the young warriors eat and drink and sing paeans all day long, evidently in the best of spirits (A 458). Feast, song, and dance are expected to propitiate the gods, better than fasting and prayer. Men not only have no idea of inherited sin or natural sinfulness, but even when they have done a wrong, they have no vivid and painful sense of guilt, and their offering of sacrifice to the gods has no deep ethical meaning. The divinity at the moment, it is true, is vexed with them, but that may be due to his caprice rather than to their fault, and they are confident that the kindliness of his nature will finally prevail over his wrath. The fact that their victims for sacrifice were eaten (A 458 ff.) proves that the sacrifice was not one of atonement.[1] Aegisthus offers his thanks and oblations after his success in persuading Clytaemestra to join him in his home (γ 273), just as he would have done after the most proper successful act,— unless we are to say that this is "a bribe to blind the eyes of deity . . . so that the divine being who is displeased

need purification from blood-guiltiness. The presence of a murderer does not pollute the sacrifice at o 222,—though this man-slayer offers not even any justification for his act. Still less did ceremonial uncleanness arise from touching a corpse or any other object.—The later ceremonies of purification are thought to have been brought from Lydia (Hdt. i. 35) or from Crete.—In one instance, however, a Homeric murderer desires to avoid shedding blood : Aegisthus does not kill directly the bard whom Agamemnon left as a counsellor for Clytaemestra, but he "takes him to a desert island and leaves him to be the prey and booty of the birds" (γ 270). This may be compared with the manner of the burial of Antigone and the unfaithful Roman vestal virgins.

[1] See page 501.—According to Stengel, sin-offerings were adopted by the Greeks from the Phoenicians long after the Homeric period.

may overlook the act," but this latter explanation is not supported by a parallel case.

Only one stated feast is mentioned by the poet: the day on which Odysseus slays Penelope's suitors is the festival of Apollo (v 156, 278, ϕ 258),—apparently the first day of its month. But the Pylians are making a great feast in honor of Poseidon when *One Stated Feast.* Telemachus reaches their shore (γ 7): nine companies are gathered, with five hundred men in each, and each company has nine bulls to slaughter. Oeneus of Calydon gave a harvest-home festival ($\theta\alpha\lambda\acute{v}\sigma\iota\alpha$, I 534) to the gods. An annual feast may be indicated for Erechtheus at Athens, where Athena gives him a place in her temple, and the Athenians win his favor by bulls and rams "as the years roll round" (B 550),—but this passage has been suspected of being of comparatively late composition.

A sacrifice, being a gift to the gods, implies the expectation of some return, and Plato's statement (*Euthyphro*, 14 E) of the ordinary view has much truth in it,—that men gave in sacrifice what they thought the gods *Sacrifice implies a Return.* wanted, in order that they might receive in return what they themselves desired,—that it was a kind of traffic ("*do ut des*").[1] In a sense, a sacrifice implied a bargain. At the time of the pestilence in the Achaean camp, Achilles seeks to learn the cause of Apollo's anger, "if haply he may please to receive the savor of lambs and goats, and ward off calamity from us" (A 66);—the lambs and the goats may be considered to be an equivalent for the wrong done. Athena rebukes Zeus for his indifference to the fate of Odysseus in spite of the latter's burnt sacrifices to Zeus on the plain of Troy (α 60). Agamemnon reproaches Zeus for sending such distress upon him, though the "king of men" had offered sacrifices to the king of the gods on every altar which the Achaeans had passed (Θ 238), and, a few verses earlier, Athena wonders that Poseidon does not pity the Achaeans, although they bring many pleasing gifts for him to Aegae and Helicé (Θ 203). In time of

---

[1] Conversely, to *supplicate* might imply a vow. So the infinitive $\rho\acute{e}\xi\epsilon\iota\nu$ (*to offer*, $\sigma\tau\epsilon\hat{\iota}\rho\alpha\nu$ $\beta o\hat{v}\nu$), λ 31, depends grammatically on $\gamma o\nu\nu o\acute{v}\mu\eta\nu$, *entreated*, as if the poet had said *vowed*.

distress in battle, Nestor appeals to Zeus, "If ever anyone in Argos, burning the fat thigh-pieces of ox or of sheep, prayed that he might return to his home, and thou didst promise it, remember this, and ward off the day of distress" (O 372); and Penelope offers a like petition to Athena (δ 763, *cf.* ρ 240) with reference to the sacrifices of Odysseus, as she begs for the safe return of Telemachus from Pylus. At the death of Hector, the heart of Zeus is sad for one who has burned many thigh-pieces of bullocks on his altars, both on the summits of Mt. Ida and on the acropolis of Ilium (X 170, *cf.* Δ 48, Ω 69); the same offerings are cited by Apollo to the gods as binding them to see to it that no ill befell the corpse of Hector (Ω 33), and old Priam attributes the gods' care for his son's body to the fitting gifts which this son had paid them (Ω 425),—not to Hector's having kept all the "commandments of the law blameless," nor to his having been a good citizen, a kind father and husband, who had "honored" his father and mother. At the opening of the *Iliad*, the old priest Chryses, on Agamemnon's refusal to set free his daughter, beseeches Apollo to remember his services in offering sacrifices and building temples, and avenge him on the Achaean king (A 39). At the Pylian festival, Athena in the guise of Mentor prays that Poseidon will grant to Nestor and all the Pylians a pleasing return for the splendid hecatomb (γ 58). The sacrifice offered immediately before an important undertaking, as before the first battle of the *Iliad* (B 400), was intended to secure the gods' favor and assistance, though sometimes, as in the last example, the divinity might receive the offering (δέκτο μὲν ἱρά, B 420), and yet not grant the prayer.[1]

Of thank-offerings, the poet says little, but, as we have seen, Oeneus offered a Thanksgiving or Harvest-home festival *Thank-offerings.* to all the gods except Artemis (I 534), whom he neglected. Nestor and his comrades offered many thigh-pieces of bullocks to Poseidon at Geraestus on Euboea after crossing the Aegean Sea (γ 178),

---

[1] Similarly, as Wellhausen says, among the Hebrews "there was no warlike expedition which was not inaugurated in this way [*i.e.* by sacrifice], no agreement that was not thus ratified; no important undertaking of any kind was gone about without a sacrifice."

as they had offered sacrifices at Tenedos (γ 159) before undertaking the voyage. On his return from the expedition by night to the bivouac of the Trojans, Odysseus places in his ship the arms which he had taken from Dolon "until he should prepare a sacrifice for Athena" (K 571). And Aegisthus, as we have seen, on his success in winning Clytaemestra's love, offers sacrifices upon the altars and hangs up votive offerings (γ 273). To say that these sacrifices really looked to the future rather than to the past, is to maintain for the Homeric Greeks the cynical view that gratitude is only a vivid sense of favors to come.

Sacrifices in confirmation of an oath were symbolical, that the violator of the oath might perish as the animal of sacrifice perished. "Whichever first breaks this oath, so may his brains flow upon the ground *Sacrifices in* as does this wine" (Γ 300).[1] A curse rested *Confirmation* upon the victim, and therefore its flesh was not *of an Oath.* eaten, but seems generally to have been buried.[2] The Achaeans before Troy, not being able to bury such a victim in their own land, cast it into the sea (T 267). The wine poured out at such a sacrifice also bore a curse, and was not drunk; therefore it was not mixed with water (*cf.* σπονδαὶ ἄκρητοι, B 341), though the wine of the two parties to the oath was mingled (Γ 295). Hera swore by the Styx, and called the divinities in Tartarus as witnesses (Ξ 271), apparently including a wish that she might join the latter if her oath was violated; again, Hera swears by heaven and earth, the water of the Styx, "which is the most dread oath for the blessed gods" (O 38, *cf.* ε 185),

---

[1] *Cf. si prior defexit publico consilio dolo malo, tum illo die, Juppiter, populum Romanum sic ferito ut ego hunc porcum hic hodie feriam*, Livy, i. 24; *ib.* xxi. 45.

[2] See Γ 310, and Eustathius *ad locum*, γεύσασθαι δὲ αὐτῶν ὅλως ἀπώμοτον ἦν. Observe that for this sacrifice no altar was at hand and no fire was used. In spite of Γ 276, the sacrifice seems intended rather for the chthonic divinities than for the Olympian gods; the blood was shed and the wine was poured upon the ground. *Cf.* Pausanias, v. 24. 10. On the Semitic custom, Wellhausen says: "In the case of the sin-offering, everything is kept far out of sight which could suggest a meal, as for example the accompaniments of meal and wine, oil and salt; of the flesh no portion reaches the altar; it all goes as a fine to the priest." *Cf.* "The flesh of the bullock . . . shalt thou burn with fire without the camp: it is a sin offering," *Exodus* xxix. 14.

by the head of Zeus, and by her nuptial couch,—but we may observe that the statement of Hera under this oath (O 36), while it may be truth, is certainly not "the whole truth." Agamemnon, making a truce with the Trojans for the burial of the dead, raises his sceptre and swears "by Zeus, the husband of Hera" (H 411). Achilles swears by Apollo, the patron god of the seer Calchas to whom he is speaking (A 86), and by the staff which he holds while addressing the assembly (A 234). The disguised Odysseus swears "by Zeus, the table of hospitality, and the hearth of the blameless Odysseus, to which I am come" (ρ 155 = ξ 158). Telemachus swears "by Zeus and the woes of my father" (υ 339). An oath by Poseidon, the god of horsemanship, while laying hold of horses (Ψ 584), seems to imply the willingness to lose these if the assertion is false,—or possibly these horses are thus called as witnesses of the facts.[1]

Perjury is punished by the gods below (Γ 279, Δ 158, T 259),—though Odysseus sees no such suffering perjurers

Perjury Punished.

on his visit to the realm of Hades (see page 469), and the expression doubtless means that the gods of the lower world punish perjurers in this life rather than that these are punished after death,— and Eumaeus checks the disguised Odysseus's readiness to take an oath (ξ 166). But Autolycus, the maternal grandfather of Odysseus, is blessed by Hermes with unusual skill "in thieving and swearing" (κλεπτοσύνη θ' ὅρκῳ τε, τ 396), which may mean that he kept to the letter of his oath while he violated its spirit, though his "thieving" implies a hardened conscience.

In a broad sense, not to be too closely pressed, every feast was a sacrifice.[2] The Greeks, as a people, were eminently

---

[1] This partakes of the nature of a wager; *cf.* ξ 393, Ψ 485. "Everywhere, to swear by what is dear implies willingness to lose what *it* implies, if the oath is false. So, in India, the warrior swears by his bow, and a farmer by his cattle."

[2] To *sacrifice* (ἱερεύειν) often means to *slaughter* (σφάζειν), and ἱερήιον ordinarily means only an animal to be killed for food. The words for slaughter and sacrifice are synonymous also in Hebrew, Aramaic, and Arabic; and the Levitical code was exceedingly strict in its prohibition that any ox or lamb or goat should be killed in the camp or out of the camp except as "an offering unto the Lord before the tabernacle of the Lord" (*Lev.* xvii. 3). Stengel, however (*Hermes*, xxxvi. 324), notes that the suitors of Penelope feast without any mention of a sacrifice, and holds that the

pious, and in early times they made no wide separation between the sacred and the secular. Not only were the Olympian games and like festivals of later times *Every Feast* sacred, but the temples and religious festivals of *a Sacrifice.* the classical period were under the direct supervision and care of the state. Certain portions of meat at every Homeric feast were set apart for the gods, and the presence and favor of these were invoked. Doubtless, then, at every meal some act was usual which corresponded to a brief "grace" before or after meat, or at least to the use of the sign of the cross in Christian times,—however formal this act may have become, and however thoughtlessly performed. Ordinary sacrifices imply thankful recognition of the gods as kindly friends, and the givers of "every good and perfect gift," who are always entitled to a share in the food and drink of mortals who have received their favors. The gods are not the hosts; they are invited to be guests,— to partake of the good cheer which ultimately *Gods are* was derived from them. The divinity who *Guests.* watched over a household was asked to share in its every meal. So the gods visited the Aethiopians to feast with them (A 423, Ψ 205, α 22), and so in former years they had shared openly in the feasts of the Phaeacians, sitting by them in the hall (η 203).[1] That the feasts of the Aethiopians did not differ in principle from those of the Achaeans, is shown by the expression of Iris, who "will go to the land of the Aethiopians, where they are offering hecatombs to the immortals, that I too may have a share in the sacrifices" (ἱρῶν, Ψ 207). By the promise of fair sacrifices (Ψ 209), Iris then persuades Boreas and Zephyrus to rouse the flames of the funeral pile of Patroclus. Athena comes to the sacrifice of Nestor "to share in the sacrifices" (γ 435), and Hermes apologizes to the nymph Calypso for

---

Homeric Greeks sacrificed to the gods only when they felt specific need of these,—in time of fear or because of a definite desire. But even the suitors had in their company one whose special duty it was to care for the sacrifices (θυοσκόος, φ 145,— see page 496).—The word θυσία for sacrificial feast or sacrifice, is not Homeric.

[1] *Cf.* Pindar, *P.* x. 34, where Apollo delights in the feasts of the Hyperboreans. So again in Pindar, *O.* iii. 34, Heracles comes with the Dioscuri to the feast (θεοξένια) of the Agrigentines.

not visiting her more frequently, by saying that not only is the way long, but no cities of men are near who offer sacrifices and hecatombs to the gods (ε 101), *i.e.* he has no refreshment on his journey. At the time of the pestilence in the Achaean camp, Achilles urges inquiry into the wrath of Apollo, in the hope that the god may "please to accept the savor of lambs and of full-grown goats" (A 66).

Every prayer, so far as possible, was accompanied by an offering of some sort, or by a reference to previous sacrifices (Θ 240), or to services which had been rendered *Prayer accom-* in the past (A 39), or by vows for the future. *panied by* If no animal could be killed at that time, perhaps *an Offering.* a libation of wine might be poured, or some other present made. Thus in the cave of Polyphemus, Odysseus and his comrades made a fire and threw into it, as an offering to the gods, portions of the curds which they found and ate (ι 231), apparently not thinking it wise to kill the Cyclops's sheep. Penelope, in distressful anxiety for her son, goes to her upper room, places barley-corns in a basket, and prays to Athena (δ 761). The barley (doubtless parched) must be merely a simpler form of sacrifice than a sheep or a cow,—it is an oblation of food, like the "meat offering" of the Israelites. The offering of Telemachus, by the stern of his ship, at ο 222, is clearly part of the luncheon which he had brought with him from the palace of Menelaus. Whether Telemachus made a fire in order to burn this offering is not clear; Penelope had no fire for her offering of barley-corns, but Odysseus seems to have had no other motive than the sacrifice for kindling a fire in the cave of the Cyclops. The earliest sacrifices of the Greeks very likely were, as Pythagoras said, of the fruits of the earth,—like that of Cain (*Genesis* iv. 3). We may compare the spirit of the modern rude tribes of Palestine, who "bring a present to God, as a man would bring a gift to an emir, and would consider it singularly impertinent to go empty handed." Thus sacrifice, including vows and oblations, is closely connected with prayer.

The importance which the divinities attach to the sacrifices offered by men, is shown by three incidents. Menelaus on leaving Egypt neglected to sacrifice to the gods, and he came no further on his way than the island of Pharos before he was checked by lack of wind for his voyage, and there his supplies of provisions were exhausted before he learned from the sea-god Proteus *Importance of* *Sacrifices.* the cause of his trouble. He returned to Egypt and offered the sacrifices which he had neglected, and then found no difficulty in sailing to his home (δ 351 ff.). A second instance is in connexion with the building of the wall about the Achaean camp, without the sacrifice of hecatombs to the gods: Poseidon called the attention of Zeus to the danger that, if this wall were allowed to stand, no mortals thereafter would think it necessary to seek the approval of the gods for their plans (H 446), *i.e.* that the gods would lose the sacrifices which generally were offered on such occasions. A third instance is the wrath of Artemis against Oeneus for neglecting to remember her at his Harvest-home festival (I 533). In anger she sent the Calydonian boar, which was the cause and occasion of many deaths. To these incidents may be added the thought of Achilles that the pestilence in the Achaean camp may have been sent by Apollo in anger because of a vow unperformed or a hecatomb unoffered (A 65, *cf.* E 178).

The poet gives no single complete account of a sacrifice, and the rites may have varied somewhat. The hearers of the poems were ready also to assume certain acts, even if these were not enumerated in detail by *No Complete* the bard.[1] In distinction from later classical *Account of* *a Sacrifice.* sacrifices, the absence of incense, music, and garlands of flowers, as well as official robes, may be noted. No fillet, either, is mentioned in connexion with the victims.

Those who were to officiate at the sacrifice must be pure in body and in raiment. Hector says that he does not dare with unwashen hands to pour a libation, "nor is it possible for one bespattered with blood and *Purity* gore to pray to the cloud-wrapt son of Cronus" *Required.* (Z 266, *cf.* Γ 270, I 174, Ω 303, γ 445). Telemachus, coming not like Hector from the field of battle, but from the assembly of the people (β 261), washes his hands in the grey sea before he prays to Athena; Achilles, though

[1] The fullest accounts are A 447-474, B 421-431, γ 430-463. *Cf.* Λ 772.

in a great emergency, which calls for immediate action, washes carefully both cup and hands before addressing his prayer, and pouring libation to Zeus (Π 230); and Penelope bathes, and dons clean raiment (δ 759 = ρ 58), before she goes to her upper room to pray.[1]

Attitude in Prayer. The attitude of prayer was standing with uplifted hands,— as Moses stood with hands supported by Aaron and Hur, praying during the conflict with the Amalekites (*Exodus* xvii. 11).[2] This attitude is so characteristic of prayer that to "lift the hands to Zeus" means to pray (H 130, Ω 301, ι 294). Similarly the sceptre is raised by the king in taking an oath, as men now "raise the right hand" when officially sworn (H 412, K 321).[3] This gesture invoked Zeus as a witness to the assertion or promise. Hera is directed by Zeus to swear by the river Styx (see page 501) with one hand resting on the "nourishing earth" and the other on the bright sea (Ξ 271). In an appeal to divinities of the sea, the arms are extended toward the water (A 351), but the notion of lifting the hands to heaven in prayer is so prevalent that Polyphemus "raises his hands to the starry heaven" in his appeal to Poseidon (ι 527). Meleager's mother, invoking the curse of the nether divinities, sits upon the ground and beats it with her hands, as though she were knocking at the gate of hell (I 568).[4]

---

[1] Hesiod, *Works and Days*, 725, warns his hearers not to offer their morning devotions with unwashen hands,—the gods *spit out* (ἀποπτύουσι) such prayers. For the change of raiment, *cf.* the "beauty of holiness" (*i.e.* holy beauty) in which the Hebrews were to appear before the Lord. *Cf.* "When they go into the tabernacle of the congregation, they [viz. Aaron and his sons] shall wash with water, that they die not; or when they come near to the altar to minister, to burn offering made by fire unto the Lord: So shall they wash their hands and their feet, that they die not," *Exodus* xxx. 20. Similarly on the death of Philip of Macedon, Demosthenes, though in deep mourning for the death of his own daughter, donned a white robe and a garland, and offered sacrifice of thanksgiving (Aeschines, iii. 77). Euripides (*Alc.* 159) represents Alcestis as bathing and taking her best array from her cedar chests before her prayer.

[2] χεῖρας ἀνασχών, A 450; *cf.* E 174, Z 257, H 130, Ω 301, ι 294, ν 355. Compare also the representations on Babylonian and Mycenaean monuments and seals.—The Homeric Greeks knew no folding of the hands, bowing of the head, or kneeling, in prayer.

[3] *Cf.* ὁ δ' ὅρκος ἦν τοῦ σκήπτρου ἐπανάτασις, Aristotle, *Politics*, 1285 b 12.

[4] *Cf.* Hom. *Hy. Pyth. Apoll.* 155; Bacchylides, v. 42; Frazer on Pausanias, viii. 15. 3; Rohde, *Psyche²*, i. 119.

A personal suppliant prostrates himself and clasps the knees of him whose favor he seeks. Thetis clasps the knees of Zeus with her left arm, and touches his chin with her right hand (A 500),[1] but kneeling in prayer to an unseen divinity was unknown.

Prayer in general was uttered, and not merely thought. The divinities were not required to read the hearts of mortals, although they often did understand without spoken words. Before his single-combat with Hector, Ajax bids the Achaeans pray to Zeus, *Prayer Uttered.* " in silence, by yourselves, that the Trojans may not hear, or even openly, since we fear no foe " (H 194) ; but the explanation of " in silence " through " by yourselves," shows that Ajax did not contemplate perfect silence, but only a contrast to a shout.[2]

The divinity was invoked from his nearest place of worship. Thus Agamemnon on the plain of Troy prays to " Father Zeus, ruler of Ida, most glorious and most great," [3] and Priam is urged by Hecuba to " pray to Idaean Zeus, who looketh down on all the plain of Troy " (Ω 291). The old priest Chryses addresses his *Divinity Invoked from his nearest Seat.* prayer to the " God of the silver bow, who dost guard (literally, *bestride*) Chrysa and sacred Cilla, and art the mighty defender of Tenedos " (A 37),—these being places near at hand. As Odysseus and Ajax go along the shore of the sea to the tent of Achilles, in the hope of persuading him to return to the conflict, they pray to Poseidon, certainly because he, in his element, is of all gods the one who is nearest to them (I 182). Yet Glaucus appeals to Apollo, " whether thou art in the rich land of Lycia, or in the country of Troy,—wherever thou art thou canst hear a man in trouble " (Π 515) ; and a few verses before this, Achilles had invoked " Dodonaean Zeus " (Π 233), —these both appealing to the divinities who were preëminent

---

[1] Thus the verb γουνοῦμαι is used for *entreat* (as I 583, *cf.* X 345), even where no physical contact was possible.

[2] Leaf thinks that, in accordance with a primitive notion, the particular form of words used in addressing a national god, was to be concealed from the enemy.

[3] Ζεῦ πάτερ, Ἴδηθεν μεδέων, κύδιστε, μέγιστε, Γ 276. " Thou who dost rule from Ida " is a possible interpretation, of course, instead of " ruler of Ida."

in their distant homes. A prayer which is very earnest, and
yet is not likely to be fulfilled, is sometimes addressed to
"Zeus, Athena, and Apollo," the three most important and
mighty of the gods of Homeric Olympus (B 371, Δ 288,

Silence during Prayer. H 132, Π 97), which may be compared with Solon's direction that an oath should be by three divinities (Pollux, viii. 142). During prayer, silence
was desired, or at least the avoidance of all words which
might be of ill omen.[1]

The horns of a bull or cow to be sacrificed were gilded
(γ 384, K 294),[2] and hair was cut from the head of the

Horns Gilded. victim[3] and thrown into the fire (T 254, γ 446, ξ 422). If several persons had part in the
sacrifice in confirmation of an oath, bits of the hair or
wool of the victim might be distributed to each, who as
it were thus held his hand on the victim's head (Γ 273).[4]
Barley-corns (perhaps mixed with salt)[5] were then taken
from a basket (γ 441, 447), and prayer was offered. After
the prayer, the barley-corns, which seem to have represented the early cereal food of the Greeks,—corresponding
in a way to the "unleavened bread" of the Israelites,—were
thrown upon the victim's head and the fire.

By the fireside of Eumaeus, the hog to be slain was
stunned by a blow with a billet of wood (ξ 425). At the

Killing of the Victim. palace of Nestor (γ 449), one of his sons with an axe cut the sinews of the cow's neck, striking
doubtless close behind the horns.[6] Then the young
men turned the head of the animal up toward heaven

---

[1] Cf. εὐφημῆσαι, I 171, though this may not have acquired as yet its full later conventional meaning of *favete linguis.*

[2] So at Eleusis, according to C.I.A. iv 27 b, a βοῦς χρυσόκερως was to be sacrificed to Athena. *Cf. velatum auro vittisque iuvencum,* Verg. *Aen.* v. 366; Tibullus, iv. I. 15; *auratis cornibus,* Livy, vii. 37.

[3] Cf. Eur. *Alc.* 74, where Death enters the home of Alcestis, in order to cut a lock of her hair and thus seal her death.

[4] Cf. "And Aaron and his son shall put their hands upon the head of the ram," *Exodus* xxix. 15.

[5] See Scholium on A 449. Stengel in *Hermes,* xxix. 627. *Cf.* "And every oblation of thy meat offering [*i.e.* unleavened cakes 'baken in the oven'] shalt thou season with salt," *Lev.* ii. 13.

[6] κόψας ἐξόπιθεν κεράων βοὸς . . . ἵνα τάμῃ, P 521.

(A 459),[1] while its throat was cut. The blood was caught in a basin (γ 444), and seems to have been then thrown on the fire.[2] At Nestor's sacrifice, when the first blow is struck on the victim, the prince's "daughters and sons' wives and his honored wife" uttered an ecstatic pious shriek (ὀλόλυξαν, γ 450), which was simply part of the ritual, not occasioned at all by the mere shock of the sight of blood, but possibly originally intended, like the shouts of Baal's worshippers, to call the attention of the divinity. This cry was their part in the sacrificial ceremony. Similarly at the vow of the Trojan matrons to Athena, the women with uplifted hands uttered a cry (ὀλολυγῇ, Z 301), to accompany the prayer of the priestess,—the uplifted hands corresponding to the modern posture of devotion, kneeling, and the cry corresponding to the "responses" of the modern ritual.

After the victim was flayed and quartered (B 422, γ 456), the nobler vitals were first roasted and tasted.[3] Telemachus, arriving at Pylus after the beginning of the great feast, takes part in the sacrifice by partaking of the *Distribution of Victim.* vitals. The thigh-bones, or at least pieces of them, were cut out, wrapped in a double layer of fat,[4] and then, with

---

[1] According to scholiasts and similar authorities, the head of the victim slain in honor of the nether gods was turned down, toward the earth. But the Homeric passage (λ 36) which has been quoted in support of this view, can easily be interpreted to mean simply that the victim's blood flowed into the pit. *Cf.* Ψ 148, ταυροσφαγοῦντες ἐς σάκος, Aesch. *Sept.* 43 ; σφάξαντες εἰς ἀσπίδα, Xen. *An.* iv. 3. 18 ; τὸν ταῦρον εἰς τὴν πυρὰν σφάξας, Plut. *Arist.* 21.—A sufficient reason for turning up the animal's head would seem to be the convenience of tightening the skin and the cords before cutting the throat.

[2] S. I. Curtiss, *Primitive Semitic Religion of To-day*, p. 183, describes a sacrifice at an Arab tent : the throat of a young goat was cut, "one of the women rushed to the victim before the blood had ceased gurgling, and caught the crimson flow in a *tannur*," a concave piece of iron which served as a basin.—Dr. Curtiss presents a strong and interesting argument to prove that, at least among the Semites, "the sacrificial meal" is not "the oldest form of sacrifice" (p. 218), but that "the bursting forth of blood" is the most important element. Certain difficulties in accepting this view for the sacrifices of the Homeric Greeks, will be made clear later in this chapter.

[3] σπλάγχνα πάσαντο, A 464, γ 9, 40. These vitals seem to have been eaten without salt, and this custom has been thought to be derived from an age when salt was not commonly used with meat.

[4] *Cf.* μηρί᾽ ἔκηε, καλύψας πίονι δημῷ | ἀρνῶν ἠδ᾽ ἐρίφων, ρ 241 ; μηροὶ καλυπτῆς ἐξέκειντο πιμελῆς, Soph. *Ant.* 1011.—That no pains were taken to leave flesh on

bits of flesh, were burned in the fire, while wine was poured upon the burning sacrifices.[1] These portions seem to have been selected as representative of the entire animal,[2] as Eumaeus threw into the fire part of every member of the hog which he had killed,[3] dredged with barley meal, which may have corresponded to the barley-corns of the more elaborate sacrifice; and the libation of wine was an offering of a share in the common drink of the company. The Homeric Greeks knew no holocausts. The rich savor of burning flesh and fat rose with the smoke (κνίση, A 317, Θ 549), and was thought to be enjoyed by the gods (cf. ε 101), to whom the flesh could be conveyed in no other way so easily and effectively. Eumaeus, the divine swine-herd, in his hut sets apart a portion of the feast (apparently a portion equal to that of each of the human guests) for Hermes and the nymphs (ξ 435), in addition to throwing bits into the fire, for the gods in general, as it would seem; and Achilles in his tent, preparing entertainment for the Achaean embassadors, but not killing any animal, bids his friend Patroclus throw into the fire the sacrificial bits (θυηλαί, I 220). The latter instance, we see elsewhere, is the only case in the Homeric poems of flesh being on hand, ready to cook: the animal doubtless was "sacrificed" when it was killed, but yet at a later hour

the bones, is indicated by Hesiod's expression (ὀστέα λευκά, *Theogony*, 540), and is emphasized by Menander in his *Dyscolus* (οἱ δὲ τὴν ὀσφὺν ἄκραν | καὶ τὴν χολὴν ὀστᾶ τ' ἄβρωτα τοῖς θεοῖς | ἐπιθέντες αὐτοὶ τ' ἄλλα καταπίνουσ' ἀεί, 129 K.), and by a poet in Clemens Alex. *Strom.* vii. 6. 34, who speaks of the credulity of a man who expects the gods to accept an offering of fleshless bones (ὀστῶν ἀσάρκων) which would be valueless even to hungry dogs.

[1] A 460 = B 423, γ 456; Λ 773. Cf. πρὸ τοῦ θοινᾶσθαι . . . ἀπαρχὰς τῶν βρωμάτων νέμειν τοῖς θεοῖς, Athenaeus, 179 B.

[2] Hesiod's aetiological story (*Theogony*, 536) of the original of this sacrifice is familiar, but not Homeric: that Prometheus, being set to divide the victim between gods and men, put on one side an attractive parcel of bones concealed in fat, while on the other side he placed most of the flesh so wrapped in the hide as to seem a mass of refuse; and that Zeus "took with both hands the fat, and anger entered his soul." According to Hesiod the original intention seems to have been to divide the animal equally between gods and men, though Zeus had his choice between the two parcels; in Homer, as in later Greek usage, only small portions of the victim are offered to the gods.

[3] πάντων ἀρχόμενος μελέων . . . καὶ τὰ μὲν ἐν πυρὶ βάλλε παλύνας ἀλφίτου ἀκτῇ, ξ 428.

Achilles thus sets apart portions for the gods, as their share in his repast.

Last of all, the tongues of the victims were burnt in the fire (γ 332),—probably, in the case of a formal sacrifice, as a present to the god in whose honor the feast was held.[1] A formal libation was then made (γ 334, 341), for which the guests may have come up in succession to the altar and poured wine upon the fire,— possibly quenching it in this way. *Tongues Burnt.*

The first libation at a feast was formal, made from a full bowl [2] by the host or a priest, originally probably at the hearth or altar, but later poured by each in his place (*cf.* αὐτόθεν ἐξ ἑδρέων, ν 56). Then the cup-bearer passed from left to right (ἐπιδέξια, Α 597, *cf.* φ 141), offering the wine to the guests who each poured a few drops upon the floor (which, as is seen elsewhere, was not kept neat) as a drink-offering. *First Libation.*

If wine was not at hand, water might be used as a drink-offering,—men presenting to the gods a share in their feast such as it was, as did the companions of Odysseus on the island of Helius (μ 357), who also used oak leaves instead of barley-corns with the sacrifices.

But drink-offerings were made not only in subordination to burnt-offerings, but also independently.[3] In general, prayer was accompanied by a libation when wine was at hand. Thus, on sending Patroclus and his Myrmidons forth to battle, when the Trojans actually have entered the Achaean camp, Achilles has no time for the formal sacrifice of a victim, but washes his hands, pours a libation on the altar of his barrack, and *Drink Offerings.*

---

[1] Similarly, the last act in the sacrifice at the outset of the Argonautic expedition, according to Apollonius Rhodius (i. 517), was to pour a libation upon the burning tongues; but this seems to be an imitation or reminiscence of γ 332. According to Athenaeus, 16 B, the tongues were offered to Hermes as the patron of heralds and the mouthpiece of the gods, but why this offering should be made at the close of the feast, he does not say, except as Hermes is ὕπνου προστάτης, and so the libation is paid to him on going to rest. See p. 435 f.

[2] Ι 175, Κ 578, γ 339, 390, η 179, ν 50, σ 423, φ 271.

[3] See Bernhardi, *Das Trankopfer bei Homer.*—The words σπένδω and λείβω (*libo*) are synonymous (Π 231, 253). σπένδεσθαι in the sense of *make a truce* (as Hdt. vii. 148) is not Homeric. So σπονδαί (Β 341, Δ 159) must be *libations*.

prays to Zeus (Π 231). The libation which old Priam
makes before going to the tent of Achilles, seems likewise
to have been at the altar of his palace (Ω 306). The
Achaean embassadors to Achilles pour a libation before
they leave the tent of Agamemnon (I 177), another as they
leave the tent of Achilles (I 657), and a third before they
separate for the night (I 712). Naturally the prayer in
each case is to be understood, when it is not distinctly
expressed. Thus Achilles calls upon the winds to aid in
the burning of Patroclus's pyre, while he pours libations
(Ψ 196). Before a voyage, too, libations might be offered
without the slaughter of victims.[1] Hecuba offers to Hector
wine for a libation, on his return from the field of battle
(Z 259), and a little later, Hector refers to the "bowl of
freedom," which the Trojans will set in their halls, if Zeus
shall grant to them to drive the Achaeans from Troy
(Z 528).

At the feasts, individual libations were customary, as well
as the more formal drink-offerings in which all took part.

Individual Libations. Thus Telemachus and Athena in the guise of
Mentor reach Pylus while the Pylians are in the
midst of their sacrifices on the shore, and Nestor's
son Pisistratus meets the strangers, and offers them bits of
the vitals of the victims, and a cup of wine that they may
pour a libation and pray,—for "all men have need of the
gods" (γ 40 ff.). The cup, given first to Athena, does not
seem to have been replenished before the libation of Telemachus; the act was formal, admitting the guests to a
participation in the sacrifice.[2] But when Odysseus comes to
the palace of Alcinoüs, near the close of the feast, a fresh
bowl is mixed for a libation (η 164), as is done likewise at
his departure (ν 50). During the feast each guest might
pour a libation at his pleasure,—very probably offering as a
rule the first few drops from each filled cup. Thus on the
night before the second day of battle of the *Iliad*, Zeus
thundered terribly, and the Achaeans were in great fear, and
"poured wine from their cups upon the ground, nor did

---

[1] As β 432; ο 222, *cf.* 258, and as Telemachus leaves the home of Menelaus, ο 147.

[2] Nothing is said here about the washing of hands; this may have been understood, or it may have been omitted in certain circumstances.

any dare sooner to drink, before he had poured a libation" (H 480).[1]

A libation before going to rest was usual (σ 419). In the palace of Alcinoüs (η 137), this is *Libation* paid to Hermes, but, in general, libations seem *before going* no more limited in direction than prayers. *to Rest.*

The hands were washed before a libation (II 230), as before a full sacrifice, but repeated washings were not necessary for each repeated libation.[2]

The wine offered in a libation was mixed with water, as the people were accustomed to drink it ; the gods enjoyed it mixed, just as men did. Only in the case of *Wine mixed* the sanction of an oath were libations used *with Water.* of unmixed wine (B 341, Δ 159), as bearing a curse,—just as the flesh of a victim slain in confirmation of an oath was neither to be eaten nor to be given to the gods. That the libations to the winds (Ψ 196) were of unmixed wine, has been suggested, since winds were wor-shipped later with chthonic rites, but this supposition is not necessary. Whether libations were paid to the dead, is not clear ; but at the pyre of Patroclus, Achilles all night long pours wine upon the ground, as he calls upon the soul of his friend (Ψ 220), and in the morning he quenches the pyre with wine (Ψ 237). In Hades, Odysseus pours into the pit, for the enjoyment of the souls, first honey and milk, then wine, and third water (λ 27).

No indication is found that a definite amount of wine was to be poured out at a sacrifice, as for the Children of Israel, the drink-offerings were to be " half an hin unto a bullock, and the third part of an hin unto a ram, and the fourth part of an hin unto a lamb" (*Numbers* xxviii. 14).

Though, in general, libations were poured from the ordinary

4

[1] When the cup of hemlock is brought to Socrates in prison, he inquires whether he may pour a libation from it (Plato, *Phaedo*, 117 B),—implying his custom to pour a libation from his cup of wine.

[2] *Cf.* H 480, σ 151, where one of the suitors had pledged the disguised Odysseus during the meal. Thus at the close of their interview with Achilles, the embassadors who had sought his return to the battle, pour a libation before their return (I 656), but had no need to wash their hands.

cups (Z 258, H *fin.*), yet for a peculiarly solemn libation, Achilles chooses a cup from which he allows no other man

Special Cup for Libation.

to drink, and with which he pours a libation to no god but Zeus (Π 225). This cup he takes from his chest, and cleanses it carefully, first with sulphur and then with flowing water, before his libation.

No libation by a woman is mentioned by the Homeric poet, but this may be mere chance, since (as is seen elsewhere) women and children drink wine themselves and so might pour it out to the gods. But Penelope (δ 759) offers in sacrifice barley-corns without any mention of a drink-offering. The offerings (θύεα, Z 270) borne with the robe by Trojan matrons to the temple of Athena, are not defined, but they are more likely to be barley than wine. Some kind of incense has been suggested for them; but incense does not appear elsewhere in the Homeric ritual. Perhaps it should be remembered in connexion with this that though Helen and Areté are present at ordinary feasts, neither is represented as drinking wine after the meal,—they sit and spin while their husbands sip their wine (δ 121 ff., ζ 305).

As for the victims for sacrifice, kine, sheep, goats, and swine were the ordinary offerings to the gods. Human

Victims for Sacrifice.

sacrifices were unknown, such as the offering of Iphigenia at Aulis by Agamemnon, according to the later myth, and that of Polyxena at the tomb of Achilles.[1] The slaughter of twelve Trojan youths at the pyre of Patroclus (Ψ 175) was not sacrifice, but vengeance, as well as the planned giving of Hector's body to the dogs (Ψ 182); Achilles had determined to make many a one of the Trojan women wipe "with both hands" the tears from her cheeks (Σ 122). The Trojans, indeed, sank horses in the eddies of the Scamander (Φ 132), but this was un-Hellenic.[2] Wild animals, fowl, and fish were not offered at the altar,—possibly because the principle of

---

[1] Eur. *Iph. Aul.* ; *Hec.* 523.

[2] For this sacrifice, *cf.* ἐς τὸν [*sc.* Στρυμόνα] οἱ Μάγοι ἐκαλλιερέοντο σφάζοντες ἵππους, φαρμακεύσαντες δὲ ταῦτα ἐς τὸν ποταμὸν κτλ., Hdt. vii. 113. See page 354 f.

life [1] had already departed from the game and the fish before they could be brought thither; while tame fowl are not mentioned as eaten. In general, however, men presented to the gods that, and only that, which they themselves enjoyed eating, since all ordinary sacrifices were feasts. Reference has been made already to Odysseus's offering of curds in the cave of Polyphemus, to Penelope's sacrifice of barley-corns, and to Telemachus's sacrifice of part of his luncheon (see page 504). A unique sacrifice is indicated in the comparison of the roar of a wounded warrior (Υ 404) with the roar of a bull dragged by young men in honor of the Heliconian king, Poseidon. This is brought into connexion with a cruel form of sacrifice which is shown by representations on gems and coins to have been known at Troy, in which the bull was drawn up a column or a tree by his head and neck. The representations show the bull in intense agony and with open mouth, which well might emit a Homeric roar.[2]

The sex of the victim as a rule was that of the divinity to which it was offered. Thus heifers were offered to Athena (as Z 93, Λ 729, γ 382), dark bulls to Poseidon (Λ 728, γ 6, ν 181), a bull to the Alpheüs (Λ 728), and rams to the river Spercheüs (Ψ 148). Odysseus in order to appease Poseidon's wrath for the blinding of Polyphemus, was to sacrifice to this god a ram, a bull, and a boar (λ 131),—the *suovetaurilia* of the Romans. A white male lamb was offered to Helius (the *sun*, Γ 103), a black ewe lamb to Gaea (the *earth*), a ram and a black ewe to the dead (κ 527). A black ram was sacrificed to the shade of Teiresias (λ 32). The age for the most part was determined by convenience; men sacrificed what they wanted to eat. New-born lambs (ἀρνῶν πρωτογόνων, Δ 120) are vowed to Apollo. The victims often were full-grown.[3] Agamemnon sacrificed a five-year-old bull to Zeus before the first battle of the *Iliad* (B 403), and another in his tent at the close of the same

---

[1] But this theory, which has been accepted somewhat widely, seems inconsistent with the practise of offering such food as curds or barley-corns.

[2] See Brückner, *Der ilische Opfergebrauch* in Dörpfeld's *Troja und Ilion*, p. 564.

[3] τέλειοι, A 66,—unless (as is improbable) this means *unblemished*. Thus has been explained also τελήσσας ἑκατόμβας, A 315.

battle (H 315). That the victim should be unblemished, may be assumed ; nothing imperfect should be offered to honored guests. To Athena, the Trojan matrons vow heifers "untouched by the goad" (ἠκέστας, Z 309), *i.e.* which had never been put to menial labor.[1] The word *hecatomb*, which seems originally to have meant a *hundred cattle*, is used in a general way of a large sacrifice. The poet speaks of a "hecatomb" of eighty-one bullocks (γ 59, *cf.* 7), of other hecatombs of bulls and goats (A 315), and of one of lambs (Δ 120). That which is sent to Chrysa in a boat rowed by twenty men cannot have been of one hundred bulls, for which no room could have been found in the boat (A 309).

No indications of "mysteries," like those of Eleusis or Samothrace, are found in the Homeric poems. The only "witch-craft" is that of Circe, who by her potent herbs transformed men into "swine or wolves or lions" (κ 212, 239, 392, 433),—but she was in fairyland.

The only instance of incantations in Homer, is the spell (ἐπαοιδή, τ 457) by which his kinsmen checked the flow of blood from a wound of the youthful Odysseus. *Incantations.* Circe had potent herbs, which could transform human beings into brutes (κ 236 f.), but she was more than mortal. Yet even her charms could be overcome by the use of the herb moly (κ 305), which was not easily dug by mortals, but was given to Odysseus by Hermes. Helen, too, had received from the wife of Thon, in Egypt, an herb *nepenthes* which dispelled care and tears (δ 221). That the cestus of Aphrodite contained all love charms (Ξ 214), is simply part of the mighty influence of the goddess. Curses were addressed to Hades, Persephone, and the Erinyes (I 454, 569).

As for votive offerings, man gave to the gods what he himself valued,—not only food and drink, but also garments, *Votive Offerings.* as a robe to Athena (Z 302 ; *cf.* γ 274) ; arms, as Hector vows the armor of his antagonist, to be hung before the temple of Apollo (H 83), and Odysseus prepares for Athena a votive offering of the arms of the Trojan scout, Dolon (K 570) ; and ornaments

---

[1] *Cf.* "A red heifer, without spot, wherein is no blemish, and upon which never came yoke," *Numbers* xix. 2 ; 1 *Sam.* vi. 7.

of gold, as those offered by Aegisthus (γ 274) and those vowed by Telemachus (χρύσεα δῶρα, π 185). These are in general thank-offerings, but the first and the last are clearly intended to secure the divinity's favor. The temple at Pytho (Delphi) was noted for its wealth (I 404), and this must have come from votive offerings.

Pandarus vowed to Apollo a hecatomb of lambs on his return to his home, if he should hit Menelaus (Δ 119) on the first day of battle, and in the shooting contest *Offerings* Meriones made a like vow to the same god, if he *Vowed.* should hit the mark and win the prize (Ψ 872). The Trojan matrons vowed to Athena that they would sacrifice twelve kine in her temple, if she would pity them and break the spear of Diomed (Z 308). Peleus vowed to the god of the river Spercheüs that Achilles, on his return from Troy, should dedicate to him his hair, and offer a hecatomb, slaying fifty rams, so that their blood should flow into its springs (Ψ 144). Odysseus was bidden by Circe (κ 522) to vow in Hades that on his return to Ithaca he would sacrifice to the dead a barren cow, and burn a pyre of treasures, and would sacrifice a black ram to Teiresias. Being weather-bound on an island, the comrades of Odysseus propose to kill some of the cattle of the sun-god for their present necessities, but as an atonement, on their return to Ithaca, to build for him a temple and put votive offerings in it (μ 345).

The only sacred animals mentioned in the poems are the 350 sheep and 350 kine of the sun-god (μ 129). These have been compared with the sacred sheep of Apollonia (Herodotus, ix. 93), the sacred horses of Hera *Sacred* (Diodorus, iv. 15), the sacred doe of Despoena *Animals.* at Lycosura (Pausanias, viii. 10. 10), and the well-known geese of Juno on the Roman capitol. (See page 346.)

The oracles at Dodona and at Delphi are mentioned expressly, each once,—both times in the *Odyssey*. The disguised Odysseus on his return to Ithaca, in his fictitious story, reports that he has heard of the *Oracles.* absent king as having set out for Dodona that he might learn from the high-crowned oak of Zeus in what manner he should return to Ithaca (ξ 327 = τ 296); and according to the song of the Phaeacian bard, Demodocus, Agamemnon consulted the oracle of Apollo at Pytho (Delphi), before the beginning of the Trojan War, and learned that the quarrel of the bravest of the Achaeans should be followed by victory in war (θ 80). But the existence of the Delphic oracle is implied further in the words of Achilles that all the wealth of the archer Phoebus Apollo at rocky Pytho (I 405) would not induce him to give up his wrath for Agamemnon,—which implies a large collection of votive offerings, possibly, it is true, bestowed for instances of the god's favor shown in other ways than by oracles,— and the existence of the oracle at Dodona is still more distinctly implied in Achilles's prayer to Zeus, whose "prophets (ὑποφῆται, II 235) dwell about Dodona, with unwashen feet, sleeping on the ground." Dodona is "wintry" (δυσχείμερος, B 750). Pytho is "rocky" (πετρήεσσα, B 519). Apollo's mother Leto was on her way to Pytho when she was assailed by Tityus (λ 581). The prophets of Dodona seem to have interpreted the rustling of the leaves of the oak. Nothing indicates the existence of any "pale-eyed" Pythian priestess or even a "prophetic cell."

In general, however, local oracles were consulted far less frequently than seers or prophets who were believed to be *Prophesy.* directly inspired by the gods, especially by Apollo, like the prophets of the Old Testament,—like Balaam the son of Beor as well as Samuel and Elijah,—a race which became extinct in later times. Thus Iamus at Olympia heard directly the voice of Apollo (Pindar, *Ol.* vi. 66), while his descendants heard no divine voice, but interpreted the omens of fire at the great altar. So Moses was favored with direct inspiration: "If there be a prophet among you, I the Lord will make myself known unto him in a vision, and will speak unto him in a dream. My servant Moses is not so. . . . With him will I speak mouth to mouth, even apparently, and not in dark speeches" (*Numbers* xii. 6). With this we may compare the saying of Balaam, "The word that God putteth in my mouth, that shall I speak" (*Numbers* xxii. 38), while a little later, in the history of the same people, we read that "the word of the Lord was precious in those days, there was no open vision" (1 *Sam.* iii. 1).

The most famed prophet of a previous generation was Teiresias, the blind seer of Thebes,—the contemporary of three successive generations, of Laius, of Oedipus, *Prophets.* and of Creon,—to whom alone Persephone granted intelligence in Hades, and to consult whom Odysseus went to the land of shades (κ 492, λ 90). The chief seer in the army before Troy is Calchas (A 69), who enjoys the favor of Apollo, and who, even without special instructive omen or guiding portent, makes known to men the will of the gods (θεοπροπίας, A 87). He had interpreted also the omen which appeared to the army while it was encamped at Aulis (B 322). That he is a warrior as well as a seer, is indicated by Poseidon's assuming his form (N 45) when he would arouse the Argives to a fiercer battle. In the Trojan army, Helenus, Priam's son, is the chief seer (οἰωνοπόλων ὄχ' ἄριστος, Z 76), and once he even overhears a conversation between Athena and Apollo (H 44). Priam's fatidic daughter Cassandra does not appear as a prophetess in the Homeric poems. The Mysian leader Ennomus was a seer (οἰωνιστής, B 858), but his omens did not save him from death at the hands of Achilles. Merops of Percote foreknew the death which would befall his sons (B 831, Λ 329), but could not save them ; and similarly Polyidus of Corinth (N 666) and the dream-interpreter Eurydamas (E 149) had warned their sons in vain. In the *Odyssey*, the old Halitherses of Ithaca appears as a seer (β 157), who at the time of Odysseus's departure for Troy, predicted his return in the twentieth year. The family of Melampus seems to have the gift of prophecy as an inherited possession (λ 291, o 225, 245, 252), and his great-grandson Theoclymenus, seeking the protection of Telemachus, displays the family power (o 531, υ 351). Theoclymenus in the midst of the feast (υ 351) sees Penelope's suitors sitting in darkness, the walls dripping with blood, and the porch full of ghosts trooping " to the infernal jail,"—while no one else beholds this scene. This is the only instance of ecstatic prophesy in the Homeric poems. Even the Cyclopes have had a seer among them, Telemus the son of Eurymus (ι 509), who foretold the blinding of Polyphemus by Odysseus. Seers, like surgeons, carpenters, and bards, are welcomed even when they come from other communities (ρ 384).

At the point of death, the dying man has a spirit's view of the future. Thus Patroclus (Π 851) *Spirit's View of the Future.* foretells the death of Hector, and Hector in turn, dying, foresees the death of Achilles (X 359).[1]

One of the immortal horses of Achilles is endowed by Hera with speech, like Balaam's ass,—just long enough to predict his master's death (T 417).

The Homeric Greeks had no astrology in the mediaeval sense, and no systematic auguries, with divisions of the *No Astrology.* heavens. No indication is found of a formal position of the observer, *e.g.* with face towards the north, unless this is found in M 239 (see p. 521).

Omens are taken most frequently from natural phenomena, especially from thunder and lightning. Athena descends to *Omens from Natural Phenomena.* the plain like a meteor (Δ 75), and men ask each other whether this is a portent of war or of peace. Serpents of lapis lazuli on the cuirass of Agamemnon resemble the rainbows which Zeus fixes in the cloud as a sign to men (Λ 28), and, again, the rainbow is a sign either of war or of cold winter (P 547). A flash of lightning on the right, as the Argives embarked for Troy, indicated the final success of the expedition (B 353, *cf.* I 236, N 242). The groans of Agamemnon at the close of the second great day of battle (K 5), after the Achaeans had been driven back to their camp, were as frequent as the flashes of lightning when Zeus is " preparing rain or hail or snow or the huge maw of devouring war." On the second day of battle, Zeus thunders from Mt. Ida and hurls a blazing thunderbolt into the midst of the host of the Achaeans (Θ 75); a little later

---

[1] *Cf.* the patriarch Jacob's predictions, *Genesis* xlix ; καὶ γάρ εἰμι ἤδη ἐνταῦθα ἐν ᾧ μάλιστ᾽ ἄνθρωποι χρησμῳδοῦσιν, ὅταν μέλλωσιν ἀποθανεῖσθαι, Plato, *Ap.* 39 c ; and John of Gaunt's prophesy, *Rich. II.* ii. 1. 31 ; and the dying Hotspur's words, " O, I could prophesy, But that the earthy hand of death lies on my tongue," *Henry IV.* 1st part, v. 4. 83. *Cf.* also Diod. Sic. xviii. 1, Cicero, *de Div.* i. 30.—Aristotle (*Frag.* 12) thought this to be one of the means by which men gained knowledge of the gods.

again he thunders terribly and hurls a gleaming thunderbolt to the ground in front of the chariot of Diomed, and
a fearful odor arises of burning sulphur (Θ 133), and while
Diomed is pondering whether to flee or to turn to the
battle, Zeus thunders thrice, indicating to the Trojans decisive
victory in the fight (Θ 170). On the next day of battle,
Zeus thunders in response to a prayer of Nestor (O 377),
but the Trojans seem to have been encouraged by the roar;
and a little later, Zeus covered Mt. Ida with clouds, thundered
loudly, shook his aegis, and put the Achaeans to flight
(P 594). In the *Odyssey*, Zeus thunders from a clear sky
in response to a prayer of Odysseus (υ 103), and again
thunders as Odysseus bends his old bow (φ 413). At the
very close of the poem, he sends a bolt to stop Odysseus
from the pursuit of the friends of Penelope's suitors (ω 539).
Bloody dew-drops are sent by Zeus from heaven at the
beginning of the third battle of the *Iliad*, as a token of the
slaughter which is to follow (Λ 53), and again when
Sarpedon is about to be killed by Patroclus (Π 459).

Omens are taken also from the flight of birds, of which
the eagle is most important and significant. Thus an eagle
is sent by Zeus "on the right" (δεξιός, Ω 320),
to encourage Priam as he sets out for the ships *Omens from Flight of Birds.*
of the Achaeans to ransom Hector's body. In
answer to Agamemnon's appeal to Zeus for the
safety of the Achaeans, an eagle is sent, bearing in its
talons a fawn which it lets fall by the altar of Zeus, the
giver of omens (πανομφαίῳ, Θ 250), and the Achaeans "saw
that the bird came from Zeus and rushed the more upon
the Trojans." An eagle skirted the army of the Trojans on
the left, as they were about to cross the trench and enter
the Achaean camp,—bearing in its talons a serpent which
it let fall in the midst of the host, "and the Trojans
shuddered as they saw . . . the portent of Zeus" (M 200).
Pulydamas urges Hector to cease at once from the advance,
but Hector replies that he heeds not whether the birds fly
"to the right, to the east and the sun, or to the left, to
the gloomy west; let us follow the counsel of great Zeus;
one *bird* [*i.e. omen*] is best,—to fight for our fatherland"
(M 238). A little later, as Ajax challenges Hector to

single combat, an eagle high in air appears on his right, and the host of the Achaeans shouted, "confident in the bird" (θάρσυνος οἰωνῷ, N 823). After the speech of Telemachus to the assembly of Ithacans, Zeus sends two eagles from the summit of a mountain, which, on coming to a point over the assembly, tore each other's "cheek and neck" with their talons, and "looked on the heads of all and boded destruction," and then darted on the right between the lines of houses of the city (β 146); this omen was interpreted by Halitherses as meaning destruction to Penelope's suitors,—but Eurymachus answers that many birds flit to and fro, and not all are fateful (ἐναίσιμοι, β 182). As Telemachus leaves the palace of Menelaus in Sparta, an eagle on his right carries away a white goose, and Helen interprets the omen as a promise that Odysseus shall return and take vengeance on his wife's suitors (ο 160). Similarly Penelope dreams that a great eagle comes from the mountain and slays the geese in her yard, and then declares himself to be her husband, who will slay the suitors (τ 538). A little later, as the suitors are planning the death of Telemachus, an eagle bearing a dove appears on their left, and they see that their plan is not to succeed (υ 242). The appearance of a hawk, "Apollo's swift messenger," tearing a dove and dropping the feathers near Telemachus, "on the right," is interpreted by Theoclymenus as meaning the safety of the Ithacan royal house (ο 525). The only other bird sent as an omen, is a heron, sent by Athena on the right of Odysseus and Diomed as they set out by night to enter secretly the bivouac of the Trojan forces (K 274); the bird is not seen, but its cry is heard, and "Odysseus rejoices in the bird." What has been said above shows that the word for bird (ὄρνις or οἰωνός) had already acquired the general meaning of *omen*.[1] "The birds were favourable" (ὄρνιθες δεξιοί, ω 311) means that the omens were propitious. Thus also Priam bids Hecuba not be to him an evil bird, *i.e.* an omen of ill (ὄρνις κακός, Ω 219). Calchas is called a "tender of birds" (οἰωνοπόλος, A 69), and "bird-man" (οἰωνιστής, B 858) is synonymous with sooth-sayer or augur.

---

[1] *Cf.* Aristophanes, *Birds*, 720, "An ox or an ass that may happen to pass . . . A name or a word by chance overheard, If you deem it an omen you call it a Bird."

In general, augury from the flight of birds is more important in Homer's time than in the classical age at Athens.

Of miscellaneous omens the most familiar is that which appeared to the Greeks while still at Aulis, while they were offering sacrifices when about to set out against Troy : a serpent appeared from under the altar, climbed the overhanging plane tree, and devoured *Miscellaneous Omens.* eight nestling sparrows and the mother-bird (B 305). This was interpreted by Calchas to mean that the Greeks should fight for nine years around Troy, and should capture the city in the tenth year.   A chance word ($\phi\acute{\eta}\mu\eta$, $\kappa\lambda\epsilon\eta\delta\acute{\omega}\nu$, β 35, σ 117) is at times accepted as an omen.   Thus the returning Odysseus, not yet recognized in his home, asks Zeus for such an omen, and straightway hears an old woman, as she is grinding at the mill, pray that Penelope's suitors may have that day their last feast in the home of Odysseus (υ 100, 120). At the opening of the second day of the action of the *Odyssey*, Telemachus calls an assembly of the Ithacans, to seek their help against his mother's suitors, and the old Aegyptius, who first rises to ask who had called the assembly, prays that the wish of this man's heart may be accomplished ; Telemachus rejoices in the omen ($\phi\acute{\eta}\mu\eta$, β 35).   A loud sneeze of Telemachus, though he was in the great hall and she was in her chamber, is interpreted by Penelope as a favorable omen in relation to the prayer for Odysseus's return which she had just uttered (ρ 541 ; *cf.* Xen. *An.* iii. 2. 9).   That, when the comrades of Odysseus had killed cattle of the Sun, the hides moved, and the flesh lowed like cows (μ 394), was naturally interpreted as a portent of ill.   Occasionally, but not often, indefinite omens are referred to (as Δ 381, 398, 408, Z 183, γ 173, π 320).   The reader observes the entire absence of omens from the inspection of the liver and the other nobler entrails, which was most important in the fifth century B.C.,[1] and that no omens are taken from the behavior of the sacrifices on the fire (*cf.* Aeschylus, *Prom.* 495 ; Sophocles, *Ant.* 1005), which was the basis of the oracle at Olympia.

[1] Some have thought such inspection implied in the name $\theta\upsilon\sigma\sigma\kappa\acute{o}os$ applied to Leodes on Ithaca (ϕ 145, χ 318, 321), particularly since $\theta\upsilon\sigma\sigma\kappa\acute{o}o\iota$ are classed with seers and priests at Ω 221.   But Leodes seems not to have been an *haruspex*, but simply to have had charge of the sacrifices of the suitors.   Certainly the gods gave to him no warning of the death of the suitors and himself.

"A dream, too, comes from Zeus," Achilles says to the Achaeans (A 63), just as in later times Socrates (Plato, *Ap.* 33 c) recognized dreams as a familiar means used by the gods in making their will known to men.[1] In sleep the mind was comparatively unfettered by the body, and had a clearer view of the future (Pindar, *Frag.* 131). But not all dreams come true. Zeus sends to Agamemnon a Delusive Dream (οὖλος ὄνειρος, B 6) in the guise of Nestor; and Penelope says that there are two gates of dreams, one of horn and the other of ivory ; the dreams which pass through the gate of ivory deceive (ἐλέφας—ἐλεφαίρω), while those which pass through the gate of horn come true (κέρας—κραίνω, τ 562). The "country of dreams" (δῆμος ὀνείρων, ω 12) lies hard by the Asphodel Plain on which the souls of the dead dwell, and ghosts and the persons of dreams behave alike (*cf.* B 20 with Ψ 68) ;[2] and we are reminded that Sleep and Death are twin brothers (Π 672). When Odysseus in Hades seeks to embrace his mother's ghost, she slips from his arms "like a shadow or a dream" (λ 207). Whether Death is a dream at K 496, is not clear. Dreams are entities. The Delusive Dream which is sent by Zeus to Agamemnon, clearly speaks to the warrior, who does not simply "see as in a dream" (B *init.*). Athena sends to Penelope the wraith (εἴδωλον, δ 796) of Penelope's sister, which slips through a keyhole, and is called a dream a few verses later. Athena herself thus appears to the sleeping Nausicaa in the form of a girl friend, behaving just like a dream or a ghost (ζ 22). The disguised Odysseus tells the story of a dream before Troy which was understood as a warning (ξ 495). Penelope, as we have seen already, dreams of an eagle which killed her geese and then declared itself to be her returning husband (τ 536), and on the

---

[1] *Cf.* the importance attached to dreams in Aesch. *Pers.* 176 ; Xen. *An.* III. i. 11. Even Aristotle held them to be a source of knowledge with regard to divine things (*Frag.* 12). *Cf.* also Joseph's dream, and those which he interpreted, *Genesis* xxxvii. 5, xl. 5, xli. 1 ; the dream of Gideon, *Judges* vii. 13 ; and those of Nebuchadnezzar, *Daniel* ii. 1, iv. 5 ; "Your sons and your daughters shall prophesy, and your young men shall see visions, and your old men shall dream dreams," *Acts* ii. 17. Xenophon (*Cyr.* viii. 7. 21) makes the elder Cyrus say that in sleep the soul appears most divine, and then sees something of the future.

[2] *Cf.* (τοὺς) νέους (viz. the shades of the children of Thyestes) ὀνείρων προσφερεῖς μορφώμασιν, *like to the forms of dreams*, Aesch. *Ag.* 1217.

morning of the day when Odysseus kills her suitors, she dreams that he is lying beside her (υ 88). Before Troy, Diomed slays two sons of a Trojan "interpreter of dreams" (ὀνειροπόλος, E 149), Eurydamas.

Another means to ascertain the will of the gods was to cast lots. The lots marked by some signs which might be known only to the makers (H 185), were put into a helmet and this was shaken by some disinterested person, or with averted face (Γ 325, H 181), until one lot "leaped forth." Thus the contestants in the chariot-race cast lots for positions (Ψ 352), the comrades of Odysseus cast lots to determine who should aid him in blinding Polyphemus (ι 331), and Hermes (Ω 400) represented himself as one of seven brothers who had cast lots to determine which of them should come to the war.[1]

Casting Lots.

---

[1] Not to speak in detail of the use of the lot for the choice of public officers at Athens, even in the New Testament the lot was thus used : "shew whether of these two Thou hast chosen, . . . and the lot fell upon Matthias," *Acts* i. 24.

CHAPTER XVII

THE TROAD[1]

THE scene of the battles of the *Iliad* was the Trojan plain, in the extreme northwestern corner of Asia Minor.[2]

The Trojan Plain. The greatest length of the plain is about nine miles, from the promontory of Sigeum, at the northwest, at the opening of the Hellespont,— the modern Dardanelles, of which the name still preserves the memory of the Dardanians, the ancient kinsmen and allies of the Trojans,—to Bunárbashi and its citadel Balidagh at the southeast, a height which rises four hundred or five hundred feet above the plain, immediately above the river Scamander, and is connected by a steep ridge with the hills to the east. The stream of Bunárbashi, as we shall see, empties into the Aegean Sea about seven miles distant, in Besika Bay, nearly due west of its sources, about five miles north of the island of Tenedos. The western shore of the Trojan plain thence stretches, nearly directly northward from the mouth of the Bunárbashi river, for about eight miles,—with limestone cliffs more than one hundred feet in height, affording no station for ships,—to the promontory of Sigeum, at the entrance to the Hellespont, opposite Elaeus in the Chersonese. Almost due east of

---

[1] The best map of the Troad is that of the British Admiralty, made by Admiral Spratt. Of this a careful revision is published in Dörpfeld's *Troja und Ilion*, and this is the basis of the map published herewith.

[2] All other works on the Trojan plain and the ruins of Hissarlik are now super- seded by *Troja und Ilion*: Ergebnisse der Ausgrabungen in der vorhistorischen und historischen Schichten von Ilion, 1870-1894, von Wilhelm Dörpfeld, unter Mitwirkung, etc. Athens, 1902. 2 vols. quarto.

this promontory, at a distance of three or four miles, lies the promontory of Rhoeteum, which like its comrade, the promontory of Sigeum, is not named by Homer, although they both are referred to at Ξ 36.

On the low sloping shore of the bay which curves slightly to the south between the two promontories, Sigeum and Rhoeteum, the ships of the Achaeans were drawn up on land at the time of the siege of Troy. But not all of this space is available for the drawing up of boats in ancient fashion. The chief river which drains the plain is wide at its mouth, and near the Hellespont are marshes and salt-water lakes or lagoons, from which in winter the water flows into the sea, but into which, in the dry summer season, water flows from the Hellespont. Near the eastern end of the shore, where the Scamander is supposed to have had its course in early times, is such a lagoon nearly half a mile in length by eight hundred feet in width. A Scotch traveller,[1] who has given a careful description of the plain of Troy, estimates that a stretch of shore about six thousand feet, or a little more than a mile, in length, is suitable for the camp of the Achaeans ; and allowing twenty feet for each boat,—(thirteen feet estimated for the width of the boat itself, and seven feet for space between it and its neighbor), he sees that three hundred such boats could be drawn up in a single line ; and that, with space allowed for places of assembly and the like, the 1186 Achaean ships must have been drawn up in four or five ranks. Other travellers have thought that the shore for an extent of about two miles may have been available for the station of the ships (ναυσταθμός),—and this would allow a thousand ships to be drawn up in two rows ; but the number of ships cannot be thought to be one of the earlier elements in the Trojan story.

The coast line of the plain of Troy does not appear to have changed materially since Homer's time. Strabo, indeed, conjectured that the bay of the Hellespont extended twelve stades, or about a mile and a *Coast Line Unchanged.*
third, further into the plain in Homer's time than in his own, but this conjecture has not been sustained by

[1] Charles MacLaren, *The Plain of Troy Described*, Edinburgh, 1863.

the scientific examination of the plain. The current of the Hellespont, which at this place is said to be of two or three miles an hour, bears away most of the alluvium which is brought into its waters by the rivers of the plain. Indeed indications have been found that in some places the sea has encroached upon the land. At least the two main promontories remain essentially unchanged, and if the bay was a trifle deeper three thousand years ago than now, the change has not been important. Herodotus, it is true (ii. 10), declares this plain to be alluvial like the Delta of the Nile, but he does not intimate his belief that this soil, any more than that of the Delta, was deposited within the historical period.

The hills on the east and the south of the plain,—the foot-hills of Mount Ida,—are not very high, and do not

Mt. Ida.   form a clearly marked boundary line. The highest summit of Mount Ida, Gargarus, lies to the south-east and rises to a height of 5740 feet above the sea, which is well above the timber-line. This summit is prominent in the Trojan landscape, though it lies farther from Ilium than a casual reader might infer; it was the station which Zeus chose, according to the poet, for his observations of the conflicts on the plain of Troy. " The oldest rocks of the Troad are an extensive series of coarsely crystalline limestones, interstratified with micaceous and horn-blendic schists. They constitute the basis upon which and out of which the framework of the Trojan peninsula has been developed. They are the chief mountain-forming strata of that region. The great mass of Mount Ida is composed wholly of them.—The structure of Mount Ida appears to be a comparatively simple anticlinal, with so short an axis extending east and west that the upper portion of the mountain is approximately a dome." [1]   Mount Ida dominates the whole of the Troad in the larger sense; the waters of the Granicus, and even those of the Aesepus, come from the slopes of Mount Ida, as well as the Scamander and its immediate neighbors.

The principal river of the Trojan plain is the Scamander,

---

[1] J. S. Diller, in *Papers of the Archaeological Institute of America*, Classical Series, i. 213.

which has its sources near one of the summits of Mount
Ida, and after a course of nearly fifty miles, empties
into the Hellespont close to the promontory of
Sigeum. The modern name of the river is *Course of the Scamander.*
Menderé, which clearly is a corruption of the
ancient appellation. Its bed appears to have been subjected
to a greater change than its name, since in Homer's time it
seems to have flowed nearer the site of Ilium · than at
present (Burnouf says within a quarter or a third of a
mile in ancient times), and to have emptied into the Hellespont at the eastern end of the bay, near the promontory
of Rhoeteum, instead of at the western end, near Sigeum,
as at present. Such a change of bed is easily explained
in a stream which overflows its banks not only every winter,
but also after every heavy rain, on a plain which abounds
in marshes. In any year such a stream is likely to find
a new way to the sea. Even a slight obstruction may
divert the stream to another quarter, and at least two or
three channels are found which appear to have served, at
different times, as beds for the Scamander. Proofs of the
earlier course of the Scamander are discovered not only in
the Homeric story, and in the present condition of the
Trojan plain, but also in masses of alluvial soil which have
been brought into and deposited in the Hellespont near
the promontory of Rhoeteum.[1]

An illustration of the change in the course of the
Scamander, has been drawn from the Satnioïs, "the next
important river of the peninsula." "Like the
Menderé, it breaks from the mountains some *Satnioïs.*
miles from its mouth, and flows to the sea through a
level and fertile plain. This plain shows no trace of any
change in the course of the stream, save one. Several

---

[1] Professor Robert of Halle, in *Hermes*, xlii. 78 ff., argues that the Scamander
flowed on the west side of the plain, in the same bed as the Menderé, and that the
Simoïs did not flow into the Scamander, but emptied into the sea, as at present,
rejecting, as by a poet who had a misconception of the situation, the evidence of
E 774 (ἧχι ῥοὰς Σιμόεις συμβάλλετον ἠδὲ Σκάμανδρος), and not accepting the interpretation of Φ 307 ff. which implies that the Simoïs joined the Scamander. Thus,
according to Robert's view, neither of the two rivers flowed between the ships of the
Achaeans and the city of Troy, and the Achaean camp lay between the mouths of
the two rivers.

hundred metres away from the present river bed are yet standing, almost intact, the arches of the Roman bridge. Within two thousand years the river has not only found a new course, but has completely effaced (doubtless by the alluvium deposited during inundations) all traces of the old channel."[1]

The Scamander is about five hundred feet wide where it is joined by the Thymbrius, not very far from Bunárbashi. *Size of the Scamander.* Lower down, its stream is only one hundred feet broad, while near the sea again it is four hundred feet in width. But not all of this bed is even covered with water during half of the year. After a long drought, in September, a traveller found it "only a series of pools," without running water ; other travellers in the same month of another year report it as having a stream about eighteen feet wide, and twenty inches deep, with plenty of fish three or four inches long, while nearer the sea were "pools haunted by turtles and frogs, but no running water was visible." Another traveller, in August of another year, found the stream thirty or forty feet broad, and nine inches deep. Another reports that he crossed dry-shod, but he may have "picked his way." Herodotus (vii. 43) says that at the Scamander first after leaving Sardis (in April or May of 480 B.C.), the forces of King Xerxes were unable to secure supplies of water sufficient for themselves and their animals. Early in June it is forded often with some difficulty by inexperienced travellers. The stream of the Scamander is compared with the Eurotas of Sparta and the Alpheüs of Elis,—which would make it about equal also to the Roman Tiber. Pliny calls it a "navigable stream" (*amnis navigabilis*, *N.H.* v. 33), but during the winter its current would seem too violent for boats, and in the summer, as we have seen, its waters are too low for navigation. In the spring season, however, large rafts of timber are brought by it from Mt. Ida. At times of flood, its water has a yellow color which justifies the alternate Homeric name, *Xanthus* or Yellow River. In Homer's time, bridges do not seem to have been used,

[1] W. C. Lawton, in *Papers of the Archaeological Institute*, Classical Series, i. 164.

but a ford is mentioned for the Scamander. Some scholars have found difficulty in the fact that the poet so seldom mentions the passage of the river by the soldiery, but Dr. Dörpfeld remarks that bare-footed and bare-legged orientals do not have the occidental man's objection to fording a stream.[1]

In some places the banks of the Scamander are steep, and eight or twelve feet high, like those under which the Trojans are represented as crouching and hiding at Φ 239. The Homeric epithets are justified: *broad* (μέγας, Φ 282), *of good stream* (εὔρροος, Φ 130), *of deep stream* (βαθύρροος, Φ 8), *with deep eddies* (βαθυδίνης, Υ 73). The flood which attacked Achilles (Φ 234) is such as the Menderé knows every winter. Men and horses have lost their lives in its currents. Julia, the daughter of the Emperor Augustus, making an unanticipated visit to Ilium, had a narrow escape from drowning in the Scamander, and the city of Ilium was heavily fined, because it had not provided for the safety of the princess, although she was unexpected. One of Dr. Schliemann's overseers was drowned in attempting to cross. So large a part of the extensive complex of Mount Ida drains directly into the Trojan plain that its rivers, and the Menderé more than all the rest, show within a few hours the effect of heavy rains or the melting of snow upon the mountain summits.[2]

The true source of the Menderé, as we have seen, is not to be found in springs on the plain, but high on Mount Ida. The springs near Ilium which the poet calls the "sources of the Scamander" (X 147) *Springs.* are no longer to be found,—or at least they no longer supply water which flows into the Scamander,—but this can occasion no surprise after an interval of three thousand years in a region which is often visited by earthquakes. Even in recent times new springs have been opened and others destroyed. Near Bunárbashi several deep springs

---

[1] See *Homeri Iliadis Carmina*, ed. Christ, page 52.

[2] A party of travellers who crossed the Menderé without difficulty, on their way to Bunárbashi, returning a few hours later, found the ford impassable, but by hard riding to another ford two or three miles below, succeeded in anticipating the flood.

break forth within a distance of a quarter of a mile. Indeed these are called the Forty Eyes (*Kirk Jos*), as forty springs. Only thirty-four have been counted by travellers. Doubtless some have escaped notice, but probably the numeral forty is used by the dwellers on the Trojan plain, as it was by the ancient Hebrews, as a round number. These springs have a nearly constant temperature through the year of about 63° F. Thus they are said to "smoke" in winter like one of Homer's springs (X 150), while in summer they seem gratefully cool. The poet's story of one hot and one cold spring may have arisen from a combination of accounts of such springs as these, in summer and in winter,— but more probably he thought of a warm or hot spring, such as are found not many leagues away in the Troad, with a temperature rising above 150 degrees Fahrenheit.

Second in importance of the rivers of the Trojan plain, is the ancient Simoïs,[1] the modern Dumbrek, which in Homer's *The Simoïs.* time emptied into the Scamander (Φ 305 f.), but now flows toward the Hellespont along what seems to have been an old bed of the Scamander. In the time of Strabo, not far from the beginning of our era, the two streams seem to have united not far from Ilium (Strabo, p. 597), and this fact indicates that the main change in the bed of the Scamander has taken place since the time of the geographer. The Dumbrek is not a mighty river in appearance and loses itself in swamps before reaching the sea ; but it is active as a true mountain torrent at the present day, just as it was in Homer's, bearing rocks and trunks of trees along by its water in winter, though it is nearly dry in summer. The Roman geographer, Pomponius Mela, says of both the Scamander and the Simoïs that they were greater in reputation than in reality (*fama quam natura majora flumina*, i. 18). Like the Menderé, the Dumbrek rises on one of the highest peaks of Mount Ida, on Cotylus, but it has a much shorter course than its sister river. At Dumbrek, where it reaches the level of the plain, it is said

---

[1] Δ 475, E 774, Z 4, M 22. *Cf. ubi tot Simois correpta sub undis | scuta virum galeasque et fortia corpora volvit,* Verg. *Aen.* i. 100; *quem . . . alma Venus Phrygii genuit Simoentis ad undam, l.c.* 618.

to be about sixty feet in width, but in April it is only six inches deep.

The river of Bunárbashi has its rise in the Forty Springs to which reference has just been made, and flows into Besika Bay to the west. Its course is about a dozen miles in length. It is about twelve feet broad, *River of Bunárbashi.* and three feet deep, and unlike the other streams of the plain, its flow is nearly constant, since it is not a mountain torrent, but is fed by deep springs. Its channel is artificial, at least in part, being in some places cut in the rocks, and is made to drain the marshes at the southeast of the plain. At times of flood, its stream joins that of the Scamander, but only for a time. Its water is pure, and is a convenience for the ships which put into Besika Bay,—this being a favorite place of anchorage for sailing vessels which are awaiting a favorable wind for the entrance of the Dardanelles. This stream was not mentioned by the poet since it lay too far out of the way of the movements of the contending armies.[1] When the channel of the river of Bunárbashi was cut, no one knows. The tradition of the inhabitants of the plain, as reported by early travellers, declared that it was made near the beginning of the eighteenth century. Schliemann, however, thought the large amount of alluvium deposited by it in Besika Bay proved that this channel had existed at least for several centuries. MacLaren held that in Homer's time this southern end of the Trojan plain, being without the drainage provided by this stream, was not only a moist meadow but the particular meadow on which the three thousand brood mares of Erichthonius (Υ 221) were pastured with their colts. These would need about six thousand acres of pasture, or ten square miles, which he finds here. During the war, MacLaren thinks, Priam kept his mares out of danger's way at Abydus (Δ 500). Since hay was not made in Greek lands, such well-watered lowland meadows were much valued for pasture (O 631).

---

[1] For a time, scholars called this river the Scamander,—when they thought Bunárbashi was the site of ancient Ilium; but the springs on which they laid great stress in the identification could not be accepted by us as the cold and hot springs of Homer, even if the ancient Ilium stood where Bunárbashi now stands.

The Thymbrius (which receives its name from Thymbré, near which the Lycians bivouacked at K 430) is a small stream which joins the Scamander opposite Bunárbashi. It is not mentioned by the poet.

The Thymbrius.

The poet's special landmarks,—the wild-fig tree, the oak of Zeus, the tombs of Ilus, of Aesyetes, and of Myrina, perhaps even Callicoloné,[1]—are hardly to be identified. The trees were dead long ages ago. Mounds upon the plain might easily have yielded to the assaults of wind and rain within three thousand years, especially since we have no reason to suppose that any of these but the mound of Aesyetes was more than a few feet in height. Schliemann tells of an ancient mound which has disappeared since 1868. Remains of the wall built around the Greek camp are not to be expected : that was only a low wall or breastwork thrown up on the shore in a single day. The rivers which we are told Poseidon brought against this wall after the departure of the Achaeans (M 19 ff.) were hardly needed for its destruction. Even Callicoloné is only Fair Hill, and the name might have been applied to almost any height, but Dr. Dörpfeld finds this near the shore on the eastern side of the Scamander. Pliny mentions an Achilleum and an Aianteum (*i.e.* tomb of Aias or Ajax), but says that these existed no longer (*fuit, N.H.* v. 30).

Landmarks.

Philostratus (*Heroicus*, p. 208) says that the oracle at Dodona directed the Thessalians to offer sacrifices to Achilles, and that these every year sailed to Troy in a vessel with a black sail, bearing twice-seven sacred messengers, a white and a black bull, wood from Mount Pelion, water from the river Spercheüs, and fire from Thessaly, and crowned the tomb, uttered a war-cry invoking Achilles, and sacrificed the bulls.

This tomb of Achilles was recognized and honored by Alexander the Great, according to Arrian (i. 12), but the identification was lost long ago. About, not on, the Trojan plain are nearly or quite a score of tumuli,—some of them being nearly one hundred feet high,— while others like them lie in the Chersonese, across the Hellespont. One of these near Rhoeteum is called by tradition the tomb of Ajax. Philostratus (*Heroicus*, p. 137)

Tumuli.

[1] E 693, Z 237, H 22; K 415, Λ 166; B 793; B 814; Υ 53, 151. See p. 604.

says that the original tomb of Ajax was washed open by the sea, and that the bones were transferred to this newer tomb by order of the Emperor Hadrian, and Strabo (p. 595) says that at Troy was a shrine of Ajax with a statue which was removed by Antony, but restored by the Emperor Augustus. A mound near the promontory of Sigeum has been called the tomb of Achilles, and another about a fifth of a mile distant has been called the tomb of Patroclus,—in spite of the Homeric story that these two warriors were to have a common tomb (Ψ 126). Another mound has been assigned

FIG. 20.—Tomb of Ajax.

to King Priam, and another, in the Chersonese, to his queen, Hecuba. But such attributions are entirely capricious. Nothing has been found as yet to prove that these mounds were constructed in exactly the Homeric period,—some of them may have been older, while others doubtless were built later than that time,—still less is it known that they contained the bones of these particular heroes. The proof is not even complete that they were tombs at all, although this seems entirely probable. That such mounds were used for tombs, is a familiar fact, and that they were held by the poet to be tombs is clear from his attributions. The tomb assigned by a modern traveller to Hector, was excavated by Sir John

Lubbock, but in it were found " neither bones nor charcoal, nor any traces of the destination of this tumulus for a funeral mound" (*Ilios*, p. 656). Schliemann on opening several of these mounds and finding no funeral remains, believed that these were cenotaphs, such as Menelaus reports that he raised for his brother, in Egypt (δ 584), and as Telemachus was advised to raise for his father if Odysseus did not return (a 291).

The main features of the Trojan landscape are clearly determined in the story by those (or by one) who knew them well. The agreement between the land and the poems is quite as great as could be expected. Sir Charles Newton wrote after a visit to the Troad in 1853 : " I took advantage of a little leisure . . . to read the *Iliad* over again in the presence of the great natural features of the scene. No one who has not seen the magnificent outline which bounds the horizon of the plain of Troy can bring home to his mind the stirring and marvellous narrative of the poet as Homer meant it to affect his readers or rather hearers." But the poet was not a topographer and had neither map nor photograph of the region before him, and his hearers for the most part had even less personal knowledge of the Troad.

Ancient Ilium [1] lay a trifle more than three miles from the Hellespont, and at about the same distance from the Aegean Sea (at which point, however, was no shore which could serve as a harbor), at the western extremity of a low continuous ridge which extends to the west from the range of Mt. Ida. The summit of the citadel before the excavations of Dr. Schliemann, which began in 1871 and were not completed at the time of his death in 1890, lay 162 feet above the level of the sea, and eighty feet above the plain. Homer nowhere declares how complete was the destruction of the city after its capture by the Achaeans. It was sacked, but the more substantial buildings and the city walls were not razed to the ground. A passage in the twentieth book of the

Ilium.

---

[1] Homer regularly uses the feminine form Ἴλιος, and only once gives a clear example of the neuter Ἴλιον (O 71), which prevails in the usage of the later Greek writers. Vergil and the Romans generally use *Ilium*. *Troy*, Τροίη, in Homer generally refers to the country, the *Troad*, but is used also of the city. *Ilium* naturally was thought to be the city of Ilus, the grandfather of Priam, while Troy was the country of Tros, who was the father of Ilus (Υ 231 f.).

Iliad (Υ 307 ff.),—the prediction by Poseidon that the mighty Aeneas and his sons' sons who should succeed him, should rule over the Trojans,—was accepted by the Romans as the basis of the story which is familiar to all from Vergil's *Aeneid*, that Aeneas was saved from the conflict, and led a company of Trojans to the Lavinian shores, and that the Romans were the descendants of the saved remnant of the Trojans. But Strabo (p. 607) knows another tradition,—that Ascanius and his Trojans removed to Scepsis, not many miles from Troy, and made their homes there. And evidently the inhabitants of the Ilium of Strabo's time claimed to be of true Trojan blood, whose ancestors had escaped slavery and death at the time of the capture of the city by the Achaeans, and had never removed far from their ancient abode.[1]

However scholars may explain the various stories of the wanderings of Aeneas and his Trojans, the ancient site of Ilium was not long abandoned, and the tradition of it was never forgotten. Herodotus says that *Site never Forgotten.* King Xerxes, in the spring or early summer of 480 B.C., on reaching the Scamander with his army, on his way against Greece, "went up to the Pergamum of Priam, desiring to see it; and having seen it and on learning from the men there the details of the Trojan story, he sacrificed a thousand cattle to the Ilian Athena, and the magi made libations to the heroes."[2] Nearly a century later (411 B.C.), Xenophon relates at the very beginning of his *History of Greece*, Mindarus, a Spartan admiral, was sacrificing to Athena at Ilium when he caught sight of the Athenian fleet advancing against his ally Dorieus, who had drawn up his ships on shore at the promontory of Rhoeteum.[3] Half a century later, an Athenian mercenary and adventurer Charidemus took Ilium, about

---

[1] Scholars are familiar with the fact that traces of the story of Aeneas and his followers, on wanderings after the capture of Troy, are found in many places,—but these details do not concern us here. See Roscher, *Lexikon der Mythologie*, i. 166 ff.

[2] Herodotus, vii. 43, ἀπικομένου δὲ τοῦ στρατοῦ ἐπὶ ποταμὸν Σκάμανδρον, . . . Ξέρξης ἐς τὸ Πριάμου Πέργαμον ἀνέβη ἵμερον ἔχων θεήσασθαι. θεησάμενος δὲ καὶ πυθόμενος ἐκείνων ἕκαστα τῇ Ἀθηναίῃ τῇ Ἰλιάδι ἔθυσε βοῦς χιλίας, χοὰς δὲ οἱ μάγοι τοῖσι ἥρωσι ἐχέαντο.

[3] Xenophon, *Hellenica*, i. 1. 4, Μίνδαρος δὲ κατιδὼν τὴν μάχην ἐν Ἰλίῳ θύων τῇ Ἀθηνᾷ ἐβοήθει κτλ

360 B.C.,—the Ilians being unable to close their gates against
him (Demosthenes, xxiii. 154).

The next appearance of Ilium in history is on the visit
of Alexander the Great, in the spring of 334 B.C. Before
crossing the Hellespont on his march for the
Visit of
Alexander. conquest of Asia and the world, he offered
sacrifices at Elaeus in the Chersonese, at the
tomb of Protesilaüs, who was the first of the Achaeans
with Agamemnon to disembark and enter Asia. Arrian
(*Anabasis*, i. 11. 6, i. 12. 1) says that the general report was
that Alexander took boat at Elaeus, and landed first of
all his army at the "harbor of the Achaeans" (ἐς τὸν
Ἀχαιῶν λιμένα),—evidently the naval station of the Homeric
Greeks on the Hellespont; that he went up to Ilium and
offered splendid sacrifices to the Ilian Athena; and that
he dedicated his panoply of armor in her temple, and took
in exchange some of the armor which had been saved from
the Trojan War, and had this borne before him in his
battles. "It was said that he sacrificed also to Priam on
the altar of Zeus,—propitiating the spirit of Priam to the
race of Achilles's son Neoptolemus, to which Alexander
belonged. He also placed a garland of flowers on the tomb
of Achilles, and his friend Hephaestion was said to honor
in the same way the tomb of Patroclus." Strabo (p. 593)
says that up to this time Ilium was a small and insignificant
village, but that Alexander not only adorned the temple
with votive offerings, but also ordered that the town should
have independence and other privileges; and that he promised
after the overthrow of Persia to make the city large and
the temple renowned, and to have sacred games held there;
and that after his death Lysimachus built a great temple,
and a wall forty stades in length about the city. Inscriptions
have been found (*C.I.G.* 3601 f.) which confirm the story
of the games. Dörpfeld, however, accepts the conjecture of
the historian Grote that Lysimachus devoted himself rather
to the development of the new city of Alexandria Troas
than to the adornment of the old city of Ilium. Grote's
conjecture is in part sustained by the fact that none of the
archaeological excavations near Ilium have brought to light
any trace of the long wall of Lysimachus, but Dörpfeld's

associate, Brückner, believes that the complete destruction
of the wall by haters of Lysimachus (and the Ilian decree
against tyrants shows the strength of their hatred) would
explain the absence of remains.

Of the great temple built at Ilium by Lysimachus, the
marks of the foundation have been preserved,—a deep bed
of sand on which the stones were laid,—and parts
of the building itself and its decoration, in par- *Temple of*
ticular a fine metope, representing the sun-god *Lysimachus.*
in his chariot,[1] which was found in the early excavations of
Dr. Schliemann.

Fig. 21.—Metope from Ilium.

In 311 B.C. Ilium was made the head of a confederacy
which held a great festival there, with games and shows
and all the accompaniments of a *panegyris,* as
well as sacrifices to Athena. About the middle *Head of a*
of the fourth century B.C., the Ilians had honored *Confederacy.*
with *proxeny* an Athenian named Menelaus, and conversely in
302 B.C., an Ilian, Nicander, received public honors at Athens,
as we learn from inscriptions. Probably on the death of

[1] Some archaeologists, however, think that this metope cannot be earlier than the
second century, B.C.

Lysimachus, 281 B.C., the Ilians passed an elaborate and exceedingly stringent law against tyrants.[1] Another inscription of the same century has preserved a fragment of a list of Ilian citizens which covers two pages. Ilium welcomed Seleucus, the conqueror of Lysimachus, and named for him one of the months of its year,—a name which endured for two centuries. Not far from 277 B.C., the Ilians in gratitude to Antiochus voted to offer prayers for him in their temple of Athena, and to set up there an equestrian statue of him in gold on a basis of white marble (*C.I.G.* 3595), and the inscription which records the vote shows that the Ilians were divided into tribes (φυλαί) and phratries. The Ilians were loyal to Attalus (220 B.C.), and were saved by

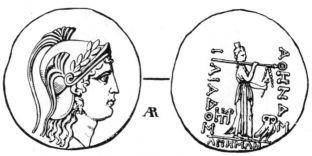

FIG. 22.—Coin from Ilium.

the citizens of Alexandria Troas from a siege of Galatians (Polybius, v. 78, 111). Not quite a generation later (192 B.C., Livy, xxxv. 43, Justin, xxxi. 8), Antiochus the Great went up to Ilium in order to sacrifice to Athena,—following the examples of Xerxes and Alexander the Great,—when he was preparing to cross into Greece to meet the Romans.

Two years after the visit of Antiochus, in 190 B.C., the general Gaius Livius was the first Roman to offer sacrifice in the temple and there to receive embassadors from the neighboring towns (Livy, xxxvii. 9). In the next year Publius Scipio came to Ilium, encamped his army on the plain under the walls (*in campo qui est subiectus moenibus*, Livy, xxxvii. 37), and went himself to the citadel and sacrificed to Athena, *praesidi arcis*. The Romans recognized Ilium as the cradle of their race, and

Romans at Ilium.

[1] See Dareste, Hausoullier, et Reinach, *Inscriptions juridiques grecques*, ii. 25.

the Ilians, on their part, welcomed the Romans as their kinsmen. Justin says that the meeting of the Ilians and the Romans was like that of parents and children after a long separation. The "great Julius," in the next century, claiming not only descent but also name from Iulus, son of Aeneas, visited Ilium after the battle of Pharsalus (48 B.C.), and gave to the Ilians additional territory, and confirmed their independence and other privileges (Strabo, 594 f.). He was reported even to have thought of making Ilium the capital of the Roman Empire.[1] The Emperor Augustus also visited Ilium, and apparently by his direction the great temple of Athena, which had been built by Lysimachus and partially destroyed by Fimbria, about two centuries later, in the first Civil War, was restored and beautified. To the same age may reasonably be ascribed the theatre, which would seat 6000 people (doubtless not so much for the inhabitants of the town as for the visitors at the festivals), a *Bouleuterion* or Senate-house, and the aqueduct, which was planned to bring a supply of water from the upper Thymbrius,—of all which structures remains still exist as evidence of the Roman interest in the Trojan story. A second theatre has been discovered, but its site has not yet been laid bare of the rubbish which has collected over it; and this too must have been built by the Romans. Nero, as a boy of sixteen years, addressed the Roman senate in behalf of Ilium. Claudius extended the privileges of the town. About 124 A.D., Hadrian visited Ilium, and restored the shrine of Ajax, and caused milestones (one of which is preserved) to be set up on the roads, or on a road. Antoninus Pius extended the privileges of the town, and Marcus Aurelius repaired the temple. Caracalla on his visit to Ilium, erected a bronze statue to Achilles, and (perhaps in imitation of Alexander the Great) took part in athletic contests (Dio Cassius, lxxvii. 16). Ilium was visited often by travellers, and a museum of relics of the Trojan War was formed there, or at least the older collection was enlarged. Among the objects shown there were the two anvils which were attached to Hera's feet, when she was

---

[1] Suetonius, *Caesar*, 79. To a like plan Horace is thought to allude in *ne nimium pii | rebusque fidentes avitae | tecta velint reparare Troiae*, *Odes*, iii. 3. 58.

hung up by her hands, by her husband Zeus (Eustathius on O 19). The Trojans were exalted in literature. Dio Chrysostomus (xi.) argued that Troy never was captured,— "this story is only one of a parcel of Greek lies,"—and that Homer in spite of his prejudices is unable to conceal the bravery and victory of Hector. The Ilian coins of the imperial period naturally honored only Trojan heroes,— Hector, and not Ajax or Achilles.

About the time of the beginning of the Roman occupation of Ilium, that town was visited by Demetrius of the *Demetrius of Scepsis.* neighboring Scepsis, who was then a mere boy. He says, according to Strabo (p. 594), that the settlement was then neglected, and that the houses did not even have tiled roofs,—doubtless being thatched, as were the houses of the rich city Sardis, when that city was burned by the Athenians and Ionians, near the beginning of the fifth century B.C. (Herodotus, v. 101).

The geographer Strabo does not seem to have visited the Troad. His description of it is dependent on that of *Geographer Strabo.* Demetrius of Scepsis, who being a native of that region, and familiar with the ground, had written an elaborate work of thirty books or chapters as a commentary on the sixty-two verses of Homer's catalogue of the Trojan forces (B 816-877), and Strabo seems to have accepted Demetrius's views without criticism. We have seen that as a boy Demetrius visited Ilium about the time when the Romans under Publius Scipio came to that town. He rejected the claim of the Ilium of his day that it occupied the site of the Homeric city, and assigned the latter to a site thirty stades, or about three and one-half miles, further east, where stood the "village of the Ilians" (τὴν νῦν καλουμένην Ἰλιέων κώμην), although he acknowledged that not a trace of the ancient city remained there. The Ilian village of his time he believed to have been founded in the reign of Croesus, or about the middle of the sixth century B.C. For the site which Strabo (following Demetrius) prefers, he presents no evidence, and modern scholars were disposed to think it an improbable position even before the excavations, which showed no prehistoric remains to exist beneath the surface, just as Strabo had acknowledged that none existed above.

The question as to the site of ancient Troy was not a new one in the time of Demetrius of Scepsis: he refers also to the work of a learned lady, Hestiaea of Alexandria,[1] who composed a treatise on Homer's *Iliad*, and at least raised the question whether the Trojan War was fought about the Ilium of her day. Strabo reports (p. 602) that the historian Hellanicus, at the close of the fifth century B.C., upheld the claim of the Ilians,—which intimates, but does not prove, that others of his day doubted it. Demetrius has been charged with prejudice, as a citizen of a rival town; and in a sense this is true, for though Scepsis did not claim to occupy the site of ancient Ilium, it maintained that the saved remnant from Ilium, under the lead of Aeneas, founded Scepsis.

Strabo (p. 596) speaks of the shrine of Achilles near Sigeum, and of the tombs of Patroclus and Antilochus, and the libations poured to the shades of these and of Ajax. He raises the question, also, why the Ilians honored these destroyers of their city, but not Heracles who had captured it in the preceding generation.

The belief of the world that the Hellenic and Roman Ilium stood on the site of the Homeric city, was not affected by the doubts of Demetrius and Hestiaea, as has been shown by the honors paid by the *Emperor Constantine.* Romans. The Emperor Constantine thought seriously of renewing the plan of Julius Caesar, and establishing at Ilium the seat of his empire, and even drew the plan of the city, and began the erection of its walls (Zosimus, ii. 30, Sozomenus, *Hist. Eccl.* ii. 3).

A letter of the Emperor Julian,[2] written apparently after he became emperor, tells of a visit made by him to Ilium when he was summoned by Constantius, in 354 or 355 A.D. He found there the remains of *Visit of Julian.* sacrifices still glimmering on the altar of Hector's shrine, and the bronze statue of Hector recently anointed. Opposite the statue of Hector, stood in the open air one

[1] She may have been of Alexandria Troas, and thus personally interested in the subject, as a neighbor, like Demetrius. She is called ἡ γραμματική in Scholion B on Γ 64, but this may mean no more than *learned* or *scholarly*.

[2] Published in *Hermes*, ix. 258.

of Achilles. The temple of Athena and its image of the goddess were still in the best of condition. The attendant of the temple, Pegasius, though he had been a "bishop of the Galilaeans" (ἐπίσκοπος τῶν Γαλιλαίων), had only feigned adherence to Christianity, and was said to worship the sun.[1] The tomb of Achilles was then undisturbed, although it had been reported to have been opened. Pegasius served as *periegete*, or official guide for visitors to the scene of the Homeric story. Clearly the heathenish elements had not been removed thoroughly either from him or from many of those to whom he showed the shrines and tombs.

After the time of Julian, Ilium was long the seat of a Christian bishopric, but it was deserted after the coming of the Turks in 1306.

A curious confirmation of the belief that Ilium was never wholly deserted, even after the sack of the city by the Achaeans, is found in the fact, reported by Polybius, Plutarch, and others, and now confirmed by inscriptional evidence, that the Locrians, even almost to the time of the beginning of our era, continued to send free maidens to Ilium, to serve as menials, with bare feet, in the temple of Athena, in satisfaction of her wrath against the Locrian Ajax for the profanation of her shrine.[2] Further support for the story has been drawn from the architectural remains of the great temple,[3] in connexion with the well, to which the Locrian maidens seem to have gone by a hidden passage, avoiding the sight of the goddess.

Locrian Tribute.

---

[1] The reference to the worship of the sun is interesting, not only in connexion with the metope of the sun-god found on the site of Ilium, but particularly because of the bronze statue of Apollo which the Emperor Constantine brought from Ilium, and had erected on a porphyry column in Constantinople, as a statue of himself, and which is said to have received the worship of the people (*Hermes*, xxxvi. 457 ff.).—Pegasius seems to have been appointed by the Emperor Julian to some pagan priesthood.

[2] Polybius, xii. 5; Plutarch, *On the Delay of the Divinity*, 557 D, Scholion to Lycophron, *Alexandra*, 1141. Strabo (600 f.) says that this tribute of the Locrians began only after the supremacy of the Persians in Asia,—but he (five hundred years later than this supremacy) names no authority, and offers no explanation why the Locrians at that late day should have begun the extraordinary custom.

[3] Brückner in Dörpfeld, *Troja und Ilion*, 557 ff.

In modern times, early travellers seem to have confused Ilium with Alexandria Troas, on the coast, several miles to the south. But Robert Wood, a friend of Lord Granville, of the British Foreign Office, in 1750 visited the Troad, and identified the general situation. The results of his observations *Modern Beliefs of the Site.* were published with a map in a chapter, "Description of the Troade," which formed a sort of appendix to his *Essay on the Original Genius and Writings of Homer*, which for the first time raised seriously the question whether the poet had the aid of the art of writing in the composition of the *Iliad* and the *Odyssey*,—a book which was translated into German, and had much influence on scholarly opinion in that country, serving as a forerunner, if not a foundation for Wolf's famous *Prolegomena* to Homer.[1] Wood rightly identifies the Menderé with the Scamander, but places Ilium much too far away, among the hills.

In February and March of 1791, M. Le Chevalier presented before the Royal Society of Edinburgh,[2] in attractive form, a general account of the Trojan plain, and an argument for the identification of Bunárbashi, the stronghold among the hills, with the site of *Le Chevalier for Bunárbashi.* Homeric Ilium, Le Chevalier claimed to have found the hot and cold springs of the twenty-second book of the *Iliad* near Balidagh, the height above Bunárbashi. The principal river of the plain, the Menderé, he took to be the Simoïs, not the Scamander, and the Dumbrek Su, which is now held to be the Simoïs, he thought to be the Thymbrius. The Bunárbashi stream, which empties into the Aegean Sea, he took to be the Scamander. His examination of the plain had been much more thorough than that of any previous traveller, and his results were generally accepted by scholars. Indeed

---

[1] Wood's book was published in Dublin in 1776, but an edition without the appendix had been privately printed in 1769, and served as a basis for the German translation, with a review by the greatest German scholar of his time, Heyne of Göttingen, as a preface.

[2] *Tableau de la Plaine de Troye, accompagné d'une Carte lévée géométriquement en* 1785 *et* 1786. *Transactions of the Royal Society*, vol. iii., 1794. Before the publication of the original, a translation by Dalzel, with notes and illustrations, *Description of the Plain of Troy, with a Map of that Region*, was published in Edinburgh in 1791.

his map was more reasonable than those of his predecessors, and for half a century it served as the basis for the maps of his successors.

The two most notable attempts during the first seventy years of the nineteenth century to overthrow the views of *Hissarlik as Ilium.* Le Chevalier and to prove that Hissarlik was the true site of the Homeric Ilium, were made independently by a Scot, MacLaren,[1] and by a German physician who resided in Smyrna, Eckenbrecher.[2] These were dissatisfied with Le Chevalier's identification of the Menderé, the most important river of the plain, with the Simoïs instead of with the Scamander, and of Bunárbashi instead of Hissarlik as the site of Homeric Ilium.

MacLaren and Eckenbrecher called attention to the fact that the distance of Bunárbashi from the Hellespont,—nine miles,—was not consistent with the Homeric story. *Bunárbashi not Ilium.* How, for example, could the Trojan army, bivouacking in front of the Achaean camp, at the close of the second day of battle, send to the city after the sun went down, for cattle and sheep and bread, for their evening meal? If the messengers had to go eight miles, after a hard day of battle, and return with the slow-paced sheep, morning would have been near at hand before the cattle arrived at the bivouac,—to say nothing of the killing, dressing, and eating of the animals. Bunárbashi, too, did not agree with Strabo's site for Ilium. And the springs near Bunárbashi were shown to be not two, as in Homer,—one hot and the other cold,—but thirty-four or forty in number, and all of the same temperature: thus these could not confirm the claim which had been made on behalf of that site. Further, Homer (X 165) tells of Hector's being pursued thrice around the walls of Ilium,— while the Scamander and the precipices would have made this impossible at Bunárbashi.[3] To this was added the thought that Hissarlik should have been mentioned by the poet, if it had lain on the route between the Achaean camp and the city

---

[1] *Dissertation on the Topography of the Trojan War*, 1822, revised and enlarged in *The Plain of Troy Described*, by Charles MacLaren, Edinburgh, 1863.

[2] *Ueber die Lage des Homerischen Ilion,* in the *Rheinisches Museum* for 1843; revised and enlarged, *Die Lage der homerischen Troja*, Düsseldorf, 1875.

[3] The Menderé flows about Balidagh "on three sides, at the base of steep cliffs."

of Ilium, and the observation that the highest peak of Mount Ida, Gargarus, is not visible from Bunárbashi, as it must have been from Ilium, according to Θ 47 ff.

On the other hand, the site of Bunárbashi and its citadel was compared to that of Mycenae ; and the great General von Moltke admitted that it seemed such a site as a Homeric soldier and statesman would have chosen, *Site of Bunárbashi Imposing.* —a summit five hundred feet in height, in a recess. It was far grander and more imposing than the hill of Hissarlik. The objections of Strabo were thought fatal to the claims of Hissarlik. Even in the geographer's time, Hissarlik had been declared to be too near the Hellespont to be the site of the Homeric Ilium. An unnatural interpretation endeavored to explain the pursuit of Hector by Achilles,— these had not run thrice around the city, but thrice in a circle in front of the city. As an answer to the objection of too great distance from the Hellespont, Strabo's theory of the formation of new land was carried still further, and one scholar maintained that the shore of the Hellespont was three miles nearer Bunárbashi in the Homeric period than at present. Naturally attention was called to the necessity of supposing a change in the bed of the Scamander, if Hissarlik was to be accepted as the Homeric Ilium, while no such change needed to be assumed if Bunárbashi were the ancient site. Finally, ruined walls were found near Bunárbashi, which indicated that it had been the seat of some settlement in olden time.

The discussion with regard to the site of ancient Ilium continued with much warmth even to the beginning of the last decade of the nineteenth century,—the contest *Discussion Continued.* during the later years being narrowed to the rival claims of Hissarlik and Bunárbashi. On the whole the balance of opinion seemed in favor of Bunárbashi,—for which, as an important military position, von Moltke's opinion was held to weigh as much as that of Alexander the Great in favor of Hissarlik,—though the historian Grote and others favored Hissarlik. Some who were dissatisfied with Bunárbashi, as not fulfilling the Homeric requirements, did not recognize Hissarlik either as fulfilling all requirements of the story, and believed that the poet or poets had been eclectic, and not entirely clear either in mind or in statement.

If the story were simply a development of the Sun Myth, according to which the Darkness came to the East to seek his fair bride the Dawn,—and if no Trojan expedition had ever been made,—clearly it was idle for scholars to discuss the site of an Ilium which had never been besieged, and indeed had never existed. Many, too, who believed that the Trojan story rested on a basis of fact, believed that this basis was very slight. In Professor Jebb's words, Homer "would retain the privilege of a poet who was adorning an ancient legend, and whose theme was a city that had long ago vanished." No "one site can be harmonized with every detail of the poem."

To Dr. Heinrich Schliemann belongs the honor of leading to a more exact knowledge of the most important Homeric sites, as well as the distinction of founding the "science of the spade," in connexion with these explorations. A thorough cosmopolitan,—a German by birth, long a resident in Russia, but a citizen of the United States of America, and making his home in Athens, with a Greek wife,—though his early training had been for trade and not for scholarship, he was early filled with a love for the Homeric poems and a desire to see Troy, and was undisturbed by modern scientific doubts as to the reality of the Trojan War. His first visit to Greece was in the summer of 1868, when he visited Ithaca, Mycenae, and the Trojan plain.[1] He reached Bunárbashi with the expectation of accepting this as the Homeric Ilium, but he saw at once that this did not satisfy two requirements,—it was too far from the Hellespont, and the pursuit of Hector by Achilles thrice about the walls, would have occupied about nine hours, which would be an absurdly long time. He hired five workmen, however, and made slight excavations at Bunárbashi, little dreaming that he was to continue excavations with hundreds of men for a score of years, before this question would be settled. At present, no one doubts, at least openly, that Hissarlik is the site of Homeric Troy. The identification of Bunárbashi,—whether it was the site of the later Gergis or Gergitha, which was given

Dr. Heinrich Schliemann.

---

[1] *Ithaka, der Peloponnes, und Troja. Archaeologische Forschungen* von Heinrich Schliemann, Leipzig, 1869. This was published also in a French edition.

to Ilium by the Romans, but soon thereafter destroyed, or Cenchreae, of which little is known,—is of minor importance.

In April of 1870, Schliemann returned to the Trojan plain, and at the suggestion of Mr. Frank Calvert, who owned part of the hill of Hissarlik as well as a large estate in the Troad, and who himself had made *Schliemann's* slight diggings on this site, made preliminary *Excavations.* excavations on the hill of Hissarlik, digging at one point to a depth of sixteen feet below the surface, and laying bare stones of a great wall. For more extensive explorations the permission of the Turkish government was necessary, and this was at length secured through the American minister to the Sublime Porte, in the autumn of 1871. Excavations were then conducted for six weeks before the cold weather compelled their cessation, and a broad trench was dug thirty-three feet deep. These excavations were resumed for four and one-half months in the spring of 1872. Again, on February 1, 1873, in spite of wind and cold, the work was resumed with one hundred workmen,—a number later increased to one hundred and sixty,—and was continued until June 17. "In order to bring Troy itself to light," as Dr. Schliemann himself wrote, he felt bound to dig down to the native rock or to virgin soil,—naturally but unfortunately believing that the Homeric Ilium of three thousand years ago would be found at the very bottom. Who could have preceded the dynasty of Priam? Was not Dardanus, the founder of this dynasty, the son of Zeus himself? And even Dardania was on the foothills of Mt. Ida. Thus Dr. Schliemann (as he himself writes) "was forced to demolish many interesting ruins in the upper strata," including massive walls, and the remains of a temple.[1] He was soon satisfied, however, that the lowest layer of remains was from a settlement which was far ruder and more primitive than the Homeric city, and after the first broad trench had been cut, he did not allow his men to dig below the remains of the second city from beneath, which bore clear indications of having been destroyed

[1] This error of Dr. Schliemann was not so pernicious as it might have been, since the greater part of the remains of the Homeric city, which interests us most, had already been destroyed by the Romans, as appears later in this narrative.

by fire, and which he identified with the Homeric Ilium.[1]
Here he brought to light town-walls and massive towers,
with a complicated mass of lesser ruins. Later he believed
the third city from the bottom to have been Homeric Ilium.
The separation into definite strata was often neither easy
nor certain, since the surface of the hill was not level, and
the layers were not everywhere of the same thickness, and
since the foundations of some structures were sunk lower
than those of other buildings of the same period. In or near
the remains of the second city from the bottom, Schliemann
found a rich treasure of gold cups and ornaments, which
he conjectured to have been on its way to a place of
safety in a time of danger, but to have been abandoned
by the bearer. It seemed to have been in a wooden box,
and the copper key was with it. Now it is believed to
have been in a cavity of the sun-dried brick wall of the
citadel, and on more careful investigation, this key "has
proved to be only a bronze chisel, with a rusty bronze
mass at one end." This treasure was promptly called the
"Treasure of Priam," for during his early excavations,
Schliemann had a strong tendency to ascribe to some
Homeric hero each important article which he found ; at
any rate, it served to justify Homer's words with regard
to the wealth of Ilium. Other gold ornaments were
found by workmen, but not delivered to the explorer,
and later eight or nine other "treasures" were discovered.

After excavations at Mycenae, the work of exploring
Ilium was resumed by Schliemann in the autumn of 1878,
Explorations and again in February 1879. The last part
Resumed. of this work was devoted to laying bare
the walls of the second or third city, and to examining

---

[1] *Trojanische Alterthümer : Bericht über die Ausgrabungen* von Heinrich Schliemann, Leipzig, 1874. With an Atlas of 218 photographs. Also published in an
English translation, *Troy and its Remains*, London, 1874.—Another explanation
has been offered for the evidence of fire in this layer. The soil was indeed saturated
with ashes and smoke, but this may be due, at least in part, to the fact that these
houses had no stone or brick hearths, and the fires, both for warmth and for
cooking, were built immediately on the ground which served as floor,—exactly as
in many a *khan* of Modern Greece. The ashes, naturally, would aid in raising
the material level of the settlement.

the tumuli in the neighborhood of the plain.[1]   Schliemann came to the conclusion that the *third* city on the hill of Hissarlik "perfectly agrees with the Homeric indications as to the site of Troy," but was obliged to grant that the culture of that early age did not agree with that depicted in the Homeric poems.   He regretted that he could not prove "Homer to have been an eye-witness of the Trojan War."   "The civilization he describes is later by centuries than that brought to light in the excavations."   "The imagination of the bards had full play; the small Ilium grew in their songs, in the same proportion as the strength of the Greek fleet, the power of the besieging army, and the great actions of the heroes."   That is, Schliemann adopted in its essence Sir Richard Jebb's view, which is quoted above.

Doubts as to the extent of the Trojan city again rose in Schliemann's mind, and in 1882 he resumed explorations in the Troad, and continued them for five months. In these he had the very great advantage of the counsel of Dr. Wilhelm Dörpfeld, who has *Excavations of 1882.* been now for a score of years the distinguished head of the Athenian branch of the German Archaeological Institute, and the highest authority on Greek architecture, on all matters pertaining to excavations, and on the topography of Athens; and in the course of their explorations of 1882, Dr. Schliemann returned to his earlier view that the second city from the native rock was the Homeric Ilium.[2]

Under the influence of an absurd charge that the records of the excavations had been falsified, and that the exact truth had been neither ascertained nor told, and a claim that Hissarlik was really an ancient *Later Excavations.* necropolis, Schliemann returned to Troy and continued excavations from March 1 to August, 1890.   He expected to resume them again in the spring of 1891, and then to carry them to completion, with the aid of

[1] *Ilios : The City and Country of the Trojans*, by Henry Schliemann.   New York, 1881.—A general view of the excavations to that time, superseding *Troy and its Remains*.

[2] *Troja : Results of the latest Researches and Discoveries on the Site of Homer's Troy*, by Dr. Henry Schliemann.   New York, 1884.

Dr. Dörpfeld.[1] But the unwearied explorer died in Naples
on December 26, 1890. Madame Schliemann loyally and
generously carried out the plans of her husband, whose
companion and helper she had been throughout the earlier
laborious and exhausting explorations, by providing means for
another summer's work, which in 1893 was conducted by
Dr. Dörpfeld.[2] These explorations proved the exceedingly
interesting and unexpected fact that the Homeric Ilium was
neither the second nor the third city built on this site,
but the sixth from the rock, or the third layer as reckoned
from above. That Schliemann should have died just before
this great discovery, was pathetic. The German Emperor
granted the money necessary for the final excavations, in
1894.

Dr. Dörpfeld's scheme of the nine cities or settlements
on this site is as follows :

(1) Lowest, most primitive settlement ; of the neolithic
age. (3000 to 2500 B.C.?)

Dörpfeld's Scheme of Successive Settlements. (2) *Prehistoric fortified city*, with strong walls
for defense, and large houses of sun-dried brick.
Thrice destroyed and rebuilt. With many objects
of bronze, silver, gold, *lapis lazuli*, and crystal.
Supposed by Dr. Schliemann to be the Homeric Troy.
(2500 to 2000 B.C.?)

(3, 4, and 5) Three successive prehistoric village-settlements on the ruins of the second city,—very probably of
the same race as that of the inhabitants of the second city.
Dwellings built of small stones and sun-dried bricks. (2000
to 1500 B.C.?)

(6) *The Homeric City*. A fortified town of the " Mycenaean
age," with substantial walls and a great tower. Large houses
of well-wrought stone. Developed monochrome pottery, and
" Mycenaean " vases. (1500 to 1000 B.C.?)

(7) Two pre-Hellenic village-settlements, with simple stone
dwellings and native polychrome pottery. During the second

---

[1] *Bericht über die Ausgrabungen in Troja im Jahre* 1890, von Heinrich Schliemann.
Leipzig, 1891.

[2] *Troja* 1893. *Bericht über die im Jahre* 1893 *in Troja veranstalteten Ausgrabungen*, von Wilhelm Dörpfeld. Leipzig, 1894. The final publication of the
results of all the excavations at Hissarlik is in Dörpfeld's *Troja und Ilion*.

of these settlements, foreigners from the north (Cimmerians?) seem to have had their habitations on this hill. (1000 to 700 B.C.)

(8) *Greek Ilium.* (700 B.C. to the beginning of our era.)

(9) Acropolis of the Roman Ilium. The top of the hill is levelled to form a plateau, and a large part of the citadel is given over to the sanctuary of Athena. (From the beginning of our era to 500 A.D.)

Very few remains are found of the Byzantine period. Some other scholars would suppose the earliest Greek settlements in the Troad and on this site to have been made at a much earlier date. The remains ascribed to the third, fourth, and fifth settlements, might be counted as merely subdivisions of one layer, but the discussion of these excavations and discoveries has been so extensive that the numeration cannot now be changed without confusion. Whether the destruction of the Homeric city was so complete that none of its inhabitants remained in the following settlements, cannot be made out from the ruins. Brückner holds that after the fall of their city the Trojan princes made no attempt to rebuild their citadel, but withdrew to the hills and dales to the east, while the Greeks may have remained masters of the plain at the mouth of the Scamander. The shrine of the Trojan goddess became for the Greeks a temple of Athena, and her worship was maintained. Friendly relations existed between the Greeks and the Trojans, and honors were paid to Hector as well as to Achilles and Ajax.

The estimates of time in the preceding scheme are manifestly not absolute, but only relative. The periods of five hundred years are convenient, but make no claim to precision.

In *Troja und Ilion*, page 32, a diagram is given of the successive strata of remains on the hill of Hissarlik. The stratum of the seventh city, the " Aeolic Ilium," reaches six feet below the surface of the hill as this *Successive Strata.* stood before the excavations of Dr. Schliemann; to the sixth city, which he called the " Lydian Ilium,"[1] the explorer assigned only a layer of six inches on the hill ; the

[1] This was changed, as we shall see, by the excavations of 1893 and 1894.

remains of the fifth city reached to a depth of thirteen feet; the fourth city to twenty-three feet; the third city to thirty-three feet; the second city to forty-five feet; and the lowest city to a depth of fifty-two and one-half feet. The native rock stands 109½ feet above the level of the sea. The assignment of one-half of the mass of accumulations, or thirty-two and one-half feet, to the third, fourth, and fifth settlements, which are estimated to have occupied the site for only five hundred years, while only six feet are thought to have been added during the last twenty-five hundred years, reminds the reader that the calculation of time on the basis of accumulations of rubbish gives a very uncertain result. Clearly rubbish accumulated and the level of the settlement was raised much more rapidly in the earlier, sun-dried brick periods, when as the rude walls tumbled to the ground they were not cleared away, but served as the "under-pinning" for the new house, and when the ashes of the household-fire accumulated on the ground which served as floor, than when the buildings were more substantial, and much rubbish was removed.

Dörpfeld's explanation of the failure of the earlier explorations to discover the Homeric city in the sixth stratum, is very

Why the Homeric City was so long Overlooked. ingenious and full of interest, as well as convincing. The central part of the site had gradually become somewhat raised, since in each settlement the new building of sun-dried brick had been erected on the ruins of its predecessor, and we remember the total increase in height to have been in places not less than fifty feet,— naturally greatest near the centre of the settlement. But when the Roman city was built, the walls were extended beyond the earlier fortifications, and the surface of the city was "graded" to one level. The upper soil of the higher parts was used as "filling" over the lower parts. This caused the ruins of the greater part of the Homeric city to be used as filling near the new walls, or to be dumped over them; while only on the earlier, lower level, near the walls, were the ruins of the Homeric town left undisturbed by the Romans. Dörpfeld compares with this work the leveling of the summit of the Athenian Acropolis, where the remains near the north wall, for example, those of the old palace, were best preserved from prehistoric times to our own.

The area of the sixth or Homeric city, according to Dörpfeld, is 20,000 square metres, or the same as that of the citadel of Tiryns, while the Acropolis at Athens is one fourth larger, and the fortress of Mycenae is one half larger than the Homeric Ilium (*Troja in* 1893, p. 46). This does not make a large city. That Achilles chased Hector three times around the Trojan city (X 165), would involve a run of only about a mile in length. This would seem to agree with the story that Heracles captured Troy under Laomedon with an expedition of only six ships (E 641). Such a city had room for only a few families; an army of five thousand men could not be quartered in it,—not to speak of the fifty thousand Trojans and allies who are assumed in the present form of the Homeric poems. The neighboring plateau has not been thoroughly examined, but no trace has been found of any fortification-wall of the Mycenaean period except about the Acropolis, and the poems send all the Trojan forces within the wall at night.

Area of the Homeric City.

Of the sixth city on the hill of Hissarlik, the Homeric Ilium, the remains are not extensive, with the exception of a rather superb wall with a great north-east tower. On the north is a wide breach in the wall, and Dörpfeld explains this by the statement of Strabo (599,—borrowed from Demetrius?) that Archaeanax of Mytilene took stones from Troy for the fortification of Sigeum, about 610 B.C. An interesting parallel to this was the requisition made on Dr. Dörpfeld by a Turkish military commander for any blocks of marble which he should find in the course of his excavations,—the officer having no thought of any archaeological value or interest in the stones. Of the ruins brought to light by Dr. Schliemann, peasants from the neighboring Chiblak have stolen many and important stones, and architectural fragments, probably from the great temple of Athena at Ilium, may be seen used as monuments in the graveyards on the plain and built into the walls of the houses in the neighboring villages. Ilium served thus as a stone-quarry, centuries and milleniums ago, and the stones for the fortifications at Sigeum naturally were taken from the side of the city which was next the harbor. So the

Remains of Homeric City.

recent excavations have afforded no information with regard to the towers and gates of the city on the side which interests us most,—the side toward the Hellespont,—where the Scaean Gate should have stood. But in general, the gates and ways in successive strata seem to have been influenced if not determined by those of the preceding settlement or city,—which indicates a certain continuity of occupation,—and these other strata suggest that the city, as we should expect, had a gate towards the harbor on the Hellespont; and, if it had a gate, it was likely to have also such a tower as stands on the northeast.

The buildings of the Homeric city lay in circular terraces rising toward the centre, which was highest of all. The houses in general had one great hall; only one had three or four large rooms. What stood at the centre of the city,—a palace or a temple,— is unknown, but the analogy of other sites makes a palace far more probable than a temple. In no one of the successive cities is any indication found of any temple in Ilium, except that of Athena.

Buildings of Homeric City.

The main approach to the Homeric Ilium was from the south. Dr. Dörpfeld observes that the approach to the town from the plain on the north or northwest, where Homer's Scaean Gate[1] must have stood,—looking toward the plain on which the battles were fought and toward the camp of the Achaeans by the Hellespont,—is too steep a slope to allow of the easy passage of chariots; but Homer makes old Priam drive forth from his Scaean Gate (Γ 263), and when pursued by Patroclus, Hector checks his horses in the Scaean Gate (ἐν Σκαιῇσι πύλῃς, Π 712), in doubt whether to turn and fight again or to order all the Trojans to come into the city,—an expression which implies that his chariot was entering by that route. The approach to the gate on the south had a much more gradual slope. This southern gate, looking towards the older Dardanian district, Dörpfeld holds to have been called the Dardanian

Gates of the City.

---

[1] Professor Robert of Halle, in *Hermes*, xlii. 80, argues that the Scaean Gate is indeed the Left Gate, but that it was on the east, not on the northwest, of the town. Robert also holds, with Aristarchus, that the Dardanian Gate was equivalent to the Trojan Gate, and identical with the Scaean Gate.

Gate (X 194),—in opposition to the scholars who have believed this to be only another appellation of the Scaean Gate. Near to this southern gate, is the spring which has been identified with that by which stood the washing-troughs of the Trojans (X 147). At the close of the last day of the battles of the *Iliad* (X 1 ff.), Priam, Hecuba, and the rest were standing on the tower by the Scaean Gate. By this gate, the fleeing Trojan soldiery poured into the city. But Achilles, after pursuing Hector thrice around the city, and heading off his attempts to enter the Dardanian Gate, at last slays him. Dörpfeld calls attention to the fact that this final conflict seems to have been near the springs (X 208) and therefore near to the gate on the south, and cannot have been seen by the Trojans who were standing on the tower by the Scaean Gate on the northwest, so that Priam and Hecuba learned of the death of their son only as they caught sight of his dead body dragged behind the chariot of Achilles on its way to the Achaean camp (X 405). That Hector should endeavor in particular to enter the Dardanian Gate, is explained by Dörpfeld from the fact that the approach was so much easier to this than to the Scaean Gate.

Belger calls attention to the following differences between the Trojan and the Mycenaean remains: At Ilium less ornament is found, and no variety of architectonic forms. The burial of the dead of the Trojan plain differed entirely from that prevalent in Greece; if the Trojan tumuli are tombs, they were intended to be seen from afar, while the Mycenaean tombs, whether "shaft-graves" or "beehive" structures, are hidden beneath the ground. The use of a vacant triangular space above the lintel of a gateway, as in the Gate of the Lions, and the so-called Treasury of Atreus, does not seem to have been known at Ilium. Great earthern jars, πίθοι, for storing grain and liquids, are found in large numbers at Hissarlik, but not at Mycenae; they are perfectly familiar, however, to the poet of the *Odyssey*, and abound in the Cretan palace of Cnosus. But the Trojans were not Achaeans, and absolute identity of indications of culture in the two cities, would testify that these were not the cities of which Homer sang.

Differences between Trojan and Mycenaean Remains.

CHAPTER XVIII

HOMERIC WAR

THE poet is not composing an Art of War,—his aim is to please rather than to teach : and Plato in his *Republic* gibes those who regard Homer as the highest authority *The* Iliad *not* on military science, saying that, if he had really *an Art of* known what was to be done in war, Homer *War.* would have been a soldier and general himself, and not a poet : he would have chosen to do brave deeds rather than to tell of them,—to be the leader who should receive praise, rather than the poet to bestow it. Still, the warriors of Plato's time were thought to draw inspiration and stimulus from the *Iliad*. Aristophanes says that Homer taught better than all others the marshalling, brave deeds, and arming of men. And the great Napoleon is quoted as saying that in reading the *Iliad* he felt every moment that Homer was a warrior himself, and had not (as most of his commentators declared) spent the greater part of his life in the schools of Chios. An enthusiastic Frenchman has even suggested that the poet was aide-de-camp or military secretary to Agamemnon. Although Homer knew no strategy in the modern sense, nor any manual of arms, nor evolutions of a squad, company, regiment, or brigade,—yet he was familiar with many brave deeds of mighty men. His interest in the conflicts which he describes, is very different from the purely literary interest of Vergil in the battles of the *Aeneid* ; while the Greek is describing scenes with which he is familiar, the Roman poet tells of conflicts such as he had never seen, based on information which was chiefly drawn from books.

In modern times and civilized countries, war is an exceptional occurrence, and comparatively few men in a generation
are called to take an active part in it. Americans
have prided themselves on their citizen soldiery *Every*
who leave the works of peace only at the stern *Achaean a*
call of duty, and who return as soon as possible *Warrior.*
to their homes and peaceful employments,—laying down
their arms and military offices gladly, like Cincinnatus. But
in the Homeric age deeds of violence were common, and
war was almost as general as peace. Even in a time of
supposed peace a hostile force might invade the land any
day or night, with no formal declaration or notice of war.
Arms were man's natural accompaniment. Athena taking the
guise of the Taphian king, on a peaceful commercial errand,
seizes her spear with sharp point of bronze (α 99), and she
tells Telemachus how his father, also on a peaceful mission,
had feasted and made merry among the Taphians " with
helmet, shield, and two spears " (α 256). At the stringing
of the bow by the disguised Odysseus, Penelope's suitors do
not wonder that Telemachus should gird his sword about
him and grasp his spear (φ 431). " All Greece wore steel,"
Thucydides tells us (i. 6), adding that the Athenians were
the first to abandon the custom, which other Greek nations
of the fifth century B.C. still retained. Doubtless the custom
long endured after the reason for it ceased, just as the sword
has continued to be a part of the " court-dress " of very
peaceable officials of our own generation, but the Homeric
poet makes the wise Odysseus declare, almost in these direct
words, that war is the proper work of man from youth even
to old age (Ξ 86 f.).

The war between the Achaeans and the Trojans was
in the main a succession of single combats between champions
(πρόμαχοι, Γ 31). The *Iliad* narrates the events
of but four days of battle, in which many leaders *A Succession*
were slain. But while, in these four days, ten of *of Single*
the fifty sons of king Priam fall, and seven sons *Combats.*
of his old counsellor Antenor, and the reader becomes
aware that the war could not long be maintained at such
a rate of loss, little is said of the deaths of the rank and
file, and this only in the most general expressions, as

where at the close of the second day of battle, Hector held
an assembly of the Trojans " by the eddying river, in a
clear place, where the ground appeared through the dead
bodies" (Θ 490). The common soldier is of little importance in the battle; he kills no " mighty man of valor."
The success or failure of the fight does not rest with him;
he is not " the man behind the gun." No " bow drawn at
a venture" smites a king between the joints of his harness.
The Homeric conflicts are not unlike those represented in
Shakespeare's *Macbeth* and the first part of *Henry the Fourth*.
The absence of Achilles from the fray is more deplored
than that of all his Myrmidons; and when his friend
Patroclus enters the battle accompanied by his followers,
the Trojans appear not to be dismayed by the advance of
the masses of common soldiery, but " when they saw the
brave son of Menoetius, himself and his squire, with glittering
armor,—then each looked about him, whither he could
escape sheer destruction" (Π 278). In the Catalogue of
the Ships, or the enumeration of the Achaean forces, stress
is laid upon the leaders, rather than on the number of
soldiers; in fact, in this catalogue, only once is the number
of men in a contingent stated, and the poet nowhere
explicitly tells his hearer how large was the force of men
before Troy.

An effort has been made to distinguish three sorts of
combats in Homer : (1) formal single-combats, like those
between Paris and Menelaus (Γ 267 ff.), Hector
Three Sorts
of Combats. and Ajax (H 206 ff.), Odysseus and Socus (Λ
428 ff.), Achilles and Aeneas (Υ 158 ff.), and
Achilles and Hector (X 131 ff.); (2) less formal combats,
like those between Agamemnon and Antiphus (Λ 104 ff.),
and between Achilles and Asteropaeus (Φ 139 ff.); (3) the
general background of *mêlées* in which only names are
mentioned, without details. But the line of distinction
between these classes of conflicts is not broad and clear,
although the poet secures a certain perspective by not
attaching equal importance to all engagements, and by
bringing a few persons into clear light in the fore-
ground.

Agamemnon, " king of men," reviews his troops at the

beginning of the first day of battle, and exhorts them to fight bravely (Δ 250 f.), but gives no directions either then or later as to the position of the several tribes or clans in the line. Each leader goes where he *No Generalship in Modern Sense.* pleases, and fights with whom he will. The chieftains boast of personal strength and valor, but not of skill in leadership or any generalship.

We are brought into serious difficulties if we assume that each leader and tribe had a definite place in the line of battle. Once, it is true, in the tenth book of the *Iliad*, which has many idiosyncrasies, we are told that the several contingents of the Trojan forces received by lot separate places in the line for their bivouac on the plain : the Carians and Paeonians are by the sea, the Lycians and Mysians received by lot the post near Thymbré, etc. (K 428 ff.), but this arrangement is not referred to elsewhere.

The poet tells of no strategic movements of an army or part of an army, as ordered or accomplished,—no manoeuvres, no flank movements, no concentration of forces at a special point in order to break the enemy's *No Strategic Movements.* line, and no surprises. No body of men is brought to the support of a hard-pressed division, or sent against a weak place in the enemy's line, or stationed for the defense of an important position. Neither Telamonian Ajax from Salamis (except, perhaps, N 709) nor his namesake the Locrian, the swift-footed son of Oïleus, is ever accompanied in the field by his own forces, but the two chieftains, though of different tribes, generally remain together (N 701, P 531, 720), and move from one part of the field to another according to the apparent need of the moment. Ajax the son of Oïleus, indeed, could not be attended by his countrymen since these were archers (N 712), while he excelled in the use of the spear ; he must be in the forefront of battle, while they must stand in the rear of the heavy-armed forces. The reader must not suppose that this Ajax may have devolved the immediate command of his troops upon a lieutenant, for while the forty ships of the Epeans had four leaders (B 615), Ajax alone led the forty black ships of the Locrians (B 527). Doubtless in many more instances than are distinctly indicated, if not as a rule, the masses of men were only lightly armed, and remained at a distance from the enemy, while their chieftains fought in the front ranks. Menestheus sends a herald to summon the two Ajaxes, when the Lycians are pressing hard upon the tower which he is defending (M 342), but no adjutant or other messenger is sent to inform the commander-in-chief, Agamemnon, or to summon a whole division or company of men for the defense of the tower.

The fact that many of the chieftains had chariots, of itself tended to separate them from their commands; like the

Leaders Separated from their Men.

Locrian Ajax, they could go where their countrymen could not follow them. Not infrequently, both on the advance and on the retreat, the warrior on the chariot is entirely out of connexion with his men. When Hector returns to his city on the first day of battle, to bid the Trojan matrons offer sacrifices to Athena, he devolves his command upon no one; he simply shouts to the troops to stand firm while he goes to the town (Z 111). In the flight before Patroclus and Ajax on the third day of battle, for a time brave Hector "stood firm and saved his comrades" (Π 363), but soon his swift horses bore him away from the Greek camp, "leaving the host of the Trojans, whom the trench detained against their will." This does not seem to have been thought an unsoldierly act on Hector's part. Each man, whether chieftain or common soldier, was following his own devices. A little later on the same day, Hector mounts his chariot and turns to flight, bidding the other Trojans also flee (Π 657),—"for he knew the sacred scales of Zeus," that the balance was against them. He leads the retreat instead of checking it, or being the last to leave the field.

On the same third day of battle, the Cretan Idomeneus and his lieutenant Meriones meet in the Greek camp,—one coming

Independence of Warriors.

from the care of a wounded comrade, and the other fetching from his senior's tent a fresh spear in place of one which he had broken in the conflict. We are surprised first to learn that the quarters of Meriones are far from those of his superior officer (N 268), so that he goes to the latter's tent rather than to his own, to fetch a spear, and again to note that when these two leaders of one of the largest contingents in the Achaean army (only Agamemnon and Nestor led a larger number of ships than Idomeneus) returned to the field of battle, they did not ask where their own men, the Cretans, were fighting, but where the Greeks were hardest pressed. They decided that the two Ajaxes and Teucer could hold the centre of the line, and therefore they betook themselves to the left (N 312). What forces were supporting the Ajaxes, is not told, and we have seen that "Ajax" could not be a brief expression for *Ajax and his men*, as when we read that our own General Grant ordered General Thomas to advance, we assume that the latter was attended by his corps; in the battle on the Trojan plain, the two chieftains by themselves are defending their position. When Idomeneus and Meriones appeared on the scene of conflict, all the Trojans advanced against them (N 330),—as if the strife were between one hundred men on a side instead of one hundred thousand. The goddess Hera says to Athena on the second day of battle that the Greeks are "perishing miserably because of the force of one man" (ἀνδρὸς ἑνὸς ῥιπῇ, Θ 355); while apparently Ilium would have been captured at once if Achilles had succeeded in entering its walls, at Φ 544. The individual and his bodily strength are clearly far more important before Troy than in modern warfare. The two Lapiths seem to be almost the only defenders of the gate of the Greek camp against the Trojan assailants (M 127). They are not simply the commanders to direct the work of defense; they themselves hurl the stones and wield the spears. When Teucer's bowstring breaks, Hector shouts to "Trojans, Lycians, and Dardanians" (O 485), that Zeus clearly is giving the victory to them,— as if the breaking of a single bowstring were to decide the issue of the battle. And again Hector shouts to all his men to stand firm while he puts on the armor of Achilles (P 184), and he runs after his comrades who are bearing his armor to the city, and changes shields. He clearly feels at this moment no immediate responsibility for the movements of great masses of men. Similarly, Meleager is urged to throw aside his wrath and defend Calydon (I 574); he is as important to the Aetolians as Achilles to the Achaeans. Not by his skill as a general, but by his personal prowess, he turns the tide of battle and drives off the enemy.

The victory is that of the leader, not of his troops, nor of the leader and his troops.   Perhaps we may compare the

Victory that of the Leader.

song of the Israelitish women, "Saul hath slain his thousands and David his ten thousands" (1 *Samuel* xviii. 7).   When Agamemnon is wounded, Diomed is downright discouraged (Λ 316), although all else is going well.   Yet Agamemnon is important only as a "mighty man of valor," not as a general, a commander-in-chief; so far as we know, he has no definite plan of battle which he is eager to carry out, and which he can direct better than anyone else.   No one receives directions from him as to his movements in all the course of the *Iliad*, but each chieftain follows his own best judgment.   Agamemnon is "more royal" (βασιλεύτερος, I 160) than any other, and brought to Troy the largest fleet of ships ; but he is not the commander-in-chief according to modern notions, after all.   He is even rebuked severely in the assembly of the soldiery by the much younger Diomed (I 32), for proposing to return to Greece.   Thus also Hector, the chief leader of the Trojans, is not kept informed of the progress of the fight at other parts of the line than his own (Λ 523, N 674) ; no official reports are brought to him, and no directions are sought from him.   When a leader is slain or wounded, or for any other reason withdraws from the field, his command devolves on no other ; he has no special post to maintain, nor special coign of vantage to gain.   When Agamemnon is wounded on the third day of battle, he shouts to the "leaders and councillors of the Argives" to defend the ships, and then bids his charioteer to drive at once to the camp (Λ 276).   He has no second in command,—neither his brother Menelaus, nor Ajax, who in bravery and might was second only to Achilles, nor Diomed.   A few minutes later, Diomed is wounded by an arrow from the bow of Paris, who had been standing by himself "in ambush," leaning on an old tombstone, and he departs from the field as unceremoniously as Agamemnon had done, to be followed shortly after by Nestor.   Paris at this time is no part of a company or regiment of light-armed troops, and Teucer also has a free bow, as well as a free lance, and follows his own devices. Even the common soldier seems left very much to himself, although subject to harsh rebuke and even punishment, if he plays the coward. On one occasion Aeneas rejoices in heart on seeing the throng follow him in the battle, as a shepherd rejoices in his flock following the ram from the pasture to the water (N 494),—he does not assume this action on their part as a matter of course; and when deprived of their personal leader, the masses of men are like sheep without a shepherd (O 325). But the movement of these men may be compared to a flock of sheep, following a bell-wether, all in a huddle, more exactly than to the regular advance of a military company or battalion. At E 235, Aeneas and Pandarus set out to attack Diomed, who evidently is at some distance from them ; they are two against one, as they think, but Diomed is joined by Sthenelus, and Pandarus is slain ; and a little later (E 571) Aeneas does not remain " when he sees two men standing side by side." According to modern notions of a battle, we should be surprised if two men did not thus stand together. That the conflict was not a mere scrimmage, however, is clear. At P 364 f., we learn that fewer Greeks than Trojans fell, since the former were ever mindful to defend each other in the throng.

Patroclus enters the conflict on the third day of battle, and at once drives the Trojans from the Greek camp, into which they had broken their way ; but a little later the Trojans again drive the Achaeans, "since Epeigeus has fallen" (Π 571), though this Epeigeus *Importance of a Single Man.* is of so little note in general that he is not even named elsewhere in the poems.[1] In the twenty-first book of the *Iliad*, Achilles seems to be almost alone in driving the Trojans to their city, and he is actually the only Greek warrior named in the twenty-first and twenty-second books (*cf.* Φ 15).[2] He calls to the "godlike Achaeans" (Υ 354) to be eager to fight; it is hard for him, mighty though he is, to press upon so many men, and fight with all ;—" not even Ares or Athena would press upon the front of so

---

[1] Nothing indicates that this Epeigeus episode is of late composition.

[2] On Assyrian and Egyptian monuments, also, a king is represented as moving against a mass of men,—the artist thus magnifying the monarch's achievements.

great a battle." Clearly the burden of the fight has been left to him.

The retreat of the forces, also, is often covered by only one or two men, who hold back the pursuers, and thus *Retreat Covered by One or Two.* allow the masses of troops to reach a place of safety. Thus after Agamemnon has been wounded on the third day of battle, Diomed and Odysseus stand firm and keep back the Trojans (Λ 310); and a few hours later, Ajax alone checked the onset of the Trojans until Eurypylus came to his assistance (*cf.* Λ 567), and at the close of the fifteenth book of the *Iliad*, Ajax alone defends the Achaean ships from Trojan fire. The retreats, however, are apt to be somewhat tumultuous, and frequently are stopped only by the interference of some divinity (as Θ 217, 246, 335). They are correspondingly disastrous : no pursuer is ever killed, while the flight is full of danger to the fugitives.

So completely is the hearer's attention concentrated on an individual or a single group of warriors, that at times, *Conversation on the Field.* before a single combat, two antagonists hold a long conversation, as if they were alone on the field. The episode of Diomed and Glaucus,— the conversation which closes with the discovery that their grandfathers were friends, and with the resultant determination not to fight against each other,—occupies one hundred and nineteen verses in the very thick of a fierce battle (Z 119-236). When Aeneas and Achilles meet, the first blow is preceded by one hundred verses, which are occupied partly by a reminder of Achilles to Aeneas of a previous occasion when the latter had fled from him, but mainly by Aeneas's recital of his family-tree (Υ 158-258),—and this was at the time when Achilles was most vehement in his anger at all the Trojans, because of the death of his friend Patroclus. With such conversations in the midst of a battle, withdrawing for the time all thought from the rest of the field of war, may be compared the second scene in the third act of Shakespeare's *Henry Fifth*, where Fluellen, after crying " Up to the breach," beseeches " a few disputations with you, as partly touching or concerning the discipline of the war, the Roman wars, in the way of argument, look you, and friendly communication," with Captain Macmorris.[1]

This habit of the poet, to give prominence to the individual, may spring from his desire to concentrate his hearer's attention, affording but a dull background for the principal figures, which are thus brought into strong relief, and have a bright light cast upon them. With this may be compared the *Hearer's Attention Concentrated.* practise of the Greek dramatic poets in presenting only two or three characters at once to their audience, although they, too, had many unnamed persons in the background. Masses of men awaken less sympathy than individuals. The poet's art also shrank from the task of narrating two contemporary actions. At the close of the last battle of the *Iliad*, as we have seen, for two whole books no other Greek warrior than Achilles is so much as named, as taking part in the fight, and the Achaean forces seem wholly forgotten for a space of six or seven hundred verses. On the visit of Telemachus to Sparta, he reaches the palace of Menelaus in the midst of a wedding-feast which the king is giving to his friends and kinsmen in honor of the double marriage of his son and his daughter,— but when the Ithacan youth has had his bath and appeared in the great hall, the other guests have disappeared entirely ; no further word is said of them (δ *init.*) ; they have served their purpose, and have been dismissed. The hearer's attention is concentrated on the chief actors. We have no reason to follow certain destructive critics who are unable to believe that the poet who invented the wedding-guests would have removed them so noiselessly ; these were invented simply to serve for the moment as the setting, in a background.

Occasionally an episode is introduced, as it would seem, chiefly in order to occupy the time of a gap in the action. Thus in the first book of the *Iliad*, the episode of the journey of Odysseus to Chrysa, for the restoration of Chryseïs to her father (A 430-487), *Episode fills Gap.* helps to occupy the time of waiting for the gods' return to Olympus from the land of the Aethopians, where they

---

[1] "Such conversations on the field are characteristic of the Hindoo epic, where also the leaders are all in all, and the common soldiers are only the 'black mass' to be routed by a single warrior."

have been feasting ; in the third book of the *Iliad*, the interview between Priam and Helen, on the tower by the Scaean Gate, occupies the time while the herald is coming from the field to the city, in order to fetch the old king and also victims for sacrifice (Γ 121-244) ; and in the sixth book, the episode of Diomed and Glaucus (Z 119-236) fills part of the time while Hector is on his way to the city. Similarly, in order to avoid the monotony of the details of the attempts by Penelope's hundred suitors to string the bow of Odysseus, a brief conference outside the great hall, between the disguised Odysseus and his two faithful men, is interposed to occupy the time (φ 188-244).

The poet's method of description of the war by single combats, doubtless, however, is not to be explained entirely
Material from Earlier Lays.
from his artistic principles, but was strongly influenced also by the fact that the earlier epic poets in their briefer lays, which furnished material and precedents for the Homeric poems and adventures, sang of much smaller armies, less elaborate and magnificent expeditions, and of single exploits, like the epic lays of the modern Tatars. These actions and episodes are retained or copied in our *Iliad*. At the opening of the third great day of battle, " the son of Atreus shouted aloud, and bade the Argives gird themselves for the fray " (Λ 15),—an action surely more appropriate to the commander of a military company than to one of an army of a hundred thousand men,—and the assemblies of Achaean soldiers which are held on the first and the last days of battle (B 86 ff., T 42 ff.), would be better adapted to a small army. At I 10 f., Agamemnon directs the heralds to summon an assembly of the troops, but without noise, calling each man separately. This general assembly is clearly distinguished from the council of chieftains which is held a little later ; it must have been intended for all the troops, but a great army cannot be summoned in such a fashion. Even the leaders of such a great camp could hardly be gathered in an hour. At H 382, when the Trojan herald comes to the Achaean camp with proposals for a truce that they may bury their dead, he finds the Danaans assembled by the stern of the ship of Agamemnon. Here,

again, we must not think of the leaders only,—it is the
agora,—but such a multitude as the Catalogue of the Ships
implies, could not gather by the stern of a single Homeric
ship. So the assemblies of the Greeks are thought of as
seated (A 101, B 99, etc.). Even for the games in honor
of Patroclus the spectators are seated ; Idomeneus bids them
"stand up" and see that the chariot of Diomed is first
(Ψ 469),—but not five thousand men, to say nothing of
one hundred thousand, could have been provided with a
"grand stand" in such a camp.

Other and similar indications may be found of the poet's
having in mind a much smaller body of men than the
Catalogue of Ships presents. For example, the
Greek camp seems to have but one gate (M 445), *Indications of*
and this is defended by but two warriors (M 127) ; *a Smaller*
and for the whole Trojan force to pass, Apollo *Army.*
tears down a portion of the Achaean wall,—but only a
spear's cast in length (O 358),—not enough for a force of
one thousand men. When Hector is wounded, all the rest
of the Trojan chieftains stand about him (Ξ 425),—gathering
in a fashion which would be impossible if the field of
battle were extended. Similarly Hector goes through the
throng looking for Deïphobus, Helenus, and the rest of the
Trojan leaders (N 758),—an act which would have been
useless and absurd in a large army which was fighting
without more military order than Homer knew. So when
Menelaus seeks Telamonian Ajax, on the field of battle,
he finds him at once (P 116), though, as we have seen,
Ajax had no regular position in the line. At K 151,
Nestor and Agamemnon find Diomed sleeping outside of
his tent, "with his comrades about him." But this does not
look like a division of five thousand or six thousand men
(Diomed led eighty ships to Troy, according to the Catalogue,
B 568), but rather like a company of fifty or a hundred,
a single ship's load. Again, when Odysseus and Diomed
by night enter the Trojan camp, on the information of
Dolon, they proceed to the quarters of the Thracian
Rhesus, and find the prince sleeping in the midst of his
men (ἐν μέσῳ εὗδε, K 474) ; Diomed slays twelve Thracians,
and Rhesus as the thirteenth. On a strict interpretation,

then, the Thracian contingent of reinforcements consisted
of but twenty-five men. Such a squad would expect but
little attention in an army of one hundred thousand. From
the tower by the Scaean Gate, Helen identifies to Priam the
Achaean warriors on the field below (Γ 161); but if an army
of 50,000 men had stood between the city walls and the
Achaean forces, and Agamemnon, Ajax, and Odysseus had
been with their army of 100,000 men,—could Priam have
distinguished these leaders from the mass of men surrounding
them? And when the commander-in-chief of the whole
Achaean expedition returns to his home, his treacherous
cousin Aegisthus lies in wait for him with a score of men in
ambush; a conflict ensues, and all the combatants on both
sides are killed in the home of Aegisthus (δ 530 ff.). Nothing
is said about any struggle outside of the palace, nor of the
absence of any of Agamemnon's men, and yet the number
engaged cannot have been large. If Agamemnon on his
return led five or six thousand men, what did these do in
their commander's defense, or after his death? Was such
an army slain to the last man in the house of Aegisthus?

To the considerations already offered, which suggest a
much smaller expedition than the Catalogue of Ships details,
*No Arrange-
ments for
Subsistence.* may be added the somewhat obvious thought
that a force of one hundred thousand men could
not subsist on the enemy's country without more
definite arrangements for the supply of food, clothing, and arms than Homer knows. Capricious expeditions
for plunder to Tenedos, Lyrnessus, or another small town
of the Troad would not suffice, nor could the warriors be
expected to capture arms in sufficient quantities to replace
those which had been broken or lost. Not every spear
which had been hurled could be recovered, and few arrows
which had been shot could be found and used again.
Commissaries are mentioned only in one passage, which is
supposed to be of rather late composition (ταμίαι, σίτοιο
δοτῆρες, T 44). Neither army has a definite arrangement
for the supply of food. No supplies were officially furnished.
Every commander must see to it that by means of forays
his men were provided with cattle and grain. Even centuries
later, in Cyrus's expedition against his brother Artaxerxes,

no regular rations were issued,—if a "market" was furnished, this was as much as could be expected; and the Athenian soldiers in the Peloponnesian War were obliged to carry their own food or to hire some one to do this service for them. The Achaeans purchased wine from Lemnian ships, giving in exchange part of the plunder of their forays and the spoils of their enemies, cattle as well as slaves, hides, and bronze (H 473). When the Trojans bivouac on the plain, they send to their homes (ἐκ μεγάρων, Θ 507) for their bread. They have no quartermaster's department, nor even sutlers. The supply of water and the sanitation of the camp for so large a body of men, also, would be difficult matters which seem never to have occurred to the poet. Moreover, as positive indications imply that the poet often thought of the forces as comparatively small, nothing in the first book of the *Iliad*, for example, nor indeed in most of the other books, indicates that the armies before Troy were large. The geographer Strabo observes that in the time of Priam's father Laomedon, Heracles came with but six ships (E 641), and took Troy. The difference between the six ships of Heracles and the twelve hundred of Agamemnon would seem more than to make up for the difference of personal might and prowess between Agamemnon and Heracles. The Argonautic Expedition for the Golden Fleece, again, had but a single ship, yet these Argonauts seem to have fought with the Colchians (Pindar, *Pyth.* iv. 212 f.).

Only in three parts of the Homeric poems are definite numbers mentioned in connexion with the size of the army before Troy: (1) the Catalogue of Ships (B 484-759),—implying in round numbers one *Definite* hundred thousand Achaeans; (2) the account of *Numbers of* Achilles's forces,—fifty ships with fifty men in *Forces.* each (Π 168-170); (3) the thousand watch-fires of the Trojans and their allies on the plain, with fifty men about each (Θ 562).

In connexion with this, it may be noted that the poet in the *Iliad* only in B 134-330, and perhaps also in Ω 765, shows knowledge of a ten-years' war, though this period is definitely fixed in the *Odyssey*, The *Iliad* contains few allusions to earlier battles of the war, and sometimes even seems to ignore the length of the war. For example, as critics have often noticed, Priam does not know by sight the Achaean leaders (Γ 166), although these have long been fighting about the walls of Troy. Shall we say again that although the action of the *Iliad* begins in the tenth year of the war, this is the beginning of the war so far as this poem is concerned? Still more remarkable is it that Helen does not know whether her brothers Castor and Polydeuces have come to the war, though she recognizes the Greek leaders readily after the ten or twenty years of separation (Γ 236). If these had been before Troy for nine years, Helen must have known about her brothers, either hearing from some captive, or failing to see them in the conflicts about the walls. And was Andromache married before the war began? Her son Astyanax is but an infant. How could Hector woo her during the war,—he a prince of Troy and she a princess of Hypoplacian Thebes? Attention has been called already to the fact that a dozen battles, as bloody as the four battles of the *Iliad*, would have left alive but few of Priam's fifty sons. The Achaeans suffer less than the Trojans from the death of their chieftains. Patroclus is the only Greek leader of prominence who is killed or seriously wounded in the engagements of the *Iliad*, but at the close of the poem, Aeneas, Paris, and Glaucus, are the only Trojans of importance left in the action. At least half of the bravest of the Trojans are slain in these four days of battle.

A Ten-Years' War?

In the fifth century B.C., the size of the Greek fleet was firmly fixed in the story;[1] Aeschylus and Euripides both speak in round numbers of the "thousand ships" of the Achaeans. Thucydides (i. 10) calls the same fleet one of twelve hundred ships, but he suggests that the poet exaggerated the numbers and importance of the expedition.

Size of Fleet Fixed in Fifth Century.

The chieftain, having no adjutants or other subordinate officers as his aids, and not even a trumpeter[2] to convey

---

[1] *Cf.* Aeschylus, *Ag.* 45; Euripides, *Iph. Taur.* 149, *Or.* 352, *And.* 106, *Rhesus*, 262, *Iph. Aul.* 174.

[2] The trumpet is mentioned by Homer but once, and that in a comparison (Σ 219); the voice of Achilles sounded clear above the tumult, "like a trumpet."

his commands to his men, needs a strong voice as well as an arm of might. "The shout of the captains" is noted also in the book of *Job* as a characteristic of the battle. "Good at the war-cry" is a frequent epithet of Menelaus (βοὴν ἀγαθός, Γ 96). The *Chieftain's Voice.* English language has received an adjective from the Achaean Stentor, "who shouted as loud as fifty others" (E 785). An evidence of difference of discipline between the two armies has been found by some in the fact that at the beginning of the third book of the *Iliad*, while the "Achaeans advanced in silence, breathing might," the "Trojans came on with clamor and din, like that of cranes," *Din of Battle.* and a little later on the same day, the war-cry of the Trojans arose as the bleating of ten thousand ewes in a farm-yard, when these hear the voices of their young (Δ 433), while the Achaeans "advanced in silence, fearing their commanders" (Δ 429), nor "would you say that so great a mass of soldiery followed with voice in their breasts." On the third day of battle, when Hector had broken open the gates of the Greek camp, the Trojans advanced in a body, following him with a mighty shout (ἄβρομοι, αὐίαχοι, Ν 41). But the Greeks could shout too. An "unceasing cry" arose from the Myrmidons (Π 267), and when the battle was once joined, then was heard

> "Of shout and scream the mingled din,
> And weapon-clash and maddening cry
> Of those who kill and those who die."[1]

Ares is called "heavy-voiced" (βρνήπνος, Ν 521); and in order to rouse the hearts of the Achaeans on the third day of battle, Poseidon shouted "as loud as nine thousand or ten thousand men shout in battle, gathering the strife of Ares; so loud a mighty voice he sent from his breast, and put great strength in the heart of each of the Achaeans" (Ξ 147). So also Athena, in order to arouse the Greeks and dismay their foe, joins in the shout of Achilles, when

But as the divinities came together in strife on the Trojan plain, the "broad earth rang and great heaven trumpeted about them" (ἀμφὶ δὲ σάλπιγξεν, Φ 388). — Recently βοή has been interpreted not as *shout*, but as *battle*; cf. βοηθόος. But this does not affect the remark above made.

[1] οἰμωγή τε καὶ εὐχωλή . . . ὀλλύντων τε καὶ ὀλλυμένων, Δ 450.

the Trojans have killed Patroclus and are pressing into the Greek camp (Σ 218). The divinities shout, too, when they come together in strife (Υ 48 ff.), and the tumult is increased by the thunder of Zeus and the earthquake of Poseidon. A ringing shout broke out as naturally in a Homeric battle as among the spectators of a modern athletic contest,—and often with a motive which is not unknown now, to encourage one's friends.

Battle-cry. The name for battle-cry (ἀλαλητός, Δ 436) indicates that the Homeric shout was the same anapaestic ἀλαλά (which corresponded in part to our "hurrah") as in later times. No watch-word or special battle-cry (like Ζεὺς σωτήρ τε καὶ Νίκη, Xen. *An.* i. 8. 16) is used; nor any pass-word, as in the Euripidean *Rhesus*, where Odysseus is allowed to pass by the Trojan pickets because he has learned the pass-word "Phoebus" from the Trojan scout Dolon, whom he has taken captive (*Rhesus*, 688).

Leader of the People. The classic Greek word for general (στρατηγός) is unknown to Homer; indeed it was impossible for his verse. The Homeric general was the *arranger, marshal* (κοσμήτωρ, Α 16) of the people, and the poet uses the cognate verb (κοσμέω) instead of the Attic verb (τάσσω) with which our "tactics" is connected. But the ordinary word for commander is *leader* (ἡγεμών, ἀγός, ἡγήτωρ, or ἀρχός).

Regiments or Companies. No indication is given by the poet of any organization of the forces, or a division into what would correspond in a way to our regiments and companies,[1] until just before the first battle of the *Iliad*, when the wise Nestor suggests that the men be divided into tribes[2] and clans, that tribe may aid tribe, and clan aid clan, and that they may know who of the leaders and which of the peoples is cowardly, and who is brave (Β 362), *i.e.*

---

[1] The clearest intimation of a company is found at the close of the second day of battle. Seven leaders of the guards go forth from their camp, for picket duty in front of the wall, and "a hundred youths accompany each, with long spears in their hands" (Ι 85).

[2] This, the reader will remember, was the principle also in the Athenian army. The members of the same *phyle* served together, and were further subdivided according to demes. *Cf.* Isaeus, ii. 42. *E.g.* at the battle of Marathon, the tribe Aeantis held the right wing. Plutarch, *Quaest. Conv.* 628.

that the responsibility may be put where it belongs. Agamemnon accepts this advice at once, with the significant
remark that if he had ten such advisers as Nestor, the city
of Priam would soon bow its head. Clearly the suggestion
was accepted as novel; the system which it contemplates
cannot have been general or universal.[1] At the first advance
of the Achaean army, each leader seems to be with his own
forces (Γ 1); Idomeneus is found with the Cretans (Γ 230),
Odysseus with the Cephallenians, and Diomed with the
Argives (Δ 251 ff.); but even here the two Ajaxes are
together, without mention of their men,—the Salaminians
and the Locrians (Δ 273), and indeed the Salaminians and
Locrians are mentioned only in the Catalogue of the
Ships and in a single passage in the thirteenth book of the
Iliad (N 686-712). Swift Iris, messenger of the gods, in
the guise of a son of Priam, gives to Hector (B 803 ff.)
advice similar to that of Nestor to Agamemnon,—that each
chieftain of his allies should command his own countrymen.
The enumeration of the Trojan forces follows (B 816 ff.),
making Hector the leader of the Trojans, Aeneas the
commander of the Dardanians, the "shaggy heart of
Pylaemenes" leader of the Paphlagonians, Sarpedon commander of the Lycians, etc. But this division is inconsistent
with that which appears in the Trojan attack on the
Achaean camp on the third day of battle (M 86), when
the Trojans advance in five sections (which division in turn
is neglected in the progress of the assault), as well as with
most of the rest of the story, in which no definite arrangement of the Trojans and their allies is recognized.

Councils of the "elders" or chiefs of the army before
Troy are held (B 53, K 195, *cf.* Ω 651), but so far as
can be seen, these discuss no particular plans of
campaign or of battle; they consider a proposal
to end the war, a truce for the burial of the dead,
Councils of War.
the placation of Achilles, the sending of a spy into the
Trojan camp, the building of a wall about the Achaean

---

[1] This passage does not easily admit the explanation that for the poet's purposes
(see pp. 572, 579), this first battle of the *Iliad* was the first battle of the war. At
least the poet seems familiar with wars in which such a division was unknown.
The praise given to Nestor for his suggestion would have been absurd if every
boy among the poet's hearers knew that this division was usual.

camp,—but not whether or how an attack shall be made or met. Perhaps the position of a contingent in the line of ships, as these were drawn up on the strand, might be thought to determine the arrangement of the Achaean forces as they advanced into battle ; but the order in which Agamemnon reaches the several contingents in his review of the Achaean line (Δ 251) agrees neither with the rest of the story of the *Iliad*, nor with the arrangement in the Catalogue of Ships (B 484 ff.) ; the last is geographical, while in the first the Athenians stand near the Cephallenians.

No flags or standards are used to designate and form the rallying centre of forces, and the commander-in-chief has no designated place in the fray, any more *No Standards or Head- quarters.* than the lesser chieftains ; he has no head- quarters,—neither at the centre as in the Persian army, nor on the right wing as in the Greek armies.

The word *phalanx* is used often (*e.g.* E 591), but the Homeric phalanxes were not of the Spartan or Macedonian *"Phalanx."* order. They knew no command to follow their file-leader, nor to "keep step," and do not seem to have been in every case (or perhaps, generally) particular divisions (*e.g.* P 285), though a technical expression was to "break the phalanx," *i.e.* the line, of the enemy (Z 6). On one occasion Hector was unable to break the ranks of the Achaeans, since these stood firmly joined (ἀρηρότες, *cf.* M 105) as a tower or rock, which withstands the assaults of winds and of waves (O 618). The rhetorician Alcidamas, in his *Contest of Homer and Hesiod*, represents Homer as repeating as his noblest verses a passage from the thirteenth book of the *Iliad* which indicates a phalanx : "About the two Ajaxes stood the phalanxes,—mighty phalanxes which neither Ares nor Athena, the rouser of the soldiery, would scorn ; for the chosen bravest awaited the Trojans and god-like Hector, resting spear on spear, and shield on well-layered shield. Buckler pressed on buckler, helmet on helmet, man on man. And their crests of horsehair touched with their bright plumes as they nodded. So close did they stand. And their spears were bent (literally *folded*) by their bold hands, as they were shaken. And these pressed straight forward, and were eager to fight " (N 126). Achilles divides his contingent of 2,500 men into five battalions, as he sends them with Patroclus into battle,— each battalion under one officer,—"and these stood closely fitted as the stones in the wall of a house,"—but even here no captains, lieutenants, or subaltern officers are mentioned or assumed (Π 168). How deep the lines were, is nowhere indicated by the poet. The columns of the army are called *towers* ($\pi\acute{v}\rho\gamma o\iota$, Δ 334). The forward movement of phalanxes, close and bristling with shields and spears, is compared to that of clouds driven by the west wind (Δ 275), or to that of waves of the sea, with one following another (N 800), while the Trojan flight before Diomed is compared to the destruction of dikes and enclosure-walls by a mountain torrent (E 87). Yet the order of the lines of battle must have been very loose, for constantly single leaders and chariots advance from the throng, and soon again retreat into the throng. To suppose that the several divisions of the army were kept in moderately close order, but that a clear space[1] was maintained between the different columns out of which clear space the champions advanced, and into which they again withdrew, is contrary to the whole impression of the poems, and would not have been imagined if it had not been for the evil habit of accepting Homeric words in Attic meanings.

Around the body of Patroclus gather warriors who form a screen about him on every side with their shields, and hold forward their spears (P 354). "Fewer of these fall than of the Trojans, for they act together." This again looks like a Macedonian phalanx ; but it was formed on the spur of the moment,—it was not an already existing body of troops which

---

[1] Some scholars have believed these intercolumnar spaces to be what the poet means by the "bridges" or dikes of war (*e.g.* Δ 371, Λ 160, Υ 427), but this expression seems to be explained better as the space between the two hostile armies, the surging tide of warriors on either side being likened to a raging sea or river. For an interesting example of the formation in columns with spaces between, see Xenophon's *Anabasis*, iv. 8. 10. But such a column would have been a "phalanx" in Homer's time, though Xenophon distinctly contrasts the two formations. Later readers naturally gave the later special meaning of the term to Homer's word.

took this position. The men who form it may never before have stood together in this order. This is "team-work," rather than "individual play," on the part of the Achaeans, but it is not a Macedonian phalanx. The reader, however, must not understand that no lines were ever formed on the Trojan plain, and that all fought in absolute confusion, but only that the armies knew no permanent divisions, and the lines which were formed were temporary organizations. At times the poet's picture is not quite distinct in its indications of formations of the troops, formulaic material which implied one kind of contest being combined with other material which assumed another manner of conflict.

Nestor and Menestheus, the leader of the Athenian forces, were the most noted for their skill as "marshals of men" (B 553). Nestor's principle of arrangement was *Nestor's Arrangement.* famous throughout antiquity: he put the chariots (which meant the chieftains)[1] first, then the worthless rabble, and behind these the best and bravest of the infantry (Δ 297). Thus the cowards were not allowed to remain in the rear and shirk, when their comrades advanced to the fray. Nestor added the injunction to "keep in line," neither advancing nor retreating too far,—but we have seen that this is not to be interpreted according to modern standards. Aristophanes probably refers to the example and precept of Nestor when he represents Aeschylus as saying that Homer is honored for teaching the arming and marshalling of men (*Frogs,* 1036).

The battles, then, were decided for the most part by a succession of single combats between heavy-armed men, though occasionally a group of two or three on a side would oppose a similar group on the other, and still less frequently a mass of men would hurl themselves upon the forces of the enemy. No other of the Achaeans interferes in the conflict between Achilles and Hector (X 131 ff.),—indeed Achilles motions to the rest to stand aloof, that he may have all the glory of Hector's defeat and death (X 205); and the fight between Hector and Patroclus may fairly be called a single-combat,

---

[1] Some scholars believe that here the poet had in mind chariots like those of Egypt and Asia, on which the warrior stood to fight. See page 350 f.

although Apollo and Euphorbus interfere against Patroclus (Π 731 ff.).

A typical example of the champion is presented in Paris, as the two armies advance for battle on the first day of conflict : " Now when these were near, advancing upon each other, the godlike Alexander stood forth as champion for the Trojans, with a leopard skin upon his shoulders, and a bent bow and *Single Combat of Menelaus and Paris.* a sword ; and, brandishing two spears, he challenged all the bravest of the Achaeans to fight against him in dire conflict. But when Menelaus perceived him advancing with long strides, in front of the throng,—as a lion rejoices in coming upon a great carcase, a horned stag or a wild goat, when he is hungry (for he devours it eagerly, even though the swift hounds and the vigorous hunters press him hard), so Menelaus rejoiced when his eyes beheld the godlike Alexander, for he thought to punish the evil-doer ; and straightway from his chariot he leaped to the ground. But when the godlike Alexander perceived Menelaus appearing among the foremost fighters, his dear heart was dismayed, and he shrank back into the throng of his comrades, avoiding death." (Γ 15 ff.) Similarly, near the close of the last battle of the *Iliad*, Hector urges forward the Trojans, and promises to go to meet Achilles, but is warned by Apollo not to stand forth in front of the rest as a champion, but in the ranks and in the midst of the throng to await Achilles's attack (Υ 365). That the war should be decided by a single-combat, a duel, between Menelaus and Paris, the two husbands of Helen, who was the source of all the trouble, is not unreasonable. This might have been expected at the very outset of the war, but the poet places it at the opening of his first day of battle, which was the beginning of the war for his story.[1] Ashamed before the rebuke of Hector, Paris says to him : " Cause the other Trojans and all the Achaeans to be seated, and bring together me and Menelaus dear to Ares, between both armies, to fight for Helen and

---

[1] With this device may be compared Nestor's advice for the division of the troops (Β 362 ff.), and Priam's ignorance of the Greek leaders (Γ 161 ff.), to which reference has been made, and for which another explanation has been suggested (pp. 572, 575).

all her possessions. Whichever of us is victorious, and proves himself the mightier, let him take all the treasures and Helen, and carry them home; but do ye others, making friendship and a faithful truce, dwell in the fertile land of Troy, while these others return to horse-feeding Argos and Achaea famed for fair women." (Γ 68 ff.) This duel had no decisive result, since the goddess Aphrodite snatched away her favourite, Paris, just as he was about to be killed by Menelaus, and conveyed him secretly to his home. The Achaeans then claimed the victory,—but this was not strictly proven since the body of Paris could not be shown, and soon, incited by the goddess Athena, who was determined that the war should not end before the destruction of Troy, the archer Pandarus, a Trojan ally, shot an arrow at Menelaus and wounded him. This flagrant breach of the truce at once set the Achaean army again in motion against the Trojans, and the general battle began.

Another single-combat which seems to be a sort of echo of the former, is fought at the close of the same day
Hector and Ajax. of battle. Hector challenges the bravest of the Achaeans to fight against him, and is met by Telamonian Ajax. But no question of moment would have been decided by the conflict if it had been fought to a bitter end, and at last it is interrupted by the oncoming of night, after blood has been drawn from Hector; the two separate on good terms,—Hector giving his sword to Ajax, and receiving from him a belt bright with purple, as a gift of friendship (H 67 ff.).

As the conflicts on the plain of Troy may be compared in general to those of the forces of David and Saul with
Cf. David and Goliath. the Philistines, so no better illustration can be given for Paris's proposition for a single-combat with Menelaus, which should decide the issue of the war, than the challenge of Goliath of Gath: "'Why are ye come out to set your battle in array? Am not I a Philistine, and ye servants to Saul? Choose you a man for you, and let him come down to me. If he be able to fight with me and to kill me, then will we be your servants; but if I prevail against him and kill him, then shall ye be our servants, and serve us.' And the

Philistine said, ' I defy the armies of Israel this day ; give me a man that we may fight together.' " (1 *Sam.* xvii. 8-10.) Goliath's first rhetorical question means simply, that a conflict of armies is unnecessary, since the issue of the war may be decided by a single-combat. The quarrel between the Achaeans and the Trojans was based on a personal wrong done by Paris to Menelaus, and might have been decided by these two. The challenge of Hector in the seventh book, however,—a challenge which aimed at nothing more than the determination of individual prowess,—resembles more closely that of a knight of the age of chivalry, and his duel with Ajax has been compared to a modern German students' duel, which is interrupted by the first flow of blood, after which the combatants shake hands and separate.

A less formal challenge to single-combat is given by Diomed to Glaucus on the first day of battle, in an episode which, as we have seen, fills the time of Hector's absence from the field when he goes to the city *Diomed and Glaucus.* in order to bid the Trojan matrons offer a special vow to Athena,—" Who art thou of mortal men ? Never before have I seen thee in the man-ennobling battle." To which the answer is given : " Great-hearted son of Tydeus, why dost thou ask of my race ? As is the race of leaves, such also is the race of men." (Z 123 ff.)

Similar single-combats will be remembered from later literature, and in the stories of other peoples. In Herodotus (ix. 26) the Tegeatan commander tells of the mythical combat between Hyllus, the leader of *Other Single-Combats.* the Heraclidae, and the chief of the Peloponnesian forces. All readers are familiar with the conflict of the Horatii and the Curatii, for the determination of the quarrel between the Romans and the Albans (Livy, i. 24 f.), and the same historian's " pictured page " tells us of a much later single-combat between the Roman leader and a Gallic chieftain.[1] Not far from the beginning of the sixth century B.C., Pittacus, the ruler of Mytilene, was challenged to single-combat by Phrynon, leader of the opposing Athenian forces,

[1] For Celtic single-combats, see D'Arbois de Dubainville, *La Civilisation des Celtes*, pp. 5 ff.

and the conflict received notoriety only because Pittacus threw a fisherman's net over his antagonist, and slew him while he was entangled therein. Apparently this caused a charge of foul play, for the single-combat did not decide the war (Strabo, p. 600).

The three main branches of the Homeric army were those of later times,—horsemen (on chariots), spearmen, and light-armed troops with bows and slings. Engineers, sappers and miners, signal-men, and the like, are unknown to the poet.

Three Branches of the Army.

The archers and the slingers, though they seem to have been far more numerous than the spearmen, were of little real importance in the battle. They stood in the rear of the heavy-armed troops, and served only as reinforcements to them. They never advanced by themselves, nor withstood an attack. The sling, indeed, is mentioned but twice, and that in the same book of the *Iliad*, and some scholars have believed that the expression, instead of meaning sling, signifies bandage in one place, and bow-string in the other, although no reason exists for doubting the use of the sling in Homeric times: it is a primitive weapon. Menelaus wounded the hand of Priam's son Helenus, but the Trojan Agenor " bound up the arm with the well-twisted fleece of a sheep, with the sling (σφενδόνη, N 600) which a comrade held"; and the Locrians, we are told, came to Troy, " trusting to their bows and the well-twisted fleece of the sheep" (N 716). "So these shooting from the rear escaped notice," the poet goes on to say, " nor did the Trojans have any thought of fighting, for the arrows drove them in confusion" (N 721). The last-quoted passage is the most distinct and emphatic of all evidence for the occasional effectiveness of the light-armed troops, which as a rule are disregarded in the Homeric account of a fray, and, partly on this ground, it has been suspected of being of later composition. That the masses of the hostile armies generally kept at a fairly safe distance from each other, must be remembered for the proper understanding of many incidents in the Homeric story.

Slingers.

In addition to the forty ship-loads of Locrians, the 350

companions of Philoctetes (B 720) are designated expressly as archers among the Achaean forces, and the Thracian Paeonians on the Trojan side (B 848). But nothing indicates that most of the rest also were *Bowmen.* not bowmen. Certainly the comrades of Achilles, during the time of his quarrel with Agamemnon, amuse themselves with shooting at a mark (B 775), and when Hector advances in order to present the challenge of Paris, many Achaeans bend their bows at him (Γ 79).

Only two of the Achaean chieftains use the bow in the action of the *Iliad*,—Teucer, the half-brother of Telamonian Ajax (Θ 266), and Meriones the Cretan leader, who kills with an arrow the son of the Paphla- *Chieftains as Archers.* gonian king (N 650). Of these, Meriones appears elsewhere regularly as a spearman, and as a bowman only here and in the contest of archery in the funeral games in honor of Patroclus (Ψ 860); while Teucer is also both able and willing to use the spear as well as the bow (*cf.* " Teucer, best of the Achaeans with the bow, and brave also in the hand-to-hand conflict," N 314), and when his bowstring breaks, he takes spear and shield (O 472). Teucer, in the earlier conflicts, remains by the side of his brother Ajax, " creeping back as a child to its mother, after shooting his arrow," and is protected by this brother's great shield (Θ 269),—just as in later times, according to Tyrtaeus (ix. 35), the light-armed troops were directed to stand under cover of the hoplites' shields, and just as archers and spear-men are found together on a Mycenaean vase. Teucer evidently is attached to no special company or division, and when his bowstring breaks, he fetches his spear, and returns to stand by his brother's side. He might have put a new string on his bow, but he was out of humor with shooting; the string which had just broken had been put on fresh that very morning, and had broken only because of the ill-will of the gods. In the *Odyssey*, Odysseus tells the Phaeacians of his skilful use of the bow on the plain of Troy (θ 215), and he makes good use of this power at the close of the poem, in killing Penelope's suitors (χ 1 ff.), but in the story of the *Iliad* he is only a spearman. In the Trojan army, Paris (Γ 17, Λ 369), his brother Helenus

(N 583), and Pandarus (Δ 88), are named as archers, but they are also spearmen, and Paris uses the spear in his single-combat with Menelaus. The poet does not seem to regard the bowman as necessarily less brave than the spearman, as was true in later times, nor does he, like Aeschylus (*cf.* the *Persians, passim*), think of the Asiatics as archers in contrast to the Greek spearmen. Was not Apollo, the god of war, a bowman, and his sister Artemis an archer (ἰοχέαιρα)? Did not Heracles vie with the gods themselves in archery (θ 225)? In later story the bow of Heracles in the hands of Philoctetes was of importance for the capture of Troy. In the *Odyssey* (λ 607), the ghost of Heracles has his bow (or the ghost of his bow) with him in Hades; and in the fifth ode of Bacchylides, Heracles in Hades, on his descent to bring up Cerberus, is about to shoot at the ghost of Meleager. Certainly Odysseus was proud of his archery (θ 219), and Teucer, with arrows from his "mighty bow," bringing the Trojans to the ground in quick succession (Θ 274 ff.), is not thought to be a mean warrior. Yet several words for the heavy-armed man, as "spearman" (αἰχμητής, X 269), "shield-bearer" (ἀσπιστής, Δ 90), "fighter-in-the-hand-to-hand-conflict," distinctly connote bravery.[1]

The brunt of the battle, then, was borne by the heavy-armed soldier, the later *hoplite*, in the Homeric period as well as in the historical times of Greece, although the proportion of these troops to the light-armed forces may have been even smaller before Troy than in Athens and Sparta at the time of the Peloponnesian war. In the hand-to-hand conflict (σταδίη ὑσμίνη, N 314), the warrior was wont to hurl his spear against a foeman who stood a rod or two away from him, and then profit by the confusion which his spear had caused, to rush forward and recover his weapon, which evidently must be regained, or the warrior would be nearly helpless, being deprived of his most important weapon of attack. Thus at N 532, Meriones recovers his spear, drawing it from the thick of the arm of Deïphobus, whom he had wounded. If

Hoplite bore Brunt of Battle.

---

[1] Compare also ἀγχέμαχοι, Π 272; ἀγχιμαχηταί, B 604; ἀσπιδιῶται, B 554; ἐγχεσίμωροι, H 134; ἐγχέσπαλοι, B 131; σακέσπαλος, E 126.

the warrior slew his antagonist by this cast of his spear, he endeavored to despoil him of his armor, or even to drag the corpse itself within the lines of his own army, and to gain possession of his chariot. The fiercest conflicts arose over the bodies of fallen warriors, whose friends desired to give them honorable burial, and whose foes would treat them with despite, and give them like the body of Jezebel to the dogs to devour. The dying Sarpedon beseeches his comrade Glaucus to gather the Lycians and fight about him ; it would be a disgrace and shame to Glaucus if the Achaeans should strip the armor from his friend's body (Π 492) ; and, a little later, Glaucus urges Hector to secure the body of the fallen Patroclus, that this may be exchanged for Sarpedon's armor and Sarpedon's corpse (P 160). The combatants sometimes stop to secure the spoils (*e.g.* Λ 246) at a time when we wonder at such an interruption of the battle, and Nestor gives the distinct command to disregard the spoils, which can be gathered after the conflict is over (Z 68). Thus also at O 347, Hector bids the Trojans to pass towards the ships and disregard the spoils. To remove the armor, as a trophy, from the slain, was so customary that this verb ($\dot{\epsilon}\xi\epsilon\nu\alpha\rho\dot{\iota}\zeta\omega$, *e.g.* Z 30) came to be used as the equivalent of to *kill*. That a foe should receive the rites of burial with his armor, was a rare exception, and a mark of great distinction (Z 418).

If the warrior's cast of his spear, on the other hand, failed of its desired effect, the two warriors would rush together with their swords, or even with stones (as H 258 ff.) ; or perhaps the one might escape *If the Spear Failed.* while the other was chasing his spear (as Λ 357). But often a very speedy retreat was necessary, if the cast of the spear was ineffectual, or if the enemy gathered in a group against a single man. For this series of operations much agility was required, and speed of foot was a much prized quality. With reference to such quick movements, Hector calls the combat a " dance in honor of Ares " (H 241). One of the most frequent epithets of Achilles is " swift-footed " ($\pi\dot{o}\delta\alpha\varsigma$ $\dot{\omega}\kappa\dot{v}\varsigma$, thirty times, and $\pi o\delta\dot{\alpha}\rho\kappa\eta\varsigma$, twenty-one times), and his friend Antilochus is praised by his father as " exceeding swift in running and a good fighter " (γ 112). Odysseus and Ajax, the son of Oïleus, are other swift runners among the Achaeans (Ψ 754 ff.), while, among the Trojans, Priam's young son Polydorus (Υ 410) and the Dardanian Euphorbus (Π 809) are noted for their speed. All of these were spearmen, not light-equipped warriors. The speed was needed naturally for the pursuit of a fleeing foe but agility was convenient in every combat.

The number of Achaeans in the army on the plain of Troy before the walls of Ilium, is nowhere definitely stated

Number of Achaeans.

by the poet. In fact, Alcidamas, a rhetorician of the fourth century B.C. who composed a " Contest ('Αγών) of Homer and Hesiod," represents Hesiod as asking his rival, as one of his most puzzling questions, " How many Greeks went against Ilium ? " The answer is given in the concluding words of the eighth book of the *Iliad*: " A thousand fires were burning on the plain, and fifty men sat in the light of each fire,"—but these were Trojans and their allies. According to the Catalogue of Ships in the second book of the *Iliad*, 1186 ships came from Greece with Agamemnon. Some of these, as those of the Boeotians, bore each one hundred and twenty men (B 510); others, as those of Achilles (Π 170) and of Philoctetes (B 719), brought each but fifty men. In round numbers the ships were reckoned by the ancients as twelve hundred, and the men (taking a rough average) as one hundred thousand. But if the Catalogue of the Ships be left out of account, as being one of the latest elements of the poems, as we have seen, only few and slight indications remain that the Greeks numbered more than ten thousand or even than five thousand men.[1] The enumeration of the troops of Achilles which assigns to him 2500 men (Π 168 ff.), has reasonably been suspected of being a late addition to the Catalogue of the Ships.

The Achaeans before Troy were all fighting men. The warriors themselves rowed and managed the boats which bore them across the Aegean ; in only one passage is the presence in the camp of " steersmen and stewards " indicated (T 43). The leaders were not attended by " body-servants " ;

[1] The only statement with regard to the number of the Trojans is at Θ 562, quoted above, in this paragraph.

they were accustomed to provide for their own ordinary wants, securing food and shelter for themselves, and they were aided by their faithful squires and heralds, *Achaeans all* who also were fighting men. The Myrmidons *Fighters.* built for their chieftain Achilles a high hut with beams of pine, and they roofed it with thatch from the meadows (Ω 449); and Achilles on going out to battle to avenge the death of Patroclus, recalls to mind how often this comrade had placed food before him as they were making ready for other combats (T 315). When Achilles, "sulking in his tent," is visited by the embassy sent by the Achaeans, begging him to return to the fight, he and his comrade Patroclus themselves cook the meat of hospitality, and serve it to their guests. No one else seems to be in Achilles's quarters at that time, and the details of the cooking are given (I 206 ff.).

The poet says that the Trojans were far fewer than the Achaeans (Θ 56). Agamemnon is made to declare that the Achaeans are more than ten times as numerous *Number of* as the native Trojans,—saying that if the Greeks *Trojans.* should be arranged in squads or messes of ten, and a Trojan assigned as cup-bearer to each mess, the Trojans would not be enough to supply these cup-bearers (B 126). But allies have come to Troy not only from the neighboring cities, but also from Lycia and from Thrace. At the close of the third day of battle, the poet tells how the Greeks are driven within their entrenchments, and the Trojans bivouac on the plain,—with a thousand fires, and fifty men about each, as quoted above. But such words of the poet are not to be pressed as if he were a military historian, or were making a formal report to a superior officer.

Of the enlistment of the Achaean forces for the expedition against Troy, we know little. Nestor reminds Patroclus that he and Agamemnon went to Phthia (Λ 776) to *Enlistment of* engage Achilles and Patroclus for the expedition, *Achaeans.* and says in another passage (H 127) that the old knight Peleus rejoiced greatly in hearing of the race and parentage of the men with whom his son was to be associated,—that he was to be a comrade of the sons of his own old comrades, Tydeus, Peleus, and the rest. In the so-called Second Nekyia (ω 115), the shade of Agamemnon, meeting the ghosts of Penelope's suitors as they troop to the realm of Hades, recognizes Amphimedon, since he had been at his house when he and Menelaus visited Ithaca to secure the aid of Odysseus. The poet is ignorant of the later stories that Odysseus[1] needed to be forced into the army by a trick of Palamedes, and that Achilles was concealed by his parents in the family of Lycomedes on the island of Scyrus, where his presence and identity were discovered by the device of displaying arms before the young people. Hera asks Zeus if he would render vain her sweat, and the toil of her horses, in gathering the Achaean army (Δ 26), thus indicating the active part which she had taken in the enlistment of the forces. Hermes, assuming the guise of a comrade of Achilles, as he convoys Priam to the Greek camp for the ransom of Hector's body, tells the old king that he is one of seven brothers, and was chosen by lot among them to accompany the expedition (Ω 400). Apparently each family was required to furnish one member of the expedition, but not more than one. If this is true, then the many brothers of the Achaeans came strictly as volunteers, for the enjoyment of the contest, for glory in what was to them man's highest employment, and perhaps some patriotic interest in the cause of Agamemnon, and also a share in the spoils. We read (B 832 ff.) of two sons of an old seer who forbade them to go from Percote to the help of the Trojans, since he knew the death which awaited them; but "the fates of black death led them on." That some obligation for military service was imposed on the Greeks is seen from N 669: Euchenor, son of Polyidus, a Corinthian seer, came against Troy, although his father warned him of the death which awaited him there,—avoiding ill-health (which would befall him at home, according to the seer's prediction) "and the grievous fine of the Achaeans," *i.e.* the penalty which these would have imposed for lack of service. Of Echepolus of Sicyon we learn that he gave to Agamemnon a mare (Aethé, which runs in the races in

---

[1] This story with regard to Odysseus was clearly born in an age when his unworthy shiftiness was contrasted with the straightforward bravery of Achilles,— as it is in the Attic drama, in which Odysseus is made contemptible.

honor of Patroclus) in order that he " might remain at home and enjoy his wealth " (Ψ 298), *i.e.* he pays a price in lieu of personal service in the field to his liege lord. The gift of a cuirass to Agamemnon by Cinyras of Cyprus (Λ 20), is the less intelligible because Cyprus seems to be out of the sphere of influence of any king of Mycenae. We are reminded also that Cyprus does not appear in the other lays of the *Iliad*, and that the Greeks of the Mycenaean age wore no cuirass.

The most remote of the allies of the Trojans are the Lycians under the command of Sarpedon and Glaucus, and the Thracians. Sarpedon speaks of the service which the allies rendered, as being free and un- *Motives of Trojan Allies.* rewarded (E 478), but Hector on the other hand refers to the Trojans as exhausted by supplying food and gifts to their allies (P 225, Σ 288). Doubtless no definite pay was given to allies in war, as indeed none seems to be given to hired helpers in time of peace, but gifts were supposed to take the place of pay. In the Achaean army, the booty from marauding expeditions supplied irregular rewards for the soldiery, but the Trojans had no such spoils, since they were not living in an enemy's country. In a simple and unreflective community, men seem more ready than in modern times to risk their lives and give of their substance for others. The tie of common interest to hold fast the alliance between the Trojans and the Lycians or the Thracians, does not seem to have been very strong. The allies were moved by general good-will and sympathy for Troy, rather than by the thought of common interest in the war. Thus in the previous generation the people of Mycenae were minded to aid Polynices against Thebes (Δ 376) without thought of either personal grievance, " balance of power," or Hellenic peace ; his cause aroused their sympathy, simply since he was thought to be wronged by his brother Eteocles. Similarly the gifts which were bestowed on Menelaus in foreign lands (δ 90, 125 ff.), and represented as given to the fictitious Odysseus (ξ 323), were more generous than a modern traveller and wanderer would expect, not to speak of the rich gifts of raiment and gold bestowed on Odysseus by the Phaeacians (ν 10 ff.).

Thucydides (i. 9) thinks that the Greeks followed Agamemnon not so much out of favor as from fear; he was
the most powerful ruler of his time in Greece;
Agamemnon's and the study of archaeology, too, shows that the
Authority. potentate of Mycenae was more powerful than
any ruler of the poet's own time.   The king whose subjects
built for him the fortress and tombs of Mycenae must have
been an absolute monarch.   Thucydides calls attention also
to the fact that the Achaeans came to Troy without any
elaborate equipment for war, and to the general lack of
material resources (ἀχρηματία) of the heroic age,—saying that
Agamemnon took with him only so large a force as he
hoped would support itself from the enemy's country, and
that after the Greeks had established themselves before the
city, they did not use all their troops in war, but from lack
of other supplies turned to till the soil of the Chersonese
(of which the poet knows nothing) and to marauding
expeditions.   He goes on to remark that this scattering of
the Achaean forces, for agriculture and for booty, explains
the long duration of the war, which might have been brought
to a conclusion much sooner if a close siege had been
maintained.   Surely battles so bloody as those of the *Iliad*
were not fought daily or weekly for nine years, or else
both armies would have been exhausted.

The battles on the plain are intended only to weaken
the power of the Trojans.   The Achaeans make no attempt
to take the city either by storm or by a close
Neither siege; and, indeed since the ancient city-walls
Storm have been laid bare by the excavations of the last
thirty years, we see plainly that without engines of war, and
projectiles more powerful than bows, an assailing army would
suffer much and accomplish little.   Andromache reminds
Hector (Z 433 ff.) that on three occasions the sons of
Atreus with Diomed, Idomeneus, and the two Ajaxes, had
assailed the city " by the wild-fig tree "; but this passage
was rejected by Aristarchus, and seems to have been composed under the influence of the later story which made
Aeacus an associate of Apollo and Poseidon in building the
walls of Troy (Pindar, *Ol.* viii. 40).   The confidence of the
Trojan Pulydamas is fully intelligible,—that " if Achilles

shall desire to come from the camp and fight about the wall of the city, he will weary his horses, but will not sack the town" (Σ 278). The poet's statement with regard to Patroclus is not to be taken literally, near the close of the third day of battle (Π 698 ff.): "Then would the sons of the Achaeans have taken high-gated Troy by the hands of Patroclus, for he raged about before it with his spear, unless Phoebus Apollo had taken his stand on the well-built tower, planning death for him, and aid for the Trojans. Thrice Patroclus set his foot on the corner of the high wall, and thrice Apollo thrust him off, striking his bright shield with his immortal hands," but when Patroclus rushed upon the wall for the fourth time, Apollo warned him off. Even if Patroclus had been left to himself, he could not easily have scaled the wall of Troy, though this wall is not every-where vertical, and a vigorous man if unmolested might climb up a score of feet.

The siege of Troy certainly was not close according to modern standards. From the first, the Trojans had accepted the defensive method of warfare, and Hector complains that the elders of the city had been *nor close Siege.* blindly infatuated in their course,—he insisting that now when the gods have granted to him to gain glory by the ships, the Trojans shall not return to the city to be cooped up within the walls (O 719, Σ 293). The allies of the Trojans, as well, seem to be quartered in the town ; they have no camp on the plain corresponding to that of the Achaeans, and when they are driven in flight by the Greeks, they retire within the wall of the city. Achilles himself says that while he was in the fight, Hector came only to the Scaean Gate and the oak-tree (I 352). Yet at night the Achaeans withdraw to their camp, three or four miles from the city-walls, and the people of the city are free to open their gates for the entrance of supplies and friends, and for the departure of those who care to go. The Trojans still have some flocks and herds pasturing on the mountains,[1] and they visit the fields and forests in order to obtain wood, although they are obliged to abandon the

---

[1] Achilles once captured two sons of Priam as they were tending their sheep on the foot-hills of Mount Ida (Λ 104 ff.).

use of the stone washing-troughs by the sources of the Scamander, " where the wives of the Trojans and their fair daughters were wont to wash their gleaming raiment, formerly, in time of peace, before the sons of the Achaeans came " (X 154). No attempt is made by the Achaeans to cut off the city's supplies of food and of water. But the wealth of the Trojans is gradually exhausted, and they cannot long continue to maintain the defensive attitude ; they must drive the enemy from the land, or yield. Hence, though fewer in number, they come forth to fight (Θ 55). Their families are safe for the present behind the city-walls, but the pressure of discomfort and shame is too heavy to bear indefinitely.

Only once does the poet refer to an Achaean ambuscade by night under the walls of the city (ξ 469), and nothing comes of this. In general, the Greeks of all times were not fond of fighting by night ; the Ten Thousand with Xenophon generally encamped at a safe distance from the enemy,—of their own preference, surely, although the Asiatics, even more than they, disliked a battle in the darkness. But forays and sallies at such a time might be successful, as they were on the visit of Odysseus and Diomed to the Trojan camp under cover of darkness (K 272 ff.), and when Achilles by night captured Priam's son Lycaon, as the latter was cutting scions of a wild-fig tree for a chariot-rim (Φ 36).

The most direct statement with regard to the forays of the Achaeans is contained in Achilles's reply to the embas-

Forays of Achaeans.

sadors who were sent by his former comrades to beg him to return to the fight : " I spent many sleepless nights, and passed bloody days in battle, fighting with men on account of their wives. Twelve cities of men I sacked with my ships, and eleven by land on the fertile Troad. From all these I took many goodly treasures, and brought them all and gave them to Agamemnon, son of Atreus. And he remaining behind, in the camp, by the swift ships, received the treasures and distributed a few, but kept many." (I 325.) On another occasion, near the opening of the poem, Achilles says to Agamemnon : " Never have I a prize equal to thine when the Achaeans sack a well-built city of the Trojans ;

but though my hands do the greater part of the work of war, if ever a division of the spoil comes, thy prize is far greater than mine" (A 163). Nestor, in telling Telemachus of the hardships of the Achaeans before Troy, is reminded of all that they "suffered, in wandering for booty with their ships, over the misty sea, wherever Achilles led the way" (γ 105).

Before the general division of the spoils, a suitable prize or gift of honor (γέρας) was set apart for each chieftain. Thus Odysseus, in the realm of Hades, tells the shade of Achilles with regard to the latter's son Neoptolemus, that after the capture of Troy he embarked upon his ship for home unharmed, with his "share of the booty, and a goodly gift of honor" (λ 534, cf. ξ 232). So the Greeks set aside the fair-tressed Hecamede from the spoils of Tenedos, as a prize of honor for old Nestor, because he surpassed all others in counsel (Λ 627). Of other definite articles which were spoils in war, the poet says little; but the lyre with which Achilles is cheering his soul when he receives the embassy of the Achaeans, and one of his horses, were part of the spoil of Thebes (I 188, II 153), and we may suppose the gifts which Agamemnon offers him in order to placate his angry spirit, also, to have been part of the booty of war,—seven tripods, ten pieces of gold, twenty basins, and twelve strong horses, as well as seven Lesbian captive women "skilled in blameless works" (I 122). The cattle captured in the forays of the army before Troy must have been kept in or near the Achaean camp, but no allusion is made to them, except when an animal is to be killed (as Ω 621), or to be exchanged for wine, as at the close of the seventh book of the *Iliad*, or where the horses given by Agamemnon to Achilles are "driven to the herd" (T 281). In the *Ajax* of Sophocles (53), the poet follows the story that the hero maddened by disappointment at not receiving the arms of Achilles, attacked the captive herds and flocks, imagining these to be his hated rivals.

The spoils taken from the slain in the battles on the Trojan plain, were of course the private property of the individual victor. Idomeneus says to ˏMeriones with much

Prizes of Honor.

satisfaction that whether he wants one or twenty spears, he will find them standing against the wall at the entrance to his barrack,—spears which he had taken from the Trojans,—and with the spears were shields and helmets (N 260). These were very tangible tokens of the chieftain's bravery, and as such have been likened to the North American Indian's collection of scalps, though somewhat less gruesome. But Nestor urges the Achaeans not to tarry for the spoils in the midst of the battle, but to press on in pursuit of the fleeing enemy (Z 68), and Hector gives a similar command to the Trojans (O 347). To refrain from stripping the slain warrior of his weapons, we have seen already, was a very unusual exertion of self-restraint, and a token of high respect for the dead. Andromache notes as a particularly generous act on the part of Achilles, that he did not despoil her father Eëtion, but buried him with his arms (Z 418); and Zeus was not pleased that Hector took the spoils from the body of Patroclus (P 205). Hector's own prayer for his infant son, however, is that men may say of him " Far braver he than his father," as he returns from the battle, and that he may gladden his mother's heart by bringing back the bloody spoils (Z 479 f.).

Spoils of War.

Little is said of the spoil from Troy itself; the Ithacans return empty-handed (κ 42). The disguised Odysseus, however, tells a made-up story, representing himself to be a Cretan who had slain a fellow-countryman who had desired to deprive him of his share in the Trojan booty (ν 262). The ordinary principle of distribution is seen in the division of the flocks of Polyphemus, the Cyclops, when the ram is granted as a gift of honor to Odysseus (ι 550), and the rest of the sheep are allotted to the ships (*cf.* ι 160), *i.e.* some object of special value is given to the leader personally, and the rest of the booty is divided equally among all. A commander at times encourages to a daring action by the offer of a special prize or part of the booty (Θ 289, P 229).

Spoils from Troy.

As in historical times, a part of the spoil from the enemy is consecrated to the gods. Thus Hector, if successful in the single-combat, proposes to hang the armor of Ajax on the temple of Apollo in Ilium (H 83), and Odysseus dedicates to Athena the spoils which he had taken from Dolon (K 570 ff.). No trophies of the later Hellenic fashion are known to Homer. *Dedication to Gods.*

The gate or gates of the Achaean camp do not seem to have been made for the passage of troops in line. So far as we can speak of a line of battle, it was formed on the Trojan side of the wall. Corresponding to the gate, a gap must have been left in the line of palisades in the trench, and a place or *Gates of Achaean Camp.* places where the banks of the trench were less steep than at others, since no indication is given of a bridge across the moat.

The Greek wall is said to be lowest by the ships of Ajax and Protesilaus (N 683); the Achaeans who were encamped there must have had most confidence in the strength of their arms.

At the close of the second day of battle, when the Trojans bivouac on the plain near the Greek camp, seven youthful leaders of the Achaeans, each with a hundred men, take their positions as guards *Guards of the Camp.* (φυλακτῆρες) along and within the line of the trench, but outside of the wall (I 66 ff.),—this, too, at the suggestion of Nestor. Clearly these guards had not been needed in the earlier period, when Achilles was active in war. Now the enemy is near, and may make an attack "even in the night" (K 101). Later in this night these guards are visited by the elders at the suggestion of Agamemnon, lest they should be "overcome by weariness and sleep" (K 97), but they are found keeping faithful watch "as dogs in a farm-yard who hear a wild beast coming through the forest" (K 181). When Hermes conducts king Priam to the ships of the Achaeans for the ransom of Hector's body, and they reach the towers and the trench, the guards are just busy about their evening meal, but Hermes pours sleep upon them (for which very purpose he seems to have brought his magic wand), pushes back the bars, and opens the gates (Ω 443). Achilles recognizes the truth that old Priam is under the gods' care, for without this no man would have dared to come, "nor could he escape the notice of the guards" (Ω 566). Whether these guards, to whom Achilles refers, were stationed simply at the gate, or were in front of the wall as a few nights before, is not made clear.

The Trojan forces, as they bivouac on the plain, leave the duty of standing guard to the native Trojans, Dolon
Trojan Guards. tells Odysseus (K 417); the allies are all sleeping. No picket is set by or for the Thracians who have just arrived at the seat of war, and thus Odysseus and Diomed have the opportunity to enter the station of Rhesus, and kill him and his comrades (K 470). Doubtless the poet would thus indicate to his hearers the confidence of the Trojans, who, exultant in their unwonted success, believe that the Achaeans are thinking only of flight, and will make no attack. The Trojans are feasting with music, according to K 13, and Hector fears that the Greeks may escape under cover of darkness, much rather than that they will seek to enter his camp. The reader is to remember also that the Trojans had not been accustomed to any sort of sentinel duty at night. Even when Patroclus has been slain, and Achilles appears to the Trojans at the trench, Pulydamas urges indeed that the Trojans should return to the city, but says that the towers and gates will protect the city through the night (Σ 274). At the close of the second day of battle, when the Trojan warriors are to bivouac on the plain, Hector directs that the city be guarded by the boys and grey-haired old men, "lest an ambush should enter the city in the absence of the soldiery" (Θ 522),—but this was a special occasion.

The poet does not provide sufficient material for a detailed picture of the Greek camp before Troy, but a
Greek Camp. general view may be gathered from the poems. The ships, nearly twelve hundred in number, according to the Catalogue in the second book of the *Iliad*, were drawn up on the shore of the Hellespont, filling the bay between the promontories of Sigeum and Rhoeteum, we are told in Ξ 31-36. This passage declares that the ships were drawn up on shore, πρόκροσσαι, which has been interpreted *like steps*, κλιμακηδόν, *en échelon*,—but the meaning of the term is disputed. The scholar Crates of Mallos believed that two rows of ships were drawn up, one behind

the other ; while Aristarchus held that the ships lay in a single line, but that some projected farther inland than others (see page 527). In an hour of despondency, when suffering from a wound, and when several of his chieftains had been disabled, Agamemnon proposed the drawing to the sea of the boats which were nearest the water (ὅσαι πρῶται εἰρύαται, ἄγχι θαλάσσης, Ξ 75), which of course implies a difference of distance.

The order of the arrangement of the several contingents of ships, is not stated by the poet, but was much discussed by ancient scholars.[1] The Catalogue of Ships seems to refer so definitely to the departure *Contingents in Camp.* from Greece[2] rather than to the arrival on the plain of Troy, that we cannot draw from it any inference as to the order of the ships on the shore of the Hellespont ; but in a curious detail the order of the Catalogue is confirmed by two other passages of the *Iliad*. In the Catalogue, the contingent of Odysseus is fifteenth in a list of twenty-nine, *i.e.* exactly in the middle ; on the second day of battle, Agamemnon, in order to stay the rout, takes his stand by " the huge black ship of Odysseus, which lay at the centre of the line (ἥ ἐν μεσσάτῳ ἔσκε, Θ 223) to shout in both directions " ;[3] and we are told in another place that the altar and place of assembly of the Achaeans, which we expect to be in the middle of the camp, were by the ship of Odysseus (Λ 806).

So far as practicable, the camp seems to have been arranged as a city, with streets, places of assembly, and altars. That the quarters of Meriones were at *Camp a* a considerable distance from those of Idomeneus, *City.* his senior officer, in command of the Cretans, has been observed already. This indicates obviously that the ships of some contingents did not lie together.

[1] See Lehrs, *De Aristarchi studiis Homericis,*[3] 221.

[2] *Cf.* νέες κίον, ἐν δὲ ἑκάστῃ | κοῦροι . . . βαῖνον, B 510. But if B 558 is original, it supplies a definite statement that Telamonian Ajax stationed his forces next the Athenian phalanxes.

[3] In modern editions this is followed by an amplification, " both to the tents of Telamonian Ajax and to those of Achilles, who had drawn up their ships at the extremities of the line," but these verses are not found in the best MSS., though also at K 112, the poet says that the ships of Ajax are most remote.

The ships were drawn well up on land, with their bows toward the sea, by means of trenches (οὖροι, B 153), which gradually became filled with sand, and so needed to be cleared before the ship was again launched (see p. 315). They were supported on either side by long props or by stones (ἔρματα, A 486), which kept them from contact with the soil which would have encouraged the rotting of the wood. The barracks were built by the side of the ships, which were prominent in the camp, and the expressions in, by, to, or from the ships are equivalent to *in* or *to* or *from the camp*.[1] Thus at the opening of the *Iliad*, the old priest Chryses comes " to the swift ships of the Achaeans " (θοὰς ἐπὶ νῆας Ἀχαιῶν, A 12), *i.e.* to the *camp* of the Achaeans, to ransom his daughter. In the night which follows the second day of battle, Menelaus finds his brother, the commander-in-chief, Agamemnon, full of anxiety " putting on his armor by the stern of his ship " (K 35), and a few moments later Agamemnon comes to Nestor who is sleeping " by the side of his hut and his black ship "[2] (K 74). Various streets and paths or alleys (κέλευθοι, K 66) lead through the camp, but this does not imply necessarily a double or a treble line of ships, for we have no exact knowledge of the arrangement of their barracks (κλισίαι). The quarters of Achilles alone are in any way described (Ω 448 ff.). These doubtless were more elaborate than most ; they are even called a house (οἴκοιο, Ω 572). The Myrmidons made for their leader, we are told, a great court-yard with thickly-set palisades, and with a gate held by a bar of pine, which needed the strength of three ordinary Achaeans to open or close it. The barrack building was high, and well-roofed with thatch from the meadows. The court-yard was at least large enough for the horses and chariot of Achilles, and seems to have contained flocks and herds also (Ω 621),—

[1] *Cf.* παρὰ νηυσί, A 26 ; ἐπὶ νηυσί, Δ 513 ; ἐν νηυσί, I 235.

[2] Evidently this was a hot night, for Diomed also is sleeping with his comrades outside of his hut (K 151). *Cf.* also K 572, where Odysseus and Diomed in this same night on returning from their nocturnal expedition cool off their sweat by the sea. This observation is important as indicating that the lion's skin worn by Agamemnon, and the leopard's skin worn by Menelaus on that night, were not so much for protection from the cold, as light armor for defense. See p. 180. *Cf.* B 388.

like the courtyard of the home of Odysseus on Ithaca. There lay the body of Hector, when Achilles had slain him and dragged him to the Greek camp, and Achilles drags this dead body thrice around the corpse of Patroclus (Ψ 13),— apparently in this courtyard. The barrack had a front porch (αἴθουσα, Ω 644) in which guests might sleep, and it probably was built on the plan of an ordinary Homeric house. The same expression is used of the place of Achilles's bed " in the recess of the well-built barrack " (Ω 675), as for the sleeping places of Nestor and Menelaus at their homes, " in the recess of the high dwelling" (γ 402, δ 304 ; see page 196). The attendants of Achilles seem to have had other quarters (Ω 473). Of course the barracks of the common soldiers were less elaborate and commodious than those of their commanders, and we must remember that the life of the Greeks at all times has been in the open air. The house served for protection against rain and unusual cold or heat,—not as a place for the reception of friends or for the ordinary occupations of the man's life. Doubtless the furniture of the barracks also resembled the very simple equipment of the soldiers' homes. Achilles had beds which might be spread for unexpected guests, but Eurypylus's pallet was of ox-hides (Λ 843), which reminds the reader of the seat which the swine-herd Eumaeus spread for Odysseus, of rushes covered with a goatskin (ξ 49), and that for Telemachus of rushes covered with a sheepskin (π 47). We are not to suppose that the common soldiers had beds and bedding. On the night after the second day of battle, Diomed and his comrades sleep outside their tents, using their shields as pillows (Κ 152). Some articles of luxury, however, doubtless, were secured on their marauding expeditions to the neighboring towns, and both Nestor and Achilles brought with them from their homes cherished silver drinking cups (Λ 632, Π 220), and other articles of value (according to our editions of Ψ 92).

The poet could not easily, and does not, state definitely the distance of the Achaean camp from the Trojan city ; he could not state this either in terms of miles or of hours. Perhaps the distance of three miles, that of Hissarlik from the shore of the Hellespont, would suit the conditions as well as any. The distance is such that the movements of the Achaean army in setting forth from their camp are not visible to the Trojans gathered before the

Distance of Camp from Troy.

city walls (B 786), and Priam takes a chariot for his visits to the forces in the field (Γ 259 ff.) and to the Greek camp (Ω 279), but yet the armies sway to and fro over the plain, between the camp and the city,—coming even to the city walls and back again,—in a manner which implies that the distance is not nearly so much as ten miles. Thus at the opening of the eleventh book of the *Iliad*, the Trojans are just before the Achaean camp (Θ 490); Agamemnon drives them to the Scaean Gate (Λ 170), but is wounded and withdraws from the conflict; Hector drives the Achaeans to their camp, and the battle is continued at the Greek ships (close of M); Patroclus enters the fray, pursues the Trojans to the city, and even sets his foot on one of the projecting buttresses of the city's wall (Π 702); but on the death of Patroclus, the Achaeans are driven back to their camp (Σ 150). Thus the distance between the wall of the city and the ships of the Achaeans is traversed by the armies in conflict four times on the third of the four days of battle of the *Iliad*, while at times every foot of progress is stoutly contested. Little stress can be laid on this argument for determining the distance, however, since the critical questions with regard to the composition of these lays of the *Iliad* are likely to remain unsettled for some time longer. The reader may remember that on this third day of battle, noon occurs twice,—at Λ 84, and again about four thousand verses later, at Π 777. When Hector leaves the battle (Z 116) in order to go to the city with a message for his mother, and then to return to the conflict, he goes on foot instead of taking his chariot,—but the distance of the armies from the Greek camp at that time is not clear, and thus this does not aid us to deduce the distance of the city from the camp. At the close of the second day of battle, after the sun has set, Hector orders cattle and sheep to be brought from the city for the Trojans in their bivouac on the plain, just before the Achaean camp (Θ 505). Clearly if these are to be brought and killed, dressed, cooked, and eaten for supper, a distance of a mile or two between the city and their bivouac would be more convenient than three or four, not to speak of eight or nine miles. Near the close of the third day of battle, Patroclus is slain near the wall of the Trojan city, but Antilochus runs to the camp to bear the news to Achilles, and does not take a chariot, as he might be expected to do if the distance were several miles (P 403, 700). In one passage the disguised Odysseus tells of lying in ambush near the city and "far from the ships," while again the Trojan Pulydamas speaks of their bivouac as by the ships and far from their city (ξ 496, Σ 256). But such expressions are comparative, and cannot be translated at once into terms of miles. That the scene of battle was at times very near the city, is indicated by the "View from the Walls" (Τειχοσκοπία, Γ 161 ff.) of the third book of the *Iliad*, where Helen recognizes the Achaean leaders on the plain, and identifies them to old Priam, as she sits by his side on the tower by the Scaean Gate,— not to speak of the rout before Patroclus when the Achaean warrior actually sets foot on a projecting buttress of the Trojan wall (Π 702).

Between the Achaean camp and the Trojan city, runs the river Scamander, according to several passages of the *Iliad*. When King Priam visits the Greek camp, to ransom the body of his son Hector, this river is *Course of the Scamander.* clearly the boundary between the territory which is under the control of the Achaeans and that which is held by the Trojans. Thus his protecting escort, the god Hermes, sent by Zeus, joins him here on his way to the camp, and leaves him again at the ford, on his return to the city (Ω 349 ff., 682 ff.). At Ξ 433, also, the Scamander flows between the city and the camp, and the wounded Hector, borne unconscious from the battle, is here bathed with water from the stream. A large part of the twenty-first book of the *Iliad* is devoted to an account of the passage of the river by the Trojans, in flight from their position before the Achaean camp (Φ 1 ff.). At the close of the first day of battle (H 329), a truce is made for the burial of those "who have been slain on the banks of the

Scamander," which naturally implies that it was crossed by the armies, and did not merely flow near their field of battle, and on one side of it. But nowhere, except in the twenty-first book of the *Iliad*, does the river form a hindrance or obstacle of any kind to the free movements of the armies.[1] Once (Λ 498) we are told that this river lay at the left of the battle, which means on the east, towards the Rhoetean promontory,—for the poet in his view of the battlefield seems to be always on the side of the Achaeans, facing toward Troy.[2] Perhaps where the river is not mentioned, the hearer was to suppose that the poet's mind was busy with another part of the field when the most of the forces were crossing the stream, as well as to remember that the forces on the plain of Troy would not mind crossing a stream so much as a modern army, being less inconvenienced by the water, and being more accustomed to movements in loose order,—not being disconcerted by being thrown out of line. Professor Robert holds that the Scamander did not flow between the camp and the city, but past both, by the side of the battlefield,—emptying itself into the Hellespont, as at present, at the western end of the bay,—but with a great bow which would make the route which crossed it the shortest course from the camp to the town. No bridges are mentioned for the Scamander, or indeed in the Homeric poems.

The Scamander. The Scamander is the chief river of the plain, which is called Scamandrian (B 465). It is said to be Zeus-begotten (Φ 2), which implies that it descends from the heights of Mount Ida, although its "two sources" are said to be near the city of Ilium, at the stone washing-troughs (X 147); we see elsewhere that the latter statement as applied to the Trojan plain can mean only that the water from these sources flowed into the Scamander (p. 531). It had a priest to offer sacrifices to it,—just as Peleus had vowed his son's hair as

[1] See *Homeri Iliadis Carmina*, ed. Christ, pp. 51 ff. Christ would consider the lays in which the Scamander is thought of as flowing between the city and the camp (H, Θ, Ξ, Φ, Ω) as of later composition than where it flows on the same side of both, as B, E, Λ. But see p. 529.

[2] This is denied by Robert, in *Hermes* xlii. 104.

an offering to the river Spercheüs of Thessaly (Ψ 146 ff.). The gods called it *Xanthus*, or Yellow River (Υ 74),—a name doubtless derived from the color of its stream in time of flood. It emptied itself into the Hellespont to the left, that is, to the east, of the Achaean camp (Λ 498; *cf.* E 36, 355). Its depth was such that not only could men swim in it, but living horses and cattle are sunk in its waters as a sacrifice (Φ 132), and its fish are thought of as large enough to tear the corpses of the dead (Φ 203). On the fourth day of battle, the Trojans in flight to their city, striving to escape from the wrath and mighty arm of Achilles, fill the stream and crouch under its steep banks (κρημνούς, Φ 26). Achilles then leaps into the river and slays his enemies, disregarding the Scamander's request that he should not clog the waters with the dead, but rather kill his foes upon the plain (Φ 214 ff.). The river in anger, arousing its stream, and calling to its aid its tributary, the Simoïs, smites the warrior's shoulders and tears the ground from under his feet. At first he aids himself by a fallen elm, which bridged (or, more properly, made a dyke into) the stream, but then the Scamander overflows its banks and would have overcome Achilles, had not Hera set her son, the fire-god Hephaestus, to oppose the river-god, who with seething waters at last ceased from the conflict. The overflow of the banks seems to represent the river in the winter season when it was a mountain torrent and flooded the plain. The Simoïs is the chief of its tributaries,[1] but this stream does not cause any *The Simoïs.* hindrance to the free movement of the armies. Its violence is thought to be indicated by a clause which follows its mention in M 22,—"the Simoïs, where shields of ox-hide and helmets fell in the dust," which was before the mind of Vergil when he wrote, "*ubi tot Simois correpta sub undis | scuta virum galeasque et fortia corpora volvit*" (*Aeneid*, i. 100). In the *Agamemnon* of Aeschylus (696)

---

[1] *Cf.* ᾗχι ῥοὰς Σιμόεις συμβάλλετον ἠδὲ Σκάμανδρος, E 774, and Φ 307. " Between the Simoïs and the streams of the Xanthus," μεσσηγὺς Σιμόεντος ἰδὲ Ξάνθοιο ῥοάων, Z 4, of the place where the battle raged, does not prove that the rivers joined,—only that their streams approached; and in this verse some ancient copies read ποταμοῖο Σκαμάνδρου καὶ Στομαλίμνης, which last was later the name of the marshy mouth of the Scamander.

the Achaean fleet, in pursuit of Helen, beach their boats on the banks of the Simoïs.

The plain seems marshy near the city (ξ 474), though elsewhere (as at Γ 13) a cloud of dust arises under the feet of the men and the horses. Elms and willows, reeds and rushes, grow near the bed of the Scamander (Φ 350). The horses of Adrastus break the pole of his chariot, which is entangled in a tamarisk shrub (Z 39), and at K 467 a "mark" is made by tying together reeds and the branches of a tamarisk.

Marshy Plain.

Several landmarks are mentioned on the plain, but are in no way described. At B 793, Polites, a swift-footed son of Priam, sits as a lookout for the Trojans on the tomb of the old Aesyetes (possibly the father-in-law of Anchises's daughter Hippodamia, N 427), in order to watch for the approach of the Achaean forces. At B 814, a high mound Batieia (*Thornhill*) is the landmark by which the Trojan forces gather and are marshalled. The immortals are said to call this the "tomb of the agile Myrina," who may have been an Amazon, as a scholiast suggests,—one of those who invaded Phrygia, according to Priam in Γ 189. The tomb of Ilus, the grandfather of Priam, for whom the city was named Ilios or Ilium, is a landmark near which Hector and the other Trojan chieftains hold a council after the battle of the second day (K 415). On the next day Agamemnon drives the Trojans past it (Λ 166), and Paris leans upon it to send an arrow at Diomed (Λ 370 ff.). At Ω 349, we see that it lay between the city and the Scamander.

Landmarks.

An oak (or a chestnut, $\phi\eta\gamma\acute{o}s$) tree [1] was one of the most important landmarks of the plain. It stood near the Scaean Gate of the city, and Achilles boasted that as long as he was engaged in fighting, Hector never ventured beyond this tree (I 354). Here the throng of Trojan women met Hector as he returned from the battle, with inquiries about the fate of their husbands and their kinsmen (Z 237). Under this tree his comrades placed the wounded Sarpedon (E 693). There Athena and Apollo

Oak of Zeus.

---

[1] Robert, in *Hermes* xlii. 90, distinguishes two oaks,—one on the plain (E 693, H 22), and the other near the Scaean Gate.

met as they were going to view the fray (H 22), and on one of its branches they "sat like cormorants" (H 60). There the Trojans first took breath in flight before Agamemnon (Λ 170), and there, apparently, Apollo inspired Agenor with courage to meet Achilles (Φ 549).

A wild-fig tree (ἐρινεός, Z 433) is mentioned as standing on a height near the walls and the Scaean Gate, where the city was particularly open to attack. At Λ 167, *Wild-fig* it is nearer the city than the tomb of Ilus, which *Tree.* was on the same route. At X 145, it stands by a "look-out," and its epithet "wind-beaten" is explained as an indication of its position on a height. This height is found by Dr. Dörpfeld on the west side of the city, and there, curiously enough, not only is the approach from the plain easier, because of the elevation, but the wall, as it remains, is of inferior construction to that of most of the city.[1] It is said to be particularly well suited to be a look-out, but for this it should be no better than the wall itself.

Callicoloné is a "Fair Hill" near the Simoïs (Y 53, 151), mentioned only as the station of Apollo and Ares, when the divinities came down from Olympus to take *Callicoloné.* part in the conflict of men. It may have stood, as Dörpfeld suggests, near the Hellespont, on the eastern side of the Scamander. A "swelling" of the plain (θρωσμός, K 160, Λ 56, Y 3) seems to have lain between the Achaean camp and the bed of the Scamander,—but it cannot have been of any considerable height. A wall is referred to as built by "the Trojans and Pallas Athena" for the defense of Heracles when he undertook to save Laomedon's daughter Hesione from the sea-monster (Y 145), but this must have been near the sea, and out of the way of the contending armies. That the highest peak of Mt. Ida, Gargarus, commanded a view of the Trojan city and plain, is clear from Θ 48 ff., where Zeus takes this summit as his post from which to watch the battles. What other heights were seen from the Trojan city, is not even indicated, except as Poseidon sat on the height of Samothrace (N 12) to watch the battle on the Trojan plain, while his elder brother Zeus was sitting on Mt. Ida. A cursory glance at the map

[1] Dörpfeld, *Troja und Ilion*, 608, 629.

shows that Imbros lies between Samothrace and the Troad, but Imbros is so much lower that it did not interfere with Poseidon's view. Tenedos also is in sight from Ilium, with Mt. Athos visible on a clear evening.[1]

Ilium. The city of Ilium lay on a height in the plain (ἐν πεδίῳ, Υ 217), which of itself would exclude its identification with Bunárbashi (see page 545). Its walls had been built for Priam's father Laomedon by Poseidon (Φ 446). The poet is ignorant of the story that Aeacus, ancestor of Achilles and Telamonian Ajax, had assisted in the building of the wall, and that the city was destined to be taken at the place where his hands had wrought (Pindar, *Ol.* viii. 30 ff.), unless a hidden reference to this may be found in the words of Andromache to Hector, urging him to station the Trojan forces near the wild-fig tree, where already the Achaeans had thrice made assault, they being impelled either by some knowledge of an oracle or by their own hearts (Ζ 438). Only one gate, the Scaean, is mentioned,—unless possibly the Dardanian Gate (Ε 789, Χ 194, 413 ;—see page 556) is another. Scholars have thought that the poet had no occasion to name any gate except that which led to the plain of the Scamander on which the battles were fought. By the Scaean Gate stood a great tower on which the women and old men gathered to watch the conflicts on the field below.[2] This was so near the scene of the battle that, from it, Helen and Priam could recognize the Achaean leaders (Γ 161 ff.), who must have been beyond the whole Trojan army. The city was surrounded by open ground, for Achilles pursued Hector thrice about it,—part of the way, at least, along a wagon road (Χ 145 ff.). The speed possible, and the effort required, clearly could not be made definite by the poet.

Of the half-dozen epithets applied to Ilium,—*lofty, well-walled, lovely, windy*, "with good steeds," *broad-streeted*, and *sacred*[3] (or *strong, cf.* p. 380),—the last is applied most

---

[1] Le Chevalier said that Mt. Athos was not only seen from the Troad, but actually cast a shadow over it.

[2] See Γ 145 ff., Ζ 386, Φ 526, Χ 1 ff., 462 ft.

[3] αἰπεινήν, Ρ 328; ἐυτείχεον, Β 113; ἐρατεινήν, Ε 210; ἠνεμόεσσαν, Γ 305; ἐύπωλον, Π 576; εὐρυάγυιαν, Β 12; ἱρήν, Η 82.

frequently, whether with reference to the sanctuary of Athena or to the walls built by Poseidon. The epithet *windy* or *wind-swept*, which is used seven times, is amply justified by the winds which blow down the *Epithets of Troy.* Hellespont. The epithet *lofty* is comparative, but is justified by the commanding position of the hill of Hissarlik. The epithet *well-walled* has been justified by the recent excavations. The epithet "with good steeds," finds illustration and confirmation in the fact that large herds of the imperial Turkish horses graze at present on the plain of Troy. The epithet *broad-streeted*, which is applied also to Mycenae (Δ 52), is clearly comparative ; it receives no clear confirmation from the remains.

Of the fortifications of the Homeric age, impressive ruins remain,—particularly at Mycenae and Tiryns, in addition to those of Hissarlik (Ilium). Those of Mycenae are not mentioned in the poems, although this *Fortifications of Homeric Age.* was the home of Agamemnon, "king of men" and commander-in-chief of the expedition against Troy. Tiryns is mentioned only in passing, as "well-walled" (τειχιόεσσαν, B 559). The Cretan Gortyna bears the same epithet as Tiryns (B 646), and the poet mentions the walls of Scheria (ζ 9), of Cilician Thebes (Z 416), of Boeotian Thebes (Δ 378), of Egyptian Thebes (I 383), and of three or four more towns ; but most other Homeric cities seem, like Sparta, to have no fortifications.[1] The twenty-three towns of the Troad which were sacked by Achilles (I 328), were doubtless very slightly defended, and probably most of them were surprised by his attack. Egyptian Thebes is said to have a hundred gates (I 383), which of course imply a wall such as never existed there. Perhaps the poet may have heard of the great portals of Thebes, which were called *pylones* (πυλῶνες) by the later Greeks.

The Achaean camp was without entrenchments until after the first day of battle of the *Iliad.* During the first nine years of the war, while Achilles took part in the conflict, the Trojans did not assume the offensive ; *Achaean Fortifications.* but when Achilles withdrew from the field of battle, the Achaeans took the advice of Nestor and built a

[1] Whether the city of Athens had walls before the Persian invasion, is disputed.

wall with towers for the defense of their camp, and dug a trench a little way in front of it (H 325, 436).[1] This work of fortification seems to be condensed into a single day, but this limit of time must not be pressed, for the trench was broad and deep (H 440), and pointed palisades were fixed in it,—not to speak of the towers and gate. The gods themselves beheld it with wonder, and Poseidon feared that it would cause men to forget the wall which he built about Troy for Laomedon (H 443 ff.). Of this wall about the camp, only one gate is mentioned (M 420), at the left of the camp.[2] This gate is broken open by Hector's throwing against it a huge stone, "which not two men of the people, such as men now are, could easily heave from the ground upon a wagon" (M 445),—which broke both vertical beams and bars. Such an entrenchment was hardly achieved in a single day. But the towers do not seem very high: the assailants heave and pull at the buttresses and the battlements (M 256), and Sarpedon, standing before the wall, strikes with his spear a defender of a tower (M 395). When Sarpedon pulls down part of the parapet, nothing but a wall, perhaps five feet in height,—a mere breastwork,— separates the two armies (M 415); and when Hector breaks through the gate, while some of his comrades follow him, others come over the wall (M 469; cf. N 50).

Twice in the *Iliad*, reference is made to an agreement between besiegers and besieged, that a city should be spared, *Surrender.*   but half of its possessions given to the enemy. This was better for the people of the city than to lose everything, and to be led into captivity them-

---

[1] Perhaps we may say of this wall, as of the organization of the army on the advice of Nestor (see page 579), that for the poet's purposes this was the beginning of the war, though in its tenth year.

[2] The expressions are not entirely clear. At M 87, the Trojans advance upon the Achaeans in five columns, which may imply five gates to the wall,—like the seven leaders against seven-gated Thebes; but against breastworks no higher than these before Troy the enemy might make a direct assault, even without scaling-ladders or battering-rams, which are foreign to our poet's experience. Some interpret M 120, 340, and H 339 as implying several gates. M 175 expressly says, "Some were fighting about one gate, and some about another," but this passage was rejected by both Aristophanes of Byzantium and Aristarchus, and was not in the edition of Zenodotus.

selves, and it well might be more profitable to the assailants than to risk an assault in which their own loss might be considerable, and the treasures of the city would in large part be destroyed. Thus in the last day of the battles of the *Iliad*, when all the other Trojans had been driven into the city, Hector shrinking from flight before Achilles, asked himself if he might not go unarmed to meet his foe, and offer to him not only Helen and all her treasures brought from Lacedaemon (which had been the cause of the war), but also half of the possessions of the city. He remembered, however, with whom he had to deal, and that the time for compromise had passed (X 111). Similarly on the Shield of Achilles, Hephaestus depicts a city beleaguered by enemies who declare that they will sack it unless half of its possessions are delivered to them (Σ 510). An indemnity for war is indicated after the single-combat between Paris and Menelaus, when Agamemnon demands not merely the return of Helen and the treasures, but also a recompense ($\tau \iota \mu \acute{\eta}$, Γ 459), which must be intended as a satisfaction for the trouble and cost of the war.

The ordinary cause of war in the Homeric times was the " lifting of cattle over the Border." Achilles had no personal grievance against the Trojans, he reminds Agamemnon (A 154); they had never driven off *Ordinary Cause of War.* his cattle or his horses, nor had they destroyed the grain in fertile Phthia. The disguised Odysseus says to Penelope's suitors, " there is no grief when a man is wounded in fighting for his possessions,—for his cattle or his white-fleeced sheep" (ρ 470). On his visit to the realm of Hades, Odysseus, wondering at the presence of the ghost of Agamemnon, asks him with regard to his death, —whether Poseidon wrecked his ships, or enemies slew him upon the land as he was cutting off their cattle or fair flocks of sheep, or fighting in defense of their city and their wives (λ 399). Near the close of the *Odyssey*, reference is made to a former occasion, on which Messenians landed on the island of Ithaca, and carried away three hundred sheep and their shepherds (ϕ 18). Athena comforts Odysseus, after his return to Ithaca, and before his killing of Penelope's suitors, by the promise of her help, and says that even if

fifty companies of men should stand around the two, eager
to slay them, yet Odysseus should drive away the cattle
and goodly flocks (υ 49). In one of several reminiscences,
Nestor calls to mind the strife between the Pylians and
the Eleans, in the time of his youth, "because of the driving
of cattle" (Λ 671). The Pylians drove from Elis fifty herds
of kine, as many sheep, goats, and swine, and one hundred
and fifty horses. Of these, Nestor's father reserved for
himself a herd of cattle and a flock of sheep, "three hundred
and their herdsmen," since a "great debt was due him in
Elis," namely, four race-horses and their chariot, which had
been sent to compete for a prize, and were detained by King
Augeas. The rest of the plundered herds and flocks were
given to the people of Pylus for distribution. Naturally
enough, the Eleans came in all haste, horse and foot, to
recover their property, and encamped about one of the
frontier towns of the Pylians, eager to sack it,—and the war
was fairly begun. Thus, also, in the *Theseus* of Bacchylides,
the chorus asks the king the ground of his anxiety,—"Has
a hostile force invaded the land, or are robbers driving away
flocks of sheep?" Sometimes a peaceful settlement of such
a quarrel might be secured. Odysseus while still a mere
lad was sent to the Messenians to ask satisfaction for the
three hundred sheep and their herdsmen which had been
taken from the island of Ithaca (φ 15).

On his way home from the siege of Troy, Odysseus lands
at the country of the Cicones in Thrace (ι 39); the Ithacans
Freebooting.   slay the men of the city, and divide among
themselves the women and the rest of the booty.
Cicones were among the Thracian allies of the Trojans
(B 846), but the poet in no way intimates that the act of
the Ithacans was in continuation of the Trojan war, or an
act of revenge, and not a simple repetition of the acts of
plundering and killing with which Odysseus and his men
were perfectly familiar before they went to Troy. They had
plundered the towns near Troy, not so much because these
were giving aid and comfort to the Trojans, as because the
Achaeans wanted the booty to be obtained. The disguised
Odysseus tells Eumaeus that, before the Trojan expedition,
he nine times had led companies of Cretans in swift ships

to other lands, and had gained rich booty (ξ 229). Clearly these were not exploits which excited horror or indignation in the mind of the hearer, or shame and penitence in the soul of the teller of the story,—they prove the latter to be "a mighty man of valor." And, the story-teller goes on to narrate, how only a month after the taking of Troy, impatient of an inactive life, he fitted out an expedition of nine ships for Egypt, where they wasted the peaceful fields, and led the women and children into captivity, until a stronger force of Egyptians appeared, and conditions changed. But even under such provocations, the leader of the expedition not only saved his life by supplication, but was accepted as a friend, and finally received many presents.

Corresponding to forays by land, were piratical expeditions by sea, which would not differ essentially from those acts to which reference has just been made. Thucy- *Piracy.* dides (i. 5) observes that a stranger in the Homeric age, on his arrival, is sometimes asked whether or not he is a pirate (as Telemachus by Nestor, γ 71, and Odysseus by Polyphemus ι 252), and that this question is neither intended nor received as an insult.[1] The historian adds that in his own time, successful piracy was honored in certain parts of northwestern Greece, and finds in such hostile expeditions as we are considering, an explanation of the fact that most of the early cities of Greece, such as Athens, Thebes, Sparta, and Mycenae, were built at some distance from the sea. The flame which Athena caused to gleam from Achilles's head, when he appears to the Trojans after learning of the death of his comrade Patroclus, is likened by the poet to the beacon fires lighted by islanders, when attacked suddenly by enemies, intended to call for help from the neighboring islands (Σ 206).

In the guerilla warfare of the epic age, ambuscades were frequent, and in these the bravery of men was thought to be most severely tried. The coward's color changed, he constantly altered his position, his heart beat hard, and

---

[1] Aristarchus, in a scholion on γ 71, says that this question is better suited to the spirit of Polyphemus than to the courtesy of Nestor, and denies Thucydides's statement that piracy brought no disgrace in the Homeric age.—In ξ 85-88, if ὄπις refers as usual to divine punishment, this is threatened to freebooters.

his teeth chattered; while the brave man's color did not change, nor did his heart fear over much (N 277). In *Ambuscades.* the quarrel near the opening of the *Iliad*, Achilles, charging Agamemnon with cowardice, says that he never dares to arm himself for battle with the people, nor to go to the place of ambush,—this seems death to him (A 226); and in Hades, the ghost of Achilles is filled with joy as he learns of the bravery of his son Neoptolemus in the ambuscade of the Wooden Horse,—how he did not pale, nor wipe a tear from his cheek, but kept handling his spear and the hilt of his sword, and, impatient for action, begged Odysseus to allow him to go forth from the horse (λ 523).

The spirit in which war was conducted in the Homeric times was much like that which is set forth in the book *Spirit of War.* of *Deuteronomy* xx. 13 : "Thou shalt smite every male thereof with the edge of the sword : but the women and the little ones, and the cattle, and all that is in the city, even all the spoil thereof, shalt thou take unto thyself."[1] In the Embassy to Achilles, Cleopatra is represented as urging her husband Meleager to defend his city, "telling him of all the woes of those whose city is taken : they slay the men, fire destroys the town, and others lead away into captivity the children and the deep-zoned women" (I 591, *cf.* ξ 264). Chryseïs was captured from Thebes and given as prize of honor to Agamemnon, whose refusal to exchange her for a ransom of countless gifts from her old father the priest Chryses, brought upon the Achaeans the wrath of Apollo and countless woes. Thus also Briseïs was "taken for a prey" from Lyrnessus ; her husband and three brothers were slain (T 296), and she was taken as a prize by Achilles, who had killed her husband. So also the royal mother of Andromache was taken with the rest of the spoil from Hypoplacian Thebes (Z 426). Hector himself looks forward to the time when sacred Ilium shall fall, and his wife Andromache be led away into captivity, to ply the loom

[1] Even in later times, under great provocation, this old rule was followed by the Greeks. Thus in the Peloponnesian War, the Athenians, on capturing Scione after a siege, killed all the men and made slaves of the women and children, and gave the land to the Plataeans (Thuc. v. 32). The Melians later were treated in the same way (Thuc. v. 116).

or to bring water from the spring, at the command of another (Z 448). And in her dirge for Hector, when his body is brought back to Troy, Andromache apostrophizes him : " Soon the city will be sacked, for thou hast perished, its guardian, who didst keep in safety the faithful wives and infant children, who now soon will be borne away in the hollow ships, and I among them. And thou, my child [turning to Astyanax], either wilt follow me to a land where thou wilt perform unseemly tasks for a harsh master, or some Achaean will seize thee by the hand and hurl thee from a tower." [1] (Ω 728.)

Clearly the male captives could not be retained in the camp as slaves ; escape or revolt would be too easy. A Homeric warrior would be an uneasy servant for a captor. Therefore if a life was spared in *Males Slain or Sold.* battle, the prisoner was sent to a neighboring island for sale,—as to Samothrace, Imbros, or Lemnos. Thus Achilles spared Priam's son Lycaon, and sold him to Lemnos, where he brought the worth of a hundred oxen (Φ 79),—doubtless not because as a slave he was so valuable, but because King Priam was sure to be willing to give a large ransom for him, as indeed he gave threefold the price which Achilles received. Other sons of Priam were similarly treated (X 45, Ω 753). A suppliant, begging for mercy, naturally tells of the stores of bronze and of gold at his home, from which his father would give gladly if he should learn that his son was alive, a prisoner, at the swift ships of the Achaeans (Z 46, K 378, Λ 131). Thus this ransom naturally takes the place of the more customary sale ; it is in effect the sale of liberty to the captive himself. Here are found the first beginnings of a code of war.

The captive was absolutely at the will of his conqueror ; only if he had spared his life on the field, the victor was not expected to change his mind. The twelve young Trojan warriors whom Achilles took captive *Position of Captive.* at the crossing of the Scamander (Φ 27), were destined from the first for an offering at the funeral pyre

[1] For the fate of conquered cities, *cf.* also, A 366 ff., B 689, θ 523, ι 40 ff., ξ 264 ff.

of Patroclus (Ψ 175), and doubtless cherished no vain hopes of safety. At the close of the first day of battle of the *Iliad*, ships arrive from Lemnos, and prisoners are among the articles of barter with which the Achaeans purchase wine (H 475). Once Menelaus is about to respect the entreaty of a Trojan whom he overtakes, but Agamemnon rebukes him with a reminder of the wrong done by Paris, and with the wish that no male of the Trojans, not even the child unborn, might escape the sword (Z 45 ff.). When Priam's son Lycaon falls a second time into the hands of Achilles, and begs for quarter, he hears an implacable voice : While Patroclus lived, Achilles took many prisoners and sold them ; but now that Patroclus has fallen, no one shall escape death of all the Trojans whom the divinity puts into the hands of Achilles (Φ 100). In these dreadful acts is no thought of special cruelty ; Achilles and Menelaus are only following the law and usage of war. Achilles continues to Lycaon : " But do thou too die. Why dost thou mourn thus ? Patroclus also died, who was far braver than thou. Dost thou not see what I too am,—beautiful and tall ? I am the son of a brave father, and a goddess was my mother, but death and mighty fate hang over me also."

Violent death was so familiar a sight to the Homeric Greeks that it lost its peculiar horror for them, as those who have been engaged in a bloody war are wont to lose respect for human life. In that primitive age, men may not have learned to feel strongly the difference between the life of a man and that of a brute. In anger, Hector planned to cut off the head of the slain Patroclus, and give his body to the dogs,—but he did not succeed. To us this seems brutal and savage ; but we remember that at the close of Shakespeare's *Macbeth*, the " dead butcher's " head was brought upon the scene, and such treatment of the dead has not been rare in rude and warlike ages. In his supreme wrath for the death of Patroclus, Achilles drags the body of Hector from before the Trojan city to the Achaean camp, and about the tomb of his comrade (X 395, Ω 16). But these are extreme cases. Zeus tells Hera that apparently her anger at the Trojans would be satisfied only by devouring them raw (Δ 35).

Brutality.

And Hecuba in her grief wishes she could eat the very heart (ἧπαρ, literally *liver*, Ω 212) of Achilles who had slain her son.   But these expressions are not to be pressed as if they were the survivals of an age of cannibalism, for they can be paralleled from later literature.   We may even compare the words of Beatrice in *Much Ado about Nothing* (iv. 1, 308): "O God, that I were a man! I would eat his heart in the market-place."   The shade of Agamemnon, speaking of his own death, says to Odysseus in Hades, "You have seen many men killed, singly and in the mighty battle," but Odysseus had never seen any sight so sad as the death of Agamemnon and his comrades at the hands of Aegisthus and his men (λ 416); and this word of Agamemnon certainly does not limit the experiences of Odysseus to the Trojan Wars.

The details of the fighting-books of the *Iliad*, particularly, perhaps, the fifth, eleventh, twelfth, and sixteenth books, are rather gory and gruesome reading for a modern man.   For example, when Peneleüs fixes his spear *Gruesome* in the eye of Ilioneus, and then cutting off his *Details* head with his sword, holds this up on the end *Given.* of his spear, "like a poppy" (Ξ 499); or where Achilles wounds Polydorus in such a manner that his bowels gush out, and the wounded man gathers these to him with his hands (Υ 418); or when Pisander is so struck on the helmet by Agamemnon that his bloody eyes fall to the ground at his feet (N 617, *cf.* Π 345); or when the Locrian Ajax chops off the head of a son-in-law of Priam, and hurls it like a ball (σφαιρηδόν, N 204) through the throng. Patroclus hurls at a son of Priam, and a charioteer of his brother Hector, a stone which crushes his forehead, and his eyes fall in the dust before his feet; the man falls headlong from his chariot "like a diver" (ἀρνευτῆρι, Π 742), and Patroclus says mockingly: "Truly he is a nimble man! How easily he turns a somersault! If he were on the fishy sea, he could provide oysters for many, even in stormy weather, by diving from the boat." Patroclus wounds another man in the jaw with his spear, and therewith pulls him out of his chariot, as a man pulls a great fish by hook and line from the sea (Π 404). Automedon, near the close of the third battle, is as bloody as a lion which has eaten a bull (P 542). Achilles drives his spear through Hector's gullet, and to his prayer that Priam may be allowed to ransom his dead body, he replies that he would fain himself devour him, and surely would give him to the dogs of the camp. Many Achaeans gather around the corpse and thrust their spears into it, saying " Hector is easier to handle now than when he was burning the ships with destructive fire," and then Achilles draws a strap through the tendons of Hector's ancles, and drags the body behind his chariot, to the camp, in full view of Hector's father, mother, and wife (X 346 ff.).

Homer certainly feels more personal interest in every detail of the battles which he narrates, than Vergil in the *Homer not Naturalistic.* conflicts of Aeneas and Turnus. The one is telling of deeds · which delight his heart, such as he has often seen with his own eyes, and has heard described by mighty men of valor, while Vergil has only a literary interest in his contests. Yet in these narratives the Homeric poet is never seeking to excite horror ; he is not naturalistic,—he is natural. His story of the Cyclops Polyphemus contains no parallel to Vergil's " *monstrum horrendum informe ingens cui lumen ademptum.*" He simply states facts, and describes scenes which are perfectly familiar to him. The accuracy of his anatomical knowledge proves his frequent sight of severe wounds. His hearers too have witnessed many such gory combats. The epic poet gives details in a perfectly objective way, rarely indicating any emotion of his own, yet avoiding such a bald statement as that *A* slew *B*. Generally he tells his hearer how and where the wound was inflicted, and what was the result, though he does not think it necessary always to report that death ensued from what would clearly be a fatal wound. For instance, to take a characteristic example, at the beginning of the fifth book of the *Iliad*, and to state the facts without any of the poetic paraphernalia : Diomed hit Phegeus on the chest, between the breasts, with his spear, and thrust him from his chariot. Agamemnon fixed his spear in the back of Odius, between the shoulders, and drove it through his breast. Idomeneus struck Phaestus with his long spear, as he mounted his chariot, on the right shoulder,—and he fell out of his chariot, and hateful darkness seized him. Menelaus struck Scamandrius, as he was fleeing before him, in the back,—and he fell prone and his armor rang over him. Meriones hit Phereclus on the right buttock, and the point of the spear passed under the bone, by the bladder,—and he fell upon his knee with a groan, and darkness covered him. Meges hit Pedaeus with his sharp spear on the nape of the neck, and the bronze (*i.e.* the spear point) pushing straight on to the teeth, cut the root of the tongue,—and he fell in the dust and seized the cold bronze with his teeth. Eurypylus struck Hypsenor with his sword, as he fled before him, on the shoulder, and hewed off the heavy arm,—and the bloody arm fell to the plain, while dark death and mighty fate came down over his eyes. Then Pandarus hit Diomed in the right shoulder with an arrow, but the wound was not serious. Diomed hits Astynoüs above the nipple with his bronze-pointed spear, and strikes Hypeiron on the collar-bone by the shoulder with his great sword, and separates the shoulder from the neck and the back; he slays two sons of Priam, as a lion, leaping into the midst of cattle feeding in a thicket, crushes the neck of a heifer or an ox; he hits Pandarus on the nose by the eye, and pierces his white teeth; he hits Aeneas with a great stone and crushes his hip-joint; he wounds the goddess Aphrodite on the wrist.—Thus in the first three hundred verses of the fifth book of the *Iliad*, twelve warriors are slain and three are wounded, but the particulars are given in every case but two. No summary statement is made, as in an official report, of so and so many as killed or wounded.

Once indeed the poet tells us (II 784) that "Thrice Patroclus rushed upon the Trojans, like to keen Ares, with a terrible shout, and thrice he slew nine men"; *Numbers* and again, "Ajax wounded twelve men in the *Slain.* hand-to-hand conflict" (O 746), while twelve of the Trojans fell in the rout when Achilles uttered his great shout from the wall of the Achaean camp (Σ 230). A German scholar (von Hahn) counts three hundred and eighteen men as definitely stated to have been killed in the

battles of the *Iliad*, including the twelve youthful Trojan
captives whom Achilles slays at the funeral of Patroclus.
Of the whole number, two hundred and forty-three are said
to be named. Patroclus kills fifty-four, including the twenty-
seven who are unnamed,—all of course on the third day of
the battles of the *Iliad*. Achilles is the next most deadly,—
killing thirty-six, all on the last day of the battles of the
Iliad. Hector slays twenty-eight ; Diomed, twenty, of whom
he kills twelve on the first day of battle ; Odysseus kills
eighteen,—nine on the first day, and nine on the third ;
Ajax and Teucer kill fifteen each ; Agamemnon kills twelve,—
four on the first day, and eight on the third ; Menelaus kills
eight, Meriones seven, Aeneas and Idomeneus six each,
Paris and Pulydamas three each, and Sarpedon and Glaucus
two each. The "charioteer of Asius" (N 394) is said to
be the only single "anonymous" of the slain,—though the
poet would not limit the imaginations of his hearers with
regard to the masses who perish.

A modern reader is surprised to observe in Homer the
predominance of fatal wounds,—more than two-thirds of the
Wounds Fatal. whole number. Without reckoning the comparatively infrequent statements of death without
details of the wound, like the killing of Priam's
two sons by Diomed, which has just been mentioned, about
one hundred and fifty cases of wounds have been counted
in the *Iliad*. One writer,[1] who counts one hundred and
fifty-four wounds, thinks that one hundred and twenty-three
cause death, while the issue of five is left doubtful. A more
elaborate discussion [2] enumerates one hundred and forty-
seven in all,—one hundred and six caused by the spear,
seventeen by the sword, twelve by a stone, and twelve by
an arrow. Of these, thirty-one were on the head,—all fatal ;
sixteen were on the neck,—of which thirteen were fatal ;
seventy-nine on the body,—sixty-seven fatal, with a small
number of doubtful cases in addition ; ten on the upper
limbs,—two fatal ; eleven on the lower limbs,—one fatal. Of
the fatal wounds on the body, fifty-nine were given by the
spear, four by the sword, three by an arrow, and one by

[1] Mr. A. G. Bentley, in an unpublished thesis.
[2] Frölich, *Die Militärmedicin Homers*, Stuttgart.

a stone. The same German scholar makes the following comparison between the ordinary place of wounds in Homeric and in modern warfare:

	Homeric Warfare.	Modern Warfare.
Wounds on the Head, - -	21 per cent.	7 per cent.
Wounds on the Neck, - -	11 per cent.	2 per cent.
Wounds on the Body, - -	54 per cent.	21 per cent.
Wounds on the Upper Limbs,	7 per cent.	26 per cent.
Wounds on the Lower Limbs,	7 per cent.	44 per cent.

From this table it is seen that the Homeric warrior aimed with the spear at the head and neck, while the modern bullet is directed from a greater distance at the whole body of the enemy. Attention has been called to the fact that the wound from an arrow is least dangerous, while all struck by a sword die.

A severed artery meant death. Homeric wounds on any part of the chest, back, or abdomen are almost sure to be fatal, and generally immediately. That a warrior so wounded should be carried to the rear for treatment, is entirely exceptional. Hypsenor, son of Hippasus, was wounded by Deïphobus in the liver, and according to our text was borne to the hollow ships (N 421-423),—but these three verses seem to be borrowed from a passage in the eighth book of the *Iliad*, where Teucer was hit by a stone on the collar-bone and then carried to the camp (Θ 332). The poet does not seem to think of the heart as a more vital organ than the liver or lungs.

In the story of one hundred and fifty wounds, we should expect to find a certain monotony, even if we were not aware of the epic poet's readiness to use the same *Variety of Wounds.* language for the description of a like situation or the narration of a like event: but the variety of incident in Homer's account of wounds is great. Hardly could the poet have covered more completely the possibilities of wounds for the human body if he had proceeded systematically and mechanically. One may naturally inquire whether different parts of the poems indicate a tendency to different wounds, but such a tendency has not been discovered, although, curiously enough, a surgical writer has observed that three of the four wounds near the groin are

inflicted by Meriones (E 65, N 570, 650; *cf.* Δ 490), and
all are given from behind. (Such wounds from the front
would in general be avoided by the shield.) Wounds are
received on the head, forehead, temple, nose, eye, ear, chin,
jaw, mouth, neck, gullet, nape of neck, collar-bone, shoulder,
arm, elbow, fore-arm, wrist, hand, chest, side, loins, liver,
lungs, heart, bowels, back, navel, belly, groin, rump, thigh,
hip, knee, behind the knee, lower leg by the ancle, flat of
the foot,—all told with so much accuracy of detail that some
classical scholars and medical writers have been inclined to
think that the poet must have been a sort of regimental
surgeon, or at least a member of a guild of priests who
paid particular attention to surgery, although no indication
is found in the poems of any connexion between surgery
and the gods. The anatomical knowledge of Homer has
been declared to be almost as advanced as that of Hippocrates. Certainly slight progress was made between the age
of the epic poets and the early fifth century B.C. The
battles of the Homeric age afforded nearly as good opportunity as the earliest dissecting-room, for the study of the
position and nature of the principal organs of the human
body, and the fact that the same men inflicted and saw the
wounds of battle, and killed and quartered animals for food,
stimulated the study of the elements of comparative anatomy.

Warriors wounded in the head are apt to fall head foremost, as is the case with Mydon, who is wounded in the
temple by Antilochus (E 584), and with Cebriones
Behavior with different Wounds. (Π 742). One who is wounded in the hip, like
Aeneas, should sink upon the knee, as he does
(E 305). In general, in the Homeric poems the
wounded behave after their hurt just as physiologists say
that they should,—in falling backwards or forwards, or
simply sinking to the ground, and in uttering a cry. Fifteen
times, according to a scholar's computation, a wounded man
falls forward, while fourteen times he falls backward. In
certain cases the direction and manner of the fall are to be
explained, most naturally, not physiologically but physically,
—not from the part of the body which is wounded, but
from the force of the weapon, as where Meges is struck in
the shoulder from behind by Menelaus, and falls forward,

evidently from the force of the spear (O 543). So Sarpedon wounds Alcmaon, and, drawing back his spear, draws with it the wounded man, who falls upon his face (M 395). Why the eyes of a wounded man should fall to the ground when he is smitten on the forehead by a sword or a stone (N 616, Π 741), has not indeed been made out. The observations that the blood flows most freely only after the weapon which caused the wound has been removed (Λ 458), and that a slight wound gives little trouble until it has become dry (Λ 266), are elementary and natural. Acquaintance with the long artery of the back (φλέψ, N 546) does not surprise us in the case of one who had seen so many wounds. The use of the verb *spurted up* (ἀνηκόντιζε, E 113) applied to blood, shows that the poet knew the action of arterial blood, although no remedy was known for a severed artery, and he does not distinguish in terminology between veins and arteries. He knew also marrow (μυελός, Υ 482), but he had no notion of nerves. That the plural (ὀστέα, Δ 521) is used of the bones of a single leg, has been noticed as significant, but is not unnatural. The account of the wound of Aeneas in the hip (E 305,—hip-joint broken, and ligaments torn) must be exaggerated greatly,—it must be a mere contusion,—or else a miracle is wrought by the care of Leto and Artemis who tend him in Apollo's temple (E 447). But Homeric wounds heal quickly and easily, if at all. Not only does Aeneas reappear on the field of battle on the same day (E 512), and Diomed continue the conflict with still greater fury after being hit on the shoulder with an arrow (E 98), but also Hector, who is hit on the breast by a great stone hurled by Ajax,—and is knocked senseless, is carried to the rear (Ξ 409 ff.), and after coming to himself vomits blood and faints again,—a little later, cheered by Apollo, returns to the conflict (O 239). On the third day of battle, Agamemnon receives a wound from a spear which pierces his arm below the elbow, and soon is obliged to withdraw from the fight (Λ 252 ff.), though he continues the battle as long as the blood is warm;[1] a hostile spear sweeps the flesh from Odysseus's ribs (Λ 437); and the flat of Diomed's

---

[1] So also a wounded stag *runs as long as* his blood is warm, Λ 477.

right foot is pierced by an arrow from the bow of Alexander (Λ 377); but these three warriors take part in the funeral games in honor of Patroclus three days later,—Diomed coming in first in the chariot race (Ψ 499), fighting in heavy armor with Telamonian Ajax (Ψ 812), and acting as second for his companion Euryalus in the boxing match (Ψ 681); Odysseus wrestling with the mighty Telamonian Ajax, who was much taller than himself (Ψ 709), and winning the foot-race over the Locrian Ajax and the younger Antilochus (Ψ 778); and Agamemnon presenting himself as a competitor in the contest of hurling the spear. Menelaus too receives a wound from the treacherous bow of Pandarus at the beginning of the first day of battle (Δ 139), but "kindly herbs" are sprinkled over the wound from which Machaon sucks or squeezes the blood, and he soon again is ready to fight (E 50). The Lycian Sarpedon is very severely wounded in the left thigh on the first day of battle (E 660), but fights desperately three or four days later (M 397). Teucer, groaning heavily, is carried from the field by his friends on the second day of battle (Θ 334), but on the next day he fights again, as though nothing had happened (M 336 ff., O 436 ff.). The poet Goethe said that the Homeric warriors were like the heroes of Valhalla, who might be cut to pieces in the morning, and yet be ready to eat a hearty dinner at night.

No surgeons or healers are named for the Trojans and their allies, and only two for the Achaeans in the army before
Surgeons. Troy,—Machaon and Podaleirius, sons of Asclepius (Aesculapius, B 732), who had learned his skill from the centaur Chiron (Δ 219), from whom Patroclus also had derived his wisdom in the art (Λ 832). But that the army had other surgeons is indicated by two passages: Idomeneus "gave directions to the surgeons" for the care of his comrade (N 213), and "the surgeons with many drugs are busy about Eurypylus" (Π 28); and the "healer of ills" (ἰητήρ) is enumerated among the "servants of the people" in the *Odyssey* (δημιοεργοί, ρ 384), who are welcomed wherever they may go. We remember, however, that the Romans in republican times had no regular medical and surgical attendance for their armies.

We might suppose that each contingent of the army would need and would have a surgeon, but the two such who are named,—Machaon and Podaleirius,—are as skilled and as active in inflicting as they are *Surgical Treatment.* in healing wounds, and only once is either of them represented as doing the work of his special office. They are sons of Asclepius, but Asclepius himself had not been admitted to Olympus in Homer's time. Podaleirius is not named in connexion with any deed of healing. But early on the first day of the battles of the *Iliad*, the truce which had been struck for the single-combat of Paris and Menelaus, is broken by the Trojan Pandarus's sending an arrow at Menelaus, who is expecting no harm. The goddess Athena, however, does not forget the warrior, and turns aside the arrow from its course, allowing it only to graze his flesh. Agamemnon at once summons Machaon, who loosens his armor, sucks or squeezes out the blood to free the wound from all extraneous matter, and sprinkles over the wound the herbs which Chiron " with friendly heart " (Δ 219,—which has been thought to indicate that the prescription was a secret) taught his father to use. On the third day of battle, Machaon himself is wounded in the right shoulder by an arrow from the bow of Paris. The wound is not severe, but Machaon is taken to the camp by Nestor on his chariot, at the reminder of Idomeneus that a surgeon is worth more than many other men (Λ 506). Patroclus being sent by Achilles to learn what wounded man Nestor is bringing from the battle, on his return meets Eurypylus, hit with an arrow in the thigh, limping from the fight (Λ 809), who calls on him for aid since Machaon himself is wounded and Podaleirius is busy fighting on the field. He conducts Eurypylus to his tent, stretches him on a pallet of ox-hides, cuts with his knife the arrow from the thigh, washes the blood from the wound with warm water, sprinkles over it a " pain-killing, bitter root," which he rubs with his hands, and which checks the pains. Then the " wound was dried and the blood ceased " (Λ 848), but the treatment continued for some time (O 393).[1]

---

[1] To ask, as scholars have done, where Patroclus obtained this healing root, seems an idle question. He may have had it with him for a like emergency;

On the first day of battle, Ares is wounded in the flank by the spear of Diomed in the hands of Athena (E 856). He withdraws to Mt. Olympus in distress and shows his hurt to Zeus, at whose bidding Paeëon sprinkles "pain-killing herbs" upon it (E 899), and it is healed immediately. Thus Aphrodite, too, when wounded in the arm by the same Diomed (E 336 f.) seeks the aid of her mother Dione who wipes off the flowing ichor, and the wound heals. As in the life of backwoodsmen in a logging-camp or on a frontier,—where accidents are not infrequent, and trained surgeons are at a distance,—every man has experience in dealing with wounds, and may be ready to give not only "first help for the injured," but as skilful treatment as Machaon himself,—drawing out an arrow or a spear, and binding up the wound. Thus Agenor binds up the wound of Helenus with a woolen sling (N 599). Sthenelus draws an arrow from the shoulder of Diomed (E 112, and a little later, Diomed draws an arrow from his own foot, Λ 398), and Pelagon draws a spear from the thigh of Sarpedon (E 694). So also when Odysseus, in his youth, visits his maternal grandfather, on the slopes of Parnassus, and, taking part in the chase, is wounded above the knee by the tusk of a wild boar, his cousins "bind up the wound skilfully and check the dark blood by repeating a charm" (τ 456),—the only mention of a charm in the Homeric poems.[1]

No special ambulance corps was needed. The comrade next at hand took charge of the wounded man (Θ 330, E 663, N 533). Hospitals naturally were un-

Primitive Appliances. known, as well as special surgical instruments and appliances. A woolen sling was used as a bandage (N 599). Patroclus, as we have seen, with his knife (μαχαίρῃ, Λ 844), cuts the arrow from the thigh of Eurypylus,—placing him on no operating table, but stretching him on a pile of ox-hides. Machaon squeezes or sucks the blood from the wound of Menelaus, and Patroclus washes

---

he may have sent for it to his tent; Eurypylus may have kept it on hand in his own tent. Patroclus and Achilles hardly had the monopoly of such simples.

[1] In the *Trachinian Women* of Sophocles, the suffering Heracles calls for one who would speak a charm *or* for a surgeon (ἀοιδός, χειροτέχνης ἰατορίας, 1000).

with warm water the wound of Eurypylus, before applying the soothing herbs (Δ 218, Λ 846). Lint was not used; the herbs served as a styptic (E 401, 900, Λ 830, O 394), just as the dust of a puffball has been used by many a rural physician in modern times. The *ichor* of Ares was stopped by the herbs of Paeëon, as milk is curdled by the sap of the wild fig tree (E 902,—Welcker thought that this meant not simply the stopping of the flow of blood, but the formation of a new skin). The herbs also quieted the pain,—being "pain-killing" (ὀδυνήφατα, E 900, *cf.* Λ 847). These herbs may have been useful also as antiseptic.

No internal medicines are directly mentioned, but Helen had learned from Polydamna in Egypt the use of a drug which prevented all sadness on the day of its use (such as opium or hasheesh? δ 228). On *Medicines.* Circe's island, Odysseus receives from Hermes the *moly* (κ 305),—a magic herb with black root and white flower which served as an antidote to Circe's drugs and spells. Of Circe's drugs themselves, served in a posset, naturally the poet gives no details. The use of poisoned arrows is mentioned once as known (α 261), but with disapproval. At β 329 f., Penelope's suitors express the fear that Telemachus may fetch drugs from Ephyra, and poison their wine. Agamede, daughter of Augeas, king of the Epeans, is said to know all the herbs (φάρμακα, Λ 741) of the broad earth. Egypt is said to be the land where the most herbs or drugs, both goodly and evil, grow (δ 230). Poisonous herbs are said to be the cause of both the venom and the anger of the poisonous serpent (X 94). That the Homeric Greeks should be more skilled in the treatment of external wounds than of internal diseases, is not strange. They had had abundant opportunity to learn the nature, and to experiment on the treatment, of the former. Elsewhere, too, (the Hottentots are cited as an example) primitive peoples have a well-developed art of surgery before they have any art of medicine. Thus for the plague sent by Apollo (A 51), the Achaeans seek not a physician nor a specific remedy, but a seer who should tell them why the god is angry; but even in more recent times processions have been made to shrines of saints for the averting of like troubles, in lieu of sanitary measures. The Achaeans "purify themselves" (a proper hygienic measure) and offer sacrifices to the god, but they take no medicine. So when Polyphemus's brothers think that he is ill, they counsel him to pray to his father Poseidon, but recommend no drugs (ι 412). At Π 28, however, the healers have many drugs (πολυφάρμακοι)—which may refer to herbs for internal remedies, for *many* herbs would hardly be used in surgery.

Illness. No case of illness is mentioned by Homer, except the pestilence which was sent by Apollo at the beginning of the action of the *Iliad*, and the most important medical observation with regard to this, is that it attacked the mules and dogs before it came upon the men. No description of it is attempted by the poet, and of course it cannot be identified with any modern plague. But wasting disease is referred to as a cause of death (λ 200), and apparently the other Cyclopes think that Polyphemus had an attack of cholera morbus (ι 411). In his accounts of battles and adventure, the poet found small place for sick men. Scholars have observed also that Hesiod does not mention physicians or surgeons. The Epic *Aethiopis*, which was ascribed to Arctinus, made of the two brothers Machaon and Podaleirius, the former a surgeon and the latter a physician, but such differentiation does not belong to the Homeric age. The freedom from disease of the army before Troy, is the more remarkable since the poet knows of no arrangements for the sanitation of the camp. Sudden and peaceful death to which no special cause could be assigned, like that from paralysis, was thought to be sent by Apollo to men, and by his sister Artemis to women (see p. 430).

Diet. Plato in his *Republic* (408 A) calls attention to the facts that the surgeon Machaon gives to Menelaus no directions as to his diet after his wound (Δ 219), and that no rebuke is administered to Hecamede for preparing a posset of Pramnian wine, goats-cheese, and barley-meal for Machaon himself when he is brought wounded to Nestor's tent (Λ 639, *Republic* 406 A). Modern German writers have wondered, too, that the wounded

Machaon and Nestor, coming heated from the battle, should stand in the breeze by the sea-shore to "cool off their sweat" (Λ 621), with no apparent fear of taking cold; and a Dutch scholar has suggested that the warming posset was intended to prevent them from taking cold after this exposure,—but the true explanation is that they ate and drank just as if no wound had been inflicted, trusting to Nature to effect the cure.

No indication is found in the Homeric poems of any communication between the Achaeans before Troy and their friends at home during the long ten-years' siege. No reinforcements arrive for them during the war, *Communica-* and no one returns from the camp to his home. *tions with* In the Catalogue of Ships (B 724), an intimation *Greece.* is given that Philoctetes, who had been left on the island of Lemnos, disabled by the bite of a water-snake, was to rejoin the Achaeans,—a suggestion which was amplified by the later epics and by the Attic tragic poets. And after the action of the *Iliad* and the death of Achilles, his son Neoptolemus was brought to Troy from Scyrus by Odysseus (λ 506),—another theme which was treated in full by the later poets,—but Neoptolemus seems to have been accompanied by no troops.

Naturally the Trojans, being nearer the homes of their allies, are in closer connexion with them. The tenth book of the *Iliad* tells of the nocturnal expedition of Diomed and Odysseus into the Trojan camp, *Reinforce-* and of their killing the Thracian Rhesus, who *ments for* had arrived at Troy but a few hours before, and *Trojans.* apparently did not know that he must guard his own camp against a night attack of the enemy. In the sixth book of the *Iliad* (Z 123), Diomed wonderingly asks the Lycian Glaucus who he is,—never before had he seen him on the field of battle. How could this be if the two had been meeting in the fray for nine years? In order to explain Diomed's ignorance of the hero Glaucus, Professor Christ offers the interesting suggestion that the introduction of the southern Lycians into the story is the work of a later poet than the author of the first and eleventh books of the *Iliad*, but possibly the theory that these were reinforcements, recently arrived, may explain the facts. On the third day of battle, the Ascanians take an active part, having arrived as " reliefs " (ἀμοιβοί, N 793) on the preceding morning. A little later, Patroclus is smitten by Euphorbus who had just come with his chariot (Π 811). And near the close of the third day of battle, Pelegon the Paeonian is questioned by Achilles, just as Glaucus had been interrogated by Diomed, as to who he is, and replies that he is from Paeonia, and that this is the eleventh day since his arrival on the plain of Troy (Φ 153). Othryoneus, who is killed by Idomeneus (N 363), has just come from his home at Cabesus, promising Priam to drive the Achaeans from Troy, and receiving in return the promise of the hand of Priam's fairest daughter, Cassandra. Some ancient manuscripts, we are told by the scholia, modified the last verse of the *Iliad*, and added another, in order to introduce a mention of the arrival of the Amazons under their queen, Penthesilea, to the support of the Trojans,—but the Amazons are not among the Trojan allies in the Homeric story as we have it. Indeed the only instances of their mention in the poems, are of their expedition against the Phrygians and Priam in an earlier period (Γ 189), and of their slaughter by Bellerophon (Z 186). The arrival of Memnon, the beautiful son of the Dawn, with his Aethiopians, to the help of the Trojans, is later than the action of the *Iliad*, and allusion is made to it in the *Odyssey* only on mention of the death of Nestor's son Antilochus (δ 187), and where Odysseus in the realm of Hades tells Achilles that the latter's son is the most beautiful man he ever saw, " next to the godlike Memnon " (λ 522). The Aethiopians and the Amazons seem to belong to quite a different sphere from most of the Trojan allies. The remark thrown out in Plato's *Laws*, (685) that Troy was a part of the Assyrian empire and trusted to its help, is wholly fanciful.

CHAPTER XIX

HOMERIC ARMS

UNTIL recent years the Homeric warrior's arms, both offensive and defensive, were supposed to have been essentially the same as those of the Athenian soldier of the fifth century B.C. But good reason has been shown [1] for believing that while the weapons of offense,—the spear, sword, bow and arrow, battle-axe, and sling,—remained without important changes the same from the twelfth to the third century B.C., with iron gradually taking the place of bronze, the defensive armor was greatly modified between the twelfth and the seventh centuries. Ordinary current representations of Homeric warriors are now seen to be highly anachronistic, projecting into the tenth or eleventh century B.C. much that was not earlier than the seventh or eighth. The excavations at Mycenae, nearly thirty years ago, brought to light so much new and unexpected archaeological material which was at variance with the previous notions based on Attic usage, that these discoveries were thought to indicate a stage of culture entirely different from the Homeric, if not absolutely un-Hellenic. The Mycenaean warrior is represented at times with no covering but a loin-cloth, and bearing such a shield

Changes in Arms.

[1] See Rossbach, *Das älteste Kriegswesen*, in *Philologus*, 1892 ; Kluge, *Vorhomerische Kampfschilderungen*, in *Jahrbücher für Philologie und Pädagogik*, 1893 ; especially, Wolfgang Reichel, *Homerische Waffen*, Vienna, 1894,—second edition, rewritten and enlarged, 1901,—to which the present treatment of Homeric arms is greatly indebted (all previous discussions of the subject have now chiefly a historical interest), and *Studien zur Ilias* by Carl Robert, Berlin, 1901, who examined Reichel's views in an acute and masterly manner.—τεύχεα and ἔντεα are general names for armor and arms.

as no modern reader or artist had imagined as carried by
Agamemnon or Achilles, and now scholars remember that
the forces of the lesser Ajax, too, had no helmets, shields,
greaves, or spears (N 715).

Similarly, in the early study of the Homeric language, the
Attic dialect was taken as the standard, and all deviations
from this were regarded as exceptions and vagaries, long
after the truth was known that the Homeric language

Fig. 23.—Silver Vase Fragment from Mycenae.

represented an earlier stage of development than the Attic;
and Attic meanings of words and constructions were accepted
and maintained by scholars in the interpretation of Homer,
even after the Homeric forms were understood and accepted
as belonging to an earlier stage of the language.

But the first impressions with regard to the Mycenaean
antiquities are seen to have been false, for these furnish
our best illustrations of Homeric life, although in dress and
other matters the Mycenaeans were not Homeric. Scenes
from the monuments of Egypt and Assyria are of comparatively little value for the elucidation of the *Iliad*

and *Odyssey*, and perhaps for our purpose must rank with the arms and implements of modern half-civilized nations, —useful only as analogies, to aid the imagination in forming conceptions of what is otherwise unknown. Scholars had projected too much of the life of the fifth and sixth centuries B.C. into *Illustrations from Mycenae.* their notions of the Homeric age, and chiefly for this reason the figures on the Mycenaean works of art appeared strangely un-Hellenic.

In this matter of the arms, as in every other of the questions before us, we must remember that all earlier material was used freely by the poet, and combined with his own composition, wherever no flagrant inconsistency existed. Thus the indications *No absolute Consistency.* of arms and armor of an early age might be handed down, as though encased in amber, and appear in a poem composed by one who was accustomed to very different arms; but in general the arms assumed in different parts of the poems have been thought to be in agreement.

Military uniforms of any sort were entirely unknown in the Homeric period, and indeed the Spartans seem to have been the only Greeks of the classical time to care for uniformity in the equipment of their *No Uniforms.* troops, though the Sicyonians, for example, in later times had a great Σ upon their shields. In the Homeric age no desire was felt to have agreement in the equipments of the men of a particular division, to say nothing of the whole army before Troy. Rather, as in the field each man fought for himself, so the size and shape of his shield, the form and material of his helmet, and the length of his spear, and whether he should use a spear or a bow or a sling, were left entirely to his own choice and ability. Very possibly, many men of the army had neither spear, sword, bow, nor sling, but fought with whatever weapon or missile, stick or stone, offered itself at the moment. In one passage, Poseidon is said to have urged the Achaeans to exchange armor (Ξ 376),—giving the larger shield to the braver man; but we do not hear of this action elsewhere, and this passage was rejected by the great critic Aristarchus. Each warrior owned his buckler and his helmet with the same right as any other of his possessions : the arms were not served to the troops by a quartermaster ; each man took to the war what he chose and had, and carried home at last what he had saved.

Of the value of the arms, but slight indication is given : Glaucus and Diomed exchange armor on learning that their *Value of Arms.* grandfathers had been friends (Z 235), and the poet adds that Zeus took away the common-sense of Glaucus, since he " gave golden arms for bronze,—arms worth one hundred cattle for those worth nine." Of the two shields, the one had a plate of gold and the other one of bronze, but these plates were not always thick, and the difference in value may have lain as much in the manufacture as in the metals. In the funeral games in honor of Patroclus, the first impulse of Achilles is to give a mare as a prize to Eumelus, who has met with an accident, but when the mare is claimed by another contestant, Achilles gives a cuirass of bronze (Ψ 560), probably of about the same value as the mare.

The principal defense of the Homeric warrior consisted in a great shield which protected the whole body, from the *Shield Chief Defense.* upper breast to well below the knee.[1] Hector's shield, as he ran from the field of battle to the city, with a message for the queen, Hecuba, struck his neck above and his ancles below (Z 117), and the shield of Ajax is compared to a tower (H 219). One epithet for the shield is " man-protecting " (ἀμφιβρότη, B 389, Λ 32, M 402, Υ 281), and another is " reaching to the feet " (ποδηνεκής, O 646, *cf.* K 24, 178). The buckler was carried by a broad strap[2] which passed over the left shoulder (*cf.* Π 106, where the left shoulder of Ajax was weary from the weight of the shield) and under the right arm, and was guided in part by this strap and partly by one of the rods which served as ribs or braces within (κανών,

---

[1] The early Celts also are said to have had no defensive armor but their very heavy and large shields. They were wont to fight naked above the waist,—with which may be compared the Mycenaean representations of Figs. 24, 25, 26.

[2] τελαμών, B 388, E 796, 798, etc.—The name of the father of the great Ajax is derived from this *telamon*,—and seems particularly appropriate in the family of the Ajax who bore a shield " like a tower."—Like other leather-work, this strap was sometimes adorned with plates of metal (M 401).

Θ 193, N 407). It might be left to hang like a fencer's *plastron*, or a base-ball catcher's breast-protector,—indeed it generally did so hang loose,—and then the warrior was free to use both hands at once. Thus the ambidextrous Asteropaeus hurls two spears at the same time (Φ 162). Hector, holding his spear in his left hand, seizes a great stone with his right (Π 734), and, a few verses later, he and Ajax each hold fast with one hand to the body of Cebriones (Π 762), while they must have borne also both shield and spear. When Hector again seizes a great stone,—greater than two men could lift, " such as men now are," when he braces himself and hurls it effectively against the gates of the Achaean camp,—he cannot be carrying his shield on one arm (M 445), and he does not seem to have laid it down ; to put off a shield which hung from a broad strap was not the act of a moment, nor a natural one at such a crisis in the midst of a conflict,—the shield must have hung free. Menelaus and Meriones carry the body of Patroclus from the field of battle (P 722),—each seeming to have shield and spear of his own, although we may conceive them to have given these to comrades to carry. Similarly, the two Ajaxes hold up the body of Imbrius, take off his armor, and behead him (N 197 ff.). The Homeric spear itself was too long and heavy to be wielded conveniently and effectively with one hand. Certainly one hand would not have sufficed to thrust at his foe Hector's spear, more than sixteen feet in length (Z 319), and still less could Ajax have wielded the great boarding-pike, twice as long as Hector's spear (O 677), if he had needed to use one hand and arm in the support and care of his shield. That the warriors often carry two spears, as at E 495, Z 104, Λ 43, M 464, may be taken as another indication that their shields hung free. Reichel draws a like inference from passages where wounded men extend their arms to their comrades, as at Δ 521, N 545 ff.

In taking his position for the fray, the warrior with a heavy shield must have stooped or crouched slightly, resting his weight chiefly on one leg, and bracing himself with the other,—allowing the lower edge of the shield to stand upon the ground, while the upper edge pressed against his shoulder or breast. In order to escape a thrust or missile aimed at his head or neck, he might crouch or kneel, or "duck" his head, as at X 274, N 405 ff., 503 ff., *Shield Rested on the Ground.* P 526. That the neck was left without protection by the shield in general, is shown by the wounds which were inflicted on that part, as at Π 339, X 322 f.

By drawing the broad strap, the *telamon* or baldric, the shield could be slipped under the right arm, and so pulled about as to hang on the back. Thus it is *Slipped upon the Back.* hanging in some Mycenaean scenes, and so Ajax carries his on the third day of battle, when several of the chieftains are disabled and he is compelled to retreat before the foe (Λ 545),—doubtless bringing the shield in front of him on each occasion when he turns to face the enemy (Λ 566 ff.). Periphetes may have been carrying his shield on his back at O 645, when "turning backward" he tripped on the edge of his shield and fell, being held in his prostrate and helpless condition by the strap of his heavy shield. So, very likely, Hector carries his shield when he hastens to the city from the plain, with directions for the Trojan matrons (Z 117), and so charioteers may wear them when they are out of the range of missiles.[1] On the Mycenaean sword (see Fig. 24), the man farthest from the lions has his shield hung behind him; thus he can hurl his spear to better advantage. The man next him has no shield at all, having laid aside the encumbrance as soon as he saw that it was not needed, and indeed to us a shield seems an odd weapon of defense in a conflict with wild beasts. When the sword was to be used, also, the shield might be thrown upon the back, in order to give more freedom to the right arm. The Homeric wounds upon the breast, where no mention is made of the shield, may certainly be explained in part by supposing that the warrior had thrown his shield back for some reason, rather than that, not appreciating the danger of the moment, he had laid it off, or that the shield did

---

[1] Gerhard, *Auserlesene Vasenbilder*, ccviii.—*Cf.* also "The superior fiend | Was moving toward the shore; his ponderous shield, | Ethereal temper, massy, large, and round, | *Behind him cast*," Milton, *Par. Lost*, i. 283.

not render the protection which it was designed to afford.

Since the shield hung from a strap, and might be moved to the right, the warriors were less necessarily defense- *Right Side Protected.* less on their right side than they were in later times when the buckler hung from the left arm. Less stress therefore was laid on the contrivance that a fortification should be assailable only by a force which exposed the right side, and a greater desire was felt to secure an approach which should allow an attack from the defenders on both sides, as at the Lions' Gate of the citadel of Mycenae. At Tiryns, however, the natural approach was with the right side toward the fortifications.

For the Homeric warrior, then, the shield was not a mere appendage to other armor, like the light round shield of later times ; it was the warrior's chief protection. It served the purpose of a cuirass rather than that of a mere buckler, and it was used as a covering when men were bivouacking in bad weather (ξ 474). The poet speaks of Hector, Aeneas, and others as "having their shoulders wrapped in their shields" (εἰλυμένω ὤμους, P 492, ξ 479), and the same verb is used for putting on a shield as for donning a garment (δῦτω, Ξ 377, ἐσσάμενοι, Ξ 372 ; *cf.* M 425). It was never used to parry a blow or a missile, though the warrior

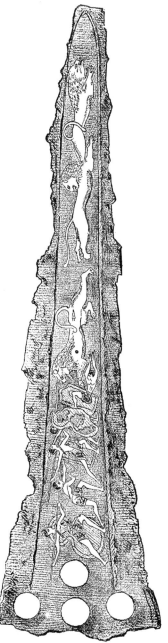

FIG. 24. Dagger.

might hide himself behind it. It could not have been carried on the left arm, and indeed Herodotus (i. 171) says that the Carians were the first to have handles (ὄχανα) for their shields. The authority of Herodotus may not settle the question of priority between the Carians and the Egyptians, but it seems satisfactory evidence for the existence of a tradition with regard to a time when the Hellenic shields were all carried by means of a strap. Strabo (154 C), indeed, says that the shields of the Lusitanians hung by straps and had no handles, though they were only two feet in diameter. Such shields served only as very imperfect breastplates.

The Homeric shield was made chiefly of ox-hide, untanned, stretched over a frame before drying. "Dry ox-hide" *Material of Shield.* is used as a synonym for shield.[1] Tanning was unnecessary for the leather of the shield, since the skin was not desired to be pliant, but rather to be as firm and unyielding as possible. Some sort of a frame was needed, since even the dry ox-hides of themselves would not be sufficiently firm in a wet season. More than a single hide might be required for full protection against blows and missiles. The shield of the greater Ajax, which is famed in literature, was made of seven bulls' hides, with an outer layer of bronze (ἑπταβόειον, H 220), and Ajax's half-brother Teucer bears a shield of four layers (τετραθέλυμνον, O 479). These layers were sometimes called circles (κύκλοι, M 297, Υ 280), as circular or oval in form; they were concentric, and the outer were smaller than the inner layers. Sometimes they were sewed together by metal thread (χρύσειαι ῥάβδοι, M 297), and in other cases by leather string (ῥαφαὶ ἱμάντων, χ 186). A rim of metal or hide gave additional strength and firmness to the shield (Υ 275, Z 117), but this had no tassels nor other pendants. Nestor's shield is said to be of gold (Θ 193), but this gold was doubtless simply an outer layer, like the bronze on the shield of Ajax, over other layers of hide, and may have been thin, and chiefly for ornament. The shield which Hephaestus makes for Achilles, it is true, seems at first sight to be all of metal (Σ 477 ff.), and its baldric was of

[1] βῶν ἀζαλέην, H 238; βόας αὔας, M 137, P 492.

silver (Σ 480), and Achilles's greaves were made of tin (Σ 613); but these may be compared with Hera's chariot, which is all of metal (E 722), and with Apollo's silver bow (A 49) and golden lyre (Pindar, *Pyth.* i. *init.*). Possibly, however, the poet would have us understand, without an explicit statement, that five of the folds or layers (πτύχες, Σ 481) of Achilles's shield were of leather, since as a rule the leather seems to have been the main reliance for protection. Sarpedon has a "beautiful bronze shield which a blacksmith forged" (M 295), but the poet goes on to say that the smith "sewed the many bulls' hides with golden wire." The "forging," in the strict sense, must have been simply of the outer layer, and possibly of the frame.

The Homeric shield is so heavy that even Telamonian Ajax is fain to give his to his men to hold for a few moments' respite (N 709,—just as a Spartan had a helot to carry his shield for him on the march), *Weight of Shield.* and it is laid off when possible (Γ 89, 114, *cf.* E 798). Hector leans his against a projecting tower of the city wall (X 97), as he awaits Achilles's approach for the final and fatal conflict. The shield of Ajax, being made of seven bulls' hides, would weigh not far from two hundred pounds, even though the hides were rather thoroughly trimmed. No wonder that it is likened to a tower, and that his shoulder grows weary beneath the load (Π 106). Clearly this could not be carried on the left fore-arm. At H 122 the armor of Menelaus is taken from his shoulders as soon as the decision is made that he is not to fight with Hector in single combat, while at H 206 Ajax has to arm himself when the lot appoints him to be the Achaean champion. Evidently Ajax had put off his shield at once when the truce was called. The weight of the shield supplies the best explanation of the use of the chariot by the leaders in the Homeric armies. Carrying their shields, they could not move easily and rapidly from the camp to the field of battle, nor from one part of the field to another; nor, with it, could they conveniently ride on horseback, since to mount without stirrups while bearing a heavy shield would have been extremely difficult, and impossible in the crisis when the chariot was most valued.

But though on ordinary occasions the combatant was glad to use a chariot for quick and easy transportation from one part of the field to another, the shield of Achilles was not so heavy and clumsy as to prevent him from pursuing Hector thrice around the walls of Troy (X 145), and Hector too must then have borne his shield,—resumed after he had leaned it against a projecting tower (X 97). The extraordinary strength and spirit of these men, and the prize before them (" they ran for the life of Hector," X 161), enabled them to do what would have been impossible for most. The poet does not tell his hearers whether these warriors wore their shields upon their backs as they ran,— but this is quite possible, since this allowed freer motion, and the poet was not bound to add such a detail. The weight and clumsiness of the Mycenaean and the Homeric shield must not lead the reader to think of it as a literal tower which could not be carried and wielded by a vigorous warrior for a considerable time, and short quick dashes were made with it (as at Λ 354, Π 342). But the action of Achilles in conflict with the river Scamander must have been particularly arduous for him while bearing a heavy shield. The stream fell upon his shield, which he may have drawn upon his back (Φ 241), and he was not able to stand firm upon his feet: the water followed him as he leaped to the shore, and the wave struck his shoulders (Φ 269), while the under-current tore the earth from beneath his feet. All this story, however, indicates rather the super-human strength of Achilles than the small size and light weight of his shield. He was unable to let his shield go, since the strap passed about his neck, and under his right arm ; so he had no opportunity to free himself.

By stooping a little, the warrior could lean upon his shield. For the protection of his neck and head, we have seen that he must crouch or kneel, and in this *Limitations of Shield.* position he could use his spear to thrust, though not conveniently to hurl. Evidently since the shield could hang as a plastron, leaving both hands free, it could not be so tall that while resting upon the ground it should protect the wearer's neck, except as he stooped. Behind it the warrior could move a little from side to side

(Γ 360, H 254, Υ 261, 278), though it hung from the shoulder. The baldric must have allowed the warrior so to stoop that he could pick up a missile or his own spear from the ground, but, as we have seen, the shield cannot have been easily put off. When Hector falls with his shield over him (H 272), Apollo is needed to set him upon his feet again. In two instances (N 543, Ξ 419), after a wound on or near the ·throat, the head sinks forward on the breast, the strap of the shield slips over the head, and the shield falls. At the death of Patroclus also (Π 802), "the shield with its strap falls to the ground from his

Fig. 26.—Oval Mycenaean Shield.

Fig. 25.—Semi-cylindrical Mycenaean Shield.

Fig. 27.—Front of the Oval Shield.

shoulders"; but here the poet leaves the hearers in doubt whether the fall of the shield is due to the sinking forward of Patroclus's head, or to the special interference of Apollo.

Two distinctly different forms of shields are represented on Mycenaean works of art (see Figs. 25, 26, 27), both supported by straps which pass around the neck and over the right shoulder,—(1) a semi-cylindrical shield,[1] made from a quadrangular piece of ox-hide,—the original skin with the extremities removed,—stretched on a curved frame, hanging nearly as close as a cuirass, but leaving free action for the arms, occasionally having a continuation at the top for the protection of the wearer's

Two forms of Shield.

---

[1] This cylindrical shield may remind the reader of some representations of those carried by Roman gladiators.

chin ; and (2) another shield much more frequently used, longer and no doubt heavier than the former, made from a round or nearly round piece of leather, but so drawn together at the sides as to seem more nearly oval. The latter, giving more space between itself and the bearer's body, allowed freer movement to the legs, and made it possible for the warrior whose shield had been pierced, more easily to escape harm by bending to one side. Either of the two forms might have an outer layer of bronze ; both seem to have had rims, or carefully sewed or riveted edges.

In addition to the two main varieties of shields, doubtless others were in use. We have been reminded that the *Choice of Shields.* Homeric warriors made no attempt to secure uniformity either in dress or in accoutrements. Individualism had not yielded to Socialism in these matters, and the warriors were equipped as individuals, and not as regiments. Some might prefer a lighter shield,— as less burdensome, although less effective,—or they might be unable to procure such a one as that of Ajax, who was recognized at a distance by his " shield like a tower." Many of the arms doubtless were made by the men who were to use them, although the name is mentioned of Tychius of Hyle, " far the best of the workers in leather," who made the shield for Ajax (H 220). At least they were not made in factories according to a single pattern, but for individuals, and according to the particular taste of the warrior.

To stretch the rods of the shield's frame directly from side to side, was impracticable. This would have interfered *Frame of Shields.* with the proper use of the shield for protection, since in that case its bearer could not stand in any sense within the shield. The semi-cylindrical shield seems to have had curved cross-ribs and straight upright rods of wood or metal. The larger shield, in addition to the vertical rod, which in this shield bent outward near the middle, had also a horizontal rod or brace, also bent outward near the middle,—or it may have had a more solid frame of a like shape. The horizontal rod was fastened to the two sides of the shield somewhat above the middle, and the sides were so far drawn together as to give the front view of the shield on primitive works of art a shape which has been compared sometimes to the Arabic figure 8, and again to the body of a violin. This shape is much like that of the *ancilia* of the Roman Salii. In other representations the shield appears much more nearly oval, with less marked incisions at the sides. The cut in the side of the shield seems to be due chiefly to the manner in which the shield was most easily made, and not to have been designed to facilitate the bearer's use of the spear ; so far as appears, the spear was thrown above, or entirely at one side of, the shield. In some cases the wooden frame seems to have been far more solid and substantial than in others. The wood may at times have been the chief element, having only a single layer of metal or of bronze upon it. In other shields, two braces, one vertical and the other horizontal, as we have seen, sufficed to give the desired firmness and solidity. The vertical brace may at times have been on the outside of the shield, as it clearly is on some Mycenaean shields ; the horizontal braces must have been in the interior. The horizontal brace may not have followed the innermost part of the curve of the hides, and thus may have served as a handle, by which the wearer could guide the shield, or hold it from him, or lift it when he desired to enter a chariot, or ascend any other steps, or to descend,—or if he wished to advance with neck and breast most fully protected.[1] Possibly in its earliest form, this "figure eight" shield may have had no frame, but consisted merely of a round or oval piece of oxhide, with a baldric fastened at either side where the rod and strap were fastened later ; then by the weight of the hide, the shield would have been contracted where the strap held it. This determined the general form. Naturally, when the hides were thicker and more numerous, the contraction of the sides would be less, and the shield would appear more nearly oval. The baldric was attached at the ends of the horizontal rod, which, as we have seen, while not fitted to serve as a true and main support for the shield, might be used conveniently as a guide for it. In

---

[1] *Cf.* ὑπασπίδια προβιβάς, II 609, N 807, *cf.* 157.

the hollow of such a shield a battle axe could hang, as at
N 611. This shield would have an obtuse projection in
front,—not an added boss, but a true "navel,"[1] caused by
the drawing together of the ends and, particularly, of the
sides. The Phaeacian island, as seen from a distance by
Odysseus in the water, appears like a shield on the surface
of the sea (ὡς ὅτε ῥινόν, ε 281),[2] and Reichel compares the
central boss to the summit of a mountain, and the folds
and creases of the shield to valleys and ridges. The boss,
naturally, is not at the exact centre of the shield, but a
trifle above this, since to increase the ease of wielding the
shield, the ends of the baldric are attached above the
middle.

To manage such a shield as that of the Homeric and
Mycenaean heroes, required both strength and skill, and
Hector in boasting of his might and prowess in
Wielding of Shields. battle maintains that he knows how to turn his
dry ox-hide to the right and to the left,—
(H 238),—possibly referring to his skill in drawing it either
to the right, upon his back, or to the left to cover the
breast. In mounting his chariot, or in turning about, or
in holding his shield for the protection of a fallen comrade
(as E 299 ff.), the warrior naturally was obliged to leave a
part of his person unprotected by the shield, as at Δ 468,
Λ 251, 423, Π 312, even when he had but a single
antagonist opposing him personally. Hector was particularly
alert in protecting himself at Π 359, where the "mighty
Ajax was ever striving to hurl his spear at Hector, but he
with skill in battle (ἰδρείῃ πολέμοιο) watched the whistling
of the arrows and the thud of spears." The shield was an
excellent defense, but it could not save a man from wounds
on all occasions, and particularly when he was attacked
from more than one direction at once.

Some passages do not indicate clearly and consistently
whether the warrior bore a heavy and clumsy shield or a
small and lighter one. Sometimes the shield does not
protect from a spear the lower part of the leg (Φ 591),

---

[1] ὀμφαλός, N 192; cf. ἀσπίδες ὀμφαλόεσσαι, Δ 448; an epithet of the shield used
eleven times in the *Iliad* and once in the *Odyssey*.

[2] ὡς ὅτ' ἐρινόν is indeed the reading of Aristarchus, but the other is more satisfactory.

and again it does not save the breast from harm by a hurled stone (Ξ 412.) At Ξ 404, Ajax seems to be saved by the dart's falling at the point on his breast where the strap of his shield crossed that of *Wounds in Spite of* his sword ; how the javelin failed to be intercepted *Shields.* by the shield, the poet does not say. That men should be wounded in battle in spite of all precautions, is not strange, and wounds are received, as we have seen, in all parts of the body. Occasionally the poet explains that a wound was inflicted upon the side, or as the warrior left himself exposed by some incautious movement (Π 400), or that the spear pierced the shield (Γ 357), but often the hearer receives no such explanation. A shield may be " man-protecting " and yet not render its bearer invulnerable. From a wound in the bowels we cannot infer with certainty that the sufferer carried no shield at all ; it may be that he bore a shield, but that through some circumstance this did not protect him at that crisis.

Homer uses two words for shield,—ἀσπίς and σάκος,— but we cannot definitely distinguish between these, and apply one name exclusively to either of the two forms which have been described as Mycenaean. The *Two Words for Shield.* great shield of Ajax, a σάκος, made of seven bulls' hides, is compared to a tower (H 219), and so might seem to be of the semi-cylindrical kind, but it has a boss (H 267). Hector's shield is thought to be of the oval descrip-tion because of an expression (ἀσπίδ' ἐνιχριμφθείς, H 272) which implies that his body in a manner entered it, but it is not necessary to assume that the Homeric poets were careful of consistency in this matter, and that they always assigned the same sort of shield to each warrior,—Ajax's shield was so noted as to be a personal characteristic, but many of the others were undetermined. The shield which Hephaestus makes for Achilles we might expect to be oval. When his former shield is taken from his fallen friend Patroclus, and he would enter the conflict to save his friend's body, the restraining thought comes to Achilles's mind that no shield in the army is large enough for him except that of Ajax, which that warrior is wearing on the field. He then would desire such a shield as he had lost. But the scenes on the shield made by Hephaestus are more easily arranged symmetrically, if we suppose the shield to be round.

The round shield was introduced into Greece in the latter part of the Epic age, or at least before the com-

Round Shield. position of the early verses of the eleventh book of the *Iliad*, which describe the shield of Agamemnon ; but these verses were composed doubtless much later than the battle scenes of the same book. The round shield may have been used by the Ionians in the seventh, eighth, or ninth centuries before our era. Reichel called attention to the facts that the shield of Agamemnon has a strap, but that this is adorned with a serpent,—a kind of decoration which does not appear elsewhere in Homer or in Mycenaean art ; that it has a main boss, but this is of blue enamel, which has nothing to do with the structure of the shield, and adds nothing in any way to its strength, while the additional twenty minor bosses of tin find no analogy in any other part of the poems ; the shield has the Gorgon's head upon it,—but just where this lies is not indicated, since at the central boss would seem the natural place for it,—and this Gorgon's head is considered a " late element in Greek art " ; and the ten circles (κύκλοι, Λ 33) are bands, not layers as elsewhere. Clearly this shield does not come into the same class as the ordinary Homeric shields, and it can be explained most easily as a round buckler. Robert holds that the round bronze shield is used far more frequently than Reichel would allow,—sometimes being held on the arm as in later times, and not infrequently hung by a strap about the neck, like the Mycenaean shields. The manner in which a wound is inflicted may argue for one form of shield or the other.

If the order of words is to be pressed, in Λ 374, Agastrophus, of whom we hear only in this passage, must have had a smaller shield than has been described as characteristic of the Homeric age, for Diomed took from him (1) his cuirass, (2) his shield, (3) and his helmet. With the heavy Mycenaean shield, the helmet must have been removed before the shield, and the shield before the cuirass. A " hysteron proteron " would not be an impossible hypothesis, but this is the only passage in the Homeric poems in which a cuirass is taken from a corpse, and this of itself suggests that the passage may be of later composition.

Evidence in favour of the use and general prevalence of the large Mycenaean shields in the Homeric age, of itself of course offers no argument against the poet's familiarity also with the smaller buckler, but the great rarity of distinct references to the round shield must be received as an indication that this was rare in the poet's mind. If the whole of the description of Agamemnon's shield is the work of one poet, we might attribute the use of the epithet "man-protecting" (Λ 32), and the mention of the strap (Λ 38), to the poet's consciousness of two characteristics of the older shield, though he passes to describe a shield of a later style. Robert, on the other hand, supposes that, in some passages, epithets appropriate to one form of shield, in the tradition of the poems, have become exchanged with metrically equivalent epithets which were appropriate to the other form of shield.

A Homeric expression which has often been translated "round" (πάντοσ' ἐίση, as Γ 347), may mean simply "well-proportioned," "well-balanced," says Reichel,—not mathematically "equal on every side." This epithet, which is used seventeen times in all, is applied at Ν 157, 803, to what are clearly the Mycenaean long shields, having been exchanged in Robert's opinion for some epithet like *well-rimmed* (τερμιόεσσα), since it would seem most appropriate to the round bronze buckler. The epithet "man-protecting" (ἀμφιβρότη), which is used four times in the poems, in Β 389 seems to be applied to all shields: "The strap of many a one's man-protecting shield will sweat about his breast."

No *testudo* is formed by the Homeric warriors. In their closest phalanx their shields rest upon the ground (Ν 128). At Μ 137, the warriors hold up their shields, but individually, because they are assailing a wall *No Testudo.* from which missiles are hurled. These would seem to be round bucklers, rather than the great Mycenaean shields "like a tower."

Peltasts or targeteers are unknown to Homer.

Devices are unknown on Homeric shields.[1] The only exception is the shield of Agamemnon (Λ 36), which had

No Devices. upon it the Gorgon's head, and Terror and Flight,— but this shield is unique in other respects also, as we have seen. Thus Aeschylus is anachronistic in assigning shields with elaborate devices to the warriors before seven-gated Thebes (*Septem*, 387, 432, etc.).

An interesting indication that the shields of at least some of the minor epic poems were of the Mycenaean

Shields in Later Story. type, was found by Reichel in the fact that in the sculptures of Gyölbashi a shield served as a bier for the corpse of Patroclus. This seems due to the tradition of the story, for the shields of the artist's time were not of a size to suggest such a use. But all remember the Spartan mother's injunction to her son as she gave him his shield,—" Either this or upon this,"—and the artist may have had a Spartan shield in mind. Other Spartans were brought home on their shields, according to Plutarch, and Tyrtaeus in the seventh century B.C. speaks of a shield which covers the lower legs (κνήμας, ix. 23) as well as the shoulders, while in the 13th fragment he urges that the shield be held forward on the left arm.

The great Homeric shield was for nobles and princes. Probably the common man had a protection which was lighter

Laiseïa. and less costly even than the small round buckler, in the *laiseïon* (λαισήιον, E 453, M 426),[2] which is mentioned twice, but in an identical line, in connexion with the ox-hide shields, but is not assigned to any chieftain. In strictness this was not a shield at all. Herodotus (vii. 91) says that the Cilicians in the army of Xerxes bore " instead of shields *laiseïa* made of untanned oxhides." In the first Messenian war " those who had neither cuirass nor shield wore goatskins and sheepskins, and some the skins of wild animals ; and especially the mountaineers of Arcadia wore

---

[1] Professor Chase, *Harvard Studies*, xiii. 62, disputes this view, and cites also E 739 and Σ 469. The three passages seem to show, however, only the decoration of shields. That metal ornaments should be laid upon shields as well as upon other works of leather, is only natural.

[2] Of uncertain derivation. Old etymologists connected it with λάσιος, *shaggy*, which would refer to the hairy surface of the skin being retained.

the skins of wolves and bears" (Pausanias, iv. 11, 3). Of these "the great mass" (ὁ ὄχλος ὁ πολύς) were light armed, as we should expect. The Homeric *laiseïon* received the epithet of winged or fluttering (πτερόεις, E 453), probably with reference to the loose ends of the skin, though it has been interpreted to mean light, in contrast with the heavy shields which had a frame and several layers. Possibly in the heroic age, two or more thicknesses of skin were used for this as well as for the shield proper. Its material is indicated by its apposition with ox-hides (βοείας). Doubtless not all *laiseïa* were alike; as great variety was possible here as in anything else. On ancient vases appear divers representations of warriors wearing the skins of animals tied about the neck by the two front paws. Thus Heracles was represented as clad in the skin of the Nemean lion, which served less as a garment, as a protection against cold, than as a shield, a defense against wounds. This particular lion's skin, the reader will remember, could not be cut by any metal. Jason, also, comes down from the cave of Chiron (Pindar, *Pyth.* iv. 81) with a leopard skin about his shoulders, but this was a protection "against bristling storms." This was the most primitive form of a shield, and appears on vases as worn by giants who are hurling stones, but it was retained in use by bowmen, and by slingers, who clearly could not manage even a light round shield together with their archery and their slings. That it did not belong exclusively to the archers, however, is shown by the scolion of Hybrias of Crete, in which the Cretan poet names as his wealth "great spear and sword, and the beautiful *laiseïon*, protection for my body" (πρό-βλημα χρωτός). At the opening of the first day of battle of the *Iliad*, Paris appears in front of the Trojan line, with "leopard skin and bent bow" (Γ 17), and the Trojan scout Dolon has a "bent bow and the skin of a grey wolf" as he sets out by night to learn what the Achaeans are doing (K 334). The goddess Aphrodite uses a fold of her garment as a warrior might use a leopard skin which hung about him, for the protection of her son Aeneas, as she carries him wounded from the field of battle (E 315), and the chlamys on the left arm of the Apollo Belvedere is conjectured to have taken the place of the earlier *laiseïon*. When after the second day of battle, which closes disastrously for the Achaeans, Agamemnon in his anxiety cannot sleep, and rises to call a council of the elders, he puts about him a lion's skin and seizes his spear (K 23), and Diomed being summoned does the same (K 177), while Menelaus takes leopard skin, helmet, and spear (K 29),—each warrior evidently taking the skin as a light shield,—and Odysseus puts on his great shield (K 149). The circumstances explain why the skins of lion and panther are worn by

Fig. 28.—Athena with Aegis.

Achaean chieftains only in this book of the *Iliad*. Elsewhere Agamemnon and Menelaus appear before the lines only as heavy-armed warriors, on their way to battle. Now they are going to a council, and do not need full armor. The light equipment suffices, but to go entirely unarmed would not have been in accordance with military etiquette. A centaur in the twenty-seventh metope of the Parthenon has a leopard skin over his left arm in the thick of the contest, in which he has just slain his foe. Clearly this was for defense and not for clothing.[1]

[1] In Professor Hopkins's *Military Caste in Ancient India*, p. 305, he describes the Hindoo shield as "of leather, adorned with figures; or a simple tiger-skin or bear-skin worn over the body, besides the brazen breastplate, served as a shield."

The aegis is supposed by Reichel to be such a skin as has been discussed,—a *laiseïon*. Thus when Athena appears to the Achaeans as they set out for battle, "with the highly honored aegis" (B 446), it is equivalent *The Aegis.* to appearing "with shield," "in armor," "equipped for battle." She takes the aegis as a mortal would take a shield, and "casts it about her shoulders" (*cf.* E 736 ff. with Γ 330 ff., T 369 ff., K 148), and on it she receives the blow of Ares's spear (Φ 400). She puts the aegis about the shoulders of Achilles in the absence of his shield (Σ 203), when he appears to the Trojans after the death of Patroclus. With the aegis, Apollo covers the body of Hector (Ω 20, *cf.* P 132). On early vases the aegis of Athena is represented as a skin which not simply lies over her breast, but also falls like a mantle over her back. The tassels or θύσανοι of B 448 may be tufts of hair, and we are reminded that the same word is used by Pindar of the tufts of the Golden Fleece (*Pyth.* iv. 231); such tufts may have been the original of the scale-like surface of the aegis as it is represented at times on works of art. The epithet "shaggy on both sides"[1] may refer to the shaggy sides of the undressed skin as it falls on either side of the wearer's arm. The figures of Flight, Strife, Defense, Rout, and the Gorgon's head, which according to E 738 were on the aegis, may be thought of as attached to the skin, just as the girdle and the baldrics of the Homeric shields and swords were often adorned with thin plates of bronze or of silver. On such plates may be based the epithet *gleaming* (μαρμαρέη, P 594), which is applied once to the aegis. The aegis of Zeus was at least in part of metal, since it was the work of Hephaestus (Ο 310), but this god makes a golden crest for the helmet of Achilles (Σ 612), and may have used more metal for the aegis than a mortal maker would have done, According to Eratosthenes (*Cataster.* xiii.), Musaeus told how Zeus had assumed for his weapon of defense the invulnerable skin of the goat which nourished him,—but other divinities may have had similar skins for

---

[1] ἀμφιδάσεια, Ο 309 ; *cf.* δασύ as applied to a goatskin in ξ 51, and δασύμαλλος of sheep in ι 425 ; also the suggested etymological connexion between λάσιος, *shaggy,* and λαισήιον.

their protection. In the Homeric poems Zeus is represented but once as using his aegis,—"Then the son of Cronus took his bright, tufted aegis, and covered Mount Ida with clouds, and, sending a lightning flash, he thundered very loudly, and shook this aegis, and gave victory to the Trojans, and put the Achaeans to flight" (P 593). The only other reference to the use of the aegis by Zeus is, after Menelaus has been treacherously wounded, when Agamemnon predicts the vengeance of the angry Zeus, who will destroy the city of the Trojans and "shake at them his gloomy aegis, in anger at this deceit" (Δ 167). Whether the aegis of Zeus was borrowed from him by Athena, or rather that she had an aegis of her own, is not definitely stated. If the contention is correct that the aegis was a *laiseïon*, as seems to be true, then the epithet "aegis-bearing" would belong to Zeus only metrically, just as the epithet "white-armed" belongs to Hera,—not that she was the only white-armed goddess, but since only to her name was this epithet particularly convenient in the verse. The other divinities may each have had an aegis of his own. Thus Athena has an aegis at B 447, E 738, Σ 204, Φ 400, χ 297,—with no indication of any kind that this was borrowed from Zeus. In the fifteenth book of the *Iliad*, it is true, Apollo has the aegis of Zeus, but this is given to him for a special purpose, when he is sent by Zeus to the Trojan plain on a special errand (O 307 ff.). At the beginning of the last book of the *Iliad*, the reader learns that Apollo wrapped the dead body of Hector in an aegis, that it might not be torn when Achilles dragged it about the tomb of his comrade Patroclus (Ω 20). This last passage was rejected by Aristarchus, who held that the aegis belonged to Zeus alone, but it evidently is entirely intelligible on the supposition that the aegis was the flexible skin of an animal, and that the indefinite article is in place before it.[1]

To say that Zeus and Athena need no shield at all, is to introduce into Homer the notions of a later and reflective age. If Athena fears no wound, why does she arm herself

---

[1] For the aegis, see Welcker, *Götterlehre*, i. 167; Bader, *Jahrbücher*, 1878, pp. 577 ff.—The warriors of the Baliaric islands went into battle ungirt, "with an aegis about the arm," αἰγίδα περὶ τῇ χειρὶ ἔχοντες, Strabo, 168 C.

for battle before descending to the field of conflict (E 737, Θ 388)? Why should she not need a shield as truly as Ares and Aphrodite, who are both wounded by Diomed (E 336, 858)? She was vulnerable, we must believe, though she may have been less likely to be wounded than the weaklings. The old usage of wearing a skin as a defense is retained by the gods, who are always thought to be conservative, just ·as old customs are retained longest by men in their worship. So Apollo, the war-god, is almost uniformly represented with bow and arrows, not as a heavy armed warrior, like a late statue of Mars, and Heracles, the mightiest warrior of men, is a bowman. In the east frieze of the so-called Theseum at Athens is depicted a conflict in which a youthful figure "with an object like a garment falling over his left arm, has an important place." This figure has been conjectured to represent Apollo, and the "garment" may have been an aegis.

No trace of any cuirass [1] or breastplate is found on any Mycenaean monument, and this piece of armor seems to be unknown in Greece even later, in the time of the so-called Dipylon vases. It has not been *No Cuirass or Breastplate at Mycenae.* found represented on vases earlier than the seventh century B.C. On a fragment of a Dipylon vase even oarsmen are depicted as rowing under the cover of shields,—clearly because they had no breastplates. So the warriors in the pediments of the temple of Aphaea on Aegina wore no cuirasses (Fig. 35).[2] Thus the cuirass in the Homeric poems is thought by Reichel to be an anachronism, though it seems to be mentioned thirty-four times. Seven Achaeans are named as wearing the cuirass: Achilles (Σ 460, 610, T 371), Agamemnon (Λ 19 ff., 234), Diomed (E 99 f., 189, 282, Θ 195, Ψ 819), Meges (O 529), Menelaus (Δ 133, 136, N 587 ff.), Odysseus (Λ 436), and Patroclus (Π 133, 804); and ten Trojans: Agastrophus

---

[1] This observation and the deductions from it were presented with emphasis first by Reichel in the work which has been often quoted.

[2] Most of these warriors wore no clothing, either; and they carried the round shield, which is associated with the cuirass. So this argument alone has not much weight. A group of statues at Olympia, by Onatas, represented Achaean warriors with spear and shield, and evidently without cuirass (Paus. v. 25. 8).

(Λ 373), Asteropaeus (Ψ 560), Hector (H 252, P 606), Lycaon (Γ 332), Oenomaus (N 507), Othryoneus (N 371), Paris (Γ 332, 358, Z 322), Phorcys (P 314). Polydorus (Y 415), and the charioteer of Asius (N 397). A cuirass is indicated also for the Trojans Alcathoüs and Antiphus, and the Achaean Menesthius.[1] This piece of armor, then, does not seem to belong specially to either Achaeans or Trojans. Ajax, Teucer, Idomeneus, and others on the Achaean side, and Aeneas, Sarpedon, Glaucus, and others on the Trojan side, have none,—as well as Ares (cf. E 857, O 125). Apparently it is not in general use, nor is it consistently worn. Odysseus seems to have one at Λ 436, but none at Λ 456, only twenty verses later; Diomed seems to have one at E 98, but none at E 112 nor at E 795 ff.; Hector has one at H 252 and P 606, but apparently not at Ξ 412, nor in the twenty-second book of the *Iliad*; Achilles has none at Y 259, and Ajax none at Ξ 404. If a cuirass seems to be used by a warrior who carries a great Mycenaean shield, we may suspect an interpolation, for the two were not necessary together, and would have been cumbrous and inconvenient,—at least if the cuirass were such a heavy corslet as became usual.

The cuirass is named neither in the *Odyssey* nor in the tenth book of the *Iliad*, the so-called *Dolonia*, of which

No Cuirass in Odyssey.

Odysseus is one of the two heroes and which bears other resemblances to the *Odyssey*,—although not a few opportunities for its mention occur there. In the *Dolonia*, for example, the poet describes old Nestor as lying in his soft couch "with his bright arms beside him,—his shield and two spears, and his bright helmet, and his gleaming belt lay by his side" (K 75). Why should the cuirass not be mentioned, if he was accustomed to wear it? That the *Odyssey*, which seems to be of later composition than the *Iliad*, and the tenth book of the *Iliad*, which is generally thought to be of later composition than most of the rest of the poem, yet contain no mention of the cuirass, which came into use after the earliest epic period, is certainly strange. The suggestion

---

[1] Alcathoüs,—χιτῶνα χάλκεον ὅς οἱ πρόσθεν ἀπὸ χροὸς ἦρκει ὄλεθρον, N 439 f. ; Antiphus,—αἰολοθώρηξ, Δ 489 ; Menesthius,—αἰολοθώρηξ, Π 173.

has been made that fighting occupies so subordinate a part in the *Odyssey* that the rhapsodists were not tempted to revise that poem for the introduction of the latest armor; another explanation is that though the tenth book of the *Iliad* is a comparatively recent lay, yet it is made up of very old material. The suggested explanation of the absence of all mention of the cuirass in the *Odyssey* does not seem satisfactory. For the tenth book of the *Iliad*, the reader may remember that in connexion with the discussion of the *laiseïon* attention was called to the unusual circumstances of the *Dolonia*: the mightiest heroes of the Achaeans on that occasion go forth from the camp not for pitched battle, as usual, but for a council, or at worst for a scouting expedition. We might ask fairly enough why Agamemnon and Menelaus needed the lion and panther skins and their spears, but the reply is reasonable,—to have gone to their military council outside of the trenches, entirely without arms, would have been unwarriorlike. But these problems give a reminder of the difficulty of applying the archaeological test in the so-called "higher criticism" of the Homeric poems.

In connexion with the question of the relation of the *Odyssey* to the cuirass, Reichel notes particularly the story told by the disguised Odysseus of the ambuscade before Ilium, who represents himself as going off for the night with only shield and loin-cloth, and suffering from the cold (ξ 469 ff.). The expedition was one of danger: why did the warrior not wear a cuirass if he had one? To this perhaps the same suggestion might be made as in the case of the scouting expedition of the *Dolonia*: agility was more important than preparation to meet a pitched battle. But in the first book of the *Odyssey* the wish is expressed that Odysseus might return and take his stand at the front door of his home "with helmet, and shield, and two spears" (a 256, *cf.* σ 376). Evidently this equipment was considered to be full armor, but the cuirass is lacking. So also on the night before the slaughter of Penelope's suitors, Odysseus and his son Telemachus remove from the great hall of the palace the "helmets, shields, and spears" (τ 32, *cf.* π 284), but no mention is made of cuirasses, nor are these brought out on the next day for the defense either of the suitors or of Odysseus and his friends (χ 110, 144). Why should not the cuirasses adorn the hall of Odysseus as they did that of the poet Alcaeus (*Frag.* 56,—see page 296) and the baronial halls of the Middle Ages? The arms did not stand and lie there for immediate use; they had been there ever since Odysseus embarked for Troy,—they were merely decorative.

In the *Iliad*, too, the cuirass is not always mentioned where it might be expected, as, for example, in the contest
Cuirass not over the Achaean wall, where the combatants
always struck each other's shields, and "many were
Mentioned wounded,—each whose back was exposed as he
where turned, and many right through the shield itself"
Expected. (M 425); and explaining the part which the Locrians took in the conflict, the poet says that these had no helmets, shields, or spears, but with their archery broke the ranks of the Trojans (N 714). At Ψ 799 the armor of Sarpedon is offered as a prize in the funeral games in honor of Patroclus,—"shield and helmet," but no cuirass. Lycaon is called stripped (γυμνός, Φ 50), when he is without helmet and shield, and Hector applies the same word to his own condition if he should lay down his "shield and heavy helmet, and lean his shield against the wall" (X 111, 124).

Just as the cuirass is not figured on Mycenaean monuments. so it is said also to be unknown on Egyptian monuments of the early empire. In the "heavy-armed" race at Olympia (ὁπλιτοδρομία), even in the fifth century B.C., the cuirass was never worn, but the equipment consisted of helmet, shield, and spear, exactly as in Mycenaean times.

With regard to the cuirass, the Homeric poems afford no distinct information, either as to how it was made or how
How was it was put on. To that which Hephaestus makes
the Cuirass for Achilles the poet gives but a single line
made? (Σ 610), although one hundred and thirty-one verses are devoted to the description of the shield (Σ 478-608). We could not expect the poet to describe the making of each piece of armor in so great detail as he does the shield,—the effect might become monotonous; but the prominence given to the shield is noteworthy in particular since the cuirass was an article which was well fitted for

decoration, as we may see from the familiar statue of the Emperor Augustus, from Prima Porta, which is richly adorned with scenes from the emperor's triumphs. The description of Agamemnon's cuirass (Λ 19-28) is elaborate, though not clear, but contains (as we have seen) serpents and parallel stripes which are said to be foreign to Mycenaean ornamentation, and which appear in Homeric works of art only here ; and this cuirass is said by the poet to have been brought from Cyprus, which is thought to have been out of the range of the earliest epic poets, although the epic poem which, next to the *Iliad* and *Odyssey*, had most popularity was called the *Cyprian Epic,* and we may suppose it to have had a Cyprian author. The Homeric cuirass had plates (γύαλα, E 99), but whether these were fastened on the side or in front (like a bodice and the later cuirass), no one knows. Reichel held that often the later word for cuirass (θώρηξ) in Homer means only armor in general. Thus in the wounding of Menelaus, when the arrow fell " where the golden fastenings of the belt joined, and the two-fold armor met it " (Δ 133),[1] the armor would refer to the fastenings of the belt which served for a protection at this point. So Iphidamas struck Agamemnon on the belt below the *thorēx* (Λ 234). But how was this possible if *thorēx* in this passage means cuirass? Reichel at first suggested that the reference might be to the shield, but later withdrew this hypothesis, probably on the ground that a wound on the belt and under the shield would assume a small shield of a very different pattern from that generally carried by the Homeric warrior. If θώρηξ meant *armor* in general, then θωρήσσεσθαι would naturally mean " arm one's self for battle," and θωρηκταί (M 317, Φ 277, 429) *armed men.* But just as to *gird one's self* (ζώννυσθαι, Λ 15) and to *helm one's self* (κορύσσεσθαι, K 37) are used in the general sense of *arm,* so to *cuirass one's self* would be a natural expression in the same sense. And as *shield-bearer* (ἀσπιστής, Δ 90) and *helm-wearer* (κορυστής, Δ 457) are used for *warrior* in general, so too

---

[1] Δ 136, καὶ διὰ θώρηκος πολυδαιδάλου ἠρήρειστο, where θώρηξ must mean cuirass, has caused great perplexity to commentators. With its omission and the interpretation of θώρηξ given above for Δ 133, the meaning of the passage becomes simple.

cuirass-wearer might be the equivalent of *soldier*. A frequent epithet of the Achaeans, used twice in the *Odyssey* and thirty-one times in the *Iliad*, is "with bronze tunic" (χαλκοχίτωνες, often translated *bronze-clad*), which may refer to small plates of metal fastened for additional protection to the linen tunic, or it may be understood most freely,— the shield with bronze plate being thought of as the protecting garment. The cuirass, which consisted entirely of plates, never reached below the hips, and so would hardly have been called a tunic. So when Idomeneus "rends with his spear the tunic of Alcathoüs, the bronze tunic which in time past warded off destruction from him" (ῥῆξεν . . . χιτῶνα χάλκεον, N 439 f.), the poet's epithet may refer to bronze plates attached to the tunic. A similar expression which is used twice, is "with bronze *thorēx*" (χαλκεοθώρηξ, Δ 448, Θ 62). No entirely satisfactory explanation has been suggested for the linen *thorēx* of B 529, 830; but we must not overlook the facts that the poet Alcaeus refers to such (θώρακές τε νέω λίνω, *Frag.* 56, 5), that Xenophon represents the Chalybes and Susians as wearing them (θώρακας λινοῦς, *Anabasis,* iv. 7, 16, *Cyrop.* vi. 4. 2), and that Pausanias[1] says that they had been dedicated as votive offerings in several temples. We know that the South Sea Islanders had cuirasses of cocoanut fibre which would be proof against a bullet from a revolver, and which doubtless did good service against spears, but the linen corslets of the Achaeans are more likely to have been linen jackets to which plates of metal have been attached, as distinguished from leather jackets so strengthened.

In twenty-five passages, even Reichel admits that θώρηξ means *cuirass*. In ten of these instances, the verse

Cuirass mentioned 25 times.

or couplet in which this word occurs is at least unnecessary, and sometimes it interrupts the connexion of thought; as at Γ 332, 358, Δ 136, Z 322, H 252, Λ 436, Π 133, 804, Σ 610, T 371. Sometimes it is in a longer episode, as at Λ 19 ff., N 581 ff., Ψ 560 ff. In other passages, as B 544, E 282, Θ 195, N 265, 342, T 361, the cuirass is mentioned in such a way that no reasonable excision can remove it.

---

[1] i. 21. 7. See Frazer's note, *Pausanias,* ii. 243.

These passages, according to Reichel, must be held to have been composed after the close of the eighth century B.C. From that time on, the rhapsodists considered the cuirass an indispensable part of the hoplite's equipment,—it became such when the heavy Homeric shield fell into disuse, being exchanged for the round shield, which could be carried on the left arm,—and the mention of the cuirass may have been added to give a more modern tone to the narrative.

The earliest and the Homeric cuirass need not have been exactly like that which is represented on ancient vases. We do not know that this piece of defensive armor was introduced from other lands already perfected ; *Development of Cuirass.* very likely it was developed in Greece itself. The plates (γύαλα) may not have been so large as in later times. The Homeric cuirass may have been in the experimental stage ; it need not have been made of two plates, nor have covered the whole breast. Sometimes it may have been made of leather or strong cloth, with several or many plates of metal attached for protection and for ornament.[1] The late historic cuirass, made of a back-plate and a front-plate, could not be donned or doffed by the wearer without assistance, and only once in Homer is such help indicated,—where the attendants of Menelaus remove the armor from his shoulders (H 122),—and this more probably refers to the removal of the heavy shield. At O 125, Athena takes "the helmet from Ares's head, his shield from his shoulders, and the spear from his hands, and bids him go and be seated." Nothing is said there about his cuirass, although it would have been no more undignified for her to assist him to remove this than to help him to doff his shield. The "argument from silence" is particularly dangerous in the interpretation of Homer, but the poet enlivens his picture by so many minor details that we may expect some reference to this service if it is actually rendered on every occasion when

[1] *Cf.* Tacitus, *Hist.* i. 79, of the Sarmatae ; *id principibus et nobilissimo cuique tegimen, ferreis laminis aut praeduro corio consertum, ut adversus ictus inpenetrabile, ita impetu hostium provolutis inhabile ad resurgendum.* Pausanias, i. 21. 6, says that these Sarmatae made as it were scales from the hoofs of horses and sewed these together to form cuirasses as good as the Greeks. Ammianus Marcellinus (xvii. 12. 2) shows that these plates of horn were sewed on linen garments.

the armor is put off or on. In connexion with the cuirass as with the shield, it is important to remember again that the warriors had no uniformity of equipment.

The *zostēr* (ζωστήρ) was a belt, corresponding to the woman's *zone* (ζώνη), to gird up the long tunic (χιτών),

Zostēr, Belt. which seems to have reached at least to the knee. This was used also in ordinary life ; with it the swine-herd girds himself when he goes to the pen for a porker (ξ 72). It lay by the side of old Nestor as he slept (K 77), where the expression "with which he girt himself when he armed himself for battle," has been taken,

FIG. 29.—Mitré.

Prof. W. Ridgeway's "Early Age of Greece."

in connexion with the absence of the mention of a corslet, to imply that this was his principal piece of armor, but it naturally refers only to "girding up his loins" for action. Sometimes the girdle is called simply a strap, as where Achilles binds the arms of his Trojan captives, with the straps which they wore over their tunics (ἱμᾶσιν, Φ 30). It was, then, of leather, but was sometimes covered with a plate of metal,[1] and served as a protection for the body of Menelaus (Δ 132), whose belt was held by golden fastenings.

The *mitré* (μίτρη) was a thin band of metal about the loins. It is mentioned only in connexion with Menelaus

Mitré. (for whom it was the chief protection at a critical moment, Δ 137, 187, 216), Ares (E 857), in an epithet (αἰολομίτρης, *with bright mitré*, E 707) of a Boeotian, and in an epithet of Sarpedon's Lycian comrades *without mitré*.[2] This *mitré* is designated distinctly as "made by a blacksmith" (Δ 187), but may have been both lined and padded with cloth. Reichel suggests that the word θώρηξ of Σ 460 may have been used in a general way, meaning the *mitré*,—such a band might be made without much circumstance by Hephaestus for Achilles. Robert thinks

---

[1] Agamemnon's belt was covered with silver, Λ 236. Bronze plates which seem to have been attached to girdles have been found in Italy and in Greece.

[2] ἀμιτροχίτωνες, Π 419. According to Athenaeus 523 D, this was equivalent to *ungirt*, ἄζωστοι.

the general expression " gird on the bronze " ($\chi\alpha\lambda\kappa\grave{o}\nu$ $\zeta\acute{\omega}\nu\nu\upsilon\sigma\theta\alpha\iota$, Ψ 130), may refer primarily to this protecting band. A broad band of metal under the tunic would hardly have been needed when the cuirass was worn. That the *mitré* was often or generally covered by the tunic, would account for the fact that it is but seldom mentioned. As a rule it would attract no attention.[1]

The *zoma* ($\zeta\tilde{\omega}\mu\alpha$) seems to have been a mere loin-cloth, and as such it is worn by the boxer (Ψ 683); strictly it is not a part of the warrior's armor. When the *Loin-cloth.* disguised Odysseus tells of his going forth in light attire for an ambuscade, he says he had only " shield and loin-cloth " (ξ 482). Naturally this, as well as the *mitré*, was concealed by the tunic, and when this was worn it did not call for frequent mention. On the Mycenaean sword (Fig. 24), the loin-cloth is in the form of " bathing trunks," like the Celtic warrior's *braca*. On the silver vase (Fig. 23), the bowmen and slingers seem downright naked. Elsewhere the *zoma* is figured rather in the fashion of the American Indian's clout (Figures 25, 26).

The *greaves* ($\kappa\nu\eta\mu\tilde{\iota}\delta\epsilon\varsigma$, *shin-guards*), according to Reichel, were not originally an independent part of the armor for defense against the missiles of the foe,—the lower *Greaves.* leg is indeed sensitive, but no more exposed to wounds than the arm,—but were simply gaiters to protect the warrior's shins from being bruised by the lower edge of his shield, which, hanging loose, would strike against one or other shin at every step. These were made of cloth or leather, and hence are not found preserved in Mycenaean graves ;—but in the Mycenaean shaft-graves were gold bands (one was found *in situ* about the knee of a skeleton) which were intended to hold these gaiters in place. The old Laërtes has leather greaves or gaiters ($\kappa\nu\eta\mu\tilde{\iota}\delta\epsilon\varsigma$, ω 229) to protect his legs against the thorns, just as he wears gloves on his hands to save these from the scratches of the brambles, when he works in the field, and this is the only mention of greaves in the *Odyssey*. Similar to these greaves would be the gaiters which were worn by Artemis as a

---

[1] For the *mitré*, see Perrot et Chipiez, *Histoire de l'Art*, vol. vi., Figs. 354, 355, 420, 422 f., 426, 428.

huntress. Greaves in the later sense are not represented in the art of the Mycenaean period, nor even on the so-called Dipylon vases, but they were an important part of the hoplite's armor during the sixth and seventh centuries B.C. So in the time of Alcaeus, about 600 B.C., metal greaves were an important defense against the enemy's missiles (λάμπραι κνάμιδες, ἄρκος ἰσχύρω βέλευς, *Frag.* 56. 4 ; *cf.* Aeschylus, *Septem*, 676, κνημῖδας, αἰχμῆς καὶ πετρῶν προβλή- ματα). Bronze greaves, like the cuirass, belong to the age when the round shield has taken the place of its Mycenaean predecessor, but remnants of them were found in a tomb of late Mycenaean times, in Cyprus, and are now in the British Museum. In the fifth and fourth centuries B.C., greaves were less used than before, though the danger of wounds in the shin would seem to have been the same, but they seem to have had a revival in the Macedonian period. The " greaves of brass " which the giant Goliath wore (1 *Sam.* xvii. 6), are part of a familiar story. In the imperial times, the Roman soldier wore a greave (*ocrea*) only on the right leg. Hephaestus makes the greaves for Achilles of tin (Σ 613),—a metal with which the poet does not seem particularly well acquainted, and which might seem ill-adapted to defensive armor, but which is pliant, and would serve as well as cloth or leather for mere gaiters. If Hephaestus is to make the greaves, they must be of some metal. In fact, this tin is made by the poet to serve a useful purpose, and repels the spear of Agenor (Φ 591),— the only passage in which a greave is said by the poet to render any service at all. The Achaeans are once called " bronze-greaved " (χαλκοκνήμιδες, H 41), but elsewhere no distinctive epithet is applied to the greaves to designate color, shape, or material.

The Homeric greaves may well have rendered a two-fold service,—protecting the wearer both from bruises by his *Useful in Two Ways.* shield, and also from the missiles of the enemy. The epithet " well-greaved " (εὐκνήμιδες) is used forty-one times in the poems, and its frequency proves that the greaves were a prominent part of the warrior's equipment,—more prominent than we should expect them to be if they were simply to serve the very commonplace office of protecting the shin from bumps of the shield. The bronze greaves appear to be making their way into use, like the cuirass and the round buckler. They could be seen even behind a large shield, and the warrior was not always seen from the front, and while bearing his great shield. The light-armed troops, indeed, seem to have worn no greaves,—they needed none on Reichel's theory,—but as usual the poet applies to all the Achaeans the adjective which belongs strictly only to the better equipped of them. We should not be surprised, then, that at Δ 517 ff., an Achaean, Diores, has his right lower leg crushed by a stone thrown by a Thracian leader, without mention of a greave to break the force of the missile ; Diores may have been an archer, or the poet may not have cared to comment upon the fact that the greave did not save the ancle ; but a gaiter of cloth or leather could not be expected to save the ancle in such a case as this, where even a greave of bronze might have proved insufficient.

Silver anclets (ἐπισφύρια, Γ 331) are mentioned five times in connexion with greaves. They have been thought to be a special protection for the ancle, *Ancle-pieces.* but more probably were gaiter-holders.

Archers, as has been said, seem to have had no greaves in the Homeric battle. They needed none, if the greaves were a protection simply against repeated hurts from the warrior's own shield, and in general the *Archers had no Greaves.* light-armed troops stood in the rear, although the bowmen Paris and Helenus were exposed to danger ; and Paris dons his greaves only when he changes from light to heavy equipment (Γ 330). The goddess Athena, too, when she puts on the armor of Zeus (E 734 ff.), puts on no greaves. We cannot explaih this fact by saying that she had no fear of wounds, for the same objection would apply to her use of the helmet which she takes. But Athena puts upon her shoulders the old-fashioned light *aegis*, and therefore needs no greaves to save her shins from the bumps of the heavy shield.

The Homeric and Mycenaean helmet (κόρυς, τρυφάλεια, πήληξ, κυνέη) gave no such complete protection to the face and head as the later, visored, so-called Corinthian helmet,

Helmet. which had cheek-pieces, and often a shield for the nose, —as is shown by the many wounds which are inflicted on these parts, without any mention of a helmet. For example, in Δ 502 the helmet seems to have had no side-pieces, and it appears to lack a back-piece in E 73. But from a wound we may not safely conclude an utter lack of defense. The temple may have been pierced in spite of a side-piece to the helmet, but we should expect the poet to mention the obstruction if one existed. Indications of the Corinthian helmet have been found in N 188 and in a few other passages. The Homeric helmet

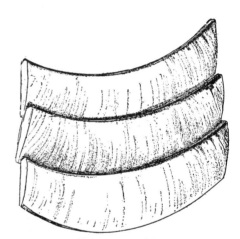

FIG. 30.—Helmet.   FIG. 31.—Boars' Teeth.

was a cap, generally of leather, but sometimes of metal, which covered only the upper part of the head. It had a rim of bronze over the temples and about the lower edge (στεφάνη, H 12, Λ 96). A leather strap, which might be ornamented, passing under the chin, held the helmet firm in place upon the head (ὀχεύς, Γ 371). It generally had a crest of horsehair (λόφος), which was sometimes dyed (O 538); for the crest of the helmet of Achilles, Hephaestus used fine gold thread (T 383). The crest of hair was sometimes fastened to the helmet directly, and sometimes on a support. Hector's helmet had three layers of leather or metal (Λ 352). Odysseus had a cap or helmet with many boars' teeth strung on the outside, evidently as a defense against blows (just as we suppose plates of metal to have been fastened to some tunics), and straps stretched within, probably to strengthen it, and a felt lining for comfort (K 261). A Mycenaean image shows such a helmet of boars' teeth, and many such teeth were found at Mycenae. Metal knob-like or horn-like projections (φάλος, Z 9 ; φάλαρα, Π 106) served not only as ornaments, but also to strengthen the helmet, and to receive and ward off blows. An ἀμφίφαλος helmet had two horn-like projections, both over the forehead (E 743); a τετραφάληρος or τετράφαλος helmet had four horn-like projections, two before and two behind (E 743, X 315),—with which may be compared a word for helmet which is used fifteen times (τρυφάλεια, [τε]τρυφάλεια = κόρυς τετράφαλος), which would imply that this ordinarily had four of these horns.[1] The epithet *bronze-cheeked* (χαλκοπάρηος, M 183) is used perhaps not of the wearer of the helmet,

FIG. 32.—Helmet.

with reference to cheek-pieces, but of the helmet itself, with reference to the parts about the temples,—although cheek-pieces of bronze could be attached to a helmet of leather. So, also, the epithet *reed-eyed* (αὐλῶπις, Λ 353) is explained by Reichel as referring to the projecting reeds or horns, which take the place of eyes for the helmet, but not for the wearer.

The helmet is called *bright* (λαμπρά, P 269) because of its metallic gleam ; it is called also *bronze-fitted* (χαλκήρης, N 714), and "of solid bronze" (πάγχαλκος, σ 378). The obvious etymology of κυνέη (sc. δορά, *skin*) suggests that the helmet was originally of dogskin, but Diomed has a κυνέη of ox-hide, "without knobs and crest" (ἄφαλός τε καὶ ἄλλοφος, K 257), Dolon has one of weasel-skin (κτιδέη, K 335), and Laërtes has one of goat-skin (αἰγείη, ω 231). We are reminded that on many representations of early art, the helmet and cap seems to be the skin of a lion's or other animal's head,—the rest of the hide hanging down the wearer's back. The length of the horn-like projections is indicated not only by the fact that they were easily hit

---

[1] Reichel distinguished φάλος, *horn-like projection*, from φάλαρα, *knobs* or *bosses*. ἀμφίφαλος has been explained, also, as not connected with φάλος, but as meaning *shining*, from the root of φαίνω.

(Γ 362, Π 338), but also by their touching when two warriors stood close (Π 216).

Offensive Weapons. The offensive weapons of the Homeric age, as has been said, differ little in principle from those of later Hellenic times,—the spear (ἔγχος, ἐγχείη, δόρυ, αἰχμή), the bow (τόξον or τόξα), the sword (ξίφος, φάσγανον, ἄορ), the sling (σφενδόνη), the battle-axe (ἀξίνη), and stones (χερμάδια).

The spear-shaft was generally of ash wood (μελίη, B 543,

Fig. 33.—Heracles and Aegis.

X 328) with a point of bronze (αἰχμὴ χαλκείη, Δ 461) in a socket which was further held in place by a ring *Spear.* or ferule (in Hector's spear, of gold, Z 320), and with a spike (σαυρωτήρ, K 153) at the butt end (οὐρίαχος, N 443), which was used to fix the spear in the ground, and to hold it upright, when it was not in use. Possibly the spike at the butt might serve a good use in battle also, if the point of the spear were broken off, as it sometimes was; that it was needed in order to make a balance of weight with the point, as has been suggested, seems hardly probable, for the weight of the point cannot have been great in comparison with that of the shaft. For its use, we may compare 1 *Samuel* xxvi. 7, "and Saul lay sleeping within the trench, and his spear stuck in the ground at his bolster."[1] Hector's spear was eleven cubits, or about sixteen and a half feet, in length (Z 319), but for the ordinary man a much shorter spear would be more serviceable, and on vases the spear is generally represented as not more than seven or eight feet long. The longest spear of the Macedonian phalanx was longer even than Hector's. Achilles's spear, which had been given to his father Peleus by Chiron, was too heavy for any other Achaean to wield (Π 141), and Patroclus left this in the tent, although he took the shield of Achilles, when he went forth to battle. The Homeric warrior not infrequently carries two spears (Γ 18, Λ 43, M 298, 464),—apparently holding one as a reserve,—and the ambidextrous Asteropaeus throws both of his at once (Φ 162). When not in use, the spear of Achilles stood in a case (σύριγξ, literally *pipe*, T 387).

The spear was used both for thrusting and for throwing, and in general the poet is perfectly distinct (as was observed by Aristarchus) in his use of the two verbs,—one for wounding by a weapon held in the hand (οὐτάζω), and the other for wounding by a missile, a weapon thrown (βάλλω).

In addition to the long lance, short javelins were used.[2] Dolon carried one of these when he set out as a spy upon the Achaean camp (K 335),—an expedition on which, as we have seen, a javelin would be far *Javelin.* more convenient than a long lance, and in general, light equipment rather than heavy armor. Agenor casts at Achilles an ἄκων (Φ 590), but this does not seem to differ from an ordinary lance (ἔγχος), and elsewhere, too, the words seem to be used without discrimination (*cf.* O 646, N 183, Ψ 622). No clear and universal distinction can be drawn between the meanings of ἔγχος, δόρυ, ἐγχείη, αἰχμή,—though the last often is the point of the spear, as distinguished from the shaft.

---

[1] According to Aristotle, *Poetics*, 1461 *a*, the Illyrians in his day used similar spikes.

[2] ἄκοντες, with a verb ἀκοντίζω, and derivatives ἀκοντισταί and ἀκοντιστύς.—No indication appears of the use of any strap or ἀγκύλη in the hurling of the javelin.

A hunting spear (αἰγανέη) which is used by the comrades of Odysseus in the chase of wild goats (ι 156), is mentioned

Hunting Spear.

also as hurled for amusement by the comrades of Achilles, while their leader was "sulking in his tent" (B 773), and for a measure of distance is named "as far as a man hurls a hunting spear (αἰγανέη, Π 589), either trying his strength in a contest or in battle."

The Mycenaean sword was not of great length,—three feet long,—and seems to have been made rather for a

Sword.

thrust than for a blow. The blade of a short sword or dagger which is preserved (Fig. 24) is highly ornamented with a scene from the hunting of lions, and the hilt is studded with gold nails. The Homeric sword of bronze must have been longer, for it seems to be used for a blow quite as often as for a thrust (*cf.* Γ 362, E 146, Λ 146), but frequently the simple expression "wounded" (οὐτάζω) leaves the manner of the sword's use uncertain. The epithet *two-edged* (ἄμφηκες) is used four times; *long-edged* (τανύηκες), five times, and the similar τανάηκες as an epithet of bronze in the sense of sword (compare the English use of *steel*) is used four times. The sword is mentioned 42 times in the *Iliad*.

The sword hung not from a belt about the waist, but from a strap (τελαμών or ἀορτήρ) which passed over the

Sword Strap.

right shoulder and crossed the baldric of the shield near the middle of the breast (Ξ 404). Odysseus received from a Phaeacian, as an atonement for a slighting word (θ 403), a bronze sword with hilt (κώπη) of silver, and sheath (κολεόν) of ivory. The epithet *silver-studded* (ἀργυρόηλον, B 45) applied to a sword, probably refers to the studs or rivets of the hilt which fastened the side-pieces of the handle to the frame, and also served as ornaments. These are prominent also on the Mycenaean swords. The Mycenaean sheath seems commonly to have been of wood or leather, since it is not found in the Mycenaean tombs, but the sheath of Agamemnon's sword was of silver (Λ 30). Fragments of linen which have been found attached to an ancient bronze sword have been understood to indicate that the sheath had a cloth lining.

The baldric, like other leather straps, was at times adorned with thin plates of precious metal, some of which have been found at Mycenae.

The mighty arm of Achilles with his sword could strike off a man's head at a single blow (Υ 481, *cf.* Π 340). In other cases the head or the arm was thus nearly severed from the shoulders. Where the head of a fallen enemy is cut off on the ground (as Λ 146), the reader does not know but more than one blow may have been required for the task.

Agamemnon carries, hanging by his side, near his sword, a large knife (μάχαιρα, Γ 271), which he uses in cutting the throats of victims for sacrifice, and doubtless also for carving at his own table; and the *Knife or Dagger.* youths who join the dance which is depicted by Hephaestus on the shield of Achilles (Σ 597) have golden knives hanging from silver straps. These would correspond to daggers or to the western American bowie-knife, but they are never used in the fight. The modern Greek peasant, also, always carries in his girdle a great knife, which is ready for divers uses.

The battle-axe is mentioned by Homer only twice (ἀξίνη, Ν 612, Ο 711). This, too, was of bronze, and in the former of these instances hung under (*i.e.* behind) *Battle-Axe.* the shield of the heavy-armed warrior. In the other case, it is mentioned in connexion with other axes (πέλεκυς, but evidently used for war), swords, and spears.

The club or mace (κορύνη) does not appear as used in the Homeric battles, but Nestor tells of the "club-bearer Areïthoüs" (Η 138), who "did not fight with the *Mace.* bow and the long spear, but broke the ranks with his iron mace,"—the only arm or weapon of iron mentioned in the poems. In Hades, too, Odysseus saw the shade of the hunter Orion with his club of solid bronze in his hands, driving over the asphodel meadow the ghosts of the wild beasts which he had slain (λ 572). A hunter, we may think, would need to be fleet of foot, if he had no other weapon than a club. This seems a very primitive arm, and as such it was ascribed in later story to Heracles. In the battle between the gods and the giants, the Moerae fought against giants who were armed with clubs (ῥόπαλοι), according to Apollodorus, i. 6. 2. But even in the sixth century B.C., the bodyguard of the tyrant Pisistratus were armed only with maces of wood (κορυνηφόροι,—not δορυφόροι, Herodotus, i. 59),—the earliest policeman's club. The club of Areïthoüs probably was of wood with iron knobs or stubs,—not of solid iron,—just as a "golden sceptre" is a wooden staff adorned with gold.[1]

The bow of the Lycian Pandarus is described more fully than any other, in the fourth book of the *Iliad* (Δ 105). It was

Bow.   made of the horns of a wild goat of the mountains which Pandarus himself had shot. The horns were sixteen hand-breadths in length. The current view has been that these horns were united butt to butt, by a wooden "grip," hand-piece, or arm (πῆχυς, Δ 375). If the hand-breadth or "palm" equalled one-fourth of a foot, as the ancients generally reckoned, such a bow would be inconveniently long even after all reasonable reductions had been made for the loss of material in the making. Apart from all other difficulties, attention has been called to the immense difficulty of bending such a bow ; "no human arm would have been sufficient," according to one authority. Yet Odysseus's bow also was of horn (φ 395), and we may suppose this to have been the usual material. A British scholar suggested that the bows "from which Homer drew his description were of composite structure, with a powerful reinforcement of sinews moulded on to the back."[2] Such bows are still used in Central Asia, and may be compared conveniently with those which were in use until recently in North America, from Mexico to the region of the Eskimo. These bows are composed of several long and thin pieces of wood, and thin layers of horn, reinforced by a mass of sinews from the back or neck of some animal,—all carefully and elaborately glued together, so as to last for an indefinite period. This bow is thick at the grip, but flattens out

---

[1] "In the Hindoo Epic, the club is of iron, plated with gold, and girded with spikes. It is used by special heroes of greatest strength."

[2] See H. Balfour, *Journal of the Anthropological Institute*, xix. p. 227 ; O. T. Mason, *Smithsonian Report* for 1893, pp. 631-679, plates lxii., lxv., lxxxviii. ; F. S. Dellenbaugh, *The North Americans of Yesterday*, p. 249.

rapidly towards the ends, and it is so formed that the "back," which is at the front in shooting, is very concave when the bow is unbent. Such a bow would justify the epithet "bent-back" (παλίντονος, Θ 266). Of these Persian bows it is said, that "after leaving the maker's hands, in order to be strung for use, they had first to be softened in a bath, and then gradually opened by cords attached to pegs in the ground." Thus the bow of Odysseus, after twenty years of disuse, had become so hard and stiff that Penelope's suitors were unable to brace it (φ 184 ff.).[1]

The horn element in the Persian bow seems to be sufficient to justify a poet in calling a similar bow one of horn, but this assumption of a composite bow for Homer's time does not seem to be absolutely required.

Bow of Horn.

The National Museum at Washington has a bow formerly used by a Sioux Indian, which is made "of two sections of cow's horn, spliced together in the middle and held by rivets. It is lined on the back with sinew. It is curved in the shape of Cupid's bow, and is three feet in length." A similar bow is in the Peabody Museum at Cambridge (Mass.). The Eskimo used "compound bows, made of reindeer antlers, and backed with sinew,"—the three pieces being fastened together by lashings of sinew, cord, or braid.

A Siberian bow is reported from the British Museum, of strongly marked "Cupid's bow" shape, with wooden base and powerful backing of sinew, and layers of horn. Dellenbaugh writes: "The chief weapon of all Amerinds was the bow and arrow. The bow was made in a number of ways and of various kinds of wood, and of horn, reinforced as a rule by a backing of sinew. . . . Amongst all the Amerind bows I have ever seen, one made from the horns of a mountain sheep, with a portion of the skull as the central part, was the finest and most graceful. It was exactly the shape of the typical bow wielded by the little god Cupid. . . .

---

[1] "In India, the horn-bow was the best. It was five feet long, and was held perpendicularly to the ear, the arrow on the level of the eye." "Bows were also of wood and cane, and arrows of iron or reed. The bows of iron and horn, united, were later. They were ornamented with designs, and sometimes were painted." "The bent bow is 'full,' and 'like a wheel,' the two ends being brought together."

I saw it in southern Utah in 1875." Clearly, then, if bows are in existence which have been made from the antlers of reindeer, and from the horns of cows and mountain sheep, the bow of Pandarus may have been made of the two horns of a mountain goat, lashed or riveted to a piece of wood, bone, or horn, which served as the grip; but the evidence is insufficient absolutely to rule out the compound bow, in which the horn served only as backing. In general, horn has been accepted as material for a bow only in default of wood which was sufficiently strong and at the same time elastic. Why the Homeric Greeks should not have found in their forests satisfactory wood for the purpose, is not easy to say. The horns of mountain goats as depicted on

FIG. 34.—Stringing Bow.

Cretan monuments (see *Annual of the British School at Athens*, ix. plate iii.) are as long as that from which Pandarus secured his bow.

When not in use, the bow of Odysseus was kept in a case (γωρυτός, φ 54), as the American Indians kept their archery, and hung on a peg. Before using it, Odysseus examined carefully his old bow, to make sure that it had not been weakened by borers (ἶπες, φ 395).

The bow-string was of ox-sinew (νεῦρα, Δ 122, νευρή, φ 410), and was caught by a metallic hook or ring (κορώνη, Δ 111) at the tip of the bow. The archer, when *Bow-String.* about to string his bow, put one end under his left leg, which served as a fulcrum, and pressed the other end upward with his right leg (see Fig. 35). In shooting, the string was drawn to the breast (μαζῷ πέλασεν, Δ 123), not to the right ear as in India and in modern archery.

The arrow of Paris had a three-barbed point (ἰῷ τριγλώχινι, Λ 507). The arrow-point of Pandarus was of iron (σίδηρον, *Arrow.* Δ 123), with barbs (ὄγκοι, Δ 151), and was fastened to the shaft of reed (δόναξ, Λ 584) by a sinew (νεῦρον, Δ 151). Elsewhere the arrow-point was of bronze,—although those which have been found at Mycenae are of stone, as were those of the North American Indians,—as is shown by the epithets applied to the arrow,—*bronze-fitted* (χαλκήρης, α 262), "heavy with bronze" (χαλκοβαρής, Ο 465). Poison is not used on them, but the fictitious Mentes says that Odysseus went to Ephyra "for man-slaying poison to anoint his arrows withal" (α 160), which shows that such use of poison was known. The arrow had a notch (γλυφίδες, Δ 122) at the butt. The epithet *winged* (πτερόεις, Δ 117) may mean simply *swift*, but very likely feathers were used in modern fashion to guide the course of the arrow; *cf.* τόξων πτερωτὰς γλυφίδας in Euripides's *Orestes*, 274. The quiver (φαρέτρη, Α 45) had a cover (πῶμα, Δ 116, ι 314), and hung from the shoulder (Α 46) or under the left arm ; not at the back, as in India.

Fig 35.—West Pediment of the Temple of Aphaea.

The bowman was wont to shoot while resting on one knee or in a crouching position. Odysseus poured out his arrows at his feet (χ 4), that he might have them conveniently at hand when he assailed Penelope's *Bowman Kneels or Crouches.* suitors. For this position, the figures of Heracles and the other archers in the pediment of the temple of Aphaea on Aegina, may serve as illustrations (see Fig. 35).

The two passages in the Homeric poems which refer to the sling (Ν 600, 716) have been considered already (page 582). The sling is of wool, not of leather. *Sling.* Nothing is known of its special form, but its use doubtless was essentially the same as in the army of Cyrus and by the youthful David (1 *Sam.* xvii. 40). Slingers are represented on the fragment of a silver vase of Mycenaean times, which portrayed the siege of a city (Fig. 23).

In default of a more convenient or effective missile or weapon, the Homeric warrior often picks up a stone

Stones Hurled. ($\chi\epsilon\rho\mu\acute{a}\delta\iota o\nu$) from the field, and hurls it at his antagonist. No chieftain holds it beneath his dignity to use such a missile. Even the goddess Athena overthrows Ares by the cast of a stone (Φ 403), and that before she has used her spear, perhaps as if in contempt,— her spear forsooth was not necessary against such an antagonist. In the midst of his bravest deeds, Agamemnon reviews the Trojan ranks "with spear, sword, and great stones" (Λ 265), which shows that the stones were accepted by all, even by the commander-in-chief, as useful and respectable missiles. A dozen wounds are inflicted by stones in the action of the *Iliad*, and five of these are fatal. Diomed, having the point of his spear still in the head of Pandarus, who had been acting as the charioteer of Aeneas, seizes a stone "which two men could not carry, such as men now are," and hurls it at Aeneas, breaking his hip-joint (E 302 ff.), and, three or four days later, Aeneas himself throws a similar stone at Achilles (Υ 285). In the single-combat between Hector and Ajax, after the two had hurled their spears in vain, each casts a great stone at his foe; Ajax throws a stone "like a mill-stone," which stretches Hector upon the ground, but Apollo raises him up, and the two warriors are about to use their swords when the heralds interfere (H 264 ff.). In the next battle, Hector throws a stone at the archer Teucer, who is aiming his bow at him (Θ 321), and again one at a Myrmidon (Π 577). Patroclus returns this last throw of Hector with a stone, not with a dart (Π 587), and with another he kills Hector's charioteer and half-brother, Cebriones (Π 734). In the same battle, Ajax hurls at Hector (Ξ 410), who had cast his spear at him, one of the great stones which served as props for the boats as they were drawn up on shore.[1] When stones are thrown by a number of men at once, we may suppose slings to have been used, as Γ 80, Λ 265, N 323, and perhaps Π 774; otherwise we have a glimpse of the survival of a very primitive manner of warfare. That stones should be thrown from a wall against assailants, is

[1] *Cf.* Δ 518, E 582, M 154 ff., 287, 380, O 250, Π 411.

natural (M 154). On another fragment of the silver vase of which part is given in Fig. 23, one warrior is represented as hurling a stone with his hand, while another is stooping evidently to take up a like missile.

This general use of stones carries us back not merely to primitive weapons, but also to conflicts of small and irregular bodies of men, rather than to systematic contests between regiments and divisions. The abundance of small stones on a field between Marseilles and the mouth of the Rhone was explained by the ancients as rained down from heaven by the gods, to furnish a supply of missiles for Heracles when he was hard pressed in battle.[1] The distinct survival of the tradition of the importance of stones in battle, is indicated by the fear of the maidens who form the chorus in Aeschylus's *Seven against Thebes*; these cry at verse 300, "The enemy are advancing against our towers; they hurl the rugged stones against the men of our city"; and at verse 676 of the same play, where the greaves are called a "protection against the spear and stones,"—αἰχμῆς καὶ πετρῶν προβλήματα. In the *Suppliants* of Euripides (503), also, stones have killed warriors before Thebes. So in Pindar, *Pyth.* iii. 49, Asclepius healed those warriors who had been wounded by the bright bronze or "by the stone thrown from afar" (χερμάδι τηλεβόλῳ), where the word used distinctly implies a stone cast by the hand rather than one hurled from a sling. The great rock cast by Alcyoneus (Pindar, *Nem.* iv. 28), which destroyed twelve chariots and the men upon them, however, was as exceptional as the summit of the mountain thrown by Polyphemus (ι 481), and the gravestone hurled at Polydeuces (Pindar, *Nem.* x. 67).[2]

The "boarding pike" (ξυστὸν ναύμαχον, O 678), twenty-two cubits in length, which Ajax wields, warding off the Trojans from the line of Achaean ships drawn up on land, is an entirely exceptional weapon. Nowhere else *Boarding Pike.* in the poems does the poet give a hint of naval warfare. This pike, however, seems not to have been intended for use in conflicts between ships, but in an endeavor to effect

---

[1] Strabo, 183 c, quoting from Aeschylus, *Prometheus Loosed.*

[2] "In the Hindoo Epic, it is especially the 'mountaineers' who are proficient in stone-throwing, but the regular troops, also, at times throw stones."

a landing, in the face of opposition, on a hostile shore. In their forays by sea, such opposition was usual. The landing of the Achaeans on the shore of Troy was vigorously opposed, as is shown by the death of Protesilaus, who was the first to leap on land (B 702).

The Homeric chariot[1] may fairly be considered among the paraphernalia of war, since its principal use was in the field of battle, for quick and easy transportation *The Chariot.* from one part of the field to another. As has been seen already, this use was conditioned chiefly by that of the heavy and unwieldy shield, and Reichel called attention to the fact that the use of chariots in battle disappeared from Greece with the great Mycenaean shields. As in India, chariots were used simply by the nobles or chieftains, and never in troops or squadrons. Each was entirely independent in its movements. They never moved in line or in close order, forming a separate and organized division of the army. The leaders were not bound to remain with their special contingents, but were free to go wherever they thought themselves to be most needed. Light-armed warriors had no chariots,—they needed none,—and at no time (as on Assyrian and Egyptian monuments) are archers found to be shooting from a chariot. Pandarus leaves his chariot at home and comes to Troy as a bowman (E 199). Occasionally a warrior, while standing on his chariot, as from a point of vantage hurls a spear upon his foe, as at O 386, where the Trojans upon their chariots fight with the Achaeans who are standing on their boats, drawn up on land,—but the chariots were not chariots of war in the Assyrian or Egyptian sense. In general the warrior descended from his chariot in order to fight,[2] while, conversely, to

---

[1] See Grashof, *Fuhrwerk bei Homer und Hesiod*; but chiefly Reichel, *Homerische Waffen*,[2] 120 ff. The names for chariot are δίφρος, ἅρμα or ἅρματα, and ὄχεα. Frequently the word for *horses*, ἵπποι, is used for *chariot and horses*, or even for *chariot* itself, so that chieftains apparently descend *out of their horses* (ἐξ ἵππων, as Θ 492), and conversely they may leap, εἰς ἵππους, as Λ 192. Thus ἀφ' ἵππων need not mean *from his horses*, but generally means *from his chariot*, as E 835. Similarly, ἐφ' ἡμιόνων, Ω 702, does not mean *on the mules*, but *on the mule-car.*

[2] *Cf.* E 494, Λ 94, 211, 423, Π 426 f. (where the Lycian Sarpedon and the Achaean Patroclus both leap from their chariots in order to fight together), 733, P 480.— Similarly the Celts, also bearing great shields, used chariots on the field of battle,

hasten to one's chariot implies that the warrior desires to leave the immediate field of action (Λ 273, 359). The charioteer was instructed to keep his chariot and horses close at hand for the warrior, ready for any emergency (as Λ 229, N 385, O 456, Π 147, P 501). Only a heedless charioteer would remain far from his chieftain. The position of the charioteer is seen to be one of danger, since he must be near the thick of the fight, and may come in the path of the missiles (P 614), while he has no shield for his defense.

The fact that chariots were not used in Greece for war-purposes in the classical period has caused perplexity to many scholars, and has encouraged the doubt whether the Achaeans ever used chariots in battle. Does Homer in this matter tell of what he had actually seen? Why did the Achaeans not use cavalry, like the Athenians of the fifth century B.C.? This doubt was ill-founded, however. Certainly the Achaeans might easily have become acquainted with the use of chariots by their neighbors on the east, and by Egyptians, and definite evidence of the Greek use of chariots in the Mycenaean age is found not simply in the system of roads between Corinth and Mycenae, but even more distinctly in the carving of chariots on rude Mycenaean tombstones. The "sacred band" at Thebes was made up of "combatants and drivers" (παραβάται and ἡνίοχοι, Diod. Sic. xii. 70) long after the use of chariots in battle had been abandoned by the Greeks,—and the names bore witness to the primitive custom. *Used in Mycenaean Age.*

The representation of the chariot on the Mycenaean tombstone seems to have been intended to indicate the knightly rank of the warrior whose bones were buried below. With it may be compared three Homeric epithets, *horse-driving* and *horse-master-ing*,[1] which mean only *knightly*, *knight*, or *cavalier*, as applied *"Knight," "Cavalier."*

but dismounted for the combat, Diod. Sic. v. 29 f. For the use of chariots by the Celts, see Darbois de Jubainville, *Civilisation des Celtes*, 327.

[1] ἱππηλάτα Πηλεύς, Η 125; ἱππότα Νέστωρ, Β 433; Ἕκτορος ἱπποδάμοιο, X 161. To translate this last epithet, *horse-taming* or *horse-breaking*, introduces a notion which is foreign to the Homeric poems. The warrior must be a horseman, in so far as he must be a master of his steeds,—but he is not to be confused with a driver or breaker of horses.

to Nestor, Peleus, Hector, and a number of others. Not every Homeric chieftain, however, is said to have a chariot. That the Salaminian Ajax never appears in one, has been explained as due to his having his home on a small island, where he would have no horses of his own. But Ajax's men helped him with his shield, and the importance of a chariot to a chieftain is indicated by the fact that Neleus hid his chariot in order to keep the youthful Nestor from going to the battle (Λ 718).

FIG. 36.—Form of Chariot.[1]

The general form of the Homeric chariot is the same as that of all the nations of antiquity,—Assyrians, Egyptians, Hittites, Celts, and Romans. In Greece this chariot was little used in later times except for races in the great festivals. No variety in form is mentioned, but doubtless, like shields and helmets, the chariots differed according to the materials at hand and the taste of the owner. The chariot had but two wheels, and was enclosed on the front and both sides, being open at the back. The body of the chariot thus resembled a large arm-chair with its back to the horses, and a name for the chariot which is used as frequently as any, means also stool or chair.[2] Above the barrier around the front and sides

Form of Chariot.

---

[1] For an explanation of the harness, see Fig. 37.

[2] δίφρος, as Γ 262. The etymology proposed, from φέρω, as *carrying two*, is doubtful.

were one or two bent rods of wood which served as a railing,[1] and must have been a convenient hold for steadying the driver and the combatant, when the chariot passed over rough ground or any particular obstacle. To this rim the reins were at times drawn back (E 262). How high the body of the chariot extended, is nowhere indicated,—except as a warrior standing on the ground wounds a man standing in the chariot, in the bowels (N 398, Π 465), which shows that the barrier did not reach above the waist, and ancient works of art show chariots with still lower bodies. Of what materials the front of the chariot was made, is not clear either, except that it was adorned, and perhaps strengthened, with plates of metal.[2] An epithet, *well-plaited*,[3] applied to the chariot, has been interpreted to mean that the front and sides were of a kind of basket or lattice work; but plates of metal would hardly be applied to this, and the epithet may refer to the chariot-board itself, since this may have been formed of woven leather straps, which would have supplied a certain amount of very desirable elasticity. Such straps were used, as we have seen (page 204), for the support of bedding. The vehicle had no springs, and the body of the chariot rested directly on the axle-tree.

The chariot was low. This was necessary if it was to serve its most important purpose, allowing the warrior with his heavy arms to enter it and to leave it easily. *Chariot Low and Light.* And in the games at the funeral of Patroclus, the horses of Diomed followed so close upon the chariot of Eumelus that each moment they seemed about to enter this (Ψ 379), and the back and shoulders of Eumelus were warmed by their breath. No step is mentioned, as facilitating the entrance of the chariot. The lightness of the chariot is shown a little farther on in the same story: Eumelus meets with an accident,—the yoke of his chariot is broken, the end of the pole falls to the ground; he is thrown from his chariot, and badly bruised; but he comes in, last of all, it is true, driving his horses before him and drawing his chariot after him (Ψ 533).

---

[1] ἄντυγες, E 728, Φ 38, made of young shoots of the wild-fig tree.

[2] *Cf.* ἅρματα ποικίλα χαλκῷ, Δ 226, Κ 322, 393; Κ 438.

[3] *Cf.* δίφρος δὲ χρυσέοισι καὶ ἀργυρέοισιν ἱμᾶσιν, E 727, of the chariot of Hera.

Another indication of the same sort is in the story of the nocturnal visit of Odysseus and Diomed to the Trojan camp ; having slain the Thracian Rhesus, Diomed is in doubt whether to draw out Rhesus's chariot, or to lift it, and carry it out from among the Thracians (K 505).

The chariot had room for no more than the combatant and his driver. On which side the combatant stood, is not *Room for Two.* made clear ; but he probably stood at the right, since he must be free to use his spear with his right hand.[1] The chariot had no seat. When the wounded son of Pylaemenes is seated in a chariot by his Paphlagonian comrades, to be taken back to Ilium (N 657 ; *cf.* ξ 280), he probably sat with his back to the horses, letting his feet hang out of the back of the car. But when Thestor "sits" in his chariot on the approach of Patroclus (Π 403), he merely crouches or squats.

When the chariot was not in use it seems to have been taken to pieces, at times. At least, when Hera prepares *When Not in Use.* to descend to the Trojan plain, Hebe aids her by putting the wheels on her chariot (E 722). On the return of Zeus to Olympus, Poseidon unharnesses his horses, and puts the chariot on a platform, and spreads a linen cloth over it (Θ 440). Similarly, while Achilles and his Myrmidons took no part in the fray, their chariots stood well covered (εὖ πεπυκασμένα, B 777) in their barracks. On the return of Hera and Athena from their second expedition, their chariot was leaned against the bright front wall of the hall of Zeus (Θ 435 ; *cf.* δ 42 ; see p. 186).

The chariot was drawn by the pole, which was firmly fixed to the axle-tree, without traces, just as an ox-cart *Drawn by the Pole.* is drawn in modern times. Thus if the pole or the yoke is broken (as at Z 40, Π 371, Ψ 392), the horses are free from the chariot. The pole appears to be most easily broken near the front end. The chariot being drawn by the pole, naturally two horses would be used. Nowhere does a chariot appear in battle as drawn

---

[1] "The combatant stood at the left in the Veda, but at the right of the driver, in later Hindoo sculpture."

by a single horse or by four horses.[1] A third horse [2] is twice mentioned as accompanying the chariot,—probably with the expectation that he shall be put under the yoke in case of an accident to one of the two yoke-horses. In both of these instances, however, it is the third horse which is injured and interrupts the course of the chariot. Menelaus offers to Telemachus three horses and a chariot (δ 590), but no hint is given as to the use of this third horse.

In driving from the Trojan city to the Achaean camp, king Priam stands in his chariot (Ω 701). Whether the Homeric Achaeans had chariot-bodies of another form, provided with seats, cannot be stated *Seat in the* *Chariot.* positively. This has been assumed chiefly because Telemachus and Nestor's son Pisistratus drove from Pylus to Sparta (γ 483—δ 1), and scholars believed that men would not stand during so long a journey. The exertion might not be greater than walking all day long, however, and the reader must remember that the chariots had no springs, and that sitting too would become wearisome. Farmers are wont to stand in their carts, often all day. But seated men are represented as driving, in early works of art, and Telemachus's chariot has a basket or box large enough to stow away not merely food for luncheon but also the presents which he receives from Menelaus and Helen,—a silver mixing-bowl and a gown for Telemachus's future bride (o 131). This journey of Telemachus and that of Helen's daughter Hermione from Sparta to her future home in Thessaly (δ 8) are the longest drives which are mentioned, but Menelaus offers to convey Telemachus on his chariot throughout Greece, visiting the cities of men (o 81). The gods often used chariots for their journeys.

---

[1] At Θ 185, however, according to our MSS., Hector addresses his steeds and names four,—but in the next verse he uses the dual imperative ; at Λ 699 Nestor's father had sent four horses to contend in games in Elis ; and at ν 81 four horses are driven together on the plain (in a comparison). This naturally agrees with the custom observed in the later Olympian games.—That the chariot was drawn at times by a single horse has been inferred, not quite certainly, from Agamemnon's words, that "many a man's horse will sweat in drawing his chariot" (B 390), and from the comparison of Achilles as he rushed over the plain with a race-horse drawing a chariot (X 22).

[2] παρήορος, *side-horse*, Π 471 ; *cf.* Θ 87.

Hera says that she wearied her horses by her efforts in assembling the Achaean forces (Δ 27), and Zeus takes a chariot when he goes from Mt. Olympus to Mt. Ida (see p. 404).

Narrow. The breadth of the Homeric chariot needed not to be great, in order to carry but two warriors, and the width of the ancient roads near Mycenae (about eleven feet) would not indicate a broad gauge for the early vehicles. Hesiod, however, in his *Works and Days* (424) advises the farmer to cut a seven-foot axletree for his wagon.

The Axle. The axle of the chariot of Diomed was of oak (φήγινος, E 838),—and it was strained when it was called to bear the weight of the goddess Athena as well as Diomed. The axletree of the chariot of the goddess Hera was of iron (E 723),—but the spokes and the tires were of bronze, the fellies of gold, and the naves or hubs were of silver,—altogether an unusual vehicle. Poseidon's chariot, similarly, had an axletree of bronze (N 30). Nothing is said of linch-pins nor of greasing the wheels.

Of no other chariot are the details mentioned so distinctly as for Hera's, as just enumerated. That the fellies some-times were made of the black poplar, is stated in a comparison which introduces that tree (Δ 486).

Yoking of Horses. The poet tells of the process of yoking Priam's mules when the old king prepares to go to the Achaean camp in order to ransom the body of his son Hector (Ω 266 ff.), and the process doubtless was essenti-ally the same as the yoking of horses to the chariot: the Trojan princes carried out the wagon, and bound a box or basket upon it. They took down from its peg the yoke of boxwood (ζυγόν,—*b* in Fig. 37), which had a good knob (ὀμφαλός,—*c*) and was well fitted with handles (οἴηκες,—*dd*); and with the yoke they carried out a yoke-strap (ζυγόδεσμον,—*gg*) nine cubits in length. They placed the yoke at the very front of the well-polished pole (ῥυμός,—*a*), and threw the ring (κρίκος,—*e*) over the pin (ἕστωρ,—*f*). Thrice on either side they bound it to the knob, and then wound the strap round and round in order, and tucked under the tongue or end ($\gamma\lambda\omega\chi\iota s$,—*h*) of the strap. The process is illustrated here by a figure borrowed from an article by Reichel,[1] who adds that the yoke doubtless rested on a cushion, and that the horses had a belt about the body which would hold the yoke-straps in place when the horses lowered their heads. Ancient monuments show that the yoke did not rest upon the withers, but much farther forward. The holes in the yoke through which passed the breast-straps by which the animals pulled the chariot or wagon, are indicated in the figure, but have no letters affixed. The combination of girt, cushion, and breast-straps, Reichel thinks to be the $\zeta\epsilon\upsilon\gamma\lambda\eta$ (P 440,

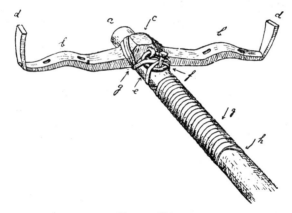

Fig. 37.—Yoke.

T 406), out of which the manes of Achilles's horses fall, as these bend their heads to the ground, in mourning for the death of Patroclus.

As for the bridle, mention is made in a comparison of ivory cheek-pieces for horses, stained with purple by Carian or Maeonian women (Δ 142). *Cheek Pieces.*

The chariot, then, was two-wheeled and was drawn by horses. The wagon,[2] on the other hand, had four wheels

---

[1] *Homerische Waffen*[2], 129, and *Das Joch des homerischen Wagens*, in *Jahreshefte des Oester. Arch. Instituts*, ii. 137.—The famous "Gordian knot" also bound the yoke to the chariot-pole (Arrian, *Anab.* ii. 3. 7), and here the end was tucked under so skilfully that it could not be discovered, but of this the strap was made of the bark of a cornel tree.

[2] $\check{\alpha}\mu\alpha\xi\alpha$ and $\dot{\alpha}\pi\eta\nu\eta$,—which are not distinguished by the poet; *cf.* ς 72, 73, where the servants made ready the $\check{\alpha}\mu\alpha\xi\alpha$ and harnessed the mules to the $\dot{\alpha}\pi\eta\nu\eta$,

and was drawn by mules or at times by kine (H 332, 426, Ω 782). A wagon, driven by an old herald, is used *Wagons.* to convey the ransom for Hector's body to Achilles's tent from Ilium (Ω 178, 275, 590), and to bring back the body to the city. The princess Nausicaa herself drives the mule-car which contains the family linen, to the river, for the work of the laundry (ζ 81). Wagons bring wood from Mt. Ida for the funeral pyre of Hector (Ω 782), and down from the hills to the city of the Laestrygonians (κ 103).

Upon the frame of the wagon might be placed a large basket or over-part,[1] in which clothing and other *Basket or Box.* things could be laid. Possibly this was large enough to receive even the body of Hector (Ω 590).

The whip was an important part of the equipment of a chariot or wagon. The animals were accustomed to it. *The Whip.* In the horse-race, Diomed regards the prize as lost by him, when the god Apollo in jealousy knocks the whip from his hand (Ψ 384), and Nausicaa with discretion applies the lash to her mules (ἵμασεν μάστιγι, ζ 316). In an earlier horse-race, old Nestor lost the prize since he was at a disadvantage in contending with twin brothers, who divided the labor,—one holding the reins and the other using the whip (Ψ 642). The epithet *shrill* or *clear-toned* (λιγυρή, Λ 532) implies that the sound of the whip-lash was familiar. Very possibly, however, the whip had a prick as well as a lash, for the goad (κέντρον, Ψ 387, 430; *cf.* Θ 396) is used in the race. The whip, or rather perhaps the whip-stock (ἱμάσθλη, Θ 43), of Zeus was of gold.

which is manifestly the same vehicle.—This is *four-wheeled* (τετράκυκλοι, Ω 324, ι 242) and *well-wheeled* (ἐύκυκλος, ζ 58, 70). " *Cf.* the Latin (Celtic?) *petoritum* (with *quattuor rotae*). In the Hindoo Epic two kinds of carts are used,—one with two wheels, and the other with four wheels."

[1] πείρινθα, Ω 267, *cf.* ο 131; ὑπερτερίη, ζ 70,—the two doubtless essentially identical in service, though possibly differing in form.

ENGLISH INDEX

GREEK INDEX